ESSAYS IN THE HISTORY OF EARLY AMERICAN LAW

The Institute of Early American History and Culture is sponsored jointly by the College of William and Mary and Colonial Williamsburg, Incorporated.

ESSAYS IN THE HISTORY OF EARLY AMERICAN LAW

EDITED WITH AN INTRODUCTION BY

David H. Flaherty

Published for the Institute of Early American History and Culture of Williamsburg, Virginia, by The University of North Carolina Press, Chapel Hill

Library of Congress Catalog Card Number 78-80020
Printed by The Seeman Printery, Durham, N. C.
Manufactured in the United States of America
THIS BOOK WAS DIGITALLY PRINTED.

PREFACE

Study of American legal history can be a stimulating experience both because of its intrinsic interest and because of the light which it sheds upon broad themes in United States history. Recently formulated hypotheses concerning the scope of legal history are moving the subject away from the old-fashioned conception of it as institutional history and making it an important avenue of approach to the study of social history. The immediate and practical concerns of an enlightened approach to legal history often provide striking insights into the essence of a society.

It is the editor's hope in presenting a selection from the finest work of the historians of early American law to encourage more general interest in the subject and to persuade others to pursue more extensive knowledge. The difficulties of writing the history of American law have been pointed out often enough to discourage many who have stood at the threshold. The result has been that, despite the existence of an impressive and valuable literature, few American historians have incorporated it into their own work.

There are obvious reasons for this. No satisfactory survey of the history of early American law exists. While there are some well-known volumes that one can turn to initially, most of these have definite limitations as studies in legal history. In some ways they are poor introductions to the subject, since their inadequacies tend to alienate a critical reader from the subject matter. In addition, much of the best work in American legal history has appeared in journals that are not readily accessible to historians. The scholars who have made the significant contributions to this subject—men such as Julius Goebel, Jr., George Haskins, Mark Howe, Richard Morris, and Joseph Smith—have done a good deal of their best work in article form. The need to make the best articles easily accessible, to integrate them into a coherent pattern, and to supply a general introduction to the subject while suggesting areas for fruitful research provides the rationale for publication of this volume, one which is directed much more to those who are historians of early America and those with a general interest in the history of American law, than to practicing legal historians.

While this collection of essays does not constitute a history of early American law as such, it does provide a substantial introduction to the subject. The reader can generate his own enthusiasms or disagreements with particular articles. Familiarity with their contents will readily suggest gaps and inadequacies in the general literature of early American legal history. Each article stands as an independent entity, with each author introducing his own topic and placing it in context. The lucidity and talent of these various authors has rendered editorial headnotes superfluous, and it has also been thought best to leave their footnotes as originally printed. The introductory essay comments on most of the articles included and places individual essays in a comprehensible whole.

With the exception of the general introduction, all of these articles have been previously published. Recent essays of high merit from the *American Journal of Legal History* and from the collection edited by George A. Billias under the title *Law and Authority in Colonial America* (Barre, Mass., 1965) have been excluded on the grounds that these were readily available. The already substantial size of this volume and the sparseness of the periodical literature account for the absence of articles on the early nineteenth-century period. The survey of the literature in the introduction, however, extends as late as 1830 in some instances, since the publication of Kent's *Commentaries on American Law* in the late 1820's provides a culmination to the early legal history of this country and a convenient starting point for the study of the development of law in nineteenth-century America. The heavy imbalance towards New England materials also deserves a word of explanation. Since legal historians have concentrated on New England and New York to the neglect of the other colonies, the literature on the legal history of the southern colonies, for example, is weak and in article form almost non-existent.

There is need to acknowledge the generous assistance given me by a variety of individuals learned in the subject. These included Joseph H. Smith, George L. Haskins, Herbert A. Johnson, Leonard W. Levy, Stanley N. Katz, and Kathryn Turner Preyer. Since their advice was not invariably followed, these scholars are in no way responsible for inadequacies that may remain. The introduction and contents of this volume inevitably reflect the current state of thinking on this subject by the editor, with all the limitations that this necessarily involves. I am grateful for the encouragement and editorial assistance provided by the Institute of Early American History and Culture, its Editor of Publications, Stephen G. Kurtz, and Joy Dickinson, the Assistant Editor. Christopher K. Seglem, Princeton Class of 1968, was my able research assistant during the preparation of the volume. My former colleague G. B. Warden tolerated my frequent desire to discuss the project with him. The Columbia University Seminar on Early American History and Culture provided me with an opportunity to present an earlier draft of my introduction to a critical and learned audience. Ultimate acknowledgment must go to the distinguished authors whose work has made this collection of essays possible.

Charlottesville, Virginia DAVID H. FLAHERTY
October, 1968

CONTRIBUTORS

CHARLES MCLEAN ANDREWS (1863-1943), one of the great names in the study of early American history, was the author of the classic *The Colonial Period of American History*, 4 volumes (New Haven, 1934-1938). Professor Andrews was an active member of the Yale history department from 1910 until 1931.

ZECHARIAH CHAFEE, JR. (1885-1957) was a prominent civil libertarian and a member of the Harvard Law School faculty from 1916 until 1956. He retained an active interest in early American legal history.

SAMUEL E. EWING is a practicing lawyer who received his degree from the University of Pennsylvania Law School in 1955.

DAVID H. FLAHERTY (1940—) is a member of the history department at the University of Virginia, where he teaches courses in the history of American law.

JULIUS GOEBEL, JR. (1892—) is currently professor emeritus at the Columbia Law School and editor-in-chief of the legal papers of Alexander Hamilton. He is the author of a distinguished series of monographs on English and American legal history.

GEORGE L. HASKINS (1915—) has been a member of the University of Pennsylvania Law School faculty since 1946 and a prolific author in the fields of English and American legal history.

MARK DEWOLFE HOWE (1906-1967) was a professor of law at the Harvard Law School from 1945 until his untimely death. His activities as the biographer of Justice Holmes were but one facet of his extensive interest in American legal history. At the time of his death Professor Howe was Charles Warren Professor of the History of American Law.

MILTON M. KLEIN (1917—) is an early American historian and Dean for Graduate Studies and Research at the State University College at Fredonia, New York.

RICHARD B. MORRIS (1904—) is a distinguished American historian who has been an active author and editor in the field of early American legal history. Professor Morris is currently Gouverneur Morris Professor of History at Columbia University.

JOSEPH H. SMITH (1913—) has been professor of law at the Columbia Law School since 1961, after many years of private law practice in New York City. He is a specialist in the history of early American law and the author or editor of several important books in this field.

JULIUS S. WATERMAN (1891-1943) was a law professor and Dean at the University of Arkansas Law School.

THORP L. WOLFORD (1918—) is a graduate of the Harvard Law School and a practicing lawyer in Louisville, Kentucky.

GEORGE E. WOODBINE (1876-1953) was a specialist in medieval English law and was active in both the Yale history department and law school from 1906 until 1944.

CONTENTS

PART ONE

General Introduction

I

An Introduction to Early American Legal History

DAVID H. FLAHERTY

The outlines of the history of early American law present a number of neatly defined problems that can serve initially to establish the dimensions of the field. A significant number of Englishmen settled in a series of different colonies in the New World in the seventeenth century. The motives and background of each group of settlers varied. The new colonies were independent of one another and enjoyed varied rates of growth in all spheres. By what laws did these residents of the New World choose to be governed? How did they envision the role of law in their society? What institutions did they create for their self-government, and what legal models did they follow? How did developments differ from colony to colony? While the colonists could not escape their legal heritage, they also were given unique opportunities for innovation and deviation from the old patterns of law and law enforcement. Such considerations shape the dominant issues in the legal history of seventeenth-century America.

After the initial establishment of law and legal institutions in each colony, there followed a period of consolidation and internal development, which extended in most instances until the eve of the Revolution. Legislatures and courts responded to the novel situations and changing requirements of law in the New World. This intervening time span was also the era of fairly rapid assimilation of some of the formalities and rigidities of the English common law system. The control and influence of the imperial authorities over each colony varied considerably, thus introducing another factor making for independent and variable development of law.

In the eighteenth century more English lawyers arrived, and the legal profession made its full-fledged appearance in each colony with an accompanying impact on the law. While most students are acquainted with such summary facts, little work has been accomplished to illuminate and substantiate them, with such noticeable exceptions as will be pointed out in the survey of the literature which follows.

The Revolution presented a crisis in the legal history of early America. Colonies that had always operated under the ultimate authority of the mother country in their legal development were now freed completely from any exterior controls over their laws and legal institutions. It became theoretically possible for the new states to throw off the yoke of the common law, which they had variously adapted from the mother country. Yet this did not really happen, despite initial murmurings about the desirability and feasibility of such action. Each colony took stock of its own relationship with the English common-law tradition, and through the so-called "reception statutes" established the extent to which the state would be formally bound by prior English legal experience.

The Revolution and the drawing up of the federal Constitution contained both starting points and elements of continuity in the history of American law. It now became possible for law to be Americanized over a couple of generations in visible fashion. The federal system introduced a completely new factor into the total picture. Anti-English sentiment stimulated a strong anti-common-law movement, accompanied by demands for codification of the laws to make them intelligible to a democratic nation. Yet by the 1830's it became once again apparent to anyone looking backward, that the United States was very much in the common-law tradition, however great were indigenous influences on that tradition. American judges continued to cite English cases, while by the middle of the nineteenth century, some of the most important American decisions were being similarly cited and printed in the English law reports. Yet industrialization in the early nineteenth century brought in its wake a whole series of novel legal problems that stimulated the building up of a truly American law.

This sketch of the development of early American law will be fleshed out by the various articles in this volume. Each author usually suggests the exact nature of his study in relation to the central questions of American legal history. If the broad outlines of this development are kept in mind, the varied interests of each essay can be fitted into the total picture.

The goals of the following bibliographical essay are relatively simple. There is no attempt to be historiographical in approach, that is to summarize early views of certain key problems and describe how the literature on the subject has developed. A few of the articles in the volume handle this task nicely. The primary aim is to direct attention to the best interpretations and scholarly productions. The focus will be on the highlights of this literature with a studied avoidance of the less adequate books and articles. The limits of an introduction also preclude consideration of some interesting areas of legal history, such as the development of admiralty law or some of the civil liberties issues, towards which so much excellent scholarly attention has been directed.

I. The Secondary Literature

1. THE LEGAL HERITAGE OF THE COLONISTS

The central theme of early American legal history, the transfer of the common law from England to America, raises some fundamental problems for the legal historian concerning the scope of the English common law in the seventeenth century and the legal heritage of the first settlers in America. Even a summary examination of such topics requires a diversion to twelfth- and thirteenth-century England and the actual origins of the English common law. One cannot begin to explain or understand the state of law in America in the seventeenth century without at least a cursory knowledge of medieval legal origins. Legal historians have of course long since recognized the importance of this early period, and the medieval era has spawned the great names in the study of English legal history. Some scholars have indeed suggested that this overemphasis on pre-sixteenth-century law in research and teaching should be corrected.

While it is perhaps unrealistic to expect the historian of American law to make extensive use of William Holdsworth's *A History of English Law*,[1] especially for introductory purposes, there are a number of survey works that provide a more gentle initiation into the intricacies of the English common law. The best known in

1. William S. Holdsworth (1871-1944), *A History of English Law*, 16 vols. (London, 1903-1966).

terms of coverage is Plucknett's *A Concise History of the Common Law*,[2] which has some especially good chapters on the literature of the law and enlightening topical chapters on such subjects as property and criminal law. George W. Keeton's *The Norman Conquest and the Common Law* (London, 1966) and Arthur R. Hogue's *Origins of the Common Law* (Bloomington, 1965) are also of value to the historian of American law. Alan Harding's *A Social History of English Law* (Pelican Books, Baltimore, 1966) is a pioneering effort covering the whole field of English legal history. However, it is written and organized in such a fashion as to make for difficult reading.

The great man of English legal history, Frederic William Maitland (1850-1906), has left us several volumes which are the best initiation to English legal history in the medieval period. With Sir Frederick Pollock, Maitland was the author of the classic *History of English Law before the Time of Edward I*, second edition, two volumes (Cambridge, Eng., 1898; Cambridge Univ. paperback, 1968). *The Constitutional History of England* (Cambridge, Eng., 1908; Cambridge Univ. paperback, 1965) is a masterly survey of the course of English public and private law. *The Forms of Action at Common Law* (Cambridge, Eng., 1909; Cambridge Univ. paperback, 1965) is a short and intelligible account of a most complex aspect of early legal history. Maitland had an extraordinary ability to explain intricate and complicated matters. Such qualities make his work of enduring value. Instead of listing some of the specialized monographs on medieval legal history, one need only mention Bryce Lyon's *A Constitutional and Legal History of Medieval England* (New York, 1960), which has thorough chapters on legal history as well as excellent notes on sources and up-to-date bibliographies.

Given the surfeit of available volumes on medieval legal history, the absence of similar studies for the sixteenth and seventeenth centuries is a major problem for students of early American legal history. Far too little is known about the state of English law, and especially English local law, in this period. The available information is much too oriented to the central courts at Westminster, which were not the dominant influence on the initial

2. Theodore F. T. Plucknett (1897-1965), *A Concise History of the Common Law*, 5th ed. (Boston, 1956). See also Frederick G. Kempin, Jr., *Legal History: Law and Social Change* (Englewood Cliffs, N.J., 1963).

establishment of laws and legal institutions in the New World. Even Holdsworth's detailed treatment of this era has been revised in recent years for subjects that have particular relevance to the colonies. Thomas G. Barnes's articles on Star Chamber in the *American Journal of Legal History* provide a case in point.[3] The only general work for this period is Charles Ogilvie's *The King's Government and the Common Law, 1471-1641* (Oxford, 1958), which is not very relevant to the interests of students of American legal history.

The extant studies of English local law, which had such a formidable influence on colonial legal development, are particularly inadequate. Sidney and Beatrice Webb's various studies of English local government[4] are informative for the late seventeenth century, and there is a slight discussion of local legal history in Wallace Notestein's *The English People on the Eve of Colonization* (New York, 1954; Harper Torchbook, 1962). There are volumes of English Quarter Sessions records in print, but these have not been studied with colonial interests in mind. Carl Bridenbaugh has recently demonstrated the successful employment of these English Quarter Sessions records in his study of the English people on the eve of the colonization of America.[5] One of the first tasks of students of colonial legal history should be to make more detailed studies of the state of English law in the early seventeenth century. A leading example of the need for early American legal historians to immerse themselves in English legal history was recently provided by Leonard W. Levy's *Origins of the Fifth Amendment* (New York, 1968), which is a brilliant foray into both English and American sources. Our knowledge of Sir Edward Coke is also limited, especially with respect to his influence on early American law. Catherine D. Bowen's biography of Coke is an excellent introduction to the entire subject in a volume that includes a substantial bibliography.[6] The scholar who attempts a perusal of Coke's

3. Thomas G. Barnes, "Star Chamber Mythology," *American Journal of Legal History*, V (1961), 1-11, and "Due Process and Slow Process in the Late Elizabethan-Early Stuart Star Chamber," *Am. Jour. of Leg. Hist.*, VI (1962), 221-249, 315-346.

4. See for example, Sidney and Beatrice Webb, *English Local Government from the Revolution to the Municipal Corporations Act: The Parish and The County* (London, 1906).

5. Carl Bridenbaugh, *Vexed and Troubled Englishmen, 1590-1642* (New York, 1968).

6. Catherine D. Bowen, *The Lion and the Throne: The Life and Times of*

Institutes will be made aware of the need for a modern scholarly edition of this seminal work.

The interests of American legal historians have been well served in recent years by studies of the seventeenth-century movement for English law reform, which was of particular importance for the establishment of legal systems in the colonies, especially in New England. The *Law Quarterly Review* has published an excellent review article by G. B. Nourse on "Law Reform under the Commonwealth and Protectorate."[7] There is also a Harvard doctoral dissertation (1957) on The Issue of Law Reform in the Puritan Revolution, by Charles R. Niehaus, and a less successful study by Stuart E. Prall, *The Agitation for Law Reform during the Puritan Revolution, 1640-1660* (The Hague, 1966).

Historians of early American law should undertake the stimulating experience of reading the great primary sources for English legal history, especially Glanville, Bracton, Coke, and Blackstone.[8] One can often learn more from direct exposure to these major figures than from tedious study of secondary sources replete with the details of controversies and encounters that are of little relevance to the particular interests of American legal historians.

2. THE SEVENTEENTH CENTURY

To a degree that varied from colony to colony the settlers of America enjoyed unique opportunities for legal innovation when they left the Old World. This suggests certain basic questions for the historian of seventeenth-century American law. What kinds of laws and what type of legal establishment did the colonists seek and create for themselves in the New World? To what extent were they inspired by the freedom, the opportunity, and the salutary neglect of the British government to make new laws, to do away with the laws and legal institutions they objected to in England, and to put into effect any of their reformist instincts in the

Sir Edward Coke (Boston, 1957). See also Samuel E. Thorne's Selden Society Lecture, *Sir Edward Coke, 1552-1952* (London, 1957).

7. G. B. Nourse, "Law Reform under the Commonwealth and Protectorate," *Law Quarterly Review*, LXXV (1959), 512-529.

8. Ranulf de Glanville (1130-1190), *The Treatise on the Laws and Customs of the Realm of England commonly called Glanvill*, ed. G. D. G. Hall (London, 1965); Henry de Bracton (d. 1268), *De Legibus et Consuetudinibus Angliae*, ed. Samuel E. Thorne, 2 vols. (Cambridge, Mass., 1967—); Edward Coke, *Institutes of the Laws of England*, 4 parts (London, 1628-1644); William Blackstone, *Commentaries on the Laws of England*, 4 vols. (Oxford, 1765-1769).

realm of law? Were the first settlers ultimately bound by the traditions of the Old World in their law-making? Did tradition overwhelm innovation in the making of laws? What regional variations affected all these questions? How did the New World alter the colonists' conceptions of the role of law in society?

Too few historians of seventeenth-century American law have posed such questions.[9] As a consequence only a handful of individuals have made significant contributions, and it is their work that has made this volume possible. The studies of certain others now serve primarily as grist for the mill of historiographers sifting the various ideas that have been put forward to explain the transfer of the common law from England to America. The late Zechariah Chafee, Jr., of the Harvard Law School provided the best analysis of these views in his article on "Colonial Courts and the Common Law,"[10] which is reprinted in this volume. Chafee's common sense and the perceptiveness of his judgments make this a very stimulating introduction to the study of early American legal history.

There are only a few general works on early American legal history. Richard B. Morris has produced a pioneering work of broad scope in his *Studies in the History of American Law*, second edition (New York, 1964). Professor Morris provided a unique and important introduction to the subject along with chapters on the land law, the rights of women, and the doctrines of tort law. A recent work by A. E. Dick Howard, *The Road from Runnymede: Magna Carta and Constitutionalism in America* (Charlottesville, Va., 1968) includes a survey of existing knowledge on the state of legal development in most of the original colonies. Francis R. Aumann's *The Changing American Legal System: Some Selected Phases* (Columbus, 1940) is the only general survey of American legal history to the present century. It provides a useful introduction to many primary sources and has an extensive bibliography.[11]

9. For a recent example of enlightened thinking concerning the initial premises of early American legal history, see Mark DeWolfe Howe, "The Sources and Nature of Law in Colonial Massachusetts," in George A. Billias, ed., *Law and Authority in Colonial America* (Barre, Mass., 1965), 1-16. Another generally important article is Stefan A. Riesenfeld, "Law-Making and Legislative Precedent in American Legal History," *Minnesota Law Review*, XXXIII (1949), 103-144.

10. Zechariah Chafee, Jr., "Colonial Courts and the Common Law," Massachusetts Historical Society, *Proceedings*, XVIII (Boston, 1952), 139-159.

11. Morris, *Studies in the History of American Law* also has an excellent

While the main themes that Aumann delineates are fairly accurate and the chapters of broad scope, the study is marred by lack of organization and the degeneration of the text into peculiarities and obscurities.

For the past thirty years George L. Haskins of the University of Pennsylvania Law School has been the most prolific and effective student of New England law in the seventeenth century. His book *Law and Authority in Early Massachusetts: A Study in Tradition and Design* (New York, 1960) is the most successful effort to date at dealing with the central legal problems of seventeenth-century America, especially in that part of his volume which deals less with general political history and more with legal issues. Haskins was one of the first to recognize the need to study law as it was involved with and shaped by the total society. In almost a dozen articles on New England law Haskins has made a further substantial and permanent contribution from this point of view. In these articles, several of which are included in this volume, Haskins has discussed such varied topics as partible inheritance, the recording system, codification, gavelkind, and dower.[12] Few American legal historians have been so productive.

Zechariah Chafee, Jr., and Joseph H. Smith of the Columbia

"Bibliographical Essay." There are two annual publications that frequently take note of the books and articles which have appeared in the field of legal history. The *New York University Law Review* has published an *Annual Survey of American Law* since 1942. The Harvard Law School Library prepares an *Annual Legal Bibliography*, 7 vols. (Cambridge, Mass., 1961—). See also Herta Prager and William W. Price, "A Bibliography on the History of the Courts of the Thirteen Original States, Maine, Ohio, and Vermont," *Am. Jour. of Leg. Hist.*, I (1957), 336-362, II (1958), 35-52, 148-154.

12. George L. Haskins, "The Beginnings of Partible Inheritance in the American Colonies," *Yale Law Journal*, LI (1942), 1280-1315; "The Beginnings of the Recording System in Massachusetts," *Boston University Law Review*, XXI (1941), 281-304; "Codification of the Law in Colonial Massachusetts: A Study in Comparative Law," *Indiana Law Journal*, XXX (1954), 1-17; "Court Records and History," *William and Mary Quarterly*, 3d Ser., V (1948), 547-552; "Precedents in English Ecclesiastical Practices for Criminal Punishments in Early Massachusetts," in Morris D. Forkosch, ed., *Essays in Legal History in Honor of Felix Frankfurter* (Indianapolis, 1966), 321-336; "Gavelkind and the Charter of Massachusetts Bay," Colonial Society of Massachusetts, *Publications*, XXXIV (Boston, 1943), 483-498; "Law and Colonial Society," *American Quarterly*, IX (1957) 354-364; "The Legal Heritage of Plymouth Colony," *University of Pennsylvania Law Review*, CX (1962), 847-859; "A Problem in the Reception of the Common Law in the Colonial Period," *Univ. of Penn. Law Review*, XCVII (1949), 842-53. Several of the above articles have been reprinted or were reprints from other journals.

Law School have furthered our knowledge of New England law in the seventeenth century by two superb introductions to volumes of printed court records for Suffolk county and Western Massachusetts.[13] These essays cover almost all aspects of the history of law in the seventeenth century, especially in terms of the structure of courts, the judiciary, criminal law, civil law, and civil procedure. Both scholars have managed to extract the meaning from the court records in a fashion that few other editors of colonial court records have matched. There is almost no parallel for the other colonies to the work of Chafee and Smith. If there is any argument to be had with these authorities, it is that their work tends to be carefully descriptive and lacking in historical analysis and generalization on a broad scale.

The history of law in colonial New York has enjoyed for many years the attentions of Julius Goebel, Jr., now professor emeritus at Columbia Law School. On the basis of his written works Goebel must be rated among the most stimulating writers of American legal history. His lifelong battle to uphold the highest standards for the study of legal history has resulted in some devastating reviews, which are recommended reading for any scholar who may become smug in his growing knowledge of this field.[14] Goebel's great work in American legal history is his *Law Enforcement in Colonial New York: A Study in Criminal Procedure (1664-1776)* (New York, 1944), written in collaboration with T. Raymond Naughton. This monumental study vividly illustrates the ultimate value of intensive and extensive manuscript research in early American legal history. Goebel has also published several seminal articles on both the seventeenth and eighteenth centuries, the most

13. Samuel E. Morison, ed., *Records of the Suffolk County Court, 1671-1680* . . . (Colonial Society of Massachusetts, *Publications*, XXIX-XXX [Boston, 1933]) Joseph H. Smith, ed., *Colonial Justice in Western Massachusetts, 1639-1702: The Pynchon Court Record, an Original Judges' Diary of the Administration of Justice in the Springfield Courts in the Massachusetts Bay Colony* (Cambridge, Mass., 1961).

14. See for example "*Ex Parte* Clio," Goebel's review of W. W. Crosskey, *Politics and the Constitution in the History of the United States*, 2 vols. (Chicago, 1953) in the *Columbia Law Review*, LIV (1954), 450-483; also his review of Charles Page Smith, *James Wilson: Founding Father, 1742-1798* (Chapel Hill, 1956) in the *University of Pennsylvania Law Review*, CV (1957), 1027-1032. A famous exchange between Goebel and Charles McLean Andrews began with a review by the former in the *American Historical Review*, XLIII (1938), 403-406, and culminated with a response by Andrews in his *Colonial Period of American History*, 4 vols. (New Haven, 1934-1938), IV, 222-223.

important being his "King's Law and Local Custom in Seventeenth Century New England," *Columbia Law Review,* XXXI (1931), 416-448. In this heavily documented work Goebel reminded scholars of the formative influence of English local law on the legal thinking of the first settlers. While this influence was not perhaps as overwhelming as Goebel argued on the basis of the Plymouth Colony experience, this aspect of early American law had been previously neglected, thus introducing a significant factor into the over-all picture.

Goebel's brilliance has been most apparent in those articles where he could combine his mastery of the sources for both England and America with his gifts for survey and summary about the developing state of Anglo-American law. An early example on a fairly standard topic would be "The Courts and the Law in Colonial New York."[15] Two broader studies are his "Introduction" to *Law Enforcement in Colonial New York,* cited above, and "*Ex Parte* Clio," *Columbia Law Review,* LIV (1954), 450-483. Goebel is particularly critical of those interpretations of American legal history which dismiss colonial legal history as unimportant and of the general ignorance of the actual state of affairs implicit in the propagation of such views. His articles emphasize the gradual reception of the English common law in New York and the quickening pace of developments in the eighteenth century. Goebel's generalizations are perceptive and sophisticated, but his use of the English tongue is occasionally overwhelming, for he does not fully share Maitland's capacity to make legal history comprehensible.

The legal history of the colonial South has been seriously neglected.[16] While there are a few monographs of varying quality, almost nothing of general distinction has appeared in article form. The first volume of Philip A. Bruce's *Institutional History of Virginia in the Seventeenth Century* (New York, 1910) is still a useful general work on Virginia. Bruce's familiarity with the manuscript sources for legal history has given the book an enduring quality.

15. Julius Goebel, Jr., "The Courts and the Law in Colonial New York," Alexander C. Flick, ed., *History of the State of New York,* III (New York, 1933), 3-43.

16. The legal history of Pennsylvania has suffered similar neglect, although Christopher K. Seglem made an excellent beginning in A Legal History of Early Pennsylvania, 1681-1701 (unpubl. senior thesis, Princeton University, 1968). See also William H. Loyd, *The Early Courts of Pennsylvania* (Boston, 1910).

While there are several other volumes on more specialized topics, all suffer from the lack of more general works in the field which could synthesize the results of their investigations.[17]

Maryland has fortunately attracted the attention of Joseph H. Smith as one of the editors of a volume of *Court Records of Prince Georges County, Maryland, 1696-1699* (Washington, 1964). While the introduction is somewhat limited in its focus, it provides an excellent survey of the legal history of Maryland, especially if used in conjunction with two recent essays by Smith on "The Foundations of Law in Maryland: 1634-1715" and "The Provincial Courts and the Laws of Maryland: 1675-1715."[18]

A major inadequacy of extant studies of the history of American law in the seventeenth century is the absence of studies that compare the colonies with the mother country and one colony with another.[19] At the present time such an approach to the study of legal history would appear to have great possibilities. Such undertakings may well do away with the traditional lament about having to study thirteen separate jurisdictions, for in colony after colony the historian is often much more impressed with the similarities than the differences. The distinctions between colonies exist, of course, but even they have not been explained or described except in the broadest terms. The uniqueness of the New England Puritans' reforms of English law can be questioned, for example, once one has examined the legal records of seventeenth-century Virginia.

The emphasis on differences in early American law has also tended to play down the traditional element and the continuities between English and American law. What kinds of restraints re-

17. George L. Chumbley, *Colonial Justice in Virginia* (Richmond, 1938); Susie M. Ames, *Studies of the Virginia Eastern Shore in the Seventeenth Century* (Richmond, 1940); Arthur P. Scott, *Criminal Law in Colonial Virginia* (Chicago, 1930); Hugh F. Rankin, *Criminal Trial Proceedings in the General Court of Colonial Virginia* (Williamsburg, 1965); Raphael Semmes, *Crime and Punishment in Early Maryland* (Baltimore, 1938); Paul M. McCain, *The County Court in North Carolina before 1750* (Trinity College Historical Society, *Historical Papers*, Ser. XXXI [Durham, N.C., 1954]).

18. Joseph H. Smith, "The Foundations of Law in Maryland: 1634-1715," in G. A. Billias, ed., *Law and Authority in Colonial America* (Barre, Mass., 1965), 92-115; "The Provincial Courts and the Laws of Maryland: 1675-1715," in Forkosch, ed., *Essays in Legal History in Honor of Felix Frankfurter*, 387-402.

19. A weak effort at a comparative study is Cyrus Harreld Karraker, *The Seventeenth Century Sheriff: A Comparative Study of the Sheriff in England and the Chesapeake Colonies, 1607-1689* (Chapel Hill, 1930).

stricted the colonist's freedom to innovate in the legal sphere? The answers to this and the myriad other questions that could be asked may not be sophisticated or far removed from the probing talents of the scholar, yet the fact remains that little of this kind of work has even been attempted. The field is not barren, as this cursory survey has indicated, yet it has not yielded a bountiful harvest.

3. *1690–1776*

In the seventeenth century the colonists had struggled with the establishment of English law in the New World. After 1689 the most difficult problems that the historian must confront arise from indigenous developments. To what extent did the experience of life in America influence changes in the law? What regional variations developed within the American colonies? What was the impact of fluctuating imperial control on the evolution of American law? Such questions assume that law was not static, but constantly changing and subject to alteration. As aids in seeking out their answers, there are only a handful of significant secondary works.

With respect to the development of law in pre-Revolutionary America, we have already mentioned several especially important survey articles by Julius Goebel, Jr. There is also an informative article by Charles McLean Andrews entitled "The Influence of Colonial Conditions as Illustrated in the Connecticut Intestacy Law."[20] Much broader in scope than the title implies, this article is one of the best studies to date of any aspect of American law around 1700. John M. Murrin of Washington University of St. Louis has recently completed an excellent doctoral dissertation, which has some particularly relevant chapters on the evolution of colonial law, the courts, and the legal profession. His work is entitled Anglicizing an American Colony: The Transformation of Provincial Massachusetts (Yale University, 1966). While one can quarrel with Murrin's thesis about Anglicization, the research involved in his chapters on legal history between 1690 and 1776 is extremely detailed and sound. Duplication of his work for other colonies should prove fruitful.

20. Charles McLean Andrews, "The Influence of Colonial Conditions as Illustrated in the Connecticut Intestacy Law," *Select Essays in Anglo-American Legal History* (Boston, 1907), I, 431-463.

The reassertion of royal control over colonial legal developments in the late seventeenth century presents legal historians with another significant theme. Joseph H. Smith has made this area his special domain in two important works. His *Appeals to the Privy Council from the American Plantations* (New York, 1950) is a monumental study in the tradition of Goebel and Naughton's *Law Enforcement in Colonial New York.* The problem presented by such comprehensive and detailed studies is that they almost defy assimilation except by the most ardent student. These works, therefore, stand unchallenged and indeed almost unread. Because of the scope and centrality of Smith's subject, his *Appeals to the Privy Council* is one of a handful of books of general importance for the history of early American law. In a learned, careful, albeit difficult fashion, Smith grapples with some of the key issues. He has developed a further aspect of this imperial problem in his article on "Administrative Control of the Courts of the American Plantations," *Columbia Law Review,* LXI (1961), 1210-1253.

The development of the legal profession in early America has attracted the attention of a number of legal historians. Charles Warren's *A History of the American Bar* (Boston, 1913) is the most frequently cited work. The continued popularity of this path-breaking volume is discouraging, because it contains many factual errors and inadequacies in interpretation. Yet the coverage of primary sources, particularly in the post-1789 period, is encyclopedic and the work provides a valuable introduction. Warren (1868-1954) was not very critical and did not pose such central questions as why, for example, a legal profession did not develop until the eighteenth century. One would expect a scholar writing fifty years later, however, to be much more sophisticated and perceptive in his broad analysis of the problems. This description, unfortunately, does not match Anton H. Chroust's *The Rise of the Legal Profession in America,* two volumes (Norman, Okla., 1965), despite the author's substantial knowledge of some primary and most of the secondary sources.[21] The series of weak generalizations and misstatements in his first volume on "The

21. See Donald P. Kommers, "Reflections on Professor Chroust's *The Rise of the Legal Profession in America,*" *Am. Jour. of Leg. Hist.*, X (1966), 201-213; Stanley N. Katz, "Looking Backward: The Early History of American Law," *University of Chicago Law Review,* XXXIII (1966), 868-873; and another critical review by Geoffrey C. Hazard, Jr., in the *University of California Los Angeles Law Review,* XIII (1966), 487-491.

Colonial Experience" should not have appeared in print. However, in his second volume beginning with the post-Revolutionary period the author's reliance on printed primary and secondary sources has not led him so far astray. Paul Hamlin's *Legal Education in Colonial New York* (New York, 1939) was a much more successful study than either of the above despite its fairly limited scope. The author's liberal use of primary sources and extensive appendixes are of genuine value for an understanding of the subject. Once again, this topic has not received similar treatment for other colonies.

The editors of the *Legal Papers of John Adams* (Cambridge, Mass., 1965; Atheneum paperbacks, New York, 1968), L. Kinvin Wroth and Hiller B. Zobel, have provided legal historians with perhaps the best study to date of the colonial lawyer in their "Introduction" to the three volumes. Coupled with two other important articles, such works do much to remedy the deficiencies of Warren and Chroust. Clement Eaton has written "A Mirror of the Southern Colonial Lawyer," which discusses Patrick Henry, Thomas Jefferson, and Waightstill Avery in their legal capacities. Milton M. Klein has published a similar article of high quality on "The Rise of the New York Bar: The Legal Career of William Livingston."[22] Eaton and Klein carry their subjects chronologically to the eve of the Revolution and center attention upon the important question of the role of lawyers in the coming of the Revolution. The problem was best posed by Richard B. Morris in his "Legalism versus Revolutionary Doctrine in New England," *New England Quarterly*, IV (1931), 195-215. In an article on "The Lawyer and the Revolution," Erwin C. Surrency, editor of *The American Journal of Legal History*, has summarized our current knowledge of this topic while concentrating on the attitude of lawyers towards the Stamp Act.[23]

22. Clement Eaton, "A Mirror of the Southern Colonial Lawyer," *Wm. and Mary Qtly.*, 3d Ser., VIII (1951), 520-534; Milton M. Klein, "The Rise of the New York Bar: The Legal Career of William Livingston," *Wm. and Mary Qtly.*, 3d Ser., XV (1958), 334-357; Klein has another pertinent article, "Prelude to Revolution in New York: Jury Trials and Judicial Tenure," *Wm. and Mary Qtly.*, 3d Ser., XVII (1960), 439-462. See also Alan M. Smith's recent study, Virginia Lawyers, 1680-1776: The Birth of an American Profession, (unpubl. Ph.D. diss., Johns Hopkins University, 1967).

23. Erwin C. Surrency, "The Lawyer and the Revolution," *Am. Jour. of Leg. Hist.*, VIII (1964), 125-135; see also Surrency's "The Courts in the American Colonies," *Am. Jour. of Leg. Hist.*, XI (1967), 253-276.

Nevertheless there remains both opportunity and need for the study of the role that lawyers played in the American Revolution. The definitive works have not yet appeared. In an age of quantification it should be noted that no scholar has kept track of every lawyer in each colony, of his activities before and during the Revolution, and which side individual lawyers chose, although a satisfactory beginning was made by Frank B. Ward in a Princeton University senior thesis (1966) entitled The American Revolution and the Legal Profession in New Jersey, 1740-1799. Curiously enough the role of law and of legal conceptions in the coming of the Revolution has similarly been little studied. There are a few suggestive articles such as those by R. A. Humphreys on "The Rule of Law and the American Revolution" and Charles F. Mullett, "Coke and the American Revolution,"[24] while Mullett has produced a catalogue of Revolutionary thinking on fundamental law in his *Fundamental Law and the American Revolution, 1760-1776* (New York, 1933; reprinted in 1966).

4. 1776–1830

The successful culmination of the Revolution had important legal implications as ultimate control over colonial laws was transferred from Westminster and London to thirteen independent states. By what laws would the various jurisdictions now choose to be governed? Would there be a wholesale rejection of the English common-law tradition? What aspects of this common-law tradition would be recognized and accepted in America? The development of an American law which had begun with the first settlements could now proceed unhindered.

Roscoe Pound (1870-1964), the famous scholar and dean of the Harvard Law School, entitled his work on the period in legal history from the Revolution to the Civil War *The Formative Era of American Law* (Boston, 1938). Although this particular volume is more a work of jurisprudence than of legal history, Pound's overriding thesis has had a significant influence on the interpreta-

24. R. A. Humphreys, "The Rule of Law and the American Revolution," *Law Qtly. Rev.*, LIII (1937), 80-98; Charles F. Mullett, "Coke and the American Revolution," *Economica*, XII (London, 1932), 457-471. See also the pertinent comments by Daniel Boorstin on the interpretation of the American Revolution in his review of the first volume of Julian P. Boyd, ed., *The Papers of Thomas Jefferson* (Princeton, N.J., 1950), in the *Wm. and Mary Qtly.*, 3d Ser., VII (1950), 596-609.

tion of the period. The major inadequacy is Pound's notion that colonial law was simple and unsophisticated to suit the society. According to this view the chief developments in American law are post-Revolutionary. As Julius Goebel, Jr., has taken pains to show,[25] such an interpretation bears little relation to the facts of the matter and contributes greatly to the neglect of colonial legal history.

At the most general level of post-Revolutionary search for an American law, legal historians have been stimulated by Perry Miller's *The Life of the Mind in America, from the Revolution to the Civil War* (New York, 1965), which devotes a major section to legal developments. This volume has even greater value if used in conjunction with a paperback collection of primary sources edited by Miller (1905-1964) under the title *The Legal Mind in America: From Independence to the Civil War* (Anchor Books, Garden City, N.Y., 1962). These documents are really the sources that Miller is interpreting in his later volume. Although Miller treats legal history primarily as an exercise in intellectual history, his contributions are important. A penetrating review essay by Lawrence M. Friedman, "Heart against Head: Perry Miller and the Legal Mind," *Yale Law Journal*, LXXVII (1968), 1244-1259, makes a strong case against Miller from the point of view of the need to study law in the context of society.

A detailed study by Elizabeth G. Brown, *British Statutes in American Law, 1776-1836* (Ann Arbor, 1964), constitutes the most satisfactory examination to date of the whole question of the "reception" statutes and the attempts made to determine what the laws were in each jurisdiction, and especially which English statutes were part of the common law that had already been brought over to America. Mark DeWolfe Howe of the Harvard Law School wrote an informative case study of the reception of English law that is a model of its kind.[26] Zechariah Chafee, Jr., used the occasion of a review of Daniel Boorstin's edition of *Delaware Cases* to investigate the state of law in the courts of late eighteenth-century Delaware

25. See Julius Goebel, Jr., "Introduction," to Goebel and Naughton, *Law Enforcement in Colonial New York* (New York, 1944), xvii-xxxix, which is reprinted in this volume.

26. Mark DeWolfe Howe, "The Process of Outlawry in New York: A Study of the Selective Reception of English Law," *Cornell Law Quarterly*, XXIII (1938), 559-579.

and to point the way toward broader generalizations and interpretations.[27]

Sir William Blackstone (1723-1780) was one of the greatest influences on the development of American law from the date of the publication of his *Commentaries* in the late 1760's, and the numerous books and articles on Blackstone are of much importance to the student of legal history. Daniel J. Boorstin presented Blackstone against the intellectual background of his time in *The Mysterious Science of the Law* (Cambridge, Mass., 1941; Beacon Press, Boston, 1958). The standard biography by David A. Lockmiller, *Sir William Blackstone* (Chapel Hill, 1938), includes a well-constructed chapter on "Blackstone in America." Walton Hamilton has indicated some of the inadequacies of this and other biographies of Blackstone in a review article, "The Law and Mr. Blackstone," *Columbia Law Review*, XXXIX (1939), 724-741. The most important article on Blackstone from the point of view of American legal history is Julius S. Waterman's "Thomas Jefferson and Blackstone's Commentaries," *Illinois Law Review*, XXVII (1933), 629-659, an excellent summary of the problems presented by Blackstone and his great influence on American law.

While this survey is not concerned with the development of law on the federal level after 1789, the neglected opportunities to study legal history on the state level deserve passing attention, particularly those which could appear in the format of studies of individual justices and famous lawyers. Leonard Levy of Brandeis provided an excellent model for such undertakings in his biography of Chief Justice Lemuel Shaw of Massachusetts: *The Law of the Commonwealth and Chief Justice Shaw, The Evolution of American Law, 1830-1860* (Cambridge, Mass., 1957; Harper Torchbook, New York, 1967). Studies should be undertaken of such important figures as Nathan Dane, Zephaniah Swift, Nathaniel Chipman, and even James Kent.[28]

The tremendous increase in contemporary writings on American law which were published after the Revolution makes the study of legal history for that period less dependent on secondary literature. It is fairly easy to return to the printed primary sources and

27. Zechariah Chafee, Jr., "Review," of Daniel Boorstin, ed., *Delaware Cases, 1792-1830*, 3 vols. (St. Paul, 1943), in *Harvard Law Review*, LVII (1944), 407-430.

28. The standard biography of Kent is not particularly helpful for his role in American legal history. See John T. Horton, *James Kent, a Study in Conservatism, 1763-1847* (New York, 1939).

draw one's own conclusions. Still there are several articles that have appeared in recent years which smooth the path for the scholar. William E. Nelson made an ambitious attempt to study changes in one area of substantive law in this period in his "Emerging Notions of Modern Criminal Law in the Revolutionary Era: An Historical Perspective," *New York University Law Review*, XLII (1967) 450-482. Maxwell Bloomfield's "William Sampson and the Codifiers: The Roots of American Legal Reform, 1820-1830," is an excellent survey of the attacks on the common-law tradition and the movement for codification.[29] Gary B. Nash has written an important study of the changing social characteristics of the legal profession in the first half of the nineteenth century.[30]

No survey touching on nineteenth-century American legal history can afford to overlook the work of James Willard Hurst of the Wisconsin Law School, who has created an entirely new school of legal historians by taking a very broad approach.[31] Hurst's efforts to discover the principles underlying prevailing statutes and common-law decisions, especially in the formulation of law by legislatures, make plain a neglected area of earlier American legal history.

II. The Primary Sources

1. GENERAL

One of the consequences of the lack of detailed research in many areas of early American legal history is that the scholar has an even greater obligation than usual to do primary research on a vast assortment of topics—this, over and above the usual need for the legal historian to delve into a massive array of sources. Attention

29. Maxwell Bloomfield, "William Sampson and the Codifiers: The Roots of American Legal Reform, 1820-1830," *Am. Jour. of Leg. Hist.*, XI (1967), 234-252. See also the following relevant articles: Erwin C. Surrency, "When the Common Law was Unpopular in Pennsylvania," *Pennsylvania Bar Association Quarterly*, XXXIII (1962), 291-300; and P. Stein, "The Attraction of the Civil Law in Post-Revolutionary America," *Virginia Law Review*, LII (1966), 403-434.

30. Gary B. Nash, "The Philadelphia Bench and Bar, 1800-1861," *Comparative Studies in Society and History*, VII (1965), 203-220.

31. James Willard Hurst's major books are the following: *The Growth of American Law: The Law Makers* (Boston, 1950); *Law and the Conditions of Freedom in the Nineteenth-Century United States* (Madison, 1956; University of Wisconsin paperback, Madison, 1964); *Law and Social Process In United States History* (Ann Arbor, 1960); *Justice Holmes on Legal History* (New York, 1964); and *Law and Economic Growth: The Legal History of the Lumber Industry in Wisconsin, 1836-1915* (Cambridge, Mass., 1964).

will now be focused on some of the most significant general sources available for the history of early American law.[32] Although almost every diarist, traveler, and chronicler said something about law, few delved deeply enough to be worthy of specific mention. The focus will continue to be upon rich sources or sources that have been seriously neglected. Fortunately several recent innovations and publications have made the legal historian's task considerably simpler. Chief among these is Clifford K. Shipton's microprint edition of *Early American Imprints, 1639-1800,* which provides a copy of every work printed in America before 1800, a collection especially useful for the eighteenth century.

There is only one general volume that contains primary sources for the entire history of early American law, Mark DeWolfe Howe's *Readings in American Legal History* (Cambridge, Mass., 1949). While it is not a volume for the beginner, and shares some of the weaknesses of most attempts to create legal history case books, this is by far the leading product of law school courses on American legal history.[33] Unfortunately the book is out of print, and copies are almost unobtainable.

For the seventeenth century there are four sources of a general nature that deserve the particular attention of the legal historian. John Winthrop's *Journal*[34] is especially central to the evolution of law in Massachusetts Bay Colony during the first two decades, when Winthrop's hand was at the helm. Winthrop had received some legal training, had served as a justice of the peace in his county in England, and had practiced as a lawyer in a Westminster court in the years before coming to America. His ideas on law are of much importance. Similarly the observations by Thomas Lechford of Massachusetts during his brief sojourn there as a lawyer deserve our

32. Readers may wish to consult Richard B. Morris, "The Sources of Early American Law: Colonial Period," *West Virginia Law Quarterly,* XL (1934), 212-223; and Eldon R. James, "A List of Legal Treatises Printed in the British Colonies and the American States before 1801," in *Harvard Legal Essays: Written in Honor of and Presented to Joseph Henry Beale and Samuel Williston* (Cambridge, Mass., 1934), 159-211.

33. James Willard Hurst pointed out some of the limitations of the Howe volume in the *Harvard Law Rev.,* LXIII (1950), 553-555. The most recent case book is Joseph H. Smith, *Cases and Materials on the Development of Legal Institutions* (St. Paul, 1965).

34. James Kendall Hosmer, ed., *Winthrop's Journal: History of New England, 1630-1649,* 2 vols. (New York, 1908). See the pertinent note on "The Rule of Law in Colonial Massachusetts," *Univ. of Penn. Law Rev.,* CVIII (1960), 1001-1036.

attention.[35] One of the best and most neglected legal history sources for the seventeenth century is a tract written in the 1690's by Gershom Bulkeley, a Harvard educated minister who had turned to the practice of law in Connecticut after 1676.[36] His "Will and Doom" reveals a royalist bias and his preference for English common law rather than the law of Connecticut. The one significant southern source of this kind is a presentation made to the Board of Trade in 1697 by three Virginia royal officials, two of whom were among the leading lawyers of their day. The authors, Henry Hartwell, James Blair, and Edward Chilton, provided the home government with a thorough survey of the legal system and institutions of Virginia.[37]

For the study of eighteenth-century legal history, printed primary sources of every type are more readily available. *An Essay upon the Government of the English Plantations on the Continent of America*, written by an anonymous Virginian in 1701, contains some excellent information for the legal historian.[38] Another important work is *The Rights of the Inhabitants of Maryland to the Benefit of the English Laws* by Daniel Dulany, Sr., first printed at Annapolis in 1728.[39]

A unique source for the eighteenth century is Charles McLean Andrews' edition of Francis Fane's *Reports on the Laws of Connecticut* (New Haven, 1915). Fane was legal counsel to the Board of Trade and from 1733 on prepared annual reports containing his evaluations of the legality and acceptability of certain colonial laws. These opinions of an English lawyer on colonial laws are of great

35. Thomas Lechford, *Note-Book Kept by Thomas Lechford, Esq. Lawyer, in Boston Massachusetts Bay, from June 27, 1638, to July 29, 1641* (American Antiquarian Society, *Transactions and Collections*, VII [Worcester, 1885]). See also Lechford's *Plain Dealing: Or, Newes from New-England* (London, 1642), reprinted in Massachusetts Historical Society, *Collections*, 3d Ser., III (Boston, 1833), 55-128.

36. Gershom Bulkeley, "Will and Doom, Or the Miseries of Connecticut by and under an Usurped and Arbitrary Power," Connecticut Historical Society, *Collections*, III (Hartford, 1895), 69-269.

37. Henry Hartwell *et al.*, *The Present State of Virginia, and the College*, ed. H. D. Farish (Williamsburg, 1940).

38. Louis B. Wright, ed., *An Essay Upon the Government of the English Plantations on the Continent of America* (London, 1701; San Marino, Calif., 1945).

39. Daniel Dulaney, *The Rights of the Inhabitants of Maryland to the Benefit of the English Laws* (Annapolis, 1728), reprinted in *Johns Hopkins Studies in History and Political Science*, XXI (1903), 543-568. See Aubrey C. Land, *The Dulaneys of Maryland* (Baltimore, 1955).

value. Another relatively unused source collection is *The Talcott Papers*, two volumes of documents and correspondence dating from the Connecticut governorship of Joseph Talcott, 1724-1741, and containing the record of important as well as famous litigation.[40] A superb new edition of James Alexander's *A Brief Narrative of the Case and Trial of John Peter Zenger* (Cambridge, Mass., 1963) has recently appeared, edited with an excellent introduction by Stanley N. Katz. The Zenger trial is more celebrated than important, yet this new edition, also available in paperback, should make its mark as a reading assignment in legal history courses.

The current publication programs of the papers of the Founding Fathers have had some direct benefits for the historian of early American law.[41] While Jefferson's legal papers will eventually be published as a separate series of *The Papers of Thomas Jefferson*, edited by Julian P. Boyd, the main volumes contain pertinent material. Professor Morris' promised edition of the Jay papers should be revealing of this distinguished legal career.[42] In two other cases rewarding volumes have already appeared. L. Kinvin Wroth and Hiller B. Zobel have brilliantly edited *The Legal Papers of John Adams* in three volumes (Cambridge, Mass., 1965). Their work is one of the most significant contributions to American legal history in recent years. The *Diary and Autobiography of John Adams* for the period before the Revolution when Adams practiced law is also informative on the making of a career at the law in early America.[43] Alexander Hamilton's legal career has begun to receive more attention since the appearance of the first volume of *The Law Practice of Alexander Hamilton* (New York, 1964), under the distinguished editorship of Julius Goebel, Jr. The topical arrangement of cases,

40. Mary Kingsbury Talcott, ed., *The Talcott Papers* (Conn. Hist. Soc., *Coll.*, IV-V [Hartford, 1892-1896]). On this subject, consult the article by Charles McLean Andrews printed in this volume.

41. See Richard B. Morris, "The Current Statesmen's Papers Publications Program: An Appraisal from the Point of View of the Legal Historian," *Am. Jour. of Leg. Hist.*, XI (1967), 95-106.

42. See also Herbert A. Johnson, John Jay: Colonial Lawyer, (unpubl. Ph.D. diss., Columbia University, 1965) and his "Civil Procedure in John Jay's New York," *Am. Jour. of Leg. Hist.*, XI (1967), 69-80. Johnson is Associate Editor of the Papers of John Marshall. His published works also include *The Law Merchant and Negotiable Instruments in Colonial New York, 1664-1730* (Chicago, 1963) and "The Advent of Common Law in Colonial New York," in Billias, ed., *Law and Authority in Colonial America*, 74-91.

43. L. H. Butterfield *et al.*, eds., *Diary and Autobiography of John Adams*, 4 vols. (Cambridge, Mass., 1961).

prefaced by an introduction to each group, is of particular value in the study of substantive law.

In both seventeenth- and eighteenth-century America many judges were not formally trained in the law, and until the early eighteenth century these lay judges were often dependent on the innumerable editions of such justice of the peace handbooks as those of Dalton and Lambarde.[44] The historian of early American law received a great boon when such handbooks for judges began to be written in America, beginning in Philadelphia in 1722 with the appearance of an anonymous volume entitled *The Conductor Generalis: or, the Office, Duty and Authority of Justices Of the Peace.* A second enlarged edition was published in Philadelphia and also in New York in 1749. In Virginia in 1736 George Webb published his *The Office and Authority of a Justice of the Peace.* Such books normally included an alphabetical discussion of all the powers and duties of justices of the peace, a collection of legal forms, and directions for the conduct of judicial proceedings. The duties of minor officials were also normally included. These volumes are of almost matchless importance for the legal historian, yet they have rarely been studied and assimilated. When it is noted that a person like George Webb was a practicing justice of the peace in New Kent County, the importance of his comments and generalizations for an understanding of Virginia law is readily apparent. The indebtedness of one American author to another in these handbooks has not been studied nor has the manner in which their works differed from one another and from their English predecessors been examined. Before the Revolution justice of the peace handbooks had also been published in North Carolina, South Carolina, and New Jersey.[45]

Sir William Blackstone's *Commentaries on the Laws of England* were published in four volumes at Oxford from 1765-1769 and in a first American edition at Philadelphia in 1771-1772. The *Commentaries* immediately became the basic text for the training of

44. Michael Dalton, *The Countrey Justice* (London, 1618), and many subsequent editions; William Lambarde, *Eirenarcha, or of the Office of the Justices of Peace* (London, 1581), and several subsequent editions. See also John Philip Dawson, *A History of Law Judges* (Cambridge, Mass., 1960).

45. William Simpson, *The Practical Justice of the Peace . . .* (Charleston, S.C., 1761); James Parker, *The Conductor Generalis: or, the Office, Duty, and Authority of Justices of the Peace . . .* (Woodbridge, N.J., 1764); Richard Starke, *The Office and Authority of a Justice of Peace . . .* (Williamsburg, 1774); James Davis, *The Office and Authority of a Justice of Peace* (New Bern, N.C., 1774).

American lawyers and retained this dominant position well into the nineteenth century, necessitating innumerable American editions of the work.[46] Attempts to Americanize Blackstone were a significant aspect of this enthusiasm. The most important and earliest such effort was "Tucker's Blackstone," edited and indeed almost co-authored, by St. George Tucker (1752-1827), a prominent Virginia judge and professor of law at The College of William and Mary.[47] This is one of the truly great sources for American legal history. Tucker grappled with many of the central problems of American law in the appendixes of each volume, which he described as "short tracts upon such subjects as appeared necessary to form a connected View of the Laws of Virginia as a member of the federal union." In the five separate volumes these appendixes on a diversity of topics totaled approximately eight hundred pages. An even more drastic reorganization of Blackstone appeared in 1831 when Judge John Reed of the Pennsylvania Court of Common Pleas published his *Pennsylvania Blackstone*.[48]

Independence from Great Britain necessitated the publication of American law reports, if the common-law tradition was to be gradually Americanized. Judges' opinions in superior court cases began to be written and kept on file in Connecticut in the mid-1780's, leading to the publication of the first volume of American reports by Ephraim Kirby in 1789.[49] The whole subject has never been seriously studied. Why were opinions not written and filed in the colonial period? Under what circumstances did Connecticut take the lead? How had cases been decided in relationship to one another at an earlier period? Why were other states collectively slow to imitate the Connecticut practice? These are but a few of the obvious questions that deserve examination.[50] The second

46. An edition of Blackstone edited by William G. Hammond and published in San Francisco in 1890 contained a "Bibliography of the *Commentaries*," I, xxi-xxvii, listing the many editions of the work.

47. St. George Tucker, *Blackstone's Commentaries: with Notes of Reference to the Constitution and Laws, of the Federal Government of the United States; and of the Commonwealth of Virginia*, 5 vols. (Philadelphia, 1803).

48. John Reed, *Pennsylvania Blackstone: Being a Modification of the Commentaries of Sir William Blackstone, with Numerous Alterations and Additions, Designed to Present an Elementary Exposition of the Entire Laws of Pennsylvania*, 3 vols. (Carlisle, Pa., 1831).

49. Ephraim Kirby, *Reports of Cases Adjudged in the Superior Court of the State of Connecticut from the year 1785, to May 1788 . . .* (Litchfield, Conn., 1789).

50. See Frederick G. Kempin, Jr., "Precedent and Stare Decisis: The Critical Years, 1800 to 1850," *Am. Jour. of Leg. Hist.*, III (1959), 28-54.

American reporter was Alexander J. Dallas of Pennsylvania, who began publishing in 1790.[51] Two other reporters, Judge Nathaniel Chipman of Vermont and Judge Jesse Root of Connecticut, included in their volumes much more than the simple reports of cases.[52] Chipman added "Dissertations on the Statute adopting the Common Law of England, the Statute of Conveyances . . ." and an appendix "containing forms of special pleadings in several cases." Judge Root prefaced his two volumes with some significant "observations upon the Government and Laws of Connecticut."

Independence also touched off a flood of important legal treatises that rapidly created a library on American law. In 1801, for example, the attorney general of Massachusetts, James Sullivan, published *The History of Land Titles in Massachusetts* (Boston), which was the first comprehensive work on real estate law in this country. In 1804 a three-volume edition of *The Works of James Wilson* appeared in Philadelphia. Wilson, in addition to being an associate justice of the United States Supreme Court, was one of the first law professors in this country. His *Works*, which have just been republished in the John Harvard Library, include his lectures on law delivered in 1790 and 1791.[53]

The post-Revolutionary attacks on the English common-law tradition and the alternative recommendations for codification can be initially viewed to great advantage in the work of Joseph Hopkinson and William Sampson.[54] Hopkinson was a supporter of the common law and attempted to demonstrate the absurdity of projects to abolish it. The much more colorful William Sampson, a successful New York lawyer and Irish emigré, was the most famous opponent of the common-law tradition and in his day a leading exponent of codification as the viable antidote.

In the 1820's massive compilations of American law made their first appearance, beginning with Nathan Dane's *General Abridg-*

51. Alexander J. Dallas, *Reports of Cases, Ruled and Adjudged in the Courts of Pennsylvania, before and since the Revolution* (Philadelphia, 1790).

52. Nathaniel Chipman, *Reports and Dissertations* (Rutland, Vt., 1793); Jesse Root, *Reports of Cases Adjudged in the Superior Court and Supreme Court of Errors 1789-1793* . . . , 2 vols. (Hartford, 1798-1802).

53. Robert G. McCloskey, ed., *The Works of James Wilson*, 2 vols. (Cambridge, Mass., 1967).

54. Joseph Hopkinson, *Considerations on the Abolition of the Common Law in the United States* (Philadelphia, 1809); William Sampson, *An Anniversary Discourse Delivered before the Historical Society of New York* . . . (New York, 1824).

ment and Digest of American Law, with Occasional Notes and Comments, nine volumes (Boston, 1823-1829). Dane's work was soon overshadowed by the publication of James Kent's *Commentaries on American Law*, four volumes (New York, 1826-1830). Kent has since been known as the "American Blackstone." His massive judicial experience permeated the pages of the text. Modeled after Blackstone's own mode of presentation, Kent's *Commentaries* provide a thorough survey of American law as it had developed by this crucial period. In one sense Kent marked a culmination, in other ways only a beginning, because after him the publication of new treatises on American law assumed landslide proportions. One need only recall Judge Joseph Story's many publications in the 1830's and 1840's as he combined his Supreme Court duties with those of professor at the new Harvard Law School.[55] With Kent and Story, American law had truly come into its own.

For those perhaps awed by the prospect of initially grappling with Kent and Story, an excellent introductory text of the 1830's should smooth the path. Timothy Walker's *Introduction to American Law* was the fruit of his labors at a law school he had founded in Cincinnati after graduating from Harvard Law School.[56] There is also a collection of well-edited source materials covering the period from 1820 to 1860, Charles M. Haar's *The Golden Age of American Law* (New York, 1960), which carries the study of early American legal history into this later period.

2. THE LAWS

Some of the most obvious, reliable, and readily available information about the state of law in early America can be obtained from the successive printed collections of statutes in each of the thirteen colonies. Examining the printed statutes of a particular colony is usually the first step in primary research in American legal history. For such colonies as Pennsylvania and Virginia, where the secondary literature for legal history is inadequate, reading their respective statutes is the essential first task of the legal historian.

Each of the original colonies compiled simple collections of its

55. Joseph Story, *Commentaries on the Constitution of the United States*, 3 vols. (Boston, 1833) includes a useful "review of the constitutional history of the colonies and states, before the adoption of the constitution."

56. Timothy Walker, *Introduction to American Law* (Cincinnati, 1837). There was a second edition in 1844 and a third in 1855.

statutes at various times. Many circulated in manuscript form prior to publication. At some point, however, every colony did publish its laws, and these publications are readily available today in one of several formats. The major research libraries have copies of many original editions of the laws. *The Early American Imprints* Series, edited by Clifford K. Shipton, makes available in microprint every legal code published in this country between 1639 and 1800. Finally several of the most famous seventeenth-century collections of laws were reprinted in the nineteenth and twentieth centuries. These collections of statutes have rarely been used for the study of even the most elementary problems in legal history. There has been almost no attempt either to compare the laws of one colony with another or to study the evolution of colonial laws. Such an important subject as the revision of colonial laws has only recently received preliminary consideration.[57]

The fame of most seventeenth-century law codes has been such that locating copies of them is not a difficult problem. By the eighteenth century legislatures were printing their sessions laws on a regular basis and major collections of statutes appeared fairly frequently. The easiest way to discover what laws were printed in such instances is to use the indexes of Charles Evans' *American Bibliography*, twelve volumes (Chicago, 1903-1934). The Greene and Morris *Guide to the Principal Sources for Early American History (1600-1800) in the City of New York* lists some of the printed sources on each colony which appeared in print before 1930.[58] Bibliographies of the laws of several New England colonies have been published.[59] The greatest single collection of colonial laws in print is The Charlemagne Tower Collection of American Colonial Laws at the Historical Society of Pennsylvania. The catalogue to this collection can serve as a handy guide to most printed editions.[60]

57. Erwin C. Surrency, "Revision of Colonial Laws," *Am. Jour. of Leg. Hist.*, IX (1965), 189-202.

58. Evarts B. Greene and Richard B. Morris, *A Guide to the Principal Sources for Early American History (1600-1800) in the City of New York*, rev. ed. (New York, 1953).

59. Albert C. Bates, Connecticut Statute Laws; *A Bibliographical List of Editions of Connecticut Laws from the Earliest Issues to 1836* (Hartford, 1900); Worthington C. Ford and Albert Matthews, "Bibliography of the Laws of the Massachusetts Bay, 1641-1776," Col. Soc. of Mass., *Pubs.*, IV (Boston, 1910), 291-480.

60. The Charlemagne Tower Collection of American Colonial Laws (Historical Society of Pennsylvania, Philadelphia, 1890).

Brief notice of some of the most famous printings or subsequent editions of colonial laws may facilitate the task of students. The most important law code in colonial America was the Massachusetts Code of 1648, which was rediscovered and reprinted in the twentieth century.[61] In the late 1880's William H. Whitmore edited reprintings of the Massachusetts collections of 1660 and 1672.[62] The Massachusetts laws from 1692 to 1780 can be found in the first five volumes of *The Acts and Resolves, Public and Private of the Province of the Massachusetts Bay. . . .*[63] *The Colonial Laws of New York from the year 1664 to the Revolution* were published in five volumes at Albany in 1894. The colonial statutes of Pennsylvania were republished in the late nineteenth century.[64] One of the best and most satisfactory editions of colonial laws is William W. Hening's compilation of *The Statutes-at-Large, Being a Collection of All the Laws of Virginia, 1619-1792,* thirteen volumes (Philadelphia and New York, 1823). The University Press of Virginia has just published a new edition of the first laws drawn up for an American colony, William Strachey's *For the Colony in Virginea Britannia. Lawes Divine, Morall and Martiall* (London, 1612; Charlottesville, Va., 1969).

3. THE COURT RECORDS

Court records constitute the major unused source for the study of both early American history in general and the history of law. This is especially true for the innumerable volumes of manuscripts that are extant for each of the original colonies. This condition reflects the difficulties inherent in both locating manuscript court records and in determining how to utilize them intelligently. The bibliographical guides to some court records which have recently appeared should facilitate their use by future scholars. Mention should be made of Michael G. Kammen's "Colonial Court Records

61. Max Farrand, ed., *The Laws and Liberties of Massachusetts* (Cambridge, Mass., 1929).

62. William H. Whitmore, ed., *The Colonial Laws of Massachusetts reprinted from the edition of 1660, with the supplements to 1672, containing also, The Body of Liberties of 1641* (Boston, 1889), and *The Colonial Laws of Massachusetts, reprinted from the edition of 1672 with the supplements through 1686* (Boston, 1887).

63. *The Acts and Resolves, Public and Private, of the Province of the Massachusetts Bay . . . ,* 21 vols. (Boston, 1869-1922).

64. James T. Mitchell and Henry Flanders, comps., *The Statutes at Large of Pennsylvania, from 1682 to 1801 . . . ,* 13 vols. (Harrisburg, Pa., 1896-1908).

and the Study of Early American History: A Bibliographical Review," William Jeffrey, Jr.'s "Early New England Court Records, a Bibliography of Published Materials," and my own "Select Guide to the Manuscript Court Records of Colonial New England."[65] A guide comparable to these has also been prepared for Maryland.[66] One of the first tasks of legal historians should be the preparation of brief guides to the court records of the Middle and Southern colonies.

Editing and publishing selected court records has absorbed the attention of a variety of persons interested in early American law. Since 1933 nine volumes of court records have been published in the *American Legal Records* series.[67] Other important publications have appeared under the sponsorship of a variety of organizations with the result that certain colonies and states have been much better served than others. Maine, Massachusetts, New York, and Maryland enjoy many printed volumes of their court records, while the opposite holds true for such important colonies as Pennsylvania, Virginia, and South Carolina. All of the Maine court records to 1718 have now been published in a series that features excellent scholarly introductions to the various volumes, and has the important virtue of continuity.[68] For seventeenth-century Massachusetts the records of the Court of Assistants, Essex County, Suffolk County, and more recently the local judicial records of the Pynchon family, are available and well known to legal historians. This is not true for eighteenth-century Massachusetts, however. The huge *Archives of Maryland* series has published innumerable volumes of court records for that colony. Professor Joseph H. Smith of Colum-

65. Michael G. Kammen, "Colonial Court Records and the Study of Early American History: A Bibliographical Review," *Am. Hist. Rev.*, LXX (1965), 732-739; W. Jeffrey, Jr., "Early New England Court Records, A Bibliography of Published Materials," *Am. Jour. of Leg. Hist.*, I (1957), 119-147; David H. Flaherty, "A Select Guide to the Manuscript Court Records of Colonial New England," *Am. Jour. of Leg. Hist.*, XI (1967), 107-126.

66. Detailed guides to all the existing court records of colonial Maryland by Louis Dow Scisco appeared in the *Maryland Historical Magazine* between 1926 and 1930. See also Morris L. Radoff, *The County Courthouses and Records of Maryland*, 2 vols. (Annapolis, 1960-1963) and H. Clay Reed, "The Court Records of the Delaware Valley," *Wm. and Mary Qtly.*, 3d Ser., IV (1947), 192-202.

67. For a complete list of volumes in the *American Legal Records* series, see the article by Kammen cited above.

68. Charles T. Libby, *et al.*, eds., *Province and Court Records of Maine*, 5 vols. (Portland, 1928—).

bia, the most successful recent editor of court records, has just added a volume for Maryland.[69] Richard B. Morris has been perhaps the most innovative of editors in his *Select Cases of the Mayor's Court of New York City, 1674-1784* (Washington, 1935). Instead of printing the records in sequence as they originally appeared, Morris has organized selected cases in topical fashion to cover many areas of general interest. Paul M. Hamlin and Charles E. Baker have edited an excellent collection of records for the *Supreme Court of Judicature of the Province of New York, 1691-1704*, three volumes (New York, 1959).

Given the current underdeveloped state of American legal history, one may argue that there has been too much emphasis on the editing of court records for publication. Whether the editing of such records should remain a major outlet for the energies of legal historians is an important question. A great deal of the editing has been much too scattered both regionally and along jurisdictional lines to be of great value. The *American Legal Records* series, for example, contains a miscellany of records from eight different colonies, including inferior court records, superior court records, and records of courts of appeals, admiralty, and equity.[70] Many of these volumes lack adequate introductions. For a collection of records of one particular court over a short span of time to make a significant contribution, the volume requires a lengthy introduction that might be profitably modeled after those of Zechariah Chafee,Jr., and Joseph H. Smith, for example. Instead of editing one volume of county court records that span a decade, the legal historian might be better advised to employ all the manuscript records of the county in an extensive monograph. Surely the editing of court records should not cease completely, but at least for the moment it is to be hoped that mature scholars will shun this outlet for their energies in favor of some of the more pressing needs of early American legal history.

Legal historians must make greater use of the manuscript court records. Too many articles and monographs on legal history fail to cite a single manuscript court record. Such sources should be

69. Joseph H. Smith and Philip A. Crowl, eds., *Court Records of Prince Georges County, Maryland, 1696-1699* (*American Legal Records* series, IX [Washington, 1964]).

70. The scattered coverage provided by published volumes in this series owes much to its unfinished and incomplete nature. Many of the planned volumes have never appeared.

studied intensively and over a considerable period of time in order that the scholar might be able, for example, to integrate file papers with the sparse notations of the court record book. Scholars can develop methods for utilizing court records effectively and should encourage plans to make the manuscripts themselves more accessible. Connecticut has provided a model of sensible procedure by centralizing its colonial court records in the State Library at Hartford, unlike Massachusetts and Rhode Island where the scholar must still make the rounds of colonial county seats. The Virginia State Library in Richmond will make available on microfilm specified colonial Virginia court records. Centralization of collection and the microfilming of court records should be championed by legal historians. One can easily belabor the need to study and utilize the court records. Yet the opportunities and sources are so great as to make this danger a negligible one, for the fact remains that few court records have ever been employed in analytical and general studies. Quantifying methods can now be used to great advantage, and there is no reason for such records to remain the preserve of the geneaologist or the individual searching for a case involving specific persons.

III. Some Conclusions

Early American legal history has been singularly fortunate in attracting the attention of a series of important scholars, and some very significant and permanently useful work has appeared. Yet too much of our legal history to date has been repetitive or superficial. With notable exceptions, we have not gotten to the heart of the matter in the study of legal history. Too little has been done to integrate legal history with the general history of early America, especially by asking broadly significant questions. The result has been that in the past the works of legal historians seem mainly to have been read by one another. The general scholar, and even the graduate student, has tended to leave legal history works in their arcane corner.

A moment's reflection should convince anyone, however, that the many basic questions involved in the study of early American law can also be of great importance for early American history in general. The history of the role of law in early American society can and should be a central theme, since law is so often at the heart of the functioning of a society. By asking the right questions legal history can introduce the scholar to the deepest workings of society as revealed at the most practical level. Enlightened legal historians can draw upon the resources of political, social, economic, and intellectual history to produce working models of the functioning of society at a given period in time. Such undertakings can evolve broad interpretations and at the same time result in concrete studies. Legal history can thus serve as the focal point for understanding a society—it can be the composite form of historical comprehension in a multidimensional fashion.

One must begin the study of legal history by posing the right kinds of questions. For what apparent or underlying reasons were certain legislative acts enacted? How did these statutes reflect the basic values of the society? To what extent did legislatures abandon control to the forces of inertia in a particular area? On what broad principles were cases being decided in the courts? Did the laws and the judicial decisions reflect the dominant forces at work in the society? To what extent did these new laws or decisions reflect changes in a developing society? Such crucial questions overlap many areas of historical specialization and an up-to-date legal history can integrate them into a coherent whole. If the tasks of legal history are construed broadly enough and the correct questions posed, the history of American law can be a major area of historical investigation and contribute substantially to an understanding of the history of an era.

In this process there are certain characteristics of earlier studies that it would be well to de-emphasize. The history of early American law has been too concerned with origins and with institutional studies. While these are important matters, they need not constitute the boundaries of legal history to the detriment of more broadly conceived studies. Professor Stanley N. Katz has recently criticized the traditional character of even the more recent work in American legal history, which has continued to abide by old-fashioned notions about periodization and has focused on a limited range of source materials.[71] Katz emphasized the need to study law broadly and to turn our concern from what law was to how law worked.

Another of the limiting postulates of American legal history to date has been that generalization is difficult or impossible because

71. Stanley N. Katz, "Looking Backward: The Early History of American Law," *Univ. of Chicago Law Rev.*, XXXIII (1966), 867-884.

of the need to study and consider each jurisdiction separately. Scholars have been so busy studying individual colonies that they have not taken cognizance of the enormous similarities in all aspects of law in the British colonies. As one studies colony after colony the dominant impression is not one of differences but of similarities. The significant deviations readily stand out. While most studies should initially begin in one jurisdiction—and the legal history of each colony might well be studied separately, especially in the format of doctoral dissertations—such difficulties should no longer be invoked as an almost sacrosanct ban on presentation of the legal history of early America from a general point of view. Indeed such a ban has constituted a major hindrance to the development of legal history, since it has made it difficult for prospective scholars to find their way into the field.

The technical nature of the law has been another major stumbling block to advances in the study of legal history. A degree of formal or informal legal training is certainly essential for serious work in the field, and the guild of lawyers has tended to reflect unkindly on those who attempted to study the history of law without prior immersion in the mysteries of the sect. At the same time the field of legal history has often been studied and defined much too narrowly by the specially trained and dominant professional group. Thus certain misconceptions need to be cleared away.

As Maitland pointed out in the late nineteenth century, legal history is history and not law.[72] The normal aims of the historian and the lawyer are totally different. The lawyer in daily practice is unhistorical and only looks to the past for the logic of authority. The historian seeks to understand the role of law in an earlier period in the pursuit and development of a scholarly discipline. Such benefits for contemporary society as may result from his work are indirect. Where the lawyer may be concerned with a single instance of usage at some earlier date and its subsequent development, the historian of law seeks a total understanding of each and every aspect of the functioning of law in the society.

The legal historian should be an historian with some legal training, whether his place in the academic community is in a law school or a history department. If, as appears likely, it is too much to ask that a person should complete law school before being trained

72. Theodore F. T. Plucknett, "Frederic William Maitland," *N.Y.U. Law Rev.*, XXVI (1951), 6-7.

as a professional historian, or vice versa, then the emphasis should be on training as a historian, coupled with some basic law courses relevant to a particular interest. The greatest danger is that the person writing legal history will not be a "historian." In the entire corpus of secondary works on early American legal history, many of the weakest productions are those of professional lawyers who have ventured into the field of legal history without comprehending the demands of historical study. While historians have sometimes committed atrocities by misunderstanding the legal aspects of their studies, their historial sense has usually saved the volume in question from total disaster. The great students of early American legal history have often had the good fortune to be both skilled historians and lawyers. Whether one is formally trained as a lawyer or historian or both, the governing consideration is the need to write legal history as history.

Some legal training is essential, then, and all legal historians should be exposed to the ways of the legal profession through study in a law school. Just as the economic or social historian requires a basic knowledge or understanding of economics and sociology, so the historian of law needs basic law courses which can be tailored to particular interests. Beyond a certain level self-education can further introduce lawyers and historians to the intricacies of their respective disciplines. Some law schools and history departments are currently planning or already have established cooperative programs to meet the peculiar needs of the legal historian.

One of the surest methods of revamping and guaranteeing the future of legal history is to have more persons teaching the history of law at a variety of levels. A growing number of major universities have legal history courses. My own experience suggests that the social history of American law is an ideal subject for undergraduates. It can be readily comprehensible and provides a fruitful field for undergraduate research, since it is relatively easy to define problems and to find manageable topics. In many liberal arts colleges a majority of male history students are inclined towards law school at the graduate level, and a course on legal history can prepare them for the actual subject matter of law in a fashion that is not normally as well satisfied by courses on constitutional history and constitutional law.

It may ultimately be decided that American legal history belongs primarily within the liberal arts curriculum for teaching purposes. Should this eventuate, it would be, in part, a consequence of the sorry state of legal history studies in most American law schools.[73] Only the best schools even list courses on legal history, and many of these "development of legal institutions" courses bear little resemblance to an historian's idea of how legal history should be studied. Attempts to teach legal history to law students over a span of time from 1066 to the present seem doomed to their current low state of reputation. If law students are too preoccupied with their professional studies to want to know much about the history of law, then this should be made available to them before they reach law school, unless some needed reforms in legal education can be instituted.

While legal history has been developing as a branch of learning, the concurrent problem of making the subject meaningful within the framework of legal education has been little recognized. Although only a few law students will ever develop a scholarly commitment to the field of legal history, many believe that lawyers should possess an understanding of the historical development and role of law in order that they may have a better comprehension of both the present and the prospects for the future. Professor Calvin Woodard of the University of Virginia Law School has recently stimulated interest in the need for an enlightened legal history in the education of lawyers.[74] In part Woodard blames negative reactions to the subject among current law students on a conception of legal history that emphasizes "legal institutions" and their "development." He perceptively observes that Maitland created "the general impression that Legal History is and must be essentially a study of medieval English legal institutions," and argues that legal history in law schools need not dwell so singlemindedly upon the twelfth and thirteenth centuries. One way to encourage student interest is to teach the history of law over the last three or four centuries and to carry it down to the present. Woodard's plea for more works of synthesis in legal history is also well grounded. In the law school itself legal history can best stimulate the minds of

73. See Edward D. Re, "Legal History Courses in American Law Schools," *American University Law Review*, XIII (1964), 45-65.

74. Calvin Woodard, "History, Legal History and Legal Education," *Va. Law Rev.*, LIII (1967), 89-121. See also Daniel J. Boorstin, "Tradition and Method in Legal History," *Harvard Law Rev.*, LIV (1941), 424-436.

students as an integral part of most courses. Yet only by studying the broad history of law as part of the legal process can legal historians begin to make headway against the ahistorical temper of current legal education. The problems of legal history as a viable discipline and as a meaningful aspect of legal education merge in the general need to expand the scope of legal history in the course of research, along the lines previously discussed.

This essay has identified areas of early American legal history where study is needed and indeed essential. I have not tried to be comprehensive in these suggestions, nor indeed am I capable of predicting the needs and possibilities of the discipline which may appear in the future. The attempt to study the development and role in society of substantive law is in its infancy. In many specific cases the impact of law on a subject—the family for example—has been almost completely neglected and stands as a major hindrance to our understanding of the topic. Research in currently obvious areas will unveil new possibilities at a rapid pace. Thus a vast field opens for research at both the graduate and undergraduate levels. It would be desirable if universities in a particular state would look upon the legal history of their state as their own responsibility and then tend it accordingly, particularly for the basic general studies that are now requisite. The vast sources are at hand and need only be cultivated. Model studies now exist for one colony or state which, if applied to other colonies and states, can result in work which contributes meaningfully to the overall study of legal history.

Legal historians should be encouraged by the continued existence of the *American Journal of Legal History*, published under the editorship of Erwin C. Surrency and his associates at the Temple University Law School. The *Journal* has now passed its tenth birthday and appears to be in a flourishing state. It has become the major outlet for articles on the legal history of those countries shaped by the common law tradition. The general level of scholarship has been high, although a few weak articles have appeared.

Ultimately the most encouraging sign for the future of the history of American law has been the appearance in recent years of a group of younger legal historians who are well trained and seriously working in this field. The kinds of work they are attempting and the questions they are posing give considerable grounds for optimism, both for the future of the discipline and for a more widespread recognition of its significance. In particular a school of legal historians has developed under the inspiration and guidance of Professor Willard Hurst of the University of Wisconsin Law School. More widespread recognition of the magnitude of Hurst's contributions and innovations in the field of American legal history would make both lawyers and historians immediately aware of the tremendous possibilities in the study of the social history of law.[75] Hurst has made all of us conscious of the need to move beyond the traditional framework in the study of the history of American law. The circumscribed approaches of the past have contributed to the subsequent neglect of this important subject. Whatever the particular period of historical investigation, the history of law must ultimately be studied with reference to the total role of law in this society, not just in terms of court decisions and changes in the field of private law. Legislatures make decisions in the form of statutes that are of central significance for the future of a society. The basic principles underlying such decisions require identification and examination. At this level of study the vital significance of the history of law is readily apparent. By his splendid work in developing and explicating hypotheses concerning the role of law in the nineteenth and twentieth centuries Professor Hurst has pointed the way to new directions in the study of early American legal history and legal history generally.

75. The best introduction to Hurst's ideas is his article "The Law in United States History," American Philosophical Society, *Proceedings*, CIV (Philadelphia, 1960), 518-526.

PART TWO

The Seventeenth Century

II

*Law and Colonial Society**

GEORGE L. HASKINS

It has been observed that if we are ever to have a competent legal history of the American colonial period, "some way will have to be found for getting scholars and colonial court archives together."[1] It may also be observed that some way must be found to familiarize historians with the nature and function of law in particular colonial societies. These two objectives are the subject matter of the present paper, which is essentially a plea for more attention to colonial law by historians and their students. Certainly the time for an artistically balanced picture of colonial law has not yet come, and it seems unlikely that that time will come until historians, economists and sociologists have given us the benefit of their techniques and special skills in the preparation of studies which are an essential prerequisite to the writing of a history of American law. Although it is obvious that some knowledge of "law" is necessary on the part of such social scientists, a formal education in law is not required. Some of the most valued contributions to American, as well as to English, legal history have been made by scholars who received no formal training in the law.

The importance of legal records in understanding colonial society is clear, and the point requires no extended comment. It is no longer possible to say, as Herbert Osgood did in 1904, that

* "Law and Colonial Society," by George L. Haskins, is reprinted with permission from the *American Quarterly*, IX (1957), 354-364, published by the University of Pennsylvania. Copyright 1957 by the Trustees of the University of Pennsylvania.

1. William Jeffrey, "American Legal History, 1952-1954," *1954 Annual Survey of American Law* (New York: New York University School of Law, 1955), pp. 866-72.

colonial legal records are fragmentary and not easily accessible.[2] Increasingly, with the compilation of bibliographies and the publication of court and other legal records, the possibilities of using the latter have increased very greatly, and historians have shown themselves entirely capable of using such records to illumine political and social history. A notable recent example is the *Introduction to the Accomack County Court Records* in Virginia, so competently edited by Miss Susie Ames. But it is only the first fruits that we have seen, and a rich harvest awaits those who will turn to legal records for illumining the subject matter of particular studies. Today "the lack is rather of workmen than of implements," as Maitland said of English legal history in 1889.[3] Some remarks made more than twenty years ago by Professor Richard Morris are almost as pertinent today as when he made them:

> Social and legal attitudes as manifest in the strivings and conflicts of social groups, in the issues between creditor and debtor, landlord and tenant, in the exploitation of labor and the treatment of poverty and unemployment, by way of example, seem clearly more significant in the history of society than old furniture, witchcraft, and dead doctors, however much we might enjoy collecting the first, psychoanalyzing the second, and embalming the third. By concentrating chiefly on the latter and failing to bring the former into clear relief, historians of early American life, with the possible exception of Philip Alexander Bruce, have failed to produce a work of the importance of Miss Dorothy George's *London Life in the Eighteenth Century*, which stemmed from the illuminating legal sources of Old Bailey and other sessions papers. The type of sources used by Miss George and by Miss Eleanor Trotter, whose *Seventeenth Century Life in the Country Parish* was so largely drawn from the records of the North Riding Court of Quarter Sessions, has been very largely neglected by American historians.[4]

The need for studies and evaluations of particular areas of the law by social scientists—for example, family law, criminal law, government regulation of business—is less easily explained. Tra-

2. Herbert L. Osgood, *The American Colonies in the Seventeenth Century* (New York: Macmillan Co., 1904) I, 182, note 2.

3. Quoted by Richard B. Morris, "The Sources of Early American Law: Colonial Period," *West Virginia Law Quarterly*, XL (1934), 212.

4. *Ibid.*

ditionally, this is the domain of lawyers, and it is terrain into which the historian without formal legal education has been especially reluctant to penetrate. Yet it is an area where the techniques and insights of historians and sociologists can be especially fruitful. At the outset, we must recognize that one reason why social scientists have been reluctant to work in legal history is the traditional isolation of law from other studies. This isolation is a regrettable consequence of the professionalization of legal study in this country. To most non-lawyers, the law is not only a science but a mystery,[5] and the uninitiated have been timid about entering upon preserves that lawyers are not loath to keep for themselves. Understandably, the complexities of legal doctrine and the intricacies of legal procedure tend to hold back the non-lawyer from investigating both the sources and the operation of law even in a past civilization. Moreover, the pragmatic view of the practitioner that law is the sum of the rules administered by courts in the settling of justiciable controversies has also tended to keep the law in isolation by obscuring the fact that law is a social product, reflecting not only social organization but the incidence of political and economic pressures at particular times and in particular places. Law is not merely a complex of rules and procedures for the settlement of controversies. Neither is it a "frozen world of arbitrary *a priori* abstractions existing in a vacuum and held together only by a formal logical consistency."[6] Law is a means of classifying and bringing into order a vast mass of human relations, and it is these human relations that constitute much of the stuff of which history is made. Writing more than one hundred years ago, Savigny stated that the phenomena of law, language, customs, government have no separate existence; "there is but one force and power in a people, bound together by its nature; and only our minds give these a separate existence."[7]

It may be helpful to attempt a definition of law that takes into account not only its nature but the fact that it is a social product and also an agency of social control. Of course, many have at-

5. This attitude may in part be the result of Blackstone's exposition in his *Commentaries*. Cf. Daniel Joseph Boorstin, *The Mysterious Science of Law* (Cambridge: Harvard University Press, 1941), pp. 11-30.

6. John Dickinson, *Administrative Justice and the Supremacy of Law* (Cambridge: Harvard University Press, 1927), p. 344.

7. Friedrich Karl von Savigny, *Vom Beruf unsrer Zeit für Gesetzgebung und Rechtswissenschaft* (Heidelberg: Möhr & Zimmer, 1814), p. 8.

tempted, from the vantage point of their particular times, to formulate a definition of law. Thus, to the school of analytical jurists represented by Austin[8] law is simply the command of the sovereign. To the so-called historical school, exemplified by Savigny, law is the unconscious embodiment of the common will of the people.[9] To the philosophical school, law is a reflection of ideas of right and derives its validity from being declaratory of idealized ethical custom.[10] Each of these schools of thought has had, and probably still has, its champions, but within the past generation or two their tenets have been challenged by views which take into account social and economic considerations as well as practical and ethical factors. In the formation of these newer views the studies of anthropologists, historians and sociologists have played a significant part, and there has developed a recognition, first, that the law of most civilizations is a product of very complex social actions and interactions, and, second, that law operates within an environment of economic, social and psychological facts whose influence is only beginning to be understood.[11]

Looking at particular societies, whether contemporary or past, one can recognize in most of them the existence of what may be termed a legal order, that is a regime—whether customary, or otherwise—of adjusting the relations of men, as well as their desires and claims with respect to each other and to things, and also for regulating conduct. Law is the central feature of this regime and consists of the body of precepts and received ideals, and the techniques of using them, consciously established or implicitly recognized by politically organized society for the delimitation and securing of interests.[12] "Interests," in the sense the word is here used, are the demands or desires which human beings, either individually or in groups, seek to satisfy, and consequently they are of the essence of what the ordering of human relations in civilized society must take into account.[13]

8. W. Jethro Brown, *The Austinian Theory of Law* (London: John Murray, 1912), pp. 16 ff.

9. Friedrich Karl von Savigny, *System des heutigen römischen Rechts* (Berlin: Veit und Comp., 1840), I, 14, 16, 38.

10. See Roscoe Pound, *Law and Morals* (Chapel Hill, N.C.: University of North Carolina Press, 1924), 92 ff. and authorities there cited.

11. See Eugen Ehrlich, *Fundamental Principles of the Sociology of Law* (Moll trans.; Cambridge: Harvard University Press, 1936), chaps. iii, v.

12. Cf. Roscoe Pound, *Outline of Lectures on Jurisprudence* (5th ed.; Cambridge: Harvard University Press, 1943).

13. *Ibid.*, p. 60.

Such a definition of law is essentially pragmatic, for it recognizes the traditional and the ideal elements in law—for example, the sense of justice and of injustice; it also takes into account the source of legal rules in custom, legislation and judicial decision, as well as their application by the courts. But the definition is also historical and sociological, since it takes into account the fact that particular rules are a function of time and place, and the further fact that the interests pressing for recognition and adjustment are ever-changing and never constant. Whether particular rules for adjusting human relations and regulating human conduct are the outcome of custom, legislation or judicial decision, by and large they reflect some need or needs of society, or of some segment of society, at particular times. Very often particular rules or the techniques of applying them become outmoded and linger on beyond their period of usefulness. But this fact does not impair the suggested definition; rather it emphasizes that the law contains elements which can be understood only in terms of its history—of past political, economic and other socio-psychological pressures. Thus, the law of any given society is a compound of past as well as of present forces, and in seeking to explain or assess its scope and function we must look to received ideals and professional techniques as well as to contemporary pressures and purposes. At the same time, because law molds society, to the extent that obedience thereto is exacted by governmental authority, law is itself a pressure upon social organization and a device for effecting social change. Legal rules thus reflect at least in some measure the picture of what men of a particular time regard as the ideal of relations among men, thereby further illumining from another standpoint our understanding of a particular society. As Dean Pound has said with his usual perceptiveness, "Law cannot depart far from ethical custom nor lag far behind it."[14] It does not seem unreasonable to predict that the day will come when no description of the New England mind will be thought adequate without reference to the colonists' ideas about law.

With a view to bringing the foregoing down to the specific, and to suggesting the fruitfulness of study of particular areas of colonial law, it may be helpful to look at certain aspects of the law of Massachusetts Bay Colony in the seventeenth century. That period is a luminous age, throwing light on both past and future,

14. Roscoe Pound, *Law and Morals*, pp. 92 ff.

and at the same time richly deserving of study for its own sake. Here it is possible to see the importance of a broad view of law and its function, and at the same time perceive the importance of historical enquiry. Examination of the legislation and the court decisions during the first twenty years of the colony's life shows very clearly that legal rules were in part the result of tradition—including received precepts and ideals—and in part the result of the developing social and economic needs of the colonists. The day has gone by when historians of seventeenth-century Massachusetts can speak of the era as "a period of rude, untechnical popular law"[15] or say that "the Scriptures were an infallible guide for both judge and legislator."[16] The printed records make it plain that these Massachusetts colonists brought with them a number of rules and principles of the English common law,[17] that is the law of the king's central courts at Westminster, and also a substantial amount of English local customs of the manors and boroughs from which they came.[18] This process of importation and rejection of law with which the colonists were familiar is illustrative of one phase of the general and very important problem of survival and adaptation in patterns of thought and habits of life in the colonies. It is well recognized that the colonists drew extensively upon their English experience in forming and developing their political and religious institutions, and that in architecture, town planning and methods of farming they patterned their ways of thinking and acting upon what had been familiar to them in the homeland.[19] That they should have availed themselves of their cultural heritage in law as well adds to our knowledge of the general problem of cultural transplantation and to our understanding of the colonists' reasons for accepting or rejecting parts of that heritage.

It is when we turn to particular rules of law as revealed in the

15. Paul Samuel Reinsch, "The English Common Law in the Early American Colonies," *Select Essays in Anglo-American Legal History* (Boston: Little, Brown & Co., 1907), I, 367-70.

16. Charles J. Hilkey, "Legal Development in Colonial Massachusetts," *Columbia Studies in History, Economics and Public Law* (New York: Columbia University Press, 1910), XXXVII, 68.

17. George L. Haskins, "A Problem in the Reception of the Common Law in the Colonial Period," *University of Pennsylvania Law Review*, XCVII (1949), 842-44 and authorities there cited; Theodore F. T. Plucknett, Book Review, *New England Quarterly*, III (1930), 156.

18. George L. Haskins, "The Beginnings of the Recording System in Massachusetts," *Boston University Law Review*, XXI (1941), 281.

19. Haskins, *University of Pennsylvania Law Review*, XCVII, 842.

court records, and especially to the innovations introduced by the colonists, that we find reflected most clearly the social organization of the colony, its general purposes and aims, and the pressures for change and adaptation resulting from political and economic needs. Here we see the law both as an anchor to accepted tradition and also as a vehicle for a change. In addition, these rules tell us much of the views people had of the ideal of relations among men. We know, of course, that in Massachusetts Bay religion was the *Leitmotiv* of the colonial enterprise[20] and that an essential purpose thereof was to build a kingdom of God in the wilderness.[21] Much of the colonial legislation at the beginning illustrates this purpose very vividly.[22] At the same time, the ideal was modified by the practical. Although we find criminal statutes enacted to secure conformity to Scripture (for example, capital punishment for idolatry, blasphemy and witchcraft),[23] we find that economic considerations helped dictate, for example, the adoption of rules respecting the descent of lands to all children rather than to the eldest son, as at common law.[24]

The first Massachusetts Code, adopted in 1648, forcibly illustrates the importance of viewing the law both as a social product and as an agency of social control. In this famous code, which came to light hardly a generation ago under the competent hands of Max Farrand, we find an authoritative compilation of constitutional provisions—regulations for the conduct of administration, courts and their jurisdiction, trade, military affairs, and the relation between church and state.[25] As such, its importance is obvious for an understanding of the formal structure of society as it was and as the colonists wished to make it. But it is from the standpoint of private substantive law that the Code has special interest, for it contains detailed provisions with respect to crime, property, domestic relations, wages and prices, and also rules governing indi-

20. Samuel Eliot Morison, *The Puritan Pronaos* (New York: New York University Press, 1936), p. 4.

21. Cotton Mather, *Magnalia Christi Americana* (Hartford, 1820), I, 219; Morison, *The Puritan Pronaos*, p. 4.

22. Especially the capital laws set forth in *The Laws and Liberties of Massachusetts* (Farrand ed.; Cambridge: Harvard University Press, 1929), pp. 5-6.

23. *The Laws and Liberties of Massachusetts*, p. 5.

24. *Ibid.*, p. 53. See also George L. Haskins, "The Beginnings of Partible Inheritance in the American Colonies," *Yale Law Journal*, LI (1942), 1280.

25. For a general analysis of the Code see Thorp L. Wolford, "The Laws and Liberties of 1648," *Boston University Law Review*, XXVIII (1948), 426.

vidual behavior and regulating the moral welfare of the community. It is a very comprehensive piece of work, far more detailed and extensive in scope than earlier codes of other colonies, and may fairly be described as the first American code.[26]

Considered as a whole, the Code reflects even more clearly than the scattered entries in the court records the basic purposes of the colonial enterprise and the colonists' general point of view toward law and its relation to society. Here was no mere compilation of English law, no haphazard syncretism of popular equity and Biblical precepts, but a fresh and considered effort to promote the purposes of settlement and to establish provisions suitable to the new conditions of a frontier society. In many respects the Code represented a clear break with traditional English law—both common and customary law. For example, it contained a new classification of crimes,[27] and the rights accorded debtors and creditors revealed a marked advance on contemporary English law.[28] To the extent that traditional elements were preserved, those elements were consciously reworked into a carefully thought out and integrated pattern, and they were modified or ignored when inconsistent with the general plan envisaged. For example, many antiquated forms of English judicial procedure were eliminated.[29] The Puritan outlook affected almost everything that the colonists thought and did, and this fact explains why to a substantial degree the Code so clearly breaks with the traditional secular law with which the colonists were familiar.

It seems doubtful whether the Code would have been prepared —at least in the form we have it—had it not been for the dissatisfaction of the colonists with the absolute authority wielded by the small oligarchic group which ran the affairs of the colony. The Puritan leaders regarded themselves as instruments in the divine hand for carrying out a great religious mission, and there was nothing democratic in their political theory.[30] The colonists gen-

26. See George L. Haskins, "Codification of the Law in Colonial Massachusetts," *Indiana Law Journal*, XXX (1954), 1; *id.*, "De la codification du droit en Amérique du Nord au XVIIe siècle," *Revue d'histoire du droit*, XXIII (1955), 311.

27. *The Laws and Liberties of Massachusetts*, pp. 5-6.

28. *Ibid.*, pp. 3, 17, 34.

29. Wolford, *Boston University Law Review*, XXVIII, pp. 437-47.

30. See generally Stanley Gray, "The Political Thought of John Winthrop," *New England Quarterly*, III (1930), 681; Herbert L. Osgood, "The Political Ideas of the Puritans," *Political Science Quarterly*, VI (1891), 1, 201; Stefan A. Riesen-

erally were eager to broaden the basis of the government and at the same time to obtain security against the arbitrary power of their leaders.[31] It was thought that the latter, who sat as judges in every one of the courts of the colony, could not be trusted to decide fairly unless the rules which were to guide their decisions were public property. The judicial functions of the magistrates also carried with them extensive administrative powers, and this discretionary power seems to have been a particular object of dislike.[32] At the same time, the colonists appear to have had a basic confidence in the aims of the sincere and earnest group of zealous leaders, and they accepted the basic aims of the colony, that is, an experiment in Christian living and the establishment of a kingdom of God on earth. This acceptance of the basic aims of the enterprise was buttressed by a vivid community spirit and solidarity which sprang up in large measure from the colonists' desire to achieve those aims.

The character of the settlement also explains the comprehensiveness of the Code, for it was not only a question of reducing to writing the existing laws of the colony but also a question of establishing comprehensive provisions suitable to the new conditions of their frontier society and religious enterprise. It must not be forgotten that, dominant as religious influences were, new conditions required the adoption of laws suited thereto. Thus, the needs of younger children in an economy where money and personal goods were scarce helped to explain the departure from rules of primogeniture obtaining in England and the adoption of a law which divided real property among all the children.[33] It must also be emphasized that a Code of this kind would not have been possible had the colony not been comprised of only a few thousand inhabitants, like-minded to a high degree and possessed of a common heritage and tradition. In such simple and self-contained communities, appreciation and understanding of the need for common action easily comes about, and the conviction readily appears that the community has the power to shape its social life by voluntary

feld, "Law-Making and Legislative Precedent in American Legal History," *Minnesota Law Review*, XXXIII (1948), 103, 110-15.

31. John Winthrop, *The History of New England* (Savage ed.; Boston, 1853), p. 322; Haskins, *Indiana Law Journal*, XXX, 1, 6-7.

32. Haskins, *Indiana Law Journal*, XXX, 7.

33. Haskins, *Yale Law Journal*, LI, 1280.

regulation.[34] The comparative isolation and lack of intercourse with other communities, except on occasional or sporadic bases, of course, strengthened these attitudes. Thus, law was viewed as a restraint on individual action in the interest of the order of the whole group to which it applied; and again, since an individual was only a member of the community, there was no aspect of his life—even his private conduct[35]—which was free of the control of the law insofar as the law was designed to further effective organization and good order in the community.

Few American colonies, at least in the seventeenth century, had so complete or so comprehensive a compilation of laws as did Massachusetts.[36] Yet even for those colonies that did not, it would be an easy and worthwhile undertaking to prepare a digest at least of the legislation, if not of court decisions, in particular colonies and to analyze the legal rules as therein revealed in terms of the particular interests which the law was designed to protect in relation to the economic and social history of that colony. Although analysis of the law in terms of such traditional classifications as crime, property, contracts and domestic relations would undoubtedly be fruitful, it might prove more helpful to look beyond such traditional categories to the kinds of interests which the law took account of in particular colonies.

It should be borne in mind that the law does not create "interests," in the sense that the word has been used in this paper.[37] The law classifies interests and recognizes a larger or smaller number of them; it defines the extent to which it will give effect to those which it recognizes, in the light of other interests and of the possibilities of effectively securing them through law; it devises means for securing them when recognized and within the determined limits.[38] As Dean Pound has said, the interests which the legal order secures may be (1) demands or desires involved in or regarded from the standpoint of the individual life immediately as such (individual interests);

34. Cf. John Dickinson, "Economic Regulations and Restrictions on Personal Liberty in Early Massachusetts," *Proceedings Pocumtuck Valley Memorial Assn.* (1927), pp. 485-87. A similar development may be found in the Greek colonies in Sicily and Southern Italy. Haskins, *Indiana Law Journal*, XXX, 11-15.

35. For example, gaming for money was proscribed, and penalties were imposed for drunkenness, profanity and the telling of lies. *The Laws and Liberties of Massachusetts*, pp. 24, 30, 35, 45.

36. Haskins, *Indiana Law Journal*, XXX, 5.

37. See text above at note 13.

38. Pound, *Outline of Lectures on Jurisprudence*, p. 96.

(2) demands or desires involved in or looked at from the standpoint of life in a politically organized society, asserted in course of political life (public interests); or (3) those wider demands or desires involved in or looked at from the standpoint of social life in civilized society and asserted in course of social life (social interests).[39] These various types of interests which the legal order secures are frequently interlocking in the sense, for example, that social interests include or take account of individual interests. But the types are nonetheless distinct. As an example of the type of inquiry that might be made, it would be valuable to determine to what extent an individual's right of privacy or freedom of association was encouraged in the legal system of particular colonies. The protection of civil liberty is another area that could bear fruitful investigation.[40]

In determining the scope and subject matter of a particular legal system, the following steps would be especially helpful:[41] (1) an inventory of the interests which press for recognition and a classification thereof; (2) a determination as to which of these interests the law recognizes and seeks to secure; (3) a determination of the principles upon which such interests are defined and limited for the purpose of securing them; (4) a consideration of the means by which the law may secure them when so recognized and delimited; and (5) a determination of the limitations upon effective legal action which may preclude complete recognition or complete securing of interests which otherwise men might wish to secure.

The foregoing is not put forward as a hard-and-fast method of proceeding but as a useful conceptual scheme for classifying legal rules and analyzing their purpose. Some such scheme is helpful in looking at law as a reflection of social forces and as an agency of social control. Such a scheme should help demonstrate that legal history is not an arid exposition of the development of doctrines and rules but should involve a careful enquiry into social structures, and into economic and such other pressures as the influence of leaders of opinion. For these reasons the techniques of the historian and the sociologist, as well as of the lawyer, are especially important.

Yet, though such studies must be made for each colony, because

39. *Ibid.*, pp. 96-97.

40. An excellent preliminary study of this topic may be found in Riesenfeld, *Minnesota Law Review*, XXXIII, 115-20.

41. Summarized from Pound, *Outline of Lectures on Jurisprudence*, p. 96.

of differing backgrounds and development, they should not be carried out without some reference to developments in other colonies. It is not enough to prepare histories of the law for particular colonies; it is essential also to compare the various legal systems with due regard to inter-colonial borrowing.[42] The scope of legal history is enlarged and its content enriched through the employment of the comparative method, which permits us to view the common characteristics of the legal systems of various and differing societies and thus to acquire a better understanding of the *processes* which affect the development of a particular system.[43] To this end, an appreciation of the aims of legal history and comparative law on the part of historians and sociologists is particularly desirable, just as for the lawyer an understanding of the techniques, methods and data of the economists and historians is required. It is the historians and to some extent the sociologists who are best suited to provide much of the data needed to trace with precision the relationships existing between social and legal developments. An appreciation of the aims of legal history and also of comparative law will permit our vision continually to be enlarged by impressing upon us the continuing significance of uniformities in human behavior in differing civilizations. It is this that gives reality to history and makes it a coherent whole.[44]

42. For example, Massachusetts Bay borrowed from Plymouth the chief features of its recording act as well as the principle of partible inheritance of land. Haskins, *Boston University Law Review*, XXI, 285; Haskins, *Yale Law Journal*, LI, 1282. Connecticut copied numerous provisions of the Massachusetts Code of 1648. *Public Records of Connecticut* (Trumbull ed.; Hartford, 1850), passim. The Duke of York's Laws in New York were based upon New England codifications. Julius Goebel and T. Raymond Naughton, *Law Enforcement in Colonial New York* (Commonwealth Fund, 1944), p. 61. Cf. Brugeilles, *Le Droit et la Sociologie* (Paris, 1910), p. 160, wherein the author says of the historical and comparative methods: "ces deux méthodes devront s'intégrer plus tard dans la science juridique à laquelle elles prêteront un concours précieux."

43. Haskins, *Indiana Law Journal*, XXX, 17.

44. Haskins, *Indiana Law Journal*, XXX, 17.

III

*Colonial Courts and the Common Law**

ZECHARIAH CHAFEE, JR.[1]

When men settle in a new land, they cannot be there long without having law of some kind to adjust their disputes and regulate important transactions. They will have to put this law in operation themselves whenever the land is vacant or thinly peopled by natives who have no power over the settlers from outside. What sort of law will the settlers establish? This is a fascinating problem. Yet, so far as I know, it has not been the subject of any comprehensive study in connection with migrations in general, and historians writing on a particular migration have so much else to interest them that they are unlikely to speculate intensively about the law which the migrants had in their new home.

Two periods in the history of the United States raise this problem in very interesting ways. The first of these periods, which I shall discuss, is the transatlantic migration from England to the colonies along the eastern seaboard. The starting-point is, of course, 1607; but it is just as well not to assign a terminal date until the investigation itself has helped to show what is the best time to stop. The other fruitful period is the opening of the gold-fields in California in 1849 and somewhat later in Colorado. Of course, the problem is presented by the entire movement into open territory in the West from the Revolution until well on in the nineteenth century. One could profitably ask, for instance, what law was set up in Iowa. Still, the gold-fields offer the most attractive opportunity for this inquiry. They brought a great many people

* "Colonial Courts and the Common Law," by Zechariah Chafee, Jr., is reprinted with permission from the Massachusetts Historical Society *Proceedings*, LXVIII (Boston, 1952), 132-159.

1. This paper was read at the December, 1945, meeting [of the Massachusetts Historical Society].

into a new region within a short time, so that law had to be established very fast. Moreover, important legal issues which demanded rapid solution were outside the previous experience of many of the settlers. A New Hampshire farmer going to fertile land in Iowa would have some notion what to do about damage done to crops by straying cows, but if he went to Roaring Camp or Cripple Creek he had to grapple with unfamiliar questions about mining and water-rights.

Leaving the Forty-niners and the Colorado prospectors to some future speculations, I shall inquire into the nature of the law which prevailed in the thirteen colonies.

At the outset it is desirable to speak briefly about the limitations of my subject. English law and American law have always been partly established by statutes, but to a considerably larger extent both have been what is called "unwritten law." The substantive rules designed to govern men's conduct are not laid down by legislatures but embodied in the decisions and action of courts. Blackstone said that the judges were maintaining and expounding law which already existed, while John Austin later insisted that the judges actually made the law in this nonstatutory area.[2] This controversy need not be settled here.[3] It is enough for our purposes to remember that a great deal of the law administered by courts does not come from statutes. This large portion of colonial law is the main object of study in the present paper.

Legislation, of course, is very important. The colonies were affected by statutes enacted on both sides of the Atlantic. Colonial legislatures were more active in making private law than Parliament was before the nineteenth century. Their output is a significant indication of the nature of colonial law and the extent of its divergence from English law. On this account I shall occasionally refer to colonial statutes in the course of comparing colonial law with English law.

At the other end of this comparison, we have to remember that several Acts of Parliament were outstanding features of the English law which conceivably governed colonial judges. Long before the emigration, enactments under Edward I and Henry VIII had en-

2. William Blackstone, *Commentaries on the Laws of England* (second edition, Philadelphia, 1766), I. 69. John Austin, *Lectures on Jurisprudence* (fifth edition, London, 1885), I. 242.

3. See Zechariah Chafee, Jr., "Do Judges Make or Discover Law?" *Proceedings of the American Philosophical Society*, XCI. 405-420

tered into the texture of land law. Personal liberties derived much of their strength from Magna Charta. In so far as the colonists brought their law with them from England, it was likely to include such basic statutes as well as the unwritten law. Nor did the possible influence of Parliament on colonial courts stop with emigration. If Parliament expressly stated that a statute was in force in the colonies, its word was pretty sure to be accepted by judges there, at least before the Stamp Act brought protests against the power of Parliament to legislate on the internal affairs of realms overseas. But suppose Parliament was silent on this subject. Here a difficult problem arises, which was explored years ago by our fellow-member, St. George L. Sioussat.[4] Take, for example, the Habeas Corpus Act of 1679, which does not say that it applies to the colonies.[5] Did this great safeguard of personal freedom nevertheless operate automatically in the Massachusetts Bay Colony, which had received its charter a half century earlier? Or did it have to be re-enacted by the General Court in Boston in order to bind colonial officials? Without trying to solve this problem, I need only say that it makes clear how important Acts of Parliament might be for colonial judges.

Still, my chief interest lies elsewhere than in either English or colonial legislation. The question for this paper may be restated thus: Was the unwritten law administered in the colonial courts the same as the unwritten law of England? If not, the question will expand into asking how far these courts diverged from English law and what they put in its place.

COLONIAL CHARTERS AND ORIGINAL STATE CONSTITUTIONS OR STATUTES

Our inquiry is bounded by two sets of indisputable documents, the royal charters at the beginning of the colonial period and state constitutions or statutes soon after its close. Anybody who speculates about the nature of law during the century and a half which

4. St. George L. Sioussat, "The Theory of the Extension of English Statutes to the Plantations," *Select Essays in Anglo-American Legal History* (3 volumes, Boston, 1907-1909), I. 416-430, reprinting extracts from his "The English Statutes in Maryland," *Johns Hopkins University Studies in History and Political Science* (1903), XXI. 17-30.

5. 31 Charles II, c. 2, 8 Stat. at L. 432; reprinted in Zechariah Chafee, Jr., *Documents on Fundamental Human Rights* (Cambridge, 1951), II. 327-340.

intervened between these two sets of documents has to reckon with the clauses therein as to law in the particular colony or state.

Colonial charters or patents commonly have two relevant types of clauses, although one of these is sometimes lacking.

First, settlers in the colonies are granted the customary rights of Englishmen. This practice began in the patent from Queen Elizabeth to Sir Humphrey Gilbert in 1578.[6] It grants to all persons travelling to such lands, and their heirs, that they

> shall and maye have and enjoye all the priviledges of free denizens and parsons natyve of England and within our allegiaunce in suche like ample manner and fourme as if they were borne and personally resiaunte within our saide Realme of England any laws custome or usage to the contrary not withstandinge. . . .

A similar grant appears, with varying language in the First Charter of Virginia (1606), the Patent of the Council for New England (1620), and several subsequent charters, although not in the Massachusetts Bay Charter of 1628/9.[7] In the Connecticut Charter of 1662 the clause runs:

> That all, and every the subjects of Us . . . which shall go to inhabit within the said Colony, and every of their Children, which shall happen to be born there, or on the Seas in going thither, or returning from thence, shall have and enjoy all Liberties and Immunities of free and natural Subjects within any the Dominions of Us, Our Heirs or Successors, to all Intents, Constructions, and Purposes whatsoever, as if they and every of them were born within the realm of *England.*

Second, the clause which empowers the chartered company or proprietors to make laws is restricted by a provision that these laws shall conform to the laws of England, as closely as possible. Here again the Gilbert Patent was a model. It provides that Gilbert shall have power to govern the inhabitants of the lands settled by him:

6. *The Voyages and Colonising Enterprises of Sir Humphrey Gilbert*, David B. Quinn, Editor, (London, 1940), I. 88-94.

7. Detailed references to the charters are omitted; these are readily accessible in Francis N. Thorpe, *Federal and State Constitutions, Colonial Charters and Other Organic Laws* . . . (7 volumes, Washington, 1909).

> according to such state lawes and ordynaunces as shalbe by him [*etc.*] devysed or established for the better government of the said people as aforsaid soe alwaies that the said statutes lawes and ordenances maye be as neare as conveniently maye agreable to the forme of the lawes and pollicies of England.

A similar limitation on colonial laws was inserted in the Second Virginia Charter (1609), the Patent of the Council for New England (1620), and many later charters. The Massachusetts Bay Charter (1628/9) says:

> That it shall . . . be lawfull . . . in any of their Generall Courts . . . from tyme to tyme to make, ordeine, and establishe all manner of wholesome and reasonable orders, lawes, statutes, and ordinances, directions, and instructions not contrarie to the lawes of this our realm of England, . . . and the forme of oathes warrantable by the lawes and statutes of this our realme of England . . . and for impositions of lawful fynes, mulcts, imprisonment, or other lawfull correction, according to the course of other corporations in this our realme of England. . . .

In the Pennsylvania Charter of 1680/81, the same restriction on laws is followed by more complex provisions. During emergencies while the Assembly is not sitting, Penn and his heirs are authorized to make ordinances with the force of law—

> soe as the said Ordinances bee consonant to reason, and bee not repugnant nor contrary, but soe farre as conveniently may bee agreeable with the Lawes of our Kingdome of *England*, and soe as the said Ordinances be not extended in any Sort to bind, charge, or take away the right or Interest of any person or persons, for or in their Life, members, Freehold, goods, or Chattles.

Then comes an interesting provision for supplying Pennsylvania with law upon important matters during the gap between the settlement of the colony and the time when express laws are adopted as to such matters:

> And . . . the Lawes for regulateing and governing of Propertie within the said Province, as well for the descent and enjoyment of lands, as likewise for the enjoyment and suc-

> cession of goods and Chattles, and likewise as to Felonies, shall bee and continue the same, as they shall bee for the time being by the generall course of the Law in our Kingdom of *England*, until the said Lawes shall bee altered by the said *William Penn* . . . and by the Freemen of the said Province, their Delegates or Deputies. . . .

If these charter clauses did in fact govern the subsequent conduct of the colonists, then English law was a predominating element in colonial law. It is true that the limitation in the second type of clauses applied in its terms only to colonial legislation and not to unwritten law. Still, when statutes had to conform rather closely to English law, it would be absurd to suppose that the home government would be completely unconcerned if colonial courts allowed their nonstatutory law to depart very far from English precedents. As for the first type of clauses, many colonists would naturally want to take advantage of those to assert their legal rights as Englishmen against arbitrary local officials. In order to do so, they would have to invoke English judicial precedents to a considerable extent, because the English liberties were established by these as well as by notable statutes like Magna Charta.

On the other hand, the colonists might have strong reasons of their own for disregarding the charter limitations and regulating their affairs according to their ideas of what was just and convenient. Such violations of the charters might go unchecked because British governments were far away, busy with other matters, and unable to interfere effectively. "A wise and salutary neglect"[8] might be their policy during most of the years before the final victory over France in 1763 unhappily led them to intensify their supervision of American matters.

In the other set of basic documents, which came at the close of the colonial period, Americans referred to English law as embodied in their law, in language more specific than the charters. As early as May, 1776, for example, the Virginia Convention which later adopted the Declaration of Rights enacted an ordinance:

> That the common law of England, all statutes or acts of parliament made in aid of the common law prior to the fourth year of the reign of king James the first, and which are of a general nature, not local to that kingdom, together

8. Edmond Burke, "Speech on the Conciliation of America," *Works* (Boston, 1881), II. 117.

> with the several acts of the general assembly of this colony now in force, [so far as consistent with action by this convention], shall be the rule of decision, and shall be considered as in full force, until the same shall be altered by the legislative power of this colony.[9]

On July 2, 1776, the New Jersey Constitution, framed by a convention, declared:

> That the common law of England, as well as so much of the statute law, as have been heretofore practised in this Colony, shall still remain in force, until they shall be altered by a future law of the Legislature; such parts only excepted, as are repugnant to the rights and privileges contained in this Charter [constitution]. . . .[10]

Many other states soon adopted similar provisions either in their constitutions or by legislation.[11] It will be observed that the passages quoted, unlike the charters, do not refer to English law in general terms, but speak of "the common law of England" and a carefully defined body of English statutes. In accordance with the limitations of this paper, we can leave aside these statutes and the problem of the status of Acts of Parliament after the settlement of each colony, and confine our attention to the statements about the rest of the law of England.

This emphasis on the common law was in accordance with the settled attitude of the colonists during the controversies with Great Britain before the Revolution broke out with fighting. Thus the Continental Congress, soon after it convened, adopted a Declaration and Resolves on October 14, 1774. One resolution was: "That the respective colonies are entitled to the common law of England. . . ."[12] And the Declaration of Independence listed among the grievances against George III his "abolishing the free system of English law" in Quebec, as a precedent "for introducing the same absolute rule" into the English-speaking colonies.

Nevertheless, we have to be cautious about regarding these

9. William W. Hening, *The Statutes at Large; Being A Collection of all the Laws of Virginia* (Richmond, 1821), IX. 127.

10. Thorpe, *Federal and State Constitutions . . .*, V. 2598.

11. For a useful discussion of some problems raised by such provisions, see Herbert Pope, "The English Common Law in the United States," *Harvard Law Review*, XXIV (1910), 6-30.

12. *Journals of the Continental Congress, 1774-1789* (Washington, 1904), I. 69.

references to the common law during our Revolutionary period as conclusive proof that the entire unwritten law of England had been continuously operating since the colonies were settled. In the first place, the patriots may have exaggerated the identity between their law and English law for political reasons, so as to strengthen their arguments against British taxes and other obnoxious proceedings. The fact that Coke and his associates were not always historically accurate in their use of Magna Charta and other precedents in their controversies with Charles I has some significance. Secondly, even if the patriots were right about colonial law in their own time, it may not have been always like that. Much greater divergencies from English law may have existed during a considerable portion of the earlier life of the colonies. Perhaps they lacked adequate information about colonial law a century before. Certainly they had no strong motives for investigating that subject and reporting about it with scrupulous thoroughness.

Finally, these documents leave us with the problem of what the men of Revolutionary times meant by "the common law of England." The words "common law" have at least four recognized meanings, varying with the circumstances in which they are used. First, they describe the legal system now prevalent in the United States and most of the British Commonwealth of Nations as contrasted with the Civil Law of Continental Europe, Scotland, and Quebec, which is derived from Roman Law. Secondly, they mean the law common to all of England. Blackstone speaks of "general customs, or the common law, properly so called; this is that law, by which proceedings in the king's ordinary courts of justice are guided and directed."[13] He distinguishes it from particular customs which, for the most part, affect only the inhabitants of particular districts, and from certain particular laws which, by custom, are adopted and used only in certain peculiar courts—the ecclesiastical courts, for instance. Thirdly, the phrase means unwritten law in contrast with legislation. Fourth, it is used with reference to the distinction between equity, applied in the Court of Chancery, and the law, applied in the Courts of Common Pleas, King's Bench, and Exchequer. Not long after the period of these documents, the United States Constitution had this meaning when it spoke in Article III of "all Cases, in Law and Equity," and in the Seventh Amendment of "suits at common law."

13. Blackstone, *Commentaries on the Laws of England*, I. 68.

This fourth sense can be eliminated while we are trying to interpret "common law of England" in early state constitutions and statutes. Probably the third sense, unwritten law, had a predominating influence. Still, the first and second meanings may have played some part. And we cannot be sure that the draftsmen had a very clear idea of what they were talking about, although they were sure it was something they liked. At all events, the words leave plenty of room for controversy, and controversy has not failed to take place.

Three Theories Which Have Been Advanced as to Colonial Law

The phrases quoted from early state constitutions and statutes treat the common law, however defined, as nothing new. Apparently the people wanted to keep something they had long possessed. But for how long?

To this question three widely different answers have been given by scholars whose judgment deserves much respect. I shall begin by stating and discussing the two theories which have received the most support. The third theory, which has been recently suggested by a single scholar of distinction, will be presented afterwards.

1. *The theory that the common law of England was substantially in force in the colonies from the time of their settlement.* This may be regarded as the orthodox legal theory, since it is the only view of the matter which has been accepted in judicial opinions. It is backed by the high authority of our former member, Mr. Justice Story. Besides voicing this theory in a decision of the United States Supreme Court,[14] he set it forth at length in his *Commentaries on the Constitution of the United States:*

> In the charters . . . either expressly or by necessary implication it is provided that the laws of England so far as applicable shall be in force there. . . .
>
> And so has been the uniform doctrine in America ever since the settlement of the colonies. The universal principle (and the practice has conformed to it) has been, that the common law is our birthright and inheritance, and that our ancestors brought hither with them upon their emigration all of it, which was applicable to their situation. The whole

14. *Van Ness v. Packard*, 2 Peters (U.S.) Reports 137 at 144 (1829).

> structure of our present jurisprudence stands upon the original foundations of the common law.
>
> We thus see in a very clear light the mode in which the common law was first introduced into the colonies; as well as the true reason of the exceptions to it to be found in our colonial usages and laws. It was not introduced as of original and universal obligation in its utmost latitude; but the limitations contained in the bosom of the common law itself, and indeed constituting a part of the law of nations, were affirmatively settled and recognized in the respective charters of settlement.[15]

A similar view was expressed from the Massachusetts bench in 1847 by our former member, Chief-Justice Lemuel Shaw. William Chapman had been indicted for a criminal libel and objected that there was no law of Massachusetts which made this punishable as an offence. Certainly there was no statute to that effect. The United States Supreme Court had held that there are no federal crimes except those established and defined by Congress.[16] A similar doctrine prevails in some states. However, Chief-Justice Shaw took the contrary position and decided that libel was a crime in Massachussets because it was a crime at common law. He said:

> It is true that there is no statute of the Commonwealth declaring the writing or publishing of a written libel, or a malicious libel by signs and pictures, a punishable offence. But this goes little way towards settling the question. A great part of the municipal law of Massachusetts, both civil and criminal, is an unwritten and traditionary law. It has been common to denominate this "the common law of England," because it is no doubt true that a large portion of it has been derived from the laws of England, either the common law of England, or those English statutes passed before the emigration of our ancestors, and constituting a part of that law, by which, as English subjects, they were governed when they emigrated; or statutes made afterwards, of a general nature, in amendment or modification of the common law, which were adopted in the colony or providence by general consent.
>
> In addition to these sources of unwritten law, some

15. Joseph Story, *Commentaries on the Constitution of the United States* (second edition, Boston, 1851).

16. *United States v. Hudson*, 7 Cranch (U.S.) Reports 32 (1812), nullifying an indictment for a criminal libel.

usages, growing out of the peculiar situation and exigencies of the earlier settlers of Massachusetts, not traceable to any written statute or ordinance, but adopted by general consent, have long had the force of law; as, for instance the convenient practice by which, if a married woman join with her husband in a deed conveying land of which she is seized in her own right, and simply acknowledge it before a magistrate, it shall be valid to pass her land, without the more expensive process of a fine, required by the common law. Indeed, considering all these sources of unwritten and traditionary law, it is now more accurate, instead of the common law of England, which constitutes a part of it, to call it collectively the common law of Massachusetts.

To a very great extent, the unwritten law constitutes the basis of our jurisprudence, and furnishes the rules by which public and private rights are established and secured, the social relations of all persons regulated, their rights, duties, and obligations determined, and all violations of duty redressed and punished. Without its aid, the written law, embracing the constitution and statute laws, would constitute but a lame, partial, and impracticable system. Even in many cases, where statutes have been made in respect to particular subjects, they could not be carried into effect, and must remain a dead letter, without the aid of the common law. . . .

When our ancestors first settled this country, they came here as English subjects; they settled on the land as English territory, constituting part of the realm of England, and of course governed by its laws; they accepted charters from the English government, conferring both political powers and civil privileges; and they never ceased to claim the rights and privileges of English subjects, till the revolution. It is not therefore, perhaps, so accurate to say, that they established the laws of England here, as to say, that they were subject to the laws of England. When they left one portion of its territory, they were alike subject, on their transit and when they arrived at another portion of the English territory; and therefore always, till the declaration of independence, they were governed and protected by the laws of England, so far as those laws were applicable to their state and condition.[17]

The fact that Story and Shaw, like many of the early state constitutions and statutes, recognized that the common law did not

17. *Commonwealth v. Chapman*, 13 Metcalf (Mass.) Reports 69 at 68-69, 73-74 (1847).

apply in the colonies when it would have been inappropriate to our circumstances does leave some leeway for a different kind of colonial law. It is always interesting to learn of any such special situation. Shaw mentions one of them in the opinion just quoted. Thomas Jefferson in his *Notes on Virginia,* written in 1781, while discussing in Query XIV "The administration of justice and the description of the laws," says: "The laws of England seem to have been adopted by common consent of the settlers, which might easily enough be done whilst they were few and living altogether." Then he mentions a statute of 1661 in which the Virginia Assembly expressly adopted these laws, unless "a difference of condition" rendered them inapplicable.[18] Jefferson goes on to describe at some length a considerable number of Virginian variations from the British model because of such "a difference of condition."

Nevertheless, the existence of some peculiarly American law to take care of local conditions does not really vitiate the theory that the English common law was substantially in force in the colonies from the beginning. Supporters of the orthodox theory regard the common law as prevailing unless there were special reasons for departing from it. This rather small exception is quite different from the position of the writers next to be considered, who have asserted that the colonists deliberately threw overboard a very large portion of English law and established in its place regulations of their own making.

2. *The theory that the colonists had in large measure their own kind of law for a long time after their settlement in America.* The first vigorous attack on the orthodox theory was made in 1899 by Paul S. Reinsch, afterwards Professor of Political Science in the University of Wisconsin.[19] Reinsch began by stating Story's view that "the common law was from the first looked upon by the colonists as a system of positive and subsidiary law," which applied whenever it was not replaced by colonial legislation or by special customs, and then rejected this view:

> On the contrary, we find from the very first, originality in legal conceptions, departing widely from the most settled theories of the common law, and even a total denial of the subsidiary character of English jurisprudence. . . .

18. Hening, *Statutes at Large . . . Virginia,* II. 43.

19. Paul S. Reinsch, "The English Common Law in the Early American Colonies," *Select Essays in Anglo-American Legal History,* I. 367-415, reprinted from the *Bulletin* of the University of Wisconsin, Volume II.

> The earliest settlers in many of the colonies made bodies of law, which, from every indication, they considered a complete statement of the needful legal regulations. Their civilization being primitive, a brief code concerning crimes, torts, and the simplest contracts, in many ways like the dooms of the Anglo-Saxon kings, would be sufficient. Not only did these codes innovate upon, and depart from, the models of common law, but, in matters not fixed by such codes, there was in the earliest times no reference to that system. They were left to the discretion of the magistrates.
>
> In many cases the colonists expressed an adhesion to the common law, but, when we investigated the actual administration of justice, we find that usually it was of a rude, popular, summary kind, in which the refined distinctions, the artifical developments of the older system have no place. A technical system can, of course, be administered only with the aid of trained lawyers. But these were generally not found in the colonies during the 17th century, and even far down into the 18th we shall find that the legal administration was in the hands of laymen in many of the provinces. Only as the lawyers grow more numerous and receive a better training, do we find a general reception and use of the more refined theories of the common law. It is but natural that, with increased training, the courts and practitioners should turn to the great reservoir of legal experience in their own language for guidance and information; the courts would be more ready to favor the theory of the adoption of the common law, as it increased their importance, virtually giving them legislative power. The foregoing statements are especially true of New England, where the subsidiary force of the common law was plainly denied; where a system of popular law (Volksrecht) grew up; and, where the law of God took the place of a secondary system.
>
> . . . we had a period of rude, untechnical popular law, followed, as lawyers became numerous and the study of law prominent, by the gradual reception of most of the rules of the English common law.[20]

A similar position was taken by Dean Charles J. Hilkey of Emory University Law School in Atlanta, Georgia, in 1910.[21] Although

20. *Ibid.*, 369-370.

21. Charles J. Hilkey, "Legal Developments in Colonial Massachusetts, 1630-1686," *Columbia Studies in History, Economics and Public Law*, XXXVII (1910), 157. See the careful examination of the situation in the early years of the

Reinsch and Hilkey conceded that the settlers were influenced by their former contact with English law, they asserted that the colonies did not consider English law binding. In so far as the settlers needed to use past experience for obtaining rules of law, they took them from the Old Testament and not from English sources.

There are two important propositions in this theory. First, the original law of the colonies was for the most part very different from English law and had a rude, popular nature. Secondly, eventually a reception of most of the rules of the English common law took place. This was a process somewhat resembling the well-known Reception of Roman Law into Germany and Holland during the Renaissance.[22]

Our fellow-member, Roscoe Pound, appears to agree in his writings with both these propositions, and he has done a good deal to expound the second of them. The following quotations indicate his position.

> . . . the history of the common law in America, begins for practical purposes, after the Revolution . . . Law made little progress in America in the seventeenth century. Social and economic conditions were such that a rude administration of justice by magistrates sufficed. . . .
>
> . . . law had made some progress in America at the outbreak of the Revolution. There had been a gradual evolution of a judicial system, and in many places there was coming to be a well-trained bar. Doubtless this would have insured a reception and development of the common law. But it happened here, as in seventeeth-century England, that the common law became useful as a political weapon. Thus a tradition arose that the colonists had brought with them the common law, as a much-prized heritage, and had clung to it and asserted it in the new world. . . .
>
> After the Revolution a reaction set in. . . . Naturally the public was hostile to England and to all that was English, and it was impossible for the common law to escape the odium of its English origin. . . . It is not too much to say that in the second decade of the nineteenth century, when

Massachusetts Bay Colony by Richard B. Morris, "Massachusetts and the Common Law: The Declaration of 1646," *American Historical Review,* XXXI (1926), 443-453.

22. See Frederick W. Maitland, "English Law and the Renaissance," *Select Essays in Anglo-American Legal History,* I. 168 and 170-175; John C. Gray, "Nature and Sources of the Law" (second edition, New York, 1921), 230-324.

Judge Story took his seat upon the Bench, the work of receiving and adapting the common law and our developing therefrom a system of American law remained yet to do.[23]

For most practical purposes American judicial history begins after the Revolution. Administration of justice in colonial America was at first executive and legislative, and these types of non-judicial justice persisted well into the last century. Again with a few conspicuous exceptions the courts before and for some time after the Revolution were made up largely of untrained magistrates who administered justice according to their common sense and the light of nature with some guidance from legislation. Until the Revolution in most of the colonies it was not considered necessary or even expedient to have judges learned in the law. . . . When James Kent went upon the bench in New York in 1791, he could say with entire truth: "There were no reports or state precedents. The opinions from the bench were delivered *ore tenus*. We had no law of our own and nobody knew what [the law] was."

Our judicial organization, then, and the great body of our American common law are the work of the last quarter of the eighteenth century and the first half of the nineteenth century. . . .

In the homogeneous pioneer or rural community of the first half of the nineteenth century, the administration of justice involved three problems: (1) To receive the English common law, or to find somewhere else a basis for legal development, and to work out upon the basis adopted a system of principles and rules adapted to America. . . .

Chief of these problems was the one first named, the problem of working out a system of rules and principles applicable to America. It has long been the orthodox view that the colonists brought the common law with them and that the English law has obtained in this country from the beginning. But this is only a legal theory. In fact the colonies began with all manner of experiments in administering justice without law and it was not till the middle of the eighteenth century that the setting up of a system of courts and the rise of a custom of studying law in England began to make for a general administration of justice according to English law. Just prior to the Revolution the wide-spread

23. Roscoe Pound, "The Place of Judge Story in the Making of American Law," *American Law Review*, XLVIII (1912), 676 and 680-682.

study of Blackstone, whose first edition appeared in 1765, gave great impetus to the reception of the common law. But as late as 1791 the law was so completely at large in New York that the genius of a Kent was needed to make the common law the law of that state.[24]

Thirty years ago I held the same theory and set it forth in the following passage, which contains more sentences I now regret than anything else I have written:

> Hostility to lawyers and case-law is no new phenomenon in this country. Puritans and Quakers arrived with unpleasant memories of the English bench and bar, who had harried them out of their homes. To them, law meant heresy trials, and the impression that these left on the minds of their victims has been set down forever by Bunyan in the prosecution of Faithful at Vanity Fair. The colonists were no more anxious to transplant some Lord Hate-good, his counsellors, and his law books to our shores, than Eugene V. Debs would strive to set up injunctions and sedition statutes if he were founding a socialistic commonwealth in the South Seas. The popular attitude toward lawyers was re-inforced by the clergy who were naturally reluctant to have their great moral and intellectual influence disputed by men who would hire themselves out to argue either side of any question. The ministers who ruled Massachusetts and Connecticut by the Law of Moses, wanted no rivals to challenge their decisions upon the authority of Bracton and Coke. And everywhere, except perhaps on the Southern plantations, the complicated structure of feudal doctrines, which constituted such a large part of English law well into the 18th century, was as unsuited to Colonial ways and needs as a Gothic cathedral in the wilderness. Life was so pressing, time was so short, labour was scarce, that the only law which could receive acceptance must be so simple that the settlers could apply it themselves. Although Justice Story has spread wide the belief that our ancestors brought the Common Law to New England on the *Mayflower*, the truth is that only a few fragments got across. These were rapidly supplemented by rules based on pioneer conditions. Much the same phenomenon occurred as in the California of 1849, where the miners

24. Roscoe Pound, *The Spirit of Common Law* (Boston, 1921), 113-116. See also, Pound, "What of Stare Decisis?" *Fordham Law Review*, x (1941), Number 1, 4-5.

> ignored the water-law of the Atlantic seaboard which gave each person bordering on a stream some share of the water, and adopted instead the custom better suited to a new country of first come, first served. Almost the earliest task of the founders of a Colony was the regulation of the disputes which arise in a primitive civilization by a brief legislative code concerning crimes, torts, and the simplest contracts, in many ways like the dooms of the Anglo-Saxon kings. Gaps in these codes were not filled from the Common Law, as would be the case to-day, but by the discretion of the magistrate, or in some Colonies, in the early days, from the Bible. Land laws and conveyances were simple,—the underlying English principle of primogeniture was abolished outright by several Colonial charters, and disputes of title were lessened by the admirable system of registering deeds. Such law did not require lawyers, and it is not surprising that even the magistrates were usually laymen. The chief justice of Rhode Island as late as 1818 was a blacksmith. Oftentimes a controversy was taken away from the court by the legislature and settled by a special statute. Thus, instead of the English and modern American judge-made law, the Colonists received for the most part executive and legislative justice, and lived under a protoplasmic popular law, with the Common Law only one of its many ingredients.[25]

Although each of these theories contains part of the truth about colonial law, as I shall endeavor to show later, both of them now seem to me to have serious shortcomings. According to the first view, the settlers transported most of their law with them from England, like cattle and furniture. By the second view, they created almost all their law afresh in America, like the houses they had to build there without stick or stone from their former abodes. Either extreme disregards the wise reflection in the Epistles of Horace: "They change their skies but not their minds who sail across the sea." Since law is the outcome of the thoughts of men in response to the conditions in which they live, colonial law was very likely to be a component of the situation of the settlers in the New World and of the ideas they carried across the Atlantic. It is essential to remember that some of their ideas had been developing for centuries in the Old World, for instance, the concepts of

25. Chafee, "The Law," in *Civilization in the United States: An Inquiry by Thirty Americans*, Harold E. Stearns, Editor (New York, 1922), 53 at 54-55.

English law, while others were the product of the Reformation, especially the more extreme aspects of it, and of their own bent as earnest individuals.

Colonial law could not be overwhelmingly English law. Some of this would be useless in a different physical environment and novel ways of life. An added factor favoring change was that many colonists were innovators by nature, notably the Pilgrims and Puritans in New England and the Quakers in Pennsylvania or New Jersey. They wanted to break away from a good deal of what they had left behind them in England. They were in close touch with the Englishmen who brought about significant legal reforms during the Commonwealth, like the elimination of Latin from court proceedings; although such reforms were mostly dropped in England when Charles II was restored to the throne, they had a better chance of persisting overseas. Some colonists had good reason to dislike parts of the English law, which had harried them with imprisonment and other penalties. By and large, the settlers were not the kind of men who shrink from change and preserve the past for its own sake.

And yet colonial law could not be overwhelmingly new law. Nobody can get outside himself to do his thinking, even after he has tossed for weeks on the Atlantic. No doubt, new surroundings do eventually produce new thoughts, but these do not wholly drive out deeply-rooted attitudes and customary methods of handling practical difficulties. It takes too much trouble to discard everything you know and start all over again. Even after a revolution, it has been sagely observed: "*Plus ça change, plus c'est la même chose.*" And the settlement of the American colonies was far from being a revolution. In spite of being innovators, the New Englanders and the Quakers had considerable continuity with the past and the remaining colonists were still closer to their English background. Here, too, there was an added factor, which in this case tended to produce compliance with English law. Officials in England and those who were sent to America kept the colonists from being completely free to make their law as they pleased. Had they wished to make it wholly unlike English law, which was not the case, the government at home would have cracked down on them in various ways. Conservatives might be scarce in the colonies, but you could find them governing in London. Although they could not produce so much legal uniformity between the colonies and England as they desired, they did have power to accomplish a good deal whenever their attention was aroused.

The *a priori* reasoning just set forth is aptly confirmed by the printed records of the proceedings in colonial courts. During the thirty years since I wrote the paragraph quoted above, my attitude toward colonial law has been much altered by editing Massachusetts Records toward the end of the seventeenth century with our fellow-member, Samuel E. Morison, and by reading Daniel J. Boorstin's publication of the elaborate notebooks which Delaware lawyers compiled of cases argued or witnessed by them between the Revolution and 1800.[26] These sources furnish convincing proof that the two theories of colonial law already set forth describe different sides of the same shield, and that the situation was much more complex than either theory recognizes.

Start with Story's theory. It is irreconcilable with the court records, if it means that the common law existed in the colonies in the same way that it did in England. English law during the seventeenth and eighteenth centuries comprised a large number of technical legal rules. These rules were worked out in a number of courts with the aid of a trained bar from which the judges had been selected. The lawyers on each side cited earlier cases in support of their respective positions, and the decision thus obtained was accompanied by one or more judicial opinions in which great attention was given to the same sort of earlier case-law. By contrast, colonial courts were simply organized and usually composed of laymen. Although the litigant frequently sent somebody else to present his case for him, this representative might be more like a business agent than a lawyer. He got his training from experience in court much more than from studying law books. Earlier decisions played little or no part in the arguments for each side, and judicial opinions were virtually non-existent until after the Revolution. Indeed, questions of law were little discussed. Decisions usually turned on issues of fact. In so far as "the common law of England" consisted of an assemblage of specific English decisions, it is hard to find anything of this sort during many decades of

26. *Records of the Suffolk County Court, 1671-1680* (2 volumes, *Publications of the Colonial Society of Massachusetts*, Boston, 1933), I. xxix and xxx; and *Delaware Cases, 1792-1830*, Daniel J. Boorstin, Editor, assisted by Frankel and Helman (3 volumes, St. Paul, 1943). The numerous cases before 1801 in these Delaware volumes are reviewed by Chafee, 57 *Harvard Law Review*, LVII (1944), 399-430.

colonial court proceedings, and the process by which disputes were adjusted by courts was much simpler in the colonies than in England.

Still, Story's theory has a good deal of truth to it if we define "the common law of England" more broadly and regard it as a system of principles and rules of action. Such a system could be learned by the colonists from a few treatises like Coke's *Institutes* and Dalton's *Justice of the Peace,* which we know they possessed. Such an "unwritten law" might gradually change with the passage of time. Colonists would go to England to study law at the Inns of Court and return with many law reports for their libraries. Proprietors and British officials would cite court decisions in their disputes with the settlers. Thus the original system of principles would eventually absorb big chunks of case-law. Yet at no point in the process would there be a sharp break or any sense of something new. The lawyers who helped put the phrases about "the common law of England" into early state constitutions may have felt that they were preserving what the colonies had always had since the first settlers landed. And it is arguable that according to the standards of a world of mutability they were right. "The test of personal identity . . . lies . . . in its life—in the continuity of its life."[27]

The Reinsch theory of an indigenous American law also conforms only in part to the recorded facts. Consider its first proposition. The colonial court records do bear this out to the extent that they reveal departures from English law, which I have already mentioned. Yet there were more English elements in colonial law than this theory recognizes. Professor Theodore Plucknett of the London School of Economics points out how much the Massachusetts Laws and Liberties of 1648 were indebted to the common law.[28]

Moreover, the view that colonial law was either rude or drawn from the Bible is dispelled by a study of the court records, at least after the earliest periods of settlement. Instead, judicial proceedings although simpler than in England do show a good deal of formality and sophistication. As for the Bible, the Massachusetts settlers did use it in their criminal statutes for capital crimes, but

27. Haldane, *arguendo,* in *Free Church of Scotland v. Overtown* [1904] A.C. 515, 609.

28. Theodore Plucknett, book review, *New England Quarterly,* III (1930), 157-158.

it had little effect upon the law they had in civil litigation. The Suffolk County Court Records do not support Hilkey's statement that "the Scriptures were an infallible guide for both judge and legislator."[29] For example, in a Boston case in 1679 where the inheritance of land of a man was disputed between the dead man's relatives on his father's side and those on his mother's side, the former group relied on a text in the Book of Numbers favoring males and insisted that they ought to get the land "according to the law of God." The opponents replied that this part of the Bible was an unsafe basis for legal decisions, since it provided for a complete distribution of land in a Year of Jubilee every fifty years, which would upset every land title in the Massachusetts Bay Colony.[30] The Delaware cases a century later ignored the Bible and paid considerable attention to English precedents, besides occasionally citing earlier decisions in Delaware.

My study of the court records makes me wonder whether the absence of professional lawyers indicates legal immaturity quite so much as Mr. Pound suggests. Men were much less specialized in colonial times than today. It is well known that they were jacks of all trades. The lack of professional architects did not deprive the country of good colonial buildings, and men who were not lawyers in our sense might attain a similar proficiency in conducting or deciding litigation or in drafting documents. Conveyances of land were technically phrased. Moreover, a good many of the lay judges occupied high official positions in their respective colonies, so that they were accustomed to act responsibly and to keep constantly in touch with statutes and other parts of the law. The arguments in the court records often seem to be addressed to thoughtful judges, in spite of their infrequent use of precedents. Additional proof that laymen among the colonies often knew a good deal of law is furnished by a famous passage in Burke's Speech on Conciliation in 1775:

> In no country, perhaps, in the world is law so general a study. The profession itself is numerous and powerful, and in most provinces it takes the lead. The greater number of the deputies sent to the Congress were lawyers. But all who read, and most do read, endeavor to obtain some smattering

29. Hilkey, "Legal Development in Colonial Massachusetts, 1630-1686," 68. Compare Introduction to *Records of the Suffolk County Court*, I. xxxii-xxxiv.

30. *Records of the Suffolk County Court*, II. 1034-1037.

> in that science. I have been told by an eminent bookseller, that in no branch of his business, after tracts of popular devotion, were so many books as those on the law exported to the plantations. The colonists have now fallen into the way of printing them for their own use. I hear they have sold nearly as many of Blackstones "Commentaries" in America as in England.[31]

Finally, the records render one very cautious in generalizing about colonial law, as if it were the same at all times and in all colonies. On the contrary, he soon sees that litigation reached different levels of maturity in the various colonies at a given period. For instance, Maryland lawyers and procedure in the middle of the eighteenth century were much closer to the English situation than was the case in Rhode Island. Another lesson is that the state of the law in a particular colony depends a good deal on the decade one is considering. After all, it was 169 years from Jamestown to the Declaration of Independence, as long a time as from 1776 until the surrender of Japan in Tokyo Harbor. Many changes are bound to occur in five generations. Thus the General Court of Massachusetts declared (somewhat inaccurately) in 1646: "Our allegiance binds us not to the laws of England any longer than while we live in England. . . ."[32] It does not follow that the same statement would have been made in the Suffolk County Court between 1671 and 1680, and its soundness would have been still more questionable. When James Otis and John Adams were arguing against writs of assistance a century later, they relied on English precedents and would have indignantly repudiated the motion that the laws of England gave the colonists no rights.[33]

Further doubts about the Reinsch theory arise from its second proposition, about the substitution of English law in place of the very different preceding system. It is difficult to find any evidence in the court records that such a "reception" took place, and yet it is an essential part of the theory. No doubt, Pound rightly stresses the increased use of English precedents after the Revolution, and the Delaware records show a good deal of it going on while Kent and Story were boys. But a reception of English case-law is not

31. Burke, *Works*, II. 124-125.

32. Quoted by Richard B. Morris, "Massachusetts and the Common Law," 452, from *Journal of the General Court*, I. 388.

33. See the material on writs of assistance in Josiah Quincy, Jr., *Reports of Cases . . . 1761-1772* (Boston, 1865), 395-540.

the same thing as the alleged reception of the common law. The important point is that lawyers during the Revolutionary period believed they were using the common law, whether or not they cited English decisions. The affirmation of the common law in the early state constitutions and statutes was made on too wide a scale to be dismissed as mere political propaganda. When the colonists eagerly bought copies of Blackstone, as Burke tells us, they did not suppose they were learning about foreign law.[34] Plainly they wanted Blackstone because he was expounding *their* law. This carries us back to my earlier suggestion that "the common law of England" meant to its users something else than case-law; it described the system of principles and rules of action which obtained in England. Then the alleged "reception" of English law in this sense must have taken place at some time before 1776.

What was the date of the big break with the past in the legal history of every colony? Here I find a great difficulty for the Reinsch theory. If a particular colony actually had a system alien to the common law for a considerable period after its settlement, a fairly obvious transition must have occurred when the new law imported from England replaced bodily the old law which the colonists had known for decades. Of course, this alleged transition was not the act of a day, like the periodic oscillations of unhappy Alsace from the Code Napoleon to the German Code and vice versa. The process of shifting over may have occupied several years, like the reception of the Roman law to which it has been compared. But we have abundant proof of the reception of the Roman law into any given country of Europe from the men who lived through it; we know what they thought about it; historians can give its approximate dates. Have we similar proof of the "reception" of the English common law in any given American colony? Do we learn from that generation or the next just when and how it happened? Unless the common law was always considered to be in force (which these modernist writers deny), one would suppose that contemporaries, especially lawyers, would be greatly impressed by the arrival of a complete new system of law from overseas and the simultaneous rejection of the law of their ancestors. They would comment on this striking event in their letters and diaries, they would get it into histories, they and their children would

34. Burke, *Works*, II. 124-125.

speak of it for years afterwards, just as they remembered the Great Awakening and we remember the Great Depression.

Taking the rather abundant court records of Delaware, I made a thorough search for any mention of the disappearance of an indigenous American law and the arrival of a new system from England.[35] Nothing of the sort was found. Instead, everybody appeared to take it for granted that the law of Delaware after Independence was the law which it had always had since its settlement.

Nobody can speak with assurance on this subject until a similar search has been made in several other colonies, but it seems fair to ask supporters of the Reinsch theory to produce some contemporaneous evidence of an awareness on the part of colonists that they had shifted from a native American law to the recently imported common law.

3. *The theory that colonial law was English local law.* In 1931 Story's theory was subjected to a different attack by Professor Julius Goebel of Columbia Law School.[36] He agreed with the Reinsch theory that for decades after settlement the English common law was largely an alien system in the colonies, but diverged widely as to what law did prevail. Instead of assuming that our ancestors left behind them practically all the legal portion of their cultural heritage and suffered a complete sea-change, Goebel concluded that they brought across the Atlantic the very law they had known in England. But *their* English law, he maintained, was not the common law. That consisted of the decisions and doctrines of the King's courts in London, which meant little to them. The law under which settlers had grown up was the customary law administered in the English local courts, which sat in county towns and boroughs and manors.

> So accustomed are we to focus our attention upon the expansion of the King's law that we have closed our eyes to the fact that at the outset of the seventeenth century local

35. Chafee, book review, *Harvard Law Review*, LVII. 416-418.

36. Julius Goebel, "King's Law and Local Customs in Seventeenth Century New England," *Columbia Law Review*, XXXI (1931), 416. See, also, the introduction to Richard B. Morris, *Select Cases of the Mayor's Court of New York City, 1674-1784* (American Historical Association, 1935); George Lee Haskins, "The Beginnings of the Recording System in Massachusetts," *Boston University Law Review*, XXI (1941), 281, pointing out the influence of borough and manorial customs.

> custom and local courts were still an immensely important part of the law administration in England.[37]

It was to the local courts that the small farmer or artisan would turn if he wished to get back his misappropriated cows or collect a bill; and it was these courts which turned upon him if his hogs had no rings in their noses or if he put his garbage in the street.[38]

This transplantation of local institutions and customary law was, according to Goebel, the basic factor in the colonial law of the seventeenth century. Eventually—here he does agree with Reinsch—as the administration of justice became professionalized, "the Leviathan common law was set in motion." Yet the seventeenth century "gave us legal institutions which the common law never succeeded in smothering."[39] But Goebel indignantly repudiated the view of Reinsch that the settlers had a rude folk law. In a later book, he says of the colonial records of the City and County of New York:[40]

> They reveal that in one outpost of Europe litigation was conducted as skillfully as at York or Bristol, and that the picture of an oafish frontier jurisprudence is a mirage of writers who have never blown the dust from indictment, pleading or judgment roll.

Goebel's theory is more persuasive to me than the theory of an indigenous and primitive law. It allows for the fact that emigrants carry their minds with them. Continuing to do justice by familiar methods was more probable than inventing a mass of novel rules and processes after arrival in America. Goebel speaks after making a comprehensive and careful study of court records, first at Plymouth and then in New York. In the Massachusetts Bay Colony, John Winthrop had been Recorder (judge) in the local court of the town of Norwich. Interesting parallels between the Mayor's Court in New York City and the Mayor's Court in London have been brought out by Richard B. Morris of Columbia.[41]

37. Goebel, "King's Law and Local Custom in Seventeenth Century New England," 417.

38. *Ibid.*, 420.

39. *Ibid.*, 448.

40. Julius Goebel and T. R. Naughton, *Law Enforcement in Colonial New York: A Study in Criminal Procedure (1664-1776)* (New York, Commonwealth Fund, 1944), xxvi.

41. Morris, *Select Cases of the Mayor's Court of New York City, 1674-1784.*

Yet before we conclude that a predominant portion of colonial law can be thus explained, we need to learn more about what went on in the English local courts and also to widen the comparison to include a greater number of colonial courts. For instance, I have some misgivings whether Plymouth was typical. Methods which adequately handled affairs in this small and simple colony may not have sufficed in the Bay Colony or Virginia. Moreover, it is not enough to show that the colonists handled small disputes in the same way that Englishmen handled small disputes. The real question is what was done in America about big litigations and serious crimes, which in England went to the King's courts and were governed by the common law.

Whatever the extent of colonial borrowings from the local English sources described by Goebel, several reasons make me conjecture that the common law was also an important element for a long time before Independence, even if not at the very beginning. In view of the assertions in the early state constitutions and statutes about "the common law of England," Goebel like Reinsch has to presuppose a sharp break between two systems of law. At what date did the English common law replace English local law in the colonies? Why is it that nobody appears to remember this significant event? Furthermore, it would have been very hard for the settlers to take over only a portion of English law from subordinate local courts and insulate themselves from the output of the King's courts. In England the local courts had no independent existence; they existed alongside the King's courts, which could control them.

It would be interesting to examine the textbooks about local procedure used in the colonies and see how extensively these bring in common-law rules as overriding. In any case, the colonists consulted treatises like Coke's *Institutes* which were permeated with decisions by the King's courts. And they must have relied on these decisions for safeguards of fundamental liberties, like the writ of habeas corpus before the Act of 1679.[42] Finally, even if the colonists desired to ignore the common law, the royal officials in England were sure to invoke it in important affairs. Goebel's theory seems a bit like drinking only the vermouth in a well-mixed Martini and avoiding the gin.

42. See note 5 above.

Suggestions Looking Toward a Solution of the Problem

It is too soon to enunciate any definite conclusion about the three contesting theories. More of the considerable materials already in print need to be subjected to a critical examination by scholars, so as to ascertain the sources of the law applied in a given colony at a given time.[43] And more court manuscripts need to be published by editors who have this problem constantly in mind.

When this process is farther advanced, we may find that all three theories are partly true. It may turn out that Winthrop and Penn and the rest brought over the common law as a body of principles, and not as the mass of case-law which Story knew; that it was always binding on the settlers, but required to be supplemented from other sources of unwritten law in order to meet their increasingly complex needs, with which local legislation could not possibly keep pace. Reinsch and Goebel and other critics of Story have supplied valuable information about these auxiliary sources of colonial law, but have perhaps exaggerated their importance and underestimated that of the common law. According to this surmise, there was no "reception" of the common law in the colonies. It was there from the start in some form, yet not the same form. I think of it as an outline map which was gradually filled in as the growth of law libraries and serious legal students brought more and more case-law and detailed doctrines from England. Law was a function of law-books.

Such a developing common law would naturally play an increasing part in the administration of justice outside the scope of colonial statutes and it would tend to displace whatever existed of homemade law or English local law. The long process can be considered at an end when the records show judges and lawyers in an American court reasoning and using precedents like their contemporaries in an English court. Yet something may still remain of the factors stressed by Reinsch and Goebel, especially in petty litigation and in situations where English rules of action are plainly unsuited to American conditions. Also new factors alien to the common law may appear, for example, the continental law which lawyers began studying in the Revolutionary period or the civil-law doctrines prevailing in territories annexed from France or Mexico.

43. Under the auspices of the Ames Foundation at Harvard Law School, our fellow-member, Mark D. Howe, is supervising the preparation of a check-list of printed sources for court proceedings in New England before 1800.

This surmise may be called the synthetic-rubber hypothesis because it endeavors to combine several elements with an elastic common law. If this hypothesis serves as a useful starting-point for future inquiries into American legal history during the seventeenth and eighteenth centuries, then an investigator can no longer be content with assembling data in support of a single monopolistic factor which he happens to favor, and grudgingly conceding a little influence to other factors. Instead, he will search for the existence of several possible factors—generalized common-law principles; English case-law; English local law; English legal reforms during the Cromwellian period;[44] homemade law, with specific reference to colonial conditions; continental law. He will endeavor to determine the relative weight of each factor, and judge whether its trend is upward or downward. He will look for the emergence of a new factor and note the signs of approaching death in an old factor. These are all phases of the central problem, the relations and divergences between the judicial process in England and in English-speaking North America.

It may be helpful to future investigators if I conclude by describing one concrete line of inquiry which is likely to prove fruitful.[45]

Since law is a function of law-books, as I have just said, scholars need more information about books on English law which were owned in the colonies. Carlyle defined a university as a great collection of books, and the same may be said of the common law when it takes the form of a system of case-law and detailed doctrines. Until very many books were available to colonial courts and lawyers, the common law must have mainly stayed a body of general principles. The law grew as law libraries grew.

The desired information about colonial law-books will have to be found in many different places. A considerable number of legal treatises were printed in America, of which Eldon R. James compiled a useful list.[46] Still, only twenty-three books appear on it as

44. See R. Robinson, "Anticipations under the Commonwealth of Changes in the Law," *Select Essays in Anglo-American Legal History*, I. 467, written in 1869 or 1870.

45. Several other interesting questions, such as the reasons for the late use of judicial opinions in this country, are suggested in Chafee, book review, *Harvard Law Review*, LVII (1944), 399.

46. Eldon R. James, "A List of Legal Treatises Printed in the British Colonies and the American States before 1801," *Harvard Legal Essays: Written in Honor*

printed here before 1765. Most treatises and all reports of decisions in English courts had to come from England. Occasionally we have official proof of overseas purchases. Thus the General Court of Massachusetts voted in 1647 to buy two copies of Coke on Littleton, Coke on Magna Charta, Coke's Reports, Book of Entries, New Terms of the Law, and Dalton's Justice of the Peace.[47]

In the court records, law-books are sometimes cited in the arguments for the litigants. The Suffolk County Court Records, 1671-1680, are meagre in this respect, mentioning only Coke on Littleton and a volume combining the treatises of Malynes and Marius on the Law Merchant.[48] By contrast, the Delaware cases a century or so later have frequent citations of treatises,[49] which indicate well-stocked law libraries. Eighteenth-century Delaware lawyers were evidently investing heavily in books imported from England, either directly or through Philadelphia booksellers.

If the accounts of booksellers in the colonies were examined by scholars, they might tell us a good deal about law-books which were sold. Those of English booksellers exporting to America would also be rewarding. Lists of subscribers printed in English law-books could be checked for American names. Thus we know that Chief-Justice De Lancey of New York was among the original subscribers to Viner's *Abridgment*.[50]

Some libraries of colonial lawyers are still extant, and we have lists of what was in others. Old law-books in university libraries and bar libraries may have the names of colonial owners inscribed on their flyleaves.[51]

Out-of-the-way sources may prove helpful. Commonplace books of the lawyers like Jefferson naturally refer to their reading. Private letters may mention the purcase or use of law-books.[52] Law-books, besides aiding litigation, can also create litigation. Thus a Providence merchant in 1741 sued a lawyer for not returning six specified law-books which he was alleged to have for safe keeping. The lawyer won by convincing the court that he had bought the

of and Presented to Joseph Henry Beale and Samuel Williston (Cambridge, 1934), 159-211.

47. *Massachusetts Bay Records*, II. 212.

48. *Records of the Suffolk County Court, 1671-1680*, I. xxx.

49. Chafee, book review, *Harvard Law Review*, LVII (1944), 420-421.

50. Goebel & Naughton, *Law Inforcement in Colonial New York*, xxxviii.

51. *Ibid.*

52. See *ibid.*, xxxvi, for an example.

books.[53] Finally, colonial wills and inventories of estates might be carefully examined for mention of law-books.

In ending this discussion of court records before a gathering of historians, I want to stress the great value of such records as a source for social history. Frequent use has been made by American historians of litigation on constitutional and political issues, like the case of Peter Zenger and the controversies over writs of assistance, but what I have in mind is less spectacular. Law-suits about contracts and private wrongs and criminal prosecutions for small offenses often tell a great deal about the way men and women lived and the transactions they carried on.[54] Sometimes matters are so much taken for granted that contemporary writers think them not worth mentioning, and yet we of a later age are eager to know about them. If such matters get into a court, they have to be set forth in considerable detail. Consequently, if the historian has the endurance to dig the nuggets out of the legal dust, he can sometimes get facts out of court records which it would be hard to find elsewhere.

53. Chafee, "Records of the Rhode Island Court of Equity, 1741-1743," *Publications of the Colonial Society of Massachusetts*, XXXV, 91 at 100 (1951).

54. For samples, see the discussion of Puritan sexual relations in the introduction to Chafee & Morison, *Records of the Suffolk County Court*, I. lxxxiii-lxxxvii; the discussion of social and economic conditions in eighteenth-century Delaware in Chafee, book review, *Harvard Law Review*, LVII. 401-407; and the cases about colonial doctors in Chafee, "Records of the Rhode Island Court of Equity, 1741-1743," 103-108.

IV

*King's Law and Local Custom in Seventeenth Century New England**

JULIUS GOEBEL, JR.

The first century and three-quarters of American legal development is bounded by two landmarks which have served as monuments to those historians who have attempted to survey the field of colonial law. The first of these is the royal charter; the second is the so-called reception statute. The former with its mandate that the law in the lands granted should be agreeable or not repugnant to the law of England,[1] is commonly regarded as a forecast of what was to transpire. The latter, with its declaration that the common law of England, in so far as it had been adopted at a particular date, was the law of a state, is held to have marked the consummation of the forecast.[2] With these landmarks before them

* "King's Law and Local Custom in Seventeenth Century New England," by Julius Goebel, Jr., is reprinted with permission from the *Columbia Law Review*, XXXI (1931), 416-448.

This article was prepared in connection with the work of the Foundation for Research in American Legal History; and was read at the annual meeting of the American Law School Association in December, 1930.

1. See, *e.g.*, the Virginia charter of 1609. *Cf.* 2 POOR, FEDERAL AND STATE CONSTITUTIONS (2d ed. 1878) 1901, 1902, 1905; the Pennsylvania charter of 1681, 2 *ibid.* 1509, 1511; the Georgia charter of 1732, 1 *ibid.* 369, 372-3; the Massachusetts Bay Charter, 1 *ibid.* 932, 940; the New York Charter of 1664, 1 COLONIAL LAWS OF NEW YORK 1, 2.

2. The so-called reception statutes vary in form, in the date chosen as a deadline, and as to the implications of the extent of reception. Compare the Virginia provision, *Ordinances of Convention* (1776) c. V (VI), 9 HENING 126, 127; 9 PA. STATUTES AT LARGE (1777) 29; MASS. CONST. (1780) c. VI, art. VI; Georgia, Act of 1784, PRINCE, DIGEST OF THE LAW OF THE STATE 310; N. Y. STATE CONST. (1777) art. XXXV, now art. I, § 16. There has been no comprehensive discussion of the relation of these statutes to the judicial elaboration of the actual details of reception. In 1926, at the meeting of the American Law School Association, the writer in a paper *Courts as Historians* pointed out that

and acting upon an assumption which I think wholly unwarranted, our historians have taken as a measure the common law of England: Coke for the outset, Hale for the turn of the century, and Blackstone for the latter years of colonial America. A technique has been established no more recondite than the process of matching colors by which Chief Judge Cardozo has so bitingly characterized the inept use of precedents. At the basis of this naïve and uninspired method for which we may not unjustly blame the low estate of colonial legal history, lies the fallacy that the sum of the law of England was the law of the King's Courts—the common law.[3]

So accustomed are we to focus our attention upon the expansion of the King's law that we have closed our eyes to the fact that at the outset of the seventeenth century local custom and local courts were still an immensely important part of the law administration in England.[4] True, these local institutions were marked for eventual doom, but they had resisted over centuries successive assaults by *quo warranto;* they were yet a part of the fabric of law and government. No one who ventures into the forbidding welter

---

judges acting on the assumption that their function to declare the law, embraces a knowledge of its history, undertook after the revolution, to decide what rules had been adopted in colonial times. Since little was known as to what actually transpired in colonial America, the results of the courts are frequently worthless as history. This theory persists. A saner view would seem to be that actual proof as to what colonial practice had been should be required. There is some discussion of the matter in GOEBEL, CASES AND MATERIALS ON THE DEVELOPMENT OF LEGAL INSTITUTIONS (1930) 293 *et seq.*

3. This is true of the earlier works and is equally true of two recent books SCOTT, CRIMINAL LAW IN COLONIAL VIRGINIA (1930), on which see 31 COLUMBIA LAW REV. 185, and MORRIS, STUDIES IN THE HISTORY OF AMERICAN LAW (1930). I believe Mr. Morris' conclusions will bear reexamination, since his method leaves much to be desired. A work which gives only superficial attention to the indigenous social and economic basis of legal development, which commits the impropriety of leaping from one colony to another as if the civilization in each were identical, which ignores the element of time in grouping cases separated by decades, and which treats the contemporary English law as a relatively static corpus of dogma appears to me unsound.

4. *Cf.* BEATRICE AND SIDNEY WEBB, ENGLISH LOCAL GOVERNMENT. . . . THE MANOR AND THE BOROUGH (1908) 7 *et seq.*, 337 *et seq.;* THE PARISH AND THE COUNTY (1906); STATUTORY AUTHORITIES (1922). The Webbs do not pretend to examine questions exhaustively before 1689. 2 HOLDSWORTH, HISTORY OF ENGLISH LAW (1922) 369 *et seq.;* and 4 *ibid.* 122. There is a serious gap in our information between the medieval period, about which considerable is known, and the seventeenth century. On the earlier period *cf.* BATESON, BOROUGH CUSTOMS (Selden Soc. Pub.) vols. 18 (1904) and 21 (1906); HENRY, CONTRACTS IN THE LOCAL COURTS OF MEDIEVAL ENGLAND (1926); Schechter, *Popular Law and Common Law in Medieval England* (1928) 28 COLUMBIA LAW REV. 369.

of contemporary charters can fail to be appalled by the multitude and extent of franchises, the tenacity with which they were clung to, and the astounding picture of jurisdictional diversities they disclose. This then is the fact to which we must cleave, that the law of England was something greater and more multiform than that of the courts at Westminster.

It is not necessary to enter upon a discussion of whether or not the provisions in the first colonial charters had reference to the statutes and the common law alone, or whether they contemplated including that part of the law of England with which the courts at Westminster rarely occupied themselves. In the last analysis the charter provisions are significant only as to the relations of a particular colony with the homeland,[5] and cannot be regarded as con-

5. It should here be pointed out that on the side of legal theory the problem of the transplantation of law during the colonial period presents three aspects, all of which underwent considerable change from 1600-1776; these are (1) the doctrine of the English Courts; (2) the doctrine of the Crown; (3) the doctrine of the Colonists. As to the first there is some discussion in GOEBEL, STRUGGLE FOR THE FALKLAND ISLANDS (1927) c. II. There has never been an adeguate study of the second. The basis of royal power undoubtedly goes back to a very ancient usage derived from the Frankish practice of treating all unoccupied lands as inuring to the King by virtue of his regality in the soil *(Bodenregal)*. *Cf.* SCHROEDER, DEUTSCHE RECHTSGESCHICHTE (7th ed. 1922) 224 *et seq.;* 3 WAITZ, DEUTSCHE VERFASSUNGSGESCHICHTE (2d ed. 1883) 141, 153: 1 INAMA STERNEGG, DEUTSCHE WIRTSCHAFTSGESCHICHTE (1879) 25-26, 108, 125; ARNOLD, ANSIEDLUNGEN UND WANDERUNGEN DEUTSCHER STÄMME (1881) 210; 2 BRUNNER, DEUTSCHE RECHTSGESCHICHTE (2d ed. 1928) 101, 103. Royal rights in regard to forests are believed to have been derived from this source. The Frankish practice in this regard was brought over to England by the Normans; *cf.* HASKINS, NORMAN INSTITUTIONS (1908) 48, 103.

In England the theory regarding the King's dominions in the Middle Ages remains to be completely studied, especially in respect to the extension of common law over conquered territory. There is some discussion of this in respect to Wales in my review of SCHUYLER, PARLIAMENT AND THE BRITISH EMPIRE (1929), in (1930) 30 COLUMBIA LAW REV. 273 *et seq.* and the references there given. See also SKEEL, THE COUNCIL OF THE MARCHES OF WALES (1904) 1-17. On the matter as to whether legislative power over Wales after 34 HY. VIII, c. 26, § 119, was a personal power of the Crown, see *ibid.*, at 138 *et seq.; cf.* COKE, FOURTH INSTITUTE, 240. The reference in some colonial charters regarding the counties palatine makes necessary a consideration of the original constitution of those regions in connection with the powers of the King in respect to his dominions. See *Le Case del Countie Palatine de Wexford*, DAVIES 59; SKEEL, *op. cit.*, at 131; LAPSLEY, THE COUNTY PALATINE OF DURHAM (1900); WHITLOCKE, READING ON THE STATUTE 21 HY. VIII, c. 13, in PRACTICE OF THE COURT OF CHANCERY OF DURHAM (1807).

In connection with this question the discussions anent Virginia are interesting, 1 BROWN, GENESIS OF THE UNITED STATES (1897) 32, 42, 64. *Cf.* also the two early patents, to Sir Humphrey Gilbert (1578) and Raleigh (1584), in 1 HAZARD, HISTORICAL COLLECTIONS (1792) at 24, 33.

stituting a reliable guide to what in fact transpired in America. While in thus casting away the charter it would appear that we had abandoned the last beacon by which to lay our course, we nevertheless retain one important light—that the colonist will avail himself of his cultural heritage whether this has to do with religion, with law, or with methods of farming. In accepting as valid this premise we must, of course, rely upon work that has been done by lay historians in fields other than the law, but I see no good reason for traversing their conclusions.[6] At the same time it should be noted that the acceptance of this premise necessarily involves the rejection of what I have already described as the technique employed in existing studies in American law. Instead of comparing the English common law with the legal monuments in the colonies, our task now becomes inevitably more complex. It is necessary for us to determine what was the cultural heritage of the first settlers, and in what form this heritage first expressed itself in the new land.

It is my purpose to single out for study one colony, not only because it was the first important English settlement north of the 40th parallel, but because the achievements of this colony were imitated by succeeding groups which settled in New England.[7]

6. Thus in respect to management of lands, MacLear, Early New England Towns (1908) 81 *et seq.;* in respect to music, Schünemann, Das Lied der Deutschen Kolonisten in Russland (1923) *passim;* in respect to architecture, Kimball, American Architecture (1928) 18 *et seq.;* in respect to poetry, Uhlendorf, *German-American Poetry,* in 22 & 23 Jahrbuch der Deutsch-Amerikanischen Historischen Gesellschaft von Illinois, 109 *et seq.*

7. I do not wish to be understood as taking the position that everything done at Plymouth was imitated, because each colony seems to have had certain peculiar social characteristics which found individual expression. This was particularly true of Massachusetts Bay, where there were a greater number of persons of outstanding intellectual force in positions of authority who had designs utterly different from those of the Plymouth men. At the same time certain major achievements of Plymouth, such as the form of church organization and the device of codification, were very certainly borrowed. Thus on the matter of Congregationalism and its acceptance in Massachusetts Bay, Bradford, History of Plimoth Plantation (1900) 315; Dexter, Congregationalism of the Last 300 Years as seen in Its Literature (1880) 413 *et seq.;* 1 Felt, Ecclesiastical History of New England (1855-62) 113 *et seq.;* Walker, Creeds and Platforms of Congregationalism (1893) 116 *et seq.;* Burrage, The Church Covenant Idea (1904) 88 *et seq.* In a later work, 1 Early English Dissenters (1912) 357, Burrage minimizes the influence of the Plymouth church, as he does not seem to relish the idea of relating the Massachusetts Bay men to Brownism. He consequently assumes the professed allegiance of these men to Anglicanism to be a candid statement of their position, which it was not. *Cf.* 1 Osgood, American Colonies in the Seventeenth Century (1904) 203-204. In

This is the colony at Plymouth, whose legal history over a period of three decades we shall examine.

If we regard the personnel of this first settlement, the picture presented to us seems relatively simple. The group was divided into two parts: those persons who were Separatists from the English church, a large number of whom had settled at Leyden, but many of whom came directly from England to America; and a number of persons who appeared to have had no religious connection with the Separatists, but who, probably for economic reasons, desired to move to the new settlement.[8] There is very little evidence that the bulk of the settlers had any intellectual contacts beyond those which their religion had given them. In other words, with the exception of a few leaders it seems unlikely that the colonists were aware of any of the literary movements of the time, of the law, or even of the politics of the royal court. Most of them were small farmers or artisans. Their leaders were exiles because of their beliefs. They were in respect of law and government footloose, maintaining with the homeland no more than a commercial relation with the group which financed them. Among their number were none who were initiated into the mysteries fostered by the Inns of Court. To suppose that they would introduce a system as complex and esoteric as that which prevailed in the King's Courts is as absurd as to expect that they would establish a religious system on the principles of the Anglican church. Unless we are willing

Massachusetts Bay, agitation for laws begins in 1635 and a committee was appointed in May, 1636; Cotton's *Judicials* were presented in October, 1636; not until March, 1637, was real work begun on the laws. The Plymouth code was enacted in November, 1636. As the *Body of Liberties* was not enacted until 1641, it seems fair to infer that Plymouth experience was drawn upon. On the pre-history of the *Body of Liberties,* see WHITMORE, BIBLIOGRAPHICAL SKETCH OF THE LAWS OF THE MASSACHUSETTS COLONY (1890). The process of imitation in respect to local custumals during the Middle Ages, as a widespread social phenomenon should be considered here. *Cf.* GROSS, GILD MERCHANT (1890) 242 *et seq.;* BATESON, *The Laws of Breteuil* in 15 ENG. HIST. REV. 73, 302, 496, 754, 16 *ibid.,* 92, 332. It should be observed that it is *after* the Plymouth code is established that the pressure for a book of laws becomes effective in Massachusetts. Note further the application to Plymouth for legal advice in 1642 by the latter after the adoption of the *Body of Liberties* (BRADFORD, *op. cit. supra* note 7, at 461). Compare with this the practice in medieval Germany of reference to the mother city by the daughter cities of difficult legal questions for decision, SCHROEDER, DEUTSCHE RECHTSGESCHICHTE, 741, 743.

8. The most detailed examination of the personnel of the early Plymouth colony is in DEXTER, THE ENGLAND AND HOLLAND OF THE PILGRIMS (1905); *cf.* ARBER, STORY OF THE PILGRIM FATHERS (1897); BANKS, ENGLISH ANCESTRY AND HOMES OF THE PILGRIM FATHERS (1929).

to resort to the frontier theory (that *pons asinorum* of American historiography)[9] we can make but one assumption: for the purpose of civil order in the colony, resort was had to the law with which the colonists had grown up.

It was inevitable that the local courts and the customary law would assume a position of transcendent importance in the life of the ordinary man. It was to these courts that the small farmer or artisan would turn if he wished to replevy his cows or to collect a bill, and that turned upon him if his hogs were unringed or if he put his garbage in the street. Except what these humble men may have known of the ecclesiastical courts, with their sompnours spying upon their amours, and the apparitors to take them to jail if they worshipped heretically, the workings of the county, manorial, or borough tribunals were the length and breadth of their knowledge of the administration of justice, the local customs the sum of their law. Since, it was men from these walks of life by

9. Thus Pound, *The Revival of Comparative Law* (1930) 5 TULANE L. REV. 1, at 3, 7, appears to lean toward this view. In his SPIRIT OF THE COMMON LAW (1912) 112, in a chapter headed "Pioneers and the Law," Pound says: "Administration of justice in America was at first executive and legislative, and these types of non-judicial justice persisted well into the last century. . . ." (113) ". . . the colonies began with all manner of experiments in administering justice without law and it was not till the middle of the eighteenth century that the setting up of a system of courts and the rise of a custom of studying law in England began to make for a general administration of justice according to English law. Just prior to the Revolution the widespread study of Blackstone, whose first edition appeared in 1765, gave great impetus to the reception of the common law. But as late as 1791 the law was so completely at large in New York that the genius of a Kent was needed to make the common law the law of that state." (115-116).

If Pound is talking about all the colonies, it may be said that the facts do not bear him out. If we take New York, with whose colonial legal records I am familiar, we start out with an elaborate code (1665). Beginning with the opening years of the eighteenth century the law rapidly becomes professionalized. Compare the memoranda of authority, in an argument on demurrer, in Clarkson v. Elphinston (1730), New York City, Hall of Records, Ms. MINUTES MAYOR'S COURT, July, 1729—October, 1734. Vernon for the defendant cited: "2 Rushworth Collections App. 176, 6; Ch. Ca. 105; Dyer 89; 1 Leonard 53; 1 Ventr. 243; 1 Salk. 290; 1 Institutes 136, 2 Ventr. 9-15; 2 Inst. 77." Murray for the plaintiff cited: "Grotius 2d Bks. 5 § 11; Wood, Institutes 58, 59; Baron and Feme 376, 377, 378; 1 Salk. 120, 121; Moore, Buntings case; Keilway 936; Brooke Abr. 79; 1 Lillie, Tit.-Abatement; Brooke, Ab. Tit.-Confession; Trials Per Pais 432; Allen 18; Ld. Raymond 84; Plowd. 440; 1 Levinz 87; 1 Salk. 284; 3 Salk. 155; Wood, Inst. 600." See also the debate of Murray and Smith *re* a Court of Chancery, *Opinion Relating to the Courts of Justice* (1734). Compare also the statement of a course of Legal Study, prepared before 1765 in N. Y. Pub. Lib. Ms. Div., *Wm. Smith Papers, Miscellanea*. It would be surprising if these developments were not paralleled elsewhere.

which the Plymouth colony was established, we must seek the secular source from which their legislative inspiration flowed in the local institutions of their native land. Historians have not failed to observe that in respect of the machinery of government the local institution was that which was first duplicated in America. Only a profound and abysmal disregard for the character of English law in the seventeenth century could have made them blind to the fact that in respect to the law conditions were no different.

The premise that colonists recruited from the lower strata of English society would put into action overseas the aspects of law and law administration which formed a part of their experience extended further than to the point of mere duplication. Much that was familiar to the settlers in New England was distasteful to them. Some things they objected to on the grounds of economic expediency. Some things were despised because they ran counter to their religious beliefs. For these they had definite notions of reform long before the idea of emigration had been ventilated. The adoption of English local customs in America is to be studied consequently in the light of these reservations.

The intellectual background of the Plymouth men, as I have stated, was determined largely by their intense concern with religion. The basis of their ideas is to some extent to be found in the theological literature of the reformed religion, transmitted to them directly or through the medium of their teachers.[10] In addi-

10. It should be pointed out that the first Separatists derived their tenets from the writings of Robert Browne as modified by Henry Barrow. Their dogma was strict orthodox Calvinism, but their idea of religious organization bears some resemblance to that of the Anabaptists whose teachings are supposed to have been familiar to Browne. It was from these notions as to church organization, an independent community of saints (*i.e.*, the predestined) established by covenant with God and by covenant with each other, that the name of the sect was derived. On the religious basis of Congregationalism, *cf.* DEXTER, CONGREGATIONALISM OF THE LAST 300 YEARS (1880); BURRAGE, THE TRUE STORY OF ROBERT BROWNE (1906); WEINGARTNER, DIE REVOLUTIONSKIRCHEN ENGLANDS (1868); 1 BURRAGE, EARLY ENGLISH DISSENTERS 94 *et seq.;* POWICKE, HENRY BARROW, SEPARATIST (1900); Loofs, *Kongregationalisten* in 10 HAUCK-HERZOG, REAL-ENZYKLOPÄDIE FÜR PROTESTANTISCHE THEOLOGIE UND KIRCHE, 680; TROELTSCH, DIE SOZIALLEHREN DER CHRISTLICHEN KIRCHEN (1912) 743 *et seq.* Especially useful on the ideology of the Pilgrims, ROBINSON, WORKS (Ashton Ed. 1851) 3 vols. See also the dreary list of theological writings contained in Bradford's library, 2 MAYFLOWER DESCENDANTS 232-3; 3 *ibid.* 146-7. Prince's library contains much the same sort of thing, but there were also three law books, two not named,

tion to these sources we must likewise take into account what may be termed the popular literature of the dissentients, the vast flood of pamphlets, many of them openly polemic, by which the anti-Anglican movement gained headway among the commoners.[11] It is in this type of writing that we find the abstractions of Calvin's *Institutes of Christian Religion* translated in terms of English institutions. Here, if anywhere, will be the rudimentary program of law reform levelled at local conditions. Here are the roots of those elements in the laws of the early New England colonists that we may describe as the results of idealism.

While I am averse to resorting uncritically and without specification to a *cliché* like the word Calvinism as an explanation of the religious ideology of the dissenting English sects, I cannot here go afield into a discussion of those details of the Calvinism which vitally affected the thinking of the early settlers. Suffice it that I am using the word with reference to the socio-religious implications imparted to it by Troeltsch and Weber.[12] Calvinism, used in

the law Dictionary of Blount (1st Ed. 1670) alone being mentioned 3 *ibid.* 208-9. The library of Miles Standish contained a volume of the *Swedish Intelligencer.* 5 NEW ENGLAND HISTORICAL AND GENEALOGICAL REGISTER, 336-7. If this volume was the one which contained the regulations of Gustavus Adolphus for his army, interesting light would be cast on early American military regulation. I have not pursued the matter. The list of Brewster's books is in 2 MASS. HIST. SOC. PROC., Ser. 5, 38 *et seq.*

11. The difficulties of determining the influences which were at work among common men in the early seventeenth century are considerable. Sermons, of course, are available, but they are too much like the anti-Red editorials in conservative newspapers to be of any help in measuring the advance of new ideas. Much more useful are tracts which were suppressed, but they are accordingly difficult to obtain. The most striking and entertaining of the tracts are the so-called Martin Marprelate tracts [*Puritan Discipline Tracts—An Epistle, etc.* (2d ed. 1843)] and the answers which were prepared in reply by various persons. There is a comprehensive list of tracts bearing on Separatism in DEXTER, CONGREGATIONALISM, App., 5. I have examined many of these, and all of the pertinent tracts published before 1640 in the McAlpin collection at the Union Theological Seminary, listed in 1 CATALOGUE OF THE MCALPIN COLLECTION OF BRITISH HISTORY AND THEOLOGY (Gillett Ed. 1927). Two tracts, the *Note-gatherer* and *Treatisour,* important because they go into the whole question of the *ex officio* oath, I could not find, but a good idea of their contents may be gathered from COSIN, AN APOLOGIE FOR SUNDRIE PROCEEDINGS (1593). All the tracts in SOMERS, TRACTS (Scott Ed.) and HARLEIAN MISCELLANY (1809 ed.) published before 1640 that bear on the development of a contemporary public opinion have been examined. It is impossible to form a judgment about these early movements for law reform without going into this type of literature.

12. TROELTSCH, *op. cit. supra* note 10; Weber, *Die Protestantische Ethik und der Geist des Kapitalismus; Die Protestantischen Sekten und der Gesit des Kapitalismus* in 1 GESAMMELTE AUFSÄTZE ZUR RELIGIONSSOZIOLOGIE (1920). The

this sense, had burned its way generally into English intellectual life during the reign of Elizabeth. Its brand is on Anglican as well as on Puritan thinking.[13] It fired the legal pietism of Coke as much as it did the outbursts of Cartwright.

former essay is translated by Parsons (1930). See also TAWNEY, RELIGION AND THE RISE OF CAPITALISM (1926).

13. So much has been made by historians of the quarrel over church discipline, vestments, and other formal differences between the Presbyterian-Puritan groups and the Anglicans, that one is inclined to assume from the ferocity of these frontal attacks that there were greater and more marked theo-philosophical differences between the two groups than in fact existed. The Anglican church parried with success these attacks on discipline and forms, but at the same time was subjected to a sort of peaceful penetration by the Calvinistic philosophy, the ultimate effect of which was the greater because it was unsuspected. Beginning with the return from Strassburg, Frankfurt, and Geneva of the clergy persecuted by Mary, the process of minor change through the absorption of Calvinistic religious dogma not incompatible with the *status quo* proceeded constantly in the face of officially approved doctrine. This particular condition is attributable to the circumstance that as the English church reckoned itself among the protestant churches, it was consequently unable to insulate itself against the intellectual forces emanating from other protestant churches. Hence, while Calvin's system of ecclesiastical discipline was constantly reproved, his doctrinal teachings were widely read and approved. Of course these influences were by no means limited to the clergy, particularly as the currents of protestant thought were flowing not only in the channels of theological discussion, but had flooded the fields of political, theoretical and social speculation. On the purely political side there has been plenty of writing: *Cf. especially* the following works which are particularly suggestive, MURRAY, THE POLITICAL CONSEQUENCES OF THE REFORMATION (1926); FIGGIS, DIVINE RIGHT OF KINGS (1914); FROM GERSON TO GROTIUS (1907); GIERKE, JOHANNES ALTHUSIUS (1880); HUNDESHAGEN ÜBER DEN EINFLUSS DES KALVINISMUS, ETC. (1842); BARON, CALVINS STAATSANSCHAUUNG UND DAS KONFESSIONELLE ZEITALTER (Historische Zeitschrift, Beiheft 1, 1924); TROELTSCH, *op. cit. supra* note 10, at 605 *et seq.;* DILTHEY, WELTANSCHAUUNG UND ANALYSE DER MENSCHEN (1924), 229 *et seq.*

On the point of popular infusion of Calvinistic ideas in England there has been no extensive or reliable study. We know, of course, that Calvin's Institutes were read and admired by all the great English churchmen, even such decided Arminians as Laud and Sanderson, MURRAY, *op. cit.*, at 111. We are aware, moreover, that the English clerics seem to have distinguished sharply between Calvin's "system of divinity" and his discipline. An example is Archbishop Edwin Sandys, one of that group of whom Heylyn [2 HISTORY OF THE REFORMATION (Robertson Ed. 1849) 176] said, "being for the most part Zuinglian Gospellers at their going hence, became the great promoters of the Puritan faction at their coming home." Sandys had been at Cambridge in the time of Bucer's stay [SERMONS OF EDWIN SANDYS (Parker Soc. Pubs. 1841) Intr. i-ii; HARVEY, MARTIN BUCER IN ENGLAND (1906) 44 *et seq.*]. Bucer's intellectual debt to Calvin is well known (TROELTSCH, *op. cit.*, at 774). Abroad Sandys lived at Strassburg and Zurich. After his return his own superior, Archbishop Parker, accused him of "Germanical nature" [1 STRYPE, LIFE AND ACTS OF MATHEW PARKER (1821) 156]. Zwinglian or Calvinist, Sandys' sermons reflect strongly the latter spirit and dogma (THE SERMONS OF EDWIN SANDYS, especially at 50 *et seq.*, 121

For our purpose we must direct attention to certain manifestations of Calvinism such as the growth of biblicism and the exaltation of the Mosaic law,[14] the embracing of Calvin's conception of

et seq.). At the same time, we find Sandys writing to Walther in 1574 disparaging Cartwright and his projected new discipline [1 ZURICH LETTERS (Parker Soc. Pub. 1842) 312]. This dualism is amusingly illustrated by the sensation caused through the publication of letters of Walther and Beza in the *Admonition* of Cartwright intending to hint at approbation. Beza, in 1572, indited a congratulatory letter to the Lord Treasurer with implications of approving the existing order. *Cf.* 2 STRYPE, *op. cit.*, at 102, 110; 1 ZURICH LETTERS, App. 362.

Via Scotland, of course, the pressure of Calvinistic ideas was very heavy. As an important phase of intellectual history the matter deserves full exploration. I have entered upon it here at such length because it seems necessary to understand the state of mind that prevailed in England in the early seventeenth century. On the spread of Calvinism during Elizabeth's reign, *cf.* also KLEIN, INTOLERANCE IN THE REIGN OF ELIZABETH (1917) at 99, 165.

14. The growth of Biblicism was to become one of the most interesting characteristics of thinking in England as well as in America. The notion that the law of England was grounded on the law of God had been indicated by Fortescue. Due largely to the influence of *Doctor and Student*, Dial. 1. c. 6, the tendency spread to make the Bible important as authority. The effects of Biblicism are seen in the growth of citations in the reports. Thus, Reniger v. Fogossa, Plowd. 8; Earl of Oxford's Case, 1 Ch. R. 1; Moore v. Hussey, Hobart, 94; Bradley v. Banks, 1 Bulstr. 141; Benton v. Trot, Moore, 529 Sherborn v. Lewis, Gouldsborough, 120; Gomersall v. Gomersall, Godbolt, 55; King v. Boreston, & Adams, Noy, 158. Colt v. Glover, 1 Rolle 451; Urrey v. Bowyer, 2 BROWNL. & Golds. 20. Coke's Reports are full of this type of citation. The same thing is true of contemporary treatises such as COKE'S INSTITUTES; PULTON, DE PACE REGIS (1609); DALTON, COUNTREY JUSTICE (1619); Selden and Spelman at large. The growth of enthusiasm for Mosaic law is in a sense part of this tendency. While during the Middle Ages an identity had been discovered by philosophers between the *lex Mosis* and the natural law, it remained for the reformers during the sixteenth and seventeenth centuries the task of attempting to put to lay uses the law of the Pentateuch. Due to Luther's insistence upon the divine origin of law, the decalogue moved into a commanding position not only as respected the theological, but also the social-ethical program of the protestants. Calvin, in turn, conceiving the Bible as a manifestation of how the Christian community should be organized to do God's work on earth, found in the Pentateuch the law for effecting this achievement (TROELTSCH, *op. cit.* 620). THE COMMENTARIES ON THE FOUR LAST BOOKS OF MOSES (4 vs. Bingham ed. 1844)—THE HARMONY OF THE PENTATEUCH—(a work owned by several colonists) is a magnificent monument to the skill with which this viewpoint was elaborated by the great Frenchman.

One of the earliest attempts to establish a definite connection between the Mosaic law and the secular law was made by the jurist Johannes Oldendorp, a disciple of Melanchton. Oldendorp finds in the decalogue the source of the Roman twelve tables and thus offered proof of his master's contention of the relation of human and natural law. 1 STINTZING, GESCHICHTE DER DEUTSCHEN RECHTSWISSENSCHAFT (1880) 311, 327; KALTENBORN, DIE VORLÄUFER DES HUGO GROTIUS (1848) 233, App. 18. The utility of this view for Protestant uses is borne out by the fact that in Calvin's HARMONY (1563) a similar technique is employed. The publication of an ancient codex, the COLLATIO LEGUM MOSAI-

the law of nature,[15] and particularly a quickening of social-ethical ideals. These things become articulate not merely in religious issues, dogmatic and disciplinary, but in definite ideas for law reform among the radical dissenting groups in England. They are the inspiration for the demands that the law of Moses be a part of the

CARUM ET ROMANARUM, by the French jurist Pithou added fire to these notions. Before 1620 this work was widely used by jurists, and in the revision of BEZA, LEX DEI MORALIS (1603), a systematic restatement of the Pentateuch, the COLLATIO is republished [*cf.* HYAMSON, MOSAICARUM ET ROMANARUM LEGUM COLLATIO, (1913) xiii *et seq.*]. The first edition of the LEX DEI MORALIS was in 1577; [see HEPPE, THEODOR BEZA (1811) 377]. In France, shortly before the appearance of Pithou's work, Francis Hotmann had demanded that the Mosaic law be enacted as the law of France. BARON, FRANZ HOTMANN'S ANTITRIBONIAN (1888) xviii. In England the agitation over the enactment of the Mosaic law took an individual form. Cromwell, while Chancellor, had ordered that the decalogue be read each Sunday [2 MERRIMAN, LIFE AND LETTERS OF THOMAS CROMWELL (1902) 152], and consequently this was the one part of the Bible universally known. [*Cf.* the *Articles of the Charge by J. Ps. at Quarter Sessions* in LAMBARD, EIRENARCHA (1619) 406. See also the trial of Udal in 1 STATE TRIALS (Cobbett ed.) 1271]. In 1567 appeared the first of the Anglo-Saxon translations whereby Archbishop Parker endeavored to establish the independent apostolic succession of the Anglican Church. The prologue to Alfred's laws, consisting of the decalogue and the two following chapters in Exodus (Liebermann, *Alfred and Mosaic Law* in 6 TRANS. JEW. HIST. SOC. 21) was included in this translation. WÜLKER, GRUNDRISS ZUR GESCHICHTE DER ANGELSÄCHSISCHEN LITERATUR (1885) 5; 1 LIEBERMANN, GESETZE DER ANGELSACHSEN (1903) XLV; TURK, THE LEGAL CODE OF ALFRED (1893) 5. The obvious deduction from this document was that there had existed at one time an identity between the law of God and the law of the land. The demand that the *lex Mosis* be regarded as binding law begins (*Cf.* Sandys the Bullinger, 15 Aug. 1573, 1 ZURICH LETTERS 294). It is not suppressed during the succeeding century, and reaches its apogee during the days of the Commonwealth in the demands of the Fifth Monarchy men [BROWN, POLITICAL ACTIVITIES OF THE BAPTISTS AND FIFTH MONARCHY MEN, ETC. (1912), 35 *et seq.*].

15. A most interesting and forthright expression of the Calvinistic conception of natural law is to be found in the "Address" to the Plymouth Code of 1658, with which compare CALVIN, INSTITUTION OF CHRISTIAN RELIGION (1634 ed.) bk. 4, c. 15, 16, 20, 22. The emphasis upon "moral equity" and the perferment of this "law" as it is expressed in Israelite models over the common law is convincing evidence of how far the Plymouth settlers had become Calvinized. This tendency was already rampant among the Separatists upon the landing in 1620. Various events in the colony had the effect of intensifying this original leaning toward Calvinism, and the successful launching of a theocratic government at Massachusetts Bay may likewise have been of influence. The Address cannot be regarded as an exact exposition of the state of mind that prevailed in Plymouth during the first two decades of its existence, but there are many collateral indications which offer support to the view that the ideas of the Address were prevalent at the time of settlement, if not so exactly articulated.

Pointing to the growth of theocratic Calvinistic ideas are the statutes regarding religious or public meetings [THE COMPACT WITH CHARTER AND LAW OF THE COLONY OF NEW PLYMOUTH (Brigham ed. 1836)—hereafter cited PLYMOUTH LAWS—at 92, 1650]; vilifying church ministry *(ibid.);* profanation of the Sab-

law of the land, for the violence with which the church jurisdiction over morality is attacked, and for the assaults upon oaths of purgation.[16] In America we shall observe their florescence in many details.

In outlining the extent to which the law was swept into the

---

bath *(ibid.)*, public worship *(ibid.*, at 93, 1651); denial of Scriptures as a rule of life *(ibid.*, at 99, 1655); admonition of the fractious *(ibid.)*; dice and cards *(ibid.*, at 101, 1656).

Early statutes not discussed in the text which contain indications of a pronounced Calvinistic spirit along the lines discussed by Weber, are those intending to get men to work in their "callings." Thus the statute making the taking of tobacco by men in the fields "to the neglect of their labors" *(ibid.*, at 59, 1638); the law prohibiting young men and laborers from resorting to inns *(ibid.*, at 62, 1638); the statute directing grand jury inquest into persons living idly and loosely *(ibid.*, at 64, 1639). Compare also the stringent workhouse section in the *Code of 1658* *(ibid.*, at 120). Compare with these the statutes 1. JAC. c. 9; 4. JAC. c. 5; 21. JAC. c. 7, *re* drinking; 3. JAC. c. 4, *re* absence from church; 21 JAC. c. 20, *re* swearing—all of which, I suspect, were reflections of the growing Puritan spirit in England.

The absence of evidence in the court records that any great problem of idleness existed in the colony such as faced Elizabeth in the early decades of her reign [LEONARD, EARLY HISTORY OF ENGLISH POOR RELIEF (1900) c. 6 and 7] points to the fact that these statutes, far from being made in response to a definite social need, were in reality expressions of religious-economic policy, and were intended to operate as "admonitions" rather than as penal statutes; otherwise we should find as many presentments for idleness as we do for drinking. At the same time it should be pointed out that the statutes against card playing (1656) and drunkeness may well have been aimed at idlers. A man was drunk within the meaning of the statute if among other things he was not able "to follow his calling." The modern rationale of laws against the use of alcoholic liquors has thus an early prototype. The gospel of work must have been preached to the Pilgrims; 1 ROBINSON, WORKS, 113 *et seq.*, *Of Labour and Idleness.* The classical English effusions are of a later date. *Cf.* 1 WEBER, GESAMMELTE AUFSÄTZE ZUR RELIGIONSSOZIOLOGIE 105 *et seq.* On the workhouse, LEONARD, *op. cit.*, at 72 *et seq.*, 223, 241 *et seq.*, 260, 272 *et seq.*

16. The first attacks on the ecclesiastical courts were formulated along two different lines. On the one hand the dissentients adhering to Pentateuchal notions of punishment, objected to the laxness with which offences against morality were prosecuted, and the inconsequential penalties inflicted. On the other hand, they were no less bitter about the severity with which heretics were prosecuted in these tribunals. Their conclusions were in both cases the same: these courts should be deprived of these jurisdictions, which should be lodged entirely in civil magistrates. This, of course, was the practice at Geneva, and the backbone of Calvin's system of controlling morality.

The movement against the courts Christian was, as suggested, closely connected with the Mosaicism of the radical sects. It becomes a focal point in the popular pamphlet literature. The popularity of Martin Marprelate, who suggested the transfer of all church jurisdiction to civil courts (*Puritan Discipline Tracts,* 68), served to intensify the fight over this issue and it continued without interruption until the Revolution. Certain issues like the attack on the oath *ex officio,* became paramount from time to time. *Cf.* BARROW, A PETITION AD-

purification activities of English dissentients, it has not been my intention to imply that here were objectives consciously before the emigrants, or that anything as pretentious as a program existed. Their ideas mark at best the limits of what we might expect would emerge in their legislation as a result of religious idealism. Moreover, these notions would normally be slow in finding expression. Foremost in the settlers' minds was their primary purpose of propagating the gospel of the Kingdom of Christ.[17] Except as practical necessity or unplanned action intervened, legal institutions and organizations were necessarily ancillary to this.

I think the growth of the law in Plymouth can be best understood if we keep before us the fact that here was a group settling on lands to which they had initially no grant and no governmental powers derived from or authorized by the crown.[18] Whatever legis-

---

DRESSED TO HER MAJESTY (1590) 48; FULLER, THE ARGUMENT OF MASTER NICHOLAS FULLER . . . (1607); COSIN, *op. cit. supra* note 11, and the tracts there analysed. The effect of these attacks was to impeach generally the whole conception of purgation, as tending to perjury, a point of great concern with the Puritan group.

Coincident with the struggle on the jurisdiction and procedure of the ecclesiastical courts occurred the long wrangle over the substantive law. After the breach with Rome there had been an abortive attempt to revise the canon law. CARDWELL, REFORMATION OF THE ECCLESIASTICAL LAWS (1850). The matter was ventilated at various times, but until the convocation of 1604 [CANONS AND ECCLESIASTICAL CONSTITUTIONS, 1604 (Wilson ed. 1923)], no successful revision had been carried through. In practice the *Corpus Juris Canonici,* minus such sections as conflicted with the reformation statutes, plus certain provincial canons, was the basic jurisprudence of the English church courts. Even after the enactment of the Canons of 1604 this must have been the case, as this new code was an exceedingly bald and meagre document. On the whole matter of the canon law, *cf.* PARLIAMENTARY PAPERS—*Report of the Ecclesiastical Courts Commission,* 1883, Appendix; Davis, *The Canon Law in England,* in 34 ZTSCH. DER SAV. STIFT. FÜR RECHTSG. KAN. ABT. 344; 1 USHER, RECONSTRUCTION OF THE ENGLISH CHURCH (1910) 359 *et seq.* The interposition of the common law courts in the matter of defining the limits of ecclesiastical jurisdiction was not without effect upon the popular movement against the church courts. On this side of the question the best statement is in USHER, *op. cit.,* and in his RISE AND FALL OF THE HIGH COMMISSION (1913).

17. BRADFORD, *op. cit. supra* note 7, 32. On the early history of Plymouth there is an excellent account in 1 OSGOOD, *op. cit.,* at 105 *et seq.*

18. *Ibid.* 109 ". . . squatters destitute of legal rights of settlement." The elaborate negotiations before departure from England of the Pilgrims are recounted in BRADFORD, *op. cit.,* at 36 *et seq.* The New England Council had a patent from the Crown to these regions. *Cf.* PLYMOUTH LAWS, 1. The Pilgrims first negotiated for a grant from the London Company. In 1619 one Jacob Wincob obtained a grant from the latter, but this was never used. BRADFORD, *op. cit.,* at 51, 41; 1 RECORDS OF THE VIRGINIA COMPANY (1906) 69 (299). As the 1620 settlement was made on the lands of the New England Council, one John

lative powers were assumed depended therefore upon some view of the inherent capacity of the group. A necessary consequence of the Separatists' ideas of church forming was that a certain corporate quality attached to the congregation formed by covenant.[19] The

Pierce, an adventurer, obtained a grant in 1621 [2 MASS. HIST. SOC. COLLS. (4 Ser.) 156] from the Council conveying also powers of government and a limited ordinance-making power, with an agreement to convey corporate capacity and full legislative powers *in futuro*. In 1629, the Council granted to Bradford and his associates the lands in question, and included in the grant a power to make laws (PLYMOUTH LAWS, 21, 25).

There can be no doubt from the terms of the royal charter to the New England Council that the legislative power conveyed by the Crown was not delegable. The charter reads to them and their successors. There is no mention of assigns. In the light of contemporary doctrines of corporations the legislative power over the lands granted conveyed by the charter was obviously conceived as a grant of by-law powers. *Cf.* Norris v. Staps, Hobart 211, "For as reason is given to the natural body for the governing of it, so the body corporate must have laws as a politick reason to govern it, but those laws must ever be subject to the general law of the realm as subordinate to it. . . ." This latter proposition was established as early as St. 15 HY. VI c. 6, and St. 19 HY. VII c. 7. Norris v. Staps contains intimations of a strict construction of by-law powers. *Cf.* the later case, Wells v. Cotterel, 3 LEV. 48; ROLLE, ABRIDGMENT 365; Rex v. Head, 4 Burr. 2515. That the power of government was not deemed delegable is brought out in the discussion over the Massachusetts Bay charter in 1677. See Lord Chief Justice Sir Richard Raynsford and Sir Francis North's report, CALENDAR OF STATE PAPERS, COLONIAL 1677-80, 110 (No. 342). Other material in *ibid.*, at 79, 102-104, 118-133. *Cf.* also 2 TOPPAN, EDWARD RANDOLPH (Prince Soc. Pub. 1898-1909) 265 *et seq.*

The nearest legal authority for the exercise of legislative powers by the Plymouth colony may be found in Davenant v. Hurdis, Moore 576, where it was said that resiants of a leet could make a by-law relative to anything concerning common interest. In the Chamberlain of London's case, 5 Coke 62b, it is laid down that the inhabitants of a town might without custom make ordinances or by-laws concerning anything which public good required should be regulated but, "corporations cannot make ordinances or constitutions without a custom or the King's charter unless for things which concern the public good." Since the legislative power here was already vested in the N. E. Council by charter, I do not see how a claim to legislative power in the colonists can be supported.

19. There has never been a thoroughgoing study made of Separatism from the angle of corporate theory, and this is all the more remarkable because of the importance of the Congregational church in New England and the close relation of state and church in that region. To comprehend the steps by which the Separatists reached their views we must remember that in England their churches were without the pale of the law; that they rejected all ideas of hierarchical organization; that the protestant doctrines of the visible church made some form of organization essential. The central and most characteristic fact in Separatism was the covenant by which a church was organized. This was a dual act, a covenant with God—a solemn promise by the body of believers to God to do His will—and a second covenant, sometimes reduced to writing, made by the believers with one another, to work for the Lord, to avoid evil, to do good, and to stand together. Only in this way could a visible church be estab-

free use by Separatist writers from Browne to Robinson of analogies drawn from English borough constitution, to fortify their conception of the corporate nature of their church, lends color to this theory. Thus, we know that before the Pilgrims left Holland, they formed by covenant a church, and that their pastor conceived this to have been simultaneously equivalent to the formation of a "civil body politick."[20] This would doubtless have been sufficient to their

lished. (BURRAGE, CHURCH COVENANT IDEA; 1 EARLY ENGLISH DISSENTERS, *passim*). That the church thus constituted was conceived of as a corporation is borne out in the Separatist writings. Thus on Browne and Barrow's views, DEXTER, CONGREGATIONALISM, at 105, 222-3; on Henry Jacobs, 2 BURRAGE, EARLY ENGLISH DISSENTERS, at 157; BURRAGE, CHURCH COVENANT IDEA, at 60: Robinson's views are in 2 WORKS 135, 440, 445; 3 WORKS 17, 64, 431. *Cf.* also the *Confessions of the Separatist church at Amsterdam of 1596,* in Walker, *op. cit.,* at 71.

The Separatists seem to have had English municipal institutions in mind, rather than ecclesiastical corporations like the Dean and Chapter. It was not until the Leyden Separatists had resided in Holland that the civil implications of their corporate theory developed, *i.e.,* an identification of the church as a corporation for civil purpose. Robinson, *Of Religious Communion* (1614) in 3 WORKS 128, believes the Dutch churches to be founded on the same principles as his. On the organization of these churches, HOFFMANN, DAS KIRCHENVERFASSUNGSRECHT DER NIEDERLÄNDISCHEN REFORMIERTEN (1902) 70, 76, 86. They were conceived as separate corporate units. In reaching this conclusion of great influence was the John a Lasco church in London, which had a charter from Edward VI [BURN, HISTORY OF THE FRENCH, WALLOON DUTCH AND OTHER PROTESTANT REFUGEES SETTLED IN ENGLAND (1846) 265, for the charter] and possessed regulations that were models for the continental congregations; see 2 RIEKER, DIE EVANGELISCHEN KIRCHENORDNUNGEN DES 16TEN JAHRHUNDERTS (1846) 99. It is curious that the circumstance that the a Lasco church had an English charter should have affected the corporate theory on the continent. At this time free association seems to have been enough to establish churches in Holland. 3 GIERKE, DAS DEUTSCHE GENOSSENSCHAFTSRECHT (1881) 724, 802; GROTIUS, DE IMPERIO SUMMARUM POTESTATUM CIRCA SACRA c. 4, § 11; HASHAGEN, DER RHEINISCHE PROTESTANTISMUS (1924) 16. On the Lutheran churches, GIERKE, *op. cit.* at 799. *Cf.* RIEKER, DIE RECHTLICHE STELLUNG DER EVANGELISCHEN KIRCHEN DEUTSCHLANDS (1893) 71 *et seq.;* 1 HOLL, GESAMMELTE AUFSÄTZE ZUR KIRCHENGESCHICHTE (3d ed. 1923) 350. On the origin of the reformed church conception of the congregation, 1 SOHM, KIRCHENRECHT (1923) 645, 648; TROELTSCH, *op. cit. supra* note 10, at 625. The close intellectual affinity of the covenant idea with the prevalent social compact theory is obvious. While the Pilgrims generally were probably ignorant of the latter, a perusal of Robinson's writings lead one to believe that he was familiar with them. Henry Jacob most certainly was.

20. The Pilgrims seem to have been fully aware of the desirability of some official countenance of their religion. An attempt in 1617 was made to obtain from the King liberty of worship. BRADFORD, *op. cit. supra* note 7, at 38. Whether they had in mind a patent like that of John a Lasco is not clear. By this time, however, their leaders' ideas of the corporate nature of their church were well developed. Had they gone to Virginia they intended to live as "a distinct body by themselves." BRADFORD, *op. cit.* at 37. "It was also agreed by

needs except for the presence of persons not members of the church. The Mayflower Compact was executed as Bradford states to keep these non-Separatists in order.[21] Since the power to legislate was the consequence of corporate character implicit in the Separatist or Congregational church, the Compact was no more than a reiteration and confirmation of this corporate association, plus an announcement of a design to "enact and frame just and equal laws."[22]

It is obvious that a group which believed it could create corporate capacity on the civil side by complying with its own formalities of ecclesiastical association, and which looked primarily to the Bible for substantive norms of conduct, was in no immediate need of comprehensive legislation. This indeed seems to be borne out

---

mutual consent and covenant that those who went should be an absolute church of themselves." *Ibid.*, at 53. This seems to indicate that a church had been formed. In the celebrated letter of Robinson occurs the phrase, "Whereas you are become a body politic using among yourselves civil government," (*ibid.*, at 81). This points to some organization before sailing, and the covenant spoken of by Bradford seems to be the only evidence of anything having been done in this direction. From what we know of the prevalent corporate ideas of these people, they had become articulate in their notion of the visible church, the evidence points strongly to the fact that their church organization was to suffice for their civil needs.

21. *Ibid.*, at 109.

22. To anyone familiar with the Separatist writings and not bemused by theories of democracy, or by hallucinations regarding the originality of the first settlers, it seems difficult to escape the conclusion that the civil order instituted at Plymouth was no more than the realization of the complete possibilities of their corporate theory of the church, and in this sense simply the consummation of their speculation regarding the church. Here is the result of growth, not an adaptation. At the outset the church in Plymouth was the state. There is no question, as Burrage, Church Covenant Idea, 68, suggests, of the use of religious forms for civil purpose. The theocratic character of Plymouth colony itself refutes this. Church and state were one and the same. The idea of Borgeaud, Rise of Modern Democracy (1894) 113, who says that the notion of free association in general was justified by custom and the common law is absurd. Whatever may have been the earlier law, in seventeenth century England corporate status could not be acquired thus, and his example of the gilds is anachronistic. (Lib. Ass. 49 Edw. III, 8; Case of Suttons Hospital, 10 Coke 22b). Nevertheless, that the colonists conceived of themselves as a corporation is clear. *Cf.* the letter of Sherley and others to Bradford, 18 December 1624, "make your corporation as formal as you can under the name of the society in Plymouth in New England." (3 Mass. Hist. Soc. Coll., 1st ser. 33). In 1632 the settlers style themselves a "society"; Plymouth Laws, 30. In 1636 they are a "colony and corporation"; *ibid.*, 35. The suggestion that the form of English trading companies may have been of influence seems to me to rest wholly on conjecture. In all the Separatist literature consulted by me, and I do not think much has been overlooked, I have seen no reference to such companies. The ideas were pretty well crystallized before the settlement of Massachusetts Bay.

by the records. Not until 1636 was there an attempt at a far-reaching establishment of laws.[23] That year was signalized by the establishment of a code intended to be a complete statement of law. Since this code was the first of a series of similar codes in New England and as I am of the opinion that the subsequent codifications in those regions were all of them influenced by this first attempt at a concise and compact statement of the law, it is necessary to inquire why such a code should have been enacted.[24]

Nowhere do the religious and experiential elements in the legal development of Plymouth merge more closely than in relation to the colonists' idea as to the form in which law was to be expressed, in their seemingly unprecedented enthusiasm for the *lex scripta*, for codification. This notion was by no means new to English law, but codification was not an idea favored by the common lawyers. The code idea as it had taken form in England was expressive of a particularistic conception of law and government utterly opposed

23. The Plymouth Laws are published in RECORDS OF THE COLONY OF NEW PLYMOUTH (Pulsifer ed. 1861)—*Laws;* and the edition of Brigham, *supra* note 15. References here are to the latter edition. During the period of Plymouth's independent existence there were, in all, four revisions of the laws: the first of 1636; the second of 1658; the third of 1671; and the fourth of 1684. Pulsifer does not mention the last. But see 6 COURT ORDERS, 1678-91, at 132.

24. There seems to have been no particular professional interest in codification during the period of the Reformation, barring, of course, the re-codification of the canon law, a matter primarily of concern to the civilians. Of course, there is a lot of talk about law reform. Woolsey seems to have had some sort of program of restatement. Bucer's suggestions in his *De Regno Christi* (HARVEY, *op. cit.*, at 77 *et seq.*) and Edward VI's *Discourse on the Reformation of Abuses* [2 LITERARY REMAINS OF EDWARD VI (Nichols ed. 1857, Roxburghe Club Pubs.) 475] are both regarded as attempts to formulate some broad and far-reaching program. None of these projects emanate from the profession and none contemplate codification.

During the Tudor period the legal literature was enriched by the publication first of STATHAM'S ABRIDGMENT, then the GREAT ABRIDGMENT OF STATUTES, FITZHERBERT'S ABRIDGMENT, and many other similar reference books. WINFIELD, CHIEF SOURCES OF ENGLISH LEGAL HISTORY (1927) 203-5 has pointed out, however, that the abridgment was a device used in manuscript form before the introduction of printing. These works were all based on a system of alphabetical arrangement of subject matter, and no attempt was made to perfect any sort of philosophical integration or coordination of the law. It is, consequently, absurd to regard any of these works as suggesting or supporting the idea of codification. The only perceptible effect that they may have had upon the colonial codes is the eventual preference for alphabetical arrangement displayed in the colonial collections of laws. The Plymouth colonists do not talk of "codes." They speak of revisions of the laws or book of laws. I do not attach any significance to the fact that the word "code" is not used, in view of the limitations in the experience and knowledge of the group.

to the centralizing tendencies of the King's Courts. In so far as codes had survived in seventeenth century England, they were the vestiges of medieval conditions, the depositaries of ancient law.[25]

I have already made reference to the diversity of franchises in England at the opening of the seventeenth century. The existence of these franchises, many of them dating back to the Norman Conquest, had favored the development of local law and customs. The latter were not universally reduced to record, but as a rule the more important the jurisdiction, the more surely were its local customs committed to writing. These custumals varied from the relatively complete statements of local law arranged in an approximately systematic way and fully deserving the name of codes, to the more primitive recordings of manorial ordinances. In all cases the active principle behind the reduction to writing was the desire to achieve certainty, to preserve the franchise, and to aid the local courts which enforced the custom. These codes existed as living law, despite the fact that they belonged to the past and not to the future. So widely diffused were they that it is difficult to avoid the conclusion that they exercised some influence upon the Plymouth planters in their choice of a code as a medium of expressing their will. This was due in part to undoubted familiarity with local conditions, and in part to the fact that the intense biblicism of the past century had given to the code idea a new vigor.

We have seen how the so-called Mosaic law had been seized upon and exploited by the radical religious elements in England as the true guide of men's ethical behavior. There can be no doubt that the great things which had been accomplished at Geneva, supposedly on the basis of Old Testament jurisprudence, had stimu-

25. The classic work on English customary law is BATESON, BOROUGH CUSTOMS. This work is made up of selections from a number of custumals. In many cases the local legal peculiarities were preserved only in the borough charters: *Cf.* BALLARD, BRITISH BOROUGH CHARTERS, 1042-1216 (1913); BALLARD AND TAIT, BRITISH BOROUGH CHARTERS, 1216-1307 (1923). Note also that gild ordinances are of no less importance: TOULMIN-SMITH, ENGLISH GILDS (1870) *passim*. Published custumals and ordinances consulted are to be found in 2 LYON, HISTORY OF DOVER (1813) 267; *Southampton Oak Book* (in 10, 11, 12, PUB. SOUTHAMPTON HIST. SOC., Studer Ed.); LIBER CUSTUMARUM: THE BOOK OF ANCIENT USAGE AND CUSTOMES OF THE TOWN OF NORTHAMPTON (Markham ed. 1895); BOYS, HISTORY OF SANDWICH (1792) 428, 495; 1 HUDSON AND TINGLY, RECORDS OF THE CITY OF NORWICH (1906) 132; BICKLEY, THE LITTLE RED BOOK OF BRISTOL (1910); WOODRUFF, A HISTORY OF THE TOWN AND PORT OF FORDWICH (1895); LIVERPOOL TOWN BOOKS (Twemlow ed. 1918); SWINDEN, HISTORY OF GREAT YARMOUTH (1772); RECORDS OF CHIPPENHAM (Goldney Ed. 1889) 4; ANCIENT USAGES OF WINCHESTER (Farley Ed. 1927).

lated this enthusiasm.[26] For it was a cardinal point of Calvin's propaganda that God's Kingdom could be realized on earth only by the adaptation of Israelite models. There was but one law in the Kingdom and that was the law of God as revealed in the Old Testament.

In addition to this more articulate aspect of biblicism a major

26. The comparison of the New England colonies with the theocracy of Calvin and Beza at Geneva has been frequently made. When one attempts to find, however, a comprehensive discussion of the legal aspects of Calvin's system, one discovers that the materials have never been assembled and thoroughly analyzed from the point of view of legal institutions and law administration. The best and most critical discussion of this phase of the Geneva experiment remains KAMPSCHULTE, JOHANN CALVIN (2 vols. 1869-99). Doumergue's voluminous, JEAN CALVIN (7 vols. 1899-1927) is not particularly useful. CHOISY, L'ÉTAT CHRÉTIEN CALVINIST À GENÈVE (1902) and his LA THÉOCRATIE À GENÉVE AU TEMPS DE CALVIN (1897) contain much useful material. Flammer, *Usage ou Jurisprudence Coutumière du Canton de Genève,* 13 BULLETIN DE L'INSTITUT NATIONAL GENEVOIS 1, and *Le Droit Civil Genevois,* 20 *ibid.,* 5 *et seq.;* Brocher de la Fléchère, *Philosophie de L'Histoire de Droit,* 33 *ibid.,* 585, 594; Du Bois-Melly, *Du Bannissement sous le Gouvernement de l'Ancienne République de Genève,* 29 *ibid.,* 45, contain some matters of importance.

The activity of Calvin falls into two periods, separated by his banishment and brief absence. On May 21, 1536, the Council voted to live according to the Holy Evangels, although Calvin had from the very first fixed as his idea the Israelite theocracy of the Old Testament and his original program as worked out with Farel had a very limited scope and contemplated cooperation of magistracy and clergy only as to specific matters. 1 KAMPSCHULTE, *op. cit.,* at 287 *et seq.;* 10 CALVIN, OPERA, 5, in CORPUS REFORMATORUM; CHOISY, LA THÉOCRATIE, ETC. 16. *The Ordonnances Ecclésiastiques* (10 CALVIN, OPERA, 15; these were never published in original forms; the text of 1561 is in 10 CALVIN, OPERA, 93; KAMPSCHULTE, *op. cit.,* at 417n) promulgated shortly after Calvin's return from banishment, lay down the foundations of the theocracy, on the principle of enacting the gospel of Christ into an ecclesiastical polity. A commission appointed to revise the criminal and civil law and procedure of Geneva, reported in 1543 the *Edits Politiques.* Compare the projects of Calvin in BRETSCHNEIDER, CALVINI ETC., ALIORUMIQUE, ETC., LITERAE (1835) 62 *et seq.,* and 10 OPERA, 124 *et seq.* A special commission was named for criminal procedure. Work upon the *Edits Civils* was tentatively begun in 1544, but this code was not completed until 1568. 2 ROGET, HISTOIRE DU PEUPLE DE GENÈVE (1870) 65; Flammer, *op cit.,* 20 BULLETIN DE L'INSTITUT, 11. In 1545, the *Ordonnances Matrimoniales* were adopted; 10 CALVIN, OPERA, 34.

In all of these projects Calvin was active. *Cf.* his drafts in BRETSCHNEIDER, *op. cit.,* at 75 *et seq.,* and 10 OPERA, 131 *et seq.* The most important parts of Calvin's program were the social and economic reforms. These are discussed in KAMPSCHULTE, *op. cit.,* at 429. By harnessing religious fervor to precisely defined social objectives, by fostering a utilitarian asceticism, and by entrusting his administration to a tightly organized machine to which the pronounced authoritarianism of his teachings gave strength and vitality, the Christian state of the great reformer became the model of all similarly disposed protestants. How far there was a popular knowledge of all this in England is difficult to estimate.

characteristic was the insistence upon a literal use of the Book[27] and an irrefragable confidence in the written word. It is here that we shall find at least a partial explanation of the desire strikingly manifested throughout New England to have the rule of law reduced to written form, the absence of judicial interpretation, the requirements for recordation of titles, and the preservation in writing of evidence. In England we see how this tendency had already been expressed in the Puritans' demands for explicit church canons that would leave no doubt as to what the law was.[28] In the later days it is exemplified in the vicious attacks upon the amorphous nature of equity jurisprudence.[29] In Massachusetts Bay the prevalence of this point of view even operated to defeat the purpose of the projectors of theocracy to have the law a growth of custom along biblical lines, so that the charter's injunction that their law be "not contrarie or repugnant" to the law of England could be avoided.[30]

27. Thus Robinson, *Of the Holy Scriptures* (1 WORKS 48): "There is in the Scripture but one proper and immediate sense. . . . The literal sense is to be followed as being the most natural." *Cf.* TROELTSCH, *op. cit. supra* note 10 at 462. Interesting sidelights on this tendency in the time of the Commonwealth are in the teachings ot Winstanley: "The bare letter of the law established by Act of Parliament shall be the rule. . . ." BERENS, THE DIGGER MOVEMENT (1906) App. c. 224. *Cf.* also Winstanley's *Law of Freedom* in *ibid.*, at 192.

28. See the instructions to the speakers at the Hampton Court Conference, in 53 HIST. MSS. COMM., *Report on the MSS. of Lord Montague of Beaulieu* (1900) 32, 33 (no. 6).

29. COCK, ENGLISH LAW (1651) 85-6; 1 COCK, AN ESSAY OF CHRISTIAN GOVERNMENT (1651) 165; Robinson, *Anticipations under the Commonwealth of Changes in the Law,* 1 SELECT ESSAYS IN ANGLO-AMERICAN LEGAL HISTORY, 467, 470.

30. 1 WINTHROP, HISTORY OF NEW ENGLAND (Savage Ed.) 322;

"The people had long desired a body of laws, and thought their condition very unsafe while so much power rested in the discretion of magistrates. . . . Two great reasons there were, which caused most of the magistrates and some of the elders not to be very forward in this matter. One was want of sufficient experience of the nature and disposition of the people, considered with the condition of the country and other circumstances, which made them conceive that such laws would be fittest for us which should arise *pro re nata* upon occasions, etc., and so the laws of England and other states grew, and therefore the fundamental laws of England are called customs, consuetudines. 2. For that it would professedly trangress the limits of our charter, which provide we shall make no laws repugnant to the laws of England, and that we were assured we must do. But to raise up laws by practice and custom had been no transgression."

"The other circumstances" include obviously the use of the Law of God. See the discussions over Roger Williams (1 WINTHROP, *op. cit.* 63 *passim;* DEXTER, AS TO ROGER WILLIAMS (1876) 26 *et seq.*). Most illuminating on the point is the discussion between Vane and Winthrop in 2 HUTCHINSON PAPERS (Prince Soc. 1865) 79 (67) *et seq.*, esp. 100.

It is not to be expected that the result of this curious union of religious objectives and lay experience, would resemble except vaguely the English prototypes, particularly as these draughtsmen had before them no copy of any local custumals. On the other hand, I find persuasive of my theory, that English custumals motivated the use of a code, the fact that the commencement of the Plymouth code resembles generally many of the English custumals.[31] It opens with a recital of authority and a specification

31. 1 BATESON, *op. cit.*, at xv gives the following characterization of these preambles in the custumals here quoted because in many cases these documents are in manuscript and are not available: "The credit for the work is frequently claimed by the writer and his purpose explained. He writes that the draft is made for his own and his successor's convenience. . . . Sometimes the clerk adduces as his authority a similar collection of earlier date . . . ; sometimes he gives clear indication that he has collected his facts from various official sources. . . . In a few cases the code is declared to be drafted and issued as a whole under the governing body of the town. Some local event has given impulse to codification; perhaps the purchase of new privileges; or a royal inquiry as in the case of the Cinque Ports in the fourteenth century. . . ." For some of these introductions *cf.* 1 BICKLEY, *op. cit.* at 24; WOODRUFF, *op. cit.* at 236; TOULMIN-SMITH, *op. cit.* at 349 for the Winchester custumal, 376 for the Worcester custumal; 1 LIVERPOOL TOWN BOOKS, 1; SWINDEN, *op. cit.* at 136, 155.

Certain superficial similarities between the 1636 preamble and those of the English custumals which may be mentioned are the following: The specification name of the committee coincides with the naming of authorities in some custumals; the prefacing or mention of the King's charter in the latter coincides with the recital of the compact and grant in the Plymouth document; finally, the express mention that the laws are made by consent both in the code of 1636 and in some of the custumals seems significant. This latter provision is not unusual in the gild ordinances. *Cf.* TOULMIN-SMITH, *op. cit.*

The preambles of statutes, and the long opening recitals of grants are not close enough in content and form for us to regard them as possible models. The statutes antedating the code of 1636 often have preambles, but these are concise statements of the facts motivating the statutes and do not resemble the code preamble.

The form of the preamble is interesting in giving some clue to the theory of legislative power. It states that the committee for the revision of the laws having read the Compact and the letters patent *(sic)* of 1629 and "finding that as free borne subjects of the State of England we hither came endewed with all and singular the priviledges belong to such in the first place, we thinke good that it be established for an act.

"That according to the . . . and due privilege of the subject aforesaid no imposicion law or ordnance be made or imposed upon or by ourselves or others at present or to come but such as shall be made or imposed by consent, according to the free liberties of the state and Kingdome of England and no otherwise."

It should be noted that the Committee goes behind both Compact and grant to the intangible privileges of the Englishmen of which these documents are treated as mere evidence. No longer, as in the Compact, is authority conferred by virtue of the fact of association. The preamble is a crudely phrased appeal

of powers. Then follow sections relating to the election of officers and the oaths to be taken by them. Precisely the same arrangement was followed in the beginning of a great many English custumals. This presents itself as evidence worth considering, for men are prone to remember how things begin, be they constitutions or laws or poems, however far they may stray from their models before they are through.

I have tried to make clear my view that in the growth of legal institutions at Plymouth we are dealing not with an exact duplication of a definite model, but with the crude imitation of inaccurately remembered things. This explains the use of the code form. It likewise explains certain aspects of law administration to which I desire briefly to advert. Thus the absence of clear-cut lines between the legislative and judicial function,[32] and the failure to

---

to the rights of Englishmen. This statement anticipates in a degree the debates which occurred shortly thereafter in England over the distinction between fundamental laws and other legislation the basis for which had been laid in the discussions over the Petition of Right. *Cf.* ROTHSCHILD, DER GEDANKE DER GESCHRIEBENEN VERFASSUNG IN DER ENGLISCHEN REVOLUTION (1902) 6 *et seq.; The Form of the Government of England, etc.* (1641) in 4 SOMERS TRACTS 121; PEASE, THE LEVELLER MOVEMENT (1916) 13; 2 COBBETT, PARLIAMENTARY HISTORY (1807) 257 *et seq.;* 6 GARDINER, HISTORY OF ENGLAND FROM THE ACCESSION OF JAMES I TO THE OUTBREAK OF THE CIVIL WAR (1893) 262 *et seq.*

If anything in the nature of a constitutional foundation for the future existed in Plymouth, it was this preamble, with the important provision that the freemen must consent to all laws. There seems, moreover, to be an implicit rejection of royal authority in the reference to the "privileges" of the subject as the source of legislation. It is possible to regard this preamble as a retort to the King's Commission on Trade and Plantations of 1634, and the projected royal government for New England. *Cf.* BRADFORD, *op. cit. supra* note 7, at 390, App. II, 540.

32. The legislature and chief tribunal of Plymouth was known as the "General Court." The earliest records are missing, but the first ones indicate no clear distinction between the two functions. *Records of the Colony of New Plymouth,* 1 & 2 COURT ORDERS (1633-1651), hereafter cited COURT ORDERS. In this series (vol. 7) the Judicial Acts begin (1636).

Sitting as a court the General Court held quarterly sessions, which it should be noted were not designated by the common law term names. In 1636, a Court of Assistants was set up, when it was provided that the governor and at least two assistants should determine cases involving less than 40 shillings (compare the County Court jurisdiction in England) and have jurisdiction over offences of small nature "as in wisdome God shall direct them" (PLYMOUTH LAWS, 42). The office of assistant came into existence very early, although it is mentioned first in 1632, where a penalty is provided for refusing to take office as councillor. The name "assistant" is applied in 1633. BRADFORD, *op. cit. supra* note 7, at 122 mentions the appointment of a single assistant (1621) and the increase (*ibid.*, at 187) of the number to five and later seven. The Court of Assistants sat in Massachusetts Bay from the very first. 1 RECORDS OF THE COLONY OF

distinguish entirely between civil and criminal[33] jurisdiction, are characteristics of Plymouth and of the country courts in England. No one who has read the records of the local courts of seventeenth century England can fail to be struck with the remarkable resemblance between the two. The eventual abandonment of what appears to have been an initial imitation in Plymouth of suit of court with judgment by the suitors, in favor of an elected and representative magistracy, tended to emphasize what I may call the essentially leet court character of jurisdiction.[34] Similarly the earliest Plymouth

MASS. BAY, 73. The term "assistant" has an origin much earlier than the joint stock companies of the late sixteenth and the seventeenth centuries. It was used by gild merchants and probably came in as an office in municipal government where a borough developed out of gild organization. 1 SCOTT, THE CONSTITUTION AND FINANCE OF ENGLISH, ETC., JOINT STOCK COMPANIES TO 1720 (1912) 7, 20; WEBB, MANOR AND BOROUGH, 363, 364.

Another interesting evidence of the concentration of function is the provision made in 1633 for proof of all wills before the Governor and Council (PLYMOUTH LAW, 32); a full inventory had to be presented before letters of administration would issue. Civil jurisdiction over testamentary matters exercised by manor courts was not unknown in some localities. HONE, THE MANOR AND MANORIAL RECORDS (1906) 22, 302; SCRIVEN, TREATISE ON THE LAW OF COPYHOLDS (7th ed. 1896) 423. WEBB, MANOR AND BOROUGH, 17, n. 3, suggests that where this custom existed, the manor may have been an ecclesiastical holding. The power of devising copyhold lands was well established. The practice was to present these wills in the lord's court in order to effect transfer of possession. Whether or not this was a probate of will in a civil tribunal need not be answered, but certainly the will of the testator could be given effect in respect to the copyhold only through due process of the lord's court. Of some bearing on the problem is the Plymouth rule that personalty was to be sold first to satisfy debts, and then the purchased lands. Lands assigned by the corporation for subsistence were exempted from seizure by creditors. The rule in England was that copyhold lands were not assets in the hands of the heir; Brown's Case, 4 Coke 21a, 22a; COKE, COMPLETE COPYHOLDER, § 50.

33. What I have reference to is not only the concentration of jurisdiction in a single court, but also the failure to distinguish sharply between a prosecution publicly initiated and a private suit. As far as the records are concerned the Court Orders are very miscellaneous in character. They contain notices of presentments, criminal and civil trials, ordinances, admissions to the corporations, marriages, recordings of personalty, inquests on special matters, grants, and many other matters. The Judicial Acts are devoted chiefly to records of civil actions, but there are also military orders, trials of traversed presentments, testimony, etc.

34. As the early records are wanting, one can only conjecture as to whether or not in the General Court judgment was given by the freemen. Certainly the religious theory of the Separatists was no bar to this, and the practice of judgment by the suitors was still prevalent in England. In 1646 a statute was enacted (PLYMOUTH LAWS, 88) which required the presence of the freemen only at the June meeting of the General Court, and the attendance of magistrates only at the judicial sessions. This leads me to believe that something like suit of court existed at one time in Plymouth. It should be pointed out

that in the seventeenth century the lawyers drew a distinction between the obligation of suit in the court leet and the county or manor courts. The difference lay in the fact that the function of judging was vested in the steward or bailiff in the former case and in the county or manor courts was exercised by the suitors. Jentleman's case, 6 Coke 11a. *Cf.* 9 COKE, PREFACE; MORRIS, W. A., THE EARLY ENGLISH COUNTY COURT (1926) 100; Maitland, *The Suitors of the County Court,* 3 ENGLISH HISTORICAL REVIEW 417; 1 HOLDSWORTH, HISTORY OF ENGLISH LAW, 72; Plucknett, *New Light on the Old County Court* (1929) 42 HARV. LAW REV. 639; Woodbine, *County Court Rolls and County Court Records* (1930) 43 *ibid.* 1083. CALTHROPE, THE RELATION BETWEEN THE LORD OF A MANNOR AND THE COPPYHOLDER (1635). On the court leet, HEARNSHAW, LEET JURISDICTION IN ENGLAND (1908); RITSON, JURISDICTION OF THE COURT LEET (2d ed. 1809).

The property and residence requirements in the rural and urban leets of England in the seventeenth century, are the decayed remainders of what was once a notion of parity implicit in the idea of suit. In Plymouth, freeholding and the religious qualifications enforced at first indirectly by the device of official approbation of residence, and subsequently by other means, made for a parity within the group along the restricted lines of special privilege, analogous to the freedom of a corporation that prevailed in many English boroughs. PLYMOUTH LAWS, 35, 36, 72, 92, 102, 112, 113.

One reason that I have used the term "leet jurisdiction" to characterize the Plymouth arrangements is that this type of local court was particularly vigorous in England at this time. It had important ordinance making power [RITSON, *op. cit.* at 39; and *cf.* BRIDLINGTON CHARTERS (1926) 271 for an example of these ordinances]. It possessed the power of appointing certain officers (WEBB, MANOR AND BOROUGH, 28). In many municipalities it was the central governing agency, with civil and criminal jurisdictions merged, and with important administrative functions (*ibid.,* at 31, 64 *et seq.,* 165, 190, 202, 337n., 338).

The resemblance between the Plymouth court records and the court leet records for the sixteenth and seventeenth centuries that I have examined is striking. *Cf.* 1 SOUTHAMPTON RECORD SOC. COURT LEET RECORDS (1906) pt. 2, 1578-1602; FIVE COURT ROLLS OF CRESSINGHAM (1885) 77 *et. seq.;* PRESTON COURT LEET RECORDS (Hewitson Ed. 1905): 2 RECORDS OF THE BOROUGH OF NOTTINGHAM (1889) *passim;* COURT LEET RECORDS OF THE MANOR OF MANCHESTER (12 vols. 1884-90); THE PORTMOTE OR COURT LEET RECORDS OF SALFORD (Chetham Soc. Pub.) 46, 48. DESCRIPTIVE CATALOGUE OF CHARTERS, ETC., OF . . . WEYMOUTH AND MELCOMBE REGIS (Moule Ed. 1883) 43 *et seq.;* RECORDS OF HENLEY IN ARDEN (Wellstood Ed. 1919); HISTORY OF BASINGSTOKE (Baigent and Millard Eds. 1889) 322 *et seq.*

For Quarter Sessions records for the period consult: HERTFORDSHIRE COUNTY RECORDS (Hardy Ed. 1905), Sessions Rolls, 5 *ibid.* (1928), Calendar of Sessions Books; QUARTER SESSIONS RECORDS OF THE COUNTY OF NORTHAMPTON (Wake Ed. 1924); LANCASHIRE QUARTER SESSIONS RECORDS (Tait Ed. 1917—Chetham Soc. Pub. 77); RECORD SOCIETY OF LANCASHIRE AND CHESHIRE (42), *Manchester Sessions* (Axon Ed. 1901); MIDDLESEX COUNTY RECORDS (Jeaffreson Ed.) vols. 1-5; WORCESTERSHIRE COUNTY RECORDS CALENDAR OF THE QUARTER SESSIONS PAPERS (Bund Ed. 1900); THE NORTH RIDING RECORD SOC., QUARTER SESSIONS RECORDS (Atkinson Ed. 1884-8) vols. 1-6. *Cf.* also SOME ANNALS OF THE BOROUGH OF DEVIZES (Cunnington Ed. 1925) 90, and compare 2 READING RECORDS (Guilding Ed. 1895), the proceedings *coram Mayor.*

The quarter sessions in England are suggested by the fact that the Plymouth assistants are styled occasionally justices of the peace. The earliest instance is

statute of 1623[35] required a jury trial in all civil actions, including debt. This was a characteristic of the undifferentiated manor courts, where civil and police jurisdiction were intermingled. In county courts and local courts exercising untarnished civil jurisdiction, wage of law was prevalent.[36] The Plymouth statute, a reflection of the dissentients' antipathy to purgation, tended to fix procedure along the indicated lines.

For our guides to pleading in English local courts we are cast upon seventeenth century handbooks like those of Dalton, Kitchin, or Greenwood.[37] Except perhaps in the county court no such uniformity existed, as these writers would have us believe.[38] We do know, however, that the primitive methods of complaint and answer[39] were usual and this seems to have obtained in the earlier

---

in 1637 (1 COURT ORDERS, 60, 69, 86). Note also that process ran in the name of the King, and even the General Court was summoned and held in the name of the King (PLYMOUTH LAWS, 41). The oath of the constable indicates an acceptance of the notion of the King's Peace [*ibid.*, at 40 (1636)] and this is borne out by the court records. In Massachusetts Bay the assistants were given powers of justices of the peace in 1630. (1 MASSACHUSETTS COLONIAL RECORDS, 74).

35. PLYMOUTH LAWS, 71. Note the changes made in 1666; *ibid.*, at 149.

36. DALTON, OFFICE OF SHERIFFS (1619 ed.) 496 states that wager of law lay for trespass and for assumpsit. *Cf.* KITCHIN, JURISDICTIONS OF COURTS LEET (1656) 255; FINCH, NOMOTEXNIA (1613) fol. 116; COKE, SECOND INSTITUTE, c. 22, f. 143; WILKINSON, TREATISE, ETC., CONCERNING THE OFFICE, ETC., OF SHERIFFS, ETC. (1657 ed.) 252; 3 SMYTH, A DESCRIPTION OF THE HUNDRED OF BERKELEY (1885) ed.) 12. Smyth, writing in the seventeenth century says "ffor there is not nor ever hath byn in any age as most ancient Court rolls doe witness any trialls by jury" in the hundred of Berkeley. See also 3 RECORDS OF THE BOROUGH OF LEICESTER (Bateson Ed. 1905) 143; THE BURFORD RECORDS (Gretton Ed. 1920) 531, 540, 541.

On the procedure in older times see Gross, *Modes of Trial in the Medieval Boroughs of England* (1902) 15 HARV. L. REV. 691, 704; HENRY, CONTRACTS IN THE LOCAL COURTS OF MEDIEVAL ENGLAND (1926) 70; 1 PALGRAVE, RISE AND PROGRESS OF THE ENGLISH COMMONWEALTH, 214-215; 2 BATESON, BOROUGH CUSTOMS, xxvii *et seq.* THAYER, PRELIMINARY TREATISE ON EVIDENCE (1898) 28, thinks wager of law was moribund in the seventeenth century, but he obviously has the King's courts in mind. Note the statement, *ibid.*, at 33, that wager of law was never introduced in America.

37. *Supra* note 36. GREENWOOD, CURIA COMITATUS REDIVIVA (1657); the 9th edition of this work (1730) is much fuller.

38. This is brought out by the Webbs, in MANOR AND BOROUGH, 11, 12.

39. DALTON, *op. cit. supra* note 36, at 463. For forms of these plaints GREENWOOD, *op. cit. supra* note 37, at 127 *et seq.*, 149 *et seq.* These did not have to be in writing; FINCH, *op. cit. supra* note 36, at 248. But see Y. B. 9 EDW. IV, 48. The theory was that trial was by all the county and need not be record, *i.e.*, all was matter *en fait.* The practice seems to have been that the shire clerk kept a book for the purpose of entering actions. *Cf.* St. 11 HY. VII, c. 15). Some clue to the pleading in Plymouth is to be found in the table of clerk's

decades of Plymouth history. On the other hand, until 1636 there was in that colony no clear conception of forms of action, at least if we may judge from the fact that only twice in the records does the clerk append a name to the action.[40] Thereafter, however, we find designation to be usual,[41] a fact which leads me to think that a book like Kitchin's *Jurisdictions of Courts Leet* may have reached these shores. There is, moreover, a remarkable preponderance of actions on the case, a characteristic of all early American procedure in the North. For this phenomenon no satisfactory explanation has ever been offered, but I venture to suggest that it was a contemporaneous condition in England. In the King's Courts, case had been on the rise. The indications are that the same thing was true in the local courts. Perhaps the emasculated action of trespass in the county courts—the trespass without allegation of force—may have had something to do with this.[42] The formal dis-

---

fees (1640-1) (1 COURT ORDERS, 170) that was inserted in the code of 1658 (PLYMOUTH LAWS, 109-110). The only items there relating to civil procedure are replevins (2s. 4d.), declarations, entering an action (6d.), an answer. I think we may assume that this was the full range of paper pleading, otherwise fees would no doubt have been required, as the clerk was feed for a warrant to summon a jury (6d.) and for recording a verdict (1s. 6d.).

40. The earliest records of the courts begin in 1633. In that year an "action of slander" is entered by name (1 COURT ORDERS, 12). In 1634 there is entered an action of trespass (*ibid.*, at 30). The records are not helpful on this point.

41. For the period January 1637 (o.s.) to May 1642 a poll of the Judicial Acts shows: actions on the case, 59; actions of slander (sic), 5; actions of debt, 5; actions of trespass, 3; actions of battery, 1.

42. On trespass in the county court, STATUTE OF GLOUCESTER, 6 EDW. I, c. 8; COKE, SECOND INSTITUTE, 311. FITZHERBERT, NATURA BREVIUM, 85, 86. Y. B. 4 EDW. IV, 15. By *Justicies* a jurisdiction in causes involving 40 shillings or more could be conferred on the county court, but there was not any allegation of *vi et armis* in these writs. *Cf.* also dictum in Wildgoose v. Kellaways, 2 Salk. 636; Walker v. Robinson, 1 Wils. K. B. 93. The plaint used is in GREENWOOD, CURIA COMITATUS REDIVIVA (1657), 154.

It seems obvious that the significance of forms of action in the county court within the limits of its competence could not have been very great. Once the allegation of force and *contra pacem* was absent from the county court trespass, the formal distinction between trespass and case was practically nil. More important from the litigant's point of view was the 40 shilling limitation. In 20 EDW. III (2 R. S. 146) a judgment in the shire court of Chester was reversed where a plaintiff had brought two actions of 39 s. 11 d. each, for a single debt. Although the position of the Chester court was in some respects different from the English county court, Coke regards the opinion as applicable to the latter (SECOND INSTITUTE, 312) and there is Yearbook authority (Y. B. 19 HY. VI, 54) bearing out this view. Nevertheless, this practice of bringing two actions for one debt seems to have continued (SCHECHTER, *op. cit. supra* note 4, at 273). By statute, 11 HY. VII, c. 15, an attempt was made to put an end to the practice, and it was provided *inter alia* that "the party Plaintiff shall have but one Plaint

tinctions between trespass and case were here totally lacking. The substantive characteristics which the form of the writ imparted to the two actions being absent, one naturally wonders whether or not, within the scope of the county courts' jurisdiction, the form of action had any significance. Until more is known of the English county court we shall not have an answer, but the early American records are highly suggestive.

Before we turn to criminal procedure it is necessary that the substantive law be briefly characterized. It mirrors in the first instance the colonists' biblicism, and the enormous concern of the English dissentients with morality. The robber is not mentioned, but the fornicator was left few loopholes.[43] The expression felony

for one Trespass or Contract." In view of the peculiar wording of this statute it is wholly possible that the complaint, for acts where trespass might lie, was thereafter formulated as an action on the case, particularly as the formal distinctions were otherwise absent. On the use of case where the formal objections interpose, Y. B. 19 HY. VI, 5, and see also the Case of the Marshalsea, 10 Coke 68b, 1 Bulstrode, 207, 208, where the trespass jurisdiction of the Court of the Marshalsea was held not to extend to case. Where an action for 40 shillings or more was brought, a *supersedeas* lay, but note that the forms of this writ were limited to actions for chattels or debts. REGISTRUM BREVIUM, 145, 146. Owing to the formal limitations of the *supersedeas* it seems unlikely that it could be resorted to where case was brought. However, it should be noted that prohibition was resorted to if trespass *vi et armis* was alleged, but after St. 11 HY. VII, c. 15, it was used where 40 shillings or more were claimed. In the few cases reported where such prohibitions were granted, there is no statement of the form of action, but the indications are that debt was used. See Anon., 1 Ventris 65; Girling v. Alders, 1 Ventris 23; Catchmade's Case, 6 Mod. 90; FITZHERBERT, NATURA BREVIUM, 46, 239 D.

I am led to the above suggestion in regard to the effect of St. 11 HY. VII, c. 15, on the use of case, by the fact that a century later a similar fate befell the statute 41 ELIZ. c. 6. This act, intended to force petty litigation back to the local courts, provided that in certain personal actions where the debt or damages "to be recovered" was less than 40 shillings, no more costs than damages could be recovered. In 1639 a petition to Parliament discloses that this statute was evaded by attorneys' laying the action in case. (Cal. St. Pap. Dom. 1639-40, cccxlix, no. 35). Consider also here Earl of Shrewsbury's case, 9 Coke 46 a, 51 a; Cooper v. St. John, Style 130. Of course, this later evasion was accomplished in the King's Courts, where the lawyers were presumably more adept than in the country. At the same time it illustrates how case lent itself to the needs of the litigant who wished to get around statutes or outmoded forms. On the prevalence of case in the sixteenth century in at least one borough, see 2 RECORDS OF THE BOROUGH OF LEICESTER, 145.

43. The list of capital crimes in the 1636 code includes treason or rebellion, wilful murder, wilful burning of ships and houses, solemn "compaction or conversing with the devill," rape, adultery, sodomy and buggery (PLYMOUTH LAWS, 43). Only four of these offences were "common law" crimes. The diabolic conversation provision had a forerunner in St. 33 HY. VIII c. 8—a witchcraft act—repealed by St. 1. EDW. VI, c. 12 and St. 1 MARY Sess. 1, c. 1, but revived by St.

used occasionally in the court records does not appear in the statutes, but misdemeanor,[44] at that time not yet established as a word of classification in the common law, is used to describe conduct, the criminal character of which the magistrate was to determine. This was thoroughly Calvinistic and entirely in line with the Puritans' notion of wide judicial discretion in penal matters.[45]

---

5 ELIZ. c. 16 and extended 1 JAC. I. c. 12. Shipburning was not made a felony until St. 22 and 23 CAR. II, c. 11, and then as to acts by mariners and officers of ships. Sodomy on man or beast was made a felony by St. 25 HY. VIII, c. 6, repealed in part by 2 & 3 EDW. VI, c. 29, and *in toto* by 1 MARY Sess. 1, c. 1, revived by 5 ELIZ. c. 17 (*Cf.* COKE, THIRD INSTITUTE 58). The listing of adultery as a civil offense is interesting as representing the consummation of the demands by the radical religious groups. There are some early indictments in England for adultery [Cleveland, *Indictments for Adultery and Incest before 1650* (1913) 29 L. Q. REV. 57], but this was a local phenomenon.

In the boroughs, jurisdiction was exercised on the nuisance theory. *Cf.* 1 LIVERPOOL TOWN BOOKS, 241; FITZHERBERT-CROMPTON, L'OFFICE ET AUCTHORITIE DE JUSTICES DE PEACE (1606) fo. 140; Y. B. 13 HY. VII, 10. See also the Star Chamber case in CROMPTON, STAR CHAMBER CASES (1881 Reprint) 19.

There is no indication whether or not in Plymouth the usual incidents of a conviction of felony attached. In only one case, 3 COURT ORDERS, 73, prior to the arrival of the Royal Commissioners (1664) was benefit of clergy claimed. There was no provision for robbery in the code, but in 1638 four men were indicted for robbery and murder on the highway. 1 COURT ORDERS, 96.

It should further be mentioned that the capital punishment was apparently not carried out against persons convicted of sexual offences. *Cf.* 2 COURT ORDERS, 35 (1642) for a case of sodomy where whipping was inflicted. For cases of adultery not punished by death, 1 *ibid.*, at 12; 2 *ibid.*, at 28; 3 *ibid.*, at 111-112; 4 *ibid.*, at 22. In 1658 the code mitigated the punishment to two whippings and wearing the letters AD.

44. The offences not capital include fornication and unclean carriages, fornication before marriage, and the stealing of ships and things of that nature. Under the rubric uncivil carriages all sort of lewdness was punished. This was due to reasons of doctrine. In 3 CALVIN, COMMENTARIES ON THE FOUR LAST BOOKS OF MOSES, 68, are collected as harmonizing with the seventh commandment all passages in the Pentateuch dealing with sexual offences. *Cf.* THE LARGER CATECHISM OF THE ASSEMBLY OF DIVINES AT WESTMINSTER (2d ed. 1658) 245. The provision regarding stealing seems to have been applied generally to all kinds of theft. Other misdemeanors were later added. In 1636 drunkeness was made a punishable offense (PLYMOUTH LAWS, 47. See also *ibid.*, at 83-84), in 1644 smoking at work (*ibid.*, at 59), and two years later a profanity statute (*ibid.*, at 65). In 1645 the fornication statute was restated (*ibid.*, at 79) and a further attempt to curb the frivolous is apparent by the statute against wearing "visors and strange apparell to lascivious ends" (*ibid.*, at 81).

Certain misdemeanors not relating to morality were named in the code of 1636, such as failure to ring swine, failure to have arms, setting traps near highways, or selling sheep out of the colony.

45. These provisions vesting so large a discretion in the magistrates appear to be of a religious origin. FLAMMER, DROIT PÉNAL DE GENÈVE (1868) 15 states that the idea of giving the magistrate discretion to inflict penalties was introduced by Calvin into the law of Geneva. *Cf.* also Dubois-Melly, *Du Bannisse-*

ment sous le Gouvernement de l'Ancienne Republique de Genève (1889) 29 BULLETIN DE L'INSTITUT NATIONAL GENEVOIS 46; GALLI, DIE LUTHERISCHEN UND CALVINISCHEN KIRCHENSTRAFEN (1879) 162 *et seq.* In his INSTITUTE OF THE CHRISTIAN RELIGION, 1. 4, c. 20, especially §§ 4, 5, 6, 9, Calvin elaborates the passages from Deuteronomy, c. 1, 16, 17 and Chronicles II, c. 19, 6, and launches upon a glorification of the judicial function as speaking in the place of God. There can be no doubt of the intellectual relation of these sections with the provision of the Plymouth Laws that the magistrates shall determine misdemeanors as in "wisdom God shall direct," as the similarity in the conception of the judicial function is too striking; *cf.* also 1 CALVIN, COMMENTARY ON THE FOUR LAST BOOKS OF MOSES, 305 *et seq.;* 3 *ibid.*, at 19, where Calvin points out that by Mosaic precedent judges should be elected (and so they were in Plymouth) and suggests that they be restrained by fixed laws. In matter of fact at Geneva it was not this latter idea which was carried out, but the notion that the judge speaking for God had necessarily great discretion in making his judgments. While this conception of vesting magistrates with a large discretion was undoubtedly a corollary of Calvin's whole theocratic system, in which the functions of civil and ecclesiastical officers were scarcely distinguishable, the notion was not original with him, but was probably derived from the practice of the Roman Catholic Church; *cf.* 2 SÄGMÜLLER, KIRCHENRECHT, 348. The indications are that this conception was derived by the Plymouth settlers as stated in the text from the practice at Geneva, and not from English precedents. The English law did not then vest in the judge particular discretion in relation to penalties or punishments for crimes. The statutes of the period were usually precise in their statements of penalties; *cf.* among others 5 ELIZ. c. 11, c. 14; 31 ELIZ. c. 4; 39 ELIZ. c. 17; but see 43 ELIZ. c. 7, where certain discretion was given judges to determine whether offenders could in fact recompense owners of destroyed corn and trees and if not, to order them whipped; 3 JAC. I, c. 13, 221; 4 JAC. I, c. 5. The theory of the law apparently was that an offense was either a felony or trespass (misdemeanor) and in either case the penalty was fixed. The fact that the form of judgment, in the event of conviction, was prescribed, is additional evidence of this point of view; *cf.* COKE, THIRD INSTITUTE, 210. The judgment was fixed and could not be altered. *Ibid.* Obviously such happenings as the imposition of whipping in place of the capital penalty for adultery as took place in Plymouth was not possible under the theory of the English courts, except through the device of benefit of clergy. The contrast between the Calvinistic theory of the judicial function and its exercise in Plymouth, particularly in criminal cases, and the wholly objective procedure of the King's Courts in England is most striking. The ossification of the judicial function in England is well illustrated by the persistence of the benefit of clergy as a mitigation of the severity of penalties (a practice not adopted generally in Plymouth), and even here the procedure was stereotype. The English practice is well summed up in the two maxims given by Coke, *loc. cit., "judicandum est legibus non exemplis,"* and "execution must be according the judgment." The form of the latter being fixed by law, there was not much play for discretion. *Cf.* 2 POLLOCK AND MAITLAND, HISTORY OF ENGLISH LAW, 461, 671. Compare the following words from the speech of Popham (Pop. 43): "The law therefore being taken from so good a ground, and working such notable and honourable effects, who can justly say otherwise, but that the profession of such a law is an honourable profession? Are not the Judges of the law professors of the law? See then what God himself in His Word hath said of Judges in Psal. 82. Speaking of judgment and justices He saith thus; I have said ye are gods, and can there be any higher name than this in heaven or earth? And

Genevese rather than English, the Plymouth criminal law indeed was, but nonetheless it was enforced by very English machinery—a strange hybrid compounded of leet and quarter session practice. Jury trial in all criminal causes was provided,[46] but this was not significant, since the magistrate was given virtually an ordinance power in respect to specifying misdemeanors.[47] The indi-

why are they so learned? But for that, they in their offices do resemble that which is the office of God, as to discern so far forth as man's capacity can reach unto between right and wrong, truth and falsehood, the just and the unjust, which is a most high, weighty and honourable charge, and therefore, 2 Chron. 19, 6 cha. Jehosophat said to the Judges, Take heed what ye do, for you do not execute the judgments of men, but of the Lord, and He will be with you in judgment. By which it is evident, that they are either grosly ignorant, or otherwise very malignant and contemptuous persons that may not be induced to be reformed, that do in any wise hold the profession to be either base or contemptible."

While in England the judicial discretion in respect of punishments for crimes was definitely restricted, it should be noted that the courts did have discretion in respect to contempts, and this power extended even to the courts leet, Y. B. 10 HY. VI, 7.

It should be noted that the discretionary power of the magistrates was reiterated in a statute of 1662, PLYMOUTH LAWS, 139. Examples of the exercise of this power are in 1 COURT ORDERS, 132, lying; vagrancy and purloining (163); harboring foreigners (106); working on Sunday (86, 87); breaking and entering (85); embezzlement (91). As to so-called extortion, *cf. ibid.*, at 61, 87, 97, 118, 128, 137. It should be noted that in the last instance the offences grouped under extortion were largely what in England was known as forestalling, ingrossing, and regrating; *cf.* COKE, THIRD INSTITUTE, 195. A statute governing the buying and regrating of goods was passed in 1638, PLYMOUTH LAWS, 60; but the power exercised by the court to punish persons who sold short measure was probably under the 1636 statute putting in effect the Winchester measure, *ibid.*, at 43. The punishment of the miller for his extortion was exercised in England by the leets and was treated as a technical extortion; Rex v. Burdett, Lord Raymond 149.

46. In 1636 the grand jury was provided for by the code, and trials by jury were to extend to all cases "as nearly as possible to English precidents" (PLYMOUTH LAWS, 41). The grand jury was to present to the court persons they found guilty or probably suspect. After 1640 presentments had to be on oath.

47. The grand jury seems to have shared to some extent the power of the magistrate in determining what constituted an offense. In the case of the latter the statute directed that in "small offences" the magistrate shall "determine doe and execute as in wisdom God shall direct them." The power of the grand jury to determine misdemeanors was broadly laid down as misdemeanors tending to the hurt and detriment of "Society Civility peace and neighborhood" (PLYMOUTH LAWS, 42, 48). There is an English analogue in the power of the leet to present public nuisances, but this was rather the determination of whether certain facts constituted an offence over which its jurisdiction was recognized, rather than a specification of new offences, particularly as the limits of the nuisance concept were well understood. *Cf.* HEARNSHAW, *op. cit. supra* note 34, at 96, 109; KITCHIN, *op. cit. supra* note 36, at 15; SHEPPARD, COURT KEEPERS GUIDE (1662) 29.

cations in the records are that a petty jury was drawn as of course only in case of a major crime. Where an offender was presented, the court proceeded apparently to sentence without further trial, the findings of the grand jury being deemed sufficient inquest.[48] In the English leets unanimous presentment except in cases where the freehold was involved operated as a conviction, and this may have been the source of Plymouth practice.[49] Occasionally the accused as well as witnesses were examined in open court, but apparently a jury was impanelled for small offences only if the presentment was formally traversed. Since the bulk of offences, drunkenness and sexual transgressions and uncivil carriage, far outnumbered more serious infractions of public order, this quasi-summary method of procedure was workable, and having pre-

48. This conclusion is reached on the basis of rather unsatisfactory evidence. The records usually indicate the fact of presentment with a marginal notation of the fine, punishment, or discharge of the accused. Since no further notation of trial is made, this circumstance taken in connection with the fact that where a jury was actually impanelled a record is made, seems to indicate that presentment was tantamount to conviction.

49. The rule in the leets was that a presentment found by twelve could not be traversed by the defendant; *contra,* if found by less than twelve or if it concerned the freehold. Y. B. 41 EDW. III, 26; 45 EDW. III, 26; Keilwey 66, 141. *Cf.* HALE, PLEAS OF THE CROWN, 153, 155; RITSON, *op. cit. supra* note 34, at 80; KITCHIN, *op. cit. supra* note 36, at 84; HAWKINS, PLEAS OF THE CROWN (1824 ed.) Bk. 2, c. 10, § 74. In England the rule was that where a presentment was traversed in a leet, a *certiorari* from Kings Bench lay. There seems, however, some doubt as to whether or not if an indictment in sessions was traversed, there could not be a trial in the sessions. LAMBARD, EIRENARCHA (1614) 542, says: "For although it be holden (2 R. 3, 11, 19, H. 8, 11 & Fitz. tit. Ass. 442 and in other books) that a man shall not be received to traverse a presentment unless it doe charge him in his freehold: yet Hussey and Fairfax said (5 H. 7, 4) that a presentment (not concerning freehold) which is found before Justices of the Peace, may be traversed: and whether they meant it of a Traverse in the Kings Bench, as before Justices of the Peace, it maketh no difference, because the reason is all one, that is, If Processe be awarded, the party may come in, and offer his Traverse, & otherwise the Processe should be in vaine.

"Hereunto agreeth Moubray (41 E. 3, 26) saying further, that in a Leet such a Presentment is not Traversable, because out of a Leete no Processe can bee awarded upon it. And this peradventure is the reason of the (booke 8 E. 4, 5 and of M. Marr.) where they say, that a presentment of bloodshed found in the Sherifes Turne, and sent as it ought to be to the Justices of the peace, cannot be traversed before them: as whereupon they can neither make Processe, nor discharge the partie by way of Plea.

"So that this seemeth a generall learning, that wheresoever any Processe *ad respondendum,* goeth out before such an Endictment as is traversable, there also the partie may offer, and ought to have his Traverse against it." If this were so, there was a good precedent for the action at Plymouth.

cedent religious and customary behind it, was not regarded as subversive of individual rights.[50]

It is not alone in the field of law administration that the experience of the planters at home is perceptible, but in the problem most vital to their existence—the land. Here the custom of England held only bitter memories, and here we shall find attempts to right those things for which at home there had been no remedies.

The Pilgrims generally came from those regions of England where the effects of the agrarian revolution of the sixteenth century had been most profoundly experienced. The bulk of the tenancies in Northern and Eastern England were copyholds,[51] and upon these had descended the full brunt of the movement for enclosure. The copyholders, as tenants at will by copy of court roll according to the custom of the manor, were roughly divisible into two groups, those who held copies of the roll establishing their tenancy, and those who relied upon oral proof of the custom.[52] Their remedy against landlord encroachment lay in the first instance in the manor court,[53] but as enclosure was usually begun by the lord, this was an illusory protection. Chancery had first taken the copyholder under its wing. Late in Edward IV's reign King's Bench had intimated he would have an action on the case against the evicting landlord,[54] and finally, upon the accession of the Tudors, the Court of Requests became his protector.[55] These courts, however, were at best available to the richer copyholder or to a group financing an action. In actual fact the copyholder was usually at the mercy of his lord.[56]

50. To anyone under illusions regarding the morality of the Pilgrim fathers, a perusal of the criminal records contained in the Court Orders will offer something of a shock. Between the years 1633-1641 offences against morals (including sabbath breach, drunkenness, lewdness, fornication) outnumbered by three to one crimes having an element of breach of the peace, and were double the number of offences against the economic order (extortion, millers' frauds, vagrancy). In the period 1641-1651 crimes involving a breach of the peace increase, the ratio as to offences against morality being one to two, the infractions of economic regulations decrease, the ratio being one to three.

51. TAWNEY, THE AGRARIAN PROBLEM IN THE SIXTEENTH CENTURY (1912) 24.

52. CO. LIT. 57 b. NORDEN, THE SURVEIORS DIALOGUE (1618) bk. 2, at 47. 2 HOLDSWORTH, *op. cit.*, at 379 *et seq.*

53. CO. LIT. 60 a.

54. Y. B. 21 EDW. IV 80 (1481). *Cf.* 3 HOLDSWORTH, HIST. ENG. LAW 208-209.

55. LEADAM, SELECT CASES IN THE COURT OF REQUEST (12 Selden Soc. Pub.) Introduction.

56. Generally on the copyholder's legal situation, COKE, THE COMPLETE COPYHOLDER (1668 ed.) esp. §§ 14-17; Savine, *Copyhold Cases in Early Chancery*

We cannot enter here into the details of the agrarian problem; it has been ably investigated by Gay, Leadam, and Tawney. I can emphasize only the wholesale character of the process of enclosure, the widespread misery which induced a succession of revolts as late as 1607,[57] and the crowding of the town by hordes of wretched beings without funds or means of livelihood.[58] Fumbling efforts by the crown to investigate and to control matters by statute were unavailing.

To the English peasant the effect of all this was to create a deep and abiding distrust of the ancient tenure; a noticeable distaste for the new economic as against the old customary rents; a suspicion of leases by which the new system of rents were put into effect; a great solicitude for the recorded title or written evidence of right in the land; and finally a nostalgia for the one type of landholding, the freehold, where the risks of tenure were slight. What transpired in Plymouth was a reflection of peasant psychosis after decades of unrest.[59]

Proceedings, 17 ENG. HIST. REV. 296; Leadam, *The Inquisition of 1517*, 6 TRANS. ROYAL HIST. SOC. (N.S.) 226. Leadam thinks the existence of a remedy implies its employment. This is traversed by TAWNEY, *op. cit.*, at 289. See also 2 ASHLEY, ECONOMIC HISTORY OF ENGLAND pt. 1, 274-282; Leadam, *Security of the Copyholder in the Fifteenth and Sixteenth century,* 8 ENG. HIST. REV. 684; the discussion of Gay and Leadam in 14 TRANS. ROYAL HIST. SOC. (N.S.) 231, 267; LEADAM, THE DOMESDAY OF ENCLOSURE. ROYAL HIST. SOC. PUB. (2VS. 1897).

57. The most serious of these was the first in 1536. DODDS, THE PILGRIMAGE OF GRACE (1915). In 1549, 1552, 1554, and 1569 there were further uprisings: RUSSELL, KETT'S REBELLION IN NORFOLK (1859); SHARPE, MEMORIALS OF THE REBELLION OF 1659 (1840). On the 1607 revolt, Gay, *The Midland Revolt and the Inquisition of 1607,* 18 TRANS. ROYAL HIST. SOC. 195. See also Gay, *Inclosures in England in the 16th Century,* in 17 QUARTERLY JOURNAL OF ECONOMICS, 576.

58. TAWNEY, AGRARIAN PROBLEM, 75; LEONARD, EARLY HISTORY OF ENGLISH POOR RELIEF, 73, 107, 125. Compare the statement of Robert Cushman, agent of the Pilgrims in England, "there is such a pressing and oppressing in town and country about farms, trades and traffic so as a man can hardly set up a trade but he shall pull down two of his neighbors. . . The country is replenished with new farms but the almshouses are filled with old laborers, . . . the rent taker lives on sweet morsels, but the rent payer eats a dry crust often with watery eyes." Full text in ARBER, STORY OF THE PILGRIM FATHERS 495.

59. One of the great difficulties which the surveyors had was to obtain views of tenants' copies. Apparently the tenants feared theft. *Cf.* TAWNEY, AGRARIAN PROBLEM, 123, and App. I, no. 4; NORDEN, *op. cit. supra* note 52, illustrates the bitterness of the tenants' feelings. The copy was not much help unless the antiquity of the custom could be proved.

It should be noted that although in 1589 Kings Bench permitted the tenant's lessee to maintain ejectment (Melwich v. Luter, 4 Coke 26 a), it was not until later that the tenant himself was given this remedy. Actually money damages

Even before removal to America the Pilgrims were involved in acrid discussion with the adventurers, who financed them, over the problem of landholding. The latter demanded that all lands be held in common, to be divided at the end of seven years.[60] They wanted security. The planters wanted homes of their own that could not be taken away at the end of a term. Since no agreement was reached before departure, the first division of land was made without reference to the adventurers' demands. Corn growing was undertaken in common on the open field cultivation system, but this was not successful.[61] In 1623 the Governor assigned to each family land in proportion to its members, from 1 to 10 acres, for purposes of tillage, a portion of the produce to be deposited in the common stock.[62]

If we attempt to describe this tenure in current legal terminology we shall have difficulty. The agreement with the adventurers had been finally executed. In 1621, Pierce, an adventurer, secured from the New England Council a grant to the lands. Title was vested in him and his associates; but the Plymouth allotees were not tenants at will, as they had a joint claim arising out of their contact, not to specific lands but to an assignment of undetermined lands to be made at the end of a term. Five years later the adventurers sold out and the debt was assumed by a few leading colonists.[63] To liquidate the debt, all heads of families and young men were made into a company, and a share allotted to each, and for each member of the family. The land assignments of 1623 were confirmed. The remaining land was then divided by lot and each share received 20 acres, besides the acre already held. This

was not what the tenant wanted, but specific relief. The helplessness of these people is indicated by the manner in which the towns were filled with destitute peasants. TAWNEY, AGARIAN PROBLEM, 275; LEONARD, *op. cit. supra* note 58, at 73 *et seq.*, 107 *et seq.*

60. BRADFORD, *op. cit. supra* note 7, at 56-8, for the terms.

61. RECORDS OF THE COLONY OF NEW PLYMOUTH, *Deeds* (hereafter cited DEEDS) 3; *Mourt's Relation*, in ARBER, *op. cit. supra* note 8, at 440-441.

62. BRADFORD, *op. cit. supra* note 7, at 162; WINSLOW, GOOD NEWS FROM NEW ENGLAND, in ARBER, *op. cit. supra* note 8, at 575-576.

63. For an account of the negotiations, *cf.* BRADFORD, *op. cit. supra* note 7, at 252 *et seq.* For the details of the scheme, *ibid.*, at 258. PLYMOUTH LAWS, 29; DEEDS, 9. It was also provided that persons who drew land nearest the town had to take a neighbor for four years, and thereafter could use the neighbor's outlying land for planting an equal length of time. Wood could only be cut with the owner's license, but hunting and fowling were free, and all men were given an easement to the water. Cattle were divided, a cow and two goats to each six shares.

was tillable land abutting the bay. The rest was designated waste and common land. The meadows were not laid out, but each year a share was allotted for mowing, based on the number of cattle each man owned.[64]

The meagre record of this transaction does not tell much. The Pierce grant had not been assigned and a direct grant was not gotten until 1629. Since the adventurers had sold out all interest and claims including lands, this purchase seems to have been regarded as having conferred title to the soil.[65] The right acquired by each shareholder was equivalent to a fee interest, although allotment was conditional upon possession of a share, which required payment in kind toward debt liquidation.

The earliest deeds, crude in form, indicate that landholding was conceived in the image of the English freehold.[66] There is evidence, moreover, that a form of Yorkshire freehold, the so-called meerstead freehold,[67] was known to the settlers. This type of land tenure obtained at Royston,[68] near the home of Bradford, and was one in which the seignorial element was almost indiscernable. Certainly it is a striking coincidence that meerstead is used for messuage in Plymouth, and that the term so far as I can ascertain was not used elsewhere in England.

64. The apparent contradiction between the confirmation of lands of the first division (1623) "to the possessors thereof and their heirs forever," and the lack of any indication how the lands of the second division were to be held, seems without importance, as subsequent deeds indicate that the holders dealt with them as freeholders of which they had the fee.

65. The text of the agreement is in BRADFORD, *op. cit. supra* note 7, at 254-256. The Pierce grant was not assigned.

66. In the Bradford grant of 1629 the land was granted as of the manor of East Greenwich, in free and common socage. *Cf.* Cheney, *Manor of East Greenwich* (1905) 11 AMERICAN HISTORICAL REVIEW 29. *Cf.* also Eggleston, *The Land System of the New England Colonies* (1886) 4 JOHNS HOPKINS UNIVERSITY STUDIES, 448. Carr, *Our Manor of East Greenwich* (1913) 29 LAW QUARTERLY REVIEW, 349. The practice of conveying lands to be held in this particular tenure appears to have dated back to the small grants made by the crown out of the monastic lands confiscated in Henry VIII's reign. One may well doubt whether any special intent lurked behind the use of this particular form. The Code of 1636 provided that future grants and conveyances be held as stated in the Plymouth grant of 1629. PLYMOUTH LAWS, 43, 49-54.

67. Of the use of the word meerstead or misted, *cf.* DEEDS, 3, and compare 1 COURT ORDERS, 16, 18, 24, 45, 57, 145.

68. Addy, *A Village Community in Yorkshire,* 10 NOTES AND QUERIES, Sec. 8, 349 *et seq.*, 470 *et seq.* The first entries in DEEDS are in Bradford's hand. In the connection note also the use of the word *falls.* This is a north country word meaning a division of arable fields attached to a village. *Cf.* BROCKETT, GLOSSARY OF NORTH COUNTRY WORDS (1846) *sub nom.*

An essential aspect of the land problem in Plymouth was the provision in the Code of 1636 requiring the recordation of all sales, gifts, mortgages, and other conveyances of houses and lands.[69] It went far beyond the limited scope of the Statute of Enrollments, with the terms of which the settlers were probably unacquainted.[70] It was motivated in part by certain borough customs and in part by the colonists' recollections of the importance of the written word as proof of the copyholder's custom, and the desire to have a means of remembrancing which would forestall the mean and petty tricks by which unscrupulous landlords had in England cheated the tenant of his property. It is to this feeling, of which great evidence abounds in contemporary English writing on enclosure, that we may attribute the early and widespread enactment of registration statutes in colonial America, for property rights had not become so involved as to make recording an economic necessity.

I desire to point out but one further aspect of the Plymouth land system that deserves attention. This was the notion of economic use expressed in laws which required the occupation of land or the consequent devolution to the government.[71] This rule had

69. PLYMOUTH LAWS, 43. The practice prevailed in some English boroughs of making entry of deeds either in a book or in court. Thus 2 RECORDS OF THE BOROUGH OF LEICESTER, 381; RECORDS OF MARSTON (1926) 82; SELECTIONS FROM THE RECORDS OF THE CITY OF OXFORD, xxxix, for a list of enrollments in the *Liber Albus.* Mention should be made here of the fact that while in Leyden some of the Pilgrims bought houses and must thereby have learned of the Dutch system of recording. *Cf.* DEXTER, ENGLAND AND HOLLAND OF THE PILGRIMS. On the Pilgrims' tenderness for records *cf.* the statute of 1645 regarding corrupting officers to deface records, see PLYMOUTH LAWS, 82.

70. Note should be made of the fact that in Yorkshire there was a practice of enrolling indentures at sessions. *Cf.* 4 THE NORTH RIDING RECORD SOCIETY, QUARTER SESSIONS RECORDS, 126 *et seq.* St. 27 HY. VIII, c. 16 provided that enrollment was to be made in the King's Courts or in the county before the *Custos Rotulorum,* two Justices of the Peace, and the Clerk of the Peace, or two of them of which the latter was to be one.

71. PLYMOUTH LAWS, 32 (1633); restated in the code, *ibid.,* at 74. Compare this with the depopulation statutes which attempted to fix not the occupation, but the sort of use to which land might be put, as the older manor custumals had fixed the proportions or arable and pasture. The statutes 4 HY. VII, c. 19; 6 HY. VIII, c. 5; 7 HY. VIII, c. 1, were the earliest of a long series. It should be noted that in practice a further mode of control was employed in the requirement inserted in original grants that where persons built houses, the lands belonged to the dwelling and were not to be sold from the houses as long as the latter were used as dwellings. 1 COURT ORDERS, 46, 49, 50, 65, 82. It is possible that this provision was suggested by the statute 31 ELIZ. c. 7, which required that all cottages erected after 1589 should have at least four acres of ground about it "to be continually occupied and manured" as long as the

its origin in the fact that a share of produce had for a period of years to be paid to the company which had assumed the debt from the adventurers.[72] The same object could have been attained by leasing, but I have mentioned that the lease was an abhorred incident of English enclosure and furthermore, where civil status depended upon freeholding, leaseholds would have threatened the stability and growth of the colony.

The picture just outlined of the law's growth in Plymouth over the early decades of the colony's existence has many flaws. It is difficult to get into proper perspective things the outlines of which have been dimmed by the preconceptions of writers and by the erasures of time. But as I have said before, if we remember that these men were English commoners and religious zealots, the records of civilization in their motherland will enable us to effect that meticulous and microscopic reconstruction essential to the true depiction of transplantation of any culture. Local custom, substantive as the Winchester measure, pretentious as the notion of the code, ineradicable as the methods of law administration, fortuitous as a form of tenure; bitter experience at the hands of a zealous bishop and his pursuivants, or a stony-hearted evicting landlord; hope and salvation in the Word of God preached by word or pamphlet, these things are the materials that went with settlers to Plymouth and out of which their law was fashioned.

The curious *mélange* of religious ideas and remnants of English local customs and practices which pervaded the Plymouth legal institutions is not without parallel, for her neighbors in Massachusetts, Connecticut, and Long Island exhibited similar proclivities. Each colony had, of course, its peculiar characteristics, but in the seventeenth century before the Leviathan common law had

---

cottage was occupied. *Cf.* COKE, SECOND INSTITUTE, 736; LEONARD, EARLY HISTORY OF ENGLISH POOR RELIEF, 73. The statute was designed to limit the number of poor settling in the country. There is no indication as to how the Plymouth restrictions were carried out.

On the Roman conception of economic use, GLÜCK-CZYLHARZ, AUSFÜHRLICHE ERLÄUTERUNG DER PANDEKTEN (Ser. Bk. 41-42) 95. See also 2 CHALMERS, OPINIONS OF EMINENT LAWYERS (1814) 44 for a similar idea in another colony.

72. The agreement between the colonists and the underwriters (BRADFORD, *op. cit. supra* note 7, at 272-3) conveyed to the latter full trading privileges for a period of six years. The colonists agreed to pay each year three bushels of corn or six pounds of tobacco. The underwriters were to purchase shoes and hose to the amount of £50, to be sold to the colonists for corn at 6s. per bushel. *Cf.* also DEEDS, 13, for other evidence of control. The eventual liquidation of the debt ended any claims arising out of this contract.

been set in motion, the basic factor was the transplantation of local institutions and customary law. Regarded from this standpoint the first century of American law no longer seems chaotic and absurd; on the contrary, the frontier theory, as I have intimated, becomes an artificial and labored explanation. We cannot brush this century aside as meaningless; neither should we invest it with greater importance for the future than it actually possesses. Yet the fact that it gave us legal institutions which the common law never succeeded in smothering is sufficient reason for devoting to it some scientific attention.

V

*The Legal Heritage of Plymouth Colony**

GEORGE L. HASKINS

More than one legal historian has more than once drawn attention to the contributions that Plymouth Colony made to American law in the seventeenth century.[1] Yet recent general studies continue to insist that Plymouth made few permanent contributions of any kind to the American heritage. Thus, Samuel Eliot Morison, dean of American colonial historians, writes that nearly all American historians are now agreed upon "the insignificance of the Plymouth Colony in the colonial era."[2] "By any quantitative standard," he says, "it was one of the smallest, weakest, and least important of the English colonies."[3] "Massachusetts Bay, rather than Plymouth Colony, was the seed bed of New England. There and in Connecticut and New Haven the distinctive New England institutions of church and state, culture and commerce were developed."[4]

* "The Legal Heritage of Plymouth Colony," by George L. Haskins, is reprinted with permission from the *University of Pennsylvania Law Review*, CX (1962), 847-859.

[This essay was] revised and developed from an address delivered on Massachusetts Heritage Day at Plimoth Plantation, Plymouth, Massachusetts, October 21, 1961, and reproduced with permission of the sponsors. The address, as originally presented, appeared in 26 SOCIAL EDUCATION 7 (1962).

1. *E.g.*, Goebel, *King's Law and Local Custom in Seventeenth Century New England*, 31 COLUM. L. REV. 416, 448 (1931); Haskins, *The Beginnings of the Recording System in Massachusetts*, 21 B.U.L. REV. 281, 302 (1941).

2. MORISON, BY LAND AND BY SEA 234 (1953).

3. *Id.* at 235.

4. *Id.* at 234. Although he concedes that Plymouth instituted civil marriage, a registry of deeds, and the first Congregational Church, Morison goes on to say that even the Pilgrim church at Plymouth was soon overshadowed by the Congregational churches that sprang up elsewhere in New England and by such learned clergymen as Hooker, Cotton, and Shepard, whose counterparts could not be found at Plymouth. *Id.* at 235. Since the publication of Professor Morison's essay on Plymouth, *op. cit. supra* note 2, he has explicitly given the colony

To this majority opinion of the court of history these pages are filed as a partial dissent. In the light of the known evidence, it is impossible to disagree with much that Professor Morison has concluded with respect to Plymouth. The Pilgrims who founded the colony were simple folk, drawn principally from a class that, in Governor Bradford's words, "followed the inocente trade of husbandrey."[5] They had little familiarity with any intellectual currents of the day except those pertaining to religion. They were not and did not become great shipbuilders, successful fishermen, or traders. They did not establish or live under democracy in any modern sense. Indeed, much that they accomplished was done after annexation to Massachusetts in 1691. In large measure, their importance lies in the example they continue to afford of courage in the face of danger, resourcefulness in the face of difficulty, and fortitude in the face of adversity.[6] In spiritual quality, the Pilgrim leaders were second to none in the New World, and in many respects, as Henry Adams said of the great Virginians at the close of the 18th century, they were "equal to any standard of excellence known to history. Their range was narrow, but within it they were supreme."[7]

At the same time, it must be recognized that Plymouth Colony made several important contributions to American legal institutions, not the least of which was an early articulation of the ideal that finds expression in the famous language of the Constitution of Massachusetts—"a government of laws and not of men."[8] At the outset, the colonists succeeded in establishing a self-governing community without benefit of a royal charter, royal proprietor, or corporate overlord, and in this respect they evinced an early political maturity which was not matched in any other American colony. They also succeeded in establishing a system of law suited to the situation and conditions in which they found themselves and to the religious purposes for which the colony had been established.

The Code of 1636

In assessing Plymouth's contribution to the American legal heri-

credit for instituting the first bill of rights. Morison, The Story of the "Old Colony" of New Plymouth 152-53 (1957).

5. 1 Bradford, History of Plymouth Plantation 28 (1912).

6. *Cf.* Morison, *op. cit. supra* note 2, at 235.

7. 1 Adams, History of the United States of America 133 (1889).

8. Mass. Const. art. 30.

tage, it should first be pointed out that to that colony belongs the credit of having established what may fairly be described as the first American constitution. At a meeting of the General Court in October 1636, the laws of the colony were read, and some "were found worthy the reforming—others the rejecting and others fitt to be instituted and made."[9] In consequence, a committee was appointed to "sertefie and prepare such as should be thought most convenient, that if approved they may be put in force at the next general court."[10] The work was accomplished within a few weeks, and the laws were drawn up in the form of a code dated November 15, 1636.[11]

Two things are remarkable about this code, which turned out to be something more than a mere compilation and revision of existing laws. In the first place, the code sets forth the general scheme or frame of government of the colony: the source of legislative power, the duties and authority of the several officers of the colony, qualifications for the franchise, provision for the holding of courts, and the source of authority to declare war. Second, it contains a rudimentary bill of rights, certainly the first in America, antedating by five years that adopted by Massachusetts Bay in the Body of Liberties of 1641.[12] These two features alone justify the statement that the 1636 code established a constitution of the type that was to become familiar in America after the Revolution. Nothing that was attempted earlier in Virginia was of the same scope; there the so-called constitution was chiefly composed of orders and instructions directed at, but not established by, the colonists, and certainly it included nothing that might be termed a general bill of rights.[13]

Significance of the 1636 Code

The 1636 code, with its revision of the colony's laws and enactment of constitutional provisions, is significant from four standpoints: first, because this codification—quite apart from its constitutional significance—was the first code of laws in any modern sense

9. The Compact With the Charter and Laws of the Colony of New Plymouth 35 (Brigham ed. 1836) [hereinafter cited as Plymouth Laws].

10. *Ibid.*

11. *Id.* at 36.

12. The Colonial Laws of Massachusetts 29-64 (Whitmore ed. 1889).

13. 3 The Records of the Virginia Company of London 12-29 (Kingsbury ed. 1933).

in North America; second, because it reveals much of the social organization of the colony; third, because it preserved and gave vitality to English legal institutions which otherwise might not have survived; fourth, because it contains laws, first introduced at Plymouth, that made lasting contributions to the present-day law of Massachusetts and, ultimately, to the modern law of the United States.

THE FIRST MODERN CODE IN AMERICA

In the history of world jurisprudence, codification of law may be said to have taken two forms, roughly described by the terms "ancient" and "modern." Of the former type are the *Code of Hammurabi*, the *Twelve Tables* at Rome, and the primitive Anglo-Saxon compilations which antedate the Norman Conquest. Of the latter or "modern" type, the *Code Napoléon* is among the most famous. The distinction between these two types of codes is essentially that the ancient code sought to reduce traditional law to writing, often as a defense against autocratic rulers, whereas "modern" codes have had as their object—beyond the necessary compilation—the revision of existing law in the light of accepted ideals for the purpose of elaborating the law and providing fresh starting points for legal development.[14] Judged by this test, and particularly in the light of its bill of rights, the first Plymouth code is modern—not so modern as the more mature and developed code adopted by the Bay Colony in 1648,[15] but a first step in that direction and certainly antecedent to it. The earlier collection of Virginia laws, enacted in 1619, cannot properly be termed a code, for it manifests no effort in the direction of either revision or completeness.[16] In any event, the later Plymouth revisions, embodied in compilations of 1658, 1671, and 1684,[17] fully justify characterization as a developed and detailed modern code. All these codes, along with that of Massachusetts Bay, provided examples that were

14. See generally Haskins, *Codification of the Law in Colonial Massachusetts: A Study in Comparative Law*, 30 IND. L.J. 1, 2-3 (1954).

15. THE LAWS AND LIBERTIES OF MASSACHUSETTS (Farrand ed. 1929). Further study of the 1636 Plymouth code has led me to revise an earlier opinion, expressed in Haskins, *supra* note 14, at 5, that because the traditional element in the code is strong it is difficult to classify the code as "modern."

16. 3 THE RECORDS OF THE VIRGINIA COMPANY OF LONDON 164-68, 170-74 (Kingsbury ed. 1933).

17. PLYMOUTH LAWS 105-21, 239-301.

looked to and borrowed from by other colonies in establishing their legal systems, including notable Connecticut and, later, New York under the Duke of York's laws.[18]

A SOCIOLOGICAL DOCUMENT

Although much neglected as source material,[19] the Plymouth laws constitute a valuable group of contemporary documents for the understanding of Plymouth's history, and they shed important and broadly diffused light upon social, economic, and institutional developments; for, whether one looks to the 17th or to the 20th century, law in its broad sense is much more than a complex of rules for settling disputes between litigants in court. Law is a command of the state, but it is also a social product and an agency of social control, a regime for prescribing countless aspects of the relations of men in organized society and for adjusting their desires and claims with respect to each other and to things. Although particular legal rules may be the outcome of legislation, executive order, or judicial decision, by and large those rules reflect contemporary pressures caused by the needs and interests of the community or of groups within the community. At the same time, legal rules reflect ethical elements—the sense of justice and injustice and the ideals of the society within which they operate. Hence, in its operation, law is both an anchor to tradition and a vehicle for change—a pressure upon social organization and a device for accommodating new and emerging forces.[20]

Viewed in this perspective, the legal records of Plymouth, as of any society, merit study as a reflection of social organization and social purpose. They aid in the identification of the groups—formal and informal—that make up the anatomy of social organization and in the delineation of the functions of those groups. They help us to assess, for example, the situation of debtors and creditors, the importance of the family unit, the extent to which environment affects the group and the individuals within the group. They shed light on the sentiments and understandings that make for

18. Haskins & Ewing, *The Spread of Massachusetts Law in the Seventeenth Century*, 106 U. PA. L. REV. 413 (1958).

19. Although only a few copies of the collections of laws printed in 1671 and 1685 survive, these and earlier laws were published twice in the last century, in PLYMOUTH LAWS and in 11 RECORDS OF THE COLONY OF NEW PLYMOUTH IN NEW ENGLAND (Pulsifer ed. 1861), and are generally available in large libraries.

20. See Haskins, *Law and Colonial Society*, 9 AM. Q. 354, 357-58 (1957).

stability or the lack of it. Hence, whether one looks to rules which prescribe that swine shall be ringed[21] or to those which prescribe the economic use of land,[22] the law is revealed as a highly specialized form of social control, regulating competing interests between individuals and groups in organized society.

The enacted laws also shed light on the problem of cultural transplantation to the extent that they were imitative or adoptive of those portions of the English legal system with which the colonists were familiar. At the same time, their conscious rejection of other portions of that system reflects, for example, their dissatisfaction with the English land law and with English criminal law and procedure and their urgent wish to effect reforms in those areas. Reliance upon and literal use of Biblical texts in framing provisions relating to crime provides, in another area, evidence not only of tradition and design, but of the continuing importance of the religious ideals which had inspired the founding of the colony.

The earliest Plymouth laws reflect concern about basic problems common to all communities: landholding, the inheritance of property, marriage, crime, court proceedings, and the like. As time went on and the colony grew, the laws reflected not only the maturing social organization, but local problems and conditions, such as those involved in legislation about bridges and ferries, highways, fairs, weights and measures, price and wage control, licensing of innkeepers, the quality of exports, and provision for the poor.

One of the most striking features of several provisions is the typically Puritan concern about the regulation of personal conduct and behavior. In the course of the 17th century, Plymouth enacted numerous laws punishing and providing specified fines for drinking, gaming, idleness, lying, swearing, and the like. They were not general prohibitions, but for the most part detailed provisions describing the offense. The tests of drunkenness, for example, are set forth with a degree of specificity which would astound many a modern police court.[23]

The significance of such provisions lies not only in their exemplification of Puritan ideas about right living but in what they re-

21. PLYMOUTH LAWS 45, 58.

22. *Id.* at 47 (land to be forfeited when not occupied by grantee).

23. "And by drunkennesse is understood a person that either lisp or faulters in his speech by reason of over much drink, or that staggers in his going or that vomitts by reason of excessive drinking, or cannot follow his calling." *Id.* at 84.

veal about the Pilgrims' views of law. To them law was conceived of in large measure as a restraint on individual action in the interest of the whole group. At Plymouth, as in the Bay Colony, the individual was essentially a member of the community, so that there was no aspect of his life, not even his private conduct, which was free of the control of the law insofar as the law was designed to further effective organization and good order in the community. To us today, such intrusions upon privacy may appear as unwarranted invasions of personal liberty, but to the Puritans such regulation seemed both proper and necessary.[24]

Lest it be thought, however, that the legal system of Plymouth was entirely an indigenous product of local conditions and of Puritan religious beliefs, it should be emphasized that the colonists drew extensively on their English legal inheritance and even on their Dutch experience.[25] There are several references to the common law of England, by which to a substantial degree they felt bound. But there are other provisions that reflect local English customs of the districts from which they had come. The terms and the forms which appear in the records are in great part the forms and procedures of manor and borough courts rather than those of the king's courts that developed the common law.[26] That this should be so is not surprising, for in the 17th century the legal center of gravity for the average Englishman was the local court of the neighborhood—the borough court, the court leet, and the county court.[27] There he would turn to collect a debt, replevy a cow, or abate a nuisance, and it is a matter of no small interest that the early Plymouth court records bear a striking resemblance to those of the English manorial courts of this period.[28] Moreover, the code of 1636 is reminiscent of many 15th and 16th century English borough customals, which probably furnish the models on which the colonists consciously framed this and later compilations. In them, for example, are the same recitals of authority, the specifications of power, the election of officers, the oaths to be taken, that are found in the English customals.[29]

24. See HASKINS, LAW AND AUTHORITY IN EARLY MASSACHUSETTS 78-80 (1960).

25. See Haskins, *supra* note 1, at 289-91, where the land registration system in force in Holland during the period of the Pilgrims' sojourn at Leyden is discussed.

26. Goebel, *supra* note 1, at 435-38.

27. *Id.* at 420.

28. *Id.* at 435.

29. *Id.* at 433-34.

PRESERVATION OF ENGLISH INSTITUTIONS

In adopting local customs and other practices of the borough and manor courts, the Plymouth colonists preserved and helped to transmit legal institutions which in the 17th century still had enormous tenacity as well as vitality. In time, those customs were to be smothered by the gradual but inexorable encroachments of the common law of the king's courts. Few of the Pilgrim settlers, however, had much familiarity with that law save on the criminal side, and the customary law of the local courts assumed "a position of transcendent importance in the life of the ordinary man."[30] Hence, it was entirely natural that the colonists should have availed themselves of their cultural inheritance in customary law, just as they did in religion and methods of farming. Their introduction of a code, of a recording system, and of a scheme of partible inheritance, to give but three instances, appears to have derived in substantial measure from English customs. The idea of a code, for example, although stemming in part from the Pilgrims' reverence for the Mosaic code of the Old Testament, was well known in the English boroughs as a device which helped to assure certainty in the application and enforcement of local law and which became increasingly popular for similar purposes in the New England colonies.[31] The example of the procedures of the English local courts, untechnical compared with those followed in the common-law courts, offered a flexibility that was advantageous to litigants untrained and largely unacquainted with the complexities of the forms of action. Thus, the introduction of half-remembered English customs at Plymouth brought into the stream of American law institutions which would otherwise have perished and which, instead, furnished in several areas a foundation on which that law would build. From another standpoint, those transplantations shed further light on the problem of survival and adaptation of patterns of thought and habits of life; at the same time they reflect, as in a glass darkly, much of the image of local England that was shortly to disappear from view.

SUBSTANTIVE PROVISIONS

The fourth distinctive contribution of the 1636 code and of other laws which were in force but not expressly incorporated

30. *Id.* at 420.
31. See Haskins & Ewing, *supra* note 18.

therein was in the development of new laws which have since had a permanent influence on the American legal system. This contribution was in two directions.

1. *A Bill of Rights*

First, the code gave expression to the idea of fundamental law embodied in a bill of rights and written constitution. That idea had already made an appearance in Massachusetts Bay in the preceding year when it was agreed to frame a body of laws "in resemblance to a Magna Charta."[32] However, except for the draft of fundamental laws prepared in 1636 by John Cotton, which was never adopted, nothing was done about the project until the Body of Liberties was enacted in 1641.[33] Thus, the Plymouth declaration of rights, rudimentary though it was, was certainly the first enactment of its kind in America. The Preamble promptly claims for the colonists the rights and liberties of Englishmen, stating that they had come "as free borne subjects of the state of Engl. . . . endewed w[ch] all and singular the priviledges belong to such. . . ."[34] Then, at intervals between other provisions of the code, come the following:

> [N]o imposicon law or ordnance be made or imposed upon or by ourselves or others at present or to come but such as shall be made or imposed by consent according to the free liberties of the state and Kingdome of Engl. and no otherwise.[35]
>
> That all trialls whether capitall or between man & man be tryed by Jewryes according to the presidents of the law of Engl. as neer as may be.[36]
>
> That the lawes and ordnances of the Colony & for the government of the same be made onely by the freemen of the Corporacon and no other, provided that in such rates & taxacons as are or shall be laid upon the whole they be without partiality so as the freeman be not spared for his freedome, but the levy be equall. And in case any man finde himselfe aggrieved, that his complaint may be heard & redressed if there be due cause.[37]

32. 1 WINTHROP'S JOURNAL 151 (Hosmer ed. 1908).
33. Note 12 *supra.* See generally HASKINS, *op. cit. supra* note 24, at 124-26.
34. PLYMOUTH LAWS 36.
35. *Ibid.*
36. *Id.* at 42.
37. *Ibid.*

As time went on, these fundamentals were elaborated and enlarged, so that by 1671 they were expressed in much more sophisticated terms and in recognizably modern form, occupying nearly three full printed pages.[38] It is not without interest that at least six provisions of that later code appear in equivalent form in the present-day Constitution of Massachusetts.[39]

2. *Innovations*

The other direction in which Plymouth made a distinctive contribution to the American legal heritage was the formulation of certain provisions of new substantive law: civil marriage, equality of descent among children, provision for widows, and recording of deeds. All these were marked advances on English law.

The introduction of civil marriage is undoubtedly the best known of Plymouth's innovations. Whereas Anglican doctrine in contemporary England, conforming to that of the Roman Catholic Church, prescribed that marriage should be solemnized in church, at Plymouth the colonists introduced marriage by officers of the civil government. Bradford speaks of the practice as having been founded on the "laudable custome of the Low-cuntries,"[40] and it appears therefore to have been one of the fruits of the Pilgrims' sojourn in Holland. The practice was also followed in Massachusetts Bay when that colony was established, and its acceptance there can fairly be attributed to Plymouth influence.[41] Civil marriage is not expressly dealt with in the first Plymouth code, but it appears to have been universally practiced. The general recognition of civil marriages in the United States today is too well known to require comment, but the practice can be traced at least in part to 17th-century Plymouth.

Among the notable advances of Plymouth law over that of contemporary England was the provision for the descent of land to all children rather than to the eldest son, as under the English rule of primogeniture.[42] As early as 1627, Isaak de Rasieres, then Acting-

38. *Id.* at 241-43.

39. MASS. CONST. arts. 4, 9, 11, 12, 15, 23.

40. 1 BRADFORD, *op. cit. supra* note 5, at 218.

41. HASKINS, *op. cit. supra* note 24, at 194-95.

42. PLYMOUTH LAWS, 43. The reference to equal descent is not explicit but may be inferred from the reference to "the comendable custome of Engl. and hold of Est. Greenwich." *Ibid.* At the manor of East Greenwich, the Kentish custom of gavelkind was believed to be in force. Lands held in gavelkind

Secretary of New Netherland, visited Plymouth and observed that "in inheritances they place all the children in one degree, only the eldest son has an acknowledgement for his seniority of birth."[43] The reference to seniority was to the practice of giving a double portion to the eldest son, pursuant to the precept of *Deuteronomy* 21:17, upon which it was ostensibly based. The rule of partible descent was expressly recognized in 1641 in the Massachusetts Body of Liberties, which apparently adopted the Plymouth practice.[44] From there it spread to Connecticut, Rhode Island, and even to Pennsylvania and thus antedated by many generations Thomas Jefferson's attack on primogeniture in 1776. In the ultimate abolition of primogeniture throughout the United States the influence of the early practice at Plymouth can hardly be ignored.

The provision for the widow was also novel.[45] Generally speaking, the common law of England at this time assured a widow a life estate in one-third of all the lands of which her husband had been seised during marriage. Plymouth also recognized a similar general right,[46] but went far beyond English law in assuring to her an absolute interest in one-third of his goods and chattels as well. In England, only by exceptional local custom could the widow share in personal property, as opposed to freehold lands, unless the husband left a will which expressly gave her such property.[47] The Plymouth law as to personal property was also followed in Massachusetts Bay, presumptively by adoption. With modifications, it ultimately became the law of the Commonwealth. In time,

decended to all sons. On this question, see Haskins, *Gavelkind and the Charter of Massachusetts Bay*, 34 TRANSACTIONS COLONIAL SOC'Y MASS. 483 (1943).

43. Letter From Isaak de Rasieres to Samuel Blommaert, in 2 N.Y. HISTORICAL SOC'Y COLLECTION, 2D SERIES 339, 352 (1849).

44. See generally Haskins, *The Beginnings of Partible Inheritance in the American Colonies*, 51 YALE L.J. 1280 (1942).

45. See PLYMOUTH LAWS 43.

46. Technically, dower at common law attached to all lands held in fee simple and fee tail of which the husband was solely and beneficially seised at any time during coverture and to which issue of the marriage might inherit. The Plymouth provision merely specified "a third part of his lands during her life" and therefore seems to have included lands owned by the husband at his death rather than during the marriage. In 1646 it was enacted that a wife must consent to a sale of land, so that there after she received some protection in lands which the husband owned and conveyed during marriage. PLYMOUTH LAWS 86. See also Haskins, *A Problem in the Reception of the Common Law in the Colonial Period*, 97 U. PA. L. REV. 842 (1949).

47. 3 HOLDSWORTH, A HISTORY OF ENGLISH LAW 552 (4th ed. 1936).

the Statute of Distribution in England[48] and its counterparts in America were to assure the widow of an intestate a share in her husband's personal estate, but these provisions came long after the early Plymouth law.

Of even greater significance was the introduction at Plymouth of a system of recording sales, gifts, mortgages, and other conveyances of houses and lands.[49] Stemming in part from a peasant psychosis bred of years of misery brought on by the inclosure movements, yet influenced by recording practices in the English boroughs and probably by Dutch example as well, the recording system furnished basic guarantees of security of land titles. As early as 1636 two features of the modern recording system were in force at Plymouth, namely, the entry of the entire deed on an official record and prior acknowledgment of the deed before a government official. These two features, subsequently adopted by Massachusetts Bay and supplemented by two further features introduced in that colony in 1640, provided the basis for modern systems not only in Massachusetts but in the United States generally.[50] Indeed, it is worthy of note that, in spite of more than twelve revisions, the present-day Massachusetts recording statute[51] goes back, substantially unchanged in form, to the Bay Colony act of 1640, which appears to have stemmed from the earlier enactment at Plymouth.

The Rule of Law

Each of these contributions of Plymouth—to its own laws, to the law of the Bay Colony, and, ultimately, to modern American law—is impressive. If Massachusetts Bay was to receive much of the credit as the vehicle of transmission, that fact illustrates the old saying that the Pilgrim saddle is always on the Bay horse. What is particularly impressive, however, is the evidence which appears early and persistently in the Plymouth enactments and court records, that the colonists were governed by and lived under a rule of law.[52] Few ideas have had so profound or so pervasive an influence in Anglo-American jurisprudence as has the idea that no

48. 22 & 23 Car. 2, c. 10 (1670).

49. Plymouth Laws 43.

50. See generally Haskins, *supra* note 1.

51. Mass. Ann Laws ch. 183 (1955).

52. See generally Note, *The Rule of Law in Colonial Massachusetts*, 108 U. Pa. L. Rev. 1001 (1960), dealing with the rule of law in the colony of Massachusetts Bay.

man is above the law. It has crystallized in the doctrine of the "rule" or "supremacy" of law, which has long been regarded as one of the central and most characteristic features of the Western legal tradition. The doctrine first found expression in mediaeval England in the course of struggles to check the threatened usurpations of kings. It also is evident in the numerous borough codes that expressly guarded the customs and franchises of townsfolk from the encroachments of the king's officers and the king's courts. In the 17th century the idea rose to central prominence both as a weapon of attack upon the royal prerogative courts and as a means of protecting the established rights of individuals from the jurisdiction of such tribunals as the High Commission and the Star Chamber, which claimed not to be bound by the accepted procedures of the ordinary courts.[53]

The rule of law was thus much more than a doctrine of lawyers and political theorists. Few had suffered more at the hands of the prerogative courts than the Pilgrims, and all Puritans were united in a belief in the overriding force of temporal law that reflected moral law. As early as the Mayflower Compact, in 1620, the signatories covenanted and combined into a body politic and declared by virtue thereof that they did "enact, constitute and frame such just and equal laws, ordinances, acts, [and] constitutions . . . as shall be thought most meet and covenient [*sic*] for the general good of the colony."[54] Note that those laws, acts, and constitutions were to be "just and equal"; note, also, that the signatories themselves covenanted to give "all due submission and obedience" thereto.[55] Later, in the code of 1636, the idea of a government of laws is reflected more explicitly in provisions such as that which prescribed that "no imposicon law or ordnance be made or imposed upon or by ourselves or others at present or to come but such as shall be made or imposed by consent according to the free liberties of the state and Kingdome of Engl. and no otherwise."[56] By 1671, when the Plymouth "Generall Fundamentals" had been elaborated into a recognizably modern bill of rights, it was ordered and declared in language echoing Magna Carta, and later to be repeated in so many American state constitutions:

53. The foregoing is elaborated in Haskins, *Executive Justice and the Rule of Law*, 30 SPECULUM 529 (1955).

54. PLYMOUTH LAWS 19.

55. *Ibid.*

56. *Id.* at 36.

> That Justice and Right be equally and impartially Administered unto all, not sold, denied or causelesly deferred unto any.
>
> [T]hat no person in this Government shall be endamaged in respect of Life, Limb, Liberty, Good name or Estate, under colour of Law, or countenance of Authority, but by virtue or equity of some express Law of the General Court of this Colony, the known Law of God, or the good and equitable Laws of our Nation suitable for us, being brought to Answer by due process thereof.[57]

Not only the provisions of the first and later Plymouth codes, but the numerous orders, fines, and judgments recorded in the court records of the colony attest to the persistent conviction that the laws must be enforced and obeyed. The conscious adoption of laws for the expressed good of the community, together with the numerous examples of restraint on individual action, reflects an overriding concern with the interest of the order of the whole group to which the law applied. As in ancient Greece, where the promotion of good order in the community was believed to give individuals a wider freedom, so in Plymouth the community was believed to thrive on the right living of its members. Indeed, there is more than a casual relation between Plymouth ideals and the recurrent statements throughout Greek literature that to obey the law is to be free. That idea was echoed and given wide currency by Cicero, and later was reinforced by Puritan doctrine which prescribed obedience to the law as a religious duty.[58] Hence it has become a priceless legacy of western civilization that we are slaves of the law as the condition of our freedom.[59]

57. *Id.* at 241.

58. FIGGIS, THE DIVINE RIGHT OF KINGS 175 (2d ed. 1914).

59. CICERO, ORATIO PRO CLUENTIO, c. 53: "Legum denique idcirco omnes servi sumus ut liberi esse possimus."

VI

*Massachusetts and the Common Law: The Declaration of 1646**

RICHARD B. MORRIS

The theory of the transplantation of the common law to this country has given rise to a moot question in American legal history. The dicta of our modern decisions, predicated in large measure on untenable historical grounds, are of little service in the study of this problem.[1] One reason for misapprehension has been the undue weight accorded to authorized statements of legal policy. In Massachusetts pre-eminently, historians, in seeking to comprehend the *rationale* of early legal development, have here encountered a decoy leading far afield. The remonstrance to the Massachusetts General Court of Robert Child and other recalcitrants in 1646 is a case in point, wherein the "vindication technique" employed with finesse by the administration has been accepted with implicit faith.[2]

* "Massachusetts and the Common Law: The Declaration of 1646," by Richard B. Morris, is reprinted with permission from the *American Historical Review*, XXXI (1925-1926), 443-453.

1. See R. C. Dale, "The Adoption of the Common Law by the American Colonies," *Amer. Law Reg.*, n. s., XXI. 554. See also opinion of West, legal advisor of the Board of Trade, in Chalmers, *Opinions of Eminent Lawyers on various Points of English Jurisprudence chiefly concerning the Colonies* (Burlington, 1858), p. 206. For the view that common law was enforced in absence of specific legislation, see Comm *v.* Churchill, 2 Metc. Mass. 123; Sackett *v.* Sackett, 8 Pick. 309; for view that adoption and usage is essential, see Comm. *v.* Leach, 1 Mass. 60, 61. In this connection, see dicta of Shaw, C. J., in Comm. *v.* Hunt, 4 Metc. Mass. 122, to the effect that "laws for the purpose of regulating wages of laborers, the settlement of paupers . . . not being adapted to the circumstances of our colonial conditions . . . were not adopted, used or approved." See *contra, Mass. Col. Rec.*, I. 109, 111; *Colonial Laws of Massachusetts* (Boston, 1889), pp. 174, 183, 184; "Andros Records," Amer. Ant. Soc. *Proceedings*, n. s., XIII. 486.

2. A popular demand for security against the arbitrary power of the judiciary

"An obscure episode in colonial history," says Charles Francis Adams[3] of the Robert Child affair; but recent critical treatment is of much value in shedding light on the motives of the petitioners,[4] men of vision and independence of spirit, willing, perhaps even anxious, to suffer official discipline for their variegated convictions. The remonstrants under date of May 6, 1646, posited these grievances against the Puritan régime: disqualification, both civil and religious, for sectarian non-conformity; and the absence of "a settled form of government according to the laws of England." They requested wholesale incorporation of English law and cast aspersions upon the colonial attempts to reform a legal system, which the English people "by many yeares experience have found most equall and just."[5] The criticism, following quickly upon the Gorton and Vassall protests to the home government, awakened apprehension on the part of the authorities as to such publicity,[6] and a threatened appeal to Parliament[7] was a fillip to immediate action. On October 7, 1646, Winthrop, Dudley, Bellingham, and Nathaniel Duncan were commissioned by the General Court "to draw up such an answer" to the remonstrance "as they thinke meete."[8] The answer which they thought meet is the Declaration of 1646. It consists of

marks the early history of Massachusetts law. Prior to 1634, such legislation as emanated from the General Court was of a desultory character. In the second half of the decade successive committees were appointed to grapple with the problem of codification. John Cotton's "Moses his Judicialls" (1636)—a proposed draft of Pentateuchal law—embraced the first fruits of this effort; the second, the Nathaniel Ward draft, bearing significant parallels to its predecessor, presumably formed the basis for the Body of Liberties (1641), the authorized code of fundamental liberties, immunities, and sanctions.

3. *Massachusetts, its Historians and its History* (Boston, 1893), pp. 59, 60.

4. See Kittredge, "Dr. Robert Child the Remonstrant," *Publications* of the Colonial Society of Massachusetts, XXI. 1-146. In justice it should be mentioned that almost thirty years prior to Adams's remarks, Marvin in his introduction to *New England's Jonas* (Boston, 1869) had cast much light on the circumstances of the petition.

5. *Hutchinson Papers* (Prince Society), I. 214 *et seq.*

6. Winthrop, *Hist. of N. E.* (or *Journal*), ed. by James Savage (Boston, 1853), II. 284. The memorial had scarcely reached the General Court before "copies were dispersed into the hand of some ill-affected people in the forts adjoining," and even as far as "the Dutch plantation, Virginia, and Bermuda." Winslow, "New England's Salamander," Massachusetts Historical Society, *Collections*, third ser., II. 116.

7. "If not [received], we and they shall be necessitated to apply our humble desires to the Honorable Houses of Parliament." *New England's Jonas*, pp. 13-15.

8. *Records of the Governor and Company of the Massachusetts Bay in New England*, II. 162.

a prefatory section in reply to the first two charges of Child *et al.*, supplemented by brief statements of the fundamental laws in England and Massachusetts, which, for convenience, may be called the *Parallels.* The specific technique is explained in the introduction:

> And because this will better appear [*i.e.*, conformity of colonial laws with English law], we shall draw them into a parallel. In the one columne we will sett down the fundamental and common lawes and customes of England, beginning with Magna Charta, and so on to such others as we had occasion to make use of, or may at present suit with our small beginnings: In the other columne we will sett downe the summe of such lawes and customes as are in force and use in this jurisdiction, shewing withall (where occasion serves) how they are warranted by our charter.

Historians have never subjected these *Parallels* to critical analysis, and have generally accepted the confident conclusion of the editors that by the *Parallels* "it may appeare that our politie and fundamentalls are framed according to the lawes of England, and according to the charter."[9] Hubbard, representing the quasi-official attitude of seventeenth-century American Puritanism, argued on the basis of this document "what little discrepancy there was, *if any*, between the fundamental laws of Magna Charta and the New England liberties."[10] In Neal's quaint account, the Hingham and Child incidents are so combined as to be seriously misleading.[11] The nineteenth-century apologists of the Puritan era are alike uncritical. "The court," says Palfrey sympathetically, "argued their case with equal circumspection and boldness."[12] Neither Ellis[13] nor Gray[14] notes any discrepancy in the *Parallels.* Even among writers like Brooks Adams[15] and Oliver, who assuredly bore no brief for the Puritan régime, there is not much serious criticism. The latter indeed suggests that at some points the *Parallels* are "liable to exception,"[16] but there is no elaboration of this point, and without

9. This is asserted also by Winthrop, *Journal,* I. 288.

10. "History of New England," Mass. Hist. Soc., *Collections,* second ser., V. 113.

11. *History of New England* (London, 1720), I. 213-215.

12. *History of New England* (Boston, 1892), II. 174.

13. *Puritan Age and Rule in Massachusetts* (Boston, 1888), p. 204.

14. "Remarks on the Early Laws of Massachusetts Bay," Mass. Hist. Soc., *Collections,* third ser., VIII. 191 *et seq.* See below.

15. *Emancipation of Massachusetts* (Boston, 1886), p. 89.

16. *The Puritan Commonwealth* (Boston, 1856), p. 427.

further investigation one might reasonably regard it in the light of the author's generally splenetic treatment. Osgood, writing with more scientific detachment, concedes that the comparison was not exhaustive, but insists upon "a very satisfactory agreement, so far as the letter of the law concerning property, family relations, and the administration of justice went."[17] Among the special students of the Child affair, Marvin[18] speaks of the ability with which the Declaration was drawn, and Kittredge in his exhaustive study of the episode dismisses the document as being "too well known to invite comment."[19] Special students of early colonial law have contributed little in this instance. Hilkey[20] mentions the rejoinder of the court, but attempts no analysis of the *Parallels*, and Reinsch[21] makes only a passing allusion to them. Washburn, Reno, and Davis, in their special treatments of the judicial history of Massachusetts, are silent. So, too, W. C. Fowler.

The most important treatment of the subject appears in F. C. Gray's monograph, "Remarks on the Early Laws of Massachusetts Bay."[22] The writer attempts to prove the authenticity of the Body of Liberties, the law code of 1641, to discredit the claim that John Cotton's earlier proposed draft, "Moses his Judicialls," might have been the basis for the Liberties, and attaches little significance to the Pentateuchal *motif* in Puritan law. He adduces the following statistics:

> In this [*i.e.*, the *Parallels*] they set forth forty-four fundamental propositions, annexing to each the authorities for it. Six times they refer for authority to their Charter,—seven times to Custom,—eight times to laws of specified dates,—once to the Bible,—and twenty-seven times to the "Liberties," citing each by its appropriate number. Now the provisions thus cited by them from the Body of Liberties, as their fundamental laws, are not to be found, in form or in substance, in this Abstract. How can this then have been the basis of their Code?[23]

17. *American Colonies in the Seventeenth Century*, I. 260.
18. *Op. cit.*, p. xxix.
19. *Op. cit.*, p. 31.
20. *Legal Development in Colonial Massachusetts, 1630-1686* (New York, 1910), p. 66.
21. "The English Common Law in the Early American Colonies," *Select Essays in Anglo-American Legal History*, I. 381.
22. As cited in note 14, above, p. 195.
23. *Ibid.*

Whitmore, editor of the Massachusetts colonial laws, pursuing the same argument as to the potency of the common-law influence on the code of 1641, accepts the Declaration as authoritative evidence of the substantial agreement between the colonial and the common law.[24]

The present writer is convinced that Gray and Whitmore were mistaken and that the question whether the Declaration with its *Parallels* is a safe guide to the study of early Massachusetts law still challenges attention. In determining this point it will be necessary to consider not only the legal materials included within the *Parallels* but also certain important legal practices which the compilers did not see fit to mention.

1. *The Parallels and the Area of Inclusion.* In the column representing the Massachusetts law, Liberty 1, wherein the word of God is adduced in defect of statutory law, is cited along with Magna Charta (a very questionable precedent). This was good Calvinism and permitted a wide field of departure from the common-law tradition.[25] Liberty 1 further provides for the infliction of capital punishment according to the word of God, and the *Parallels* extend this rule to include all criminal cases for which there are no specific penalties, rather audaciously citing the charter as authority.[26] The *Parallels* concede that under the common law in such cases penalties should be prescribed "according to the nature and merit of the offences." In either case the judge's discretion was given a dangerous latitude.[27] In the light of Winthrop's plea in his *Arbitrary Government* (1644) that the legislature should provide no definite penalties except in capital cases—the adjudication to be

24. *Mass. Col. Laws,* p. 19.

25. In early English law resort to the law of nature was not characteristic. Holdsworth, *History of English Law,* II. 512, 513. But see *Doctor and Student,* Dial. I., c. XI.; *Parl. Hist.,* I. 1046. A more plausible analogy than in the *Parallels* is offered by Eliot in his injunction "to fetch out of the Word of God making that their only Magna Charta." "Christian Commonwealth," Mass. Hist. Soc., *Collections,* third ser., IX. 144. For a similar observation during the Commonwealth period in England, see Keble, in Howell, *State Trials,* V. 172.

26. Yet in reply to a query propounded by the elders in 1644, the court confessed "we do not find by the patent they are expressly directed to proceed according to the word of God," but maintained the privilege nevertheless. *Records,* II. 91.

27. Among the offensive charges in the letters of the "Gortonoges," which Winslow summarizes, appears this: "That the whole Word of God is a parable to them, as their conversation in all points daily declare it." *Hypocrisie Unmasked,* ed. by H. M. Chapin (Providence, 1916), p. 40.

made in each individual case by the magistrate, proceeding according to the word of God as revealed specifically in the Mosaic dispensation[28]—the full significance of this attitude can be appreciated.

Liberty 65 provides: "No custome or prescription shall ever prevaile amongst us in any morall cause, our meaneing is maintaine anythinge that can be proved to be morrallie sinful by the word of god." The editors, averse from including anything which might detract from the desired effect, prudently omitted the second clause. The Puritan theory of the identity of law and morality, sin and crime, was proposed in substance in England by the law committee of 1653,[29] but was hardly common-law practice.

Liberty 81, in accord with Deuteronomy 21:15-17, provided for inheritance by the eldest son of a double share of the real and personal estate in case the parent died intestate.[30] This was at variance with general common-law practice;[31] but the *Parallels* claim the authority of English law for the rule that "the eldest sonne is preferred before the younger in the ancestors inheritance." In this connection the assertion has frequently been made that the colonists repudiated the inapplicable rule of primogeniture, and the charter of 1629, providing as it did for tenure as of the "Manor of East-Greenwich, in our County of Kent, in free and common Socage, and not in Capite, nor by Knights' Service,"[32] has been interpreted to signify gavelkind tenure, which, by presumption of law, was the common law of Kent.[33] This tenure provides for equal inheritance among the sons.[34] The authority of the crown to create gavelkind

28. *Life and Letters,* II. 445 *et seq.*

29. Robinson, "Anticipations under the Commonwealth of Changes in the Law," *Select Essays,* I. 483.

30. The assertion of Andrews that "for more than sixty years it [*i.e.,* the intestacy law] existed as a custom in no way binding on the people," and that "it did not become a law in Massachusetts until 1692" ("The Influence of Colonial Conditions as Illustrated in the Connecticut Intestacy Law," *ibid.,* p. 437), appears untenable in view of the specific provisions of the codes of 1641, 1648, and 1660. For some instances of judicial enforcement in the early period, see *Records of the Court of Assistants,* II. 97, 286; *Essex County Court Records,* I. 206, 387; VII. 180; Suffolk Court Files, no. 333.

31. Blackstone, *Commentaries,* IV. 214.

32. Poore, *Federal and State Constitutions,* etc., I. 926.

33. Somner, *A Treatise of Gavelkind,* second ed. (London, 1726), p. 44; *Robinson on Gavelkind, the Common Law of Kent,* fifth ed., edited by C. I. Elston and H. J. H. Mackay (London, 1897), p. 44; Randall *v.* Wrettal, 3 Keb. 214, 216.

34. Littleton, *Treatise of Tenures,* ed. by T. E. Tomlins (London, 1841), bk. III., ch. II., p. 305, for Custumal of Kent.

and its customary decedent rules has been challenged,[35] but in any case, neither primogeniture nor gavelkind partible descent was in force in Massachusetts Bay at the time of the Declaration.

Similarly misleading was the claim of common-law authority for paragraph 13 of the Massachusetts "Fundamentals," which reads as follows: "Treason, murther, witchcraft, sodomie, and other notorious crimes are punished with death: But theft, etc. is not so punished, because we read otherwise in the scripture. Capitalls, etc." In the common-law column it is asserted that "simple theft and some other felonies are not punished with death, if the offender can reade in Scripture." High treason, the highest crime at common law, consisting of various acts of disloyalty to the sovereign, was not then capital in Massachusetts. Capital law no. 12 in the Body of Liberties recognizes only treason against the commonwealth. Such disloyalty to a corporation could hardly be comprised within the meaning of petit treason at common law. Larceny above the value of 12 *d.* was a capital felony in England.[36] The colonial punishment generally enforced was whipping in minor cases of theft[37] and double or treble restitution to the injured party, in accord with Exodus 22:4.[38] The editors of the Declaration missed an excellent opportunity, honestly and without equivocation to evince a reformatory interest in the criminal law and refute the insinuation of the petitioners: "We likewise desire that no greater punishments be inflicted upon offenders than are allowed and sett by the laws of our native country."[39] In contemporary England

35. Robinson, *op. cit.,* p. 55. The present writer has considered the contention of Egleston ("Land System of N. E. Colonies," *Johns Hopkins University Studies,* IV. 558) that the words "as of the manor of East Greenwich" were used, not with reference to gavelkind, "but simply to negative the otherwise necessary inference that the grant was to be held *in capite,* or, to speak more accurately, *ut de corona.*" His authority, Lowe's case (*Works of Francis Bacon,* London, 1730, IV. 113-120), does not seem to apply to this sort of grant. For colonial attitude, see, *e.g., Col. Records,* V. 199.

36. Coke, *Third Part of the Institutes of the Laws of England* (London, 1809), p. 109. Here petit larceny, a non-capital felony (Coke, *First Institute,* Phila., 1826, III. 109), should not in extenuation of the colonial position be identified with "simple larceny," defined by Blackstone as "plain theft unaccompanied with any other atrocious circumstance." *Comm.,* IV. 229. Despite the common-law penalty for larceny, the *Middlesex* (England) *Session Rolls* for the period, 1625-1668, reveal that benefit of clergy was effectually pleaded in 67 instances, whereas the death penalty was imposed in but 27.

37. See *Rec. Ct. Assistants,* II. 9, 13, 19, 32, 40, 59, 66, 81, 83, 86, 97, 118.

38. See *ibid.,* pp. 32, 66, 70, 83, 108, 118, 134, 137; *Col. Records, Mass.,* II. 180.

39. *Hutchinson Papers,* p. 220.

robbery[40] and burglary[41] were non-clergyable felonies. In Massachusetts, by the law of 1642, capital punishment in either case was not inflicted until the third offense.[42]

In other cases the Massachusetts criminal law was more severe. Fundamental 14 reads: "Adultery is punished according to the canon of the spiritual law, *viz.*, the scripture. Capitalls, etc." and in neat juxtaposition we find this vague reference to the common law: "Adultery is referred to the canon or spiritual lawe." Adultery was a statutory felony in Massachusetts, triable in the civil courts and punishable by death.[43] In England the spiritual courts punished this offense in a most desultory way, if at all.[44] Likewise blasphemy[45] and perjury endangering life[46] were punished capitally in Massachusetts, contrary to English precedent.[47] In short, there is considerable discrepancy between non-clergyable felonies in England and capital crimes in Massachusetts Bay. As to the *Parallels* themselves, the conclusion seems necessary that such statements of

40. Coke, *Third Instit.*, pp. 67-69, a "crimen improbissimum"; 1 Edw. VI., c. 12: 10; 8 Eliz. c. 4: 3; 39 Eliz. c. 15. Dalton, *Countrey Justice*, p. 231.

41. 1 Edw. VI., c. 12 and 18 Eliz., c. 7 took clergy away from the principals. Dalton, *op. cit.*, p. 231.

42. *Col. Records*, I. 22. Not only is there no distinction between day and night, but the vital common-law provision requiring felonious intent is absent. See, for non-capital penalties, *Rec. Ct. Assistants*, II. 79, 132.

43. *Col. Records*, I. 301, and Liberty 94, s. 9. For actual enforcement, see *Rec. Ct. Assistants*, II. 286 (1643-1644).

44. Pollock and Maitland, *History of English Law* (Cambridge, 1895), II. 542, 543; Coke, *Third Instit.*, p. 205. A distinct reflex of the Puritan point of view is found in the Commonwealth act of 1650 making adultery a non-clergyable felony with mitigating circumstances. Scobell's *Acts*, pt. 2, p. 121; Blackstone, *Comm.*, III. 139.

45. Not capital at common law. *Comm.*, IV. 49.

46. Although perjury at common law was punished by fine and imprisonment (Coke, *Third Instit.*, p. 163), the Massachusetts law providing the death penalty for one who perjures "wittingly and of purpose to take away any man's life" (Deut. 19: 16-19) is directly repugnant to the common law, which makes the "monstrous exception" of exempting from penalty a perjurer in a capital trial for reasons of dubious public policy. Stephens, *History of the Criminal Law of England* (London, 1883), III. 246, 247; *Comm.*, IV. 197. For a colonial criticism, see charge of Hutchinson, C. J., to grand jury, 1768. Quincy, p. 281.

47. As an earnest of "good faith," on the very day that the Declaration appears to have been ratified, Nov. 4, 1646, the court reiterated its assertion that blasphemy was capital and added two more capital offenses without parallel at common law—cursing or smiting parents and incorrigible behavior of sons above sixteen (Exod. 21: 15, 17; Levit. 20: 9; Deut. 22: 20, 21). *Col. Records*, II. 179; *The Book of the General Lawes and Libertyes* (Cambridge, 1648), capital laws, nos. 14, 15, pp. 5, 6.

important law as are included are often incomplete, garbled, and misleading.

2. *The Area of Exclusion: Neglected Legal Practices.* Among the Liberties which the editors neglect to include in the *Parallels* several diverge markedly from the common law: Liberty 43, providing for forty as the maximum number of stripes to be inflicted, "gentlemen" exempted (Deuteronomy 25:2, 3); Liberties 85-88, the four laws of servitude, humanitarian in character, and based on Deuteronomy 23:15, 16; Leviticus 25: 39, 40, 43; Exodus 23:12; 21:2, for which common-law precedent could not be conveniently found; Liberty 80, protecting the wife from bodily correction;[48] and Liberties 92 and 93 for the protection of animals against cruel treatment, significant in their divergence from the hard common-law concept of animals as possessed of no rights.[49]

Certain important legal practices, not necessarily included in the Liberties and prudently omitted from the *Parallels,* deserve mention. In legal procedure there are evidences that the privilege of testifying in one's own behalf was sometimes extended to parties in civil suits contrary to the common law.[50] Deeds required signature in the presence of witnesses,[51] while at common law it is still a debatable issue whether the Statute of Frauds (1677) made a signature essential to the validity of a contract under seal.[52] The courts, contrary to Dean Pound's theory as to the Puritan abhorrence of equity,[53] early assumed chancery jurisdiction.[54] Such chancery jurisdiction was exercised in decreeing the cancellation and re-execution of a deed, in redemption of land from mortgages, in cases of charitable trust, specific performance of executor of a testator's contract, sequestration of lands, mistake, and fraud.[55]

48. Common law granted the husband the privilege of moderate chastizement, *Comm.*, I. 444. See dicta, Braley, J., in Nolin *v.* Pearson, 191 Mass. 283.

49. Bishop, *New Criminal Law,* I. 595. For observation as to the English point of view in 1700, see Botsford, *English Society in the Eighteenth Century as influenced from Oversea* (New York, 1924), pp. 313, 314.

50. Sherman *v.* Keayne, *Col. Records,* II. 40; Winthrop, *Journal,* II. 83, 143. *Contra:* Morris *v.* Chamberlayne (Virginia, 1735), *Va. Col. Dec.,* II. 51, where the common-law rule was invoked.

51. Hilkey, *op. cit.,* p. 119.

52. That it does, see *Comm.*, II. 306. The better view it seems is that the Statute of Frauds did not in its requirements of a signature include instruments under seal. Aigler, *Titles,* p. 275.

53. *Interpretations of Legal History* (Cambridge, 1923), pp. 103, 104.

54. Lechford, "Plain Dealing," in Mass. Hist. Soc. *Collections,* third ser., III.

55. See Woodruff, "Chancery in Massachusetts," *Law Quarterly Review,* V. 370-386, and cases cited.

Marriage, in England an ecclesiastical function, came under civil purview in Massachusetts in accordance with the Calvinist attitude; ecclesiastical jurisdiction over suits for breach of promise of marriage[56] and divorce was assumed by the civil courts. Grounds which in England would have been considered merely cause for a separation *a mensa et thoro* were in Massachusetts sufficient for a decree *a vinculo matrimonii*. Desertion,[57] adultery,[58] refusal to perform the marital obligation,[59] and cruelty[60] were all grounds for divorce, whereas in England, even after the act of 1653 providing for civil marriage, that union was accorded "all the inviolability of a sacrament," nor was there any "trace of any proposal to introduce . . . any system of divorce."[61]

The identification of untruth with malicious criminal defamation was a forward-looking legal practice, rarely, if ever, credited to the American Puritans. "It is not material whether a libel be true," said Coke in 1609.[62] Indeed at common law the old maxim was, "The greater the truth, the greater the libel." Yet the Massachusetts law of 1645, antedating the Zenger trial by almost ninety years, made it a criminal offense for any person at the age of discretion (fourteen years) "to wittingly and willingly make or publish any *lye*, which may be pernicious to the public weal, or with intent to deceive and abuse the people with false news and reports."[63] The truth, no justification at common law in criminal libel, was a good defense.[64] Slander as well as libel could be criminal,[65] although

56. Howard, *History of Matrimonial Institutions*, II. 200-203.

57. Bachiler's case, *Rec. Essex Ct.*, I. 191; *Col. Records*, IV. 282.

58. Clarke's case, *Col. Records*, II. 86.

59. Clement's case, *Col. Records*, IV. 259, 269.

60. See testimony of Governor Hutchinson, *History of Massachusetts*, I. 393, that "in matters of divorce they left the rules of the canon law out of the question."

61. Inderwick, *The Interregnum* (London, 1891), p. 46. There were, however, instances of annulments. *Middlesex County Records*, III. 233, 234, 264.

62. *De Libellis Famosis*, 5 Rep. 125a; Hudson, Treatise of the Court of Starre Chamber, pp. 138, 139 (MS., Columbia Law School Library).

63. *Col. Records*, II. 104; *Laws, 1648*, pp. 35, 36; *Col. Laws*, p. 171.

64. Comm. *v.* Farrington, *Rec. Essex*, I. 171 (1649); Comm. *v.* Fowler, *ibid.*, p. 224 (1651); and see also Rex *v.* Dyer, *Records of the Court of General Sessions of the Peace of Worcester County*, 1736-1737, p. 173.

65. See *Rec. Assistants*, II. 109; *Rec. Essex*, I. 156, 196, 224; *id.*, II. 196; see also Torrey *v.* Rex, *Worcester Records*, 1733-1734, p. 97, and Rex *v.* Parsons, *ibid.*, 1734-1735, p. 120, which affords interesting comparison with Rex *v.* Stonehouse, 3 Salk. (1696) 188. These precedents would be of interest to Justice May, who in his *Law of Crimes*, p. 176, says: "No instance has been found of an indictment for mere verbal slander against an individual in this country, nor is

not in the ordinary sense at common law.[66]

Not alone in the abstracts of laws included in the *Parallels* do we find evasion, but the very absence from the Declaration of many important legal practices of a pioneer character bears eloquent testimony to its apologetic nature. The *Parallels* are by no means comprehensive. When the Massachusetts common and statute law differed from English precedent, any allusion thereto is generally excluded. Only twenty-two of the ninety-eight Liberties are referred to, and, taken by themselves, the Liberties, as we have seen, are by no means inclusive statements of legal theory and practice. The pronounced disinclination to confess a legal policy at variance with English law is reflected in a memorandum noted by Winthrop under date of November, 1639, in which he admits that the delay in acceding to the will of the people in their demand for codification was due to the belief that laws "should arise *pro re nata* upon occasions" and that specific legislation "would professedly transgress the limits of our charter, which provide we shall make no laws repugnant to the laws of England, and that we are assured we must do."[67] The Declaration bears evidence throughout of considerable ignorance of the common law on the part of its sponsors—this despite the fact that all of the members of the drafting committee had had some form of legal training abroad.

The obvious conclusion, then, is that the Declaration of 1646 is not a fair presentation of fundamental law in this constructive period. Disingenuousness marks the document. Far more courageous was the reply of the General Court to the petitioners themselves:

> Our allegiance binds us not to the laws of England any longer than while we live in England, for the laws of the Parliament of England reach no further, nor do the king's writs under the great seal go any further. . . . And whereas they seem to admit of laws not repugnant, etc., if by repugnant they mean, as the word truly imports, and as by the charter must needs be intended, they have no cause to complain, for we have no laws . . . contrary to the law of God and of right reason, which the learned in those laws have anciently and still do hold forth as the fundamental basis of their laws, and

it indictable in England." Slander was also indictable in Virginia (*Lower Norfolk County Records,* 1632-1640, p. 22) and in Pennsylvania. (See Gipson, *Journal Amer. Instit. of Crim. Law and Criminology,* VI. 325, and cases cited.)

66. Coke, *Third Instit.,* p. 198.

67. *Journal,* I. 388, 389.

> that, if anything hath been otherwise established, it was an error, and not a law, being against the intent of the law-makers, however it may bear the form of a law (in regard of the stamp of authority set upon it) until it be revoked.[68]

An allegiance such as the court describes "involved privileges without corresponding duties," is the trenchant summation of Osgood.[69] The Declaration of 1646 was one of the principal documents employed by Winslow in his successful presentation of the colonial attitude before the home government,[70] and when the true nature of this paper is even dimly perceived, much light is cast upon the statement of Captain Johnson that the authorities "thought meet to send over this year the honored Mr. Winslow *to manifest and declare the naked truth of things.*"[71]

68. *Ibid.*, II. 352. For a similar honest renunciation of English law, see Winslow, "New England's Salamander," *op. cit.*, p. 137. Indeed, the practical effect of the attack on Massachusetts law was to make the law code committee of 1647 more assertive. In the preamble to the code of 1648, we find the codifiers asserting that the rules of civil polity were framed according to the law of God, and further: "*That distinction which is put between the Lawes of God and the lawes of men, becomes a snare to many* as it is mis-applyed on the ordering of their obedience to civil Authorities; for when the Authoritie is of God, and that in way of an Ordinance Rom. 13.1, and when the administration of it is according to deductions, and rules gathered from the word of God, and the clear light of nature in civil nations, *surely there is no human law that tendeth to common good (according to those principles) but the same is mediately a law of God, and that in way of an Ordinance which all are to submit unto and that for conscience sake.* Rom. 13.5."

69. *Op. cit.*, p. 262.

70. "It is ordered that a copy of the petition of Doctor Child, etc., and our charge and their answers, or sentence thereupon, and declaration of the Courts apprehension of their petition, etc., be delivered to Mr. Winslow *to make use of in England* as occasion may require." (Nov. 4, 1646.) *Col Records*, II. 175.

71. *Wonder-Working Providence of Sions Saviour in New England*, ed. by W. F. Poole (Andover, 1867), p. 203. Here again "truth" was triumphant, for in 1648, Winslow was able to write that their "hopes and endeavours . . . had been blasted by the Special providence of the Lord who still wrought for us." Winthrop, *Journal*, II. 321.

VII

*The Laws and Liberties of 1648**

THORP L. WOLFORD†

In 1906 the *New York Evening Post*, under the heading, "The Most Valuable American Printed Book," announced that a copy of the long lost *Lauues and Libertyes Concerning the Inhabitants of Massachusetts*, of which six hundred had been printed in 1648, had been found in a library in distant Rye, England.[1] If not then, at least after the book was reprinted in facsimile type, with introduction by Max Farrand,[2] one might have expected considerable historiography to follow. Such has not been the case.[3]

This remarkable apathy on the part of legal historians can in no way cast doubt upon the importance to their profession of the *Laws and Liberties*. As "the first attempt at a comprehensive reduction into one form of a body of legislation of an English-speaking country"[4] it signified the culmination of a general movement for codification which began in Massachusetts Bay almost from the first moment of debarkation, and which was one element in the heterogeneous movement to bring about legal reform in England before and throughout the period of Interregnum.

* "The Laws and Liberties of 1648," by Thorp L. Wolford, is reprinted with permission from the *Boston University Law Review*, XXVIII (1948), 426-463.

† The writer is indebted to Professor Mark DeWolfe Howe of the Harvard Law School for the inspiration for this article and the valuable counsel he gave throughout its preparation.

1. *New York Evening Post*, July 7, 1906. The copy which was found is now in the Huntington Library, San Marino, Calif.

2. *The Laws and Liberties of Massachusetts* (introduction by Max Farrand), Cambridge, Mass., 1929.

3. See, however, Theodore F. Plucknett, "A Review of the Laws and Liberties of Massachusetts," *New England Quarterly*, 1930, III, 156-159.

4. *Laws and Liberties*, viii.

Historical Development

From the beginning the colonists revealed an interest in political and legal rights. In 1630 over one hundred sought admission as freemen, and by 1634 it was established that the colonial lawmaking power was vested, not solely in the assistants, but in the General Court, which was composed largely of deputies, elected by the freemen of each town.[5]

An early result of this more representative government was a demand that the laws be written to limit and define the discretionary power of the magistrates.[6] A committee of four assistants, appointed by the General Court in 1635, "to frame a body of grounds of laws, in resemblance to a Magna Charta," apparently did nothing.[7] Another, appointed in 1636 for the same purpose, included also Cotton, Peters and Shepard, who being ministers were ineligible to be assistants.[8] Assistants dominated this committee, too, however; and its failure was indicated by the appointment of a

5. *Records of the Governor and Company of the Massachusetts Bay in New England* (edited by Nathaniel B. Shurtleff), Boston, 1853, I, 79-80, 87, 16, 117. (Herein cited as *Records.*) See also John Winthrop, *The History of New England* (edited by James Savage), Boston, 1853, I, 153.

Assistants, like deputies, were elected annually by the freemen, but unlike deputies were elected at large and did not represent particular towns. Nearly all assistants were university trained men of good families. Their number varied, twelve being the greatest number to hold office at one time. They acted as judges in county courts, as well as on the Court of Assistants. When acting in a judicial capacity they were usually called magistrates.

6. Winthrop, *op. cit.*, I, 191. Distrust of discretionary power in England led to the revolt against Chancery, where equity was characterized by Selden as being measured by the Chancellor's foot. F. A. Inderwick, *The Interregnum (1648-1660)*, London, 1891, 223. Reformists argued that "the law which so much concerns every man, ought not to be a mystery." Even the written law—being in French or Latin—was attacked as being "so close lockt up in an unknown tongue" that it was unknown even to wise men. Anonymous, "Certain Proposals for Regulating the Law . . ." in *A Collection of Scarce and Valuable Tracts . . . particularly that of the late Lord Somers* (edited by Walter Scott), 2d edition, London, 1810, V, 534-535. (Herein cited as Somers, *Tracts.*) John Warr, "The Corruption and Deficiency of the Laws of England . . .", London, 1649, reprinted in *Harleian Miscellany*, London, 1810, VI, 222. An early reform under Cromwell was the enactment that all law treatises, writs, judgments and records be written in English. Inderwick, *op. cit.*, 204.

7. *Records*, I, 147. Winthrop, *op. cit.*, I, 191. In 1648 "an impartial well-wisher" advocated various legal reforms in England so that England might have "instead of a vast body of law, a few plaine brief laws, like a Magna Charta." C. P. Gooch, *English Democratic Ideas in the Seventeenth Century*, Cambridge, Eng., 1927, 310.

8. Hugh Peters is of particular interest because he later served on a law reform committee in England in 1651. See John W. Thornton, *The Historical*

third in 1637-8,[9] to survey and abridge the laws and make a code as complete as possible, not merely a Magna Charta of fundamentals.

The change in sentiment which had taken place during these years was reflected in two codes which were submitted. As early as 1636 Cotton had presented to the General Court, upon request, a body of fundamental laws, based upon Moses' "judicials,"[10] upon which action had never been taken when Rev. Nathaniel Ward submitted another draft, the *Body of Liberties*, in 1639.[11] Ward, unlike Cotton, had practiced law before his ministry, and revealed in his draft some legal, as well as religious influences.[12]

It is now clear, since the discovery of a manuscript copy of the *Body of Liberties* of 1641 by Francis C. Gray, that after some revision it was this and not Cotton's draft which the Court accepted.[13]

Relation of New England to the English Commonwealth, Boston, 1874, 75 footnote. Many ideas expressed in his *Good Work for a Good Magistrate*, London, 1651 (Herein cited as Peters, *Good Work*), bore a marked resemblance to colonial practice and theory. Peters, *Good Work*, 28-32, 39, 42, 43, 51. Even in his simplification of the problem, Peters reflected a colonial way of thinking. In 1647 he could "look above all present agitations" in England "knowing if we enter into our chambers, and shut our doors for a little moment, the indignation shall be overpast." Hugh Peters, "A Word to the Army and Two Words to the Kingdom, . . ." London, 1647, reprinted in *Harleian Miscellany*, London, 1810, VI, 73 (Herein cited as Peters, *A Word*.)

9. *Records*, I, 222. Where double dating occurs in this article, the first figure represents the legal year, which began March 25th, and the last represents the historical year, beginning January 1. For a fuller explanation of colonial calendar peculiarities, see *Records*, I, x-xi.

10. Winthrop, *op. cit.*, I, 240-241. This was called *Moses his Judicials*. Fifth Monarchists, in the Interregnum, urged complete abolition of English law and substitution for it of a simple code based on the law of Moses. Samuel R. Gardiner, *History of the Commonwealth and Protectorate 1649-1660*, London, 1897, II, 265. Reformists argued that "the Law of God contained in the holy Scriptures ought to be the foundation of all laws"; and even the lawyer, Sheppard, accepted this as a major premise. Booth, *Examen Legum Angliae, or the Laws of England Examined by Scriptures*, . . . London, 1656, 4 ff. William Sheppard, *England's Balme*, London, 1657, 2, 7.

11. Winthrop, *op. cit.*, I, 388.

12. For brief facts about Ward's legal background, see *The Colonial Laws of Massachusetts* (edited by W. H. Whitmore), Boston, 1889, 18-19. (Herein cited as Whitmore, *Laws*.)

13. An earlier widely held belief to the contrary stemmed from the anonymous publication of *Moses his Judicials* in London in 1641 under the title "An Abstract of the Laws of New England as they are now established." The error was persistent and even supported by Thornton, *op. cit.*, 76. That it should have gained so much force before Gray's discovery is surprising, however, in view of the evidence against it cited in Mr. Gray's article and Whitmore, *Laws*, 6 ff. See Francis C. Gray, "Remarks on the Early Laws of Massachusetts Bay," Boston, 1843, in *Collections of Historical Society of Massachusetts*, 3d Series, VIII, 7 ff.

Although the provisions of the *Body of Liberties* were transcribed and sent to various towns, they may never have been enacted technically; for many colonists were fearful of violating the Charter by enacting laws possibly repugnant to the laws of England.[14]

The codification movement was now growing. Ward's *Liberties* had been accepted on a temporary basis, but was apparently unpublished with the exception of the criminal section. On November 4, 1646, a committee was appointed to "peruse, examine, compare, transcribe, correct and compose in good order all the liberties, lawes, and orders extant with us" with a view toward publication.[15] The code resulting from this was largely a matter of "scissors and paste," but marked an attainment of the immediate objective.[16] It was far more complete than the *Body of Liberties* of 1641. Also, by 1648 the colonists, encouraged by the success of the *Liberties*, and, no doubt, by current unrest in England, now frankly called this a book of laws as well as liberties. On the title page it plainly stated that it was published by authority of the General Court.

Originally, the Code was to have been published in 1647, which was the date printed on its title page. Records of the period disclose, however, that considerable delay was experienced; and when it was actually published in 1648, it had been amended to include

14. *Records*, I, 340, 344, 346. Whitmore, *Laws*, 61. Professor Reinsch states that the word "liberties" was used instead of "laws" to avoid passing laws contrary to the charter. Then, he says, having technically refrained from enacting any law, the Court did "with one consent fully authorize and entreat all that are and shall be in authority to consider them as laws." Paul S. Reinsch, "The English Common Law in the Early American Colonies" in *Select Essays in Anglo-American Legal History*, Boston, 1907, I, 373. Winthrop in particular wished to avoid enactments. Winthrop, *op. cit.*, I, 389. The practical aspect of this problem was illustrated in 1646 when Maverick and Child complained to England that the colony was not adhering to English common law as the patent stipulated. See Richard B. Morris, "Massachusetts and the Common Law: The Declaration of 1646" in *American Historical Review*, 1926, XXXI, 443-453. Professor Morison attributes to the Child episode indirect credit for the *Laws and Liberties*, published two years later. Samuel Eliot Morison, *Builders of the Bay Colony*, Cambridge, 1930, 261.

15. *Records*, II, 168.

16. Professor Morison characterizes it as an "arrangement of statutes" but "not a code." Morison, *op. cit.*, 264. It was successful, however, in stating in one instrument the general colonial public policy and the limits within which its officers could act. Although it was not comparable with the works of Justinian or Napoleon, it was the kind of document colonial exponents of codification had demanded.

some additions of that year.[17] Its discovery in England has shown that the notion advanced by Whitmore that the first edition was published in 1649 was erroneous.[18]

For two and a half centuries the *Laws and Liberties* of 1648 was lost. This may have been the result of a deliberate effort to prevent its being circulated too freely because of possible repercussions in England. It was discovered in Rye only after many had despaired of its ever being found.[19]

Plucknett describes the *Laws and Liberties* as a "lawyerly piece of work."[20] It was in an alphabetical form familiar to lawyers of the day, and purported in its introductory Epistle to contain all the general laws of the colony, repealing all former laws not contained therein. It was an important milestone in the effort to curb, by written law, the discretionary power of magistrates. Pointing to the legal confusion in England, the legislators said perfection should not be expected of them:

> For if it be no disparagement to the wisedome of that High Court of parliament in England that in four hundred years they could not so compile their lawes, and regulate proceedings in Courts of justice, etc: but that they had still new work to do of the same kinde almost every Parliament: there can be no just cause to blame a poor Colonie (being unfurnished of Lawyers and Statesmen) that in eighteen years hath produced no more, nor better rules for a good, and setled government then this Book holds forth.[21]

It has been argued strongly that the colonists did not feel bound by the common law. This is substantiated by a perusal of the codes of 1641 and 1648. In many respects the draftsmen departed from well-established common law principles. They felt perfectly justified in putting God's express law above all other law. All except one of the capital laws in the *Laws and Liberties* were supported

17. *Records*, II, 209, 217-218, 246, 263. *Laws and Liberties*, 38.

18. Whitmore, *Laws*, xvii, 11, 79.

19. See George L. Moore, *Memoranda Concerning the Massachusetts Laws of 1648*, New York, 1889. Whitmore, *Laws*, xvii.

20. Plucknett, *op. cit.*, 156. *Contra*: Morison, *op. cit.*, 264. That it was not entirely lay in character is illustrated by a comparison with Cotton's *Moses his Judicials.*

21. *Laws and Liberties*, Epistle. The law reform following in England has been noted for its "poverty of principle" and "abundance of anomalies." R. Robinson, "Anticipations Under the Commonwealth of Changes in the Law" in *Select Essays in Anglo-American Legal History*, Boston, 1907.

by Biblical authority, and the distinction between capital and other crimes by no means corresponded with the English line of demarcation between felonies and misdemeanors.

On the other hand, it is possible to overemphasize this thesis. Whether by necessity or desire, these colonists, being Englishmen, found it natural in very many instances to follow the English common law. They ordered English treatises on the common law even while the *Laws and Liberties* was in preparation.[22] If they accepted God's law as a subsidiary system in absence of statutory law, that was no complete rejection of common law traditions, for they admitted no valid conflict between the two. Indeed, it was their intention to formulate a statutory system which would as completely as possible provide the regulation necessary for their colonial affairs so that resort to subsidiary systems would be minimized.

It is true, too, that English common law was under attack at the same time in England,[23] and legal treatises liberally annotated it with Biblical authority. Dalton's *Countrey Justice*, one of the English treatises ordered by the General Court, was typical, citing Biblical authority throughout.[24] When the colonists did the same in their own codes, they did only what the compilers of English legal abridgements of the day were doing on a larger scale.

Reinsch calls codification "a general trait of early colonial law."[25] This was particularly true in Massachusetts. But it was a trait not peculiar to America. A glance at England in 1648 reveals a similar movement gaining strength there,[26] where there were men

22. *Records*, II, 212.

23. The violence of this attack ranged from constructive suggestions of reformist lawyers, such as William Leach and William Sheppard, to the demands of Winstanley and his Diggers that all law books be burned. Gooch, *op. cit.*, 308-311, 186-187. W. S. Holdsworth, *A History of English Law*, London, 1924, VI, 412-415.

24. Michael Dalton, *The Countrey Justice*, London, 1643.

25. Reinsch, *op. cit.*, 410.

26. Winstanley proposed that Parliament establish "the bare letter of the Law" and bar from public office any who sought to add to or diminish from it. *The Works of Gerrard Winstanley* (edited by George H. Sabine), New York, 1941, 591, 512. (Herein cited as Winstanley, *Works*.) The Army regarded law reform as one of the great objectives it had fought for, and, in 1647, urged the appointment of a committee to codify the laws. Gooch, *op. cit.*, 124-129. Inderwick, *op. cit.*, 210. In 1648 Bulstrode wished "to file off the rust" from the laws and reduce them "into a sound and solid body," and others said that all laws repugnant to God's should be cleared away as had been done in New England. Robinson, *op. cit.*, I, 481. Parliament in 1653 appointed a committee to codify the law, the objective being to reduce "great volumes of law . . . into the bigness of a pocketbook." Gardiner, *op. cit.*, II, 253, 253 footnote. Shep-

trained in the law, and where an established judiciary and bar resisted the demand to the utmost,[27] even more than did the assistants —who were judges as well as legislators—in Massachusetts Bay.

THE CODE

The *Laws and Liberties* of 1648, with its revisions in 1660 and 1672, was the basis of civil and criminal administration in the Bay Colony until the charter was taken away. In this one instrument the Puritan legislators sought to provide a foundation for colonial administration, civil and criminal procedure, church government, registry of important instruments, property rights, domestic relations, regulation of trade, and criminal law. Being more detailed than the *Body of Liberties*, it purported to inform the colonists of all their major rights and reduce the number and importance of disputes. It added weight to an appraisal by Thomas Lechford, an early colonial lawyer and critic, who wrote in 1641:

> I think that wiser men than they, going into a wildernesse to set up another strange government differing from the setled government here [in England], might have falne into greater errors than they have done.[28]

CIVIL ADMINISTRATION

In the section on "Magistrates" in the Code,[29] the colonists tried to solve one of their most controversial problems: how much discretionary power should be vested in the assistants? Subsection 3 provided that on urgent occasions the Court could be called into session by the governor, deputy governor, or majority of the assistants; but no act or sentence was to be valid unless so voted by the

pard advised Cromwell not to "be satisfied with particular Acts, but proceed to a Settlement and Reformation (at least in the main things) of the whole." William Sheppard, *op. cit.*, Introduction. The impetus for this movement came largely from New England, which has been called "its regenerating influence." Thornton, *op. cit.*, 75, 77. Gooch, *op. cit.*, 79-80.

27. There were in England about 30,000 lawyers, who opposed this movement as a class. William Cole, *A Rod for Lawyers* . . . , London, 1659, reprinted in *Harleian Miscellany*, London, 1810, VII, 28. Holdsworth attributes the failure of the reform movement in England largely to the fact that "reformers of this period had not learned . . . that it is only those who understand a technical system who can restate it or reform it effectively." Holdsworth, *op. cit.*, VI, 423.

28. Thomas Lechford, *Plaine Dealing*, London, 1642 (edited by J. Hammond Trumbell, Boston, 1867), 7-8.

29. *Laws and Liberties*, 36.

majority of both deputies and assistants. It was this issue that had caused the controversy over the negative voice in the famous Goody Sherman case. Although the magistrates were soon to lose their negative voice in judicial disputes,[30] they retained it in questions of a legislative nature. Thus, without nobility, the colony was quick to establish a bicameral legislative system.

While the colonists learned from the British the advantage of bicameral assemblies, they wisely rejected other precedents. In England the Parliament sat at the pleasure of the king, and during the Interregnum Cromwell could dissolve Parliament at will.[31] To avoid any such forced adjournment in Massachusetts, it was provided in 1641 that no General Court should "be dissolved or adjourned without the consent of the major part thereof," and this provision was continued in 1648.[32]

The power of the governor was more limited than is generally realized. Although the governor was frequently mentioned throughout the Code, under the title "Governour"[33] there were only four lines, providing that he should have a casting vote in the event of an equal division of the General Court or Court of Assistants. In another section was a provision that if the particular business to be done was not important enough to warrant his calling the Court into session, the standing council was authorized to handle it.[34]

In contrast to the short section on the "Governour," the one on "Courts"[35] occupied nearly a full page. It embodied the development of central and local justice in a comparatively detailed form. Four Quarter Courts of Assistance were established, and four County Courts were to be held at Boston. Quarter Courts were also to be held by Essex magistrates. Appeal was allowed from the County Courts to the Court of Assistants, and all divorce cases were to be heard originally before the latter. Extraordinary courts were provided for civil or criminal suits to which a stranger was a party.

The familiar American governmental pattern today prescribes a separation of legislative and judicial power. Such was not the case

30. A vote was passed October 19, 1649, providing that in judicial matters the vote of the General Court as a whole should be determinative. *Records*, III, 180. As the deputies far outnumbered the magistrates, this virtually gave the former the controlling power.

31. See Gooch, *op. cit.*, 56, and Inderwick, *op. cit.*, 212.

32. *Laws and Liberties*, 24.

33. *Laws and Liberties*, 24.

34. *Laws and Liberties*, 14.

35. *Laws and Liberties*, 14.

in 1648; hence it was natural that under the title, "Courts," were inserted the provisions governing legislation. It was stated that experience showed it inexpedient for the magistrates and deputies to sit together. The two Houses, therefore, were to sit separately, and legislation could originate in either. Enactment required a majority approval of both Houses, but the governor had no veto power.[36]

The subject of elections and voting was treated in considerable detail.[37] Freeman could delegate power by electing deputies to the General Court. The sparsity of freemen of the day was indicated in the provision that no town was entitled to more than two deputies even if its population exceeded twenty freemen. Towns having ten to nineteen freemen were allowed one deputy, and those with fewer than ten could combine their vote with that of the next town. Because they could not foresee far in advance what variety and importance of legislation might arise, deputies were not to be chosen for more than a year "that the Countrie may have an annual liberty to doe in that case what is most behoofeful for the best welfare thereof."[38]

Many of these provisions superficially suggest a most democratic society—the requirement that deputies approve all legislative acts, the substantial control they obtained in 1649 of the highest judicial review, the limitation of deputies' terms to one year, and the lack of veto power in the governor. It must be borne in mind, however, that the judicial power below the level of the General Court was almost solely in magistrates, and that the largest segment of the community was non-freemen, who were not allowed to vote for members of the General Court.[39] Their consent to all this was implied from their continued presence in the community.

36. This gave practical application to the natural law theories advanced in England. Early in the reign of James I, Coke opposed the absolutism of the king, and Henry Parker, a spokesman in Parliament under Charles I, asserted that the king had "no negative voice." Prynne's *Sovereign Power of Parliaments*, 1643, was a very influential book, and began by declaring that Parliament was above the king. Thomas Edwards, in the first volume of *Gangraena*, appearing in 1646, wrote in a similar vein. The House of Commons, early in 1649, declared its acts to be law without the consent of the king. Gooch, *op. cit.*, 54-56, 92, 99, 116-117, 146. See Warr, *op. cit.*, 214.

37. *Laws and Liberties*, 16-17, 20-21. Voting for assistants was to be by "indian corn and beans."

38. The Levellers, who were most truly the people's party in England in the early 1650's, urged annual elections to Parliament as "the only right rule for regulating the laws and liberties of the people of England." Gooch, *op. cit.*, 169-173. Gardiner, *op. cit.*, II, 178.

39. Class distinctions were preserved throughout, and fines were frequent for

The colonists considered the privilege of petition a sacred right. Hence, on the local level, "everie man whether Inhabitant or Forreiner, Free or not Free" had a common "libertie to come to any publick Court, Counsell, or town-meeting; and either by speech or writing, to move any lawfull, seasonable, or material question."[40] The right to be silent was protected, too. A freeman called "to give any Advice, Vote, Verdict or Sentence in any Court, Council or Civil Assemblie" could do so "inoffensively" or, if in doubt, had "libertie to be silent."[41]

The Code defined civil responsibilities as well as civil liberties. Every inhabitant was required to contribute to the support of the State and Church in proportion to his ability; and in case of non-compliance, his lands and estates were subject to assessment and distress.[42] "Bondslavery, villenage or captivitie" was forbidden except for "lawfull captives, taken in just warrs, and such strangers as willingly sell themselves, or are solde to us" and any others "who shall be judged thereto by Authoritie."[43]

At the instigation of an assistant and overseer, laborers could be demanded of a town for "all ordinary publick works of the Commonweal."[44] They were to be compensated as said assistant and

wearing attire above one's social status. A typical case was that of Richard Knight's wife, who was "presented for wearing a silk hood" but "discharged, her husband being worth about two hundred pounds." *Records and Files of the Quarterly Courts of Essex County, Massachusetts*, Salem, Mass., 1911, I, 303. (Herein cited as *Essex County Records.*) See also *ibid.*, I, 272, 273, 274, 276. The fines for cursing and swearing in England in 1650 varied according to the status of the offender in his community, the oath of a peer being nine times as valuable as that of an ordinary person. Interwick, *op. cit.*, 46. Henry O. Wakeman, *The Church and the Puritans*, London, 1887, 173. *Acts and Ordinances of the Interregnum 1642-1660* (edited by C. H. Firth and R. S. Rait), London, 1911, II, 393. (Herein cited as *Acts and Ordinances.*)

40. *Laws and Liberties*, 35. Mere criticism, as distinguished from petition, however, was not countenanced. In 1649 at Salem, Mary Oliver was sentenced to be whipped not more than 20 stripes for saying the Governor was unjust. *Essex County Records*, I, 182. Only a few months after the colony was established, Philip Ratliffe was severely punished and banished for speaking against the government and Church, and Henry Lynn was whipped and banished for writing to England against the government and justice of Massachusetts Bay. *Records*, I, 88, 91.

41. *Laws and Liberties*, 51.

42. *Laws and Liberties*, 10.

43. *Laws and Liberties*, 4. See *Essex County Records*, I, 181.

44. *Laws and Liberties*, 9. It is significant that throughout the Code, the Bay Colony was referred to as a commonwealth. Also, except for the rather uncomplimentary reference to the English Parliament in the Epistle, the mother country was ignored. In the 25 oaths prescribed for the highest to the lowest

overseer judged their work to be worth. Civil and church officers were exempt, and for ordinary work none were to be kept away from home longer than a week—a provision which was doubtless fostered by considerations of morals as well as justice.

Even on the higher level there was forced labor. Experience had shown that many church members chose to remain non-freemen rather than accept certain civic responsibilities. In 1647, therefore, the General Court removed their exemption if they were chosen by freemen to serve as constables, jurors, selectmen or surveyors of highways. On refusal to serve, they might be fined up to twenty shillings.[45]

In the Code the Court placed considerable responsibility upon local government. Necessary expenses of the governor, deputy governor, assistant or juryman at any court, deputy for the General Court, or commissioner to maintain order at their local meetings were to be borne by the town or shire in the service of which they acted.[46] Towns of over fifty householders were required to appoint one within the town to teach children to read and write, and those with one hundred or more families were to provide a grammar school to prepare students for the University (i.e. Harvard).[47]

Harvard, not unnaturally, was subject to close State supervision. The governor, deputy governor, magistrates and the teaching elders

officials—from governor to viewers of pipe staves—there was not once a reference to England, the King, Parliament, nor English law. This was also true of all forms to be used for summonses, attachments and replevin. The Epistle was addressed to the "Brethren and Neighbours, the Inhabitants of Massachusets, the Governour, Assistants and Deputies." One unacquainted with history would not learn from reading the Code that a relationship existed in 1648 between the two countries. The colonists at this time were in no defiant mood. They could not afford to be, and had no reason for defiance; but they had always shown some inclination for independent thought, which was encouraged by internal political strife in England in the 1640's. Their silence here was that of a small boy who has just stolen an apple, unnoticed.

45. *Laws and Liberties*, 23. Fines for unexcused absence from jury were not unusual. See *Essex County Records*, I, 236, 374, 387. Laws such as this became a source of substantial revenue in later New England town meetings as various wealthy townsmen were appointed in succession to positions they did not desire in the expectation that they would refuse, pay the fine, and help replenish the town coffers.

46. *Laws and Liberties*, 9.

47. *Laws and Liberties*, 47. Towns were also held responsible for the upkeep of roads. In 1650 the town of Ipswich was presented at court to repair a highway within three months, but was "acquitted for not laying out a highway to Gloster, upon proof that it was already completed. *Essex County Records*, I, 188. See also *ibid.*, I, 223, 224, 230.

of the six adjoining towns were given "full power and authoritie to make and establish all such orders . . . as they shall see necessary for the . . . guiding . . . of the said Colledge, and several members thereof . . . in Pietie, Moralitie and Learning, as also to . . . manage . . . all gifts . . . as . . . have been . . . bestowed."[48]

These representative provisions from the Code reveal that already an embryonic system of checks and balances had been instituted in Massachusetts government. The balances were not so equalized nor was the representation so democratic as in twentieth century Massachusetts, but considered as a whole they marked a step forward from the England of Charles I. All the people might be heard at town meeting. All the freemen might vote for deputies and assistants. Assistants exercised important judicial as well as legislative power, but in the General Court their judicial decisions could be reversed and their legislative proposals rejected by deputies.

Many improvements could have been made in the substance, arrangement and language of the Code; but when it is viewed *in toto*, Lechford's commendation of the colonists appears to have been justified. On administrative structure, Ward's *Liberties* had had less to say than Cotton's *Judicials*, even though the approach was more legal. The lost ground was more than regained in 1648.

JUDICIAL PROCEDURE

While colonial society did not stress the separation of administrative or legislative from judicial power, it is interesting to notice separately the feeling in Massachusetts regarding judicial procedure, and the technique prescribed by the Code for initiating and maintaining legal proceedings. The line of demarcation between civil and criminal procedure was less distinguishable than in England. Power given courts and magistrates in the Bay Colony to try civil and criminal suits, as distinguished from the power given Justices of the Peace in England to try only criminal cases, is just one instance of a colonial departure from English tradition at a point where it was experiencing much criticism.[49]

A much larger proportion of the Code pertained to judicial proceedings than administration. These provisions in large mea-

48. *Laws and Liberties*, 12.

49. Hugh Peters advocated substantially the same system for England. Peters, *Good Work*, 51.

sure dispensed with outworn legal hurdles which caused so much delay and expense in England and which were the subject of most violent attack by legal reformists there at the time.[50]

Common barratry was a common law crime in England, which the Justice of the Peace could punish at his discretion. A common barrator was described as one "who is either a common mover and stirrer up (or maintainer) of suits in Law in any Court."[51]

Having removed many of the obstacles to litigation in Massachusetts, it was particularly necessary to discourage unnecessary suits. Several provisions for this purpose were written in the *Laws and Liberties.* The basic prohibition against common barratry, enabling the tribunal to reject the cause and punish the offender, was copied almost verbatim from the *Body of Liberties.*[52] Another provision, also carried over from 1641, imposed treble damages to be paid the defendant and forty shillings to be paid the "Commonwealth" upon any one who wittingly did wrong to the defendant by commencing or prosecuting his suit.[53] If the plaintiff had a cause of action, he might still be fined for falsely pretending that damages or debts were greater than he knew they actually were.[54] Further protection was provided on the first page of the Code in the provision that every person impleading another in a County Court or the Court of Assistants must pay a minimum of ten shil-

50. Cole argued that "there may be as much injury suffered from the delay of justice as from the denial of justice." Cole, *op. cit.*, 31. Replevin was said to be so dilatory an action that a plaintiff could delay his case two or three years. Anonymous, *Certain Proposals of Divers Attorneys . . . Presented to the Honourable Committee for the regulating proceedings in Law*, London, 1650, 3. (Herein cited as *Attorneys' Proposals.*) The Little Parliament found in 1653 "twenty-three thousand Causes of from five to thirty years continuance lying undetermined in Chancery." Thomas Carlyle, *Oliver Cromwell's Letters and Speeches*, N. Y., 1845, II, 62. Booth complained that it took at least seven months to get judgment in England, whereas "at new England . . . most causes are ended upon the hearing at the same court." Booth, *op. cit.*, 111. Cromwell attempted with more zeal than skill to remedy this by his proclamation in 1654 that no case should last over one day. *Acts and Ordinances*, II, 958. Robinson, *op. cit.*, 471. See also Warr, *op. cit.*, 221, and Sheppard, *op. cit.*, 20.

51. Dalton, *op. cit.*, 43, citing Coke on Littleton, 368. Sheppard, *op. cit.*, 102.

52. *Laws and Liberties*, 3-4. Whitmore, *Laws*, 41.

53. *Laws and Liberties*, 49. In a review of Saltingstall v. Payne "it appeared to the court a vexatious suit, the jury and 'standers by' finding no evidence," and the plaintiff was ordered to pay a fine to the county and treble damages to the defendant. *Essex County Records*, I, 187. Peters proposed a fine in England for any plaintiff who "sue's and impleads another unjustly," with a stronger penalty for any one suing basely "out of plaine deceit." Peters, *Good Work*, 44.

54. *Laws and Liberties*, 16.

lings into court before the case was entered unless allowed to sue *in forma pauperis*.

The hostility to lawyers, so loudly proclaimed in England in the Interregnum,[55] was also present in Massachusetts, where there were no practicing lawyers when Thomas Lechford arrived in June, 1638. In England he had been a mere solicitor. "I am no pleader, by nature," he told the colonial magistrates in 1640; "oratory I have little." But he had solicited in the cause of Mr. Prynne in England, lived at Clement's Inn in the company of chancery clerks and lawyers; and in Massachusetts he incurred the ill will of both parties in the Goody Sherman affair by his efforts to make peace. From the moment of his arrival he was viewed with distrust because of his profession. Winthrop, Bellingham, Humphrey, Dudley, Downing, and perhaps Pelman and Bradstreet had all been students of law in England, but made no direct use of it in America. Lechford not only used it, but used it unethically a year after his arrival, going to the jury and pleading with them out of court. For this he was expressly disbarred "from pleading any mans cause hearafter, unless his owne."[56] He freely acknowledged his offense in a petition to the General Court, being "so much the more inexcusable . . . inasmuch as he knew it was not to be done by the law of England," yet found some extenuation in the fact that it was not done for embracery. The General Court thereupon allowed him to return to his profession with the usual limitations, presumably that he must not practice advocacy for money.[57]

Lechford was employed to transcribe the breviats of the *Body of Liberties* to be sent to towns for approval. It may well be that

55. Lawyers were accused of perpetuating their profession by keeping the law a mystery to laymen, largely at the expense of the poor. Wealthy men, too, such as Henry Robinson, accused them of pretending it was harder than it was. W. K. Jordan, *Men of Substance*, Chicago, 1942. Even Sheppard, who was a lawyer and had written many books on law, proposed that judges should not sit alone, but with an honest man who was not a lawyer. Sheppard, *op. cit.*, 45. See Holdsworth, *op. cit.*, VI, 421. Cole asked, "Who will expect ease from oppression from the masters of oppression, the lawyers?" Declaring that their profession stemmed from William the Bastard, he demanded to know why men should travel to London courts "where the lawyers shall baffle and confound witnesses and jury by their impudent sophistry and prattle." Cole, *op. cit.*, 29. Scant attention was given proposals to "procure some learned in the laws . . . to argue . . . the inconveniences on the one side, with the profit . . . on the other" of various suggested legal reforms. Somers, *Tracts*, V, 538. See also Lechford, *op. cit.*, 68.

56. *Records*, I, 270.

57. Lechford, *op. cit.*, xiv ff.

in the transcription he felt impelled to do some editing, for he was not one to withhold his legal talents. If so, the *Liberties*, from which the Code of 1648 eventually grew, bore the imprint of another legal mind than Ward's.[58]

Lechford's legal criticism was quite orthodox despite his own most unorthodox breach of ethics. His chief complaints were that precedents were regarded too little, matters of fact and law were not distinguished in jury trials, and records were not duly kept.[59]

Had Lechford come to Massachusetts a few years later, he might have fared better. The stipulation in the *Body of Liberties* that an attorney must not receive pay for his advocacy[60] was omitted in 1648. After that, the influence of lawyers grew so rapidly that the General Court found it necessary to enact in 1663 that no common attorney should be admitted to it as deputy.[61]

With the admission of paid lawyers in courts, another evil was corrected. A practice had grown up of going to magistrates for advice before commencing suit. Reprehensible as this would seem today, it was justified by Winthrop on the ground that if it were not allowed "we must then provide lawyers to direct men in their causes." However, the practice was denounced by Ward, and the Code of 1648 did not prohibit advocacy for pay. In the revision of 1660, therefore, pre-trial consultation with magistrates was forbidden.[62]

Written pleadings were mentioned in the *Body of Liberties*, and a statute late in 1647 required them in civil actions; but Professor Chafee has pointed out that only a handful of cases in Suffolk County Records show that there were any written declarations. That the statute may have been a dead letter is further evidenced by the fact that it was omitted from two revisions of the *Laws and Liberties*.[63]

58. Morison attributes to Bellingham, a former lawyer and judge in England, the principal work of compiling the Code. Morison, *op. cit.*, 265.

59. Professor Reinsch uses these complaints to support his thesis that the colonists deliberately disregarded the common law. Reinsch, *op. cit.*, 382.

60. Whitmore, *Laws*, 39.

61. See Zachariah Chafee, Jr., "Introduction to Records of Suffolk County Court" in *Publications of the Colonial Society of Massachusetts*, 1933, XXIX, xxiv. A proposal was made in Parliament in 1653 that no pleading or practicing lawyers should be admitted to sit in that body and that no counsel should be allowed more than £5 for any one case. Somers, *Tracts*, VI, 184. Inderwick, *op. cit.*, 201-202. See Robinson, *op. cit.*, 477.

62. Whitmore, *Laws*, 141. See Lechford, *op. cit.*, 69.

63. Whitmore, *Laws*, 39. *Records*, II, 219. Chafee, *op. cit.*, xlii. More simpli-

Forms of action played a far less important role in Massachusetts than in England at this time. The Code provided that "debt, accounts, slaunder, and Actions on the case concerning debts and accounts" should be tried in the jurisdiction of the plaintiff or defendant at the plaintiff's option.[64] All other actions were to be tried where the cause arose. With the intricate distinctions between feudal forms of action little understood by magistrates or litigants, courts felt little compulsion to insist upon them; and when in doubt, action on the case was brought and permitted.[65] Thus, one of the reasons for righteous indignation against courts, becoming increasingly audible in England, was avoided. Each town maintained a clerk to issue writs of attachment or summonses and grant replevin on receiving security to prosecute suit. Fees were nominal.[66]

The era was full of paradoxes on both sides of the Atlantic. In England, where suits were tedious and fitted into the rigid traditions of an antiquated law system, the protest against Chancery was even greater than against courts of law. Many of the reformists urged complete abolition of Chancery, not a revision to make it fulfill more fully its true function as a complementary system to soften the hardships of the common law.[67]

---

fied pleadings were urged in England. See Peters, *Good Work*, 42, Sheppard, *op. cit.*, 196, and Somers, *Tracts*, VI, 217, 234-235.

64. *Laws and Liberties*, 1.

65. The lack of insistence upon form was illustrated by many mixed actions. On March 1, 1647-8 Richard Praye was fined for swearing, cursing, wife beating and contempt of court. *Essex County Records*, I, 136. Avis Chubb was admonished for slander and idleness, *ibid.*, I, 174; and John Hardman was fined for swearing, name calling and drunkenness, *ibid.*, I, 181.

66. *Laws and Liberties*, 47, 12. Fees were so numerous and so great in England that courts were said to be shops with a monopoly on justice. Anonymous, *Proposals Concerning the Chancery . . .*, London, 1650, 1, 4, 5. (Herein cited as *Chancery Proposals.*) Robinson, *op. cit.*, 478. Warr, *op. cit.*, 220. Somers, *Tracts*, VI, 179. As most of these fees went, not to the clerks who did the menial work, but to judges, who had often bought their offices at a considerable price which they had to recoup, there was a demand that judges be given fixed salaries. Peters, *A Word*, 70. By an Act of January 27, 1651-2, the House ordered that "no fee prerequisite, or reward shall be taken by any of the judges of Westminster Hall or their servants but such salary as shall be allowed them by the State." Inderwick, *op. cit.*, 206.

67. Feeling against Chancery became so strong that on August 5, 1653, the House, after a single day of debate, voted to abolish it. Gardiner, *op. cit.*, II, 241. This was never effected, but its powers were greatly reduced. Robinson, *op. cit.*, 471. Inderwick, *op. cit.*, 224-225. Somers, *Tracts*, VI, 207. Even its friends were forced to admit that it had become "unsupportable." *Chancery Proposals*, 2. Its more moderate critics proposed some kind of combined law

In Massachusetts there was a like attitude. The *Laws and Liberties* was printed largely to reduce the equity powers of the magistracy. At the same time, courts of law, presided over primarily by magistrates, exercised a combined law and equity jurisdiction. The preamble to the Code stated that no man's life was to be taken, honor stained, person arrested, or wife, children or goods taken from him "unles it be by the vertue or equity of some expresse law" or the word of God.[68] Proof that equity was deliberately embodied in the Code is found in specific provisions, such as the one that "if there be any matter of apparent equitie as upon the forfeiture of an Obligation, breach of covenant without damage, or the like, the Bench shall determin such matter of equitie."[69]

The demand for law reform in England was not purely a revolt of the poor against the rich. While it was true that with the assistance of innumerable delays, primarily in Chancery, a wealthy litigant might exhaust his opponent, it was also costly for him. Because there was something fundamentally wrong, "men of substance" joined the poor in urging that the law be brought up to date in a world turning increasingly from the manor to town and industry.[70] Creditors, as well as debtors, wanted reform.

Here, too, the Code was in advance of English law. Land was subject to execution as well as personal property, in contrast to England, where it could be taken to pay judgment only to a very limited extent.[71] Professor Chafee finds in the liberal use of attachments in the Bay Colony the explanation why they are comparatively easy to obtain in Massachusetts today.

Another departure from traditional English law was the provision that debts, bills and other specialties could be assigned and the assignee could sue on them as fully as the original creditor could have, provided the assignment was made on the back.[72] England had more commerce and greater interests in free negotiability

---

and equity jurisdiction. Somers, *Tracts*, V, 537. Sheppard, *op. cit.*, 145. Booth, *op. cit.*, 46 ff.

68. *Laws and Liberties*, 1.

69. *Laws and Liberties*, 32.

70. Henry Parker and Henry Robinson exemplified this. See Jordan, *op. cit.*

71. *Laws and Liberties*, 22, 3. Chafee, *op. cit.*, xliii. Particular criticism was directed at the fact that in England an heir could escape liability for his ancestor's debt by alienating what he had inherited before action was brought. *Attorneys' Proposals*, 11. Parliament proposed to make even future interests in land subject to execution. Somers, *Tracts*, VI, 221. See Sheppard, *op. cit.*, 88.

72. *Laws and Liberties*, 4.

than the Bay Colony at that time, but was also more bound by tradition and hence less progressive.[73]

At the same time there were provisions to protect the debtor from arbitrary action by his creditor. No corn nor hay nor anything subject to decay was to be taken in distress unless it was put where it could not spoil or unless security was given.[74] A man's necessary bedding, apparel, tools, arms and essential household implements were exempt from a levy of fines even though his person was not.[75] Special precautions were taken in cases where a foreigner wanted to attach property of a settled inhabitant.[76]

Reinsch's statement that imprisonment for debt was not in use in the Bay Colony unless property was concealed has been challenged on the ground that cases proved the contrary.[77] Certainly it was permitted where there was reason to believe property was being concealed; but even then other methods were preferred, and debtors were even sold. The whole tenor of the Code strongly suggests that the legislators intended what Professor Reinsch states as true,[78] but ways were found to circumvent it. Even if the Code provision was not compelling, it revealed the general disapproval of debtors' prisons in Massachusetts—a feeling which was reflected in England.[79]

Jury trials were held in both civil and criminal actions. Shortly

73. Five years later, however, Barebones Parliament proposed to make specialty debts more negotiable in England. Somers, *Tracts*, VI, 189. Plucknett, *op. cit.*, 159.

74. *Laws and Liberties*, 17.

75. *Laws and Liberties*, 34.

76. *Laws and Liberties*, 3.

77. Chafee, *op. cit.*, xliv. See *Laws and Liberties*, 2-3.

78. *Laws and Liberties*, 2-3, 28.

79. Two centuries before Dickens, many groups were loud in their opposition to debtors' prisons but disagreed on the remedy. Peters preferred forced labor until the debt was paid, suggesting some colonial influence. Peters, *Good Work*, 23, 46. Peters, *A Word*, 72. Leach, a lawyer, proposed freedom from prison upon the debtor's agreeing to pay double the debt. William Leach, *Proposalls for An Act for speedy setting at large all prisoners both for damages and debt . . . as well for the benefit of their creditors as of themselves*, London, 1649, 1 ff. (Herein cited as Leach, *Prisoners*.) Sheppard wanted bankrupts punished and barred from public office. Sheppard, *op. cit.*, 147. Robinson, the wealthy merchant, advocated releasing all debtors from prison after six months confinement, free of all liability if they were unable to pay. Jordan, *op. cit.*, 198. Barebones Parliament proposed, if the debtor was insolvent, to require him to work in a work house, half his earnings to go to the creditor and half to his family. Somers, *Tracts*, VI, 185, 221. Debtors who swore they had no more than £5, got some relief under Cromwell. Inderwick, *op. cit.*, 107-108. Holdsworth, *op. cit.*, VI, 427. *Acts and Ordinances*, II, 240, 321, 398, 753.

after Winthrop arrived, a jury was chosen;[80] and Lechford observed in his book that matters of debt, trespass, case, equity and heresy were tried by juries, which could bring in a general verdict.[81] Reinsch has pointed out that some time between 1642 and 1652 juries may have been abolished; but they could not have been for long, because the Code of 1648 provided for both grand and traverse juries and inquests were to be held in cases of unnatural death.[82]

Massachusetts allowed jurors more latitude than did England. If the evidence was so obscure or defective that the jury, whether grand or petty, could not give a positive verdict it had "libertie to give a *Non liquet* or a special verdict, in which last, that is, a special verdict the judgment of the Cause shall be left unto the Bench." In matters of fact, "if they cannot finde the *main issue,*" they were to "finde and present in their verdict so much as they can."[83] If neither bench nor jury could reach a verdict, the General Court was to take the controversy and decide it as an original case. Furthermore, there was a provision that wherever "Jurors are not clear in their judgments or consciences, concerning any Case wherein they are to give their verdict, they shall have libertie, in open Court to advise with any man they shall think fit to resolve or direct them, before they give in their verdict." Parties were ordinarily allowed to decide by mutual consent, in civil or criminal cases, whether the trial should be by jury or bench.[84]

The section on "Appeale"[85] provided for appeals from judg-

80. *Records,* I, 77-78.

81. Lechford, *op. cit.,* 66.

82. Reinsch, *op. cit.,* 378. See also *Records,* II, 28; IV (1), 107. *Laws and Liberties,* 31-32, 16. Charles J. Hilkey, *Legal Development in Colonial Massachusetts, 1630-1686,* New York, 1910, 76, suggests that the 1652 order reinstating juries probably repealed an earlier order of that year in *Records,* IV (1), 81. As late as October 7, 1651, the Quarterly Court at Hampton fined James Wall for absence from the grand jury. *Essex County Records,* I, 236. Some English reformists wanted juries abolished in small cases because jurors were reluctant to serve and there was no remedy against a wrong verdict. Sheppard, *op. cit.,* 43, 46. Jordan, *op. cit.,* 196, 197. *Contra:* William Walwyn, *Juries Justified, or a Word of Correction to Mr. Henry Robinson . . . ,* London, 1651.

83. *Laws and Liberties,* 32. Plucknett, *op. cit.,* 159. *Cf.* Henry Robinson's statement that juries should be dispensed with in many cases for it was foolish to think that all could always come to a unanimous verdict independently. Jordan, *op. cit.,* 197. *Contra:* Walwyn, *op. cit.,* 1-14. The provision permitting Massachusetts jurors to bring in a non liquet verdict caused so much trouble and delay in civil proceedings that it was repealed in 1657. *Records,* IV (1), 291.

84. *Laws and Liberties,* 51.

85. *Laws and Liberties,* 2.

ments of magistrates to shire courts and from inferior courts to the Court of Assistants. In the case of criminal appeals, only those resulting in a capital sentence or a difference among judges were heard. No such limitation was put upon civil appeals.

This appellate court undertook to decide cases on their merits, singly if only an issue of law was appealed, or with a jury if there was an issue of fact.[86] Although the Code provided that an appellant who lost could be charged costs and also fined as a deterrent to appeals, this seems to have had little effect in accomplishing its express purpose. Reviews and appeals were very frequent, often being obtained merely to get the matter before a different jury.[87]

The doctrine of primary jurisdiction was insisted upon, and there were many courts on the lower level.[88] A magistrate sitting without jury could decide cases in his own town where the alleged debt, trespass or damage did not exceed forty shillings. To assure quick and close justice where no magistrate lived, or where he was disqualified by self-interest to sit, freemen were appointed to administer justice.

Justice being cheap, the colonists went to extremes in exercising their legal rights. A litigant could sue and lose in one court, get a bill of review in the same court on the ground that he had new evidence or new matter to plead, and on losing a second time, could still appeal to a higher court. Also, a plaintiff always had the liberty to withdraw his action or be non-suited any time before

86. Chafee, *op. cit.*, xliv-xlv. By 1648 at least some differentiation was made between issues of fact and issues of law. Lechford's complaint that juries decided both was probably truer in 1641 than in 1648, but the dividing line was always less certain in the colony than in England.

87. To discourage unwarranted appeals in England, Sheppard proposed that the appellant be required to forfeit to the State as much as he had to pay the appellee in costs and that second appeals be forbidden. Sheppard, *op. cit.*, 82-83, 111. As punishment for those who sued *in forma pauperis* and appealed without merit, Parliament favored confinement one month at the work house and whipping. Somers, *Tracts*, VI, 243. Cromwell took a more moderate course, requiring the appellant first to do the act appealed from and pay £50 security for costs. Inderwick, *op. cit.*, 185.

88. *Laws and Liberties*, 8-9, 51. More local justice was demanded in England especially in the administration of estates. Cole, *op. cit.*, 29, 31-32. Somers, *Tracts*, VI, 198, 199, 201. A Justice of the Peace heard only criminal cases, and to prosecute a civil action, plaintiffs frequently were forced to travel to London. The demand for more courts in the county or hundred was widespread. Warr, *op. cit.*, 221, 223. Sheppard, *op. cit.*, 20. Peters, *Good Work*, 39. Peters, *A Word*, 72. Gooch, *op. cit.*, 167.

the jury gave a verdict, and upon paying costs, sue in another court.[89]

A current grievance in England was that prisoners were frequently held in long confinement while awaiting the slow moving of the law.[90] Various provisions were made to prevent that in the Bay Colony. Every man accused, whether he was in jail or out on bail, was to be tried at the next court having proper cognizance.[91] No man was to be imprisoned before sentence if he could provide bail unless the alleged crime was capital or contempt in open court.[92] This is but one instance where the colonial law has come down to the present day substantially the same.

The right of confrontation of witnesses was given limited application in criminal cases. If the witness lived over ten miles from court or was otherwise unable to come, a deposition could be taken and used; but if the indictment was capital, no deposition was permitted as evidence. Testimony of two or three witnesses was required for a death sentence, a person of fourteen years with sufficient understanding having capacity to testify.[93]

A system of inter-town rendition was established, the prisoner being conveyed from constable to constable until he reached the place where he was to be tried. Any one indicted for a capital crime forfeited his lands and goods for refusal to appear before the magistrate, his unexcused absence taking the place of one required witness at trial.[94]

The Code provided that there should be "no inhumane, barbarous or cruel" punishment, and whipping should be resorted to for only the most shameful crimes, and even then should be no more than forty stripes. This limitation was of Biblical origin, not present in the common law. The penalties inflicted seem cruel by

89. *Laws and Liberties*, 1.

90. Peters recommended that no householder who had lived in a place a year "bee liable to bee arrested till after sentence, and execution be out against his goods." Peters, *Good Work*, 23.

91. *Laws and Liberties*, 16.

92. *Laws and Liberties*, 28. *Cf.* Sheppard's suggestion that rather than keep a man in prison long before his trial, English courts should release him on bail unless he was held for treason or wilful murder. Sheppard, *op. cit.*, 197.

93. *Laws and Liberties*, 54. Leach urged wider use of depositions in England to speed up and reduce the cost of trials. William Leach, *Proposals Concerning the principall Courts of England, London*, 1652 (?), 36. (Herein cited as Leach, *Courts.*)

94. *Laws and Liberties*, 13, 29.

modern standards, but by English standards of that day they were moderate.[95]

The complaint in England was not so much that the punishments were cruel as that they did not fit the crime.[96] The Code marked an advance in this respect.[97] It must be borne in mind that the choice of punishment was more limited in 1648 than in 1948 and more restricted in the colony than in England. Imprisonment may be less cruel today than mayhem, but long confinement at that time would have cost the colony much, made families destitute and deprived the community of much needed labor. Even being sold into servitude was preferable.

Reinsch finds in early colonial law an anticipation of some of the most far reaching American law reforms, noting its simplified pleadings, recorded evidence, and inclusion of land in property creditors could reach.[98] It was not unnatural that Englishmen, coming to a new land to set up a new and better government, should disregard many traditional forms of judicial procedure which were under attack in their native land and even less applicable in America than there. In his emphasis on the change, however, Professor Reinsch seems to slight the fact that those common law traditions which were applicable in the new colony were pre-

95. The penalty for perjury drafted in Parliament in 1653 was that the convict "shall stand in the pillory, and have both his ears cut off, and also have his nostrils slit and seared with a hot iron, so as they remain a perpetual note or mark of his falsehood, and suffer six months imprisonment in the workhouse . . . and be liable to satisfy the party damnified treble the value." Somers, *Tracts*, VI, 237. Little improvement was found in the provision that "where a woman was burnt before, henceforth she shall be hanged." Somers, *Tracts*, VI, 236. The punishment of *paine fort et dure*, or pressing to death, inflicted upon defendant on trial for life who refused to plead, was especially criticized. Barebones Parliament proposed to let them plead, "I abide my lawful trial," or upon refusal so to plead, be punished as if convicted. Sheppard favored entering a plea of "Not Guilty." Somers, *Tracts*, VI, 235. Sheppard, *op. cit.*, 196.

96. Warr, *op. cit.*, 221. Sheppard, *op. cit.*, 2, 16,17. There were objections that a man could be put to death for a trivial theft, forging a deed or transporting sheep, beyond the sea and not for manslaughter, which was any killing without malice aforethought. Sheppard, *op. cit.*, 134, 195. A law on the lines of Lord Campbell's Act was proposed to make the offender liable civilly for wrongful death. Holdsworth, *op. cit.*, VI, 421. Sheppard, *op. cit.*, 148. One who killed in self defense or by chance was required to forfeit all his goods and had to sue for pardon. Sheppard, *op. cit.*, 196. In Massachusetts in 1647 necessary defense of a human being was made a complete defense. *Laws and Liberties*, 37. The same policy was proposed by Barebones Parliament in 1653. Somers, *Tracts*, VI, 235.

97. *Laws and Liberties*, 46, 50. Chafee, *op. cit.*, lxxix.

98. Reinsch, *op. cit.*, 412.

served. The result was that colonial Massachusetts was in many ways the kind of society toward which English legal reformists were even then striving. Many of the procedural antiquities which caused so large a measure of their discontent never crossed the Atlantic.

THE CHURCH

One of the most difficult problems the early settlers of the Bay Colony had to solve was the division between Church and State. The difficulty was accentuated by the fact that religion played so tremendous a part in men's lives in that day and the colonists had for years been combatting religious oppression.[99] Yet they could not afford to be completely tolerant of all religious faiths, or they might soon find themselves under the domination of the same religious factions again as new immigrants came from England. The objection to religious equality was political as well as religious.

Accordingly, one of their first acts was to prescribe a religious standard for all freemen.[100] The State was to approve each church, and each church was to approve its members. Generally, only freemen were eligible to be magistrates, officers or jurymen. A church was permitted to elect its own officers, if orthodox, and admit and expel members. No injunction was to be put upon any church prescribing doctrine, worship or discipline "besides the institutions of the Lord." Thus the civil government put some limitation upon its authority over the Church, reserving at the same time considerable latitude.[101]

Limitations were also placed upon the secular power of the Church. No church could depose a man from public office.[102] Churches could excommunicate members, but that had no effect upon the capacity of the excommunicate to make a will or alienate

99. There were many sects in England in the 1640's—largely overlapping—and feeling ran high. Goodwin was called "a compound of Socinianism, Arminianism, Antinomianism, Independency, Popery and Scepticism." Gooch, *op. cit.*, 113. Presbyterianism was made the state religion in 1645. When toleration came, it was a secular victory, opposed by the various sects. Even under "toleration," a Committee of Triers could reject prospective ministers and a Committee of Scandalous Ministers could eject incumbent ones for such offenses as using the Book of Common Prayer and encouraging dances and plays. Gooch, *op. cit.*, 105. Jordan, *op. cit.*, 5. Wakeman, *op. cit.*, 173-174, 180-181.

100. *Laws and Liberties*, 18. *Records*, I, 87.

101. *Laws and Liberties*, 18.

102. *Laws and Liberties*, 20.

land if he was otherwise able.[103] According to Thomas Lechford, other consequences of excommunication varied with the locality, Boston allowing the excommunicate far more privileges than New Haven, where he was treated with more severity, as in England.[104]

Churches were allowed conferences but were to impose no authority upon one another. This was made a part of the Code expressly to prevent any church authority similar to that of the Presbyterians in England, "that the truth may be searched out to the satisfying of every mans conscience in the sight of God according to his word."[105]

The civil government, while abstaining from the actual administration of churches, supplemented their police power. If a so-called Christian acted contemptuously toward the minister or reproached the doctrine, he could be punished by a magistrate. A fine was imposed for absence from worship without reason,[106] and all townsmen—church members or not—were assessed to provide a habitation for the minister.

Lechford summarized the solution found to this problem, saying:

> The Magistrates and Church-leaders labour for a just and equall correspondence in jurisdictions, not to intrench one on the other, neither the civill Magistrates to be exempt from Ecclesiasticall censure, nor the Ministers from Civill: and whether Ecclesiasticall, or Civill power first begin to lay

103. *Laws and Liberties*, 1.

104. Lechford, *op. cit.*, 32. He wrote: ". . . it hath been declared at Boston in divers cases, that children may eate with their parents excommunicate; that an elected Magistrate excommunicate may hold his place, but better if another were chosen; that an hereditary Magistrate, though excommunicate, is to be obeyed still in civill things; that the excommunicate person may come and heare the Word, and be present at Prayer, so that he give not publique offense by taking up an eminent place at the Assembly: But at New-haven . . . the excommunicate is held out of meeting at the doore, if he will heare, in frost, snow, and raine." In England as late as 1813, excommunication barred one from serving as juryman, bringing actions, appearing as witness in any cause, practicing as an attorney in any court, or doing any act "required to be done by one that is *probus et legalis homo*." Lechford, *op. cit.*, 32 footnote.

105. *Laws and Liberties*, 19-20. See footnote 99, *supra*.

106. Roger Scott was severely whipped for sleeping at meeting "and for striking him that wakened him." Emory Washburn, *Sketches of the Judicial History of Massachusetts*, Boston, 1840, 58. In a single day at Salem five were presented, admonished or fined for absence from meeting. *Essex County Records*, I, 414. This was paralleled in England; and in 1650, when the Elizabethan statutes enforcing church attendance were repealed, the repealing statute itself enforced attendance at some place of worship. Robinson, *op. cit.*, 479.

hold of a man, the same to proceed, not barring the other to intermeddle.[107]

The lack of such a compromising spirit on the part of Lechford, himself, was a contributing factor in the difficulty he experienced in living under the government of Massachusetts.[108] In July, 1640, he wrote to England, "I thank God that: Christians cannot live hapily without Bishops, as in England, nor Englishmen without a King."[109] To him "the Government of New England seemeth to make so many Churchmembers so many Bishops . . . and in time their Churches will be more corrupted than they are now."[110] As it was, Massachusetts was surprisingly tolerant of this lawyer, who was not a freeman nor church member nor householder. He questioned the validity of non-episcopal ordination, refused to recognize the established policy of Church and State, and did not hesitate to point out to Winthrop and Cotton the error of their ways.[111]

Massachusetts was realistic in seeking to regulate acts rather than thoughts. This was noticeable in the provision that jurors should not be forced to agree upon a verdict. The fact that the colonists had formerly been persecuted and many of them driven from England for their beliefs was not forgotten. Accordingly, the section on "Heresie"[112] began by stipulating that "no humane power be Lord over the Faith and Consciences of men, and therefore may not constrein them to beleive or professe against their Consciences."

At the same time, for reasons already stated, it would have been dangerous to allow heretics free rein. Subversive activities and words could be curbed even if subversive thoughts were not. Banishment was the penalty for denying that the soul was immortal, the body resurrected, that Christ gave Himself for a ransom, or that justification was by His death and not works. Anabaptists could be banished for teaching against infant baptism or war;[113] and Jesuits ordained by the Pope were forbidden ever to come, the "Court taking into consideration the great wars . . . in Europe: and

107. Lechford, *op. cit.*, 35-36.

108. It was his criticism of the Church more than his being a member of the legal profession that prevented his appointment as clerk. Lechford, *op. cit.*, xxv.

109. Lechford, *op. cit.*, xxx.

110. Lechford, *op. cit.*, 6.

111. Lechford, *op. cit.*, xxxii, xxx.

112. *Laws and Liberties,* 24.

113. *Laws and Liberties,* 1-2.

that the same are observed to be . . . fomented chiefly by . . . those of the Jesuiticall Order."[114]

Puritans in Massachusetts as well as in the English Commonwealth made statutory crimes of what are now considered minor violations of the moral code. Punishment for the first offense was frequently light, but as the number of offenses grew greater, so did the punishment. The eighth offense of wilful lying by one fourteen or over could be punished by forty stripes.[115] A magistrate could impose a fine upon one guilty of swearing rashly or vainly, and upon non-payment, commit the offender to the stocks for one to three hours.[116] Shuffleboards in public houses were forbidden, both the keeper and player being subject to a fine; and if the accused played for money, he might lose three times his earnings, half to go to the informer.[117] Church doctrine was further bulwarked by a provision that no custom or prescription should ever prevail to maintain anything sinful by the Word of God.[118] The moral code

114. *Laws and Liberties,* 26.

115. *Laws and Liberties,* 35. In practice, the penalty for lying was usually a fine, admonition or public admission. In a single day the Essex County Quarterly Court fined five persons for lying. *Essex County Records,* I, 224-227.

116. *Laws and Liberties,* 45. See *Essex County Records,* I, 136, 181. *Cf.* Dalton, *op. cit.,* 171, which the Colony ordered while preparing the Code: "If any person shal profanely sweare or curse . . . every such offender shall for every time so offending, forfeit and pay to the use of the poore" a fine, his goods being subject to distress to collect it. Upon failure of such action, the offender "shall . . . be set in the Stocks by three whole houres," or if under twelve, whipped. Sheppard wanted the English law against swearing enlarged to make clear it included swearing by the "Sun, Light bread, Troth, Faith, Plague," etc. He proposed to prevent swearing, cursing, whoring, drunkenness and other such crimes by punishing any who saw but did not report them and by arresting for the offense without warrant. Sheppard, *op. cit.,* 160, 26-28, 35. Barebones Parliament would have made it "lawful . . . for any person . . . upon hearing any person profanely swear, curse, or blaspheme . . . to apprehend . . . every such offender" and get a reward upon conviction. The penalty could be twelve hours in stocks or twelve days in the work house. Somers, *Tracts,* VI, 190. Profane swearing and cursing are still punishable by fines in Massachusetts. Mass. Gen. Laws (Ter. Ed., 1932), c. 272, sec. 37.

117. *Laws and Liberties,* 24. See *Essex County Records,* I, 91. In England by an Act of June 26, 1657, the penalty was made double the earnings with similar provisions for rewarding the informer even if he was the loser. *Acts and Ordinances,* II, 1249. *Cf.* Sheppard, *op. cit.,* 163.

118. *Laws and Liberties,* 45. The English Commonwealth, also, was guardian of public morals. In 1650, publication of books and pamphlets was put under severe censorship, and as early as 1647 a bill passed both Houses totally prohibiting all stage plays as dangerous to morals. Cock fighting was banned. Wakeman, *op. cit.,* 174, 173. *Acts and Ordinances,* I, 1070; II, 861. *Cf.* Sheppard, *op. cit.,* 182.

was applied not only to colonists but also to Indians, who could be punished for profaning the Sabbath or false worship although they were not compelled to embrace the Christian faith.[119] Whether through fear of motal or immortal retribution, these petty crimes seem to have been generally prevented.[120]

The Code and other historical records show a very great synchronization of effort on the part of the Church and State to attain definite theological objectives. The State lent power to the Church, and elders were ever present to advise the governor and assistants. But it would be incorrect to say that Massachusetts was a theocracy.[121] In the final analysis it was the State which governed. Its stipulation that only church members could be freemen and its refusal to recognize churches with doctrines abhorrent to those of the community were supported by political necessity as well as religious polity.

The civil government exercised authority over churches in matters of doctrine and faith under the provincial as well as under the earlier colonial government. The civil government in Massachusetts handled many affairs which had been under the control of ecclesiastical authority in England, such as recording births, marriages and deaths, performing the marriage ceremony and granting divorces.[122] Burials were without religious ceremony; and religious holidays, including Christmas, were not observed. Ministers gave advice but could hold no important civil office. However much they might work together for common purposes, the Church and State were separate.[123]

119. *Laws and Liberties,* 28-29. *Records,* II, 176.

120. In a sermon preached April 2, 1646, called "God's Doings and Man's Duty," Hugh Peters said, "I have lived in a Country [Massachusetts Bay] where in seven years I never saw a beggar, nor heard an oath, nor looked upon a drunkard." Eleanor B. Peters, *Hugh Peters,* New York, 1902, title page. Ward wrote, "I have lived in a Colony . . . these twelve years . . . and I have never heard but one oath sworne, nor never saw one man drunk. . . ." Nathaniel Ward, *The Simple Cobler of Aggawam,* London, 1647, reprinted in *Publications of Ipswich Historical Society,* Salem, Mass., 1905, XIV, 65. Lechford admitted that swearing, drinking and begging were rare. Lechford, *op. cit.,* 69.

121. Horace E. Ware, "Was the Government of the Massachusetts Bay Colony a Theocracy?", *Publications, Colonial Society of Massachusetts,* Boston, 1907, X, 163 ff.

122. By 1653 most of these functions had been removed from ecclesiastical authority in England. Inderwick, *op. cit.,* 46. Robinson, *op. cit.,* 474. Gardiner, *op. cit.,* II, 242. *Acts and Ordinances,* II, 715.

123. Ware, *op. cit.,* 152. Lechford, *op. cit.,* 39 footnote. Gooch argues that the moral influence of ministers was so great that they were in effect supreme, but Ware's analysis is more thorough. Gooch, *op. cit.,* 68.

PUBLIC RECORDING

Puritans on both sides of the Atlantic demanded certainty in secular as well as spiritual affairs. They found the answer to religious questions in the Bible. To satisfy their desire for more positiveness in secular transactions they took increased interest in public recording. The demand for recording extended beyond those functions which the colonial government had taken from the Church.

Lechford had criticized the failure to record colonial judicial proceedings. In June, 1639, apparently by request, he made certain specific proposals to the General Court. All actions between parties should be entered in a book before the court sat. Declarations and answers should be in writing. A public notary should record all the proceedings and enter executions of commands done and satisfactions acknowledged. This, he said, would enable the jury to see the point more easily and give a verdict sooner, would produce more uniformity of decisions, and would enable the parties to ascertain their rights in advance.[124]

The following September the General Court ordered that "henceforth every judgment, with all the evidence, bee recorded in a booke, to bee kept for posterity."[125] This did not go far enough to satisfy Lechford, who still complained, in *Plaine Dealing*, that "for want of proceeding duly upon record, the government is clearly arbitrary, according to the discretions of the Judges and Magistrates for the time being."[126]

Further progress in the direction of Lechford's ideas was shown in the Code of 1648, however, where it was ordered that both the judgment of any court and the reasons therefor should be recorded. Even in small towns where there was no magistrate, the three freemen, appointed to hear and decide cases involving less than forty shillings, were to keep a record of all such cases.[127] Every man was assured the privilege of having all testimony given under oath and all legally confirmed evidence publicly recorded. Another belated triumph for Lechford came in 1650 with the order that evidence should be presented in writing as it was hard to make a perfect

124. Lechford, *op. cit.*, 69-71.

125. *Records,* I, 275.

126. Lechford, *op. cit.*, 67.

127. *Laws and Liberties*, 46. *Cf.* Sheppard's recommendation to Cromwell that all courts of justice, great and small, be courts of record and all their proceedings be printed and posted where the courts sat. Sheppard, *op. cit.*, 20.

record of testimony in court. This represented an advance beyond contemporaneous English procedure.[128]

More progress was shown in the direction of modern land recording. Professor George Haskins made an analysis of this phase of Massachusetts legal history and concluded, in accord with the Reinsch thesis, that the colonists more probably derived their ideas from the practice of recording conveyances, leases, and wills in English boroughs than from the common law.[129] It is doubtful that the Statute of Enrolments[130] was their source, for it applied only to lands passing by bargain and sale and soon became a dead letter as freeholds began to be transferred by lease and release without enrolment.[131]

The recording provision in the 1648 code originated in an ordinance passed by the General Court in 1640. The usual features of modern land recording are four: (1) the instrument must first be acknowledged before a public officer; (2) title passes with the deed, not the recording; (3) the first grantee who records generally has legal priority; and (4) the deed is recorded in full. At least the first two of these features were present in the ordinance of October 7, 1640, and the provision which is contained against recording in full was omitted in the 1648 code.[132] Thus the colonists were ahead of their English contemporaries in recording land transactions.[133]

128. *Records,* IV (1), 27. Reinsch, *op. cit.,* 378.

129. George L. Haskins, "The Beginnings of the Recording System in Massachusetts," 21 B. U. LAW REV. 291 ff. (1941).

130. 27 Henry VIII c. 16 (1536).

131. In England it was not regarded in one case out of a hundred. Robinson, *op. cit.,* 486.

132. *Records,* I, 306-307. Haskins, *op. cit.,* 282, 283, 288. In 1648, however, the applicability of the recording provisions was restricted to transactions "where the Graunter remains in possession" and this restriction survived throughout the colonial period. *Laws and Liberties,* 13-14. On this ground Professor Howe has recently attacked the soundness of the Beale-Haskins contention that substantially the same recording system was continuously in force in Massachusetts from 1640 to the present. Mark DeW. Howe, "The Recording of Deeds in the Colony of Massachusetts Bay," 28 B. U. LAW REV. 2-4 (1948). *Cf.* Joseph H. Beale, "The Origin of the System of Recording Deeds in America," 19 Green Bag 335 (1907). In view of the fact that colonial legislation was often inartistically drafted, Professor Howe suggests that even the 1640 Act may have been intended to be applicable only where the grantor retained possession. If so, the only change in land recording effected in 1648 brought the colony somewhat nearer the present system. *Cf.* Mass. Gen. Laws (Ter. Ed. 1932) c. 183, secs. 4 (amended, 1941) and 29.

133. See Chafee, *op. cit.,* lxiii-lxiv. There were, however, many demands that deeds, conveyances and encumbrances be recorded in English counties. Peters, *Good Work,* 28. Sheppard, *op. cit.,* 115, 121. Somers, *Tracts,* V, 535.

PROPERTY

Property was another segment of law in which the colonists departed significantly from the common law of England. Their charter had been granted "as of our Mannor of Eastgreenwich, in the County of Kent, in free and common Soccage." This manor was a favorite of the Tudors and was commonly used in sixteenth century grants to make plain that the grantee was not to be burdened with military tenures. It is unlikely that its use here was a deliberate effort to avoid the rule of primogeniture in the colony. The same provision in the Virginia charter was not so construed, and it is not even clear that in this part of Kent gavelkind was in force.[134]

From this provision in their charter, however, the colonists argued that gavelkind was an incident of their tenure and primogeniture was not intended to be in force. They went still farther. Strictly, gavelkind meant that all sons of an intestate shared equally, daughters inheriting nothing if they had brothers. The colonists departed from gavelkind, letting daughters share with sons, and departed from primogeniture, letting the eldest son take only a double portion.[135] They put the Biblical law of descent above common law. A declaratory section forbade feudal incidents.[136]

Significantly, Massachusetts applied this doctrine to personal property as well as real estate.[137] The section on "Escheats"[138] provided that an heir could claim his share of "houses, lands, tene-

---

536; VI, 191-196. Unfortunately, the Parliamentary committee charged with legal reform was composed of laymen; and after trying three months, without success, to define encumbrances, they admitted defeat and left registration merely permissive, hence nugatory. Robinson, *op. cit.*, 486-487.

134. See Chafee, *op. cit.*, lxvii-lxviii. Gavelkind was not necessarily an incident of free and common socage. In England the Long Parliament abolished all feudal burdens. After the Restoration all tenures were turned into free and common socage, but that did not abolish the doctrine of primogeniture.

135. Hugh Peters urged England to do likewise, that "all entails may be cut off for ever, and men hav libertie to bestow what they have to whom they pleas, the eldest having a double portion." Peters, *Good Work*, 31. Sheppard was among those who wanted primogeniture abolished. Sheppard, *op. cit.*, 3. The Levellers and, even more violently, the Diggers opposed unequal property distribution. In "A Declaration from the Poor Oppressed . . . ," 1649, Winstanley declared, "We have a free right to the land of England, being borne therein as well as elder brothers." Winstanley, *Works*, 276. He would have gone farther and denied complete ownership to any one.

136. *Laws and Liberties*, 32.

137. *Laws and Liberties*, 53-54.

138. *Laws and Liberties*, 21.

ments, goods or chattels" which had escheated conditionally, indicating that here, too, no distinction was to be made between real and personal property. In the absence of lineal descendants, intestate distribution was left uncertain, "heirs" not being defined.

The same disregard for the difference between realty and personalty was shown in the section on "Dowries."[139] The widow had dower right to land her husband was seized of during the marriage except land conveyed away for valuable consideration before the end of "the ninth month now last past." She also had a dower interest in "one-third part of all such monie, goods and chattels, real and personal of what kinde soever as her Husband shall dye possessed of."

The word, "wills," like the word, "heirs," was given no technical definition. Holographic wills were common, and their contents and execution required little proof.[140] This was in accord with the lax practice existing concurrently in the mother country.[141]

DOMESTIC RELATIONS

Domestic relations were subject to strict Puritan surveillance. In England at this time common law marriages were valid, and the practice was adopted so widely in the American colonies that such marriages are valid in half the states today. Massachusetts was the first colony absolutely to require ceremonial marriages. The importance still placed upon the formal marriage ceremony by Massachusetts may be attributed in large measure to her Puritan founders.[142]

Most modern marriages, however, would not comply with standards of the *Laws and Liberties*.[143] The ceremony was required to be performed by a magistrate or other person appointed by the

139. *Laws and Liberties*, 17-18. In England dower was more limited, allowing the widow a life estate in one-third of her husband's real estate in possession during coverture. Sheppard urged that she should be permitted to get a one-third division in Chancery speedily. Sheppard, *op. cit.*, 199.

140. See *Essex County Records*, I, 126, 127.

141. The first English statute requiring that wills concerning land be signed was the Statute of Frauds, 29 Charles II, c. 3, sec. 5 (1677), which did not apply to the colonies unless they accepted it. Wills of personality did not require witnesses until the Wills Act, 7 W. IV & 1 Vict., c. 26 (1837). See Chafee, *op. cit.*, lxvi.

142. Chafee, *op. cit.*, lxxxvi. *Cf.* Mass. Gen. Laws (Ter. Ed., 1932), c. 207, sec. 38. See Comm. v. Munson, 127 Mass. 459 (1879).

143. See *Laws and Liberties*, 37-38.

General Court or Court of Assistants.[144] No suitor could endeavor, directly or indirectly, to draw away the affections of any maid until he had the consent of her "Parents or Governours (or in the absence of such) of the neerest Magistrate."[145] An Act, passed in 1648 and inserted in the Code, provided that no parties were to be joined in marriage until their names were published according to law.[146]

> . . . after due publication heerof no persons shall be joyned in marriage before the intention of the parties proceeding therein hath been three times published at some time of publick Lecture or Town-meeting, in both the towns where the parties or either of them doe ordinarily reside; or be set up in writing upon some post of their Meeting-house door in publick view, there to stand so as may easily be read by the space of fourteen dayes.[147]

Once solemnized, however, every effort was made to preserve the union.[148] It was strengthened by a stipulation that spouses must not be separated long for public duties and by the policy against long imprisonment. Married men and women whose spouses were in England were required by the Code to return or show cause why they must be away from their mates.[149] Such per-

144. *Cf.* Mass. Gen. Laws (Ter. Ed., 1932), c. 207, sec. 39. From 1653 to 1657 all marriages in England not solemnized by a Justice of the Peace were void. *Acts and Ordinances,* II, 715-718, 1139.

145. Theophilus Salter was fined at Salem in 1653 "for making love to Mary Smith and seeking to marry her without the consent of her friends." *Essex County Records,* I, 287. Richard Graves was fined and whipped upon his confession that he had kissed Goody Gent twice and "spoke foolish & base words" to her. *Ibid.,* I, 34. See also *ibid.,* I, 387.

146. Fines imposed for offenses may be found recorded in *Essex County Records,* I, 142, 143, 191. Even before this insertion it was an offense to marry without prior publication of intention three times. *Essex County Records,* I, 128 footnote.

147. Peters proposed that the names of parties to be married be posted at the church door in England and remain there three weeks or a month before the ceremony. Peters, *Good Work,* 115. *Cf.* the Parliamentary draft of 1653, providing that a "person so intending to be married shall first (three weeks before such intended marriage be consummated) deliver . . . unto the register" the names of the parties and their parents or guardians, and the register should fix the names on the door of the meeting place, or chapel, for three weeks; then the Justice of the Peace should marry them if there was no complaint. Somers, *Tracts,* VI, 179. See *Acts and Ordinances,* II, 715.

148. Nicholas Russell was fined for remaining in the house of Nicholas Penyon, who "had ordered him to keep away, being jealous of his wife." *Essex County Records,* I, 134. In 1650 it was made a crime to strike a spouse of either sex. *Records,* III, 212.

149. Separation cases were numerous, and a reunion of spouses was ordered

sons were found to have a corrupting influence on local youths. Original jurisdiction to grant divorce lay in the Court of Assistants, not local courts, and the divorces granted were not *a mensa et thoro* but *a vinculo*.[150] Remarriage was encouraged for practical reasons, and a long waiting period was not essential for respectability.[151]

A parent was not permitted arbitrarily to deny his child a suitable marriage.[152] The child in such a case could get redress from local civil authorities. Selectmen had a duty to see that families taught their children and apprentices to read English, know the capital laws, and learn some short orthodox catechism and some trade, calling or husbandry. If, after warning, any of these duties continued to be violated, the selectmen could put the child or apprentice under the control of a master—boys until they were twenty-one and girls until they were eighteen.[153]

BUSINESS REGULATIONS

If this Code of fifty-nine pages were divided into topics of law as they are studied today, a surprisingly large part of it would fall into the classification, "Government Regulation of Business." Not only would the sections under this classification be many, but as a rule they would be longer than the others. Only four lines were required under the title, "Governour"; but under the title, "Inkeepers," one hundred ten were needed. Detailed regulations speci-

---

unless the defendant could prove that he had done all within his power to effect a reunion and that his spouse still refused to live with him. See *Essex County Records*, I, 135, 152, 158, 191, 207.

150. *Laws and Liberties*, 15. Thomas Hutchinson, *The History of the Colony and Province of Massachusetts Bay* (edited by Lawrence S. Mayo), Cambridge, Mass., 1936, I, 375. Dorcas Hall was granted a divorce in 1654 upon proof, by her husband's confession, that he voluntarily left and refused to cohabit with her. The court stated that she was at liberty to remarry. *Records*, III, 350. Jewish law permitted and regulated divorce; and in England, Milton, for personal reasons, urged a system of divorce, but the Commonwealth never enacted one. Inderwick, *op. cit.*, 46. See, however, Somers, *Tracts*, VI, 181.

151. The Salem Court in 1648-9, appointed as executor of Abraham Robinson's estate "William Browne, who married the widow." *Essex County Records*, I, 159.

152. The Parliamentary draft in 1653 provided for forfeitures to be imposed if an English infant married without the consent of his father or guardian. Somers, *Tracts*, VI, 181. Sheppard proposed that the infant should inherit nothing from the parent until reconciled, and that Chancery should have power to annul the marriage, but only if the parent was reasonable in withholding his consent. Sheppard, *op. cit.*, 156. Cf. *Laws and Liberties*, 12.

153. *Laws and Liberties*, 11.

fied how much bakers might charge, where and when fairs might be held, what rights fishermen had in pursuing their business, how fur trade with the Indians must be carried on, what regulations tanners were to observe, what part a miller might keep for his pay, how viewers of pipe-staves were to be appointed, and what rates might be imposed for wharfage.[154]

Taking an excessive wage was a wrong for which the offender might be fined or imprisoned.[155] In an effort to assure a uniform reasonable wage for servants, town freemen were to agree upon what was reasonable; then all were to be bound by the agreement. If one town complained that its neighbor was allowing an unreasonable rate, the Quarterly Court was to settle the dispute. Plucknett, in his review of the Code, points out that compulsory wage fixing was derived from the Statute of Labourers, while control of leather trades and prohibition of tanners from currying and shoemaking was in the tradition of a long line of English cases.[156]

Certain provisions were designed to protect the laborer.[157] After serving faithfully seven years he was not to be sent away empty handed. If the servant had an eye or a tooth knocked out or was otherwise maimed by his master, he was to get his freedom and damages. The master could assign him to another, but for not more than a year unless with the consent of a court or two magistrates.

Other regulations were for the purpose of protecting the public.[158] Weights and measures were standardized,[159] and interest above eight per cent was deemed usurious and illegal. Tobacco was not permitted to be taken nearer than twenty poles from any house because of the danger of fire. Bread had to bear the mark of the

154. *Laws and Liberties,* 3, 21-22, 23, 26-27, 32-34, 43, 44, 53. The English Commonwealth, too, had price and wage control. It specified the price of corn and bread and the quantity of cattle a man might keep, ordered bakers to put their mark on bread to facilitate enforcement, forbade any to undersell another, punished shoemakers who did not use good leather, and fixed the price of meat, cheese, rabbits, sheep, oxen, hay, straw, shirts, labor of women and other items. Inderwick, *op. cit.,* 58 ff.

155. *Laws and Liberties,* 43. See Essex County Records, I, 247 footnote. As early as 1636 three laborers were fined at Salem for taking excessive wages. *Ibid.,* I, 3.

156. *Laws and Liberties,* 38-39. Plucknett, *op. cit.,* 159.

157. *Laws and Liberties,* 38.

158. *Laws and Liberties,* 52, 50, 3, 6.

159. Presentments for neglect to provide weights and measures were frequent. *Essex County Records,* I, 144, 178, 184, 196, 273.

baker, and inspectors of bread and butter weights were rewarded for all wrong weights they found. Cattle was to be branded and fenced in, and selectmen were to appoint two townsmen to inspect common fences in order to protect the corn from trespassing animals.

Monopolies, which were attacked by newly forming democratic groups in England,[160] were allowed for few enterprises in the colony. Ferrymen had a protected privilege of transporting passengers where they ran their ferries, but were subject to detailed regulations, even specifying the order in which passengers should be taken on board. Disagreeable persons could be excluded for safety at the demand of a magistrate, deputy, elder, the ferryman or the majority on board.[161] This kind of business was not within the colonial concept of a monopoly, however, for another section of the Code stated flatly that "there shall be no *Monopolies* graunted or allowed amongst us, but of such new inventions that are profitable for the Countrie, and that for a short time."[162]

Idleness was a crime, particularly in America where work was so much in demand.[163] In time of special need laborers could be pressed into service. Even a craftsman could be drafted to do labor in the busy season when the harvest of hay, corn, hemp and flax all came close together.[164] On the other hand, there was some protection of individual rights. No man could be compelled to do public work unless the order was based on an Act of the General Court and he was given fair compensation. None were to be compelled to go out of the jurisdiction in any offensive or voluntary war, but only in "vindictive or defensive wars."[165] Even a man's cattle could not be used for any public service unless under warrant based on an Act of the General Court and at the usual rates.

160. See Peters, *Good Work,* 37.

161. *Laws and Liberties,* 22.

162. *Laws and Liberties,* 43. *Cf.* Gooch, *op. cit.,* 128, and Peters, *Good Work,* 37.

163. *Laws and Liberties,* 25-26. *Essex County Records,* I, 174. *Cf.* Peters, *Good Work,* 18; Winstanley, *Works,* 591; and Sheppard, *op. cit.,* 25.

164. *Laws and Liberties,* 55. *Cf.* Dalton, *op. cit.,* 94: "Every Justice of Peace, upon request, may cause all such Artificers and other persons as be meet to labour, (by his discretion) to work by the day in Hay-time, and Harvest-time, for the saving of corn and hay, and may upon their refusal imprison them in the Stocks by the space of two days and one night."

165. This may have influenced Peters to recommend that in England no one should be pressed into service against his will "unless in some verie great exigent." Peters, *Good Work,* 26. See *Laws and Liberties,* 28.

It is apparent from these provisions that the civil authorities of that day exercised a large degree of control over individual commercial enterprise. Government regulation of wages, prices and trade practices began early in colonial America and was likewise considered necessary across the Atlantic. But the exercise of this power in the Bay Colony was not unreasonable. Forced labor in Massachusetts was the result of necessity. Servitude was frequently enforced when a colonist could not pay his debts, but the forced laborer in Massachusetts was a more favored person than the debtor in enforced idleness in a London cell.

CRIMINAL LAW

The colonists nowhere revealed their independence of English common law more than in their classification of capital crimes. It is not surprising that this independence was asserted at a point where English common law was most severely criticized in its native land. The criticism came not only from irresponsibles or men with comparatively few followers like Winstanley. Cromwell, himself, told the second Protectorate Parliament in 1656:

> The truth of it is, there are wicked and abominable Laws, which it will be in your power to alter. To hang a man for Six-and-eight pence, and I know not what; to hang for a trifle, and acquit murder,—is in the ministration of the Law, through the ill-framing of it. . . . And I wish it may not lie upon this Nation a day longer than you have an opportunity to give a remedy.[166]

In dealing with crimes, particularly capital offenses, the colonists looked to the law of Moses. The result was not so much to add new capital crimes as to eliminate the more petty ones. There were far more felonies in England than capital crimes in Massachusetts.[167]

Death was the penalty for worshipping other gods than the Lord God, for being a witch and for blasphemy.[168] Witchcraft is associated in modern thought with Salem, but it was by no means a crime peculiar to that village. Dalton listed it as a felony in England and went into great detail to define familiar spirits and

166. Carlyle, *op. cit.*, II, 241.

167. Cromwell proposed in 1656 that capital offenses be limited to murder, treason, and rebellion; but Parliament never acted upon the recommendation. Inderwick, *op. cit.*, 231.

advise how they could be recognized;[169] and Exodus 22:18 said, "Thou shalt not suffer a witch to live." The blasphemy law of 1646 is still in the Massachusetts statutes although the penalty is no longer death.[170]

Premeditated or cruel murder was, of course, a capital offense, as was slaying suddenly in anger.[171] Killing by guile, as by poisoning, specifically brought a death penalty in accord with Biblical law; but involuntary manslaughter and killing in self defense were not criminal. Buggery with man or beast was punishable by death, not only for the man, but also for the beast.[172] Cases were not uncommon. Children above sixteen could be put to death for unprovoked cursing or smiting of parents, as could a rebellious and incorrigible son at the instigation of his parents. Some of these penalties were very severe by modern standards, but were in fact less severe than contemporaneous English practice. Also, there were few convictions in proportion to the number of capital trials.[173]

There was some hesitation among Puritans to inflict capital punishment without scriptural authority. In the *Body of Liberties* rape was not a capital offense. It was soon made one, however, and was the only offense listed among the capital crimes in 1648 without a Biblical citation. Significantly, the death penalty for this was not mandatory.

Adultery with a married or espoused wife was a capital crime for both parties; but if a married man and single, unbetrothed woman committed the act, it was considered no more than fornication—a distinction which was paralleled in grounds for divorce.[174]

168. Capital crimes were collected on pages 5-6 of *Laws and Liberties.*

169. Dalton, *op. cit.,* 348 ff. The first execution for witchcraft in New England was in Charlestown in 1648. Washburn, *op. cit.,* 58.

170. *Cf.* Mass. Gen. Laws (Ter. Ed., 1932), c. 272, sec. 36. See Chafee, *op. cit.,* lxxxix.

171. Dalton, *op. cit.,* 297, defined manslaughter as killing "upon present heate, and yet without any malice aforethought."

172. *Cf.* Leviticus 20:13, 15, 16. Dalton included among common law felonies "carnalis copula contra naturam . . . home ou feme, ove brute beast . . . home ove home, feme ove feme," but said nothing about deodand. Dalton, *op. cit.,* 337-338. Execution of the offending animal before the eyes of the guilty person was sometimes ordered to increase his penalty as well as to punish the animal.

173. Hilkey, *op. cit.,* 98.

174. Adultery, not a common law felony in England, became a felony by statute during the Interregnum. See *Acts and Ordinances,* II, 387, 50. Wakeman, *op. cit.,* I, 479. Convictions under the Adultery Act were rare. Sheppard, *op. cit.,* 159. Gardiner, *op. cit.,* II, 10, says there was only one in ten years

The punishment for fornication could be marriage, fine or corporal punishment in the discretion of the Court.[175]

Many of these offenses, while founded on Mosaic law, were in considerable conformity with the common law of England. Some of the outworn English distinctions, however, were wisely ignored. Burglary and theft were serious crimes in Massachusetts, although not capital; and the accused could not escape justice merely by proving on a burglary indictment that he had committed the offense in daylight.[176] Parents and masters of thieves could be whipped for refusing to pay the penalty of their child or servant, the conviction apparently being regarded as proof of their own inadequate instruction.[177] The same offense, committed on Sunday, frequently brought an additional punishment, such as the loss of an ear. On the whole, however, Massachusetts criminal law represented an advance over the technicalities which had evolved from centuries of English legal history.

Conclusion

That was true, in general, of the *Laws of Liberties*, itself. It was by no means a model code. It contained many ambiguities, was detailed about such minor matters as the order of admission to ferries, and slighted or ignored many far more fundamental legal problems. In its very simplicity, however, the Code avoided many outmoded feudalistic defects of the more staid English law. It cut the Gordian knot of the Chancery problem by establishing no separate court of equity but giving law courts certain equity

after its passage. Inderwick lists three, one involving a woman and priest. Inderwick, *op. cit.*, 34.

175. *Laws and Liberties*, 23. Fornication cases were tried in Quarterly Courts. In 1649 Mathew Stanley and Ruth Andrews were ordered whipped for the offense, and, unless they married, were also fined. *Essex County Records*, I, 180. Another couple the following year was fined, "a child fully grown in the opinion of the women then present, having been born twenty-eight weeks after their marriage." *Ibid.*, I, 196. Indians and negro servants, too, were punished for the offense. *Ibid.*, I, 337, 196.

176. *Laws and Liberties*, 4-5. Common law burglary required (a) a breaking (b) and entering (c) into another's dwelling (d) at night (e) with intent to commit a felony. English reformists objected that the punishment was too harsh if all elements were proved and too easy to escape when they were not. Gardiner, *op. cit.*, I, 178-179. If all were proved, a death penalty was mandatory. Dalton, *op. cit.*, 308. In Massachusetts the death penalty could be invoked only after the third offense.

177. *Laws and Liberties*, 5. Frequently the father or master paid the penalty for moral infractions, too. See *Essex County Records*, I, 387, 196.

powers. It was intensely practical in its insistence that voters must be of an orthodox faith, thus preventing immigrants from imposing English standards of religion and politics upon those who had fled their oppression.

Many of the complaints against English law were never voiced in America, for the causes were left behind. In general, the colonists did not go so far as extremists in England were advocating—they did not set up a communistic government, as Winstanley wanted; they did not abolish all but God's law; nor did they adhere to the principle that natural law was the only test of true government—but in making a definite advance in the direction of English reformists, they may have forestalled a movement of similar intensity in Massachusetts. At the time when lawyers were under most attack in England, they began to emerge in the Bay Colony.

It is in this light that the *Laws and Liberties* must be evaluated. It has been considered in some detail here, with particular reference to its most characteristic and significant provisions, because this has never been done before. The major books on Massachusetts colonial law were published before the Code of 1648 was found and reprinted in 1929, and necessarily ignore its laws, which are important both as they contribute to a better understanding of the reform movement leading to the Interregnum in England and as they throw more light upon legal concepts which have come to be taken for granted in modern America.

It would be unjust and naive to disregard the three hundred years that have now passed and criticize the *Laws and Liberties* of 1648 severely for its alphabetical arrangement, which would be most awkward today, its legalistic defects, which resulted from its being drafted by men not skilled in legislation, or its simplicity, which was regarded by many as its greatest virtue. For colonial society, Ward and Bellingham could have found in the Revenue Act of 1948 no improvement upon "Charges publick" of three centuries ago.

VIII

*The Spread of Massachusetts Law in the Seventeenth Century**

GEORGE L. HASKINS AND
SAMUEL E. EWING

No history of the colonial period will be complete until the spread of ideas from colony to colony has been fully investigated. Intercolonial relations have received considerable attention,[1] but the processes by which, and the extent to which, patterns of life and thought were carried from colony to colony still await detailed exploration.

A significant chapter in the history of those processes is the spread of legal ideas and institutions. One phase of that topic can be illumined by an investigation of the effect of the legislation of one colony upon that of others. Thus, it is clear that certain of the laws of Plymouth Colony were adopted by Massachusetts Bay,[2] that certain laws of the latter colony found their way to Connecticut[3] and eventually to New York,[4] to New Jersey,[5] to Dela-

* "The Spread of Massachusetts Law in the Seventeenth Century," by George L. Haskins and Samuel E. Ewing, is reprinted with permission from the *University of Pennsylvania Law Review,* CVI (1957-1958), 413-418. Copyright 1958 by the University of Pennsylvania.

1. *E.g.,* 1 OSGOOD, THE AMERICAN COLONIES IN THE SEVENTEENTH CENTURY 392-423 (1904).

2. For example, divisible inheritance of land: Haskins, *The Beginnings of Partible Inheritance in the American Colonies,* 51 YALE L.J. 1280, 1281 (1942); recording of deeds: Haskins, *The Beginnings of the Recording System in Massachusetts,* 21 B.U.L. REV. 281, 285 n.19 (1941).

3. See notes 18-23 *infra.*

4. GOEBEL & NAUGHTON, LAW ENFORCEMENT IN COLONIAL NEW YORK 16, 61 (1944); 1 COLONIAL LAWS OF NEW YORK 6-71 (1894).

5. See 23 NEW JERSEY ARCHIVES xiv-xv (1901).

ware[6] and to Pennsylvania.[7] However, no attempt appears to have been made systematically to determine the precise extent of such intercolonial borrowing. It is the purpose of this paper to attempt to trace the provisions of the Massachusetts Code of 1648 which were adopted by the colonies of Connecticut and New Haven.

The Massachusetts Code of 1648[8] was the product of several years of effort to reduce to writing the laws of Massachusetts Bay.[9] When published, it was regarded as a complete statement of the laws, privileges, duties and rights in force in the jurisdiction, and, as such, it was the first comprehensive code of laws in the New World.[10] That alone gives it special significance. But it derives added significance from the fact that many of its provisions were adopted by other New England colonies. As the ensuing discussion will show, the Massachusetts Code had an indisputable influence on the codes of the neighboring colonies of Connecticut and New Haven enacted in 1650 and 1656 respectively. That influence is not surprising since the two Connecticut colonies were strongly Puritan and were founded by men who had been closely identified with the Massachusetts enterprise.[11] The Connecticut government, in fact, was established under authority from Massachusetts,[12] and examination of the Fundamental Orders adopted in Connecticut in 1639 reveals an essential identity between the systems of government obtaining in the two colonies.[13] New Haven Colony, although independent of other colonies, adopted a form of government similar in its principal respects to that of Massachusetts and Connecticut.[14]

At the outset, it may be noted that the codes of Connecticut and New Haven are briefer and more condensed than that of Massachusetts. This was so chiefly because they contain few references to political matters, which had been dealt with earlier by

6. *E.g.*, 1 DELAWARE BODY LAWS 1700-1749, at 297, 298 (1752).

7. *E.g.*, 1 ACTS OF ASSEMBLY OF THE PROVINCE OF PENNSYLVANIA 33 (1775).

8. THE LAWS AND LIBERTIES OF MASSACHUSETTS (Farrand ed. 1929).

9. These efforts are outlined in the MASSACHUSETTS COLONIAL LAWS 1660-1672 (Whitmore ed. 1889).

10. See generally Haskins, *De la codification du droit en Amérique du Nord au xvii*e *siècle*, 23 REVUE D'HISTOIRE DU DROIT 311 (France 1955); Haskins, *Codification of the Law in Colonial Massachusetts: A Study in Comparative Law*, 30 IND. L.J. 1 (1954).

11. 1 OSGOOD, *op. cit. supra* note 1, at 301-03, 321.

12. *Id.* at 303.

13. *Id.* at 309-11.

14. *Id.* at 325.

various enactments of their respective general courts;[15] moreover, a number of Massachusetts provisions were discarded in Connecticut as unsuitable to local conditions. On the whole, however, the Massachusetts influence is clear.

The Connecticut colonists had been aroused by the efforts of the Bay colonists to prepare the 1648 code, and in April, 1646, the General Court requested Roger Ludlow, former deputy governor, to draw up a code.[16] That this was completed in 1650 is shown by a further reference, in the *Connecticut Records* on 5 February, 1650/51, to the effect that the code had been concluded and established in the previous May.[17] The Connecticut Code of 1650 contains, in all, seventy-eight provisions, including the preamble. Of these, twenty-two provisions are practically the same as certain sections of the Massachusetts Code.[18] The wording was copied so completely that it is clear that the Connecticut codifiers had before them a copy of the Massachusetts Code and did not hesitate to borrow freely from it. Thirty-six provisions of the Massachusetts Code were adopted with deletions[19] or amendments.[20] There are only twenty new topics in the Connecticut Code,[21] but examination of these provisions shows that six had been included under other Massachusetts provisions,[22] and all but a few of the remaining fourteen were concerned with purely local matters.

15. *E.g.*, THE FUNDAMENTAL ORDERS OF CONNECTICUT.

16. 1 THE PUBLIC RECORDS OF THE COLONY OF CONNECTICUT, 1636-1665, at 138 (Trumbull ed. 1850).

17. *Id.* at 216.

18. These twenty-two provisions are the Preamble, Ability, Age, Arrests, Ballast, Barratry, Burglary and Theft, Cruelty, Dammages pretended, Death untimely, Escheats, Fyre, Forgerie, Fornication, Idlenes, Inditements, Lands, freelands, Levyes, Manslaughter, Poore, Pound, pound breach, and Profane Swearing.

19. These are Actions, Cattel Cornfields Fences, Children, Constables, Conveyances fraudulent, Ecclesiasticall, Gaming, Lying, Magistrates, Straies, Wolves, and Wrecks of the Sea.

20. These are Attachments, Bills, Bounds of Townes and Persons, Capital Lawes, Cask & Cooper, Fines, Hygh-wayes, Indians, In-keepers, Juries Jurors, Marriage, Masters Servants Labourers, Marshal, Militarie Affairs, Rates Fines, Records, Schools, Secretaire, Straies, Swyne, Tobacco, Trespasse, Votes, Watching and Weights & Measures.

21. These twenty provisions are Cattle to bee Marked, Common Fields, Caveats Entred, Dissorder in Courte, Secreets in Courte, Delinquents, Execution uppon Delinquents, Fences, Guards at Meetings, Grand Jury, Ministers, Meintenance, Peage, Timber, Treasurer, Verdicts, Wyne and Strong Water, Vessells, Forreigners, and Home Lotts.

22. These six provisions are Cattle to be Marked, Common Fields, Fences, Grand Jury, Ministers Maintenance, and Wyne & Strong Water.

All in all, there was little departure from the pattern set by the Massachusetts Code. Although sixty-six provisions of that code were missing from the Connecticut Code, some of those related to governmental matters already provided for, and others were incorporated as parts of various sections of the Connecticut Code.[23] That Connecticut did not strike out on its own, except for a half dozen of its seventy-eight provisions, is an indication both of the completeness and comprehensiveness of the earlier Massachusetts statute and of its suitability to the conditions of Puritan society elsewhere. By and large, Mr. Ludlow and his assistants were content to take the provisions of the Massachusetts Code, modify them where necessary, shorten them where wordy, and thus adapt them to the needs of the Connecticut Colony.

A similar process of adoption and adaptation can be seen in New Haven. There, an enactment of 1643 had established the structure of colonial government.[24] However, this scheme was not made part of the code that New Haven later adopted, and it remained separate from the rest of the colony's law. When it was determined to collect the New Haven laws into one body, the General Court assigned the task to the governor. His use of the Massachusetts Code is made plain in the New Haven records.[25] The New Haven Code was drawn up, approved and then sent to

23. These sixty-six provisions are Ana-Baptists, Appeale, Appearance Non-Appearance, Bakers, Benevolence, Bond Slavery, Causes Small causes, Charges publick, Clerk of Writs, Colledge, Condemned, Councill, Courts, Criminal causes, Deeds and writings, Deputies for the Generall Court, Distress, Dowries, Drovers, Elections, Farms, Fayrs & Markets, Ferries, Fish Fishermen, Freemen Non-Freeman, Fugitives Strangers, Generall Court, Governour, Heresie, Hydes & Skins, Jesuits, Impost, Impresses, Imprisonment, Justice, Leather, Liberties common, Mills Millers, Monopolies, Oaths Subscription, Oppression, Payments, Pipe-staves, Powder, Prescriptions, Prisoners Prisons, Protestation contra Remonstrance, Punishment, Replevin, Secresie, Ships Ship-masters, Strangers, Summons, Suits vexatious suits, Tile-earth, Torture, Townships, Treasure, Trespasse, Tryalls, Usurie, Wharfage, Wills intestate, Witnesses, Wood and Workmen.

24. Records of the Colony and Plantation at New Haven, 1638-1649, at 112-16 (Hoadley ed. 1857).

25. "The Gouernour being formerly desired by this court to view ouer the lawes of this jurisdiction, and draw up those of them which he thinkes will be most necessary to continew as lawes here, and compyle them together fitt to be printed, which being done, were now read, considered, and by vote confirmed, and ordered to be printed with the articles of confederation also, and the court further desired the gouernour to send for one of the new booke of lawes in the Massachusetts colony, and to view ouer a small booke of lawes newly come from England, which is said to be Mr. Cottons, and to add to what is already done as he shall thinke fitt, and then the court will meete againe to confirme them, but in the meane time, [when they are finished] they desire the elders of the jurisdiction may haue the sight of them for their approbation also." 2

England to be printed in the fall of 1655.[26] The completed code of 1656 contains only sixty-seven provisions, as contrasted with the one hundred and twenty-three sections of the Massachusetts Code; but in the heading of the New Haven Code specific acknowledgment is made to the Massachusetts laws,[27] and their influence can be detected in the great majority of its provisions.

Twenty-seven sections of the Massachusetts provisions are contained in the New Haven Code, some of them combined with others.[28] Twenty-nine of the New Haven provisions are modifications of Massachusetts provisions,[29] and only thirteen are topics original to New Haven,[30] although even some of these latter were included in the Massachusetts Code under other headings. New Haven, as well as Connecticut, failed to include sixty-five of the Massachusetts provisions,[31] but these omissions do not mean that

RECORDS OF THE COLONY OR JURISDICTION OF NEW HAVEN, 1663-1665, at 146-47 (Hoadley ed. 1858).

26. *Id.* at 154.

27. "Certaine Lawes, Liberties, and Orders, made, granted, and established, at severall times, by the Generall Court of New-haven Colony, for and to the Inhabitants of that Jurisdiction, now Collected, and further Published, for the use of such as are concerned in them, wherein they have made use of the Lawes published by the Honourable Colony of the Massachusetts." *Id.* at 571.

28. These twenty-seven provisions are Age, Appearance Non-Appearance, Attachments, Bakers, Barratrie, Bills, Burglarie and Theft, Cask & Cooper, Conveyances fraudulent, Damages pretended, Suits, Distresse, Dowries, Fyre, Fornication, Gaming, Imprisonment, Arrests, Inditements, Levies, Man-slaughter, Oppression, Pound Pound breach, Replevin, Straies, Trespasse, and Witnesses.

29. These twenty-nine provisions are the Preamble, Actions, Appeales, Ballast, Capitall Lawes, Cattell Corn Fields Fences, Charges publick, Childrens Education, Courts for Strangers, Ecclesiasticall Provisions, Escheates, Forgery or Falsifying, Heresie, Impost, Indians, Inkeepers Tipling Drunkenness, Leather and Shoo-makers, Lying, Magistrates, Marriage, Marshall, Masters and Servants &c, Military Affairs, Rates Fines &c, Records, Strangers Sojourners and Servants, Weights and Measures, Wills, and Wolves.

30. These thirteen provisions are Disturbers of the publick Peace, Divorce or a Marriage declared a Nullity, Horses, Incest, Laws without penalty, Mayning wounding, Plantations, Prophanation of the Lords Day, Seamen, Sentences of Judgment, Single persons, Strangers complaining, and Stripes.

31. These sixty-five provisions are Abilitie, Ana-Baptists, Benevolence, Bondslavery, Bounds of townes and persons, Causes small causes, Clerk of writs, Colledge, Condemned, Constables, Criminal causes. Crueltie, Death untimely, Deeds and Writings, Deputies for the Generall Court, Drovers, Elections, Farms, Fayrs & Markets, Ferries, Fines, Fish, Freemen Non-Freeman, Fugitives Strangers, Generall Court, Governour, Hydes & Skins, Hygh-wayes, Idlenes, Jesuits, Impresses, Juries Jurors, Justice, Lands Free lands, Liberties Common, Mills Millers, Monopolies, Oaths Subscription, Payments, Pipe-staves, Poor, Powder, Prescriptions, Prisoners Prisons, Protestation contra Remonstrance, Punishment, Schools, Secresie, Secretarie, Ships Ship-Masters, Summons, Swyne, Tile-earth, Tobacco, Torture, Townships, Treasure, Tryalls, Votes Usurie Watching, Wharfage, Wood, Workmen, and Wrecks of the Sea.

New Haven any more than Connecticut was making a fresh codification of New England law; the same reasons for omission already referred to apply to both colonies.

Thus, it is clear that the Connecticut and New Haven Codes drew primarily on the earlier Massachusetts legislation. However, the influence of the latter code did not end in New England. When, after the conquest of the Dutch, it was desired to frame a code of laws for the Province of New York, the New England codes were studied as precedents.[32] In this way, substantive provisions of Massachusetts law spread southward to New York both directly and via Connecticut. Since, for a number of years, the Duke of York's laws were in effect in parts of New Jersey[33] and Pennsylvania,[34] the effects of the New England legislation went even further. Although this further spread of Massachusetts influence is beyond the scope of this paper, it is worth observing that, although the Massachusetts Code was framed to meet the conditions of Puritan society, many of its provisions were thought suitable to colonial conditions elsewhere. For example, among the important Massachusetts provisions which migrated southward to the Middle Atlantic colonies was that prescribing that, in intestacy, fee simple lands should descend equally to all children rather than to the eldest son by primogeniture as at common law.[35] This basic rule of modern intestate distribution was thus in force in several localities well before Thomas Jefferson's attack on primogeniture in 1776.[36]

The foregoing demonstrates that detailed investigation of the legislation of the various American colonies can provide a fruitful source of information as to the means and extent of intercolonial legal borrowing. Supplemented by studies of local conditions affecting the acceptance or rejection of the legislation of a sister colony, such investigations can also shed much light on the patterns of life and thought in particular localities.

32. See GOEBEL & NAUGHTON, *op. cit. supra* note 4.

33. See 23 NEW JERSEY ARCHIVES xiv-xv (1901).

34. See generally LOYD, EARLY COURTS OF PENNSYLVANIA 13 (1910); CHARTER TO WILLIAM PENN AND LAWS OF THE PROVINCE OF PENNSYLVANIA iv (1879).

35. MASSACHUSETTS COLONIAL LAWS 1660-1672, at 201, cl. 3 (Whitmore ed. 1889); 1 DELAWARE BODY LAWS 1700-1749, at 297, 298 (1752); 1 COLONIAL LAWS OF NEW YORK 9 (1891); 1 ACTS OF ASSEMBLY OF THE PROVINCE OF PENNSYLVANIA 33 (1775). These colonies all provided for a double portion to the eldest son, following the Massachusetts provision which appears to have been based on the Mosaic law as set forth in *Deuteronomy:* see DEUTERONOMY XXI, at 17.

36. 1 JEFFERSON, WRITINGS 43, 139 (Washington ed. 1853).

IX

*The Suffolk County Court, 1671-1680**

GEORGE E. WOODBINE

During the past year two notable contributions have been made to the hitherto much too neglected field of American colonial legal history. Under the auspices of the American Historical Association Judge Bond brought out the Proceedings of the Maryland Courts of Appeals, and now Professors Chafee and Morison make available for us these Massachusetts documents of a full generation or more earlier.

Though some court records of this general nature have long been accessible in printed form, they have been slighted by most of those who have written on the subject of colonial law in favor of the seemingly more definite bodies of written laws, statutes and enactments, which also have, in large measure, been for a long time in print. The insufficiency and misleading character of this latter sort of material when used alone has been either overlooked or unrecognized by most of the writers. As the late Professor Tout has said of the medieval English statutes, these colonial codes are "too often the mere enunciations of an ideal."[1] The idealistic, even Utopian, forces operating in the English colonization of America are well enough known. That this idealism may have so influenced both the spirit and the content of colonial codes of law as to have made them impracticable is more than a possibility; some of the laws which were on the books may have been as unworkable as the ideal Assizes of Jerusalem or much of our own legislation of the

* George E. Woodbine's book review of Samuel E. Morison, ed., *Records of the Suffolk Court, 1671-1680 . . .* (Colonial Society of Massachusetts, *Publications,* XXIX-XXX [Boston, 1933]) is reprinted by permission of The Yale Law Journal Company and Fred B. Rothman and Company from the *Yale Law Journal,* XLIII (1936), 1036-1043.

1. 3 POLITICAL HISTORY OF ENGLAND (1905) 378.

prohibition period. Yet, almost without exception, the writers on colonial history have taken the statements in the colonial laws at their face value, apparently oblivious to the importance of the question of the enforcement or the non-enforcement of any particular provision, or of the interpretation given to the wording of it by the courts. In the matter of legal history, historians, and even lawyers largely, seem to forget that the law under which the people of any particular time or place live must be sought for, in the last analysis, not in what the written laws, or even the courts, *say*, but in what the courts *do*.

In these two volumes of Suffolk County Court Records we have a perfectly clear picture of what the court is doing in the decade that ends approximately the first fifty years of the colony's existence. The picture is made so complete by a wealth of collateral documentary material, that it would be hard to conceive of a more real and welcome contribution to our knowledge of colonial legal history. Though comparatively little progress has actually been made in the study of that history, there have already developed two schools of thought on the question of the exact extent to which the colonists were knowingly and intentionally using English law. Both sides admit that in the eighteenth century, at least for the generation before the revolution, colonial law in all its fundamental aspects was substantially and soundly English. In regard to the seventeenth century opinion has been divided. Some writers have asserted that in these earlier days the colonists consciously and deliberately developed a law of their own which was different from English law, and that they took over the latter law only after the practice and the administration of law came into the hands of lawyers who had been trained in England. To others it seems clear that from the beginning the colonists used, and thought they were using, English law. These two volumes of records strongly support the latter view; they show that this county court, within the specified time limits, was using English law to the best of its knowledge and ability.

That knowledge was none too great, especially in regard to details, presumably because the district was devoid of lawyers. As Mr. Chafee says in his excellent introduction, "the practice of the law was far from being recognized as a profession or even a reputable calling."[2] The only man of legal training in early Boston who

2. p. xxiii.

might have given the community the benefit of his technical knowledge as a practicing lawyer "was practically frozen out by the refusal of the courts to allow him to practice." In place of the professional lawyer and the modern attorney at law, there appeared a character much more ancient than either of these in the history of English court procedure, one to whom our earliest legal treatise devotes a whole book[3]—the *attornatus* of the old plea rolls, a person for whom we have no exact modern equivalent, but who may be described as an attorney in fact for purposes of litigation. If merely for the reason that he represents his principal in court we call him an attorney at law, we must be very careful not to give a modern connotation to that term. He was an important factor in court proceedings; it was legal for the litigant whom he represented to pay him for his services; he could, and did, bring an action in his own name instead of in the name of his principal; as in the case of his English prototype, certain prescribed ceremonies were necessary to constitute him an attorney. For the most part and normally, a man's attorneys, like his foes, were then of his own household. A litigant who could not himself appear would usually appoint his wife or son or brother or father or some other relative, or a close friend, to represent him in court. The business agent in the colony of a merchant in England would often act as the merchant's attorney in the colonial court as a part of his regular duties.

On the other hand we find a number of men who are acting as common attorneys—men who for pay will represent any litigant in court. In this very limited sense they are professional, but still they are not attorneys at law in our modern sense of the word; they do nothing, and can do nothing, which the wife or son or brother who acts as attorney may not do. From these county rolls (and from such records of the higher Court of Assistants as the reviewer has been able to consult), it is quite clear that none of these attorneys does enough legal business to make a living from that source alone. Even those who appear most frequently figure in so few cases over this long ten year period that it is manifest that they must have had some other means of livelihood. Their legal work is incidental. Ultimately these men and the class of agent which they represent will give way to the professional lawyer, not because it was necessary for the attorney to be a lawyer, but because the trained lawyer naturally made the best attorney. The men who

3. GLANVILL, DE LEGIBUS Lib. xi.

appear in the Suffolk County records at this time most emphatically are not professional lawyers. They are not lawyers of any kind unless we wish to dignify by that name laymen who have picked up a smattering of legal knowledge through contact with courts and litigation—just as today in certain parts of rural New England there are town clerks and judges of probate who are not lawyers, and who are not thought of as lawyers, but who have a limited working knowledge of real property law and testamentary law from the very exigencies of their positions. Professor Chafee does wish to call these lay attorneys lawyers. Perhaps it is difficult for any one who has done as much as he to help make Suffolk County populous with lawyers at the present day to think of the same region as being a total vacuum in regard to lawyers in the 1670's. At any rate he would believe that "despite the absence of any recognized bar and of any systematic professional training, the Bay Colony probably contained many a man who might have been described, like Benjamin Mussey, as a 'Subtle Lawyer'."[4] To him they "correspond to the lawyers of today." When we read what the index calls the "disbarment" of Peter Goulding, we are inclined to agree that some of them did, in certain respects, correspond to some of the worst lawyers of today. There are a number of points of analogy: "Peter Goulding, convict of antedating Writings and stirring up persons to goe to law, and buiing of Debts to Vexe others with Suites. The Court Sentanceth him to bee disinabled for pleading in any Court as an Attourney or Assigne (except in his owne case) and that hee doe not undertake to draw up any writings for others without allowance of Authority."[5] But the fact remains that Peter Goulding was not a lawyer, but a layman without any professional or technical training in law. Yet it was he and others like him who were drawing up legal writings, pleading, and doing delegated legal work in general. (Note, in passing, that the English distinction between attorney and pleader does not obtain in this Massachusetts court.) The magistrates, except for the training derived from their experience in official duties, were as innocent of legal education as the attorneys."[6] This being the personnel of the court, we must not expect too much of either its knowledge or its ability. Its records contained in these two volumes must necessarily seem crude

4. p. xxv.
5. p. 186.
6. p. xxvii.

and untechnical in many respects when compared with English records of a similar kind or with the later colonial law reports written by trained lawyers.

It must be admitted, too, that there is in these volumes, in regard to both substantive law and procedure, not a little which is not entirely consonant with the English common law. It is a fact which at first sight would seem to support the contentions of those who argue that the early colonists were using a law of their own that was not English, especially as the same general situation existed in the other colonies. But the fact by itself is worthless as a proof of a non-English element in colonial law. All the distinct and separate parts of the earlier England from which the colonists came likewise had local laws, again in regard to both substantive law and procedure, which were not in agreement with the common law. For in the England of pre-colonial times the common law was not a law that took in all England to the exclusion of all other law, but it was only a part of the non-statutory law under which the great mass of Englishmen lived.[7] Throughout England the common law was impinged upon, modified and even annulled, by local law. In a way the situation was analogous to that which obtained in the case of the manors—in their broad fundamentals all manors were alike, but in the matter of the innumerable details which most directly affected the every day lives of the men on the manors, the custom of each individual manor determined what should or should not be done. Almost from the beginning our legal literature states and restates the fact—which all our courses and text books on common-law actions consistently refused to recognize—that local law was just as much an integral part of the living law of England as the statutes or the common law. Glanvill, after repeatedly pointing out the necessity of recognizing the validity of local law, even when it differed from the law of the king's court, in one place flatly refuses to discuss the customs of the county courts touching a few pleas which he has just mentioned, because of the conflicting customs of these counties, each of which has its own law on the subject.[8] At the very beginning of his treatise, Bracton, in words which would have been perfectly true until comparatively recent times, says, "In England there are many and dif-

7. See Schechter, *Popular Law and Common Law in Medieval England* (1928) 28 COL. L. REV. 269.

8. GLANVILL, DE LEGIBUS Lib. xii, c. 23.

ferent customary laws according to the diversity of places. For the English have many things by custom which they do not have by the law of the land (*ex lege*), as in different counties, cities, boroughs and towns, where it will always be necessary to enquire what the custom of the place is, and how they who allege the custom use it."[9] Throughout his great work he time and time again points out, always as a matter of plain fact, how local law and custom override the common law.

These facts are most fully substantiated by the cases themselves. Thus, for example, there may be a certain local law in regard to a marsh which even the great common-law action of novel disseisin will have to take into account;[10] an act or judgment to be legal must be "according to the custom and the law of the marsh."[11] A custom of Cornwall may be pleaded not only in the local court, but in the king's court before the itinerate justices.[12] The king's justices can not take the usual murder fine when one is found slain in Malvern Forest, "and this by ancient custom.[13] Inextricably connected with the murder fine was the presentment of Englishery; one might well suppose that this practice at least would be uniform in all England. Actually the practice varied greatly in the different counties; in five of them, and in the district beyond the Severn, there was no presentment of Englishery.[14] Instances of this kind could be cited ad infinitum. The best lawyers in England would plead these local laws in support of their cases in the king's court; "the law of the ancient demesne in the court of Cokam" might be just as potent as the common law in determining an issue in the court of Common Pleas.[15] Even in the great court of Exchequer Chamber most of the discussion in a lengthy case could center around the question of the validity of a certain custom, a validity that was not to be determined by the mere fact as to whether or not the particular local law was opposed to the common law—"there are many customs observed in this country which are more opposed to the common law than this is"; "these customs are good, and yet they are contrary to common law."[16]

9. BRACTON fol. 1.
10. SELECT CIVIL PLEAS (Seld. Soc.) no. 98.
11. 6 CURIA REGIS ROLLS 1.
12. SELECT PLEAS OF THE CROWN (Seld. Soc.) no. 3.
13. *Ibid.* no. 128.
14. 11 SOMERSET RECORD SOCIETY lxxvii-lxxx.
15. Y. B. 11-12 Edw. III. 328. (Rolls Series).
16. SELECT CASES IN EXCHEQUER CHAMBERS (51 Seld. Soc.) 114-32.

This local law and custom was still an important factor in the general administration of law in England at the time when the English colonization of America began. Unfortunately there is very little printed material dealing with the subject for this particular date. For the earlier period enough has already appeared to give us a good idea of the extent and scope of these local laws, most of which, like the colonial laws, were put in writing. They are so extensive, so far reaching in so many directions, that the local laws of the colonies sink into comparative insignificance in comparison with them. Any one who is well acquainted with the contents of the four volumes of the *Hunimenta Gildhallae Londoniensis* and with Bateson's two volumes of *Borough Customs*—to mention only the two largest of the repositories of printed source material on this subject—will have difficulty in regarding the laws of the colonies as non-English. The colonists merely did what their English ancestors for hundreds of years before them had been doing—the very English thing of every community developing as much local law of the kind it wanted as its purse and its privileges would allow. The fact that the various colonies had laws which differed from the common law and from the laws of the other colonies does not make them unique in the world of English law. But they would have been unique if their law had been only English common law with no admixture of conflicting local law.

Inasmuch as in England itself we find the courts adapting themselves to local customs inherently repugnant to the common law rule relating to the same matters—as gavelkind and borough English, for example—we should be prepared to find the same sort of thing in the colonies. On our Suffolk County rolls there are a good many grand larceny cases. The crime is not treated as it would have been treated by common law. It is not, as in England, a capital offence, but the thief is held to threefold restitution. Now this penalty is quite in line with our oldest set of laws. Yet no one would for one moment maintain that the Massachusetts law was English because it agreed with Ethelbert's law, or that the makers of it had been influenced by the Kentish king's dooms. Just as readily might one claim for it a Roman origin because it was similar to the Roman law which demanded a fourfold restitution from the manifest thief. It was English because it was an accepted local custom in a community dominated by English law, which found acceptable even such a local law of theft as that mentioned by

Nedeham in the case before the court of Exchequer Chamber already referred to: "In the Isle of Man there is a certain custom that if a man steals a horse he shall not be hanged, but he shall pay a fine for it and shall go quit, inasmuch as the owner can have the horse back, because it can not be eaten. But if he steals a hen or a capon, etc. he shall be hanged for that, because it shall be presumed that he took it to eat, and therefore the owner shall never have them back again, and this custom is good."

In England the amount of divergence of the local custom from the common law was seemingly a matter of little concern; the one essential thing was that the privilege of using the local law should be recognized. According to Chief Justice Prisot the real test to be applied to a local law was that of reasonableness: "I think that a thing can not lie in custom unless that same thing can be within reason, and if it can be within reason, notwithstanding that it may not be in accordance with the common law, yet it may quite well lie in custom."[17] By this test, how many of the colonial laws were non-English? It is clear that the English character of the colonial laws is not to be determined merely on the basis of whether or not a number of these laws are in agreement with the common law. Actually we need not greatly concern ourselves with particular laws of any given colony if only we can be sure that the fundamental law of that colony was based on English law. On that point there is no question in the case of Suffolk County. These records of its county court prove conclusively that the broad foundation on which the administration of law in that court rested was English in nomenclature, rules and procedure.

The terminology is characteristically English. All the usual technical words appear in settings and with a significance that leave no doubt as to their source. The very English special verdict, that salvation of the troubled jury, is met with frequently; we even find that other technicality of the jury system, the double jury of attaint. A large part of the court's business is connected with the very practical matters of trade, contracts, transfers of realty, testamentary affairs, and the administration and settling of estates. The treatment and legal aspects of things of this sort are, in spite of some minor irregularities, clearly and basically English. The effect of English influence is just as marked in many situations of lesser legal importance. Thus, inter alia, the finder must "cry" lost property

17. *Id.* at 127.

which he has found.[18] As in Bracton's time, the man who is proved unoathworthy loses his law.[19] The man who borrows a horse to ride four miles and rides him all the way to Boston, where he sells him, is apprehended by "hue-en-cry" in the good old English way.[20] Even more medieval English in its wording is the story of the constable complained of "for not prosecuting of a hue-en-cry," but "letting it fall in his hands."[21] The husband must pay for his wife's necessaries.[22] Men "purge themselves by oath," as for centuries they had done in England, though here with a local variation in the procedure.[23] The spirit of the Assize of Clarendon is certainly present in the jury that finds John Starkey "suspitiously guilty."[24] Suspicion alone is a sufficient ground on which to base an indictment.[25] Numerous cases of branding found in these records bring to mind the similar practice introduced into the procedure connected with the claim of benefit of clergy by the statute of 18 Elizabeth.[26] The inspection of a woman's body to ascertain whether or not she is pregnant, a procedure which regularly would be initiated by the writ *de ventre inspiciendo,* and one in operation from before the time of Bracton until after the time of Blackstone,[27] is several times mentioned in these records.[28] As in English law from medieval times, the penalty of the pregnant woman who is to suffer corporal punishment is respited till after the birth of her child.[29] In an action for wrongful death, the result is as it would have been in England until after the passage of Lord Campbell's Act.[30]

The forms of action are English. We find Debt (for both money and chattels), Replevin, Trespass, an action for assault and battery, but most of all the Action on the Case. Maitland has described Case as the great residuary action.[31] In Suffolk County it is the

18. pp. 782-83, 847, 847-48, 916.
19. p. 786; BRACTON fol. 185.
20. p. 913.
21. p. 956.
22. p. 694-95.
23. pp. 181, 491, 559, 1013, 1066.
24. p. 258.
25. pp. 521, 524, 808, 844, 1067, 1100.
26. pp. 88, 91, 235, 548, 557, 1163.
27. BRACTON fol. 69b; BRACTON'S NOTE BOOK pl. 137; 1 BL. COMM. 456.
28. pp. 91, 185-86, 189, 690.
29. pp. 233, 424, 521.
30. pp. lx, 166.
31. MAITLAND, EQUITY AND THE FORMS OF ACTIONS (1909) 361.

residuary action par excellence. Not only is it used in cases of negligence, slander, nuisance, undertakings (assumpsits), but for almost every other variety of circumstance as well. Behind many of these unusual cases the basic principle seems to be that of non-feasance. There is Case for non-performance of a contract, "for breach of promise upon a bargain," for breach of a covenant, for not observing the terms of a lease. Case is brought against a keeper who allows a prisoner to escape; it is the action used to obtain redress for false arrest. Not only do we find Case used where Covenant would normally apply, but it is used in place of Account and Ejectment. This perhaps is not so much to be wondered at after all. Both of these actions at common law are highly technical, Account because of its double character—the judgment that there be an accounting followed by the actual accounting before auditors, —and Ejectment because of the employment of the fiction of the casual ejector. In one case at least Trespass, "an action of review upon a trespass," is brought, instead of Case, for a three foot encroachment upon land, which the plaintiff recovers.[32] This may possibly be an actual case of Ejectment whose identity is obscured by the way in which the clerk has enrolled the action. In one of the actions in Case involving an accounting, three men are appointed by the court "to Auditt the Acompts."[33] Here, again, an obscurity in the enrollment may possibly be hiding an accounting before auditors. Mr. Chafee would lay much at the door of the untutored and untechnical clerks who made up the records: "The clerks, . . . on looking at the writ would merely get a pretty good notion of the nature of the claim. Once in a while some such word as 'debt,' 'trespass,' or 'slander' would catch their eyes and be set down in the record as the form of action, but ordinarily these clerks would describe the action as 'case' and let it go at that."[34] This is at least a plausible explanation, and one in keeping with the statements as to the legal knowledge and ability of the personnel of the court which have been made above. It makes quite understandable why we should have a surgeon bringing Case to recover money due him for professional services, while on the very next page we find a cooper bringing Debt to recover money owing him for work done.[35]

There is no separate Court of Chancery in this colony, though

32. p. 287.
33. p. 5.
34. p. xli.
35. pp. 648-49, 650.

there is, by statute, a slight exercise of equity jurisdiction by the law court. This subject of Equity is discussed in detail in the introduction.[36]

The presence of biblicism and Scriptural law is very little in evidence in these records. Much has been written on the effect of the Mosaic law upon the legal situation in the New England colonies. Undoubtedly the influence of that law as an active legal force in their civilization has been greatly overstated. King Alfred's laws contain whole chapters of Old Testament law taken verbatim from the original, but the law of his day was little, if at all, affected thereby. In the colonies the result would seem to have been almost the same. The inclusion of Biblical law in the laws of colonial New England was in itself the manifestation of a trend that was almost as evident in England as in the colonies. This particular phase of Calvinistic influence was, as Professor Goebel has already shown, noticeable in both places.[37]

These Suffolk County records are just as valuable for the student of economic, social and cultural history as they are for the legal historian. Among other things we get a vivid impression of the importance of the colony's sea trade; the vessels were small, but carried an almost unbelievable amount of mixed cargo. The colonists still speak of "the wampum value" of things; some of them utter pewter counterfeit money, and others forge notes. Widows and other indigent women operate something analogous to the tea shops of our own motor age and dispense coffee, chocolate and bottled cider. There are a good many "cook shops" and plenty of taverns. Some of these taverns get their owners into trouble because the bars are kept open on Sunday, which begins on Saturday evening and ends on the next evening. There is much brawling and fighting and an excessive amount of drunkenness, Madeira wine, rum, brandy, beer and cider being responsible. Incidentally, one Henry Tyte is a common drunkard. An unexpected amount of night life shows up in the records, singing, dancing, riotous carousing—even married women are found "drinking and danceing" and sitting in the laps of men who are not their husbands. Much tobacco is used, but smoking in public is forbidden. A considerable number of Indians, already debased by contact with the white

36. pp. l-lvi.

37. Goebel, *King's Law and Local Custom* (1931) 31 COL. L. REV. 416, 423, n. 14.

man, hang around the settlements, do a little petty thieving, seek oblivion in cellars where cider or rum is stored. Negro slaves are not uncommon, but are far outnumbered by indented white servants. Both the slaves and the servants are unruly elements in the community; the latter most often try to run away from their masters. Quite the most striking thing of all is the existence of something we do not ordinarily associate with Puritanism, a widespread and excessive sexual irregularity. This apparently affects all classes; it is hardly connected with prostitution, of which there is very little. There is at least one case of incest, and another having to do with the use of aphrodisiacs. Amazingly frequent are the cases in which married people confess to having committed fornication before marriage. Whatever else Puritanism may or may not have been, in Suffolk County it most certainly was no effective antidote for the biological urge.

"A number of documents have been printed simply because they record the common speech of the day." Briefly we may pick out Collonell,[38] which, as in Milton's sonnet, "Captain or Colonel, or Knight in Arms," is a word of three syllables. As in Elizabethan England, bin and ben occur. Our modern clerk is either clarke or clerke. A pronunciation still maintained in modern England is found in numerous Leiftenants and Leftenants.

All in all the reviewer considers these volumes two of the most interesting books on American colonial history that it has ever been his pleasure to study.

X

*The Beginnings of Partible Inheritance in the American Colonies**

GEORGE L. HASKINS

Thomas Jefferson's attack on primogeniture in 1776[1] is generally considered to have led the way in America for the laws abolishing the descent of fee simple estates to the eldest son. Under these statutes for well over a hundred years the rule has prevailed in the United States that when a person dies intestate, seised of real property in fee simple, such property descends equally to his or her children, subject to the rights of the surviving spouse. Variations appear with respect to succession by the next of kin according to the state statutes of distribution, but among children entitled the general principle of equality of division is preserved. As a recent writer has said, the attitude of this country "may be attributed to the social philosophy in the colonies, and an experience which has been universally unfavorable to the preservation of primogeniture."[2]

In some of the American colonies, however, opposition to the English rule of primogeniture considerably antedated the Jeffersonian offensive of the late eighteenth century.[3] In the early New

* "The Beginnings of Partible Inheritance in the American Colonies," by George L. Haskins, is reprinted by permission of the Yale Law Journal Company and Fred B. Rothman and Company from the *Yale Law Journal,* LI (1941-1942), 1280-1315.

1. JEFFERSON, WRITINGS (Washington's ed., 1853) 43, 139.

2. Morris, *Primogeniture and Entailed Estates in America* (1927) 27 COL. L. REV. 24.

3. Criticism of the English rule, for example, is found in tracts for the purpose of attracting settlers to New Jersey. See WHITEHEAD, EAST JERSEY UNDER THE PROPRIETARY GOVERNMENTS (2d ed. 1875) 324, 389; MORRIS, STUDIES IN THE HISTORY OF AMERICAN LAW (1930) 77-78. For criticism of primogeniture in England itself, see note 255 *infra*.

England colonies, and in Pennsylvania, partible descent was observed, as a result both of custom and enactment, from the seventeenth century on.[4] The practice may be traced first to Massachusetts, where, in the colonies of Plymouth and Massachusetts Bay, an intestate's property descended in this way from the time of the earliest settlements. Throughout the colonial period the law provided, subject to the claims of dower and creditors' rights, for equal division among the children, with a double portion to the eldest son.

It is thus apparent that equal descent of realty among an intestate's children in this country has a dual origin. On the one hand it is to be traced, particularly in the southern colonies, to the Jeffersonian offensive and the influence of the back-country party;[5] on the other hand, in New England and Pennsylvania, it is to be traced to the early practices in seventeenth-century Massachusetts.[6]

4. These colonies—Pennsylvania, Connecticut, Plymouth and Massachusetts Bay—provided for divisible descent, with a double portion reserved to the eldest son. In the eighteenth century it is also found in Delaware. 1 DEL. BODY LAWS 1700-1749 (1752) 297, 298. In Rhode Island both primogeniture and divisible descent were in force, at different times. MORRIS, *op. cit. supra* note 3, at 78, states that except for the years 1718 to 1728 land descended to the eldest son. See 4 R. I. COL. RECORDS (1859) 238, 417; R. I. COL. LAWS (1719) 95, 96. There seems to be some reason to question this. In 1647 it was enacted "that in case a man dyeth intestate . . . they shall make an equal and just distribution of his Estate among those to whom it does belong." 1 R. I. COL. RECORDS (1859) 189-190. In 1667 the Council of the Town of Providence is found making a provision for equal distribution. 1 EARLY RECORDS OF THE TOWN OF PROVIDENCE (1892) 30-34. There is also a suggestion that the large estates in the Narragansett area descended partibly. Channing, *The Narragansett Planters,* in 4 JOHNS HOPKINS STUDIES IN HISTORICAL AND POLITICAL SCIENCE (1886) 16. Further material may be found in Eaton, *The Development of the Judicial System in Rhode Island* (1905) 14 YALE L.J. 148, 158.

For New Hampshire, see MORRIS, *op. cit. supra* note 3, at 103 n. 2, 115.

5. Thus, Georgia in 1777, 19 GA. COL. RECORDS (1912), pt. 2, 455; North Carolina in 1784, 24 N. C. STATE RECORDS (1905) 572-577; Virginia in 1785, 12 VA. STAT. AT LARGE (Hening, 1823) 146; Maryland and New York in 1786, 2 MD. LAWS (Maxcey, 1871) 16, 1 N. Y. LAWS (Greenleaf, 1792) 206; and South Carolina in 1791, 5 S. C. STAT. AT LARGE (1839) 162.

6. Massachusetts disposed of its vestigial suggestion of primogeniture, *i.e.,* the double portion, in 1789. Acts and Resolves, 1788-1789 (May Session), in 1 ACTS AND LAWS OF THE COMMONWEALTH OF MASS. (1894) 395-396. New Hampshire followed suit in the same year; 5 N. H. LAWS (1916) 384; Pennsylvania in 1794: 15 PA. STAT. AT LARGE (1911) 83; Rhode Island in 1798: R. I. LAWS (1798) 287. These statutes were not completely effectual in abolishing primogeniture, since in some jurisdictions today entailed estates descend to the eldest son. This persistence of primogeniture is discussed in relation to its historical background by Morris, *loc. cit. supra* note 2. As to primogeniture in entails in Massachusetts, see note 68 *infra.*

For this reason the sources of partible inheritance in Massachusetts deserve investigation. Their study will aid, moreover, in shedding light on the growth of an indigenous law of probate in the United States. This mode of descent developed early in the Massachusetts colony among relatively homogeneous groups of people and preceded by well over a century the general opposition to primogeniture; thus its growth has a considerable significance in the legal and social history of the seventeenth century.

The earliest indication of the existence of partible inheritance of land in the American colonies is found in the colony of Plymouth. In 1627, Isaak de Rasieres, then Acting-Secretary of New Netherland, visited Plymouth,[7] and observed that "in inheritances they place all the children in one degree, only the eldest son has an acknowledgment for his seniority of birth."[8] Fourteen years later in the neighboring colony of Massachusetts Bay a similar custom was given recognition in two provisions in the Body of Liberties of 1641. In Articles 81 and 82 it is enacted that

> When parents dye intestate, the Elder sonne shall have a doble portion of his whole estate reall and personall, unlesse the Generall Court upon just cause alleadged shall Judge otherwise.[9]
>
> When parents dye intestate haveing noe heires males of their bodies their Daughters shall inherit as copartners, unles the Generall Court upon just reason shall judge otherwise.[10]

How much before 1641 the practice had made its appearance in the Bay Colony the records do not tell. In one or two instances it is plain that each child took something, though in what proportions is not clear.[11] The early entries as to administrations are very brief,[12] and it is sometimes even difficult to tell whether the deceased left a will or died intestate. It may well be that the Plymouth experience was drawn upon in the Massachusetts codifica-

7. 2 BRADFORD, HISTORY OF PLYMOUTH PLANTATION (Ford's ed. 1912) 41-43.

8. In a letter to Samuel Bloomaert, one of the directors of the West India Company. 2 N. Y. HIST. SOC. COLL. 2d Ser. (1849) 339, 352.

9. MASS. COL. LAWS 1660-1672 (1889) 51, c. 81.

10. *Id.* at 51, c. 82.

11. 2 RECORDS OF THE COURT OF ASSISTANTS (1904) 51 (1634-1635), 54 (1635); 1 ESSEX PROB. RECORDS (1916) 11.

12. *Ibid.*, and see note 17 *infra*.

tion.[13] But in any case it is plain that the simple provision in the Body of Liberties formed the basis for the interpretation in the courts, and for later more elaborate acts.

Although Plymouth colony was founded first and had an intestacy law similar in many respects to that of Massachusetts Bay, the latter has been chosen for study because the records are more accessible and the picture we can form is consequently more complete.[14] The period selected for study are the years from the founding of the Bay Colony in 1630 to the establishment of the Province of Massachusetts Bay in 1691, for during this time the chief features of the law of partible inheritance were worked out and may best be seen in operation.[15] No attempt will be made to pursue all the details of the colonial intestacy law, except insofar as is necessary to explain the subject at hand.

Sources for the study are to be found partly in the enactments of the colony, and partly in the interpretation and application of these laws in the records of the courts having jurisdiction in testamentary matters. The former include the acts of the General Court of the Colony;[16] the latter, generally speaking, the records and proceedings of the county courts.[17] The colonial laws cannot be con-

13. Several achievements of Plymouth seem to have been taken over by Massachusetts Bay—for example, Congregationalism, the recording of deeds, the device of codification. See Haskins, *The Beginnings of the Recording System in Massachusetts* (1941) 21 B. U. L. REV. 281, 285 n. 19.

14. The Plymouth intestacy law from the founding of the colony until its coalescence with Massachusetts Bay in 1691 has been reserved for treatment elsewhere. Its possible influence on the Massachusetts intestacy law has not, however, been overlooked. See Part II *infra*.

15. The changes during the brief period of the Andros administration, 1686 and following, have not been given special attention.

16. These enactments are to be found in 1-5 RECORDS OF MASS. (Shurtleff's ed. 1853-1854); MASS. COL. LAWS 1660-1672 (Whitmore's ed. 1889); MASS. COL. LAWS 1672-1686 (Whitmore's ed. 1887); and LAWS AND LIBERTIES OF MASS. (Farrand's ed. 1929). English statutes of the period are not an important source, as will appear.

17. For reasons stated below most of the material used in this study is based on the records of the county and probate courts of Essex and Suffolk.

The Suffolk County Court records survive in two manuscript volumes. One, covering the years 1680-1692, is in a bad state of preservation and is in the office of the Clerk of the Superior Court of Suffolk County. The other, covering the years 1671-1680, is preserved in the Library of the Boston Athenaeum; most of it has been printed in *Records of the Suffolk County Court 1671-1680* (hereafter cited *Suffolk County Records*) in 29, 30 MASS. COL. SOC. COLL. (1933). This material must be supplemented by the Suffolk Files (hereafter cited S. F.), preserved in the office of the Clerk of the Supreme Judicial Court of Suffolk

sidered independently of the court records, since the legislative and judicial functions were really undifferentiated. For, although the county courts were judicial tribunals in name, in a sense they also made law; and conversely, like the assemblies in other colonies, the General Court (the forerunner of the modern legislature) included in its business much that we should today call judicial. Since the seventeenth-century records thus show a fusion of powers entirely characteristic of the day, it should be no cause for surprise when we find the lower courts administering estates in ways unsanctioned by legislative act. Indeed, with regard to several aspects of the law of descent, the enactment by the General Court merely crystallizes existing practices in the county courts.

Attention has been focused particularly on the courts of the seaboard counties of Essex and Suffolk, although other localities have not been neglected. This is partly because many of the records here are available in print, partly because, due to their greater wealth and population, these counties present during the early period of the colony's history more material than the counties to the north and west.[18] It should be stated, however, that the operation of the intestacy law in Essex and Suffolk is entirely typical of the courts elsewhere in the Bay Colony.[19] A major obstacle, how-

---

County, and by the early records and inventories of the Suffolk Probate Court (hereafter cited *Suffolk Prob. Records*).

Most of the material relating to probate matters in Essex County from 1635-1681 has been collected in 1-3 ESSEX PROB. RECORDS (1916-1920), or may be found *passim* in the COLLECTIONS of the Essex Institute.

Appeals from the county courts are in general to be found in 1-3 RECORDS OF THE COURT OF ASSISTANTS (1901-1928), and 1-5 RECORDS OF MASS. *supra* note 16.

18. Suffolk, for example, by an act of 1643, embraced the towns of Boston (including what is now Brookline, Chelsea, Revere and Winthrop), Roxbury, Dorchester, Dedham, Weymouth, Hingham, Braintree, Nantasket (Hull). 2 RECORDS OF MASS. 38. By 1680 it included many more towns in what is today Norfolk County. Essex included, by the same act, Salem, Lynn, Ipswich, Rowley, Newbury and Gloucester. To the north was old Norfolk County, comprising Salisbury, Hampton, Haverhill, Exeter and Dover; slightly to the west was Middlesex, comprising Charlestown, Cambridge, Watertown, Sudbury, Concord, Woburn, Medford and Reading.

19. For example, the probate and administration proceedings in the records of Middlesex County are very similar to those of Suffolk. See *Papers in Cases Before the County Court of Middlesex County, 1649-1663* (unpublished photostatic copy in Harvard Law School Library) 355, no. 837; 487-493, nos. 1181-1183; 494-495, no. 1186; 620-622, nos. 1517-1518; 646-647, no. 1582. See also the unpublished manuscript *Notebook* of Walter Pynchon, a magistrate of Agawam (Springfield). Even here, in frontier Massachusetts, the process of collecting inventories, granting administrations, etc., is very like the practices in the counties to the East. See, *e.g.*, *Notebook* 16 (1641), 18-19 (1641), 68 (1654-1655), 80 (1659). The

ever, to effective investigation in this, as in other branches of colonial law, is the manner in which many of the printed records have been edited.[20] Genealogy, names of persons, inventories have loomed large in the eyes of the compilers, so that the details of administrations, formalities of wills and other valuable data are often omitted.[21] Moreover, in other cases, the records themselves are all too brief in their information.

Before proceeding to a description of the intestacy law, something more must be said of the courts which had jurisdiction in testamentary matters. Unlike the prevailing practice in contemporary England, where such causes belonged to the ecclesiastical courts, the administration of estates was handled in secular courts. Although probate jurisdiction was not conferred on any court by any colony charter until 1691,[22] it had been assumed almost at once by the General Court[23] and by the Court of Assistants,[24] where it remained until the establishment of the first county courts of 1635/36. Shortly thereafter the county courts had begun to take over probate jurisdiction, and in the 1640's the county court became the normal tribunal for such matters. This power was confirmed by enactment of the General Court[25] which by a law of 1649 ordered that

manuscript is in the Harvard Law School Library. [Ed. note: see Joseph H. Smith, ed., *Colonial Justice in Western Massachusetts, 1639-1702* . . . (Cambridge, Mass., 1961)].

20. Notable exceptions are the RECORDS OF MASS., *supra* note 16; RECORDS OF THE ASSISTANTS, *supra* note 17; *Records of the Suffolk County Court, supra* note 17.

21. Even the three volumes of the ESSEX PROB. RECORDS, *supra* note 17, are open to this criticism. More flagrant are the omissions in 3, 4, 5, 40, 41 ESSEX INST. HIST. COLL. (1861-1905); 1, 5, 6, 7 PUTNAM'S MONTHLY HIST. MAG. (1892-1899); 4 ESSEX ANTIQUARIAN (1900). All these contain extracts of wills or administrations which would be of value if only the record had been fully copied. Professor Goebel has recently commented on some of the unfortunate results in entrusting legal research to laymen. Book Review (1938) 43 AMER. HIST. REV. 403, 404-405.

22. 3 THORPE, FEDERAL AND STATE CONSTITUTIONS (1909) 1870, 1881.

23. Examples may be found in 1 RECORDS OF MASS. (1853) 151, 153, 259, 278-279.

24. See 2 RECORDS OF THE ASSISTANTS (1904) 34, 35, 46, 51, 52, 55, 56, 57, 58, 59, 72, 74, 77, 81, 85, etc.

25. For dower, in 1647, see LAWS AND LIBERTIES OF MASS. (1929) 17-18; generally, in 1649, see 2 RECORDS OF MASS. (1853) 281, 3 *id.* at 170; MASS. COL. LAWS 1660-1672 (1889) 200-201. These powers were greatly extended in 1685. See MASS. COL. LAWS 1672-1686 (1887) 122-123.

> . . . when the husband or parents dy intestate, the County Court of that Jurisdiction, where the party had his last Residence, shall have power to assigne to the Widdow such a part of his estate as they shall judg just & equal, as also to divide and assigne to the Children or other heires their severall parts and portions out of the said estate. . . .[26]

Thus it was to the county court that the executor or the next of kin had to go to present the inventory of the deceased's lands and goods. It was here that the validity of the will was tested, the absence of one shown; here that the division of the property was made, subject to the considerable discretion which rested with the court.[27] An appeal would lie to the Court of Assistants in cases where "any person shall finde himselfe greived" with the decision of the county court.[28] That court also had original jurisdiction in at least one case, namely in a matter of dower where the deceased's land lay in more than one county.[29] On particularly difficult questions, an appeal would lie to the General Court, either directly from the county court, or by way of the Court of Assistants.[30] The General Court had original jurisdiction at least in cases to relieve a widow who had not been left a competent portion,[31] or to vary the extent of the shares of the children in instances of hardship.[32] As will appear, however, these matters were generally taken care of under the broad discretion enjoyed by the county court.[33]

When a person died intestate it was the duty of the next of kin or near friend to give notice of the decease to the county court within one month. A schedule of fines adjusted the penalty for not

26. MASS. COL. LAWS 1660-1672 (1889) 201, c. 3. See also 2, 3 RECORDS OF MASS. (1853), *loc. cit. supra* note 25. Administration might be granted of the estates of "merchants, seamen and other strangers" dying within the county before any two of the magistrates of the court. 3 RECORDS OF MASS. (1853) 280-281; MASS. COL. LAWS 1660-1672 (1889) 201, c. 2.

27. This flexibility seems to have been assumed as a delegation from the General Court under cc. 81 and 82 of the Body of Liberties. MASS. COL. LAWS 1660-1672 (1889) 51.

28. 1 RECORDS OF MASS. (1853) 169 (in 1635/36), 238 (in 1638).

29. LAWS AND LIBERTIES OF MASS. (1929) 18 (1647); MASS. COL. LAWS 1660-1672 (1889) 146. For examples, see 3 RECORDS OF THE ASSISTANTS (1904) 90-93, 208.

30. *E.g.*, a will made by a minor. 2 RECORDS OF MASS. (1853) 183. See also 2 *id.* at 266.

31. Body of Liberties of 1641, in MASS. COL. LAWS 1660-1672 (1889) 51, c. 79.

32. *Id.* at 51, cc. 81-82.

33. See note 27 *supra*.

doing so according to the length of the delay.[34] Administration would then be granted by the court, usually to the surviving spouse, next of kin, or near friend of the deceased. Severe fines were meted out to administrators for delay in bringing in the inventory;[35] and an administrator who was found to have sold or "embezzled" any lands or goods before submitting the inventory was, in addition, held personally liable for the debts of the estate.[36] The last two provisions, to judge from the preamble, were enacted in the interest of creditors, who seem to have suffered from the concealment or non-recording of wills and inventories.[37]

The early courts evinced great anxiety to avoid when possible having recourse to the intestacy law, and in all cases of possible intestacy they made every effort to discover the intent, or presumed intent, of the deceased and to administer the estate accordingly. There was a notable lack of insistence on formalities. In fact no formalities of execution seem to have been prescribed by law, and nuncupative wills were allowed freely. Unhampered by the English Statute of Frauds[38] or the Statute of Distribution,[39] the courts could and did look to the deceased's intent and interpreted his will accordingly.

Intestacy resulted in seventeenth-century Massachusetts when a person died (1) leaving a will defective as to some formality of execution, (2) leaving a will without naming an executor, (3) leaving a will which disposed of a part only of the estate, (4) without

34. 2 RECORDS OF MASS. (1853) 287-288.

35. 2 *id.* at 287 (1649); MASS. COL. LAWS 1660-1672 (1889) 200-201, c. 1. There are several cases in which the widow entered on the inheritance in this way before the estate was settled. See "Reasons for Appeal" in Suffolk Files 470/4.

36. 2 RECORDS OF MASS. (1853) 287; MASS. COL. LAWS 1660-1672 (1889) 201.

37. "Whereas it is found by two often experience, that, some men dying and making wills, sajd wills are concealled, & not prooved & recorded, &, others dying intestate, no administration is sought for nor granted, and yet, in either case, the wiues, children, kindred, or freinds of the deceased, or some other, doe enter vpon the lands, & possess themselues of the goods, of the sajd deceased, & the same are many times sould or wasted, before any creditor to whom the deceased was jndebted know of whom to demand, or how to recouer, their just debts, for prevention of such vnjust & fraudulent dealings. . . ." 2 RECORDS OF MASS. (1853) 287.

The recording of wills, administrations and inventories was first ordered in 1639. 1 RECORDS OF MASS. (1853) 276. Apparently ineffective, the order was re-enacted in 1643/44, with penalties attached for non-compliance. 2 *id.* at 59.

38. 29 CAR. II, c. 3 § 5 (1677).

39. 22 & 23 CAR. II, c. 10 (1670). These statutes were applicable in the colonies only so far as accepted.

leaving a will. It is at once apparent with regard to the formalities of executing a will that the sections of the colonial laws concerned with wills say nothing as to whether wills must be in writing or signed or witnessed.[40] It is not strange, therefore, to find so little insistence by the court on such formalities. Several Essex wills, allowed by the court, are unsigned;[41] at least two in Suffolk are unwitnessed;[42] and many others have from one to four witnesses.[43] Unwitnessed codicils are occasionally tacked onto the end of a will,[44] and changes in the will itself are sometimes made merely by blotting out a line.[45] Very often a seal was attached after the signature,[46] but its presence or absence seems not to have affected the validity of the instrument.[47] Such formalities as were observed, in other words, were far from being uniform or consistent. Capacity to make a will was construed somewhat less liberally, for infants were excluded;[48] but there was no prohibition against women's wills,[49] although in one case the consent of a woman's husband is mentioned.[50]

In short, the courts seem to have been little interested in formalities. Provided they were satisfied that the will represented the intent of the testator, they were prepared to overlook such defects as the absence of signature or witnesses. For this reason it was not even insisted that the will be in writing. Nuncupative wills (orally

40. MASS. COL. LAWS 1660-1672 (1889) 35, 121, 140, 200-201; MASS. COL. LAWS 1672-1686 (1887) 32, 157-158.

41. 2 ESSEX PROB. RECORDS (1916) 81, 90, 122, 190, 242, etc. 1 *Suffolk Prob. Records* 210-211. A study of the original wills might, however, show that more wills were signed than the probate records indicate.

42. 1 *Suffolk County Records* 132-133, 230-231.

43. One witness: 1 *Suffolk Prob. Records* 409, 1 *Suffolk County Records* 429; four witnesses: 2 *id.* at 1033.

44. 1 ESSEX PROB. RECORDS 146, 2 *id.* at 36, 51.

45. 1 *id.* at 137.

46. 1 *id.* at 20, 77, 133, 307, 310, 319, etc.; 2 *id.* at 34, 36, 71, 79, 100, etc.

47. See, however, the case of the will of Bozoone Allen (1652) where a seal was accidently torn off and the will promptly taken before the magistrates for inspection. 1 *Suffolk Prob. Records* 287-289.

48. "All persons which are of the age of 21 yeares, and of right understanding and meamories, whether excommunicate or condemned shall have full power and libertie to make there wills and testaments, and other lawfull alienations of theire lands and estates." Body of Liberties, 1641, in MASS. COL. LAWS 1660-1672 (1889) 35, c. 11. See also LAWS AND LIBERTIES OF MASS. (1929) 1; MASS. COL. LAWS 1660-1672 (1889) 121.

49. 1 ESSEX PROB. RECORDS (1916) 3, 12, 24, 40, etc. Women's wills are not frequent, however. See note 86 *infra*.

50. 2 ESSEX PROB. RECORDS (1917) 195.

made in the presence of witnesses) are often found.[51] Equally common are depositions by friends as to the "mind" of the testator: the court, if convinced by the witnesses, thereupon ordered a distribution accordingly.[52] By the same token, the courts even allowed a written will to be varied by oral evidence.[53]

Such practices as to lack of formalities seem less strange when it is remembered that even in England the Statute of Frauds was not enacted till 1677.[54] Besides, with respect to English wills of the time, it has been pointed out that a nuncupative will may be impossible to distinguish from a written will.[55] English wills at this time were very often written on the deathbed. As Swinburn says, "it is received for an opinion amongst the ruder and more ignorant people, that if a man should chance to be so wise, as to make his will in his good health, when he is strong and of good memory, having time and leisure, and might aske counsell (if any doubts were) of the learned; that then surely he should not live long after."[56] It was the "last words" which were all important, and we know that a testator sometimes died before he was able to sign the document.[57] It must also be recalled that even by the seventeenth century the mediæval notion had not quite disappeared that a writing was not dispositive but merely evidentiary.[58] Again, it must be emphasized that the courts were anxious to carry out the deceased's wishes as far as possible, so as to avoid the more mechanical distribution by the intestacy law. The evidence or testi-

51. The earliest we know of in Massachusetts Bay was in 1633. 1 RECORDS OF MASS. (1853) 153. See also 2 RECORDS OF THE ASSISTANTS (1904) 57; 1 ESSEX PROB. RECORDS (1916) 44, 50, 388, 389, 446.

52. 1 ESSEX PROB. RECORDS (1916) 86-87; 2 *id.* at 159-160; 2 *Suffolk County Records* 996.

53. 1 ESSEX PROB. RECORDS (1916) 301-302.

54. 29 CAR. II, c. 3 § 5 (1677).

55. *Early Lincoln Wills, II,* 10 LINCOLN RECORD SOC. PUBL. (Foster's ed. 1910) xvii.

56. SWINBURN, BRIEF TREATISE OF TESTAMENTS (1611) 28.

57. Thus, a will in the Lincoln Consistory Court, dated 1635, which is nuncupative in form, has a note to this effect. See *Early Lincoln Wills, II, supra* note 55, at xvii. See also Brown v. Sackville, Dyer 72 a, pl. 2, 73 E. R. 152 (K. B. 1552), where a dying man's will was taken down in the form of notes; later the will was drawn up, but the man died before he saw it. It was held to be valid.

For an oral revocation of a written and spoken will, see *Early Lincoln Wills, II, supra* note 55, at 14.

58. See *id.* at xvii, and *cf.* Haskins, *Charter Witness Lists* (1938) 13 SPECULUM 319, 322, n. 3.

mony offered might not always be convincing,[59] or it might be disputed.[60] But if it were believed, the defects in the instrument would generally be supplied; and the court would order a distribution "as neere as may bee according to the minde of the deceased."

Intestacy also resulted, as indicated above, when a testator neglected to name executors in a will. This requirement for the validity of a will dated back to a time when the naming of the executor was the heart and core of a will, and was as important as the will itself.[61] By 1600, however, it had become merely a technicality even in England; that is, an administrator was appointed by the ordinary, but the "imperfect" will was annexed to the letters of administration.[62] So, too, in Massachusetts: although the court recognized the will as defective for want of executors, an administrator was appointed and the estate ordered to be distributed according to the will.[63] Such a result is even less surprising in view of the court's attitude toward formalities of execution and the general desire to give effect to the deceased's intent.

No cases have been found of wills which disposed of only part of the estate, with a resulting partial intestacy. The reasons are perhaps not hard to find. In the first place a will was generally written in a testator's last sickness when he had not long to live.[64] Hence the question was not likely often to arise. The fact that

59. 2 ESSEX PROB. RECORDS (1917) 174-175. Compare the case of John Endecott's will in 1659, to which there had been no witnesses. It was voted "by the whole court together that they doe not approove of this instrument to be the last will & testament of the late Jno. Endecott Esqr. Governor." 40 ESSEX INSTIT. HIST. COLL. (1904) 212. A contemporary (1663) Maine case is interesting. Deceased had made a "deede of gyft" which he had signed and sealed. It was presented as a will by his son, but rejected by the court. 2 LIBBY, PROVINCE AND COURT RECORDS OF MAINE (1931) 383-385.

60. 3 ESSEX INSTIT. HIST. COLL. (1861) 190-191.

61. *Cf.* FLETA (Selden's ed. 1647) bk. II., c. 57, § 13; BRITTON (Nichols' ed. 1901) c. 29, § 35. Swinburn repeats the notion explicitly, although he elsewhere qualifies its operation. The naming of an executor, he says, "is said to be the foundation, the substance, the head, and is indeed the true formall cause of the Testament." SWINBURN, *op. cit. supra* note 56, at 8. The early executor is not unlike the *institutio heredis* in Roman law; "testamenta vim ex institutione heredum accipiunt et ob id veluti caput atque fundamentum intellegitur totius testamenti heredis institutio." Institutes of Justinian: II. 20. 34.

62. SWINBURN, *op. cit. supra* note 56, at 340.

63. 1 ESSEX PROB. RECORDS (1916) 200, 226, 314; 3 *id.* at 198; 1 *Suffolk Prob. Records* 407, 409.

64. A comparison of the dates of wills and of the inventories presented after death brings this out clearly.

realty was in effect treated as personalty would further exclude the doctrine as to after-acquired property. In the second place, the legatees were often left their shares in portions—one half, one third, or the like; this was particularly so in the case of near relatives. In addition, residual clauses, the catch-all for oversights, were very common.

For all the lack of insistence on form in early probate procedure, and the effort to discover the deceased's intent, intestacy was common. It has been pointed out that wills were generally made on the death-bed or in the last sickness, despite the scriptural injunction to "Set thine house in order; for thou shalt die, and not live." The wills, for example, very frequently begin with a statement that the testator is "weak in body but of perfect understanding and memory";[65] and, again, a comparison of the dates of wills with the dates of probate shows little time intervening.[66] It was in cases where a man died without leaving a will, or where the formalities of his will were considered too defective, that the Massachusetts intestacy law operated.

The basic rules for distribution were the sections of the Body of Liberties of 1641, and the enactment of 1649 already quoted.[67] These remained substantially unchanged during the period under consideration, although the interpretation was very often fitted to the particular case in hand. Contrary to the common law of England, where the real estate went directly to the heir and did not come within the jurisdiction of the courts of probate, land and personal property in Massachusetts Bay were valued together and were administered in one indiscriminate mass. The surviving inventories of decedents' estates, of which there are a very large number, show this practice in operation. It is within this framework that the custom of partible inheritance among descendants operated with respect to fee simple land.[68] It remains to consider its application in further detail.

65. For example 1 ESSEX PROB. RECORDS (1916) 25, 28, 43, 67, 73, 76, etc.

66. The same is true at an earlier day in England, in spite of the supposed horror of intestacy in the Middle Ages. See Gross, *The Medieval Law of Intestacy* (1904) 18 HARV. L. REV. 120.

67. MASS. COL. LAWS 1660-1672 (1889) 51, 201. See *supra* at 1282.

68. There is some confusion in the records and the early authorities as to whether the rules of partible inheritance extended to a fee tail in Massachusetts, or whether primogeniture prevailed. In Baker v. Mattocks, Quincy 69 (Mass. 1763), the court construed the Province Statute of 1692 as not extending to estates tail, thus holding that the common law rule of primogeniture prevailed.

The first claim against the estate, before the children could participate, was the widow's share. Following the common law rule of dower, the widow's basic portion from almost the beginning seems to have been a one-third interest in her husband's lands for life. By enactment in 1647, a widow received a one-third interest for life in the houses, lands, tenements and hereditaments of which her husband had been seised during coverture.[69] This included also one-third of the personalty absolutely, but the addition was dropped in 1649.[70] A widow was entitled to take in three cases only: (a) when she had lived with her husband, (b) when she had not lived with him but was absent by his consent, through his "meer default," or "inevitable providence," (c) when they had been divorced and she was the innocent party.[71] This interest was free from the claims of creditors.[72] Prior to 1647 there had been no

Cf. THE CHARTER AND GENERAL LAWS OF THE COLONY AND PROVINCE OF MASSACHUSETTS BAY (1814) 230-232. Earlier in the century, however, the court reached an opposite result in two cases: see MORRIS, *op. cit. supra* note 3, at 100-101. Yet in 1723 the council passed a declaratory resolution that the Statute of 1692 did not apply to estates tail: 5 JOURNALS OF THE HOUSE OF REPRESENTATIVES OF MASSACHUSETTS (1924) 279. The real difficulty is that the Statute of 1692 refers explicitly to fee simple estates. The earlier enactments, in 1641 and 1660, in providing for descent to all children, make no distinction between fee simple and fee tail estates: MASS. COL. LAWS 1660-1672 (1889) 51, cc. 81, 82; 201. MORRIS, *op. cit. supra* note 3, at 102, has concluded that partible descent existed as to fee tail estates during the seventeenth century. It is noteworthy that Plymouth enacted in 1685 that "all Lands heretofore Intailed, and that shall be Intailed hereafter, shall descend and enure as by the Law of England the same ought to do." BRIGHAM, COMPACT AND CHARTER (1836) 299. This parallel might tend to weigh in favor of the view that in the Bay Colony rules of partible inheritance applied to estates in fee tail, since no contrary enactment exists. But the use of the words "fee simple" in the 1692 statute equally supports an opposite view. The question must remain an open one until more evidence than the enactments comes to light.

69. LAWS AND LIBERTIES OF MASS. (1929) 17-18.

70. 2 RECORDS OF MASS. (1853) 281, 3 *id.* at 169-170: amendment to the 1647 law to strike out the clause "a third part of her husbands money, goods, & chattels, reall and personall." The effectiveness of the amendment is perhaps open to question. Thus, 3 RECORDS OF THE ASSISTANTS (1928) 91: "by A third part for the wife to be ment a third part of the whole." This declaration was made in 1656 by Governor Endecott. See *id.* at 208, where a committee was appointed by the court "to lay out the peticon[r] hir Just *Thirds* as the law directs." (Italics mine). Curiously enough, the excision in 1649 was voted at the same session (May 2) at which Endecott was elected Governor. 2 RECORDS OF MASS. (1853) 265.

71. LAWS AND LIBERTIES OF MASS. (1929) 17.

72. ". . . freely discharged of and from all titles, debts, rents, charges, judgements, executions and other incumbrances whatsoever had, made, or suffered by her said Husband during the said marriage between them." *Id.* at 17.

provision for dower, as the preamble to the act shows.[73] But a section in the Body of Liberties of 1641 had provided she should not be destitute:

> If any man at his death shall not leave his wife a competent portion of his estaite, upon just complaint made to the Generall Court she shall be relieved.[74]

Evidently this enactment continued in force even after the enactment of the law concerning dower. The courts interpreted the provision as meaning the widow was to have, in addition to dower, whatever more was necessary for her support.[75] The practice was given the added force of enactment in the law of 1649, whereby the county court was given power to assign to the widow "such a part of his personall estate as they shall conceive just and equall."[76] In fact, there are a few indications that the widow was thought in some sense her husband's heir.[77] In the famous Patten litigation, for example, the courts maintained the right to give intestate land to the widow in preference to the collateral heir of her husband.[78] Normally this added share of the widow's would not be exempt from creditor's claims,[79] but there are one or two instances where the widow's entire share—dower and added portion—was first set aside and the creditors thereafter paid proportionately.[80]

When the widow received a disproportionate share of the estate, it was very frequently because there were young children to be

73. "Forasmuch as no provision hath yet been made for any certein maintainance for Wives after the death of their Husbands. . . ." *Id.* at 17. The earlier provision of 1641 was of a very general character and was clearly "uncertain." See note 74 *infra.*

74. MASS. COL. LAWS 1660-1672 (1889) 51, c. 79.

75. 1 ESSEX PROB. RECORDS (1916) 50, 67, 91, 106.

76. 2 RECORDS OF MASS. (1853) 281; 3 *id.* at 170; MASS. COL. LAWS 1660-1672 (1889) 201, c. 3.

77. As when the widow takes the entire estate with apparent disregard of the rights of lineal or collateral heirs. 1 ESSEX PROB. RECORDS (1916) 287-288; 2 *id.* at 130, 165. The 1649 law speaks of "children or other heires" but is completely indefinite as to who are heirs. MASS. COL. LAWS 1660-1672 (1889) 201, c. 3.

78. Patten v. Dyer, 1 RECORDS OF THE ASSISTANTS (1901) 4.

79. See 1 ESSEX PROB. RECORDS (1916) 366.

80. S. F. 245. Also, 2 ESSEX PROB. RECORDS (1917) 162; *cf.* 1 *id.* at 243. The fact that the courts were occasionally petitioned for permission to sell land suggests the added portion may have included some sort of homestead exemption. See S. F. 530, 536. See also 1 RECORDS OF MASS. (1853) 278, 292; 2 *id.* at 254.

reared,[81] or because the children had left home and did not need their portions.[82] Frequently she was required to give security to administer the estate in case of remarriage,[83] or for the portions of the children to be given them at age or marriage.[84] Thus the children's interests would be amply safeguarded. In short, the settlement of the estate with regard to the widow's share shows concern for the maintenance of the home and for fair adjustments in the individual case. The share would apparently vary according to need, and might be anywhere from the basic one-third up to the whole estate.[85]

After the widow had received her allotted share,[86] and the debts of the estate had been paid, the remainder went to the children. If no widow survived, the children took all.[87] From the start, the courts provided a share for all the children.[88] The first enactment on the matter came in 1641, in the sections of the Body of Liberties already quoted.[89] By this law, when parents die intestate, the eldest son is to have a double portion; when there are no heirs male (*i.e.*, sons) the daughters are to take as coparceners. Equality of shares is fairly to be understood from this enactment, both in the calculation implicit in the double portion and in the provision as to coparceny. This manner of division, already operating by the time

81. 1 Essex Prob. Records (1916) 50, 67, 91-92, 363-364, 365.

82. 1 *id.* at 287-288, 2 *id.* at 280. This again emphasizes the suggestion, note 77 *supra*, that the widow was sometimes thought of as her husband's heir.

83. See, *e.g.*, S. F. 530. See also 4 Essex Instit. Hist. Coll. (1862) 64.

84. See, *e.g.*, 1 Essex Prob. Records (1916) 188; 2 *id.* at 110, 146. The new husband might also be required to furnish the security. 2 *id.* at 258, 271.

85. The following are roughly calculated as examples of the varying share of widows in intestates' estates: (a) one-third, 1 *id.* at 294-295, 324, 377, 434; (b) one-half, 1 *id.* at 327, 353, 2 *id.* at 138, 188; (c) two-thirds, 1 *id.* at 173, *bis.* (d) whole, 1 *id.* at 287-288, 357, 363; (e) whole for life or until remarriage, 1 *id.* at 314-315, 2 *id.* at 129-130.

86. The question of the rights of a surviving husband does not seem to have come up in the seventeenth century. No cases in which a husband took on a wife's dying intestate have been found in the material examined. Curtesy was not mentioned in any of the enactments of the Bay Colony. Indeed, it seems to have been unusual for a husband to survive his wife. Almost all the estates of women probated in Essex were those of widows. It is unlikely, also, that many women had property of their own unless they had survived their husbands. At any rate, it is worthy of note that only 8% of all the estates administered in Essex in the ten years from 1675-1685 were those of women. For an eighteenth century case involving a husband's interest in his deceased wife's realty, see Morris, *op. cit. supra* note 3, at 164, n. 7.

87. See, *e.g.*, 2 Essex Prob. Records (1917) 146-147.

88. 2 Records of the Assistants (1904) 51 (in 1634).

89. Mass. Col. Laws 1660-1672 (1889) 51, cc. 81, 82, *supra* at 1282.

the law was enacted,[90] remained the basis of the intestate scheme of distribution throughout the colonial period. An act of 1649 impliedly lodged power in the county court to vary the portions, by authorizing it to "devide and assigne to the children, or other heires, their severall partes and portion out of the said estate."[91] The probate records, at least, show variations in cases of hardship, or where some of the portion had been already received.[92]

The early provision as to the coparceny of the daughters has sometimes been interpreted as meaning that the daughters were to take only in the absence of the heirs male, *i.e.*, of sons. Much evidence in the records shows clearly that daughters and sons took together, both before and after 1641,[93] and that the section merely provided how the daughters were to hold the property in the absence of sons.[94] The ambiguity was removed by the language of the 1649 act which speaks of "children or other heires."[95]

The cases arising during the succeeding years indicate that the law was administered in conformity with the provisions of the early act. Realty was first assimilated to personalty, and the total estate was then divided among the children equally,[96] with a double portion to the eldest son.[97] It made no difference that the intestate might be the mother and not the father,[98] for the 1641 law had spoken of *parents* dying intestate.[99] The portions were often determined with reference to the needs of the child, or of the family

90. See 2 RECORDS OF THE ASSISTANTS (1904) 97.

91. 2 RECORDS OF MASS. (1853) 281, 3 *id.* at 170; MASS. COL. LAWS 1660-1672 (1889) 201, c. 3.

92. See notes 104, 108, 109 *infra.*

93. 2 RECORDS OF THE ASSISTANTS (1904) 97; 1 ESSEX PROB. RECORDS (1916) 11, 62, 91, 118, 173, 201, 325-326; 2 *id.* at 92, 103, 193, 271, 307-308, etc.

94. It does not appear from the records whether or not coparceny was always followed. See 1 ESSEX PROB. RECORDS (1916) 371, where there was an equal division between two daughters, but one took the realty, the other the personalty. However, there may have been an agreement between them to this effect.

95. 2 RECORDS OF MASS. (1853) 281, 3 *id.* at 170; MASS. COL. LAWS 1660-1672 (1889) 201, c. 3.

96. See, *e.g.*, 1 *Suffolk County Records*, 119, 223, 225; 2 *id.* at 996, 1015, 1017, 1067, 1167.

97. See, *e.g.*, 1 ESSEX PROB. RECORDS (1916) 44, 62, 91, 201, 325, 353, 377, 384. See also references cited *supra* note 96, and 1 *Middlesex County Papers, supra* note 19, at 481, no. 1178. *Cf.* 2 LIBBY, PROVINCE AND COURT RECORDS OF MAINE (1931) 335, 429.

98. Examples of the partible rule applied to a mother's estate may be found in 1 ESSEX PROB. RECORDS (1916) 57-58, 62, 201, 371; 2 *id.* at 94, 96.

99. MASS. COL. LAWS 1660-1672 (1889) 51, cc. 81, 82.

as a whole. Thus, the taking might be postponed till age or marriage,[100] or the widow might be given a greater share in order to rear the children.[101] Provision might be made for increasing the portions in case the widow remarried.[102] If the estate were small, the eldest son might not receive the double portion.[103] In two cases, after making the distribution, the court ordered "the overplus to be given to the eldest daughter, she being a lame child."[104] The doctrine of advancements was well recognized in the colony. Although not effectively a part of English law until 1670,[105] it was recognized by Littleton[106] and is spoken of by Coke as being characteristic of distributions in the City of London.[107] As early as 1638/39 it was decided that children who had received their portions were excluded from the distribution.[108] Other instances have been noted during the period.[109]

Specific agreements among those entitled under the intestacy law might further vary the portions,[110] or might confirm them in cases where the law might otherwise not have been followed.[111] Such agreements indicate that the provisions of the intestacy law were treated as directory only, and that the courts were primarily interested in fairness and in an adjustment satisfactory to the parties.

When no children survived the parent, it is not entirely clear how an intestate's estate was divided. The third chapter of the intestacy law speaks of the shares due "children or other heires."[112] What "heires" meant, who were heirs, the Massachusetts enactments do not say. As already indicated, it is conceivable that a wife was thought in some sense her husband's heir.[113] In one case the mother and father became the heirs of an intestate who seems

100. See, *e.g.*, 1 ESSEX PROB. RECORDS (1916) 395, 455; Pynchon's *Note-Book*, *supra* note 19, at 68.

101. See note 81 *supra*.

102. ESSEX PROB. RECORDS (1916) 423.

103. 3 *id.* at 186.

104. 2 *id.* at 171; 2 RECORDS OF THE ASSISTANTS (1904) 91.

105. 22 & 23 CAR. II, c. 10, § 5.

106. CO. LIT. *179b.

107. *Id.* at *176b. For York, where similar rules prevailed, see SWINBURN, *op. cit. supra* note 56, at 117 *ff*. See also Exeter, 2 BATESON, BOROUGH CUSTOMS (1906) 133.

108. 1 ESSEX PROB. RECORDS (1916) 11.

109. 2 *id.* at 142; 2 *Suffolk County Records* 992.

110. 2 ESSEX PROB. RECORDS (1917) 142-143, 160, 162, 176, 398; 3 *id.* at 373.

111. 2 *id.* at 96; 3 *id.* at 199.

112. MASS. COL. LAWS 1660-1672 (1889) 201, c. 3.

113. See note 77 *supra*.

to have died without children;[114] in another, where the parents were dead, the brothers and sisters took equally.[115] In the famous Patten litigation, already referred to,[116] the deceased's nephew—son of a younger brother—was preferred to the deceased's older brothers.[117] The judgment was affirmed by the Court of Assistants,[118] but was modified later by the General Court in such a way as to divide the part not assigned to the widow between the two claimants, nephew and uncle, in equal shares.[119] Such evidence seems to confirm Professor Chafee's statement that the principle of equality among the children extended to others who took in their stead. "If primogeniture was rejected for children, it would also be rejected for collateral heirs."[120]

Thus from the earliest days of the colony, we can see in operation a law of intestacy of which the most marked characteristic was partible descent of realty and personalty among the children.[121] This scheme of intestate succession was a clear departure from the common law of England, where the realty went to the eldest son. It was also unquestionably a violation of the charter of 1629, which gave the colony power to make laws "not contrarie or repugnant to the Lawes of this our Realme of England";[122] and for this reason the system was subjected to censure from the Government in England.[123] In the revision of the Province laws in 1692, the General

114. 2 ESSEX PROB. RECORDS (1917) 132.

115. 2 *id.* at 132. Here, however, the man's estate consisted of the portion left him by his father. But see 2 *id.* at 193.

116. See note 78 *supra.* See generally Chafee, *Professor Beale's Ancestor*, in HARVARD LEGAL ESSAYS (1934) 39.

117. Patten v. Winsley, 1 *Suffolk County Records* 377 (1673).

118. 1 RECORDS OF THE ASSISTANTS (1901) 4.

119. 5 RECORDS OF MASS. (1854) 23-24. *Cf.* the agreement preserved in S. F. 1403/5 in execution of this order.

120. Chafee, *supra* note 116, at 55.

121. Professor Andrews is mistaken in thinking the intestacy law did not become a law in Massachusetts until 1692. Andrews, *The Influence of Colonial Conditions as Illustrated in the Connecticut Intestacy Law*, in 1 SELECT ESSAYS IN ANGLO-AMERICAN LEGAL HISTORY (1907) 431, 437.

122. 3 THORPE, FEDERAL AND STATE CONSTITUTIONS (1909) 1853.

123. For example, the objections by the Attorney General in 1667, replied to by the General Court, in 5 RECORDS OF MASS. (1854) 199. See comment in 1 HUTCHINSON, HISTORY OF THE COLONY AND PROVINCE OF MASSACHUSETTS BAY (Mayo's ed. 1936) 377.

In an earlier day, when objection was made by the colonists in 1646 to the arbitrary power of the magistrates, Winthrop and others felt called upon, in justifying the correspondence between colonial law and common law, to claim the highly dubious authority of English law for the eldest son's double portion.

Court felt obliged to insert in the chapter on wills and intestacy a long preamble justifying divisible descent and the departure from English law.[124] In the eighteenth century a controversy arose over the legality of the Massachusetts law of intestate distribution. This was the case of *Phillips v. Savage*, which began in the Suffolk County Court in 1733 and was ultimately appealed to the Privy Council in 1738/39.[125] Primarily it put in issue the constitutionality of the section of the Act of 1692 dealing with intestacy.[126] Although the latter was in general declaratory of prior enactments and of the law long administered in the courts, the earlier acts had never been passed on in England.[127] The Connecticut intestacy law, which apparently was based on that of Massachusetts Bay, had been declared illegal only a few years before by the Privy Council in *Winthrop v. Lechmere* (1728).[128] Nonetheless in *Phillips v. Savage* the distribution made in accordance with the 1692 act was affirmed. In recommending this result to the King, the report emphasized the approval of the Massachusetts laws in 1695 and 1731 by the Lords Justices in Council.[129] In also emphasizing that the intestacy law was of long standing, the Committee implied that it had had its approval by use and custom.[130] No doubt they were impressed by the respondent's brief, which stressed the reasonableness of the law with reference to the social and economic conditions of the col-

---

Morris, *Massachusetts and the Common Law* (1926) 31 AMER. HIST. REV. 443, 447.

124. "Whereas estates in these plantations do consist chiefly of lands, which have been subdued and brought to improvement by the industry and labour of the proprietors, with the assistance of their children, the younger children generally having been longest and most serviceable unto their parents in that behalf, who have not personal estate to give out unto them in portions, or otherwise to recompense their labours. . . ." THE CHARTER AND GENERAL LAWS OF THE COLONY AND PROVINCE OF MASSACHUSETTS BAY (1814) 230.

125. The report of the Privy Council is in 3 ACTS OF THE PRIVY COUNCIL, COL. SER. (1910) 433. The decree is in no official report, but may be found in 13 MASS. HIST. SOC. PROC. (1873-1875) 101-103.

126. THE CHARTER AND GENERAL LAWS OF THE COLONY AND PROVINCE OF MASSACHUSETTS BAY (1814) 230.

127. Except for the objections to the provisions against forfeitures by the Attorney General in 1667, note 123 *supra*.

128. 3 ACTS OF THE PRIVY COUNCIL, COL. SER. (1910) 139-151. The decree is printed in 5 MASS. HIST. SOC. COLL. 6th ser. (1892) 496-509. Further papers connected with the case may be found in 5 CONN. HIST. SOC. COLL. (1896) 418 *ff.*

129. 3 ACTS OF THE PRIVY COUNCIL, COL. SER. (1910) 435, 436. *Cf.* 5 MASS. HIST. SOC. COLL. (1862) 78-80.

130. 3 ACTS OF THE PRIVY COUNCIL, COL. SER. (1910) 436.

ony.[131] In this way the Massachusetts intestacy law was approved by the royal authority.

The law of partible descent seems on the whole to have achieved fair and desirable results. The absence of formalities allowed the courts to give effect to the deceased's intent, insofar as that intent could be ascertained, and the courts seem to have administered estates wisely and well. All members of the family were in some way provided for, and the flexibility of the law permitted adjustments to the needs of the individual case. Thus, those children who had received their portions or who had left home were excluded from the distribution. If the children were young, the importance of preserving the family unit was recognized by giving the widow the bulk of the estate. Again, in cases where the need of the widow or of a particular child was very great, an additional share was allotted.

That the law met with approval we cannot doubt. Not only was it consistently reaffirmed and corroborated by enactment and court practice, but many wills followed exactly the provisions of the intestacy law as to equality of distribution and the double portion to the eldest son.[132] This general acceptance is proof of the law's close adaptation to the colonists' needs. But when this is admitted, we are led to inquire how partible descent came to be adopted in the first place. To this question, in the absence of any direct evidence, no final answer can be given. Analysis of the various forces at work will, however, clarify the possible solutions of the problem.

* * * * *

Several theories have been advanced to explain the existence of partible inheritance in Massachusetts and other New England colonies. Among legal writers, it has often been said that the American scheme of partible inheritance is based on the English Statute of Distribution,[133] but this notion is clearly false as far as New England is concerned. The obvious objections are that the early Massachusetts laws of 1641 and 1649 long antedate this statute

131. 5 MASS. HIST. SOC. COLL. (1862) 78-80.

132. See 1 ESSEX PROB. RECORDS (1916) 81, 124, 167, 238, 368, 399. See also, S. F. 120, 333/10; 1 *Suffolk Probate Records* 287-289; 4 ESSEX INSTIT. HIST. COLL. (1862) 68; 40 *id.* at 214.

133. 22 & 23 CAR. II, c. 10. See REPPY AND TOMPKINS, HISTORICAL AND STATUTORY BACKGROUND OF WILLS (1921) 81; 1 WOERNER, THE AMERICAN LAW OF ADMINISTRATIONS (3d ed. 1923) § 64.

in providing for equal distribution, and that the statute concerned personalty and not land. On a more serious level, several historians have urged that partible inheritance is the necessary consequence of the provisions in colonial charters by which the land was granted to be held as of the royal manor of East Greenwich, Kent, in England, in which inheritances were supposedly partible by the custom of gavelkind.[134] Others have found the source in Mosaic law[135] or the economic and social conditions in the colonies.[136]

The theory which looks back to gavelkind and the charter merits some discussion.[137] Its proponents have contended that land in Massachusetts was attached to the Kentish manor for the express purpose of making gavelkind an incident of the tenure.[138] The chief peculiarity of this system of tenure was that the lands of a decedent, instead of descending to the eldest son, were divided equally among all the sons. Because of a general presumption at common law that gavelkind attached to all lands in Kent,[139] it was thought to follow that it obtained in East Greenwich and was therefore extended to New England by the seventeenth century charters. The apparent similarity between this mode of descent and that in seventeenth-century Massachusetts led to the easy conclusion that the Massachusetts custom was gavelkind.

134. Lands included in the grant to the Massachusetts Bay Company were to be held of the king, as of the manor of East Greenwich in the County of Kent, "in free and common Socage and not in Capite, nor by Knights Service." 3 THORPE, FEDERAL AND STATE CONSTITUTIONS (1909) 1849. The clause is found in contemporary New England grants: New England Council, 3 *id.* at 1834; Maine, 3 *id.* at 1627; Connecticut, 1 *id.* at 536; Rhode Island, 6 *id.* at 3221.

135. MORRIS, *op. cit. supra* note 3, at 111-112; Eggleston, *The Land System of the New England Colonies* in 4 JOHNS HOPKINS STUDIES, *supra* note 4, at 56. Of the same opinion was Peter Oliver, Chief Justice of Massachusetts, in 1773. I LITERARY DIARY OF EZRA STILES (1901) 331.

136. Notably Andrews, *loc. cit. supra* note 121; and Chafee, *supra* note 116, at 50.

137. For a complete discussion of the "gavelkind theory" see a paper by Haskins, *Gavelkind and the Charter of Massachusetts Bay*, in the forthcoming volume of TRANSACTIONS of the Colonial Society of Massachusetts. [Ed. note: see Col. Soc. of Mass., *Trans. and Colls.*, XXXIV (Boston, 1943), 483-498].

138. A partial list of these writers may be found in MORRIS, *op. cit. supra* note 3, at 106, n. 2.

139. Browne v. Brokes, 2 Sid. 153, 82 E. R. 1307 (K. B. 1659): "fuit agrée per touts que si terre soit alledge d'estre en Kent, serra presume d'estre Gavelkind, si non que le contrary soit prove." Again, Wiseman v. Cotten, 1 Sid. 135, 138, 82 E. R. 1015, 1017 (K. B. 1661): "touts terres in Kent sont suppose destre Gavelkind." See also, ROBINSON, GAVELKIND (1897) 44.

Comparison of the incidents of gavelkind with the customs of descent in Massachusetts provides convincing evidence that gavelkind did not exist in the Bay Colony. There are roughly five main characteristics of gavelkind.[140] (1) On the death of a proprietor, the lands were divided equally among his sons or their representatives. (2) The wife's dower, instead of being one-third as at common law, one-half of the lands of which her husband had been seised during coverture. (3) The husband's right of curtesy extended to merely one-half, instead of all, his wife's lands. (4) The heirs came of age for purposes of alienation at fifteen. (5) The proprietor's estate was not forfeited for felony, as it was at common law, but the heirs succeeded.

Equal succession was a marked characteristic of the law of descent in Massachusetts Bay; but, as shown above, sons and daughters took equally without discrimination as to sex.[141] Also, the Massachusetts provision for the double portion to the eldest son again varies the gavelkind formula. In the matter of dower, it is clear that the widow received one-third of the lands for life, and for a time one-third absolutely of the personalty.[142] Curtesy is not mentioned in the laws or records;[143] and the age of alienating land was twenty-one, as at common law.[144] In only one respect, namely, that lands were not forfeited for felony, is there a close resemblance to gavelkind. It seems probable, however, that this is to be traced not to the Kentish custom but to a Puritan mistrust of the feudal system and its incidents.[145] This interpretation is borne out by the fact that the section of the laws providing that there shall be no forfeitures includes the prohibition with a long list of other feudal privileges.[146] In short, it is impossible to accept such a contention as that of Judge Gray that "the Body of Liberties contained articles upon each of the principle points distinctive of the Kentish tenure of gavelkind."[147]

140. For full discussion of these and other incidents, see especially ROBINSON, GAVELKIND (1897) bk. II; ELTON, TENURES OF KENT (1867) 39-44; Neilson, *Custom and the Common Law of Kent* (1925) 38 HARV. L. REV. 482.

141. See note 93 *supra*.

142. See notes 69, 70 *supra*.

143. See note 86 *supra*.

144. MASS. COL. LAWS 1660-1672 (1889) 35, c. 11; 45, c. 53.

145. On this distrust of the English land system, see Haskins, *The Beginnings of the Recording System in Massachusetts* (1941) 21 B. U. L. REV. 281, 301-302.

146. MASS. COL. LAWS 1660-1672 (1889) 35, c. 10.

147. Jackson v. Phillips, 14 Allen 539, 561 (Mass. 1867).

A further weakness in the gavelkind theory is that this system of tenure almost certainly never prevailed in East Greenwich itself. The common law presumption that gavelkind attached to all lands in Kent was merely a general rule to aid the courts; it was a rebuttable presumption.[148] There is ample evidence that many lands in Kent were not gavelkind lands.[149] Much of it had never been subject to the custom, and more was disgavelled by Act of Parliament in the sixteenth century.[150] It is true that there is no direct evidence in the Greenwich records or elsewhere that gavelkind did not prevail there.[151] However, the absence of such evidence is significant[152] in view of the fact that at the time of the Norman Conquest East Greenwich was held in frankalmoigne or free alms, as appurtenant to the manor of Lewisham, by the Abbot of St. Peters at Ghent in Flanders.[153] Admittedly gavelkind did not attach to lands held since the Conquest in frankalmoigne.[154] Since the manor remained in the hands of the Abbot in this tenure until the suppression of the alien priories in 1413,[155] by which time the limits of gavelkind were well fixed, there can be little question that it was not subject to gavelkind.

Finally, there seems good reason to question how far descent in one set of lands would affect that in another set. Elton, a high authority on gavelkind, states categorically that the tenure of gavel-

148. ROBINSON, GAVELKIND (1897) 38-39.

149. *Id.* bk. I, ch. v.

150. Notably by the statute 31 HEN. VIII, c. 3 (1539), and 2 & 3 EDW. VI, c. 1 (1549).

151. The best general account of the history of Greenwich is in 1 HASTED, HISTORY OF KENT (1797) 383. There is nothing on our point. The charters and royal grants of the manor are silent in this respect, as are the court rolls and Domesday Book. For the charters, from the Anglo-Saxon period on, see 1, 2 VAN LOKEREN, CHARTES ET DOCUMENTS DE L'ABBAYE DE SAINT PIERRE (1868) *passim.* For the court rolls, see Barnes, *Land Tenure in English Colonial Charters of the Seventeenth Century* in ESSAYS IN COLONIAL HISTORY PRESENTED TO CHARLES MCLEAN ANDREWS (1931) 4, 33. See also 1 DOMESDAY BOOK (1783) 12 b (under "Levesham").

152. See a survey of the customs of the manor in 1695 in KIMBELL, AN ACCOUNT OF THE LEGACIES, GIFTS, RENTS . . . OF THE PARISH OF ST. ALPHEGE, GREENWICH (1816) 183, 206.

153. The pertinent charters and grants may be found in 1 VAN LOKEREN, *op. cit. supra* note 151, nos. 38, 124, 159, 170, 215. They are discussed further in Haskins, *Gavelkind and the Charter of Massachusetts Bay, supra* note 137, at n. 54.

154. ROBINSON, GAVELKIND (1897) 73-75, ELTON, TENURES OF KENT (1867) 236 *ff.*

155. By the statute of 1 HEN. V, c. 7 (1413).

kind could not be created out of the bounds of Kent; "nor can any custom," he says, "whether borough-English, partition in descent, or anything else, be newly imposed upon land by any royal grant."[156] On its face, therefore, it would not seem possible that gavelkind could be extended to the colonies by royal charter, even supposing that gavelkind existed in East Greenwich.

The explanation of partible inheritance in Massachusetts is not, then, to be sought in a transplantation of gavelkind customs from the manor of East Greenwich. Proponents of this view have been deceived by the superficial resemblance between different rules of partible inheritance. The approach, however, has merit insofar as it brings into consideration the influence of the colonists' English background. We must not forget that a number of the settlers did come from Kent[157] and that the general gavelkind analogy of partibility might for that reason have suggested itself to them. At the same time, partible descent existed in many places in England outside of Kent,[158] and there is little in Massachusetts history which leads us to derive its intestacy law necessarily from that of Kent.[159] This caution is even more cogent in view of the marked differences in the details of the two laws of descent. It is rather to elements in the colonists' background that we must turn in order to obtain further light on their adoption of a scheme of partible inheritance.[160]

It seems fair to say that the scheme of partible inheritance in cases of intestacy, which we find in the colonies of Plymouth and Massachusetts Bay in the seventeenth century, had its origin either

156. Elton, Tenures of Kent (1867) 157. He is supported by Robinson, Gavelkind (1897) 55, 61, who is explicit to the effect that gavelkind customs cannot be imposed on land which had never been subject to them. For a consideration of early cases, see Haskins, *Gavelkind and the Charter of Massachusetts Bay, supra* note 137, at n. 60.

157. *Cf.* Hoar, in Amer. Antiq. Soc. Proc. (1883-1885) 369.

158. This is discussed pp. 1302-1304 *infra.*

159. See, however, the reply by the General Court in 1667 to certain objections by the Attorney General, in 5 Records of Mass. (1854) 199. The assertion may merely be a legal argument which they hoped would stick. It is worth noting here that partible inheritance, whether in or outside Kent, was frequently termed gavelkind in the sixteenth and seventeenth centuries. Elton, Tenures of Kent (1867) 53-54.

160. The notions that Mosaic law or economic conditions in the colony are to be looked to as the origin of the practise are not discussed independently from the main exposition below. Neither has ever been worked out in any detail, so that it seemed advisable to include such references as there are to the theories in the general treatment.

in the ideas or experience growing out of the settlers' previous backgrounds, or in the environment in which they found themselves, or in a combination of both. Five possible sources of the practice may be suggested. (1) The Dutch or Roman Law scheme of intestate succession, with which the Plymouth settlers, at least, were acquainted from their sojourn in Leyden. (2) Manorial or borough customs of inheritance in those parts of England from which the colonists came. (3) Practices of intestate distribution of personalty made by the courts of the ordinaries in England. (4) The Mosaic rule of descent laid down in the Old Testament and interpreted in relation to Puritan social and religious ideals. (5) The exigencies of social and economic life in the new frontier community in which the settlers found themselves.

The Dutch scheme of intestate succession cannot be ignored, but it is difficult to assess its rôle with any certainty. While it could not have influenced the settlers in Massachusetts Bay directly, it might have done so indirectly through Plymouth. More than one of the achievements of Plymouth Colony seem to have been borrowed by its neighbor:[161] for example, Congregationalism,[162] the device of codification,[163] and the elements of the recording system.[164] The possibility that Massachusetts Bay drew upon Plymouth experience is therefore one which throughout the discussion must not be overlooked. Moreover, it will be remembered that the characteristic feature of colonial partible inheritance—equal succession among all children, and a double portion to the eldest son—made its first appearance in Plymouth.[165] Many of the Pilgrims had lived in Holland in close contact with the Dutch.[166] Many

161. Morison, *The Pilgrim Fathers* (1937) N. H. MAYFLOWER SOC. PROC. 5, dissents from this proposition, except possibly for Congregationalism. But see notes 163, 164 *infra*.

162. *Id.* at 5.

163. Goebel, *King's Law and Local Custom in Seventeenth Century New England* (1931) 31 COL. L. REV. 416, 418-419, n. 7.

164. Haskins, *The Beginnings of the Recording System in Massachusetts* (1941) 21 B. U. L. REV. 281, 285 n. 19. Such inter-colony borrowing was by no means exceptional. Thus, Connecticut and Pennsylvania seem to have borrowed their intestacy law from Massachusetts Bay, and Delaware in turn from Pennsylvania. As Professor McIlwain has shown, it can be seen in constitutional doctrine as well as in private law. *Cf.* MCILWAIN, CONSTITUTIONALISM AND THE CHANGING WORLD (1939) 237.

165. See note 8 *supra*.

166. See generally DEXTER, THE ENGLAND AND HOLLAND OF THE PURITANS (1905). For real estate transactions, see *id.* at 601-641; and *cf.* PLOOIJ, THE PILGRIM FATHERS (1932) 60, 102.

had died there. Before 1620, there were 288 known members of the Pilgrim group in Leyden, of whom 33 became citizens of Leyden;[167] and between 1620 and 1633, 81 members of Plymouth Colony migrated from Leyden.[168] There would therefore have been opportunity to learn of the Dutch system of intestate succession.

Although there was great confusion in the Dutch law of intestacy in the sixteenth century,[169] and it varied greatly from place to place,[170] we know with considerable certainty the features of the law obtaining in the two Pilgrim havens, Amsterdam and Leyden, in the early seventeenth century. The Political Ordinance of 1599, accepted by these two towns along with others, provided for: (1) equal division among children, male and female alike; (2) failing children, equal division between the deceased's parents, if both were living; (3) if only one parent survived, then one-half to such parent, one-half to the brothers and sisters who were children of the deceased parent; (4) if neither parent survived, then to the deceased's brothers and sisters on the two several sides.[171] The obvious resemblance of this scheme to that in use in Massachusetts Bay must not lead us to accept a hasty analogy. While the double portion for the eldest son is conspicuously absent from the Dutch law, the points of resemblance are noteworthy. In Massachusetts the children, male and female, took equally, as under the Dutch Ordinance; and, in cases which have been noted, where the intestate had no children, Massachusetts seems to have followed a rule similar to points (2) and (4) above.[172] Moreover, it is very likely that under the Ordinance of 1599 a widow might under some circum-

167. DEXTER, *op. cit. supra* note 166, at 648-649.

168. *Id.* at 650-652.

169. Excellent brief treatments of the Dutch intestacy law at this time may be found in LEE, AN INTRODUCTION TO ROMAN-DUTCH LAW (1915) 327 *ff.;* 1 VAN LEEUWEN, COMMENTARIES ON THE ROMAN-DUTCH LAW (Decker's ed. 1921) bk. III, ch. xii.

170. Generally speaking there were two laws of intestacy, the Aasdoms-recht in North Holland, and the Schependoms-recht in South Holland. The districts are separated by the river IJssel. An attempt was made in 1581 to establish a common law of intestate succession for the two districts. 1 GROOT PLACAET-BOECK (1658) 335; also, an "interpretation," 1 *id.* at 342. But the northern towns refused to adhere to the new scheme, which was based largely on the Schependoms-recht. The Political Ordinance of 1599 was based partly on the old Aasdoms-recht, partly on the Schependoms-recht, and partly on Roman law. 1 *id.* at 343.

171. *Ibid.*

172. 2 ESSEX PROB. RECORDS (1917) 132, cited in notes 114, 115 *supra.*

stances share in the deceased's estate as an heir.[173] Such—outside of customs like freebench[174]—had never been the law of England. Yet in some Massachusetts cases the widow seems to have been thought in some sense her husband's heir.[175] The analogy is not to be pushed too far. But it is worth noting that in another field of law, namely, the adoption of the recording system, Dutch influence may well have been a factor of weight.[176] It is conceivable, therefore, that we may look for at least one root of partible inheritance in the Dutch law of intestacy obtaining in Amsterdam and Leyden.

Turning to local customs in the districts in England from which the colonists came, we find a perhaps more obvious source of the Massachusetts law of partible inheritance. The generalization that in England land invariably descended to the eldest son is an inaccurate one and subject to many qualifications. For example, since the early Middle Ages land had been divided in many manors and towns throughout England among all the children of the deceased. These customs were by no means restricted to Kent. Partible descent, in fact, seems to have been the normal manner of descent of lands in England until the Normans, for military and governmental reasons, began to force on land-owners the system of primogeniture.[177] In spite of the steady pressure of the royal courts to eliminate exceptions, such customs persisted beyond the Middle Ages in various manors and boroughs among certain classes of tenants below the top brackets of the feudal system.[178] For our purposes it is significant that such customs of partible descent were well-known in districts from which the early New England settlers came, and were not confined to Kent.

173. Lee, *The Intestate Succession of Husband and Wife in Roman-Dutch Law* (1911) 12 J. SOC. COMP. LEG. 310, 315. The Ordinance of 1599, of which the provisions are considerably more elaborate than sketched above, provides in Article 14 that in all cases not expressly covered, Roman law is to control: "Eyntlick alle andere Successien daer van hier vooren niet en is ghedisponeert, sullen ghereguleert worden nae de waerlijcke beschreven Rechten." The pertinent provision in Roman law is D. 38, 11.

174. See note 207 *infra.*

175. See note 77 *supra.*

176. Haskins, *The Beginnings of the Recording System in Massachusetts* (1941) 21 B. U. L. REV. 281, 289-291.

177. 2 POLLOCK AND MAITLAND, HISTORY OF ENGLISH LAW (1895) 260-262. Tacitus noted the existence of partible descent among the Germans in the second century. TACITUS, GERMANIA, XX.

178. *Cf.* PLUCKNETT, CONCISE HISTORY OF THE COMMON LAW (3d ed. 1940) 471-472.

Instances of partible inheritance are found most extensively in manors in the East of England, particularly in Norfolk and East Anglia.[179] It is also found in Cambridge,[180] Dorset,[181] Gloucestershire,[182] Leicestershire,[183] Middlesex,[184] Nottinghamshire,[185] and Suffolk[186] not to mention other counties.[187] Such customs were not confined to manors, but existed in many boroughs and towns,[188] as Dover,[189] Exeter,[190] Ipswich,[191] Torksey,[192] and Wareham.[193] Much of the evidence is from the mediæval period; and until more of the later court rolls have been studied, it is not possible to say with certainty how late some of these customs persisted. At the same time, the tenacity of mediæval local customs throughout England until well into the modern period is a factor of importance which is frequently overlooked.[194] There is good evidence that partible inheritance was well known by local custom in the sixteenth and seventeenth centuries;[195] indeed, it had not entirely disappeared by the time of the First Report of the Commission on Real Property in 1829.[196]

179. 2 POLLOCK AND MAITLAND, HISTORY OF ENGLISH LAW (1895) 268; Douglas, *The Social Structure of Medieval East Anglia* in 9 OXFORD STUDIES IN SOCIAL AND LEGAL HISTORY (Vinagradoff's ed. 1927) 260 *ff.;* GRAY, ENGLISH FIELD SYSTEMS (1915) 337; Homans, *Partible Inheritance of Villagers' Holdings* (1937) 8 ECON. HIST. REV. 48, 51-55; Hudson, *Three Manorial Extents of the Thirteenth Century* (1901) 14 NORFOLK ARCHAEOLOGY 46, n. 1.

180. Homans, *supra* note 179, at 53, n. 2.

181. TAYLOR, GAVELKIND (1663) 101.

182. ELTON, TENURES OF KENT (1867) 54, 170, n. m.

183. Homans, *supra* note 179, at 55, n. 1.

184. ELTON, TENURES OF KENT (1867) 169.

185. *Id.* at 54.

186. *Ibid.* Homans, *supra* note 179, at 53, n. 2.

187. ELTON, TENURES OF KENT (1867) 54, 169-170.

188. CO. LIT. *110 b.

189. 2 BATESON, BOROUGH CUSTOMS (1906) 133.

190. 2 *id.* at 132, 133.

191. 2 *id.* at 132.

192. 2 *id.* at 133.

193. TAYLOR, GAVELKIND (1663) 101.

194. This is particularly true in the boroughs, where the customs were early reduced to writing. A very good general treatment of the importance of local custom in mediaeval and early modern England may be found in Schechter, *Popular Law and Local Custom in Medieval England* (1928) 28 COL. L. REV. 269.

195. See Sympson v. Quinley, 1 Vent. 88, 86 E. R. 61 (K. B. 1670), Newton v. Shafto, 1 Sid. 267, 82 E. R. 1097 (K. B. 1665). In some places partible descent was changed by royal acts similar to disgaveling statutes. Thus, Oswaldbeck, Notts, 32 HEN. VIII, c. 29 (1540); Exeter, Devon, 23 ELIZ., c. 12 (1581); Stepney, Hackney and Mile End, 21 JAC. I, c. 6 (1623).

196. FIRST REPORT REAL PROPERTY COMM. (1829) 254. The Report indicates

Special incidents might sometimes attach to such customs—as in several places near London, where, if the land were worth under £5, it descended to the youngest son, but, if over that value, it was partible among all sons.[197] Yet it should be noticed that these customs were not gavelkind and seldom carried with them any of the characteristics of gavelkind. In most of these cases land merely descended in equal shares among the children. Sometimes "children" meant sons,[198] sometimes it meant that daughters as well as sons were included to every degree of relationship.[199] The details might vary indefinitely from place to place,[200] but the underlying idea of partibility maintained itself with extraordinary tenacity.

In order to make the connection between English and colonial customs plainer, the sources of New England immigration in the seventeenth century must be considered. Bearing in mind the possibility that Massachusetts Bay borrowed the basic idea of its intestacy law from Plymouth, we consider first the districts in England from which the latter colony was settled. The Pilgrims were predominantly from manors and towns in East Anglia, particularly from Norfolk and Essex; nearly one-half of those whose origins are known came from these counties.[201] Yorkshire, Nottinghamshire, Lincoln and Kent were also strongly represented.[202] It becomes apparent at once, in comparing these sources of origin with the places where partible inheritance prevailed, that many of the Plymouth settlers—countrymen and townsmen—had had opportunities of knowing of these customs. Particularly is this likely when it is remembered that by and large the Pilgrims were men and women of humble origin, for the most part townsmen or of the poorer copyhold class.[203] Hence, had any of them lived on manors or in

that these were "gavelkind," but most of them are outside Kent. ELTON, ORIGINS OF ENGLISH HISTORY (1882) 193.

197. *Id.* at 193.

198. ELTON, TENURES OF KENT (1867) 169.

199. *Id.* at 169-170; 2 BATESON, BOROUGH CUSTOMS (1906) 133 nn. 1, 2; BLOUNT, TENURES OF LAND AND CUSTOMS OF MANORS (Hazlitt's ed. 1874) 355; Newton v. Shafto, 1 Sid. 267, 82 E. R. 1097 (K. B. 1665).

200. Thus, partibility among daughters only. BLOUNT, *op. cit. supra* note 199, at 174; Roe d. Raper v. Lonsdale, 12 East 39, 104 E. R. 16 (K. B. 1810).

201. DEXTER, THE ENGLAND AND HOLLAND OF THE PURITANS (1905) 650. The classification is necessarily very imperfect, for few records survive.

202. *Id.* at 650. Dexter estimates that probably scores of those who fled to Holland came from Lincolnshire, Nottinghamshire and Yorkshire, but points out that the Dutch records give only scant information.

203. *Cf.* Goebel, *King's Law and Local Custom in Seventeenth Century New England* (1931) 31 COL. L. REV. 416, 443-444.

boroughs and towns where partible inheritance obtained, they would have had firsthand acquaintance with the custom.

The immigrants to Massachusetts Bay came mostly from the towns and manors of two groups of counties: East Anglia (Norfolk, Suffolk and Essex) and the West Country (Cornwall, Somerset, Dorset, Glouchester and Wiltshire).[204] Again, the predominance of the East county element suggests, as in the case of the Pilgrims, acquaintance with customs of divisible descent in England. Moreover, such customs prevailed in several of the counties of the West Country from which the settlers came. Unlike the Pilgrims, the Massachusetts Puritans were of greater wealth and substance than the Plymouth settlers, but their opportunities for acquaintance with such customs were no less considerable.

The hypothesis that local customs in England may have furnished prototypes for partible inheritance in this country is given substance by resemblances between the English and colonial practices. Even in seventeenth century England partible inheritance seems to have been comparatively well-known, and to have extended in some cases to daughters as well as sons.[205] Moreover, in some parts of England the widow might, as in Massachusetts Bay, take all or part of the deceased husband's property, either in addition to dower[206] or in place of it.[207] The notion of prolonging the family community is also common to Massachusetts and to certain English borough customs.[208]

204. Banks, *English Sources of Emigration to the New England Colonies in the Seventeenth Century* (1927) 60 MASS. HIST. SOC. PROC. 366.

205. See note 199 *supra*.

206. As at Ipswich, in Suffolk. 2 BATESON, BOROUGH CUSTOMS (1906) cix.

207. This was usually freebench. See CO. LIT. *110 b-112 b; 2 BATESON, BOROUGH CUSTOMS (1906) 121-122, 126. Freebench was well known by custom in copyholds, and was really a rule of succession to property. The portion varied considerably from place to place and might be one-fourth, one-third, or the whole. 2 WATKINS, TREATISE ON COPYHOLDS (1799) 87-90. See also an excellent discussion by Gomme, *Widowhood in Manorial Law* (1888) 2 ARCHAEOLOGICAL REVIEW 184. In some custumals the wife is explicitly spoken of as her husband's heir: SHILLIBEER, ANCIENT CUSTOMS OF THE MANOR OF TAUNTON DEANE (1821) 42; *cf.* Martin v. Wentworth, Noy 1, 74 E. R. 974 (Q. B. 1596). Again we wish to emphasize how many of the New England colonists were of the copyhold class in England. This fact may in part explain why the widow seems to be treated sometimes as an heir; such practices in Massachusetts Bay may be no more than survivals of the custom of freebench. Freebench should be clearly distinguished from dower, for in some localities the widow took one-half or the whole by way of dower. See CO. LIT. *33 b, *111 a; Baker v. Berisford, 1 Keble 509, 83 E. R. 1081 (K. B. 1663).

208. 2 BATESON, BOROUGH CUSTOMS (1906) cviii.

Customs by which the eldest son was given preference in certain districts of partible descent in England further hint at the influence of the homeland on the colonies. While only one example of the eldest son's receiving a double portion has been found,[209] there are many instances of some sort of preference for the eldest from the twelfth century on.[210] In Bracton's day, in places where the inheritance had been divisible from ancient times, if there was only a single messuage, that remained entirely for the eldest son, though the others received up to its value from the general property.[211] Where there were several messuages, the eldest among several coheirs had the first choice.[212] The custom of giving of heirlooms and principals to the eldest son, found in impartible[213] and partible[214] districts alike at least as late as the seventeenth century, are instances of the same preference for the eldest. This tendency can again be found in the occasional preference of the eldest daughter, either among coheiresses,[215] or by herself on the analogy of primogeniture.[216]

In short, certain resemblances between the colonial intestacy law and those of places in England from which the settlers came suggest that Massachusetts Bay may have drawn on English customs—either directly or by way of Plymouth—in working out the beginnings of its law of partible inheritance.

A third possible source of the Massachusetts law may be found in the customary distribution of personalty in England. Since realty and personalty were assimilated in the administration of estates in Massachusetts Bay, it has been suggested that the whole was distri-

209. Hudson, *Manorial Life* (1923) 1 HISTORY TEACHERS' MISCELLANY 161, 162.

210. GLANVILL, bk. VII, c. 3.

211. BRACTON, fol. 76 a. *Cf.* 2 POLLOCK AND MAITLAND, HISTORY OF ENGLISH LAW (1895) 262; 2 BATESON, BOROUGH CUSTOMS (1906) 133. An entry in British Museum Cot. MS. Tib. B, II, f. 198 (Ely custumal, 1222) seems to show one brother getting three times what the other got. I owe the reference to Mr. G. C. Homans.

212. BRACTON, fol. 76 a. This custom of first choice in the eldest son was known as *ainescia* and was well recognized from the twelfth and thirteenth centuries. GLANVILL, bk. VII, c. 3; BRACTON, fols. 76 a, 76 b, 77 a; FLETA (Selden's ed. 1647) bk. V, c. 9; CO. LIT. *166 b.

213. CO. LIT. *18 b.

214. 2 BATESON, BOROUGH CUSTOMS (1906) 143, 144.

215. CO. LIT. *165 a; ELTON, ORIGINS OF ENGLISH HISTORY (1882) 203-204.

216. *Id.* at 204. See also BLOUNT, *op. cit. supra* note 199, at 219 (Northampton) 265 (Herts.). For the custom in the border counties of the north in the nineteenth century see Doe d. Hamilton v. Clift, 12 Ad. & E. 566, 113 E. R. 927 (Q. B. 1840); Doe d. Foster v. Sisson, 12 East 62, 104 E. R. 25 (K. B. 1810).

buted as if it had all been personalty. This notion received support from the fact that realty and fixtures constituted at first the greater part of the wealth of the early settlers; but it is difficult to analyze the situation adequately, in view of the obscurity of the English law of intestate distribution of chattels before the time of the Statute of Distribution.[217] Estates were administered for the most part by the ecclesiastical courts according to certain general rules to the effect that the children and the wife of the intestate had some rights in the property. If he left a wife and no children, she took half; if he left a wife and children, they took respectively one-third. The remainder was used by the administrator for the good of the deceased's soul. From an early date the wife and children could get their shares by bringing the writ *de rationabile parte bonorum* at common law. While York and London had this custom till a late date,[218] we cannot tell how widely it persisted in the seventeenth century[219] until more ecclesiastical registers are available for study. In a great many towns, however, where estates were frequently administered before the town officers,[220] it had become established by the end of the fourteenth or fifteenth century that the chattels of an intestate should go to his wife and children, or, failing these, to his kinsmen. These in turn might be expected to devote a portion of the property to pious works.[221] Since at first in the colonies there were no fixed proportions into which estates were divided, and the widow might not share in the personalty at all,[222] the influence of the English ecclesiastical or borough schemes of distribution may not have been very great.[223] Still, the possi-

217. 22 & 23 CAR. II, c. 10 (1670).

218. In York till 1692; 4 WM. & MARY, c. 2 (1692); in London till 1724; 11 GEO. I, c. 18 (1724).

219. 3 HOLDSWORTH, HISTORY OF ENGLISH LAW (4th ed. 1935) 554 *ff*.

220. See, *e.g.*, London, 2 BATESON, BOROUGH CUSTOMS (1906) 194-195, 196; Oxford, 2 *id.* at 195-196; Exeter, 2 *id.* at 196; Fordwich, 2 *id.* at 200; Sandwich, 2 *id.* at 200, n. 6; Dover, 2 *id.* at 201. That this was recognized in the seventeenth century can be seen from Selden, *The Disposition or Administration of Intestates' Goods* in 3 OPERA OMNIA (1726) 1677.

221. Gross, *The Medieval Law of Intestacy* (1904) 18 HARV. L. REV. 120, 131.

222. The laws of 1641 and 1649 contemplate merely that the widow shall be adequately provided for. MASS. COL. LAWS 1660-1672 (1889) 51, c. 79; 201. Several cases show the widow taking only her dower. It will be remembered that the provision of 1647 giving the widow one-third of the personalty in addition to dower was repealed in 1649. See note 70 *supra*.

223. Contrary to the general opinion that until 1857 all estates were probated or administered in the ecclesiastical courts, there were in addition to secular administrations in the towns some places in which estates were admin-

bility remains; and since it seems true that much of the procedural law of succession in this country stems from the practice of the ecclesiastical courts,[224] some of the substantive law as well may come from this source.

The instinct to imitate or to reproduce the familiar is seldom a complete explanation of social phenomena, and it is not enough merely to emphasize laws and customs in England and Europe with which the colonists were familiar. It must be remembered that the men who settled in Plymouth and Massachusetts Bay had been deeply affected by Calvinism and the contemporary renaissance of biblicism and the exaltation of the Mosaic Law.[225] Their intellectual background was dominated by religious idealism. To the majority, if not all of them, the word of God was law, and the source of this law was found in the literal Scriptural word. With the teachings of Calvin the New England Puritans were thoroughly familiar, both through their ministers and through the flood of dissentient pamphlets current in England. Calvin had taught that the kingdom of God could be reproduced on earth only by closely following the Hebrew models.[226] Encouraged by the practical success of Calvin in Geneva in framing laws and a form of government on the basis of Old Testament law, the Puritans in this country attempted to give his theories concrete application. Cotton himself asserted that "the more any Law smells of man, the more unprofitable" it is.[227] The dominant position of the clergy in New England helped achieve these ends. Thomas Lechford, writing in

istered before manorial courts. "By prescription," says Scriven, "a court baron might have jurisdiction as a court peculiar, to grant probate and administration and to take cognizance of testamentary causes." SCRIVEN, TREATISE ON THE LAW OF COPYHOLDS (7th ed. 1896) 423. Upwards of fifty such manors having this jurisdiction in the sixteenth, seventeenth, and eighteenth centuries are listed in HONE, THE MANOR AND MANORIAL RECORDS (2d ed. 1912) 302-304. *Cf.* Nicholson v. Shirman, 1 Sid. 45, 46, 82 E. R. 960 (K. B. 1661): "Testamentary causes . . . fueront prove devant Seigneurs del Mannors . . . come ore sont in ascun lieus." But of the details of such administrations we know practically nothing.

224. In general, see the forthcoming edition of WOERNER, ADMINISTRATIONS, by Mr. T. E. Atkinson. The seventeenth century was well on its way before the writs of prohibition hampering the jurisdiction of the ecclesiastical courts began to issue. Thus, Slawney's Case, Hob. 83, 80 E. R. 233 (K. B. 1616), Frotherbie's Case, Cro. Car. 62, 79 E. R. 657 (K. B. 1627), Lavanne's Case, Cro. Car. 201, 79 E. R. 777 (K. B. 1631).

225. This background is sketched briefly but admirably by Goebel, *King's Law and Local Custom in Seventeenth Century New England* (1931) 31 COL. L. REV. 416, 423-432. See also MORRIS, *op. cit. supra* note 3, at 21-41.

226. CALVIN, INSTITUTES, bk. I, cc. 7, 8; bk. IV, cc. 8-10.

227. Quoted by MORRIS, *op. cit. supra* note 3, at 35.

1642, pointed out that not only did the ministers advise in making the laws, but they were frequently present in court.[228] The Plymouth and Massachusetts criminal codes bear the strong impress of their ideas, for many sections are clearly modeled on rules laid down in Exodus, Leviticus and Deuteronomy.[229]

With the general influence of the Bible on colonial law we are not here concerned.[230] There is good reason to believe that, insofar as partible inheritance is concerned, the Massachusetts law may have been based on Mosaic law. John Cotton, as a member of a committee appointed in 1636 to "make a draught of laws agreeable to the word of God,"[231] presented a proposed code of laws entitled "Moses his Judicialls."[232] Most of the provisions were based on texts of the Pentateuch. Among them were two dealing with inheritance. So close are they in wording to the two provisions in the Body of Liberties of 1641, that it is hard to believe that the latter were not copied from Cotton's draft.

> V. Inheritances are to descend naturally to the next of kinne, according to the law of nature delivered by God. Numb. 27, 7, 10, 11.
>
> VI. If a man have more sonnes than one, then a double portion to be assigned and bequeathed to the eldest sonne, according to the law of God, unlesse his owne demerit doe deprive him of his birthright. The like for personall estates. Deut. 21, 17; Chro. 5, 1.[233]

228. LECHFORD, PLAINE DEALING OR NEWS FROM NEW ENGLAND (1867) 62.

229. See, for example, the Body of Liberties, MASS. COL. LAWS 1660-1672 (1889) 55, c. 94.

230. The general thesis that law in New England was mainly Biblical has been argued by Reinsch, *English Common Law in the Early American Colonies* in 1 SELECT ESSAYS IN ANGLO-AMERICAN LEGAL HISTORY (1907) 367, 372-386, and HILKEY, LEGAL DEVELOPMENT IN COLONIAL MASSACHUSETTS, 1630-1686 (1910) 5, 66 *ff.*, 144. The view has not received much support. Later studies have shown a surprising amount of English local custom and common law in use. It is interesting to note that the Bible is frequently cited in English cases in the sixteenth and seventeenth centuries. See Bradley v. Banks, 1 Bulstr. 141, 142, 80 E. R. 834, 835 (K. B. 1611); Sherborn v. Lewis, Gouldsborough 120, 123, 75 E. R. 1037, 1038 (Q. B. 1601); Ratcliff's Case, 3 Co. Rep. 37a, 40a, 76 E. R. 713, 726 (Q. B. 1592); Reniger v. Fogossa, 1 Plow. 1, 8, 75 E. R. 1, 12 (K. B. 1551). *Cf.* WINFIELD, CHIEF SOURCES OF ENGLISH LEGAL HISTORY (1925) 146.

231. 1 RECORDS OF MASS. (1853) 174. See also *id.* 175: "& where there is noe law, then as neere the lawes of God as they can."

232. 1 HUTCHINSON PAPERS (Prince Soc., 1865) 181-205. *Cf.* Ford, *Moses his Judicialls* in 16 MASS. HIST. SOC. PROC. 2d ser. (1902) 274; Calder, *John Cotton's "Moses His Judicials"* in 28 MASS. COL. SOC. TRANS. (1935) 86.

233. 1 HUTCHINSON PAPERS, *supra* note 232, at 191.

As the notations indicate, these provisions were taken from the Books of Deuteronomy and Numbers. While the Body of Liberties modified these, both by making the division turn on intestacy and by adding the provision about the coparceny of the daughters, the similarity between the proposed code and the law actually adopted is striking.

The "Judicialls," with their chapter and verse citations to the Books of Moses, cannot explain the Plymouth inheritance scheme which had adopted the same principles of descent at least three years before the colony of Massachusetts Bay was founded. The law of the former may therefore have influenced the latter. At the same time, the scheme of equal descent to children and a double portion to the eldest son is sufficiently unusual so that the Plymouth law may in turn have been based on the Mosaic code. The strong Calvinistic leanings which infected the social and religious beliefs of the Pilgrims lend support to such a theory. Although evidence fails us, the fact remains that the Plymouth settlers, like those of Massachusetts Bay, were thoroughly acquainted with the Old Testament[234] and with Calvin's writings.[235] In fact Calvin had written a sermon, as well as comments, on Deuteronomy XXI, in which the Hebrew law of descent was discussed.[236] Although Calvin's own scheme of intestate succession exists only in imperfect draft form,[237] the law of Geneva, with which the Pilgrims seem to have had some acquaintance, followed a scheme of divisible descent.[238]

Yet, except for these two general characteristics, equality of descent and the double portion, the Massachusetts law of descent was not the Mosaic law of descent. For example, under the Hebrew law, daughters were excluded from the inheritance as long as there

234. Many leading men in the colony were seriously engaged in Hebrew studies and had a profound reverence for Hebrew. See NEWMAN, JEWISH INFLUENCE ON CHRISTIAN REFORM MOVEMENTS (1925) 635-645. The Jewish law of descent was also well known in England in the seventeenth century. For example, see ROBINSON, GAVELKIND (1897) 12-13; Selden, *De Successionibus in Bona Defuncti ad Leges Ebraeorum* in 2 OPERA (1726) cc. 5-8, 12, 13. Selden's exposition of the Jewish law of succession is based on a thorough study of the sources and of Rabbinical interpretations.

235. For example, a copy of Calvin's Institutes was in the library of Miles Standish. 5 NEW ENGLAND HISTOR. AND GEN. REG. (1851) 337.

236. 27 CALVIN, OPERA (1864-1900) 663-676. See also 24 *id.* at 709-710; 25 *id.* at 310-311.

237. 10 *id.* at 133. For Calvin's influence on the law, see generally BOHATEC, CALVIN UND DAS RECHT (1934).

238. FLAMMER, LE DROIT CIVIL DE GENÈVE (1875) 17-18.

were either sons or any descendants from sons,[239] whereas under the Massachusetts intestacy law daughters often took equally with sons.[240] Again, if a son died without issue, his inheritance under Hebrew law never went to his mother; she and her ancestors were completely excluded.[241] Yet there is at least one case in the Essex records where mother and father both shared in a deceased son's estate.[242] Or again, by Hebrew law a grandchild of a deceased eldest son would never take a double portion,[243] whereas in at least one case in Massachusetts he seems to have done so.[244] Lastly, according to Hebrew law, an eldest son could receive a double portion only from his father, and never from his mother;[245] yet the Body of Liberties and the Act of 1649 say that when *parents* die intestate, the eldest shall have a double portion.[246] This is borne out in several Essex cases, where the eldest son took a double portion from an intestate mother.[247] In short, we can go no further than to say that the notion of equality of shares, with a double portion reserved to the eldest son, may easily have been based on similar features in the Hebrew law of inheritance as laid down in the Books of Deuteronomy and Numbers. The colonists certainly did not attempt to re-enact the detailed rules of the Hebrew law.

Prominent among other ideas which may have played a significant part in shaping the rules of partible descent was the notion of equality, a strong one among the settlers of both Plymouth and Massachusetts Bay. In part this was a result of theories of natural law and equality of rights with which the colonists were deeply imbued.[248] Thus, John Robinson had said, "we are not over one another, but with one another."[249] An early town record of Lan-

239. SELDEN, *supra* note 234, at c. 8; HALE, HISTORY OF THE COMMON LAW (1779) 243.

240. For references, see note 93 *supra*.

241. SELDEN, *supra* note 234, at c. 12; HALE, *op. cit. supra* note 239, at 244.

242. 1 ESSEX PROB. RECORDS (1916) 57-58, 62, 201; 2 *id.* at 94.

243. SELDEN, *supra* note 234, at c. 6-7; HALE, *op. cit. supra* note 239, at 245.

244. 1 ESSEX PROB. RECORDS (1916) 395.

245. SELDEN, *supra* note 234, at c. 6.

246. MASS. COL. LAWS 1660-1672 (1889) 51, c. 81; 201, c. 3.

247. 1 ESSEX PROB. RECORDS (1916) 57-58, 62, 201; 2 *id.* at 94.

248. 1 OSGOOD, THE AMERICAN COLONIES IN THE SEVENTEENTH CENTURY (1904) 425.

249. Quoted in POUND, THE SPIRIT OF THE COMMON LAW (1921) 42-43. In his sermon in 1621, at New Plymouth, Cushman spoke out strongly against inequality; he finished saying, "Did not Satan, who was not content to keep that equal state with his fellows, but would set his throne above the stars?" Quoted in 1 BRADFORD, HISTORY OF PLYMOUTH PLANTATION (1912) 300, n.

caster, Massachusetts, speaks of "that Equallitie which is the rule of God."[250] The idea found expression, for example, in the early allotments of land. In Plymouth the land was allotted according to the numbers in a family, each person thus being thought entitled to an equal share.[251] Equality in economic status was sought to be maintained by limitations on alienations, and by even distribution of common obligations, such as the burden of taxation and the care of fences and highways.[252] Quite apart from social theory, these ideas were rooted in a long experience in equality in the sharing of obligations and duties in the routine of English agricultural life which they knew so well. The physical appearance as well as the organization of the New England towns afford striking resemblances to those of the villages and manors of seventeenth century England. It is hard not to conclude that much of the local English agricultural system, carrying with it implicitly the idea of equality, was imported to this country.[253] At the same time many of the settlers had keenly felt the effects of the inequalities of the English land system which became so apparent in the accumulations of land by a few in the inclosure movement.[254] Even in the England of that day there was criticism of the inequalities of primogeniture and the unfairness to younger sons.[255]

It seems to have been apparent to the colonists that primogeniture was ill adapted to conditions in New England. It would have encouraged the growth of accumulated estates, which they had learned to distrust. It would also have meant the impoverishment of younger sons who, deprived of a share in their family's lands,

250. 1 HURD, HISTORY OF WORCESTER COUNTY (1889) 6.

251. 1 BRADFORD, HISTORY OF PLYMOUTH PLANTATION (1912) 299-300. For other instances, see AKAGI, THE TOWN PROPRIETORS OF THE NEW ENGLAND COLONIES (1924) 107-108; Andrews, *Die Stadt in Neu-England* (1893-1894) 2 ZEITSCHRIFT FÜR SOCIALUND WIRTHSCHAFTSGESHICHTE 103, 224.

252. Andrews, *supra* note 121, at 434-435.

253. See MACLEAR, EARLY NEW ENGLAND TOWNS (1908) 81 *ff.;* 1 OSGOOD, *op. cit. supra* note 248, at 426.

254. This was particularly true of the Plymouth colonists. Haskins, *The Beginnings of the Recording System in Massachusetts* (1941) 21 B. U. L. REV. 281, 299-300.

255. PAGE, JUS FRATRUM, THE LAW OF BRETHREN (1638); NORTHTONUS, THE YOUNGER BROTHERS ADVOCATE (1655). In the latter, many of the arguments in favor of partible descent are drawn from Mosaic law. Typical is the statement, "So that I cannot see, but that a more equall division, than is generally practised with us amongst brethren, is more agreable to scripture, right, reason, naturell justice, and no prejudice to the flourishing condition of a Nation, and true happiness of a Commonwealth." *Id.* at 15.

would have had no means of support in a frontier community. It would have meant the depletion of the population on which the very success of the colony depended. These matters are expressly recognized in the preamble to the section dealing with intestates' estates in the Act of 1692:

> Whereas estates in these plantations do consist chiefly of lands, which have been subdued and brought to improvement by the industry and labour of the proprietors, with the assistance of their children, the younger children generally having been longest and most serviceable unto their parents in that behalf, who have not personal estate to give out unto them in portions, or otherwise to recompense their labours. . . .[256]

It is apparent that there was much sense in applying the same rules to realty and personalty. Land and houses in the beginning were the chief form of property,[257] and there was little else for a man to leave to his children. If one son had received the land, there would be nothing for the others. The alternative of seeking work in the towns, as in England, would not be possible in sparsely settled communities. Similar reasons might explain why the County Courts should have varied portions according to need, or allotted to the widow more than her mere dower. Such reasons, too, were pressed by counsel in the arguments before the Privy Council in *Phillips v. Savage*.[258] The foundation and growth of the colony, it was said, depended on equality of descent, "for the whole estate consists in lands, stock, buildings, and such other improvement."[259] The personal estates were insufficient provision and recompense for the long labor and industry of younger children, in subduing and improving the settlements of their ancestors. "If they were to receive no share at all of those lands which they themselves have cultivated, all future culture must cease, and the unsubdued part of the Colony eternally remain, as it is, a wilderness, and younger children must rove about the world for bread, the Province be depopulated, and so the very intentions of the charter destroyed."[260]

256. THE CHARTER AND GENERAL LAWS OF THE COLONY AND PROVINCE OF MASSACHUSETTS BAY (1814) 230.

257. This would be less true of Massachussetts Bay than of Plymouth. The inventories in the former show fairly sizeable personal estates.

258. See note 125 *supra*.

259. 5 MASS. HIST. SOC. PROC. (1860-1862) 78.

260. *Id.* at 78.

Altogether, therefore, there seems to have been much in the social and economic conditions in the colony to support the settlers' theories of equality.

The main features of the colonists' background, social and intellectual, can be discerned with some certainty. That the Plymouth settlers had some knowledge of the Dutch law of descent; that they, in common with the Massachusetts colonists, had some acquaintance with customs of partible inheritance in the manors and towns of England, seems highly probable. That both groups entertained theories of law and government which might cause them to adopt the Mosaic scheme of succession seems likewise very probable. Their religious and social theories, together with the environment from which they came, gave them a strong bias in favor of equality of ownership. Economic conditions in a part of the world which was still wilderness must have had much to do with the adoption and the continuance of rules of partible descent. But it is no easy problem to separate these strands of influence. The records show no single answer.

That the Massachusetts law of inheritance was based neither on the Statute of Distribution nor on gavelkind we can be certain. We may therefore begin by again suggesting that the principles of the Massachusetts Bay scheme of partible inheritance were borrowed directly from Plymouth. The latter colony had had ten years of experience on New England shores, and this experience may well have been drawn upon by the sister colony. This is the more likely, given the other instances of inter-colony borrowing which have already been noted. However, even if we accept this hypothesis, the question is hardly advanced, for we are forced to ask in turn why Plymouth adopted partible inheritance. Here the possibility of Dutch influence may not be neglected in view of the similarities of the two schemes of intestate succession. Beyond this was the common background of both groups of colonists in rural and urban England where customs of partible descent were well known. There had also been first-hand acquaintance with the customary distributions of personalty in the ecclesiastical courts. Although neither the Dutch system, nor the ecclesiastical system, nor the local customs of partibility were reproduced exactly, there are nevertheless hints of all of them. There is much reason to suppose that the colonists availed themselves of their cultural heritage in law, just as they did in religion and farming. The social system of colonial New England was first and last English. Many instances of English common law, both substantive and procedural, can be found in the law of colonial Massachusetts in the seventeenth century.[261] Practices akin to those of the ecclesiastical courts are also found; indeed, the flexibility of probate procedure and the absence of insistence on formalities in wills in contemporary England[262] bear striking resemblance to features of the Massachusetts law which have been observed. But above all, the similarities between New England practices and customs in the parts of England from which the settlers came are most noticeable.[263] It is to be remembered that until well on in the seventeenth century there were few professional lawyers in the colony,[264] and there were few English law books.[265] In the days before the common law had acquired its universal dominion, local customs and local courts loomed large in the eyes of the average Englishman. It was these that formed the larger part of the legal heritage of the persons who settled New England in the early seventeenth century. It was the half-remembered notions of customs in other lands which, together with the needs of a frontier community, seem to have been of high significance in the early law of the New England colonies.

In stressing such features, we must not forget the significance of the belief that the word of God, as exhibited in the Old Testament, was to the colonists law in a fundamental sense; nor that ideas about equality played a highly important part in their outlook. The Mosaic analogy, because of the double portion, is a particularly tempting source for the intestacy law. Even if it were not the source itself, the passages in the Books of Deuteronomy and Numbers would provide the settlers, as they did John Cotton, with a ready rationalization of the inheritance scheme.

No single "source" can be pointed to without distorting the facts as they were. Professor Goebel has pointed with some acuteness to

261. See Morris, *Massachusetts and the Common Law* (1926) 31 AMER. HIST. REV. 443; Chafee, in 1 *Suffolk County Records* xxx-xxxii, xxxviii; Plucknett, Book Review (1930) 3 NEW ENGLAND QUARTERLY 159. *Cf.* 4 RECORDS OF MASS. (1853) pt. ii, 554-555, where in 1673 the question arose as to whether the heir of an intestate might enter by attorney, and a committee was appointed to discover the law of England in the matter.

262. See 3 HOLDSWORTH, HISTORY OF ENGLISH LAW (1935) 538-539, 541.

263. For further discussion, see Goebel, *King's Law and Local Custom in Seventeenth Century New England* (1931) 31 COL. L. REV. 416, 434 *ff*.

264. Chafee, in 1 *Suffolk County Records* xxiii-xxvii.

265. *Id.* at xxx-xxxii.

the curious *mélange* of religious ideas and the remnants of English local customs which pervaded the laws and institutions of Plymouth and Massachusetts Bay.[266] It seems altogether possible that in the beginnings of the law of partible descent in Massachusetts there may have been some such mixture of custom and ideal. But in the last analysis, the answer is that it proved a wise method of distribution which produced on the whole fair results. Whatever the reasons for its original adoption, its suitability to colonial conditions is why in the long run it survived and became one of the roots of the modern law of intestate division of realty.

We cannot close without pointing out that this study has a wider import than as a chapter in legal history. Stressing as it does the social and intellectual background of the colonists, it takes on significance as a study in survival and adaptation of patterns of thought, habits of life. Important for what light it sheds on the sources of colonial law in general, it further shows the law adapting itself to the needs of the colonists in New England. It reveals the beginnings of an indigenous American law, not overly hampered by tradition, growing up in response to the social and economic conditions of a new civilization.

266. Goebel, *King's Law and Local Custom in Seventeenth Century New England* (1931) 31 COL. L. REV. 416, 447-448.

XI

*The Courts and the Law in Colonial New York**

JULIUS GOEBEL, JR.

Law a Factor in Social History

It is only in recent years that what men said and did in law courts has come to be regarded as an important source of information for social history. Our attention has been focused upon the more material evidences of how our ancestors lived, and we have preferred to look aside when we came upon their quarrels or their lapses from grace, except in so far as these incidents may have had some bearing upon political developments. Moreover, the circumstance that useful facts are often concealed by the murky penumbra of technical legal detail has made the laymen reluctant to undertake the examination of legal records; and the lawyer, indifferent to the past, has not lent his aid. These factors have conspired to keep us ignorant of the course of legal development in the colonies, so that for no one of the American colonies has the story of the law been told in its entirety.

There is no doubt that a great deal of what went on in the courts and legislative halls of the colonies was and will ever remain arid and unfruitful for an understanding of the life and times of the participants. But, if in point of detail it is not always essential to know the workings of a specific rule, there can be no doubt that the law, both civil and criminal, played a considerable rôle in the affairs of the settlers and that the attitude of the colonists with reference to both the judicial establishments and the substantive

* "The Courts and the Law in Colonial New York," by Julius Goebel, Jr., is reprinted with permission of the Columbia University Press from Alexander C. Flick, ed., *History of the State of New York*, III (New York, 1933), 3-43.

rules there enforced was closely involved in questions of social and political progress.

To no colony do these remarks apply with greater force than to the province of New York. Beginning with efforts of certain English settlers on Long Island to have their law conform to Biblical precept, through the assembly at Hempstead in 1665, the effort to overthrow the Duke's Laws in 1691, the quarrels with Bellomont over the power to establish courts and with Cosby over the chancery, down to the battle over writ of error and appeal under Colden, there was no lessening of the public concern with the basic questions: What law obtains in the colony? Where is its source? How far is English precedent operative? These questions acquired from the very first a strong political color, but they derived broader social importance from the circumstance that the New Yorkers, being extraordinarily litigious, professed and demonstrated the keenest interest in the law, so that far from being a matter of mere professional concern, the rules of law were the subject of frequent lay discussion. And it is precisely this fact of the law's direct effect upon the lives of the people at large that has lent an enduring interest to the story of how their law was molded.

Courts and Law under the Dutch

Our earliest notices of judicial institutions in New Netherland occur in the governorship of Peter Minuit. The governor together with a Council of five, and the schout fiscal, an officer who combined the duties of prosecutor and sheriff, constituted the first judicial tribunal. Under Kieft, a regular session of the Council, sitting in a judicial capacity, was provided, though the methods of procedure appear to have been summary, and by various repressive devices appeals to the Amsterdam chamber of the West India Company were completely stultified. A series of protests by the colonists against this practice of the court eventually led to certain changes after Stuyvesant had succeeded Kieft (1647). Stuyvesant established a court of general jurisdiction, presided over by Van Dincklagen, who was learned in the law; and associated with the latter were other officers of the company. When Stuyvesant finally conceded partial popular participation in the government, certain judicial powers in civil cases were exercised by the Nine Men chosen by the governor from an elected panel of eighteen.

The mollifying effect of the concessions made by Stuyvesant was frustrated, partly because of political reasons, and partly because of the personality of the governor. In 1650, the Nine Men succeeded in obtaining from the States General an order for changes in the machinery of justice, but, as this order was resisted by the Amsterdam chamber of the West India Company, two years elapsed before it was put into effect. Based upon the custom of Amsterdam, the new arrangements provided for a court of justice composed of a schout, two burgomasters, and five schepens from whose judgments an appeal lay to the supreme Council. This court was in fact instituted at New Amsterdam. And in succeeding years similar courts were established in the Dutch settlements of Long Island.

The records of the New Amsterdam court disclose a state of legal development in many respects remarkable. Some of the officers were of considerable legal learning, and as a consequence the reception of Dutch law was not hindered by lay incompetence or ignorance. In the Dutch of the Long Island towns, of course, there was not the same sophistication, and in many respects the proceedings there bear close resemblance to the town courts in the adjacent English settlements.

Under the influence of our theory of precedent, it has become almost a convention of our thinking in legal history that the events of the past which bear the most palpable relation to the present are most worthy of remembrance. And it is thus that for the law the line between chronicle or antiquarianism and history has come to be drawn. It is for this reason that we have dealt somewhat perfunctorily with Dutch law and courts. As far as later developments in the colony are concerned, the significance of the Dutch occupation is slight. This was due in the first instance to the terms of the surrender in 1664. But even without the interposition of the articles of capitulation, it is obvious from the state of English law in respect to the dominions that a doom had been pronounced which spelled the obliteration of alien jurisprudence in any lands which the Britons might make their own.

A few years before the enterprising Dutchmen built their first fort on Manhattan Island, in the Court of the Exchequer Chamber, the assembled benches of the Court of Common Pleas, the King's Bench, and the Exchequer sitting with the Lord Chancellor, had come to a determination with respect to the nationality of the king's subjects born in Scotland. In the course of the argument on this important matter, the whole question of the status of king's dominions and the law that obtained therein had been well ventilated. Reported in *Calvin's Case* (7 *Rep.* I) by the learned Coke, the doctrines on which the court was presumably agreed formed the foundation of all future action by the courts in respect to the American plantations. Briefly stated, the consensus of opinion supported the proposition that where a country was conquered, the law was what the king willed. The great significance of this pronouncement, at the very moment of the first English settlement in America, lay in the circumstance that the crown's rights in the dominions were by a legal fiction attributed to conquest, and that old medieval dogma respecting the King's prerogative of legislation in his dominions by conquest was reasserted. Even the limitation advanced in this case, that once the common law was introduced by the crown, a *pro tanto* surrender of the prerogative ensued, so that acts of Parliament were extensible to the dominions, did not affect the major premise that lands not of the realm were dominions of the king and that any depositions regarding the law in these dominions emanated in the first instance from the crown. From the very first then, as far as the courts were concerned, the question of title to the land and the law that was to obtain there were inextricably linked. And it is reasonably clear from the charters which passed the seals, both before and after the judgment in *Calvin's Case*, that there was in fact no doubt as to where the lawmaking power was lodged. So it appears in the charter by which Charles II conveyed to his brother the territories which he was presently to conquer. To the Duke of York was granted, along with the land, powers in essence regal, and among them that of making laws in so far as these laws were not repugnant to the common law.

From the terms of the grant to James, it appears not only that the legislative power was the king's to delegate, but also that the acts of the grantee, in exercise of this power, were to be subject to the express limitation of agreeing with, or at least not being repugnant to, the laws of England. This charter to the Duke of York may be said to reflect the administrative viewpoint regarding royal rights. This view, considered in connection with the doctrine of the judicial branch of the government expressed in *Calvin's Case*, furnishes strong evidence in support of the conclusion that even before the reduction of New Netherland the crown had foreclosed the possibility of preserving Dutch law, and that not the common law but a system which was to resemble the latter was planned. Indeed, it is difficult to see how a recognition of Dutch law could have taken place, because the crown, since 1620, had in its diplomatic relations steadfastly asserted its sovereignty over New Netherland and had insisted that the Dutch settlers were intruders without right.

The leaders of the English expedition, when they reached the scene of operations, lost no time in communicating to the "enemy" the intentions of their sovereign. A proclamation addressed to the inhabitants promised, to those who would submit, protection "in His Majesty's laws and justice," and we must assume that this assurance was likewise a statement of what Colonel Nicolls and his associates thought was the true legal situation: *i.e.*, that, once they took possession of the land, English law would obtain. In any event, the articles of surrender apparently were drawn on some such assumption, for what the conquerors were willing to preserve of the legal institutions of the vanquished were but meager remnants. Contracts made before the signing of the articles of surrender were to be settled according to Dutch practice; no judgments hitherto passed were to be reopened; and inferior civil officers were to continue until new elections. One important saving of Dutch custom was made: that the Hollanders who remained should continue to enjoy their customs concerning inheritance.

The summary action with respect to the Dutch law disposed of one problem confronting the Duke of York. The disposition to be made of the institutions that had been established by the English colonists on Long Island was another and more difficult problem, since the character of the inhabitants and their political leanings promised a possible collision with the forces of centralized administration which James and his advisers proposed to set up. Moreover, the Long Island settlements were emanations of a spirit, reputedly rebellious, that prevailed in New England, a spirit of which the crown was fully aware and to investigate which Colonel Nicolls and his associates were commissioned by the king.

Influence of the Long Island English on the Law

We must pause at this point to examine briefly the peculiarities of the English settlements on Long Island. These settlements professed a variety of political allegiance. At Newtown and Gravesend, proximity to Manhattan involved a closer control by the masters of the province. In the center of the island, the control was less sure, but by patent and by ordinance the Dutch had conceded a power to hold courts of a limited jurisdiction. The colonists of eastern Long Island, however, acknowledged no foreign suzerainty. After shifting briefly for themselves, a loose relationship with Connecticut had been established, an example which some of the middle-island colonists followed shortly before the conquest. Despite these efforts to secure the protection of their fellow Englishmen across the Sound, however, the system of law administration as it appears in the records seems to have been unaffected by changes in political ties. It was a manifestation of impulses that operated without the field of administrative affiliation, in response to factors which we may observe at work in law among the mainland Puritans.

The most striking of these factors was an attempt to realize in lay legislation divine precept, especially as it appears in the Old Testament. From the time of Calvin's experiment in theocracy at Geneva, the notion that the "judicials" of Moses were binding upon men and should be incorporated in man's law had obsessed the more radical Protestant groups, both in England and on the Continent. When opportunity at last came to these zealots to regulate their affairs without episcopal or royal interference, there was no hesitation in setting these ideas forth in their codes. We can observe this in the Plymouth laws, in the Body of Liberties of Massachusetts Bay, and in the New Haven code. It was in the main the source of the brief and ferocious criminal law drawn in Southhampton in 1641. In addition to this more obvious phase of Biblicism, we may observe further among these people the infiltration of the whole mode of Puritan thought, especially in relation to questions of social control of behavior whether matters political or economic were at stake.

But this was not the only substance from which was drawn the early law of the dissenters in America. Even the most intensely devout churchgoer would have been hard put to extract from the Bible sufficient guide for the details of judicial establishment and procedure. Nor have we any evidence that the Puritan Biblicism in America was ever so broadly conceived, even among the holy men of New Haven. For these matters of detail, and where the incidents of daily life did not impinge upon religious belief, these people did what one would expect: they imitated the institutions and practices with which they were familiar. The models that they imitated were not, however, the great courts of the king at Westminster which dominated the judicial scene in England, nor did they use the law which was practiced in those courts and about which Coke wrote so learnedly when the first Puritans settled in New England. For it was not these courts and their law with which the small artisans, merchants and peasants were familiar. Their contacts had been for the most part with those relics of ancient local jurisdiction which still functioned in seventeenth-century England—the courts baron and leet on the manor, the borough courts in the city, the county courts and the quarter sessions. All but the last of these institutions had their roots in the feudal jurisdiction of the Middle Ages. They were already marked for destruction but, as we know from their extant records, they still handled the bulk of petty litigation. Here was administered old custom embodied in the rolls of the court or in the custumals of the boroughs, customs that are as hoary as the common law, and to which the latter in specific instance or on occasion gave recognition and validity. Here were observed practices in pleading and procedure long since outmoded in the central courts. Here may be found the striking parallels between the law of old England and the law which the settlers, where there were no barristers to lead the way, presently put into operation for their civil litigation. For their criminal jurisprudence, where they were not bound by substantive provisions culled from the Bible, the colonists' models were the court leet (the police court of the manor), or the quarter sessions (the courts held by the justices of the peace in the county). The latter alone in England were endowed with the vigor of going concerns with a future ahead of them and were pushing out of the picture the moribund court leet. They were definitely part of the central royal authority and at the same time were local institutions, manned largely by laymen, and maintaining practices that had no more in common with the older methods of petty police administration than with the practices of the assizes or of the King's Bench.

We have entered upon this lengthy characterization of the law on Long Island, not only because it affected the steps taken by Colonel Nicolls to establish a unified system of jurisprudence in the province, but because the same motives which had guided the English settlers before the conquest persisted throughout the colonial period among certain classes of the population, manifesting themselves in claims to autonomous legislative power, and in the never wholly quiescent opposition to an unmitigated reception of all the details of the English legal system.

Shortly before the reduction of New Netherland, Colonel Nicolls, to secure the coöperation of the English colonists, promised to convene an assembly for the enactment of laws. Some months later steps were taken to execute this engagement, but in a manner that was not pleasing to the province. On February 8, 1665, the Long Island and Westchester towns were summoned to send deputies to Hempstead to advise with the governor in settling "good and known laws" for the province. The convention met on February 28, and Nicolls presented the assembled members with a code previously prepared by himself and his counselors. This proceedings by no means corresponded with the inhabitants' idea of lawmaking, and there was consequently considerable dissatisfaction expressed. Nicolls shrewdly accepted a few amendments, but rejected the major demands of the deputies. On March 1, 1665, the code, thereafter known as the Duke's Laws, was promulgated.

In view of the manner in which the Duke's Laws had been compiled, it is not strange that they should have evoked opposition. Both the governor and Matthias Nicolls, the secretary of the province, had been trained as lawyers, and Thomas Willet, who may have advised in the work, had had practical experience in the Plymouth colony government. The code represented in a sense a compromise between these points of view—between the New England conception of what a body of laws should contain and what a man schooled in the common law might think desirable. The major portion of the Duke's Laws was drawn from various New England codes which Nicolls had obtained for the purpose or for perusal, as commissioner, to inspect their coincidence with the laws of England. The "Capitall Laws," for example, were a restatement of the familiar Puritan rules extracted from the Pentateuch, and we can recognize the American paternity of countless other provisions. On the other hand, the appointment of magistrates by the governor was copied from crown practice in England, and was an exercise of power in bitter conflict with the tradition of the colonists. Similarly, the duty vested in the churchwardens of presenting in the sessions courts offenses against morals was an unwelcome adaptation of English ecclesiastical practice.

Merely listing the offensive details of the Duke's Laws does not completely explain the attitude of the English inhabitants. Their chief objection to the code was that the legislative initiative had not been theirs. Consequently it was immaterial that an effort to draw on American sources had been made, since in their eyes this was no virtue, and since the whole code was regarded as infected by the sections which emphasized prerogative or interfered with their infant traditions. The Long Islanders were, indeed, rebels against the theocratic tendencies of New England, as much as against the royal-episcopal system. What was undoubtedly intended as a gesture of propitiation did not excite their loyalty. For this Nicolls, a wise and moderate executive, cannot be blamed—to him, no doubt, one Puritan resembled another.

The Courts under the Duke's Laws

The judicial machinery set up by the Duke's Laws deserves some attention. At the pinnacle of the structure stood the court of assizes, a body composed of the governor, his Council (*ex officio* justices of the peace), and the several justices of the peace in New York. Originally the court of assizes was to meet annually on the last Thursday in September, but a subsequent amendment provided that it could be convened at other times on special warrant of the governor. The original jurisdiction of the court of assizes comprehended criminal justice, civil suits where the amount in controversy exceeded £20, and "matters of Equity." It was an appellate court from all inferior jurisdictions. Appeals were initiated by petition. The record was certified, but the court could consider the testimony of witnesses who were not available at the time of trial. In criminal cases an appeal was allowed, apparently in the form of a new trial. It likewise possessed a curious form of residual jurisdiction, which is to be considered really as a manifestation of its legislative rather than of its judicial function, in the power conferred upon it of determining what should be done in the case of crimes not specified in the laws or for which proper punishment was not established.

The bulk of ordinary litigation in the colony was evidently designed to be heard in the courts of sessions. The territory of Long Island and Westchester had been divided into three ridings, in each of which a court of sessions was to sit in March and June. The court was held by all the justices who resided in a riding and, in the absence of the governor or a councilor, the oldest justice presided. It possessed both civil and criminal jurisdiction—the former in cases at law involving more than £5 and less than £20, the latter in matters not capital. Where a capital offense took place, the governor could issue a special commission of oyer and terminer. All cases in sessions were tried by jury, and the judgment was final unless the amount in controversy exceeded £20 or there was doubt as to the law. An amendment of 1666 mentions a power of "review"—in effect a rehearing at which fresh evidence could be considered, a provision palpably patterned after the practice in Plymouth.

At the bottom of the judicial system were the town courts. Here Nicolls had seen fit to employ an existing institution, but he limited the jurisdiction of these courts to cases involving less than £5. The town courts were to be held every two or three weeks or at the instance of an individual if he paid the necessary charges. The court could be presided over by a justice of the peace, but six overseers with a constable (elected by the town), or seven overseers without the latter, composed a quorum. In the original code it was clearly intended that the causes brought before the town court were to be tried by arbitration, the arbitrators to be named by a justice of the peace where the parties could not agree. But a later amendment indicates that an alternative form of judgment by the majority of the bench was sanctioned.

When this machinery was set up, there still remained to be handled the Hudson River towns and New York City itself. In the former, the Dutch institutions were apparently not rooted out. The Duke's Laws did not expressly repudiate the Dutch arrangements in the Hudson Valley, and consequently Dutch law continued to be administered by Dutch methods in the Dutch language, with certain modifications, in towns like Albany and Esopus. For instance, in 1665 the manorial court of Rensselaerswyck was consolidated with the court of Albany, and again in 1671 Governor Lovelace made a slight change in the number of magistrates. The next year Schenectady was permitted to have a town court to try minor cases, major cases going as hitherto to the court of Albany. On the other hand, in 1671, in orders issued to regulate affairs at Esopus, it is apparent that a partial introduction of the Duke's Laws was intended there, and certainly a Council order of June, 1673, does not leave room for doubt. But Dutch ideas dominated the upcountry judicial system and law until 1674, when after the reconquest of New Netherland it was assumed by the English that the liberal provisions of 1664 had been nullified.

The Dutch inhabitants of New York were of a different opinion, however, and indeed as late as 1759 Cadwallader Colden said that the Dutch thought that the original terms of surrender in 1664 were still in force. The question was hotly debated for many years. The historic fact is that magistrates chosen by the Dutch inhabitants for a long time after 1664 decided cases according to Dutch law. It was only gradually, as English settlers became more numerous, that English law crowded out Dutch law in practice, although theoretically it had been in operation. A study of the court minutes of Fort Orange, Beverwyck, Albany, Rensselaerswyck and Schenectady, which are in Dutch and extend to the year 1685, clearly reveal the persistence of Dutch influence. The Dutch notarial papers, which extend to the year 1696, show the same influence. It should be pointed out, however, that those parts of the Duke's Laws definitely relating to town government were translated into Dutch; and furthermore that in the court of assizes sat commissaries from Albany. How far we can deduce from the facts an extension of the Duke's Laws over the whole province is, of course, problematical.

In Manhattan the old court of the burgomasters and schepens was transmuted into the mayor's court, with the mayor and aldermen exercising the function of judges. From Nicolls' proclamation of June 12, 1665, which instituted this change and put in force the new laws, it is obvious that far from merely changing the names of the courts and "style" of the court, he had definitely in mind the erection of a court similar to those of the same name that flourished in various great English boroughs.

The judicial arrangements which have been sketched were intended to satisfy the basic needs of the inhabitants at large without too great a disturbance of existing institutions. There were no exact English analogues for any of the courts, unless on the basis of this procedure we can see in the town courts an imitation of the courts baron that handled a not dissimilar type of business in the manors of old England, or of the borough courts in the smaller cities. The merger of law and equity powers, however, was without contemporary precedent and, being admirably designed to serve the needs of an attenuated and practically lawyerless society, might have given rise to a distinctive form of jurisprudence had not the early judicial structure been subsequently altered.

In one particular, however, Nicolls made a deliberate effort to import into New York a familiar English institution, and, while it was not destined to play a rôle in the administration of the law, it was of considerable consequence in the growth of the land law. This was the introduction of the manorial system.

It is unnecessary to enter into the long-since buried argument as to whether or not the statute of *Quia Emptores* (1290) was ever law in New York. This famous statute forbade subinfeudation in England and, while it did not bind the king, persons taking from the king's immediate grantee were bound and could not create the feudal bond between themselves and their tenants. In the seventeenth century, lawyers took the view that a manor could not be created in England, since at least one essential—tenants owing homage to the lord and suit to his court—could not lawfully be constituted. In the nineteenth century, the New York court of appeals, by claiming that this statute had been in force in New York colony, was able to deny that feudal tenure had ever been introduced into the province. There is no doubt that, in view of the seventeenth-century doctrine of the crown's complete power to legislate for conquered territories, the introduction of this statute depended entirely upon some royal act. The grant of James and the conduct of Colonel Nicolls under his instructions negative any idea that, so far as New York was concerned, the limitations of *Quia Emptores* were ever intended to operate. Certainly the lawyers' deduction that the statute would bar the creation of a manor could not have weighed seriously with Colonel Nicolls, since he created several manors and confirmed certain grants with powers that transformed into manors the holdings of the grantees. These grants were made to persons most likely to be attached to the cause of the duke, in places where Nicolls expected trouble, whether from Englishmen, Indians, or Dutch. They conveyed to the grantees immunity from local jurisdiction and, by combining a grant of township privileges with rights incident to the manors, impressed on the lords of the manors the duty of maintaining a military establishment.

An incident of the manor was the court baron, the tribunal which in seventeenth-century England still handled questions of tenancy and the small civil litigations of the tenants. This privilege was either granted in terms or was implicit. In many of the grants, the franchise to hold a court leet—the police court of the manor—was also included. How far these rights to hold courts were ever exercised we do not know, since there is extant only one record referring to a single manor court (Fordham). The significant phase of the matter is that the efficiency of the ordinary governmental arrangements was such as to submerge the possible political usefulness of the manor system, and even the multiplication of the manors under Nicolls' successors did not alter the situation. At the same time this type of land holding must have seemed a very ominous portent to those who were freemen of the towns where the New England system of land ownership prevailed, since it brought to the New World the possibility of the very economic evils which the settlers had sought to escape and which had caused the agrarian discontent in Tudor England.

When we scrutinize the list of grantees, we see listed many of the men who were powers in the community for years to come, and to this extent Nicolls' policy was successful. The introduction of the policy of conveying to a single individual large tracts of land, where there was no prospect of immediate settlement by redistribution in freehold form, became in a short time a serious abuse, a temptation to venal governors as well as to adventurous speculators. Since the crown received for these patents no respectable *quid pro quo*, and since, even as to quitrents to which it was entitled, its claims were persistently flouted, the land question remained for nearly all parties the subject of political manipulation and endless litigation.

The Courts under Dongan

Except for the brief period of Dutch reoccupation, there were no changes of consequence in the judicial arrangements that prevailed in New York until the governorship of Dongan. After the withdrawal of the Dutch, the Duke's Laws were again put into operation and were subjected to occasional amendment by the court of assizes under Governor Andros. Upon the accession of Dongan to the governorship, however, came the institution of a provincial Assembly. With the change in legislative control, one might normally expect that a considerable renovation of the law would have ensued. Yet, despite popular participation in legislation, the latent resentment to many articles of the Duke's Laws did not find expression in any effort for a general repeal. The high spirits of the populace were diverted into the enactment of a very pretty charter of liberties which, alas, failed of confirmation. This same Assembly, however, managed successfully certain important statutory additions, not the least of which was an act for the reform of the judicial system (November 1, 1683).

The old town courts were confirmed, but their jurisdiction was limited to cases of debt or trespass to the value of 40 shillings. The act particularly specified that the causes were to be tried by persons commissioned for this purpose, without a jury; but if the parties desired and paid for the latter form of trial, it could be had. The courts of sessions for civil and criminal causes in each of the newly constituted counties were confirmed, but apparently without jurisdictional limit as before. At least three justices of the peace were necessary for a quorum.

The most radical change introduced by the new act was the institution of a regular court of oyer and terminer and general gaol delivery with a "Capitall and Criminall" jurisdiction as well as power to try cases civil and "causes tryable at Common Law." To this court could be removed all suits where the debt or damage alleged was £5 or more; and by warrant, writ of error or certiorari any "Judgment Informacion or Indictment" was likewise removable. The oyer and terminer court possessed, therefore, both a transfer and error jurisdiction. It sat once a year in each county. The equity jurisdiction, heretofore distributed among the several courts, was vested in a court of chancery to be made up of the governor and the Council. A special right of appeal to the crown, where a case involved £100 or more, was fixed in the statute. It should be noted, however, that, by the terms of the commission which Dongan received after James ascended the throne, the governor and the Council were to act as a final court of review in these cases, and appeal was allowed to the crown only when £300 or more was in controversy.

Two important courts established under the previous laws were not touched by the new legislation, the court of assizes and the mayor's court of New York City. The former was abolished in 1684, and pending business turned over to the chancery for settlement. The criminal jurisdiction of the mayor's court was severed and exercised by a court of quarter sessions. Under the charter granted by Dongan to the city, however, a court of common pleas for civil suits was set up, which continued the name, as well as the civil jurisdiction, of the mayor's court. A court held by the recorder, at that time instituted, was abandoned after three years.

In the interval between the conquest of New York and the Revolution of 1688, the law, as it developed in the courts, presents many interesting and curious features. In the town courts, there is little perceptible change in jurisprudence, if we can dignify by such a sonorous term the primitive practice and idea of law there. Here we find active the methods which were still usual in the English local tribunals of the period, and if anything the jargon of the professionals is even less apparent. In the sessions courts the records reveal a certain crystallization of the procedure, which on the criminal side resembles greatly that of the quarter sessions in England. Taking due account of the variations introduced in the colony by code and statute, such as the issuance of writs by the clerks of court, the civil practice, at first extremely amorphous, acquired a certain regularity and in some details had the aspect of a crude imitation of the king's courts. Of the sessions in the country, it is difficult to form any decided judgment, since the records preserved are extremely meager. On the whole, their practice was on a somewhat higher level than that of the town courts. But even the most professional of the civil tribunals—the mayor's court of New York City—cannot fruitfully be compared with the Common Pleas at Westminster. During the years immediately following the conquest, the records of this court read but little differently from those of its predecessor, the court of the burgomaster and schepens. There is at first only an occasional use of the jury, but this method of trial becomes more usual. The exercise of what we may call its equity functions is constant; and the frequent administrative action, strongly reminiscent of the English justices of the peace, but performed *en banc*, adds to the difficulty of describing the early New York practice in terms of any single piece of English judicial machinery.

The Judiciary by Act of Assembly and Governor's Ordinance

There is no purpose in attempting to detail the vicissitudes of the courts during the Leisler régime, or the innovations which were then attempted. For it was not these events, but the reconstruction of the judiciary effected in 1691, which determined the course of institutional development during the eighteenth century. On May 6, 1691, was passed the well-known Act for Establishing Courts of Judicature. For the town courts were substituted justices of the peace, with power to try cases of debt or trespass to the value of 40 shillings. The justices were to act without a jury, but were to sit with one freeholder of the town or place where the cause of action should arise. A jury would be summoned, however, on the demand and at the cost of either litigant.

For the "Increase of Virtue and the discouraging of Evildoers," in every city or county a court of sessions of the peace was to be held at stated intervals during the year. The civil jurisdiction, however, was intrusted to courts of common pleas, to be held in the various cities and counties immediately after the sessions adjourned. One judge with three justices was to be commissioned in each county to hold the common pleas, with jurisdiction over all actions and matters "tryable at Common Law." In Albany and New York City, the mayor's courts were to function as the courts of common pleas. Judgment in matters up to £20 was to be final.

The chief court of the province was established as the supreme court of judicature. To hold this court at New York City and not elsewhere, five justices at least were to be commissioned, of which two, together with the chief justice, were to constitute a quorum. The supreme court was to have cognizance in all cases civil, criminal and mixed, as "fully and amply" as the courts of King's Bench, Common Pleas, and Exchequer in England "have or ought to have." In this supreme court could be begun, or to it removed, any "action or suit the death or damage laid in such action or suit being upward of twenty pounds." The statute is not clear on the limits of criminal jurisdiction. It provides for the removal by warrant, writ of error or certiorari of judgments, indictments or informations from common pleas or sessions there had or depending, and gives the supreme court power to correct errors in judgment or to reverse the same. At this same time, in England, a writ of error did not lie as of right in criminal cases. The New York act, therefore, must be understood to confer upon the supreme court no more than the power of the King's Bench to remove by certiorari indictments or informations from the country to be heard *en banc*. It may be added that the language of the act of November 11, 1692, enacted to continue the 1691 statute, bears out this interpretation.

Two other important features of the new establishment were

the provisions for a court of chancery, and for appeals from the supreme court to the governor and the Council, when the amount of the judgment exceeded £100, and from the latter to the king in Council when more than £300 was involved.

The judicial system thus set up was confirmed by various statutes in the ensuing six years, all of the acts being temporary. Only one noteworthy addition was made in the arrangements, and this by the act of 1692. Provision was made for a justice of the supreme court to "goe the circuit" once a year in each county of the province and to hold the supreme court assisted by two or more justices of the peace, to hear and determine all process and pleas there depending and issued. In this rather maladroit manner the English *nisi prius* system was introduced. We may surmise from the language of the statute that the judge on circuit was by its terms competent to hear both civil and criminal causes, but in practice, following the English usage, he was armed with a commission of oyer and terminer to enable him to function in the latter case. In England, owing to extensions of the jurisdiction of justices of the peace, the quarter sessions courts were competent to try practically all felonies. Nevertheless, as a matter of practice in the late seventeenth and during the eighteenth century, capital cases were not there tried, but the prisoner was held for the assizes. It was likewise possible for a defendant by certiorari to have his cause removed directly to the King's Bench and to be tried at Westminster. An examination of the remaining records of the New York supreme court indicates that the criminal jurisdiction of that court was built up roughly on this pattern. The defendant would be normally tried at sessions, yet by certiorari his case could be removed to the supreme court, and his trial would take place at the circuit term. Of course it was always possible for a special commission of oyer and terminer to issue, and this in fact was frequently done.

The striking thing about the legislation after the Leisler revolt is the fact that a definite effort was made to Anglicize the judiciary. In England all three of the king's courts, the King's Bench, Common Pleas and the Exchequer, were vying with each other for business. The King's Bench alone had cognizance of criminal causes and by various fictions it had built up a tremendous civil jurisdiction. The Common Pleas had exclusive jurisdiction over real actions—the oldest forms of land actions—and competed with the

King's Bench for civil business of other sorts. The Exchequer, originally a court for revenue cases, had evolved both an independent common law and an equity branch. In New York there was, of course, no sensible reason for duplicating these courts when in many particulars they had overlapping powers, or merely offered alternative writs or procedure. Nevertheless, the intent of the legislature was clear—that the New York courts were to be formed in the image of the courts at Westminster.

When we contrast the English courts with those of New York, there emerge many curious points of similarity and difference. Thus on the civil side there were many features of the English *nisi prius* system that made it useful in New York, for the conditions under which the English system had grown up were in some respects similar to those in the colony. In England a series of courts of high professional skill existed in the metropolis, but tribunals with a crude and outmoded procedure functioned in the country. In New York, the supreme court and the mayor's court, as we shall see, had acquired in the early eighteenth century a technical perfection in doing business, comparable to the king's court, but in the counties the courts of common pleas were manned by men of little learning and, as we know from the Council minutes, not always above reproach. Even the circumstance that the leading barristers of the province did in fact practice in these courts on occasion was not in itself sufficient pressure to overcome the handicap of a lay judiciary. In these circumstances, the circuit term of the supreme court enabled litigants whose cases came within the jurisdictional limits of that court to have their causes tried by a professional judge without the trouble and expense of a journey to New York. It is to be noted also that the supreme court was liberal in permitting the trial of cases *en banc*. If a litigant desired to have the full bench of that court sit on his case he was not subjected to the same restrictions that would have applied in England for the same advantage. This is apparent from the ruling in *Jackson ex dem. Terboss v. DuBois* (MS Min. Sup. Ct. 1764-1766): ". . . it appearing to the court that an impartial Jury cannot be had in Ulster [County] . . . and that the cause will require great examination both on account of the value of the Lands in controversy and the length and difficulty of the tryal; and because *from the peculiar state of this country to which the Practice of this Court has been adapted* for the advancement of Justice, tryalls at Barr have been frequently allowed on reasons not so urgent as those now offered."

All of the legislative acts relating to the judiciary at this time were temporary. This rendered each reënactment subject, of course, to possible disallowance; and the recurrent necessity of such reënactment was a fruitful source of political dispute. Thus in 1695 the common pleas courts in the country were given power to try titles, a provision which caused the governor to remark bitterly that it was "a thing unpresidented for the county justices to have the power of trying title of land where the construction of deeds and writeings is necessary and requires more skill in the law than any of them can pretend to." It is a curious commentary on the English conception of justice that laymen could be intrusted with the trial of men's lives, but not of their lands.

The final act of the Assembly relating to the judiciary expired in 1698. At that time a prolonged wrangle between Bellomont and the Assembly was under way. The former dissolved the legislature before a reënactment of the judiciary act was put through, and in the ensuing year a bill was passed which Bellomont thought so incoherent and repugnant to the laws of England that he refused to give his assent to it. The objection was addressed to that portion of the act which endeavored to set up a supreme court of judicature in every city and county. This, Graham, the attorney general, and William Smith, the chief justice, regarded as contrary to the common law and a restriction on the king's prerogative. Their opinions formed the basis of the governor's refusal to assent. The Assembly thereupon declined to take further action, and was adjourned. The situation thus precipitated threatened to become critical, since the province was without courts. Bellomont, however, refusing to be dragooned by his legislature, decided to take advantage of his commission authorizing him to erect and establish a judicial system. He had already sharply declared that "the people must not be deceived. The province is subject to the Crown of England." Having reminded the New Yorkers whence his power emanated, by an ordinance dated May 15, 1699, he reëstablished the judicial system theretofore existing. This ordinance was in effect until superseded by a similar ordinance of Lord Cornbury, promulgated in 1704. The latter remained the legal foundation of the judicial system up to the Revolution, except in so far as it was modified by ordinances relating to the circuit system.

It is well to consider at this juncture the judicial arrangements for dealing with probate and admiralty cases, for here the exercise by the governor of his prerogative does not appear to have excited opposition.

In England, during the seventeenth and eighteenth centuries, jurisdiction in matters testamentary was vested in the ecclesiastical courts. Such a system was, of course, impractical in colonial New York. Under the Duke's Laws, the courts of sessions were vested with jurisdiction over probate matters. At the same time, this code required all wills to be registered at New York in the office of the secretary of the province. This led to the practice of the latter issuing letters of administration. Matters of probate consequently fell into the hands of the governor, whose jurisdiction was in theory exercised as a part of his prerogative. In 1692, an act for the probate of wills was passed by the Assembly, providing that in every town two freeholders should be chosen to take charge of intestates' estates. Probate of wills was to be made before the governor, and he or his delegate was to issue letters of administration under the seal of the prerogative office. In outlying counties, the common pleas courts were to take proof of wills and then transmit the record to the secretary.

Pursuant to this act, the governor appointed a delegate, and a court known as the prerogative court was established, to which appeals lay from the common pleas courts and from the acts of town officers. In due course, delegates subordinate to the governor's delegate were appointed for outlying counties, but their powers were slight, for, if any litigation arose, it was settled in the prerogative court or in the chancery.

Another important jurisdiction, which in England was administered outside the common law tribunals, was the admiralty jurisdiction. In New York the first governors derived their authority to set up admiralty courts from their commissions and instructions. The first court of this sort was held by Colonel Nicolls shortly after the conquest, and in this early period the mayor's court in New York City exercised jurisdiction in certain admiralty cases, and laid the basis for its claims to take cognizance of these matters. From time to time special admiralty courts *ad hoc* were set up, but until 1692 no serious attempt was made to settle the matter on a permanent basis. Governor Fletcher apparently did not think his general commission sufficient for him to set up a permanent court of admiralty. Accordingly he applied to the Lords of Admiralty, who by warrant empowered him to appoint a judge, registrar and marshal. Under Bellomont, the admiralty issued a commission to Chief Justice Smith, and the brief practice of having the chief justices act as admiralty judges was thus initiated; but in 1721 this practice was discontinued by the appointment of Francis Harrison.

In 1697, the British government organized the vice admiralty for the dominions and set up various districts. When Mompesson came over, he was commissioned admiralty judge for New York, New Jersey, Connecticut, Rhode Island and Massachusetts, but in 1721 the jurisdiction was cut down to include only New York, New Jersey and Connecticut. Crimes on the high seas were tried by virtue of special commissions of oyer and terminer for the admiralty jurisdiction. The admiralty courts were useful during the privateering of the early eighteenth century, and had, therefore, a certain popular support. Subsequently, when the chief business was the enforcement of the navigation acts, they were abominated, and the fact that the crown kept control over appeals tended to increase this feeling.

It has been remarked that executive initiative in setting up courts for probate and admiralty was not opposed, and the reason for this undoubtedly lay in the circumstance that these were not matters of common law. On the other hand, in respect to the ordinary judicial establishment, the action of the governors in executing the powers of their commissions was not viewed by the people at large with complaisance. Since 1683, they had undertaken themselves to regulate their judicial institutions and personally regarded the execution of the governors' commissions in this matter as dependent upon their mandate. But the ground on which they rested their opposition to the governor's actions was the technical one that the king without Parliament could not establish courts. This was blunt and tactless talk for the late seventeenth century, since even Coke (*Jentleman's Case*, 6 *Rep.* XI) had never ventured so far as to deny royal power to set up courts. It is true that in 1641, when various Tudor prerogative courts were abolished, the English Parliament sought to check the future formation of courts by the crown out of Privy Council by enacting a prohibition upon "English bills," as the petitions to the latter were called; and certainly the Revolution of 1688, which established the supremacy of

Parliament, accomplished in fact the result for which the colonists were contending. Nevertheless, this was still a controverted question among lawyers and Nathaniel Bacon, some twenty years after Bellomont's ordinance, is very careful, in his *Abridgment*, not to be categorical on the question. Whatever interpretation may be set on the constitutional results of the English Revolution upon the crown's power to erect courts in England, it is certain that as respects the over-sea dominions this power was not conceived to have sustained any diminution. Indeed, the persistence of the practice of the king reviewing in council both colonial legislation and judicial decision, testifies to the fact that the curtailment of his domestic privileges did not extend to his majesty's pleasure abroad. The colonists, however, had their own ideas about the common law. They resented the distinctions between the king's prerogative at home and abroad, and it is patent from Bellomont's reports that their notions and those of the royal administration were essentially irreconcilable.

In the matter of the common law courts, the governors succeeded in frustrating popular initiative, although there was a periodic effort to regain, by the passage of acts "settling" courts of justice, what in effect amounted to lost prestige. Indirectly, a certain measure of control was exercised by the Assembly through its power of voting salaries to the justices of the supreme court and its practice of voting these sums to the justices personally by name, and not to the officers for the time being. This was clearly a device designed to restrict the governor's choice when an office was open. Clinton, in 1748, remonstrated against the form of grant and the Assembly promptly told him that it was done to keep out unworthy persons.

The issue between governor and people on the power to establish courts eventually became focused upon the establishment of chancery. By his commission, the governor had the power to erect a court of chancery and to sit as chancellor. Although the court was set up from time to time, it does not seem to have functioned effectively or with regularity, since, as Bellomont complained, he needed five of his councilors to sit with him and he could never round up that number. After Cornbury's arrival, some of these defects were remedied, but there developed a very bitter opposition to the court, in part attributable to the fact that, equity jurisprudence being a highly technical branch of the law of England, a layman was utterly unqualified to sit as chancellor. Although the lawyer members of the Council could, and on occasion did, sit with the governors, there seems to have persisted in the breasts of the latter an unconquerable desire to "play the Chancellor," as Francis Bacon once remarked of the common law judges.

During the Cosby régime, an effort was made to secure a capable equity court by taking advantage of the fact that the supreme court had been given the powers *inter alia* of the court of the exchequer. In England, the tribunal of this name had developed an independent equity jurisdiction, and on the strength of this fact the notion of building up in the supreme court these functions was actually put into operation. The crown was interested in developing the revenue jurisdiction of the exchequer chiefly because of the quitrent situation. In this the wishes of the crown and the desires of the governors were in opposition, since, under the accepted legal theory of the period, it would have been difficult to have in active operation a separate exchequer court, or even a regular exchequer term of the supreme court, without implicitly admitting that all the equity functions of the English model were exercisable as necessary and proper. This would have led to a division of equity business, and would undoubtedly have deprived the governors of a valued jurisdiction. Entries in the minute books show that the supreme court did sit as a court of exchequer, but this experiment, with an exchequer term, eventually proved abortive. As far as the general public was concerned, the advantage of a trained bench did not compensate for the vitiation of their fundamental tenet that a chancery court could not be established without a legislative act.

The Common Law and Political Propaganda

The matter reached a climax when the issue was debated before the Assembly, pursuant to resolution, by William Smith and Joseph Murray, the two leaders of the bar. No legislative action ensued, and the governor continued to act as before: indeed, as the manuscript minute books and dockets testify, the business of chancery waxed. Nevertheless the debate, preserved in a contemporary pamphlet, was important and illuminating, for it brought into sharp relief the popular and official views. Of these, the former is by far the more interesting, since the opposition in New York to chancery did not entirely abate until the court was abolished nearly a century later.

The arguments of Smith and Murray are cast in the legalistic mold; but, if we read them in connection with other sources of information, the basis of the division over chancery becomes obvious. The royal officials were in the habit of blaming the odium of chancery upon landholders who did not desire their patents to be inquired into, or who resented the persistent attempt to collect quitrents. In this their observations were not at fault. There were many dark chapters hidden in the books of land patents which leading citizens would have been reluctant to have dragged into the light. With the same avidity with which they clung to their domains in the wilderness, they held on to the bushel of wheat, or the two beaver pelts, owed to the crown as quitrent. At the same time, one must not underestimate the deep-rooted popular aversion to chancery because it was regarded as an instrumentality of prerogative, and consequently not subject to the controls that were believed to exist over the common law courts. A scrutiny of the great variety of occasions upon which a vociferous appeal was made to the common law, shows that a great deal of misapprehension existed among the colonists at large concerning the nature of the common law, its function in the English legal system, and its genius as the guardian of human liberty. The popular beliefs can be explained only if we realize that the chaplet of political liberalism, which Coke and his contemporaries had woven about the common law, was as yet untarnished in the colony. The common law still retained its repute as a palladium of liberty, and the later quarrels of the eighteenth century in New York are carried on, by one side at least, in much the same idiom as the political Puritans in the reign of Charles I conducted the early parliamentary battles.

The persistence of this illusion can be explained in large measure by the fact that the early seventeenth-century books were more current than those of late vintage, and by the extraordinary vogue which Coke's *Institutes* enjoyed up to the dawn of the American Revolution. In such an intellectual atmosphere, the tenor of mid-eighteenth-century debate in England is rarely heard. In New York reverberate the echoes of the older battle cries. This mixture of common law as liberty, and common law as a better system of law than any other, we encounter most decidedly in the movement for a charter of liberties during the Dongan régime.

It is again sharply apparent in the effort made to repeal the Duke's Laws at the 1691 Assembly, since these were considered as an heritage from the days of tyranny. The Assembly passed a resolution to this effect, but the Council and the governor did not give their assent. This resolution consequently never became law. Nevertheless, the impression has until lately prevailed in our courts that the Duke's Laws were thereafter not observed, and that the resolution was in fact as effective as if it had had statutory force. This view is not borne out by the records, since we find that various provisions of the Duke's Laws, such as the registration of conveyances, were in fact observed for years after the Assembly's abortive action; that a trial for adultery, not an offence at common law but made so in the Duke's Laws, actually was held in the quarter sessions of New York City in 1694; and that in the early eighteenth century the Duke's Laws were offered in evidence by counsel in the supreme court, in the same manner as are other statutes. Indeed, in the wrangle over the governor's power to establish courts of justice, the argument was advanced that the legislation of 1683 regarding courts had been revived by the expiration of the colonial act of 1697, because the early act was permanent and later statutes were temporary only. Again, in 1741, there was a proposal for the repeal of all acts prior to the "Happy Revolution." In view of such contemporary evidence, we cannot deny that, except where repealed in specific cases, these laws in fact retained their validity, and they continued likewise to serve the needs of political expediency.

The episode of the "repeal" of the Duke's Laws is instructive, chiefly because it testifies to the existence of an almost nostalgic desire for common law rather than manufactured colonial law. When we say the people desired the common law, however, we do not mean that they thought of it in the bald terms of an action of trespass, a plea in abatement, a special traverse, a writ of entry in the *cui* or any of the other constituents that went to make up the lawyer's idea of what this law was. It was to them a sanctuary which beckoned when there threatened some black evil from which they suffered, whether the Duke's Laws, a governor's ordinance, or a royal disallowance of a provincial act. Reduced to its lowest terms, we may say the colonists' desire was to enjoy the same privileges and rights with reference to the crown that were enjoyed by the residents of England. That these rights and privileges seemed from the American woods much more delectable than they in fact were is comprehensible. Inured to democracy, we of the twentieth century smile when the Spaniards drive out their king. The discontented seek rights where they will find only duties.

The desire for the common law was fulfilled with the advent of lawyers from home, and in their hands the amorphous jurisprudence of the new courts presently took shape. There was a certain mordant humor in the situation. The common law as an ideal was devoutly prayed for; the law in fact—a tangle of technicalities—was what the lawyers brought. In the early days, with a lay chief justice like "Tangier" Smith, there was little hope for an intelligent application of the tortured darkness of the *Book of Entries*, but there was a rough and substantial justice accomplished. The metamorphosis from country justice to common law perfection begins with the turn of the century.

The profound change which took place in the whole technique of law administration is in many ways astounding. There was never really any necessity for abolishing the Duke's Laws or the acts of the Dongan Assemblies, for upon the arrival of really learned barristers the crudities that had become the rule in the practice of the law were by mere force of example swept into the discard. There have been preserved some notes of memoranda of authority in various arguments on demurrer in the provincial courts about the year 1733, which demonstrate that the New York bar was not far behind that of England in profundity of learning and adeptness in dealing with common law precedent. Indeed one need only examine the account of the Bayard trial (1702), one of the most fully reported cases of the early eighteenth century, to realize how the professionalization of the law was advancing. And if one turns to the Zenger trial (1735), it is apparent that the practice of the law had acquired a high degree of technical perfection.

The Lawyers and the Law

The men who practiced as attorneys during the first decade of English government in New York were undoubtedly self-taught. After the revolution of 1688, somewhat more skillful persons appear at the bar, and we may well surmise that they were men who at home had been articled as clerks in law offices. Judged by English standards, they were not ornaments of the profession, but the blanket indictment of the bar penned by Lord Bellomont in 1698 we may dismiss as altogether too prejudiced. The thoroughgoing metamorphosis of practice which ensued after 1700, and particularly after 1714, we can attribute only to the new lawyers who came during this period. We have biographical details of only a few of these men; two or three of them we know were trained, as were their English contemporaries, in the Inns of Court. Others, about whose lives we know little, exhibit such learning as to justify an assumption that they too were trained in the Inns. It was not long before their store of learning was a part of the provincial law. The lawyers drew up the pleadings and forms necessary to an orderly practice, adapting the English models to colonial conditions. These "precedents" they carefully preserved, and when they died, these manuscripts were almost invariably passed on to brother barristers. In the course of the eighteenth century, the leading practitioners, constituting a "Law Society," made provision for the study of law in their offices. An agreement was drawn up with reference to this matter, by which it was stipulated that the prospective clerks must have two years of college education and must bind themselves as clerks for five years. No attorney was to take in more than two clerks at a time, and the fee established was £500.

In both the Smith and the Livingston papers, is preserved a document dealing with law study, that probably represents the typical method of training in an eighteenth-century New York law office. It tells us that

> The sciences necessary for a lawyer are 1. The English, Latin and French Tongues. 2. Writing, Arithmetick, Geometry, Surveying, Merchant's Accounts or Bookkeeping. 3. Geography, Cronology, History. 4. Logick and Rhetorick. 5. Divinity. 6. Law of Nature and Nations. 7. Law of England.

Explicit instructions were given as to the books to be used in the various fields of knowledge. The directions for the study of the law itself are exceedingly interesting, since the student is first expected to ground himself in the legal philosophy of the period, and only then to master the leading English text writers. Many of the leading lawyers of the later eighteenth century were trained in this way, and one can understand why these men were superior in learning to those of a later generation, whose chief pabulum was the cloying text of Blackstone.

The chief result of the lawyers' achievement in bringing about a more or less complete reception of the common law in the province was the certainty and stabilization of practice. But the reception of English common law tended toward a certain ossification. The reason for this appears to have been that, in the substantive law of the province, there was little or no growth of native precedent. English cases and English statutes served as a sort of *corpus* to which reference was made for support of legal arguments, much as the *Corpus Juris Civilis* was contemporaneously used on the continent. Thus in the same or ensuing terms of the supreme court, the same point might be adjudicated, the later case not referring to the precious provincial determination, but depending upon the identical English precedents used before. This the manuscript remains of the colonial courts clearly and unanimously demonstrate. Unless some important find in the way of provincial judicial opinions should be made, any other conclusion is unlikely. Under the circumstances, the dependency of the legal profession upon the output of the English was considerable, yet we do not find that there existed the same passion for the latest case that is one of the ludicrous by-products of our modern system of over-reporting. Bracton and Coke were venerated names, and many of the New York lawyers owned and used the old *Year Books* at a time when they were rapidly going out of fashion in England. Indeed, the colonial reliance on the older monuments of the law lends to the New York practice an air almost Jacobite.

There is no doubt that the New York bar during the eighteenth century was learned; but the law, as practiced by it, was not flexible and, in spite of certain occasional changes, it did not have that close relation to the life of the community, nor did it make that steady and minute adjustment to circumstances, which was one of the prime attributes of the judge-made law of England, and which gave to English law its constant vitality. In New York, the task of adjusting the common law to the American wilds was an accomplishment of the legislature, and not of the judiciary; and in the statutes enacted within a period of one century lies the real record of the execution of the crown's behest that colonial law should conform "as nearly as may be" to the law of England. It is this record which discloses to us how genuine was the interest and the concern of the inhabitants in the problems of the law. If the courts lacked flexibility in response to the changes in social needs, social pressure was bound to manifest itself elsewhere. It is perhaps this phase of the law's development in the colony that may account for the extraordinary predominance of the legislature in the government during the early years of the Republic.

Conditions at the Close of the Colonial Period

It is not to be assumed from what has been said that colonial legislation was, in matters of private law, either radical or progressive. It took the initiative in law-making, but it was dominated by certain familiar taboos. Of these, opposition to the royal prerogative and veneration for the common law, in what may be called its "rights and interests" phase, were predominant. This temper is most admirably demonstrated in the controversy which raged in 1764 and 1765 over the question of whether cases could be carried from the supreme court to the governor and Council on appeal. The question was one dealing with the technicalities of appellate review. It was made to bristle with public law implications regarding the rights of subjects and the integrity of the common law.

One Forsey brought an action of trespass for assault and battery against Waddel Cunningham. The jury found for the plaintiff and damages in excess of £1,000 were awarded. Cunningham's attorney applied to Cadwallader Colden, acting governor, for a writ directing the chief justice to bring the proceedings in the cause before the governor and the Council. This was granted. Previously a "writ of inhibition" had been issued to stay all proceedings by way of execution.

This is the first time an appeal was attempted in a common law case in New York. Theretofore, the practice had been to obtain review by writ of error, whereby only errors of law on the record or as noted in the bill of exceptions came before the appellate court. The appeal was the method employed in England to secure a review of an interlocutory order or final decree in chancery. Since in chancery the evidence was in writing, the appeal permitted an investigation into the merits of the controversy and was not limited, as in the writ of error, to mere errors of law that appeared on the record. Colden, an inveterate enemy of the lawyers, informed the crown that he acted as he did because he felt that on a writ of error the merits of a cause seldom appeared. Moreover, he discerned, in the opposition to the appeal, the influence of the great landed proprietors of the province who, he asserted, were hand in glove with the judges and provincial lawyers. He urged the form of appeal, as against the writ of error, as a means of strengthening the hand of the crown.

The excitement caused by the case ran high. The issue really turned on the construction of the instructions to the governor. In 1753, in the clause of these instructions which gave permission to appeal from any of the courts of common law in the province, the words "in case of error only," previously inserted, were left out, and succeeding instructions followed this form. This was undoubtedly the technical basis for Colden's action. On January 11, 1765, the Council ruled that there could be only an appeal in error under article 32 of the king's instructions. Justice Horsmanden prepared for this occasion an elaborate opinion. He saw beneath the innocent and just design of having an appellate review, which would inquire into the merits of an adjudicated case and not merely of errors on the record, a villainous thrust at the jury. The inevitable response to this challenge was revival of old libertarian arguments for the preservation of the integrity of the jury's function.

The provincial Council's interpretation of the instructions was supported by the attorney and solicitor generals of England, who were of the opinion that the alteration of the wording in the instructions did not alter the sense, and that a jurisdiction in error only could be meant. In the instructions then drafted for Sir Henry Moore, the old words "in error" were inserted, so that in future there could be no doubt.

The reaction of the Assembly to Colden's action was typical. Influenced by the arguments regarding the governor's attack upon the jury system, on November 12, 1765, a resolution directed toward the preservation of this system was passed—"trial by jury is the right of the subject not only by common law, by statute law and the laws of this colony, but essential to the lives, liberty, and prosperity of the people." This was coupled with a reprimand to Colden and compliments to the justices of the supreme court. On the Assembly's record, the common law had once more appeared holding the bright sword of liberty. It had, in fact, triumphed because two of his majesty's counsel preferred a lawyer's interpretation of the governor's instructions to that of a politician.

The fidelity with which the New York colonists adhered to the common law may well have something to do with the failure of a native precedent to develop in the courts. In any event, the law of New York bore the aspect of a mere parasite grafted on the law of England, and one would not suppose that at the hands of the judges a distinctive American jurisprudence was ever to emerge. Despite these factors, however, which tended to retard the spirit of initiative and independence in the judiciary, there were springs which fed the colonial law and from which it drew a philosophic life that was eventually to be not without its effect. This was the great body of Continental writings on natural law and the law of nations. During the seventeenth century in England, there was a certain infiltration of ideas from this source, and some Roman law doctrine in the guise of natural law was in this wise received. In New York province, however, works like Grotius' *De jure belli ac pacis*, Ducks' *De usu et authoritate juris civilis*, and Pufendorf's *De jure naturae*, appear to have become domiciled. They were frequently cited in argument, beginning as early as 1729, and with no less reverence than the monuments of the common law. Indeed works of this type appear to have supplied a deeply felt need in the literature of the English law, which was strangely lacking in philosophical grounding, and had but rarely formed the basis of philosophical speculation.

The American lawyer's esteem of the learning and discipline to be derived from the natural law treatises pervades the document relating to the study of the law which we have already mentioned. The philosophical grounding of the apprentice begins with the study of Pufendorf's *De officio hominis et civis*, to be followed by Tyrrel's treatise on the law of nature, Pufendorf "at large" and Grotius' *De jure belli ac pacis*. It was no mere accident that the first professorship of law in America, established at King's College in New York, should have been denominated a chair of "Natural Law."

It is difficult for us to judge precisely how far the fermenting juices of the natural law, and the union of these with the libertarian traditions of the common law, produced in the practice of New York province a definable result. The political consequences we know were vast: the effect upon conceptions of public law was revolutionary. Yet when independence had been declared and some pronouncement had to be made with respect to the private law, it was enacted that such parts of the common law and statutes of England and of the colonial legislature as did together form the law of the colony on April 19, 1775, "shall be and continue" the law of the state, subject of course to legislative addition. In the practice of the courts and in the ordinary problems of daily life that might be litigated, there was no intention of abandoning the certainty of the past for the dreams of philosophers. But for all this, the common law did not escape unscathed. Some readjustments took place. Men had inveighed against the prerogative in all its manifestations, so the power of purveyance disappeared, but, in the guise of Grotius' phrase—the power of eminent domain—it crept into the Constitution. The theory of corporate creation as a grant by royal prerogative was metamorphosed into a doctrine of contract, under the influence of notions of social compact, then greatly in fashion. The horrors of judgment of felony gave way to restricted punishments toward which men were led by the humanitarianism of the rationalists. The changes were many. The record of post-revolutionary trials and appellate argument discloses a continual pounding with weapons from the civil law and the law of nations. Yet when a generation had passed and the foundations of an autochthonous precedent had been laid, it was clear that, from whatever source innovation might spring, these matters would be tributary to the main stream, the common law, by whose currents men's thinking about law would continue to move.

Select Bibliography

This chapter is based chiefly upon manuscript records of the New York colonial courts. The bulk of this material, preserved in various county and state offices in regions settled before 1776, was examined by the writer in the years 1925-26. This examination included all MS minute books of the several courts, dockets, parchments, loose papers and miscellaneous files. Where the present account differs in matters of detail from versions in the secondary works listed below, such differences are based upon documentary sources.

Crump, Helen J., Colonial Admiralty Jurisdiction in the Seventeenth Century (London, 1931).

Daly, Charles P., History of the Court of Common Pleas, in E. D. Smith's Common Pleas Reports, I, xvii (New York, 1855).

—— The Nature, Extent and History of the Jurisdiction of the Surrogate's Courts of the State of New York (New York, 1863).

Fowler, Robert L., Historical Introduction. Grolier Club Facsimile of the Bradford Laws of 1694 (New York, 1894).

——— History of the Law of Real Property in New York (New York, 1895).

——— Organization of the Supreme Court of Judicature of the Province of New York. Albany Law Journal, XIX, 66, 87, 106, 149, 189, 209, 229, 309, 349, 389, 430, 489.

Goebel, Julius, Jr., Cases and Materials on the Development of Legal Institutions (New York, 1932).

——— King's Law and Local Law in Seventeenth Century New England. Columbia Law Review, XXXI, 474.

——— Some Legal and Political Aspects of the Manors in New York (Baltimore, 1928).

Hoffman, Murray, A Treatise upon the Practice of the Court of Chancery (1835).

Hough, Charles M., Reports of Cases in the Vice-Admiralty of the Province of New York (New York, 1925).

New York (state), The Colonial Laws of New York. 5 vols. (Albany, 1896).

O'Callaghan, E. B., Documentary History of the State of New York. 4 vols. (Albany, 1849-51).

——— Documents Relative to the Colonial History of the State of New York. 15 vols. (Albany, 1853-87).

PART THREE

The Eighteenth Century

XII

*Administrative Control of the Courts of the American Plantations**

JOSEPH H. SMITH

Studies of the imperial control of the administration of justice in the American plantations in the seventeenth and eighteenth centuries have tended to concentrate on the appellate jurisdiction of the King in Council or the Privy Council over the various colonial courts—common law, chancery, probate, and admiralty.[1] Yet an important adjunct to the control of the various plantation judiciaries by conciliar appeals was the regulation exercised by the disallow-

* "Administrative Control of the Courts of the American Plantations," by Joseph H. Smith, is reprinted with permission from the *Columbia Law Review*, LXI (1961), 1210-1253.

1. For the literature see J. SMITH, APPEALS TO THE PRIVY COUNCIL FROM THE AMERICAN PLANTATIONS (1950); WASHBURNE, IMPERIAL CONTROL OF THE ADMINISTRATION OF JUSTICE IN THE THIRTEEN AMERICAN COLONIES, 1684-1776 (1923); SCHLESINGER, *Colonial Appeals to the Privy Council*, 28 POL. SCI. Q. 279, 433 (1913); Andrews, *The Connecticut Intestacy Law*, 3 YALE REV. 261 (1894) (the same article in modified form entitled *The Influence of Colonial Conditions as Illustrated in the Connecticut Intestacy Law*, is also found in 1 SELECT ESSAYS IN ANGLO-AMERICAN LEGAL HISTORY 431 [1907] and in CONNECTICUT TERCENTENARY COMMITTEE PUBLICATION NO. 2 [1933]); Hazeltine, *Appeals from Colonial Courts to the King in Council with Especial Reference to Rhode Island*, 1894 ANN. REP. AM. HIST. A. 299; Davis, *The Case of Frost vs. Leighton*, 2 AM. HIST. REV. 229-40 (1897) (another version appears in 3 PUBLICATIONS OF THE COLONIAL SOC'Y OF MASS. 246-64 [1896]); Scott, *The Constitutional Aspects of the "Parson's Cause,"* 31 POL. SCI. Q. 558 (1916); G. Smith, *The Parsons' Cause, 1755-1765*, 21 TYLER'S Q. HISTORICAL & GENEALOGICAL MAGAZINE 140, 291 (1940); DICKERSON, AMERICAN COLONIAL GOVERNMENT, 1696-1765 at 274-81 (1912); LABAREE, ROYAL GOVERNMENT IN AMERICA 407-19 (1930); KEYS, CADWALLADER COLDEN, A REPRESENTATIVE EIGHTEENTH CENTURY OFFICIAL 300-11 (1906); 1 HAMLIN & BAKER, SUPREME COURT OF JUDICATURE OF THE PROVINCE OF NEW YORK 1691-1704, at 422-38 (The New York Historical Society 1952); GOEBEL, CASES ON THE DEVELOPMENT OF LEGAL INSTITUTIONS 281-95 (1946); KNOLLENBERG, ORIGIN OF THE AMERICAN REVOLUTION: 1759-1766, at 53-64 (1960).

ance of colonial legislation by the King in Council. While the appellate process was of greatest importance for individual litigants, the legislative review process had far greater effect upon colonial judicial organization and procedure. In but few appeals did the conciliar determination affect the form of the judicial organization below or the procedure adopted by colonial judiciaries. It should be noted at the outset that, in the case of disallowance, acts were void and of no effect only from the date of communication of the royal disallowance to the colony; in the case of a declaration of nullity upon judicial review, acts were declared null and void *ab initio.*[2]

During most of the seventeenth century, the various councils and committees in England charged with the administration of plantation matters exercised no systematic control over colonial legislation.[3] It was not until the establishment in 1696 of the Lords Commissioners for Trade and Plantations, commonly known as the Board of Trade, that legislative review, specifically delegated to this body, attained an important role in imperial administration. While the Privy Council's Order in Council was the instrument of disallowance, and such orders were invariably based upon the advice of the conciliar committee charged with plantation affairs, the decision as to disallowance basically resided in the Board of Trade. However, in some areas of legislative review the Board placed great reliance on information and advice emanating from other governmental agencies. In its review of legislation relating to the colonial judicial establishments, the Board, until 1718, relied primarily on the opinions of the crown law officers, the Attorney General and the Solicitor General. With the appointment of its

2. See also the declaration of nullity upon legislative review under An Act for Plantation Trade 7 & 8 Will. 3, c. 22, § 9 (1696), J. SMITH, *op. cit. supra* note 1, at 526-37, 578-85, 592-93, and the hearing before the Board of Trade on some New York acts regulating the Indian trade, COMMISSIONERS FOR TRADE AND PLANTATIONS JOURNAL 1722/23-1728, at 166, 177 [hereinafter cited as JCTP].

3. See RUSSELL, THE REVIEW OF AMERICAN COLONIAL LEGISLATION BY THE KING IN COUNCIL 15-32 (1915); ANDREWS, BRITISH COMMITTEES, COMMISSIONS, AND COUNCILS OF TRADE AND PLANTATIONS, 1622-75 *passim* (26 Johns Hopkins University Studies in Historical and Political Science Nos. 1-3, 1908); BIEBER, THE LORDS OF TRADE AND PLANTATIONS, 1675-96 *passim* (1919). A charge levelled by Edward Randolph against Massachusetts Bay was that some of its laws were derogatory and contradictory to those of England. 3 OSGOOD, THE AMERICAN COLONIES IN THE SEVENTEENTH CENTURY 316-33 (1907); 2 TOPPAN, EDWARD RANDOLPH 232-34, 266, 271-72, 278-79, 281-84, 293-94, 312-18 (Prince Society Publication 1898); 3 *id.* at 39 (1899).

own counsel, termed "King's Council," in that year, primary responsibility for passing on such legislation "in point of law" shifted to such counsel—successively Richard West (1718-1725), Francis Fane (1725-1746), Matthew Lamb, knighted while counsel (1746-1768), and Richard Jackson (1770-1782). Over a span of more than fifty years, the opinions rendered by this counsel probably shaped the colonial judicial establishments more than any other single factor.[4]

This shaping was not, of course, confined to the mainland plantations; it also extended to the West Indian possessions, such as Jamaica, Barbados, and the Leeward Islands (Antigua, St. Christopher, Nevis, and Montserrat), then regarded in some quarters as more important components of empire than the continental colonies. In addition, it was not uniform in application. In the royal provinces there was no constitutional hindrance to legislative review. Of the proprietary colonies, only Pennsylvania was made subject to such review, and of the chartered colonies, only Massachusetts Bay. In the royal colonies, the gubernatorial commissions and instructions served not only as standards for legislative review but also as instruments to stifle undesirable colonial enactments in their incipiency. In some colonies, for certain periods, establishment of judicial systems and procedure by ordinances of the Governor and council made control by disallowance unnecessary. From time to time, however, patterns of resistance to legislative review developed; in addition, in some royal colonies control of the purse by the colonists served to blunt the force of gubernatorial objections to acts deemed to contravene imperial policy.[5]

4. The authoritative treatment of legislative review of colonial legislation is contained in RUSSELL, *op. cit. supra* note 3. It is, however, largely confined to the mainland colonies. Other discussions appear in DICKERSON, *op. cit. supra* note 1, at 225-74; Andrews, *The Royal Disallowance*, 24 AMERICAN ANTIQUARIAN SOC'Y PROCEEDINGS 342 (n.s. 1914) Dorland, *The Royal Disallowance in Massachusetts*, DEPARTMENTS OF HISTORY AND POLITICAL SCIENCE, QUEENS UNIVERSITY, BULLETIN NO. 22 (Kingston, Ontario, Canada, 1917). None of these contains an integrated treatment of the disallowance as it affected the colonial judicial establishments. For additional material on the organization and functions of the Board of Trade see 4 ANDREWS, THE COLONIAL PERIOD OF AMERICAN HISTORY 272-317 (1938); BASYE, THE LORDS COMMISSIONERS OF TRADE AND PLANTATIONS . . . 1748-1782 *passim* (1925); JACOBSEN, WILLIAM BLATHWAYT 296-354 (1932); Clarke, *The Board of Trade at Work*, 17 AM. HIST. REV. 17 (1911).

5. See 3 ACTS OF THE PRIVY COUNCIL OF ENGLAND, COLONIAL SERIES NO. 75, at 105-11 [series published from 1908 to 1912: date of volume will be omitted; hereinafter cited as APC, COL.]; BURNS, CONTROVERSIES BETWEEN ROYAL GOVERNORS AND THEIR ASSEMBLIES IN THE NORTHERN AMERICAN COLONIES 26-27, 304-

The legislative disallowances under consideration fall into two categories—those concerned with the establishment and regulation of courts and those concerned with judicial procedure. In the first group of disallowances, two policies emerge: (1) the desirability of centralized administration of justice, culminating in an appeal to the King in Council, and (2) the necessity of guarding against any diminution or infringement of the royal prerogative. In the second group, a wide range of procedural matters was tested for conformity with such standards as the laws of England, the common law, acts of Parliament, reason or justice, and colonial "constitutions." Disallowance was also employed to set aside acts that attempted to limit or restrict appellate recourse to England, and to exclude the colonial legislatures from exercising judicial powers; these subjects have been treated elsewhere.[6]

The present examination of the disallowance power is also related to the exercise by the Privy Council of appellate jurisdiction over the plantations in its judicial capacity. Conciliar attitudes in judicial matters proper were undoubtedly influenced or shaped by information gleaned from review of colonial laws. In the second place, legislative review fixed, to some extent, the conditions precedent for the exercise of appellate jurisdiction by the King in Council. Third, such review possibly explains why a number of "constitutional" questions, grappled with on administrative levels, never came before the Privy Council in its judicial capacity.

The Colonial Judicial Establishment

In general, the colonial judicial arrangements were fabricated locally without benefit of much or any direction from England, for in most cases these arrangements stemmed from the seventeenth century, when the Crown's controls had not yet been settled. This lack of administrative direction was in many respects a boon, since the picture of jurisdiction in England was one of bewildering complexity when the first plantation courts were established. Not only

13, 323-26, 340-56, 417-18 (1923); 6 Documents Relative to the Colonial History of the State of New York 460-61, 466-69, 472-73 (O'Callaghan ed.) [published from 1856-1887: date of volume will be omitted; hereinafter cited as Doc. Rel. Col. Hist. N.Y.]; Labaree, *op. cit. supra* note 1, at 269-373; 4 Osgood, The American Colonies in the Eighteenth Century 194-200 (1924); Spencer, *The Rise of the Assembly, 1691-1760*, in 2 History of the State of New York 185-91 (Flick ed. 1933).

6. See J. Smith, *op. cit. supra* note 1, at 174-77, 637-53.

was the common law civil jurisdiction divided at its fountain head among three courts—King's Bench, Common Bench, and Exchequer —of roughly coordinate power, but also the equitable phases were handled in Chancery and in Exchequer, probate was vested in ecclesiastical tribunals, and certain matters of commerce resided in the Admiralty. Criminal jurisdiction was superintended by King's Bench, but was largely exercised at assizes or in courts of quarter sessions. As one descended into the nether regions of local courts, a veritable bedlam came to view, with duplication of function because of the occasional creation of new agencies without liquidation of the old, jurisdiction by feoffment or by franchise, and authority exercised regionally by special courts. No effort had been made by English statesmen to rationalize and simplify, except during the Puritan revolution, because jurisdiction was a source of profit and was dominated by notions of property.

The colonists approached the problem of their judicial settlement primarily as one of providing an economical system of law enforcement, and were little concerned with property concepts of administering justice. Not wishing to sacrifice any heads of jurisdiction as these existed at home, they telescoped into single courts the powers that were diffused in England, and produced in certain localities, as for example Massachusetts, a fusion of powers that was sensible but scarcely made in the image of English justice.[7]

Toward the close of the seventeenth century, when imperial administration assumed significant stature, the posture of the Crown toward the colonial arrangements was, generally, to freeze the *status quo* as to the common law jurisdiction, and to reserve the chancery and ordinary (probate and administration) powers to the Governors. It manifested, furthermore, decided hostility to further colonial legislative activity in establishing courts, tossing to these perennial watchdogs of liberty a scrapless bone in the shape of privilege to deal with courts for small causes.[8] Even in this limited area the disallowance could be employed to ensure the right of

7. For a description of the Massachusetts Bay judicial system from 1639 to 1702 see COLONIAL JUSTICE IN WESTERN MASSACHUSETTS (1639-1702) 65-88 (J. Smith ed. 1961).

8. For the instructions concerning courts for small causes see 1 LABAREE, ROYAL INSTRUCTIONS TO BRITISH COLONIAL GOVERNORS, 1670-1776, No. 435 (1935) [hereinafter cited as LABAREE, ROYAL INSTRUCTIONS].

appeal[9] or to protect the trading classes.[10]

We are concerned primarily with the policy after 1696, but as this had its roots in the work of the Lords Committee of Trade and Plantations (1674/75-1696) it is desirable to advert briefly to this earlier period. The first royal commissions to Governors did not mention the power to erect courts, but the early Virginia instruc-

9. In 1706 a New Hampshire act to compel constables to perform their duties in collecting rates was disallowed. The Board of Trade objected that provision for imprisonment when no estate was visible was unreasonable, there being no appeal to the justices against the rates. 1 Laws of N.H. 559, 866 (Batchellor ed.) [published from 1904-1922: date of volume will be omitted]. In 1751 a Virginia act of 1748 was disallowed because, *inter alia*, it limited the appellate jurisdiction of the General Court to the putative detriment of trading subjects. 4 APC, Col. No. 155, at 139; 5 Statutes at Large . . . Va. . . . 1619-1792, at 467 (Hening ed.) [published from 1809-1823: date of volume will be omitted; hereinafter cited as Stat. at Large Va.]. Acting in 1764 to disallow a Georgia act concerning partition of lands, the Committee on Trade and Plantations stated that the corresponding act of Parliament, An Act for Partition of Land, 8 & 9 Will. 3, c. 31 (1696), had reserved an appeal from judgments upon writs of partition in cases of infancy and other disabilities. The Georgia act was so loosely worded as to be incomprehensible as to the effect of the act of Parliament. 4 APC, Col. No. 569. In 1770 a New Jersey act for settling claims to common lands in Bergen township was disallowed after complaint that it deprived petitioner of the right to judgment of the supreme court of judicature and appeal therefrom if necessary. 5 *id.* No. 152; Colonial Office Papers 5/979/L 5, L 9 (located in Public Record Office, London, England) [hereinafter cited as CO]. In the next year, another New Jersey act was disallowed which provided that in certain actions before a single justice of the peace no appeals would be permitted and, in actions in which the real debt or demand exceeded the sum of forty shillings, either party might demand a jury, with its verdict to be final. 5 APC, Col. No. 191. A 1770 West Florida act was disallowed in 1772 because, among other things, it established a county court of common pleas with a jurisdictional amount of thirty pounds sterling and no provision for appeal. 5 *id.* No. 200. In 1774 Richard Jackson advised disallowance of an act granting the selectmen of Boston certain regulatory powers, which might be used for oppressive purposes, without reserving an appeal. CO 5/895/PP 66. See also the 1700 disallowance of a Massachusetts Bay act as dilatory and vexatious in allowing three trials in each cause with liberty of three years delay between trials. 2 APC, Col. app. at 844; Calendar of State Papers, Colonial Series, America and West Indies, 1700, No. 825 [hereinafter cited as CSP, Col.].

10. In 1728 an Antigua act of 1724 establishing a court to hold pleas of foreign attachments according to the custom of the city of London was disallowed on the advice of the crown law officers. It was concluded that the act might occasion many inconveniences in commerce and might discourage British merchants from giving credit to persons residing in Antigua or from entrusting them with their effects. 3 APC, Col. No. 139. In Virginia, by a 1736 act, the jurisdiction of the Court of Hustings of Williamsburg was enlarged to include all actions cognizable in any county court. 4 Stat. at Large Va. 541. Subsequently, a 1769 act limited the court's jurisdiction to all transitory actions and suits at common law and in chancery "which should actually arise within the limits" of Williamsburg. 8 *id.* at 401. When it was reported to the Board of Trade that the

tions to Wyatt (1639) and Berkeley (1641) apparently intended a preservation of the *status quo*.[11] In 1673, the practice was initiated of incorporating a provision in the commissions to the effect that the Governor, ordinarily with the advice and consent of the council, could establish such courts as were thought necessary for hearing and determining all causes, both civil and criminal.[12] This authority, which persisted in the eighteenth century commissions, was apparently intended to settle the exclusion of provincial assemblies from creation of courts, and also to delegate to the Governors the necessary prerogative to issue occasional commissions, alter terms, fix fees, and the like. This commission formula was generally subjected to limitation by instruction. These limiting instructions, sent first in 1680 to Barbados and then in succession to Jamaica, the Leeward Islands, and New York, prohibited erection of any court or office of judicature not previously erected or established, or dissolution of any established court or office without special royal direction.[13] The prohibition that became common form after 1696 has particular significance in that it was designed to prevent further local meddling with judicial systems and, despite all the putative objections to early colonial legislation, was a recognition that the *status quo* was preferable to further experiment.

This expression of royal policy did not pass unchallenged, and in some royal provinces there were sustained struggles between the Governor and the assembly over the right to establish courts. In certain instances, as in New York, provincial legislation was frustrated

former extensive jurisdiction facilitated recovery of debts by English creditors since proceedings in the county courts or the general courts were dilatory and the county judges seldom qualified to exercise any extensive jurisdiction, the act was disallowed. 5 APC, COL. No. 201.

11. 17 RYMER, FOEDERA 618 (2d ed. 1727); 18 *id.* at 311 (2d ed. 1726); 2 VA. MAGAZINE OF HISTORY & BIOGRAPHY 281 (1895); 11 *id.* at 54-55 (1903). Since 1634 the monthly or county courts had exercised final jurisdiction in civil causes not exceeding ten pounds sterling. 1 Stat. at Large Va. 125, 224; COUNCIL AND GENERAL COURT OF COLONIAL VIRGINIA, MINUTES 481 (McIlwaine ed. 1924).

12. 2 LABAREE, ROYAL INSTRUCTIONS app. at 812. Col. Edward D'Oyley, first Governor of Jamaica, was authorized by his commission in 1661 to erect "such and so many civil judicatories" as he and his council should deem necessary. The same clause was contained in Lord Windsor's commission in the same year. 1 ASSEMBLY OF JAMAICA, JOURNALS app. at 2, 4 (journals published from 1811-1829; date of volume will be omitted). The more expansive instructions appear in 1 *id.* app. at 3, 5-7. See also 1 CHALMERS, OPINIONS OF EMINENT LAWYERS ON VARIOUS POINTS OF ENGLISH JURISPRUDENCE 207-09 (1814) [hereinafter cited as CHALMERS, OPINIONS].

13. 1 LABAREE, ROYAL INSTRUCTIONS No. 421.

by the resident crown officials, but in others acts were passed and not all of these were disallowed.[14]

The cases of disallowance reveal grounds that on the whole have more legal substance than mere political antipathy to assembly activity. In certain instances the objection was to infringement of the royal prerogative. A Jamaica act of 1753 appointing commissioners of nisi prius was disallowed for this reason,[15] as were North Carolina acts of 1746 and 1754 establishing courts, a St. Christopher act of 1766 constituting a court of chancery, and a New Hampshire statute that conferred on the Governor power to erect courts.[16] Commenting in 1725 to the Board of Trade on a Massachusetts act, Richard West stated that the "power of erecting Courts of Judicature is the unalterable prerogative of the Crown"; although the courts were probably held in the King's name, "there seems to be a kind of industry to avoid naming the King even upon those occasions where there is a kind of legal necessity."[17] The conception of prerogative infringement was, moreover, not confined to what were conceived as general attacks upon it but was applied to details, for we find disallowance because particular provisions conveyed probate powers to common law courts,[18] or attempted to interfere with the authority to commission justices of oyer and terminer.[19] A 1734 South Carolina act for better regulating the courts of justice was disallowed after being characterized as an infringement of the prerogative, repugnant to the laws of

14. For some of these instances see GREENE, THE PROVINCIAL GOVERNOR IN THE ENGLISH COLONIES OF NORTH AMERICA 138 (1898).

15. It was stated that the act would make an extensive change in the constitution of the government with respect to the administration of justice, was a great encroachment on the royal prerogative, to which the establishment of courts of justice belonged, and would not be beneficial to the subjects. 4 APC, COL. No. 216. For the act see 4 Laws of Jamaica 81-82 (ms.) (preserved in the Jamaica Record Office, Spanishtown, Jamaica, B.W.I.).

16. 4 APC, COL. app. at 807; 5 *id.* No. 50; 5 COLONIAL RECORDS OF NORTH CAROLINA 108 (Saunders ed.) [published from 1886 to 1907: date of volume will be omitted; hereinafter cited as COL. REC. N.C.]; 6 *id.* at 26; 1 Laws of N.H., 660, 862, 866-67. See also the 1771 disallowance of an Antigua act for determining differences by arbitration, which excluded the jurisdiction of the court of chancery without any exceptions such as those contained in the 1698 act of Parliament in cases of fraud, corruption, or misbehavior of the arbitrators. 5 APC, COL. No. 249.

17. CSP, COL., 1734-1735, No. 569.

18. PRIVY COUNCIL REGISTER 2/86/99 (located in Public Record Office, London, England) [hereinafter cited as PC]; CSP, COL., 1717-1718, No. 168 (Jamaica).

19. 3 APC, COL., app. at 844; CSP, COL., 1720-1721, Nos. 610, 626 (Antigua).

Britain and prejudicial to private property and the public administration of justice.[20] Obviously, the commission and instructions to the Governor were considered an expression of royal pleasure of supervening importance, and since these were the means of delegating royal prerogative to the Crown's representative, any interference with their letter was an intolerable diminution of the Crown's right.[21]

Unlike the case of chancery and ordinary powers, which the Crown could monopolize on a theory of prerogative alone, colonial attempts to trespass on the Admiralty jurisdiction were assailable on a somewhat broader basis because the prerogative was supplemented by the specific authority of the Acts of Trade, notably that of 1696.[22] In two cases in which interference was surmised, a Rhode Island act of 1696 and a Pennsylvania act of 1775, disallowance was grounded on the fact that the charters did not authorize the attempted extensions of jurisdiction.[23] On the other hand, a 1697 Massachusetts Bay act for erecting courts, which attempted to provide generally for jury trials, was set aside because it would have affected Admiralty Court trials under the Navigation Acts.[24] In 1705/06 and again in 1714 and 1719, Pennsylvania efforts of a like nature met a similar fate.[25] A 1749 North Carolina act met disallowance because, in effect, it excluded the courts of the province

20. 3 APC, Col. No. 299; CSP, Col., 1734-1735, No. 452 (i).

21. For an example of the usual recital in an Order in Council disallowing acts in royal colonies see the language of a January 15, 1772 order: "Whereas by Commission under the Great Seal of Great Britain the Governor Council and Assembly of His Majesty's Province of New Jersey are Authorized and impowered to make constitute and ordain Laws, Statutes and Ordinances for the Publick Peace Welfare and good Government of the said Province; which Laws Statutes and Ordinances are to be as near as conveniently may be agreeable to the Laws and Statutes of this Kingdom and are to be transmitted for His Majesty's Royal Approbation or Disallowance. . . ." 18 Documents Relating to the Colonial History of the State of New Jersey 282-83 (Archives of the State of New Jersey, Ser. 1) [published from 1880 to 1949: date of volume will be omitted; hereinafter cited as Doc. Rel. Col. Hist. N.J.].

22. 7 & 8 Will. 3, c. 22.

23. 2 APC, Col. No. 917; CSP, Col., 1699, No. 1002; *id.*, 1702-1703, No. 1415; 5 APC, Col. No. 298.

24. 1 Acts and Resolves, Public and Private, of the Province of the Mass. Bay 283-87 [published from 1869 to 1922: date of volume will be omitted; hereinafter cited as Acts & Res. Prov. Mass. Bay].

25. Charters and Acts of Assembly of the Province of Pa. 17-19, 51, 74 (1762) [hereinafter cited as Charters & Acts Assembly Prov. Pa.]; 2 Statutes at Large of Pa. from 1682 to 1801, 18, 128, 359, 479, 481, 550 [published from 1896 to 1915: date of volume will be omitted; hereinafter cited as Stat. at Large Pa.]; 3 *id.* at 31, 463.

from exercising the powers of a court of exchequer, if granted by the Crown.[26]

The disallowances already mentioned were scattered and obviously did not shape the judicial establishment of any one colony; their effect was largely peripheral.[27] In the case of the colony of Pennsylvania, however, the legislative efforts to settle a judicial system brought on a long and bitter contest between Crown and colony in which the weapon of disallowance was wielded to defeat provincial desires for a decentralized system of law administration and to compel an establishment that would centralize justice and thereby facilitate the appellate process. Although there were some earlier piecemeal enactments relating to the judicial system in this province,[28] the first comprehensive act was not passed until October 1701. In substance it provided that county courts should exercise jurisdiction over all pleas of the Crown or criminal causes (except major capital offenses), all common law actions, and all equity matters. Appeals and writs of error were to lie from the county courts to a Provincial Court sitting at Philadelphia and also on circuit; this court was also vested with original jurisdiction over the criminal causes excepted from the jurisdiction of the county courts.[29] When the act came before the Board of Trade in 1705, Attorney General Northey raised no objection in point of law to the enactment. Nevertheless, the Board of Trade advised disallowance of the act, stating that "this act is so far from expediting the determination of law suits that we conceive it will impede the same." Accordingly, on February 7, 1705/06,[30] the act was disallowed by the King in Council.[31] Apparently, the rationale of disallowance was opposition to the exercise of wide original jurisdiction by the

26. 4 APC, Col. 807; 5 Col. Rec. N.C. 105-106.

27. The Board of Trade recognized this in the case of South Carolina in February 1755 in its recommendations to Governor Lyttleton concerning the judicial establishment. JCTP, 1754-1758, at 114.

28. See Shepherd, History of Proprietary Government in Pennsylvania 371-73 (1896); Lewis, *The Courts of Pennsylvania in the Seventeenth Century*, 5 Pa. Magazine of History and Biography 141-74 (1881).

29. Charter to William Penn and Laws of the Province of Pennsylvania Passed between the years 1682 and 1700, at 311 (George, Nead & McCamont ed. 1879) [hereinafter cited as Charter & Laws Prov. Pa.]. For an assertion that this act was written by David Lloyd, see Lokken, David Lloyd, Colonial Lawmaker 103-07 (1959).

30. All dates from January 1 to March 24 inclusive, prior to the calendar reform of 1752, are given in both Old Style and New Style, reflecting the fact that the calendar year then commenced on March 25.

31. 2 Stat. at Large Pa. 449, 456, 471-72, 477, 482, 488.

county courts, and limitation of the Provincial Court to virtually an appellate function.

When the disallowing Order in Council was received, Deputy Governor John Evans, in September 1706, laid before the Pennsylvania Council a bill for establishing courts in the province.[32] The assembly conceded that the Governor or his deputy, with some of the council, should have power to hold a court of equity with general jurisdiction over the province and that there should be a Provincial Court held in each county twice a year, which should hear and determine all causes brought before it by habeas corpus, certiorari, or writ of error.[33] In turn, the council resolved that provision should be made for a fair trial when the subject feared to put himself upon the county in which the action was commenced. If a cause were removed by habeas corpus or certiorari to the Provincial Court, so that the trial would take place there, the subject should have an appeal in the colony before removal to England. The Governor and council would constitute a proper appellate body, since they should have notice of every appeal to England.[34]

In conference, the speaker of the house asserted that the chief difficulty arose from the objection of members from outlying counties that the judicial function would center in Philadelphia. To this the council replied that it did not seek to remove all judicial business to Philadelphia, but that it merely proposed a province-wide jurisdiction (transfer and concurrent original) for the Provincial Court, so that it would be of more service in inducing uniformity of proceedings. Under existing practice in civil causes, only matters of law upon writ of error were brought before it. As to the proposed appellate jurisdiction of the Governor and council, the house thought this proper in equity cases, but not convenient in common law cases, in which the determination of a chief justice skilled in the law was most fitting. No agreement was reached on

32. 1 PROVINCIAL COUNCIL OF PENNSYLVANIA, MINUTES 251-53 (Colonial Records, 1683-1790 [volumes 1 & 2 published from 1838 to 1840: date of volume will be omitted; hereinafter cited as MINS. PROV. COUN. PA.]. See also 2 *id.* at 188, 208, 222-23.

33. 2 *id.* at 253-54. *Cf.* 1 HOUSE OF REPRESENTATIVES OF THE PROVINCE OF PENNSYLVANIA, VOTES AND PROCEEDINGS, pt. 2, at 88 [published from 1752 to 1756: date of volume will be omitted; hereinafter cited as VOTES & PROC. PROV. PA.].

34. 2 MINS. PROV. COUN. PA. 254-55. As to Assembly reaction see 2 *id.* at 256; 1 VOTES & PROC. PROV. PA., pt. 2, at 88.

the crucial points and the courts were further adjourned until the matter could be laid before the next assembly.[35]

To expedite matters at the next assembly, the council drafted a bill that provided that county courts should be established with jurisdiction over all causes, except matters of life and death, such matters to be tried by commissions of oyer and terminer granted to Provincial Court judges or others on occasion. A Provincial Court should be held at Philadelphia, going on circuit in the other counties twice a year; in common law matters involving more than ten pounds this tribunal would exercise concurrent original jurisdiction with the county courts, transfer jurisdiction by habeas corpus or certiorari, and appellate jurisdiction by writ of error. The Governor and council would constitute a court of equity of original jurisdiction.[36]

When Evans communicated this bill to the house without specifying the reasons for the recent disallowance, the house, under the influence of David Lloyd, was inclined to follow the disallowed act rather than the council suggestions. It therefore resolved that a Supreme or Provincial Court should be held twice a year in each county with power to issue all remedial writs, except original. No one was to remove any cause to the Supreme Court before judgment in the inferior court. Courts of common pleas with original jurisdiction over all manner of actions were to be held in each county, writ of error lying to the Supreme Court. Courts of equity were to be held similarly, with an appeal to the Supreme Court in causes involving ten pounds or more. An appeal to the Queen in Council was reserved for final recourse.[37]

After this house bill had been submitted to the council in November 1706 and found to vary widely from the council proposals, an ordinance following the earlier council proposals was ordered drafted. A last opportunity was afforded the house to pass a bill along the lines of the proposed ordinance, under threat that a judicial system would be established by virtue of the gubernatorial ordinance power.[38] In its answer, the assembly rejected the charge

35. 2 MINS. PROV. COUN. PA. 257-59; 1 VOTES & PROC. PROV. PA., pt. 2, at 89-90.

36. 2 MINS. PROV. COUN. PA. 259, 280.

37. 1 VOTES & PROC. PROV. PA., pt. 2, at 94-100; LOKKEN, *op. cit. supra* note 29, at 166-67.

38. 2 MINS. PROV. COUN. PA. 261-66. The house admitted that the Supreme Court should exercise transfer jurisdiction as well as appellate. To the Governor and council acting as a court of equity, it was answered that the council

that it had merely interpolated the disallowed act and challenged the power to settle the judicial establishment by ordinance without assembly concurrence.[39] By this time, the original purpose of the exchange of bills had become obscured by a constitutional struggle between the assembly and the Governor and council. The only important mention of jurisdiction in the reply of the Deputy Governor and council was a defense of the equity jurisdiction of the Governor and council, and a rejection of the suggestion that it exercise jurisdiction in common law causes.[40] Although opposed to employment of the ordinance power, the assembly evidenced a conciliatory attitude.[41] Therefore, it was decided to further adjourn the courts, and to enjoin the lower house to proceed with the bill as far as it related to the establishment of courts.[42]

The ordinance power having been questioned, Evans was reassured by the council, in January 1706/07, that authority existed under the charter to establish courts of judicature without assembly concurrence. After a month of fruitless exchange of sentiments

should not meddle in private causes (on the theory that the prohibition of the Act Regulating the Privy Council, 16 Car. 1, c. 10 [1640], applied) but that jurisdiction should be lodged in commissioners. As to alleged double trials by county justices of the same cause in both law and equity, it was answered that authority existed for the same personnel adjudging a cause twice in an act of Parliament for Wales whereby common law judges determined equity matters at the same sessions. 2 MINS. PROV. COUN. PA. 266-70.

39. 2 *id.* at 266-70; 1 VOTES & PROC. PROV. PA., pt. 2, at 103-110. As to double trials see SHEPHERD, *op. cit. supra* note 28, at 379.

40. 2 MINS. PROV. COUN. PA. 261-75; 1 VOTES & PROC. PROV. PA., pt. 2, at 110-13; LOKKEN, *op. cit. supra* note 29, at 167-76.

41. 2 MINS. PROV. COUN. PA. 277-79; 1 VOTES & PROC. PROV. PA., pt. 2, at 113-15. In answer, the house resolved that its proposal was well adapted to the circumstances of the province and for the most part warranted by the laws of England, and that the parts of the council's scheme that embodied the practice of neighboring provinces might produce the same inconveniences. A law settling equitable jurisdiction in the Governor and council would suffer the same fate as that part of the Ordinance of Wales that gave the President and council chancery powers and was suppressed by The Court of Marches of Wales Act, 1 W. & M., c. 27 (1688), but the settlement of chancery in the respective counties of Wales, the foundation of the assembly bill, had been established since Henry VIII. In a later communication to the assembly, the Governor declared that the equitable jurisdiction of the President and Council of Wales had been suppressed as intolerable to the subject in its operation. Yet the Queen had established equitable jurisdiction in the Governor and council in many colonies, such as New York, Maryland, Virginia, and the insular possessions. This precedent was regarded as overruling the county equity practice derived from Welsh sources and advocated by the assembly. 2 MINS. PROV. COUN. PA. 284-88. Compare the Assembly answer, 2 *id.* at 290, 295.

42. 2 *id.* at 279-80; 1 VOTES & PROC. PROV. PA., pt. 2, at 118-19.

and of conferences, the Deputy Governor resolved the impasse on February 22, 1706/07, by issuing an ordinance for establishing courts.[43] It provided for the establishment of a Supreme or Provincial Court, to be held semi-annually in each county, exercising jurisdiction over all causes removed from the inferior courts by writs of habeas corpus, certiorari, error, prohibition, injunction, *audita querela,* or any other remedial writ. This Supreme Court was also to exercise equitable appellate jurisdiction in every county. Inferior county courts were to consist of courts of general quarter sessions, courts of common pleas, and courts of equity, with special commissions of oyer and terminer for determining all capital offenses.[44] This exercise of the ordinance power was challenged by the assembly as unauthorized, but in vain.[45]

In April 1709, while affirming the regularity of judicial establishment by ordinance, Colonel Charles Gookin, who had replaced Evans as Deputy Governor, recognized defects in the existing system and expressed willingness to consider reasonable proposals for permanent settlement of the judicial establishment using the ordinance as a working basis.[46] However, the process of arriving at any agreement was prolonged and an act establishing courts was not passed until February 28, 1710/11.[47] It provided for a Supreme Court sitting semi-annually in each county and exercising transfer and appellate common law jurisdiction and appellate jurisdiction in equity. The inferior courts were substantially the same as existed under the recent ordinance.[48]

This statute suffered the same fate at the hands of the imperial authorities as the earlier enactment. The Solicitor General, consulted by the Board of Trade, could see no occasion for establishing such a Supreme Court. He was of the opinion that since comprehensive jurisdiction continued in the inferior courts, the Supreme Court was erected only to draw from them what business it thought proper by certiorari, writ of error, habeas corpus, etc., which would only serve to multiply suits or make proceedings at

43. 2 MINS. PROV. COUN. PA. 296, 301-37; 1 VOTES & PROC. PROV. PA., pt. 2, at 132-52.

44. CHARTER & LAWS PROV. PA. 319.

45. 2 MINS. PROV. COUN. PA. 350-53.

46. 2 *id.* at 438, 479; *cf.* 2 *id.* at 443, 454, 483, for expressions of house opinion.

47. For the course of the bill see 2 *id.* at 485-87, 489-91, 503, 519, 522-23, 526-29. This bill is said to have been prepared by David Lloyd. LOKKEN, *op. cit. supra* note 29, at 192.

48. CHARTER & LAWS PROV. PA. 323.

law more dilatory and expensive. As a result, the act was disallowed by the King in Council on February 20, 1713/14.[49]

Immediately upon receipt of the disallowance in July 1714, an ordinance to revive the courts was drafted and put into effect. In its jurisdictional outlines it closely followed the earlier ordinance.[50] In February 1714/15, five assembly bills for establishing and regulating the judicial system of the province were laid before the council,[51] and after the usual legislative adjustment process, enacted in May 1715.[52] Two of these acts provided for the usual county courts of general quarter sessions and courts of common pleas. A third established a Supreme Court at Philadelphia exercising original jurisdiction in law and equity, and transfer and appellate jurisdiction from the county courts.[53]

Although these acts had the support of the Proprietary, the Board of Trade found all of them objectionable. The acts establishing courts of general quarter sessions and of common pleas were faulty in giving too wide a latitude to the judges, while the act establishing a Supreme Court was open to the same objection as that made by Solicitor General Raymond to the earlier act of 1710/11. Accordingly, they were disallowed by an Order in Council on July 21, 1719.[54]

When this conciliary order was sent to the Pennsylvania Council in November 1719, Deputy Governor Keith, who had succeeded Gookin, issued new commissions to the justices of the several courts, which in effect continued the disallowed judicial establishment.[55]

49. 2 Stat. at Large Pa. 543-44, 548-49. It was also reported: (1) that the justices of the peace were given a very arbitrary power in making persons find sureties for threatening anyone in body or estate, with no requirement that the charge be on oath or affirmation; (2) that the provision that a certain act of Parliament was to apply as far as circumstances would permit was very improper; and (3) that the provision that issues of fact in equity causes should be tried at law would make proceedings in equity "insufferably dilatory and multiply trials at law in the plain cases to no manner of purpose."

50. 2 MINS. PROV. COUN. PA. 571; 2 Stat. at Large Pa. 556. The reasons for the disallowance were not transmitted, leaving the Assembly without guide in reenactment. JAMES LOGAN LETTER BOOK, 1712-1715, at 237 (ms., Historical Society of Pennsylvania) [hereinafter referred to as HSP].

51. 2 MINS. PROV. COUN. PA. 577; 2 VOTES & PROC. PROV. PA. 161-62.

52. 2 MINS. PROV. COUN. PA. 578-81, 583, 585, 595-96; 1 PENNSYLVANIA ARCHIVES 165-67 (1st ser., 1852). See also LOKKEN, *op. cit. supra* note 29, at 194-95.

53. CHARTER & LAWS PROV. PA. 356, 359, 362.

54. 3 Stat. at Large Pa. 439-40, 445-54, 464.

55. 3 MINS. PROV. COUN. PA. 75-76, 90. For specimen commissions see CHARTER & LAWS PROV. PA. 382, 385.

In one aspect, however, centralization of justice was obtained. Upon representations as to the need for an equity court, Keith was advised by lawyers that the office of chancellor could be performed only by the King's representative under the Great Seal. Nevertheless, in a message to the house in May 1720, Keith declared that the opinion of that body would principally govern his conduct. The house thereupon determined that Keith should hold a court of equity with the assistance of such of the council as was thought fit, excluding those who had heard the cause below. In August it was decided in council that the Deputy Governor, with all the council in or near Philadelphia as assistants, should constitute a court of equity for the province, and the court was then announced by proclamation.[56]

Since the other courts would continue by virtue of commissions, it was observed in council on May 12, 1722 that the constitution of the courts would be more regularly and effectually established by ordinance. When this sentiment was conveyed to the assembly, a bill was shortly forthcoming that became law on May 22.[57] In outline, the judicial system established by this act was similar to that established by the 1715 acts. The Supreme Court's common law jurisdiction was both transfer and appellate; whether or not original jurisdiction was conferred provided the subject of later controversy. Although this court was to continue to sit at Philadelphia, issues joined there were to be tried by the judges on circuit in the county from which the cause was removed.[58] Although apparently not satisfying the earlier criteria of jurisdictional distribution, this act was not disallowed.

The next alteration in the Pennsylvania judicial system evolved from an attempt to frustrate operation of the Navigation Acts within the province. Enforcement of these acts presented a recurrent problem to the imperial authorities. Earlier, from about 1699 to 1702, considerable heat had been generated by several condemnations by Robert Quary, sitting as judge of the vice-admiralty court in Philadelphia.[59] In the autumn of 1724, John Moore, the collec-

56. *Id.* at 386; 3 MINS. PROV. COUN. PA. 91, 105; 2 VOTES & PROC. PROV. PA. 270-71.

57. 3 MINS. PROV. COUN. PA. 171-74; 2 VOTES & PROC. PROV. PA. 322-26.

58. CHARTER & LAWS PROV. PA. 387.

59. For the problems of enforcement generally see HARPER, THE ENGLISH NAVIGATION LAWS 109-47 (1939). For Quary's activities see 4 *House of Lords Manuscripts* (*n.s.*), *1699-1702*, 331-37, in 17 ROYAL COMM. ON HIST. MANU-

tor at Philadelphia, who had been King's Advocate in the colony at the time of the Quary condemnations, seized the ship *Fame* for illegal importation, but the seizure was released by force, and the prohibited goods landed. Deputy Governor Keith then made a new and pretended seizure, and a collusive condemnation took place in the county court of Philadelphia. When this was communicated to London, the collector was advised to prosecute upon the seizure in the proper Pennsylvania court, the Supreme Court, which under the 1722 act possessed like power and jurisdiction as the courts of King's Bench, Common Pleas, or Exchequer at Westminster.

Pursuant to this advice, the seizure was prosecuted and a condemnation obtained. A *qui tam* action was then brought in the Supreme Court against one Lawrence as principally concerned in the running and concealment of the prohibited goods, to which suit Lawrence appeared and gave bail.[60] While the suit was pending in November 1726, Lawrence and others objected to the assembly that subjects were detained in gaol by unlawful issuance of original process from the Supreme Court. The assembly thereupon resolved that the 1722 law for establishing courts should be amended and that no original process should issue out of the Supreme Court in civil causes.[61] Accordingly, an act incorporating these resolutions was passed in August 1727.[62] By this retrospective act, the action against Lawrence was allegedly discontinued and all remedy lost.[63]

In the regular review process, the act was not laid before the

SCRIPTS, REPORT; 1 MINS. PROV. COUN. PA. 541-46; 1 Lewis, *supra* note 28, at 177-81; LOKKEN, *op. cit. supra* note 29, at 81-87; J. SMITH, APPEALS TO THE PRIVY COUNCIL FROM THE AMERICAN PLANTATIONS 178-80 (1950).

60. 4 Stat. at Large Pa. 422-23, 429-30.

61. 4 Stat. at Large Pa. 424; 3 VOTES & PROC. PROV. PA. 8, 11.

62. CHARTER & LAWS PROV. PA. 395; 4 Stat. at Large Pa. 424; 3 VOTES & PROC. PROV. PA. 14-15, 25, 32-35. It has been alleged that Francis Rawle was the leader in the movement. KONKLE, BENJAMIN CHEW, 1722-1810, at 21 (1932). Collector Moore made an unsuccessful attempt to insert a provision that all actions, *qui tam* suits, informations, and prosecutions in which the Crown was interested might be commenced or prosecuted originally in the Supreme Court. 3 MINS. PROV. COUN. PA. 278-79. The enactment, however, provided that the court of common pleas have jurisdiction of "informations and actions upon penal statutes."

63. 4 Stat. at Large Pa. 424, 430. Presumably, the discontinuance was a negative inference from a provision that no indictment found or depending before the Supreme Court, or removed thereto from any other courts, or any other matter legally removed from any other court and depending before said court should be discontinued. CHARTER & LAWS PROV. PA. 401.

Board of Trade until April 1730, when it was referred to counsel Francis Fane.[64] At the same time collector Moore petitioned the Privy Council for repeal of the offending act. To this petition the proprietors objected.[65] Finding that the act was before the Board of Trade, the committee suspended further consideration until the usual representation would be made. The Board of Trade pressed Fane for his opinion on the act, but no report was rendered until November 1730. After hearing solicitors for both sides, Fane reported that it did not plainly appear that discontinuance of collector Moore's action was the sole reason for the act, although there was ground for assuming that the legislature had such prosecutions in mind. Fane was of the opinion that there was nothing in the earlier act of 1722 giving the Supreme Court unquestionable original jurisdiction, and that the assumption of such jurisdiction by the court in Moore's case was scarcely conclusive. The contention that the act of 1727 was repugnant to several acts of Parliament allowing prosecutions under the Acts of Trade in any court of record was rejected on the ground that the act was passed under a supposition that the Supreme Court was merely a court of error, which, although technically a court of record, did not come within the reason of the parliamentary acts. As to the disadvantages of having primary appellate jurisdiction in England, it was answered

64. 4 Stat. at Large Pa. 428-29. Surveyor General of the Customs Fitzwilliam had represented to the Board of Trade in December 1727 that the act deprived of jurisdiction the court most competent for the trial of suits in which the King was concerned. The choice of going to trial in the Supreme Court rather than in the inferior county courts was based largely on the differences in training and inclination of the respective judges. Furthermore, the act was directly repugnant to An Act for Plantation Trade, 7 & 8 Will. 3, c. 22 (1696), which gave the prosecutor an election to sue for breaches of the Acts of Trade in any of the King's courts in the plantations that he thought fit. 4 Stat. at Large Pa. 424-26.

65. 4 Stat. at Large Pa. 431-40. After asserting that Moore had initially attempted to vest an original jurisdiction in the Supreme Court, the Proprietary dwelt on the inconvenience of such practice to the province and to the Privy Council. Under the circumstances of the colony, it would be ruinous to force distant settlers to attend courts at Philadelphia in all actions and from thence to face an appeal to England; such practice varied from that of other colonies in which the Governors and council formed courts of error. Their constitution gave the Pennsylvania Governor and council no error jurisdiction, for it resided in the Supreme Court; consequently, if actions were to be commenced originally in the Supreme Court, an appeal would lie without intermediate colonial review to the King in Council. Since no minimum limitation for appeals existed in Pennsylvania, the Council Board would be harassed and the poor litigant oppressed.

that an appellant from a colonial appellate body was in no better position than one from a court of original jurisdiction. Moreover, in the vice-admiralty courts there was no review but by appeal home. After sundry other objections, Fane concluded that without a clause reserving the right to commence crown actions in the Supreme Court the act would be of very great prejudice to the revenue.[66]

A hearing on the act by counsel finally took place before the Board of Trade in June 1731. Finding that some Supreme Court jurisdiction was conferred on inferior courts and that officers of the revenue were apprehensive about revenues being affected by abridgment of their statutory right to sue in any court of record, the Board proposed repeal. In its representation the Board stated that continuance of the act might prove highly prejudicial to the revenue and encourage illicit trade by placing crown officers under great difficulties in prosecutions upon seizures. Finally, by an Order in Council on August 12, 1731, the act was disallowed.[67]

Upon notice of the order, both Deputy Governor Patrick Gordon (the successor to Keith) and the assembly characterized as false the representations by which disallowance had been obtained.[68] In November 1731, a bill for reviving and continuing the proceedings of the courts of judicature was introduced in the assembly and passed into law; it merely revived the provisions of the 1722 act.[69] In later years the Supreme Court assumed wide original jurisdiction under the 1722 act; the trend to centralization was probably most complained of in the mid-eighteenth century under John Kinsey, chief justice and for many years speaker of the assembly.[70]

The efforts of the Board of Trade and the Privy Council to prevent diffusion of judicial administration were not confined to Penn-

66. 4 *id.* at 441-47.

67. 4 *id.* at 421, 447-50; 3 MINS. PROV. COUN. PA. 397-98. *Cf.* Letter From Thomas Penn to Deputy Governor Gordon, July 23, 1731, in 1 PENN LETTER BOOKS, 1729-1742, at 32 (ms., HSP).

68. 3 MINS. PROV. COUN. PA. 418-19; 3 VOTES & PROC. PROV. PA. 167-69; 2 PENN OFFICIAL CORRESPONDENCE, 1728-1735, at 214-15 (ms., HSP).

69. 3 MINS. PROV. COUN. PA. 422; CHARTER & LAWS PROV. PA. 404; 3 VOTES & PROC. PROV. PA. 170.

70. For the jurisdiction exercised see SUPREME COURT APPEARANCE DOCKETS (Office of the Supreme Court Prothonotary, Philadelphia, Pa.). See also 3 PENN LETTER BOOKS, 1750-1754, at 12, 33 (ms., HSP); 4 PENN OFFICIAL CORRESPONDENCE 1744-1749, at 203 (ms., HSP); 5 *id.*, 1750-52, at 36, 89; PENN SUPP., 1720-1766, at 35 (ms., HSP).

sylvania. Numerous scattered acts that conferred varied civil and criminal jurisdiction on inferior courts were disallowed. The grounds advanced in justification were diverse; to some extent the low repute that courts of inferior jurisdiction had in England may have contributed to the result.[71] In some cases, acts were disallowed because they entrusted jurisdiction over real property or testamentary matters or femes coverts without support of English precedent.[72] In some cases, the method of proceeding provided by the act was regarded as too summary for the subject matter in question,[73]

71. As to the status of courts of inferior jurisdiction in England in the seventeenth and eighteenth centuries see 1 WEBB, ENGLISH LOCAL GOVERNMENT FROM THE REVOLUTION TO THE MUNICIPAL CORPORATION ACT 287-91, 321-37, 343-50 (1906); 2 *id.* at 31-80, 114-26, 200-11 (1908).

72. In 1705/06 a Pennsylvania act for determining debts under forty shillings, 2 Stat. at Large Pa. 43, was disallowed because titles to land might be arbitrarily and finally determined. 1 Charters & Acts Assembly Prov. Pa. 18; 2 Stat. at Large Pa. 493. A 1770 act of the same colony, 7 *id.* at 334, which allowed trial of title to realty by two justices, was disallowed in 1771. 5 APC, COL. No. 187. The Board of Trade objected to a North Carolina act of 1755 that gave county courts cognizance of all filial portions, legacies, and the distribution of intestate estates for any sum. This jurisdiction was contrasted with county court jurisdiction in England, "which being generally matters of fact and seldom complicated with any intricate circumstances are easily determined, without much mischief to the parties at worst." 6 COL. REC. N.C. 27-28; 4 APC, COL. No. 465. The Board noted that the jurisdiction of county courts in England was limited to causes under forty shillings. Another North Carolina act was disallowed as giving county courts jurisdiction over orphans and their estates not warranted by any English law or practice. 4 *id.* app. at 807. A Georgia act, disallowed in 1760, was deemed unnecessary and inexpedient in that it departed from English practice in transferring the security of femes coverts into the hands of justices of the peace. 4 *id.* No. 453; 18 COLONIAL RECORDS OF THE STATE OF GEORGIA 417-20 (Chandler ed. 1910).

73. A Barbados act was disallowed in 1726 on the ground that the recovery of the penalty provided before justices of the peace was too summary a way of proceeding on so penal a law, and that the matter should undergo the most regular and strict inquiry that the nature of the offense would allow. 3 APC, COL. No. 98. Another was disallowed in 1735 for the reason, *inter alia*, that penalties were to be recovered in a summary way before the Governor and one justice of the peace on the oath of a single witness. 3 *id.* No. 309; CSP, COL., 1734-1735, No. 124. See also the 1717 opinion of Attorney General Northey characterizing as "unreasonable and unjust" several Barbados acts of a similar nature. 2 CHALMERS, OPINIONS 47-49. In 1748 a South Carolina act of 1747 that established jurisdiction in two justices and three freeholders or a majority of them to try and determine all actions of debt for any sum not exceeding seventy-five pounds current money, equal to twelve pounds sterling, was disallowed. This was considered by the Board of Trade "a sum too large to be determined in so summary a way." 4 APC, COL. No. 78. For objections to the act see CO 5/371/H 111; for Lamb's opinion thereon, see 2 CHALMERS, OPINIONS 160-64. In 1768 Lamb questioned whether causes not exceeding twenty pounds

or dangerous to commerce,[74] or inquisitorial and not conforming to the principles of British justice.[75] In other cases it was objected that the jurisdiction conferred embraced causes of too great importance, considering the qualifications of the bench.[76] The two objections as to method of proceeding and qualifications of judicial personnel were combined, and acts disallowed as subjecting parties to petty tyranny and their property to partial determinations.[77] In some cases, disallowance was based on the consequent infringement of the jurisdiction of royal courts and the prequisites thereof.[78]

---

should be tried by circuit court judges without a jury as provided in a South Carolina act. CI 5/379/O 1.

74. A Bahamas act of 1762 was disallowed in 1772 on this ground. 5 APC, Col. No. 212. See also the disallowance of a Massachusetts Bay act subjecting the Crown and merchants building ships in the province to the inconvenience of inspection by overseers appointed by justices of the peace. 2 *id.* app. at 844; CSP, Col., 1700, No. 824.

75. West Florida act disallowed in June 1771. 5 APC, Col. No. 193.

76. A North Carolina act of May 1760 (An Act to Establish Inferior Courts of Pleas and Quarter Sessions in the several Counties in this Province) was disallowed in December 1761. The courts established were given jurisdiction in all common law causes exceeding forty shillings and not exceeding fifty pounds, and in all cases of petty larceny, assaults, batteries, trespasses, and breaches of the peace, and of filial portions, legacies, and distribution of intestate estates for any sum. The Board of Trade advised that the causes cognizable were causes "of too great Consequence and Importance to be adjudged and determined in those Courts, Considering what must be the Qualification and Abilities of those who Compose them. . . ." 4 APC, Col. No. 465. It was further described as a "still greater Absurdity in restraining the Jurisdiction of these Courts in Common Actions at Law, to a limited value and giving them an Unlimited Jurisdiction in other Causes of a more Important and delicate Concern, which is upon the face of it, altogether inconsistent with reason and Justice. . . ." In disallowing a South Carolina act of 1747, it was advanced that execution of the act might be attended with difficulties for want of persons in all parts of the province properly qualified for that purpose. 4 *id.* No. 78. In reporting on a New York act in 1772, Richard Jackson declared that "it cannot but frequently happen, that in the execution of the jurisdiction given by the act titles will come in question before those, who cannot be competent." 5 *id.* No. 226, at 506. The Board of Trade, in commenting on a 1755 North Carolina act enlarging the jurisdiction of the county courts to forty pounds, stated that "it is well known that those who generally Act as Justices in the County Courts are unlettered Persons and chiefly guided by some popular Lawyer in the neighbourhood. . . ." 6 Col. Rec. N.C. 27.

77. A Georgia act of 1756 made all causes of the value of ten pounds sterling triable by justices of the peace without juries, excluding the jurisdiction of any other count. Sir Matthew Lamb observed that by the act "the Properties of Your Majestys Subjects [were] made liable to partial Determinations." 4 APC, Col. No. 379, at 407; JCTP, 1754-1758, at 428. See also Jackson's comments on a New Jersey act of 1769 erecting courts in the several counties for the trial of causes of ten pounds and under. 5 APC, Col. No. 191.

78. Two New Jersey acts, Acts of the General Assembly of the Province of

The exercise, by inferior courts, of concurrent jurisdiction with establisher superior courts was disallowed as introductive of confusion, operating to the obstruction of justice and prejudice of private property.[79] Another reason advanced for curtailment of the creation of numerous inferior judicatories was the destruction of legal uniformity and certainty inherent in a diffuse judicial system.[80]

There are instances of disallowance in which it was generally declared that the jurisdiction of inferior judicatories was extended by provincial statute too far or further than by any other colonial act.[81] In advising disallowance of two New York acts, one em-

---

New Jersey (1776), chs. 53, 66, were disallowed in 1721/22 as destructive of the jurisdiction of the Supreme Court. 3 APC, COL. app. at 849; CSP, COL., 1722-1723, No. 7; 14 DOC. REL. COL. HIST. N.J. 238-41. Two later acts of the same nature were disallowed in 1731. 3 APC, COL. No. 242. In the 1748 disallowance of a South Carolina Act of 1747, it was reported that the jurisdiction conferred on justices and freeholders over all actions of debt between twenty and seventy-five pounds current money included most of the actions brought in the province, and thus greatly lessened the jurisdiction of the court of common pleas, wherein all actions above twenty pounds current money had hitherto been determined by juries. 4 APC, COL. No. 78. A 1756 Georgia act making all causes of ten pounds sterling triable exclusively by justices of the peace without juries infringed "the authority of Your Majesty courts and the rights of the officers thereto belonging. . . ." 4 *id.* No. 379. A New York act was disallowed in 1772 because, *inter alia*, it was too great an invasion of the jurisdiction of the Supreme Court. 5 *id.* No. 226; 5 Colonial Laws of N.Y. from the Year 1664 to the Revolution 204 (1894) [hereinafter cited as Col. Laws N.Y.].

79. See the Board of Trade comment on a 1760 North Carolina act establishing inferior courts of pleas and quarter sessions in the several counties. 4 APC, COL. No. 465.

80. Richard Jackson, commenting on a 1769 New Jersey statute erecting courts in the several counties for the trial of causes of ten pounds and under, declared:

> That nothing is of greater importance to every Country, than that its Laws should be certain, and depend as little as possible on a Man's discretion or affections; That without this certainty Law ceases to be what it ought to be an universal measure of Justice, and no longer answers the End of its institution; That the Laws of a country cannot be certain unless they are uniform, and they can neither be uniform nor certain, where probably more than one hundred Judges are to determine, each according to his own Notions of Justice; that the uniformity is necessary to the publick welfare in all Countries, it is much more so in a Colony, where, without it it is evident, that a conformity of the Laws of Great Britain, cannot long be preserved, for that the continuance of this Conformity can only be hoped for from frequent determinations of the Supreme Court, affecting the property in every part of the Colony.

5 *id.* No. 191, at 310. See also the May 17, 1775 report of Jackson on a North Carolina act. 9 COL. REC. N.C. 1251, 1254; CO 5/304/K 4.

81. See the 1756 Georgia act disallowed in 1759, wherein all causes under ten

powering justices of the peace, mayors, recorders, and aldermen to try causes to the value of ten pounds, and the other prohibiting the bringing of actions under fifty pounds in the Supreme Court of the colony, Richard Jackson, counsel for the Board of Trade, reported that the acts ran counter to the juridical policy of England (having in mind perhaps the forty shilling limitation of the county courts and courts baron in personal actions) and could not but occasion mischievous effects under the specious appearance of facilitating justice.[82] Jackson proved himself a relentless opponent of extension of the jurisdiction of inferior judicatories; probably the most comprehensive criticism of such extension appeared in his unfavorable report on a New Jersey act of November 1769 that made cognizable before any one justice of the peace actions of debt and other demands to the amount of ten pound proclamation money. It read in part as follows:[83]

> That Summary and Domestick Justice, under the specious pretext of facilitating the Recovery of Debts necessarily encourages a litigious Spirit, and frequently the practice of perjury, both highly pernicious in every Country much more so in a commercial one and the last Subversive of every public and private Benefit derived from the Institution of civil Society; that it serves too often to favour the establishment of much petty Tyranny in men altogether unfit to be intrusted with such power, and that these Reasons have weighed so far with the Legislature of Great Britain, that this kind of Jurisdiction has been always given with caution, sometimes with reluctance, and never hitherto to his knowledge, extended beyond the Sum of forty Shillings Sterling. . . .[84]

pounds were to be tried by justices of the peace, 4 APC, Col. No. 379, and the 1762 Bahamas act disallowed in 1772, giving justices of the peace jurisdiction in suits to the amount of six pounds, 5 *id.* No. 212.

82. 5 *id.* No. 168. For the acts see 4 Col. Laws N.Y. 1079, 1088.

83. The act made cognizable before any one justice of the peace actions of debt and other demands to the amount of ten pounds proclamation money. 5 APC, Col. No. 191. This disallowance gave the assembly "very sensible regret," since in the short time the act had been in force it "had answered the ends proposed, and proved beneficial to the people we represent." 18 Doc. Rel. Col. Hist. N.J. 219, 260-64. See also the earlier attitude of Attorney General Northey characterizing as unreasonable a provision in a disallowed New York act of 1719 requiring plaintiff to pay defendant's costs if a suit for under twenty pounds current money was brought in the Supreme Court. CSP, Col., 1717-1718, No. 293; CSP, Col., 1719-1720, No. 201.

84. 5 APC, Col. No. 191.

The imperial authorities were forced to proceed cautiously in allowing inferior courts in any one colony to assume jurisdiction in causes involving substantial amounts. Although differentiation in jurisdiction could easily be justified by differing conditions in the various colonies, such allowance was apt to be regarded by other colonies as carte blanche for similar enactments, regardless of dissimilarity of conditions. In 1760 a North Carolina act increasing the jurisdiction of inferior courts to fifty pounds was justified by judicial officers on the basis of Virginia precedent, despite gubernatorial qualms raised by the disallowance of an earlier act conferring a forty pound jurisdiction on such courts.[85] When the act was disallowed, the assembly accused the Board of Trade of being misinformed concerning the jurisdiction of inferior colonial courts, which was represented as being unlimited in some colonies.[86]

The reviewers also sought to protect the subject by disallowance of acts granting unreasonable or arbitrary judicial powers. In 1706 two New Hampshire acts met with disallowance because they granted unreasonable powers of commitment to justices of the peace.[87] The Board of Trade severely criticized a 1758 New Hampshire statute aimed at preventing the killing of deer out of season. In advising that the powers granted were very extraordinary and totally inconsistent with the principles of the constitution, the Board adverted to the provisions permitting self-incrimination and double jeopardy. Furthermore, a grand jury might take cognizance of an offense under the act and yet the court could proceed to summary conviction without a petty jury. The act was accordingly disallowed on July 29, 1764.[88] It is somewhat ironic that while the colonists were commencing to urge their "constitutional" political

85. 6 Col. Rec. N.C. 253, 256. For the Virginia act see 6 Stat. at Large Va. 325. From 1710 on, 3 *id.* at 504; 5 *id.* at 489, county courts in Virginia had jurisdiction in all civil causes except those of less value than twenty shillings, Chitwood, Justice in Colonial Virginia 80-81 (23 Johns Hopkins University Studies in Historical and Political Science Nos. 7-8, 1905). It was stated by the Board of Trade in 1771 that the jurisdiction in the Virginia county courts "is by the Constitution of that Colony unlimited. . . ." 5 APC, Col. No. 201.

86. In advising disallowances the Board of Trade stated that "the amount of fifty pounds value [is] . . . greatly beyond what is allowed in most, if not all other colonies. . . ." 4 *id.* No. 465, at 505-06. The assembly alleged that jurisdiction was in reality twenty-five pounds sterling (fifty pounds proclamation money), a jurisdiction possessed by inferior courts in most colonies. 6 Col. Rec. N.C. 987-88.

87. 1 Laws of N.H. 568, 680, 860-63, 866.

88. 3 *id.* at 172; 4 APC, Col. No. 560.

liberties in a flood of polemical literature, the Board of Trade should be cast in the role of protector of individual rights in the colonies themselves.

While not entirely consistent, the Privy Council generally disallowed laws extending the Habeas Corpus Act[89] to the colonies.[90] In this connection it should be noted that in several instances the Privy Council disallowed, as irregular or improper, reception *en masse* of acts of Parliament in particular colonies. Portions of such disallowed acts were criticized as allowing too much judicial discretion in determining what laws of England were in force in the colony.[81]

In the case of uncertain delegation of judicial power, acts encountered disallowance because they fostered arbitrary conduct.[92] Disallowance of three Pennsylvania acts was predicated on the fact that the offenses were too loosely defined. Thus, there was too great an opportunity to punish by arbitrary judicial construction.[93]

89. Habeas Corpus Act, 31 Car. 2, c. 2 (1680).

90. 1 Acts & Res. Prov. Mass. Bay 95-99; 3 APC, Col. No. 45 (Jamaica); CSP, Col., 1734-1735, No. 15; J. Smith, Appeals to the Privy Council from the American Plantations 475 (1950). Compare the Bermuda act disallowed in 1704 as not containing sufficient safeguards against illegal imprisonment. 2 APC, Col. app. at 831; CSP, Col., 1704-1705, No. 495. See also Goebel & Naughton, Law Enforcement in Colonial New York 502-06 (1944); 1 Hamlin & Baker, Supreme Court of Judicature of the Province of New York 1691-1704, at 389-404 (The New York Historical Society 1952); Carpenter, *Habeas Corpus in the American Colonies*, 8 Am. Hist. Rev. 19-27 (1902).

91. 2 APC, Col. app. at 837; CSP, Col., 1693-1696, No. 2230 (as to a 1696 Maryland act the Attorney General was of the opinion that it was not reasonable to have a general clause declaring all the laws of England to be in force in Maryland); 2 APC, Col. app. at 831, 836; CSP, Col., 1702-1703, No. 1356; *id.*, 1716-1717, No. 422; 3 APC, Col. No. 45 (if all the laws of England were in force in Jamaica, there would be instances in which such laws were not competent or might cause mischief; if all the laws of England did not become the laws of Jamaica, it would cause great doubt and vexation as to what laws governed persons and property); 5 *id.* No. 168 (the reception in New York of a number of acts of Parliament passed after the establishment of a legislature in the colony would occasion great difficulties of construction, some of which ought not be left to a court of justice to decide); CSP, Col., 1702-1703, No. 1356; 2 Chalmers, Opinions 75.

92. Richard West commented, on a New York act of 1721, that the power given two justices to commit an offender until he "made fine and ransom," being very general and unlimited, was too arbitrary. CSP, Col., 1735-1736, No. 179.

93. 1 Charters & Acts Assembly Prov. Pa. 18, 51-52; 2 Stat. at Large Pa. 4, 45, 419, 480, 489, 551. Francis Fane found several Connecticut acts faulty in this respect. Fane, Reports on the Laws of Connecticut 67, 70, 79-80, 84-85, 97, 164-65 (Andrews ed. 1915) [hereinafter cited as Fane, Rep. Laws Conn.].

A 1704 Nevis act provided for the establishment of a court merchant to hear and determine without a jury all causes between transients not exceeding one hundred pounds current money, according to law, equity, and good conscience. Objection to the act was made by the Board of Trade on the ground that it was arbitrary and uncertain; it was not clear whether the judges were to proceed according to law or equity.[94] In 1772 a Nova Scotia act conferring on the judge of probate large and undefined power to punish for contempt was disallowed, Richard Jackson having stressed the danger inherent in loose, and consequently arbitrary, delegation of judicial power.[95]

After courts had been established in the colonies, the necessity

94. CSP, Col., 1708-1709, No. 264. See also Fane, Rep. Laws Conn. 99.

95. 5 APC, Col. No. 221. With adequate transportation facilities frequently lacking in the colonies, the location of courts was often important in the administration of justice. But imperial authorities were loath to permit changes in location unless cause was shown. In 1735 a New Hampshire act of 1730 removing inferior courts from Portsmouth to inland towns was disallowed. It was related that no reason appeared for the removal, and further, that the inland towns being timbering centers, it would be difficult to secure impartial juries in prosecutions for cutting timber reserved to the Crown. 3 APC, Col. No. 328; CSP, Col., 1734-1735, No. 423; 2 Laws of N.H. 525; Fry, New Hampshire as a Royal Province 459-63 (1908). Usually colonial courts were located in the earliest settled towns, but later developments might leave these courts relatively inaccessible to the majority of the population. In Jamaica, where such conditions allegedly existed, an attempt was made to remedy the situation by passage of an act removing the Supreme Court of Judicature from St. Iago de la Vega to Kingston, the principal trading center. 4 Laws of Jamaica 119-21 (ms.). There was some opposition manifested to passage of this bill, see 4 Assembly of Jamaica, Journals 505, 510-11, resulting in an act appointing commissioners to inquire into losses sustained by removal of the court, 4 Laws of Jamaica 122-23 (ms.). See also 4 Assembly of Jamaica, Journals 514-17; Anonymous, An Account of the Trial of Francis Delap, Esq., Late Provost Marshal-General, Upon An Information for a Misdemeanor *passim* (1755). Further alleviation was sought in passage of an act extending the jurisdiction of the inferior courts of common pleas over personal actions of the value of two hundred pounds. 4 Laws of Jamaica 123-24 (ms.); 4 Assembly of Jamaica, Journals 466, 468, 490, 492-93, 505, 510. *Cf.* the resolutions that were embodied in an earlier bill of a similar nature, which did not become law. 4 *id.* at 325. Despite an address to the King, both acts were disallowed as lacking necessary suspending clauses. The first act repealed several confirmed acts, and the second was of an unusual and extraordinary nature and importance, whereby the property of subjects might be prejudiced. 4 APC, Col. No. 236; JCTP, 1754-1758, at 98-100, 180-81, 211-12; 4 Assembly of Jamaica, Journals 586-87. When Governor Ellis urged the need for a 1760 Georgia act providing for the more easy and speedy recovery of small debts, removing the necessity of resort to the general court in Savannah, the Board let the act "lie by" until the colony "was in a situation to admit of more constitutional and less exceptionable regulations" to such end. JCTP, 1759-1763, 202.

of appointing judges still remained. The usual eighteenth century Governor's commission authorized appointment of judges, commissioners of oyer and terminer, justices of the peace, and other necessary officers and ministers for the better administration of justice.[96] The power thus conferred did not, however, exclude the Crown itself, for, on occasion, it might designate persons for the judiciary whom the Governor commissioned by mandamus or sign manual. The Governor's power was further restricted by certain instructions primarily devoted to preventing arbitrary removal from office, referring to the commissions "which you are to grant with the advice and consent of the Council."[97] From 1753 on, this power was more directly modified by instruction that appointments of judges or justices of the peace were to be with the advice and consent of at least three of the council or in some cases a majority thereof.[98] In Massachusetts the appointing power was vested, by charter provision, in the Governor with the advice and consent of the council; therefore, commissions and instructions were silent on the subject.[99]

A scattering of acts that attempted to interfere with the prerogative of judicial appointment were disallowed. The Attorney General objected to a Nevis act of 1704 on the ground that it annexed to the office of Commander in Chief the power of appointing judges. Even though the Crown often delegated such power of those appointed Governors, it was represented as more convenient for the Crown to retain the power to direct the form of commission. Later, an Antigua act of 1728 provided that a court of chancery should be held on the island by designated officers in the progressive ab-

96. In some, the commissioners of oyer and terminer were omitted. For sample commissions see 3 DOC. REL. COL. HIST. N.Y. 378, 539, 625, 829, 857; 4 *id.* at 268; 5 *id.* at 95, 837; 6 *id.* at 192; 2 LABAREE, ROYAL INSTRUCTIONS app. at 821, 830; 2 Laws of N.H. 7, 162, 214, 414, 463, 604; 3 *id.* at 246, 417.

97. 1 LABAREE, ROYAL INSTRUCTIONS No. 512. In 1754 Governor Popple of Bermuda pointed out the conflict of the instruction with the commission power and the disadvantages of a limitation on the gubernatorial appointing power. 2 *id.* app. at 865-66.

98. 1 *id.* No. 513. The Board of Trade, in a June 1754 representation on instructions to Governor Dobbs of North Carolina, declared that although this was "plainly implied in the former Instructions the Governors have not strictly adhered" thereto. 5 COL. REC. N.C. 1104.

99. 1 Acts & Res. Prov. Mass. Bay 12. See the commissions set out in 2 COLONIAL SOC'Y OF MASS., PUBLICATIONS (1913); for the instructional omission, see 1 LABAREE, ROYAL INSTRUCTIONS No. 513. Yet Solicitor General Hawles, in reporting on two acts establishing courts, 1 Acts & Res. Prov. Mass. Bay 369, 370, questioned "whether the power of nominating the Chief and other Justices of the said courts ought not to be reserved to his Majesty," 1 *id.* at 418.

sence of higher appointees. In reporting on the act, the Board of Trade stated that since the appointment of judges and chancellors was a very material part of the royal prerogative it should always be exercised by the Crown immediately or by persons specifically delegated by the Crown to exercise it. Royal appointment would permit alteration or addition at pleasure, whereas an act of assembly establishing judicial offices could not be repealed without popular consent, regardless of the inconveniences that might ensue.[100] In South Carolina in April 1733, an act was passed by which the Governor was empowered to nominate two or more assistant justices to sit in judgment and to hear and determine all causes together with the chief justice. Incumbent Chief Justice Wright complained to the King in Council that the act was an encroachment on the royal prerogative and that ignorant appointees thereunder overruled petitioner in all judicial acts. In March 1735/36, the act was disallowed as objectionable, particularly in that the appointment provision encroached on the royal prerogative. An additional instruction to the Governor in August 1735 directed appointment of two assistant judges in each law court in the province, thus constitutionally satisfying the legislative desire.[101] A 1754 North Carolina act that created the office of associate judge, leaving to the Governor only the formality of naming and commissioning such judges, was disallowed. In 1761 a May 1760 act of the same colony, which provided that no person should be appointed a Supreme Court judge unless certain professional qualifications were met, was disallowed. The Board of Trade had asserted that the act would operate to preclude royal appointments and was also an unconstitutional restraint on the power of judicial appointment delegated to the Governor under the Great Seal.[102] A South Carolina act was disallowed in 1768 for the reason, among others, that the matter of granting judicial offices was constitutionally in the Crown's discretion. A provision for the appointment of sheriffs left the Governor no discretionary power to reject nominees for office, contrary to

100. CSP, COL., 1708-1709, No. 250; 3 APC, COL. No. 238. See also the disallowance of a 1695 Massachusetts Bay act that distinguished between Suffolk and other counties in providing that justices of the peace in Suffolk were to be specially appointed by the Governor with the consent of the council. 1 Acts & Res. Prov. Mass. Bay 37.

101. CSP, COL., 1734-1735, No. 89(i); 3 APC, COL. app. at 852; JCTP, 1734/35-1741, at 52-53; 1 LABAREE, ROYAL INSTRUCTIONS No. 520.

102. 7 COL. REC. N.C. 26, 28-29; 4 APC, COL. No. 465.

usage in England and the original constitution of the Carolinas.[103]

The essence of the objections to attempted interference with judicial commissions was the well-founded suspicion that unless appointment to judicial office depended on the Crown, colonial libertarian tendencies in any matter involving crown right could not be properly restrained. During the seventeenth century in England, the Crown's fight to protect prerogative and to safeguard royal policies had been aided on various occasions by control over judicial appointment. These halcyon days had been terminated in England in 1700 by the Act of Settlement,[104] which established the rule that judicial commissions should be granted during good behavior. Since this act did not apply overseas and since the prerogative there was not subject to other restraints, it was an obvious maxim of administration that the judiciary in the dominions should be kept in the same state of dependence as it had been in Stuart days.

This matter of the terms of commissions did not become an issue engaging English officials until after the middle of the eighteenth century. Then, prompted by an episode in Jamaica, an overhauling of instructions took place that precipitated a series of sharp conflicts in various colonies. The details of this struggle are too lengthy to include here; it is necessary to note merely that the Crown maintained its position that judicial commissions issued "at pleasure."[105] In a related area, the Council used its disallowance power to prevent invasion of the prerogative by colonial legislative action removing crown appointees from clerical offices in the judicial establishments, by assuming the right to make such appointments, or by regulating fees, thus reducing the value of such offices.[106]

103. 5 APC, Col. No. 86.

104. 12 & 13 Will. 3, c. 2, § 3 (1700).

105. See 4 APC, Col. Nos. 216, 465, app. at 807-08; 5 *id.* No. 86; Russell, The Review of American Colonial Legislation by the King in Council 190 (1915); Goebel, *Constitutional History and Constitutional Law*, 38 Colum. L. Rev. 555, 565 (1938).

106. Acts were disallowed from Barbados, 2 APC, Col. No. 1093 & 3 *id.* No. 309; Georgia, 4 *id.* No. 379; Jamaica, 4 *id.* No. 469; New Jersey, 3 *id.* app. at 849 & CSP, Col., 1722-1723, No. 7; North Carolina, 3 APC, Col. No. 559; and South Carolina, 3 APC, Col. No. 396 & CSP, Col., 1734-1735, No. 124 & 5 APC, Col. No. 86. See also the argument that a North Carolina act of 1740 depriving Nicholas Rice of the office of clerk to all the courts, which was granted by the Crown under the Great Seal, was "a nullity in itself and void ab initio, it not being a matter proper for the exercise of their power." CO 5/296/B 56. In

In so far as any consistent lines of policy governed administrative action respecting colonial statutes dealing with the judiciary, they appear to have been chiefly concerned with maintaining a centralized judicial system, keeping the channels of appellate review free from obstruction, and preventing any attenuation of the royal prerogative—which meant, usually, any encroachment on executive authority.

Control Over Judicial Procedure

The attitude of the Crown toward colonial legislation in the closely related field of procedure was differently motivated, for here the governing consideration was the question of repugnancy to the laws of England or some substantially equivalent standard. To a certain extent, the ancient tradition that the accepted common law ways of proceeding constituted "due process" colored the official attitude, for certain disallowances can not otherwise be explained.[107] In a few cases political reasons are apparent; in others the desire to protect merchants resident in England controlled. On the whole, however, the testing of provincial statutes in the procedural domain approached, in Judge Cardozo's phrase, a mere matching of colors.[108]

The effect of disallowance in the field of judicial procedure was uneven; some areas emerged unscathed, in others the incidence of disallowance was high. In the area of process and its service, in both civil and criminal causes, a significant number of laws met disallowance. In several colonies, the use of an affirmation instead of an oath by witnesses, jurors, and judges was the subject of close administrative scrutiny. A number of disallowed acts provided for

1773 Richard Jackson, reporting on two Pennsylvania acts (one establishing a new county, the other dissolving a marriage), stated: "If these last two laws are not within the extent of the power of the provincial legislature, I conceive they are void of themselves and therefor proper subjects for the determination of a court of justice, in the meantime neither receiving the sanction nor the condemnation of the crown." CO 5/1278/L 42.

107. This attitude is reflected in Jackson's report on a New York act of 1772 that provided for more effectual prevention of private lotteries. This act, he reported, gave one justice of the peace power to compel anyone whom he should have reasonable cause to suspect to be privy to a lottery to answer on oath, a power very much unlike that given to any judge by the English constitution and certainly not to be entrusted to any person unless on some occasion of the highest importance. 5 APC, Col. No. 266. For the act see 5 Col. Laws N.Y. 351.

108. Cardozo, The Nature of the Judicial Process 20-21 (1921).

methods of proof differing from accepted English usage or for objectionable limitations on execution following judgment in civil actions. On the criminal side, a substantial number of acts were set aside as providing penalties regarded as differing from those prescribed by the laws of England or as too severe, unreasonable, or superfluous. Other subjects touched upon included restrictions on crown process, limitation of actions, qualifications of and contempt on the part of jurors, damages in civil causes, and obliteration of the distinction between civil and criminal causes.

Anyone who has examined provincial judicial records of the seventeenth and early eighteenth centuries is aware of the great difficulties that beset law enforcement officials in the matter of process and its service. Apart from the fact that it was at first impossible to create any but the rudest equivalent of the Chancery and the teeming clerical apparatus of the English courts, there also existed the problem of paper and parchment, the obstacles to travel, and the inadequacies of technical knowledge. Certain initial practical adjustments, which eventually gave way to a more general acceptance of English methods, were made. In certain particulars these left a great deal to be desired and in some plantations there were occasional legislative efforts to introduce reform. Such attempts were not favored.

A Massachusetts Bay act, which provided for establishment of precedents and forms of writs and processes in civil cases, was disallowed in 1700 as establishing a practice of attachment of the appellee in civil appeals that seemed very incongruous and unreasonable.[109] A Nevis act that sought to make changes in initial process incurred the objection of the Attorney General in 1704 because summonses were to be issued by judges rather than from the secretary's office, only three or four days were given to locate and serve defendants, and because it was felt that the substituted service provided was unjust to absentee defendants.[110] In 1716 the Attorney General considered an Antigua act unreasonable because it allowed judgment to be obtained against inhabitants of Great Britain and other dominions by affixing a summons upon the court house door.[111] Similarly, a South Carolina act of 1732 that altered initial process from a summons to a capias was disallowed upon

109. 2 APC, Col. app. at 844; CSP, Col., 1700, No. 824.
110. *Id.*, 1708-1709, Nos. 250, 264; PC 2/81/226.
111. CSP, Col., 1716-1717, No. 422; *id.*, 1717-1718, No. 337.

the complaints of merchants trading with residents of the province.[112] In keeping process conformable to English practice, in 1764 the King in Council disallowed a New Hampshire act of 1758. This enactment had established a regulation, with respect to the service of summons, *scire facias*, and other writs, contrary to the practice of England.[113] Richard Jackson, reporting in 1772 on a New Jersey act enabling creditors to recover debts against absent members of a partnership, stated: "It is essential to justice that no judicial determination shall affect any man who has not an opportunity of making a defense."[114]

A recurring theme in procedural disallowances was the protection of nonresidents against discriminatory enactments. In November 1698, a Massachusetts act of 1695 was disallowed because it provided that all persons commencing suit who were neither freeholders nor settled inhabitants should give security before process would be granted. English merchants trading in those parts were particularly aware that the act would operate to their prejudice.[115] A North Carolina act granting settlers immunity against English creditors was disallowed as not consonant with reason nor agreeable to the laws and customs of England.[116] A South Carolina act, disallowed in 1733 on the protests of Bristol merchants, provided that no person should be arrested for any debt contracted prior to arrival in the province until resident therein for five years.[117] In addition, acts unreasonably protecting certain classes within a colony from process were disallowed. The Board of Trade had objected to a disallowed 1719 Antigua act that exempted all freeholders from arrest, including criminal arrests by the Crown.[118] In July 1726 the King in Council disallowed, as an unreasonable privilege, a Pennsylvania act of March 1723 regulating the process of summons against freeholders. The Board of Trade had represented that

112. 3 APC, Col. app. at 852; CSP, Col., 1732, No. 124.

113. 4 APC, Col. No. 560; 7 Documents and Records Relating to the Province of New Hampshire 2 (New Hampshire State Papers ser., 1867-1873); 3 Laws of N.H. 175.

114. CO 5/979/L 29.

115. PC 2/77/271; CSP, Col., 1697-1698, No. 1008; 1 Acts & Res. Prov. Mass. Bay 222-23. In 1734 Francis Fane objected to the hardship caused by a Connecticut act compelling foreign suitors to give sufficient security when process issued. Fane, Rep. Laws Conn. 114-15.

116. 2 APC, Col. app. at 832; CSP, Col., 1706-1708, No. 1189.

117. 3 APC, Col. No. 285; CSP, Col., 1733, Nos. 425, 426.

118. *Id.*, 1720-1721, Nos. 610, 626.

the act exempted from arrest all freeholders who owned fifty acres of land but that such freeholders might contract debts to a much greater value and possess considerable personal property with which to abscond.[119] In 1773 an Antigua act that exempted militia men from arrest for their just debts was disallowed as improper.[120]

On several occasions the King in Council acted to disallow statutes concerned with attachments that might operate to the prejudice of inhabitants of Great Britain. In 1705/06 a 1700 Pennsylvania statute relating to attachments was set aside after Attorney General Northey had given his opinion that it would prejudice all owners of land and traders resident in England.[121] A North Carolina act was set aside as attempting to vary or alter application of the 1732 act of Parliament[122] that provided for the easier recovery of debts in the plantations.[123] In 1771 two West Florida acts were disallowed because attachment was not confined to debtors who absconded or remained outside the province to avoid payment of debts.[124] In the same year a New Jersey act of 1770 that made the realty and personalty of persons who had never resided in the colony liable to attachment for recovery of debts was disallowed. As a result of this action, a circular instruction issued ordering Governors to refrain from assenting to any bill making realty and personalty of persons never resident in their respective provinces liable to attachment for the recovery of debts otherwise than was allowed in England.[125] In January 1772 a Montserrat act of June 1767, of the same nature as the above, met disallowance after a vigorous representation by Richard Jackson as to the iniquity of such acts.[126] In 1774 a Bahamas act of 1770 was disallowed as it

119. PC 2/89/250; 3 APC, COL. No. 97; CSP, COL., 1726-1727, No. 142; 1 Charters & Acts Assembly Prov. Pa. 97. *Cf.* 1 *id.* at 106-07.

120. 5 APC, COL. No. 300.

121. 1 Charters & Acts Assembly Prov. Pa. 2; 2 Stat. at Large Pa. 27, 492.

122. An Act for Recovery of debts in American plantations, 5 Geo. 2, c. 7 (1732).

123. 5 APC, COL. No. 16, at 39; CO 5/300/F 4.

124. 5 APC, COL. No. 193. Richard Jackson noted the universality of this type of law in the colonies, but advised against increase in their number or introduction into a new colony.

125. 5 APC, COL. No. 203; 1 LABAREE, ROYAL INSTRUCTIONS No. 472.

126. 5 APC, COL. No. 196. In 1773 Richard Jackson urged disallowance of a North Carolina act granting attachment against the goods of persons residing outside the colony as being expressly contrary to the gubernatorial instructions and inconsistent with the true commercial interest of the colony. CO 5/303/I 13. In this connection Governor Martin commented on the affection the people of North Carolina had for an act whereby they could attach the lands and

granted an attachment against the goods of absentees whatever the cause of absence and whether or not they had ever been within the colony. In advising disallowance, Richard Jackson characterized the act as contrary to the principles of the English laws and highly dangerous to commerce. Despite this disallowance and the 1772 instruction, another act was passed in 1774 that, because of its loose terminology, was susceptible of application to all persons absent six months though never present in the islands. The Board of Trade finding that the objections to the former act were equally applicable, the law was disallowed.[127]

In several instances the disallowance process was invoked against colonial outlawry statutes. As part of the celebrated Bayard and Hutchins incident, an April 1702 New York act provided for the outlawry of Phillip French and Thomas Wenham, who had been indicted for high misdemeanors and had withdrawn from the province, if they did not surrender within ten days of the enactment. Outlawry upon proclamation was also provided for all persons who in the future evaded jurisdiction in civil and criminal causes by withdrawal from the province for a six-month period following notice of process. Governor Cornbury termed the act "very unjust," and it was disallowed in December 1702.[128] It was obvious that this act deviated greatly from the English practice, an elaborate

goods of persons who had never resided in the colony, an act based on the municipal custom of foreign attachment obtaining in London and other commercial cities. In a message to the assembly, he characterized this method of attachment as "unconstitutional." CO 5/303/I 27, I 40. For a memorial containing arguments of agents of the assembly thereon and the opposition of Jackson see CO 5/304/1, and K 4. In connection with attachment it should be noted that the Attorney General in 1716 had termed unreasonable the provision of a disallowed Antigua act that prevented alienation of realty or personalty by defendants in law or equity. CSP, COL. 1716-1717, No. 422; *id.*, 1717-1718, No. 337.

127. 5 APC, COL. Nos. 281, 328.

128. 1 Col. Laws N.Y. 476; PC 2/79/282. See GOEBEL & NAUGHTON, *op. cit. supra* note 90, at 83-85, 231-35, 274-76, 443-44; J. SMITH, APPEALS TO THE PRIVY COUNCIL FROM THE AMERICAN PLANTATIONS 295-306 (1950). Cornbury remarked that either the people of the province were entitled to the laws of England or they were not. If the former, they ought to be outlawed only according to the laws of England. If the latter, "it ought to be declared that the people may know what they are to trust to and that an English Governour may know how to behave himself. But by this act here are men outlawed in ten days without any manner of proceedings before had against them." 4 DOC. REL. COL. HIST. N.Y. 999-1000. The Board of Trade described the act as unjust and repugnant to the laws of England, which allowed a much longer time in cases of outlawry. CSP, COL., 1702-1703, No. 100.

process of original writ, capias, alias, pluries, exigent, proclamation under 31 Eliz., c. 3,[129] and finally *utlagatum capias.*[130] A North Carolina act of 1764 authorized outlawry of all persons refusing to surrender within a certain time after indictment or presentment for a crime punishable by death, for counterfeiting or for knowingly passing counterfeit money, or for escaping after apprehension for any such crime. The act was disallowed, being characterized as extraordinary and dangerous in giving an unprecedented power, liable to unfit use.[131] In 1771 another act was passed in North Carolina to meet riotous conditions caused by the Regulator movement; it provided that recalcitrants were to be deemed outlawed upon failure to surrender within sixty days of indictment or presentment for certain designated crimes. Although the Board of Trade represented the act as irreconcilable with the principles of the constitution, it was not disallowed because repeal might endanger the peace of the province and the act by its terms was on the verge of expiration.[132] However, an additional instruction was dispatched to the Governor that care be taken that any new law passed for the same purpose be framed as near as might be agreeable to the laws of England.[133]

In March 1774 an act was passed in New York to supply the colony's lack of outlawry process to cope with certain riotous boundary dispute conditions. The act provided that persons indicted thereunder who did not appear within seventy days of gubernatorial proclamation requiring surrender would be deemed convicted of the crimes with which they were charged.[134] The act, which ex-

129. Act for Avoidance of Secret Outlawries, 31 Eliz. 1, c. 3 (1589).

130. For the process in outlawry see The King v. Yandell, 4 T.R. 521, 100 Eng. Rep. 1153 (K.B. 1792); 2 HALE, PLEAS OF THE CROWN 194-209 (1847); 2 POLLOCK & MAITLAND, THE HISTORY OF ENGLISH LAW 449, 580 (2d ed. 1923). See also the facetious summation of process in ANSTEY, PLEADER'S GUIDE pt. I, lecture VI (1884).

131. 5 APC, COL. No. 16; 23 COL. REC. N.C. 616; CO 5/300/19.

132. 5 APC, COL. No. 222; CO 5/302/H 22. The Board stated that this clause was "highly Exceptionable, as being full of Danger in it's operation, and irreconcileable to the principles of the Constitution, depriving withal the crown of its prerogative of extending Mercy to Offenders, by committing the Execution of the Law into the hands of the Subject." For the background of the act, 25 COL. REC. N.C. 519a-19d, see Bassett, *The Regulators of North Carolina, 1765-1771*, 1894 ANN. REP. AM. HIST. A. 141-212.

133. 1 LABAREE, ROYAL INSTRUCTIONS No. 415. The 1771 act was characterized as "irreconcilable with the principles of the constitution, full of danger in its operation, and unfit for any part of the British Empire."

134. 5 Col. Laws N.Y. 647. As to the statement, "want of Process to Outlawry

pired in December 1775, was never passed upon by the imperial legislative review agencies. However, those subject to the act declared "that the legislative authority of the province of New York had no constitutional right or power to make such laws and consequently they are null and void, from the nature and energy of the English constitution. . . ."[135] What the Board of Trade and other reviewers failed to realize was that colonial conditions, frequently riotous, called for sterner measures than the diluted outlawry procedure operating in England.

Colonial legislatures at times endeavored to restrict unpopular crown prosecutions by procedural limitations. Pennsylvania acts of 1706 and 1709 limiting grand jury presentments were disallowed as excluding crown informations.[136] A New York act of 1727 concerning oppressive informations by the Attorney General quashed all such existing informations; it then provided that misdemeanors should not be prosecuted other than by grand jury presentment or by information upon a signed order from the Governor in council.[137] Fane, counsel for the Board of Trade, characterized the act, passed by the same assembly that made a vicious attack on the chancery establishment, as a violent and extraordinary attack on the prerogative. He submitted that the right of the Attorney General to file informations was delegated by the King and was an

(which is not used in this Colony)," see generally GOEBEL, CASES ON THE DEVELOPMENT OF LEGAL INSTITUTIONS 402-04 (1937); GOEBEL & NAUGHTON, *op. cit. supra* note 90, at 442-47. A similar situation appeared in Jamaica. A May 1747 act, 3 Laws of Jamaica 183-84 (ms.), contained a recital that "no process of outlawry hath ever been in use in this island to compell persons to appear and answer in any causes criminal or civil." But in a 1671 account of the state of Jamaica by Sir Thomas Lynch it was set forth as part of the instructions to the court of common pleas "that all acts of assembly be published gratis, and also all process against persons that are outlawed, the coroner being present, to be directed to the judges of this court, to be published ex officio, which shall be as sufficient in law as the like publications in England and the same shall be recorded there and a certificate of such publications returned." 1 ASSEMBLY OF JAMAICA, JOURNALS app. at 36. Among the orders and rules of the Grand or Supreme Court it was related that when persons for whom a summons had issued could not be found, "a capias, and so process to outlawry, shall issue." 1 *id.* app. at 38.

135. CONVENTION OF THE REPRESENTATIVES OF THE NEW HAMPSHIRE SETTLERS, PROCEEDINGS 16 (1775).

136. 2 APC, COL. app. at 851.

137. 2 Col. Laws N.Y. 406. For the legislative background see 1 GENERAL ASSEMBLY OF THE COLONY OF NEW-YORK, JOURNAL OF VOTES AND PROCEEDINGS 1691-1745, at 566, 568-70 (1764); 1 LEGISLATIVE COUNCIL OF THE COLONY OF NEW-YORK, JOURNAL 1691-1743, at 560-62 (1861). See also 5 DOC. REL. COL. HIST. N.Y. 844, 847; GOEBEL & NAUGHTON, *op. cit. supra* note 90, at 372-73.

essential and necessary power with respect to the security of the public tranquillity as well as to protection of the revenue. If no delinquent was to be prosecuted without such solemn inquiry as to expediency, encouragement would be given to perpetrate crimes in hopes of escaping punishment by delay of justice. The crown law officers concurring, the Board of Trade advised disallowance, which took place in November 1728.[138] In a related area, a Virginia act was disallowed as weakening the process available to the Crown in recovery of forfeitures and arrears of quitrents. Later, two New York acts were disallowed as rendering collection of quitrents by crown officers more difficult and limiting the courts in which they could sue therefor, an encroachment on the royal prerogative.[139]

It was chiefly in connection with legislation respecting the conduct of trials that the Council's concern with restraining repugnancy to the laws of England became emphatic. The most basic of the issues here encountered was the matter of oath taking, and it was basic because the whole functioning of a trial depended thereon—the oaths of the judge, the jurors, the witnesses—and because the religious beliefs of large sections of the colonial population made the matter one of intense political importance.[140] Inevitably, since the province was dominated by Quakers, the major struggle centered in Pennsylvania where doctrinal rejection of the usual oath in legal proceedings and insistence on an affirmation produced a disagreement lasting over two decades.

In England in 1696 it had been enacted that Quakers might make an affirmation in the form provided in cases in which the law

138. CSP, Col., 1728-1729, Nos. 236, 357, 415, 451; 2 Chalmers, Opinions 180-84. See also 6 Doc. Rel. Col. Hist. N.Y. 17-18.

139. 3 APC, Col. No. 46; 4 *id.* No. 4; Bond, The Quit-Rent System in the American Colonies 271-73 (1919). See also Fane's opinion that a Montserrat act prohibiting trade with the French was unreasonable in that it required the expense of prosecuting any offense to be taken from the Crown's share of the forfeitures; "this appears to me to be an unusual regulation and I believe there cannot be produced two instances here or in the Plantations where the same has been done." CSP, Col., 1735-1736, No. 431.

140. The necessity of an oath in legal proceedings is seen in a Board of Trade report on a disallowed Antigua act of 1719. Although the act provided for jury trials in all cases, there was no oath prescribed for jurors nor any remedy provided against a false verdict. CSP, Col., 1720-1721, Nos. 610, 626. In the seventeenth and eighteenth centuries entire practice books were devoted to various forms of oaths. See for example, The Book of Oaths and the Severall Forms thereof, Both Ancient and Modern Faithfully Collected out of sundry Authenticke Books of Records, not heretofore extant (1649).

required an oath, but no Quaker or reputed Quaker was thereby qualified to give evidence in any criminal cause, serve on any jury, or occupy any office or place of profit in the government.[141] The Frame of Government adopted in Pennsylvania in the same year was to the same effect, but contained none of the parliamentary exceptions.[142] In November 1700 an act was passed in the province that provided that judicial and other officers should be qualified to act in their respective offices upon taking the attestations mentioned in the statute. Forms of attestation were also provided for grand inquests and traverse juries; any magistrate not scrupling to do so might administer the oath in the name of the court to those free to take it.[143]

The Anglican elements in the province, fearful of Quaker domination and oppression, hastened to complain to England. William Penn was thereupon ordered by the Board of Trade in May 1702 to answer whether all persons in judicial and other offices in Pennsylvania and the Lower Counties on the Delaware took the oath directed by the law of England or the affirmation allowed to Quakers. Further, he was to report whether all persons who in England would be obliged, and were willing, to take an oath in any public proceeding were permitted to do so in Pennsylvania.[144]

141. Quaker Affirmation Act, 7 & 8 Will. 3, c. 34 (1696).

142. CHARTER & LAWS PROV. PA. 247-48. See also the 1693 law on the manner of giving evidence. *Id.* at 228. Early instances of avoidance of the oath occurred. 1 MINS. PROV. COUN. PA. 148, 398. Nonextension of the act of Parliament to the colonies was brought to imperial attention in connection with enforcement of the Navigation Acts. Under 7 & 8 Will. 3, c. 22, § 17 (1696), English-built ships had to be registered and proof made on oath before the collector of the customs. In Pennsylvania the collector was not suffered by his superior to permit Quakers to register vessels upon affirmation. CSP, COL., 1700, Nos. 168, 366. Furthermore, a clause in the Frame of Government provision as to affirmation stated that no person should be excused from swearing who by the Navigation Acts was or should be required to take an oath. CHARTERS & LAWS PROV. PA. 249. By a 1698 act this exception was eliminated. *Id.* at 271-72. In justifying his assent to this provision, Deputy Governor Markham informed the Board of Trade that he took encouragement from the indulgence of the English act of 1696, and that greater reason for the act existed in that Quakers were a greater proportion of the people in Pennsylvania than in England. CSP, COL., 1700, No. 176. However, parliamentary intervention was still desired, *id.*, 1700, Nos. 158, 366, 734; *id.*, 1701, No. 219, and this 1698 act was declared null and void *ab initio* by the Privy Council on legislative review, J. SMITH, APPEALS TO THE PRIVY COUNCIL FROM THE AMERICAN PLANTATIONS 531-32 (1950).

143. 2 Stat. at Large Pa. 39. Much of the act repeated Frame of Government provisions.

144. For the complaint of the vestry of Philadelphia's Christ Church see CSP, COL., 1701, Nos. 101, 404. For the attitude of William Penn toward the

Penn replied that since the province was largely settled by Quakers the solemn attestation was employed in pledging allegiance to the Crown and proprietor and in giving evidence, but that from early times oaths were administered to those so desiring.[145] The Board of Trade thereupon recommended to the King in Council that all persons in judicial or other offices in Pennsylvania and the Lower Counties should be obliged before entrance into office to take the oath directed by the law of England or the affirmation thereby provided, and that no judge should be allowed to sit unless this condition were met. Likewise, all persons willing to take an oath in any public or judicial proceeding should be permitted to do so by the proper judges and officers; in default thereof or in case of refusal to administer oaths, judicial proceedings should be declared null and void. This was accordingly ordered by the King in Council.[146]

Anglican element in the colony see 1 PENNSYLVANIA ARCHIVES 141-42 (1st ser.). The inveterate foe of the proprietary government, Colonel Quary, also joined the chorus of complaint. CSP, COL., 1702-1703, No. 305. See also *id.*, 1702-1703, Nos. 580, 638 for the complaint of Thomas Byfield, among the Quary charges against Penn, as to the illegality of proceedings and verdict when the jury was not sworn. Quary also declared that the name of God was not used in the attestations. 1 *Correspondence between William Penn and James Logan, Secretary of the Province of Pennsylvania, and Others, 1700-1750*, in 9 & 10 MEMOIRS OF THE HISTORICAL SOCIETY OF PENNSYLVANIA 164 (1870-1872) [hereinafter cited as *Penn-Logan Corres.*]. For the Board of Trade order see CSP, COL., 1702-1703, No. 508. For further complaint by Quary see *id.*, 1702, No. 782. The imperial authorities themselves diverged from the terms of the 1696 act, for in the 1702 instructions to Lord Cornbury as Governor of New Jersey, Quakers were to be allowed to hold office, provided they took and signed the declaration of allegiance in the form used by Quakers in England, An Act for Exempting Dissenters from Penalties of Certain Laws, 1 W. & M., sess. 1, c. 18 (1688), together with a solemn declaration for the true discharge of their respective trusts, LEAMING & SPICER, GRANTS, CONCESSIONS AND ORIGINAL CONSTITUTIONS OF THE PROVINCE OF NEW JERSEY, 1664-1682, at 633-34 (1881).

145. CSP, COL., 1702-1703, No. 1207. This answer was not "altogether satisfactory" to the Board of Trade. *Id.*, 1702-1703, No. 1208.

146. *Id.*, 1702-1703, Nos. 218, 219. Penn objected to the validity of the conciliar order, requesting an instruction instead, since "the law of the country cannot be augmented any more than diminished without a law, and sent to Col. Hamilton to be past into a Law; or I am sure it cannot answer the end, for the Law here is none there, being Locall, till made so by the Assembly of the Country." *Id.*, 1702-1703, No. 234. To this objection the Board of Trade retorted that it saw no reason for any alteration in the Order, "the matters therein contained relating equally to the due administration of Justice and to the good Government of the Province of Pennsylvania." *Id.*, 1702-1703, Nos. 256, 258. Later Penn wrote that "the opinion of all lawyers is that . . . those statutes only reach you that mention you, and therefore you are not obliged to take either affirmation or abjuration." 1 *Penn-Logan Corres.* 259. For the opera-

Further complaint, emanating from Anglican sources and transmitted by Lord Cornbury, was then made that people in Pennsylvania were condemned to death by Quaker judges and juries not acting under oath.[147] On the basis of the Cornbury description of these trials, the Board of Trade ordered Penn to give particular directions to his Deputy Governor and use all other means for putting a stop to such undue proceedings.[148]

When the 1700 act finally came before Attorney General Northey in October 1704, he found nothing therein disagreeable to law or justice, or prejudicial to the royal prerogative. But the Board of Trade objected that none of the officers mentioned were obliged to take an oath for the due execution of their places, but

tion of this order in Chester and Bucks counties see 1 *id.* 215; CSP, COL., 1702-1703, No. 1407(i). For use of the order by Quary to embarrass the proprietary government upon the death of Deputy Governor Hamilton and Penn's reaction thereto, see JANNEY, THE LIFE OF WILLIAM PENN 452-53 (1852). See also Penn's later comments on this incident. *Id.* at 461.

147. CSP, COL., 1702-1703, No. 761. The version reaching Penn was that the jury was not only not sworn, but also not attested according to the 1696 act. 1 *Penn-Logan Corres.* 205. *Cf.* 1 *id.* at 193, for Quary's version that the jury was impanelled without an oath and on only a single affirmation. The events leading to this complaint originated in February 1702/03. In that month a particular commission of oyer and terminer and gaol delivery was issued, directed to those capable of taking and administering oaths, rather than the standing commission to the judges of the provincial court. 1 *id.* at 175-76, 193, 196; CSP, COL., 1702-1703, No. 1407(i). But the judges acting under this commission were frustrated by the anti-Quaker faction, and failed to secure anyone to take an oath for the grand jury. This was allegedly done to provide such faction with a complaint of delay of justice. 1 *Penn-Logan Corres.* 194. Quary alleged that the potential grand jury "gave their reasons [for refusal to serve] that since the Quakers had engrossed and did exercise all the powers of Government, they should trey the criminalls too; and not thinke to put that part of the drugery on them." In addition, the commission was unsatisfactory to the grand jury. CSP, COL., 1702-1703, No. 368(i). In April, three provincial court judges, who scrupled to take an oath, held the court and impanelled a grand jury by affirmation "according to the law of England." 1 *Penn-Logan Corres.* 194-95 (7 & 8 Will. 3, c. 34, § 6 [1696] was apparently disregarded). It was declared that by the charter the law for felonies, etc. was to be the same as in England until altered by exercise of the legislative power. Since the charter gave full power to make laws, the laws of England could not be ruling in the province after such alterations were made. Laws made under the charter and not disallowed must be guiding; thus, action taken under a law directing how juries should be qualified was legal. Accordingly, the grand jury was again attested according to the provincial law and the session proceeded. At this session one man was burned in the hand for manslaughter, pleading benefit of clergy, and a woman condemned to death for murder of her child, but probably not executed. 1 *Penn-Logan Corres.* 195.

148. CSP, COL., 1702-1703, No. 941.

only to make an attestation in the form provided, which was insufficient. Thereupon the act was disallowed February 1704/05.[149]

In the colony some courts had been regularly held with an exact observance of the Order in Council; in other cases a failure of justice had resulted from Quakers quitting the bench and from adoption of an uncooperative attitude by opposing elements.[150] Some proceedings in violation of the counciliar order had even been declared void by proclamation of Deputy Governor Evans.[151] The main failure of justice occurred in cases in which there was no judge present who was able to administer an oath when evidence was offered on oath.[152] In December 1705 the assembly resumed the legislative offensive with a bill for taking in all cases the affirmation prescribed by Parliament in lieu of an oath. A controversial clause provided that when no magistrate or other officer able to administer an oath was present, it would be lawful for the magistrate or officer present to administer the affirmation in lieu of an oath.[153] When the Governor and council recommended that the bill be drawn more in conformity with the royal order, great debate ensued.[154]

First debated was the question whether legislative power existed to enact a law that an affirmation should in all cases, except when the Navigation Acts required oaths, be equivalent to an oath. It was finally resolved that the power was sufficient and that such an act was not contrary to law, reliance being placed on the failure of the Attorney General to object in point of law to several acts altering the method of proceeding in capital crimes from that employed in England. As to the expediency of such an enactment, the assembly asserted that the bill complied with the conciliar order, but the Governor objected that according to the bill an oath could not in all cases be administered to willing persons because of the provision that, when the magistrate could not admin-

149. *Id.*, 1704-1705, Nos. 604, 1278; 2 Stat. at Large Pa. 449, 465. See also Penn's reply to the Board of Trade. CSP, Col., 1704-1705, No. 1324.

150. 1 *Penn-Logan Corres.* 221, 236-39, 244-46. Quary wrote in October 1704 that the conciliar order "hath been noeways complyed with." CSP, Col., 1704-1705, No. 605, at 282.

151. *Id.*, 1704-1705, No. 605(ii); 1 *Penn-Logan Corres.* 318; 2 Mins. Prov. Coun. Pa. 160-61.

152. 2 Stat. at Large Pa. 508.

153. 1 Votes & Proc. Prov. Pa. pt. 2, at 70-71; 2 Stat. at Large Pa. 266-72.

154. 2 Mins. Prov. Coun. Pa. 219, 225-26; 1 Votes & Proc. Prov. Pa. pt. 2, at 74-75.

ister an oath, the affirmation should be taken in lieu thereof. The assembly in reply indicated that it was primarily concerned with the problem of evidence on oath before a single judge or a bench without a judge able to administer an oath, but asserted that to cause failure of justice in such case could not be the incongruous intent of the royal order.[155] Since the assembly was intent upon the act, the Deputy Governor in January 1705/06 agreed to its passage with a clause suspending operation until September 1706.[156]

The enactment instantly evoked a storm of protests, principally from Anglican sources.[157] Attorney General Northey, asked for his opinion on the act, favored affirmance in view of Quaker predominance in the province and the failure of the English act to extend to the plantations. The objection to the absence of magistrates on the bench able to administer an oath could be obviated by stipulation with the proprietor requiring their presence, but fault was found with the provision allowing depositions in criminal cases when persons were sick or departing the province. The Board of Trade, upon receiving this opinion, agreed to advise disallowance unless assured by Penn that the assembly would immediately pass a corrective act.[158] Whatever Penn's reaction to this proposition, the matter lay dormant until November 1706, when "some gentlemen of Pennsylvania" petitioned against confirmation of the act. The Board then advised disallowance on the basis of Northey's objections, and the act was disallowed on January 8, 1707/08.[159]

The repeal left the province with only the conciliar order for

155. 2 MINS. PROV. COUN. PA. 226-28. Compare 2 *Penn-Logan Corres.* 240, that it was for "want of a jury of the vicinity more than that of magistrates, that . . . the preamble of that law declares that there might be a failure of justice."

156. 2 MINS. PROV. COUN. PA., 229-32; 2 Stat. at Large Pa., 508. See 2 *Penn-Logan Corres.* 98, in which Logan asserted that he thought it necessary to defend the act to Penn, since "it introduces the affirmation as by Act of Parliament, and takes notice of the Queen's orders." He was of the opinion that "a less security than that affirmation, among so very loose a people as in many places here shelter themselves under the name of a profession, would be very dangerous." See also 2 *id.* at 187. For the attitude of Penn on affirmations see CSP, COL., 1704-1705, No. 810.

157. ROOT, THE RELATIONS OF PENNSYLVANIA WITH THE BRITISH GOVERNMENT, 1696-1765, at 244-45 (1912).

158. 2 Stat. at Large Pa. 512-14; JCTP, 1704-1708/09, at 272-73. As to the act being contrary to the laws of England, Northey stated: "By the English act, affirmation is not to be allowed in criminal cases; but is allowed by this in Pennsylvania, for which there may be some reason, because the greatest part of the inhabitants are Quakers. . . ." 2 Stat. at Large Pa. 513.

159. 2 *id.* at 506, 514-18, 521-23.

guidance; however, the form of affirmation as used in England was not only opposed by the Anglican faction, but was also disliked by some Quakers. Finally, in February 1710/11 an act was passed directing the use of an affirmation by those who for conscience's sake could not take an oath.[160] This act, which established the form of affirmation in giving evidence, provided that nothing therein should be construed to hinder any magistrate or officer from administering an oath to any person not scrupling to take it. Several Anglican judges showed reluctance to act pursuant to the act,[161] and the Anglican faction in New Jersey, fearing legislation imitation, petitioned in England against the act.[162] The Board of Trade thereupon advised disallowance, observing that the affirmation provided differed from that enjoined by act of Parliament, particularly in that the name of God was not mentioned, and that evidence under affirmation might be given in a criminal cause, contrary to the Parliamentary enactment. Royal disapprobation was manifested on December 19, 1711.[163] When report of the disallowance reached the province in May 1712, the assembly immediately set about to remedy matters by a supplementary act to the 1693 law concerning the manner of giving evidence. The new act, in effect the same as the disallowed enactment of 1710/11, was found objectionable by Solicitor General Raymond for the same reasons as the earlier statute and disallowance followed on February 20, 1713/14.[164]

This disallowance was countered by passage of two acts in May 1715; one provided for an affirmation containing the divine name, another provided an affirmation lacking such name for those scrupling to take the affirmation as allowed in England.[165] But before these two acts were put on the statute books, the parliamentary act of 1696 had been extended to the plantations by a 1714

160. 2 MINS. PROV. COUN. PA. 524-25, 529; 2 *Penn-Logan Corres.* 430; 2 Stat. at Large Pa. 355; 2 VOTES & PROC. PROV. PA. 76, 82, 88, 90, 93.

161. The attorney general of the colony was asked to give his opinion whether there was "any danger to the Justices in acting and Receiving Evidences in pursuant to that Law." 2 MINS. PROV. COUN. PA. 531.

162. HILLS, HISTORY OF THE CHURCH IN BURLINGTON 134-35 (1876); JCTP, 1708/09-1714/15, at 317; 2 Stat. at Large Pa. 536-38.

163. 2 *id.* at 535, 538-40.

164. 2 MINS. PROV. COUN. PA. 553; 1 PENNSYLVANIA ARCHIVES 158-59 (1st ser.); 2 Stat. at Large Pa. 425, 543-44, 549-50; VOTES & PROC. PROV. PA. 113, 115-17, 121. For the effect of the passage of the act upon the church party see JAMES LOGAN LETTER BOOK, 1712-15, at 12, 15-16 (ms., HSP).

165. 2 MINS. PROV. COUN. PA. 591-96; 3 Stat. at Large Pa. 39, 58.

act of Parliament.[166] The conflict between the terms of this act and the provincial enactments inevitably resulted in a constitutional controversy between Deputy Governor Gookin and the assembly. Upon receiving complaints of great delay in criminal trials, the house resolved that under the charter provincial acts were absolute until royal repeal, that laws of the province had sufficiently settled the qualifications of magistrates and officers, and that the parliamentary enactment of 1714 did not repeal or make void any laws of the province.[167] Gookin agreed with the assembly as to the force of provincial laws, provided they were not repugnant to the laws of England. He asserted, however, that the provincial laws as to affirmations prevailed only until publication of the act of 1714 relating thereto.[168]

In a December 1716 reply to Gookin, the assembly presented lengthy argument that the provincial acts as to affirmation were still in force. In the first place, no repeal had taken place under the charter provisions. Second, the repugnancy intimation of Gookin was refuted. The term "repugnant" meant "an absolute opposition or contrariety in matter," which was not the present case. If any variation from the laws of England was repugnant, then the power in the charter to alter the laws of England in certain respects was meaningless. Third, as to the presumed main contention of Gookin that the provincial acts were, by the superior force of the act of Parliament, repealed and made void, the negativing clause of the parliamentary act only prevented qualification by virtue of said act and did not prevent qualification by virtue of provincial acts already enacted or to be enacted.[169] When Sir William Keith assumed the government and the administration of criminal justice was resumed, an appeal to the King in Council was sought from proceedings held in accordance with the provincial law. Although the appeal was denied by the Deputy Governor, the assembly was alarmed into a crude attempt to give a constitutional basis to trial

166. The Quaker Act, 1 Geo. 1, st. 2, c. 4 (1714).

167. 2 VOTES & PROC. PROV. PA. 191, 194-95.

168. 2 *id.* at 195; 2 MINS. PROV. COUN. PA. 614-15.

169. 2 *id.* at 616-29; 2 VOTES & PROC. PROV. PA. 201-04. Blankard v. Galdy, 2 Salk 411, 91 Eng. Rep. 356 (K.B. 1694), and Wey v. Yally, 6 Mod. 194, 87 Eng. Rep. 948 (Q.B. 1705), were cited for the proposition that laws in the plantations might differ from the laws of England. 2 VOTES & PROC. PROV. PA. 207. For the excitement generated by imposition of the death sentence on two offenders as the result of a trial at which some judges and jurors took the affirmation see JAMES LOGAN LETTER BOOK, 1717-31, at 17, 20, 30 (ms., HSP).

by jurors under affirmation only. By an act for the advancement of justice of May 1718 it was provided that, in the administration of criminal law, qualification for judges, justices, inquests, and witnesses was to be either by corporal oath or by solemn affirmation as allowed by the act of Parliament.[170]

When the Board of Trade considered this 1718 act, it determined that the act allowed greater indulgence to Quakers than did the laws in England; however, since the Quaker population predominated and since the administration of justice would be rendered difficult without the qualification proposed, the act was recommended for approbation. On May 26, 1719, conciliar approval was obtained.[171] In the meantime, attention was directed to the delay in presenting for royal approbation the two acts of 1715.[172] In March 1718/19 counsel Richard West pointed out that the affirmation in which the name of God was omitted was materially different from that used in Great Britain, and the Board of Trade agreed to advise disallowance, circumstances not rendering it necessary to extend toleration to Quakers further than provided by the laws of Great Britain. On July 21, 1719, this act was disallowed; the companion act regarding affirmations became law by lapse of time under the charter provision.[173]

But matters were on the mend for the Quakers, for in England in 1721 an act was passed that allowed a form of attestation omitting the name of the deity.[174] In Pennsylvania, a 1724 act provided for the new forms. No objection to this act was voiced by counselor West or by the Board of Trade, and the King in Council expressed approbation on March 27, 1725.[175] The question of oaths and affirmations in Pennsylvania dropped from administrative notice, until in May 1739 an act was passed providing, for the relief of Presbyterians, the method of administering oaths used in Scotland.

170. 3 MINS. PROV. COUN. PA. 40-42; 3 Stat. at Large Pa. 200-01; 2 VOTES & PROC. PROV. PA. 233-34, 237. As an inducement to favorable consideration of the provisions relating to affirmations, changes were made in the criminal law, making it more consonant with the laws of England and less consistent with Quaker ideals. Fitzroy, *The Punishment of Crime in Provincial Pennsylvania*, 60 PA. MAGAZINE OF HISTORY & BIOGRAPHY 242, 250-52 (1936).

171. 3 Stat. at Large Pa. 437-39.

172. 3 *id.* at 441-45, 448-49, 451.

173. 3 *id.* at 40, 439-40, 456-58; JCTP, 1718-1722, at 44.

174. Quaker Affirmation Act, 8 Geo. 1, c. 6 (1721).

175. 3 MINS. PROV. COUN. PA. 235; 3 Stat. at Large Pa. 427, 514, 516-17; 2 VOTES & PROC. PROV. PA. 345, 347, 362, 367-68, 378, 384, 385, 387, 396-97.

Although the Board of Trade found no objection to the act, the crown law officers adverted to the act's loose, uncertain draftsmanship and the danger of yielding to new scruples about oaths. Therefore, the act suffered disallowance in May 1740 upon committee advice.[176]

Although the main struggle took place in Pennsylvania, in March 1759 a Georgia act of 1756 easing the plight of dissenting Protestants scrupling to take an oath in the accustomed manner was disallowed. Sir Matthew Lamb, counsel for the Board of Trade, had observed that the degree of indulgence granted (all dissenters were allowed to take affirmations whether as jurors, witnesses, or parties in all causes, civil or criminal) was not conformable to the laws of England. This was so because the Act of Toleration did not exempt Protestant dissenters from taking oaths and by the 1696 act Quakers were disqualified from giving evidence in criminal causes or from serving on juries.[177]

The representations against this Georgia act included objections to its failure to deal with other qualifications for jurors. From an early date the English administrators had dispatched instructions directing passage of acts fixing property qualifications for jurors, a matter that the English had always regarded to be no less important than the "lawfulness" of the juror and the oath that made his share in the verdict the true voice of the country.[178] Lamb viewed as improper the prevailing Georgia practice of impanelling only those seised of fifty acres or more, since it excluded urban inhabitants of substance. It was further objected that the time fixed for jury balloting gave too great an opportunity for tampering, and that balloting for grand jurors was unusual and unnecessary.[179] The policy that forbade deviation from English standards as to how a jury should be constituted is illustrated further by an earlier disallowance grounded on the fundamental necessity that jurymen be of the vicinage. In 1738 a South Carolina act of 1731 obliging persons living in any county and precinct to serve as jurors in Charleston was rejected as unreasonable.[180]

176. 3 APC, Col. No. 493; 4 Stat. at Large Pa. 337, 482-84.

177. 4 APC, Col. No. 379. For the act see 18 Colonial Records of the State of Georgia 157-59. See also Fane's objection in 1738 to a South Carolina act as not prescribing a particular form of affirmation. CO 5/366/F 94.

178. 1 Labaree, Royal Instructions, Nos. 417, 418.

179. 4 APC, Col. No. 379.

180. 3 *id.* No. 448; CO 5/366/F 94; 3 Statutes at Large of S.C. 287 (Johnston ed. 1838).

In the area of the jury system it should be noted that a disallowed Nevis act of 1704, found objectionable in several respects, had provided that all extraordinary contempts of jurors were to be punished by the bench by fine. The Board of Trade objected that contempt might be construed to include refusal to find a verdict according to the court's direction, recalcitrance for which jurors by law were not to be fined. It was also objected that the act unreasonably provided that in all cases after verdict the defendant should be barred from moving in arrest of judgment.[181]

A further type of procedural legislation to encounter resistance at Whitehall was that relating to alterations in accepted methods of proof. This is particularly interesting, since the English had not yet developed a systematic law of evidence, and certain rules, such as those respecting hearsay, were in an embryonic state. The disallowed provincial acts covered a variety of matters. In February 1705/06 a 1700 Pennsylvania act providing for confirmation of nuncupative wills was disallowed as unreasonable in requiring witnesses of such wills made in England to come to the province in order to prove the will. At the same time, another 1700 Pennsylvania act, which required two credible witnesses in all criminal cases in order to proceed to judgment, was disallowed. Attorney General Northey had argued that no reason existed to require two witnesses when by the law of England one was sufficient, except in cases of treason and noncapital criminal matters.[182] In 1706 a New Hampshire act allowing the taking of affidavits without notice to the adversary was disallowed as unreasonable.[183] To a disallowed Antigua act of 1716, the Attorney General had objected that it unreasonably allowed the certificate of a public notary to be evidence of the execution of a deed, although a public notary could not administer an oath.[184] Richard West, reporting on a 1723 Massachusetts act for preventing trespasses, stated: "This act introduces a strange kind of . . . [wager] of law, by the single oath of either plaintiff or dependant [*sic*] in cases of trespasse, and as it manifestly tends to the encrease of prejury and is a practice not known to the Law of England," was not proper to be passed into law.[185] In 1761 a South Carolina act of 1759 for supplying defects

181. CSP, Col., 1708-1709, No. 264; PC 2/82/226.

182. 1 Charters & Acts Assembly Prov. Pa. 18; 2 Stat. at Large Pa. 47-48, 493.

183. 1 Laws of N.H. 689, 862, 866-67.

184. CSP, Col., 1716-1717, No. 422; *id.*, 1717-1718, No. 337.

185. *Id.*, 1734-1735, No. 568. Presumably, West was commenting on Chapter

in evidence when original wills could not be produced was disallowed as establishing a method of proving wills not permitted by the practice of the English courts. The act, directed to the case in which wills devising realty within the province were probated outside the province, allowed such wills to be evidenced by duly authenticated probate or by a properly attested copy in any court of law or equity in the province. It was advised that since the province had the same method of proving wills disposing of realty in chancery *per testes*, and of exemplifying the wills to make them evidence as in England, no alteration was advisable.[186] In 1762 a North Carolina act to the same effect was disallowed.[187]

In connection with the matter of judicial proof, one act that was ex post facto in nature was disallowed. In Antigua in 1737, an act was passed empowering slaves to give evidence against two free Negroes charged with an intended insurrection. Since such admissibility was contrary to unvaried island practice, and since the act was passed long after commission of the crime charged, it was described as a law of very extraordinary nature and a dangerous precedent to the lives and properties of free Negroes. It was therefore disallowed in November 1738.[188]

Certain acts providing punishment for perjury were also disallowed. A Pennsylvania act of 1700, disallowed in 1705/06, provided that every witness convicted of perjury should suffer the same penalty as the person testified against would have suffered if found guilty. This was more extreme than the law of England, for a witness convicted of perjury after a felony acquittal would be hanged, since the act was not confined to civil causes.[189] In November 1706 a New Hampshire act was set aside as unreasonable in discouraging prosecutions for perjury. The act, which allowed convicted perjurors to recover damages against their prosecutors in the event of reversal of judgment, was objectionable in that reversal might be on formal grounds.[190]

In this connection it should be noted that colonial legislators

10 of the Acts of 1723-24, which was not, however, disallowed. See 1 Acts & Res. Prov. Mass. Bay 299-301, 310.

186. 4 APC, Col. No. 452; 4 Statutes at Large of S.C. 101 (Johnston ed. 1838).

187. 4 APC, Col. app. at 807; 6 Col. Rec. N.C. 749.

188. 3 APC, Col. No. 443.

189. 1 Charter & Acts Assembly Prov. Pa. 18; 2 Stat. at Large Pa. 133, 497.

190. 1 Laws of N.H. 677, 862, 866-67.

did not always distinguish carefully between civil actions and criminal prosecutions. However, such failure did not escape the scrutiny of the legislative review process. In 1773 a Virginia act of 1772 aimed at preventing malicious maiming and wounding was disallowed; in counsel Jackson's opinion the act displayed a tendency "to confound the principles of legal proceedings, by giving the effect . . . [of] a Criminal prosecution to an Action upon the Case."[191] In 1774 a New York act of the previous year was disallowed on the ground that it provided for purgation by oath in a criminal matter, which was "contrary to the Genius of the Laws of this Country" and an irresistible temptation to perjury.[192]

In several instances disallowance or gubernatorial instruction reached acts concerned with execution upon judgments in civil actions. In 1703 Solicitor General Harcourt found a Bermuda act giving jurisdiction to justices of the peace in causes not exceeding twenty shillings unfit for confirmation. The arbitrary power granted a justice to put a defendant out to service, when judgment could not be satisfied from personal property, was termed not agreeable to any execution that could be awarded according to the law of England. The Board of Trade accordingly ordered Lieutenant Governor Bennett to have the act "rectified" at the first assembly.[193] A 1719 Antigua act providing that in case of execution the oath of the agent or attorney of defendant as to nonconcealment of effects would be admitted to stay execution was characterized as unjust and conducive to perjury. A provision allowing return of goods taken on execution after posting a bond in double their value was termed unreasonable in affording no security when the defendant's entire effects, which might be concealed and made away with, were worth less than the amount of the debt and charges. Furthermore, no execution was to issue upon any judgment for debt contracted prior to passage of the act, unless plaintiff forbore to levy execution for two years after the date of the act. The act

191. 5 APC, Col. No. 247; 8 Stat. at Large Va. 520. See the comment that, "quite obviously, the Assembly would not have passed the act of 1772 unless there had been a considerable amount of gouging-out of eyes and biting-off of ears." Scott, Criminal Law in Colonial Virginia 205-06 (1930).

192. 5 APC, Col. No. 299; 5 Col. Laws N.Y. 458.

193. CSP, Col., 1702-1703, No. 1356; *id.*, 1704-1705, No. 529; 2 Chalmers, Opinions 73-74. See also the objection to a 1704 Nevis act limiting those authorized to administer an oath to appraisers upon execution. CSP, Col., 1708-1709, Nos. 250, 264.

was accordingly disallowed.[194] In Jamaica an act for the further regulation of the Provost Marshall's proceedings was passed in 1751; it prohibited issuance of writs of execution until the next court day. The act was disallowed in 1753, in part because this provision was an unnecessary and dangerous delay of justice and might afford great opportunities for fraud, concealment, and embezzlement.[195] A North Carolina act was disallowed as providing an improper and inadequate method of appraisal of goods taken on execution.[196] A desire to protect trading interests is manifest in the conflicts over application of the statute of limitations[197] to colonial conditions; especially objectionable was the extension of limitations to judgments in addition to causes of action.[198]

194. CSP, Col., 1720-1721, Nos. 610, 626.

195. 4 APC, Col. No. 216; 4 Laws of Jamaica 72-74 (ms.). The crown law officers in a 1753 opinion characterized as "unjust" a Jamaica act that permitted execution on the lands of the heir or executor of the original debtor without regard to the qualification contained in the English laws. 2 Chalmers, Opinions 107.

196. 4 APC, Col. app. at 807. See also the 1747 opinion of the crown law officers that a 1715 North Carolina act giving priority to country debts "was contrary to reason, inconsistant with the laws and greatly prejudicial to the interests of this kingdom; and therefore, unwarranted by the charter, and, consequently void." CO 5/296/B 73; 2 Chalmers, Opinions 61-62.

197. Act for the limitation of certain actions, 21 Jac. 1, c. 16 (1623).

198. In 1729 a Virginia act of 1705 that limited actions on judgments to seven years and on bonds or bills obligatory to five years was disallowed, being termed repugnant to the English act and of bad consequences to the trade of the kingdom. 3 APC, Col. No. 171; CSP, Col., 1728-1729, No. 637; 3 Stat. at Large Va. 377. See also the 1748 act, 5 *id.* at 513, that met disallowance for procedural reasons, 4 APC, Col. No. 155; 6 Stat. at Large Va. 215. Later, it was objected to a Connecticut statute of limitations that it contained none of the savings of the English act in favor of infants, persons beyond the seas, etc. Fane, Rep. Laws Conn. 70-71. A Jamaica act of 1751, that provided that all judgments dormant for twenty years were to be deemed satisfied was disallowed on other grounds in 1753. 4 APC, Col. No. 216; 4 Laws of Jamaica 72-74 (ms.). A 1766 act providing a twenty-one year period also met disallowance. 5 APC, Col., No. 59. *But see* An Act for the further quieting possessions, and preventing vexatious suits at law, Acts of the Assembly of Jamaica 143 (1738), which was confirmed on May 5, 1715. PC 2/85/220. In 1759 an Antigua act of 1754 for preventing wrongs and inconveniences arising from dormant judgments was disallowed as being of an unusual and extraordinary nature and no more warranted in Antigua than in England. It was declared that the act could only operate in favor of careless and ignorant debtors and might in particular cases defeat just creditors of their rights. 4 APC, Col. No. 383. Some colonial acts sought not to extend the statute of limitations but to partially suspend its operation. In 1771 a North Carolina act was disallowed because it contained a dispensation from the law of limitations, counsel Jackson representing that no law was more essential to the quiet of property. 5 *id.* No. 190; CO 5/301/G 48. Yet the attitude of the Board of Trade was not entirely con-

In the same procedural area, a New York act that provided double damages and treble costs for taking or levying on specialties more than the principal, interest, and costs of suit was disallowed because the common law courts in the province provided a remedy and the act would encourage law suits.[199] Earlier, a 1708 Maryland act determining damages allowable on protested bills of exchange was rejected as working hardship on English merchants.[200] A Pennsylvania act was set aside in 1706 as granting double damages for false imprisonment even in cases of probable cause.[201]

In the field of criminal law, the Privy Council strove to maintain colonial sanctions consonant with the laws of England. In Massachusetts Bay particularly, deviations from English standards existed because of the influence of the Scriptures on punitive legislation.[202] A 1692 act of this colony against counterfeiting or clipping of coins was disallowed in 1695 on the ground that the crimes were not punished as in England. At the same time an act for the punishing of capital offenders was disallowed as not conformable to the laws of England in several respects. Witchcraft, blasphemy, incest, slaying by devilish practice, and unpremeditated homicide had been made punishable by death. The treason provision failed to punish counterfeiting of the Great Seal of England or the province seal, nor was it agreeable to the act of Parliament enumerating those offenses that should be adjudged treason.[203] An act against conjuration, witchcraft, and dealing with evil spirits was also disallowed as not agreeable to the English law that provided penalties for practicing invocation or conjuration,[204] whereby dower was saved to the widow and the inheritance to the heir of the party

---

sistent. In several earlier instances, reception of 21 Jac. 1, c. 16 (1623) in individual colonies was discouraged. CSP, COL., 1696-1697, Nos. 735, 803, 1405. See also the disallowance of Montserrat and Jamaica acts as providing too limited times for making claims to land. 2 APC, COL. app. at 835, 845; CSP, COL., 1708-1709, No. 834.

199. 3 APC, COL. app. at 850; CPS, COL., 1731, Nos. 181, 201.

200. 2 APC, COL. app. at 838. For the act see 27 MARYLAND ARCHIVES 364-65 (1907).

201. 2 APC, COL. app. at 851.

202. HASKINS, LAW AND AUTHORITY IN EARLY MASSACHUSSETTS 124-27, 141-59 (1960); HILKEY, LEGAL DEVELOPMENT IN COLONIAL MASSACHUSETTS 93-111 (1910); HOWE, READINGS IN AMERICAN LEGAL HISTORY 181-89 (1949); Goebel, *King's Law and Local Custom in Seventeenth Century New England*, 31 COLUM. L. REV. 416 (1931).

203. Treason Act, 25 EDW. 3, c. 2 (1351).

204. Witchcraft Act, 1 Jac. 1, c. 12 (1603).

convicted.[205] Two Pennsylvania acts against firing and breaking into houses encountered disallowance as providing for sale of offenders into servitude, a punishment not allowed by the laws of England.[206] A Virginia act that punished assembly of Quakers was disallowed in 1718, since such assembly was permitted by the laws of England.[207]

The Privy Council also made some attempt to guard against undue severity in colonial sanctions.[208] Pennsylvania acts of 1700 against robbery and scolding were disallowed in February 1705/06 as providing too severe punishments for the crimes in question. An act against riotous sports was disallowed for the same reason in February 1713/14. In September 1760 an act for recording warrants and surveys was disallowed, one ground being that the penalties imposed on negligent officers were too severe. An act appointing wardens for the port of Philadelphia, disallowed in 1773, was characterized as providing penalties of a severity contrary to the laws of England.[209] A Massachusetts act for preventing the spread of infectious diseases met disallowance in 1700 for severity of penalties.[210] A New Hampshire act providing the death penalty for willfully killing one's negro servant was disallowed as too severe in the absence of a requirement of malice.[211] In 1762 a Jamaica act of the previous year was disallowed; it had provided that any person importing, contrary to a 1759 act, sugar, rum, or molasses of foreign growth or produce should be deemed guilty of felony and suffer death as a felon without benefit of clergy. The Board of Trade had expressed great concern at this departure from established principles of justice, equity, reason, and the laws of England and had represented the act as null and void in being repugnant thereto.[212] In 1765 a Quebec ordinance for the better observance of the Sabbath met disallowance, because observance was enforced

205. 1 Acts & Res. Prov. Mass. Bay 55-56, 70-71, 90-91; CSP, COL., 1693-1696, No. 1874.

206. 1 Charters & Acts Assembly Prov. Pa. 18; 2 Stat. at Large Pa. 11-12, 491.

207. 2 APC, COL. app. at 853; CSP, COL., 1718, No. 281.

208. Compare the several instances in which Francis Fane was of the opinion that sanctions provided by Connecticut laws were not severe enough. FANE, REP. LAWS CONN. 77-78, 195-96.

209. 4 APC, COL. app. at 808; 5 *id.* No. 298; 1 Charters & Acts Assembly Prov. Pa. 18, 51; 2 Stat. at Large Pa. 9, 85, 360, 481, 491, 550; 5 *id.* at 448, 719.

210. 1 Acts & Res. Prov. Mass. Bay 376-77; CSP, COL., 1700, No. 824.

211. 2 APC, COL. app. at 847.

212. 4 *id.* No. 468; 5 ASSEMBLY OF JAMAICA, JOURNALS 347-50.

with severer penalties than were prescribed by the laws of England.[213] In 1768 a Virginia act of 1766 compelling infected ships conveying convicts or indentured servants to perform quarantine suffered disallowance; the severity of the penalties provided for violation of the act was found liable to great objection. A similar act, passed in 1772, received the same condemnation.[214] Inhumane penalties, particularly castration, were proscribed; three Pennsylvania acts, a New Jersey and a Bermuda act were disallowed on that score.[215] A Bermuda act providing for the banishment of free Negroes under certain circumstances was termed "unprecedented, and founded upon unjust and unconstitutional principles" and not proper for confirmation by the Crown.[216]

Acts providing "unreasonable" penalties, as opposed to "too severe" penalties, were also subject to disallowance. Two Nevis acts regulating the militia were disallowed in 1701 on that ground.[217] A 1700 Pennsylvania act for making debtors undergo servitude was disallowed in 1705/06 as unreasonable in subjecting visitors to the province to slavery. Another 1700 act against bigamy suffered the same fate as unreasonably providing for divorce of the first wife and subjecting the guilty husband to life labor for such wife's benefit.[218] Acts against counterfeiting seals and against adulterating strong liquors were disallowed as being unreasonable in not making intent an essential element of the crimes. An act against murder met disallowance for not restricting the death penalty to premediated homicides.[219] A New Hampshire act also failed to confine the death penalty to cases of premeditation and similarly suffered disallowance.[220] A Maryland act regulating the tobacco trade was

213. 4 APC, Col. No. 622.

214. 5 APC, Col. Nos. 83, 247; 8 Stat. at Large Va. 260, 537.

215. For the Pennsylvania acts see 2 Stat. at Large Pa. 7, 8, 77. For the 1705/06 disallowance and the Attorney General's opinion see 1 Charters & Acts Assembly Prov. Pa. 18; 2 Stat. at Large Pa. 490, 495. For the New Jersey act disallowed in October 1709 see PC 2/82/450; 3 Doc. Rel. Col. Hist. N.J. 473-74. For the Bermuda act, disallowed in April 1705 see PC 2/80/333; CSP, Col., 1704-1705, Nos. 1071, 1074, 1081.

216. JCTP, 1759-1763, at 296.

217. 2 APC, Col. app. at 846; CSP, Col., 1701, Nos. 816, 1020.

218. 1 Charters & Acts Assembly Prov. Pa. 18; 2 Stat. at Large Pa. 8, 129, 490, 496.

219. 1 Charters & Acts Assembly Prov. Pa. 18; 2 Stat. at Large Pa. 14, 17, 84, 491, 495.

220. 1 Laws of N.H. 570, 861, 866-67.

rejected in 1708 on the ground of unreasonable penalties.[221] A Virginia act concerning servants and slaves was disallowed in 1748/49 as having tendencies contrary to the design of the laws of England relating to felons.[222]

The Council strove equally to prevent superfluous legislative sanctions. Virginia, in November 1766, passed an act for the punishment of persons aiding prisoners for debt to escape or attempt to escape from prison. The law was disallowed in 1768; one reason for such action was that the remedies provided were unnecessary and superfluous, the common law remedies being sufficient.[223] A Barbados act of 1762, disallowed in July 1764, rendered one John Adams incapable of being elected to the assembly or of exercising any office in the island government after he had been tried for misdemeanor and had suffered the usual punishment therefor.[224] Several Jamaica acts, and one of West Florida, were disallowed as infringing upon the royal prerogative of granting pardons or *non vult ulterius prosequi*.[225]

The reverse of the coin is seen in the 1695 disallowance of a 1692 act setting forth the privileges of the inhabitants of Massachusetts Bay. This act abolished all escheats and forfeitures, except in the case of high treason. It also provided that bail be taken in all cases except those in which treason and felony were plainly expressed in the warrant of commitment. With this and "with other priviledges proposed by the said Act not having been as yet granted by his Majesty in any of the plantations," it was not thought fit to allow the act.[226]

Conclusion

The disallowance of acts relating to the courts and to procedure formed only a part of a much more extensive activity, the exact scope of which can not be accurately measured until some study is devoted to the acts that were approved or escaped disallowance. The legislative control exercised from Whitehall was perhaps most

221. 2 APC, Col. No. 1056. For the act see 27 Maryland Archives 157-59 (1907).

222. 4 APC, Col. No. 155.

223. 5 *id.* No. 83; 8 Stat. at Large Va. 240. The act was also termed of an "oppressive Nature and tendency," and by its loose terminology liable to arbitrary extension and abuse.

224. 4 APC, Col. No. 570.

225. 2 *id.* No. 1278, app. at 835; 5 *id.* No. 200; CSP, Col., 1718, No. 168.

226. 1 Acts & Res. Prov. Mass. Bay 40-41.

effective in the matter of judicial structure. The restraint upon experiments with procedure was less so, since much could be and was accomplished in the practice of provincial courts without the intervention of local legislatures. At the same time it may be inferred from the cases that came judically before the Privy Council that disallowance achieved something in reducing substantially the range of procedural questions that might otherwise have been raised on appeal—the sort of questions that were to occupy the courts of the young Republic under the due process guarantees of the several constitutions. Whether or not the colonists were guided into notions as to what was proper procedure by a policy exemplified mainly in dissent is open to some doubt, but it is certain that administrative review played no small part in determining the character of the Council's judicial work.

It is also a fair inference that the recurrent administrative testing of colonial statutes against a "constitutional" standard exemplified in the laws of England helped pave the way for acceptance of the doctrine of judicial review in the new nation. Certainly, many more politicians, lawyers, and administrators were familiar with legislative disallowances than with the limited role of the Privy Council in judicial review.

XIII

*The Influence of Colonial Conditions as Illustrated in the Connecticut Intestacy Law**

CHARLES McLEAN ANDREWS[1]

The colonial era of our history has generally been treated with an insufficient appreciation of its economic forces, and, in consequence, there has been a tendency to minimize the importance of certain periods of that history which show little political activity and are to the world at large dull and uninteresting. Such a period is the first forty years of the eighteenth century, and in the following paper I hope to show why I think that, from the point of view of the English policy toward the colonies and their economic development, this period will in the future stand much higher in the estimate of historians than it does now. The discussion that follows involves a number of points of law, and carries us through a controversy which, although of immediate importance to Connecticut only, was of exceeding interest to all New England, and indirectly touches the general subject of colonial history.[2]

* "The Influence of Colonial Conditions as Illustrated in the Connecticut Intestacy Law," by Charles McLean Andrews, is reprinted from *Select Essays in Anglo-American Legal History* I (Boston, 1907), 431-463.

1. These passages are extracted from an essay on "The Connecticut Intestacy Law," Yale Review, 1894, Volume III., pp. 261-294.

2. My attention was originally directed to this subject by the publication of the first volume of the Talcott Papers by the Connecticut Historical Society and the remarks of Judge Mellen Chamberlain upon them as printed in the Proceedings of the Massachusetts Historical Society, March, 1893. The second volume of the Talcott Papers is now in press, but I am indebted to the editor, Miss Mary K. Talcott, a descendant of the old Connecticut governor, for ad-

The starting point of the controversy and its underlying cause was the agrarian system of New England. It is well known to students of the subject that the methods employed in the division of lands by the proprietors of the various towns involved certain principles based on the necessities of a new country. We may believe, if we wish, that these methods were the expression of deep-seated racial traits, but it is more rational to take into account two influences only; first, the agrarian environment in which the settlers had been reared; and, secondly, the conditions and necessities that govern the settlement of a new and uninhabited country. These two considerations will concern us here.

Those who settled the New England colonies were—save in a very few cases—men of the burgher and freeholder class, to whom the detail of the English agricultural life was familiar. They had been inhabitants of towns and villages located on feudal estates and subject to a superior, the King or the lesser lay or ecclesiastical lord; they had in a large number of cases been reared in the midst of the English agricultural system, of which the village community with its long streets, its homesteads, its open fields divided into shots or furlongs and subdivided into what were originally acre and half acre strips, its meadows, pastures, common and waste, was the local unit and that part of the system with which they were in daily contact. To this system that of New England bears a striking resemblance. One cannot compare the old manor maps of the seventeenth and eighteenth centuries with any plan based upon the land records of a New England town without feeling that the similarities are more than coincidences. There is the same village street, the same homestead plots, the same great fields, the same shots and furlongs, and the same subdivision into smaller strips; there are the enclosed meadows held by a few, the pasture and the waste common to all, and there are numbers of trifling manners and customs which show the English origin. It was the local, non-feudal land system which was transplanted with important changes to New England, and formed the basis of the law of real property.

But were we to be satisfied with this statement of the case, we should be guilty of accepting a hasty analogy. There were other reasons why the local agrarian system of England was in its out-

---

vance sheets as far as completed. [Ed. note: see Mary Kingsbury Talcott, ed., *The Talcott Papers* (Conn. Hist. Soc., *Coll.*, IV-V [Hartford, 1892-1896])].

ward form reproduced by the New England settlers. Had it not accommodated itself to their notions of equality and equity, and to the economic needs of a people settling in a new and uninhabited country, it might have been altered and changed beyond recognition. But the local land system of England was pre-feudal in its origin, and probably grew out of a primitive system of agrarian equality, a fact which the equal strips, the scattered holdings and the common rights serve to attest. The New England settlers were entering an environment similar to that out of which the English village came, and they therefore found it necessary to change the English local system but little in order to apply the methods of allotment demanded by a new country. The colonists took no retrograde step; all changes from the existing system at home were in keeping with the higher ideas of property and equality which the New Englanders brought with them. The principles which governed their action were three: first, that of preventing the engrossing of lands and their accumulation in the hands of a few, the dangers of which in England were familiar to the colonists;[3] secondly, that of subserving the law of equity by treating every man fairly, not only in giving him a share in conquered or purchased lands, but also in so allotting that share that he might be subject to all the advantages and drawbacks that bore upon his neighbors;[4] and thirdly, that of hastening settlement and the im-

3. "Whereas much experience shows that sundry inconveniences do arise to the burdening, disturbing or depopulating of smaller plantations, were either sundry lotts or accommodations are engrossed into one hand or possessed or held by unsuitable or unfit persons," etc. *Guilford Mss. Book of the More Fixed Orders.* "Where as there hath been a great abuse in several towns and plantations in this colony in buying and purchasing Home-lotts and laying of them together by means whereof great depopulation may follow," etc. *Laws of the Colony of Connecticut* (ed. 1715), p. 51.

4. I have discussed this question briefly in an article entitled "Die Stadt in Neu-England," in the *Zeitschrift für Social-und Wirthschaftsgeschichte,* vol. ii. pp. 103-131, 224-240, especially p. 232, note 58. To the instances there quoted I will add two others, as the question is an important one.

"And whereas by the Law of Natural Equity and Right all those that joyned in making the conquest and those that joyned in subdueing the country from a Wilderness (as it then was and in a great measure still is) to a condition fit for tillage and Profit should also joyntly and share in the advantages that arise from this their Conquest and Industry and accordingly the first Planters did devide the lands thus obtained among themselves," etc. "An Act for the Settlement of Intestate Estates," *Conn. State Archives, Foreign Correspondence,* II, p. 146, Cf. *Talcott Papers,* I, p. 148.

"It is a fundamental agreement that all lands whether upland, meadow or home lotts should be made equal, that if it was not equall to other mens in

provement of land.[5] Land was therefore divided[6] by the towns or by the bodies of proprietors into fields, called "squadrons" in Worcester, "furlongs" in Middletown, "shots" in Milford, and "quarters" in New Haven, and these were subdivided into smaller strips ranging from one acre[7] to forty or more in size. Various methods were employed for obtaining equality,[8] and every effort was made to hasten cultivation and to increase industry. Removal was discouraged by liability to forfeiture;[9] alienation was limited by laws common to nearly every town in New England;[10] the burden of

the quality of it it should be made up in quantity, or if it unequall in distance of place it should be made equall in quantity also. So that where you find any parcell to exceed in number of acres more than it is charged with rate you may know that it is allowed for satisfaction to equall his lands to other mens." *Milford Mss. Town Records*, Dec. 28, 1646. For all the extracts from the Milford Town Records I am indebted to Miss J. L. Brownell.

5. "It was inhabitants and not land that was wanting." *Talcott Papers*, I, p. 145, Cf. *Conn. Col. Rec.* II, pp. 185, 187. Palfrey estimates the value of land in 1713, at 6 farthings an acre. *History of New England*, IV, p. 364.

6. There was greater regularity and uniformity than in England. One system was new, the other old. But by curving the allotted strips, by running the shots and fields a little more irregularly, by throwing in a few gores and headlands, we should have what would be in its main features the same system.

7. "It is agreed by vote that the remainder of the Dreadful Swamp . . . shall be laid out into acre lotts." *Milford Town Records*, I, p. 62.

8. The "Purchase Right" which each proprietor had in the town was determined not only by the amount of money subscribed to the purchase of the lands but also by the number of heads in each family. I have discussed the "Purchase Right" at some length in "Die Stadt in Neu-England," and have endeavored to show that its scattered character was due to the desire to obtain equality. This principle permeated the system as the following will show: "Ordered that in this division every one shall have his division in two places, half in the nearest field and the other half in the furthest." *Milford Town Records*, I, p. 10. "The field was divided into two parts lengthwise and the order of holders in one tier would be reversed in the other thus making the distribution more equal." *River Towns of Connecticut*, pp. 44-45, J. H. U. Studies, VII.

9. Rules to this effect are to be found in every book of Town Records. *Milford Town Records*, I, p. 13. *River Towns*, p. 50.

10. "Ordered that no man shall sell his house but first he must propound his person and chapman to the town and within twenty days after his propounding it the town to answer his desire to take it off or let him take his chapman always provided the Inhabitants may buy and sell within themselves notwithstanding this order." *Milford Town Records*, I, p. 11. I have quoted this law from the Milford Records, because it contains some new points supplemental to the many others printed before and has itself never been printed. A similar law passed by the Colony of Connecticut came to the notice of the legal advisor of the Board of Trade who commented on it thus: "This Act would be very extraordinary in England but whether it may not be proper in a country where they are encompassed with enemies is humbly submitted to your Lordship's consideration." The limited range of this law, which grew,

taxation and the care of the fences, highways, etc., was distributed as evenly as possible; and every effort was made to increase the amount of land brought under cultivation. All this was characteristic of New England in general and of Connecticut in particular. The life in the latter colony was predominantly agricultural, the industrial and commercial aspects had hardly begun to appear, the government was republican—and for a hundred and fifty years of all the colonial governments it was the one most independent of the mother country[11]—the laws made were adapted to the con-

as did the intestate law, out of the necessities of the settlement, and the brief period during which it was enforced, prevented it from assuming so important a place in the relations between England and the colonies.

11. The colonies most exempt from English interference and control were of course Maryland, Pennsylvania, Connecticut, Rhode Island, and Massachusetts. Massachusetts, however, had a royal governor and was obliged to deliver her laws for the approval of the Council within three years after they had been passed, though if they were not repealed within that time they could not be repealed at all. Pennsylvania had a five years limit. But the laws of Connecticut and Rhode Island were not repealable by the Crown; these colonies never lost their charters as did Massachusetts, never came into direct dependence upon the Crown as did Maryland for a short time, and were almost outside the knowledge of the Privy Council and the Board of Trade. There is, however, one difference in the attitude of these colonies toward English law which is interesting. Rhode Island, by referring herself to the law of England in cases where she had none of her own, made some of the laws of England to be her own laws. Connecticut, on the other hand, in case of doubt referred to "some plain and clear rule of the Word of God." In 1665 the Deputy Governor and the Assistants desired the advice of the General Court concerning incest, whether the law of the colony "that orders in defect of a law we should have recourse to the Word of God for our law" were binding or not. The Court decided that the colony should act according to the Word of God. *Conn. Col. Rec.*, II, p. 184. Robert Quary commented on this statement in the Book of Laws as follows: "The people are of a very turbulent, factious and uneasy temper. I cannot give their character better than by telling your Lordships that they have made a body of laws for their government which are printed; the first of which is that no law of England shall be in force in their government till made so by act of their own. Having told your Lordships this, I think there is no further room to admire at any extravagancy acted in the government." Quary to the Board of Trade, *B. T. Papers, Plantations General, Entry Book*, D. fol. 201, Cf. *Milford Town Records*, I, p. 1; *Talcott Papers*, I, p. 143, II. Appendix. "Instructions to Agent." Gershom Bulkeley in his "Will and Doom" complains that "by this Law all the Law of England (Common or Statute or other) is exploded at once." (From MSS. copy of the transcript sent over by Lord Cornbury in the possession of the Conn. Hist. Society. The transcript is in *B. T. Papers, Proprieties*, N. 20). I know of but two Connecticut Acts directly taken from the English Statute law before 1750. First, "Act about Bastards" from 21 Car. c. 27 and second, "Act for Ease of those who soberly Dissent" from 1 Wm. and M. c. 18 commonly called the Toleration Act. Five others, however, are probably based on English Statute law. 1. "Act concerning the Dowry of Widows." 2. "Act concerning forms of Writs." 3. "Act concerning

veniences of the inhabitants rather than to the common and statute law of England, and the policy of the colony at all times was to remain hidden as far as possible from the notice of the home authorities. It is no wonder, therefore, that there should have grown up under the conditions—agrarian and economic—attendant on the settlement of a new, partly uninhabited, partly unconquered territory, laws based not on legal theory but on custom, laws that either were not known to English law[12] or were not in accord with it.

Of all these laws none was more important, more an organic part of the life of the colony or fundamental to its welfare, than that which governed the disposal of intestate estates. It is manifest that people influenced by the principles already mentioned in their distribution of land would apply the same principles to the distribution of the realty of an intestate. They certainly would not have undermined the colonial structure by admitting into its construction methods foreign to the general plan. Primogeniture, favorable to the accumulation of estates, but unfavorable to a rapid increase of the inhabitants, a furtherance of agriculture, and a cultivation of the soil, and opposed to the natural law of equity, was not in accord with the principles of the New England settlers. The intestacy law was, therefore, the unavoidable and logical outcome of the principles which underlay the land-system of New England. This becomes the more apparent when we realize that for more than sixty years it existed as a custom in no way binding on the people, and that it did not become a law in Massachusetts until 1692, or in Connecticut until 1699.[13] By the English common law the

Deputies Salary." 4. "Act for Regulating Juries and Witnesses." 5. "Act relating to Sureties upon Mean Process in Civil Action." In 1750 the Colony printed all Acts passed by Parliament which were considered to be binding on the colony. There are ten Acts in all, and none of these had been reënacted by the colony. *Conn. Col. Rec.* viii. p. 352.

12. Two laws certainly were not known to English law. 1. "Act for the punishment of Lying." 2. "An Act for the preventing of Oppression."

13. *Conn. Col. Rec.*, IV, p. 307. "I have observed," writes Lieut. Governor Law, "the law to be of no ancienter date than 1699 and our old law book, dated in 1672, prescribes no rule excepting the righteousness and equity lodged in the breast of the County Court." Law to Talcott, *Talcott Papers*, I, p. 119. Also I, pp. 122-123, 144, 392-394. II, pp. 225, 244-245. The October Orders of 1639 contain the earliest form of the law, as follows: "But when any prson dyeth intestate the sayd orderers of the affayres of the Towns shall cause an Inventory to be taken and then the Public Court may graunt the administrac̄on of the goodes and chattels to the next of kin, joyntly or severally, and divide the estate to wiefe (if any be) children or kindred as in equity they shall

eldest son was the sole heir and was entitled to the whole estate exclusive of all other children; whereas the colonial law[14] directed that the real estate of an intestate be distributed in single shares to all the children except the eldest son, to whom, following the ruling of the Mosaic Code, the law assigned a double portion.[15] The Connecticut law was not the arbitrary act of the assembly of the colony; it was the sanctioning of a custom which had grown out of the consent of heirs to an intestacy, and which had been proved by experience to be the best adapted to the needs of the colony.[16] Governor Talcott gives in brief the reasons for the intestate law in his instructions to Belcher:—"And much of our lands remain unsubdued, and must continue so without the assistance of the younger sons, which in reason can't be expected if they have no part of the inheritance; for in this poor country, if the landlord lives, the tenant starves: few estates here will let for little more than for maintaining fences and paying taxes. By this custom of dividing inheritances, all were supply'd with land to work upon, the land as well occupy'd as the number of hands would admit of, the peo-

meet." *Conn. Col. Rec.*, I, p. 38. This was repeated verbatim in the Code of 1650. In the Revision of 1673 to which Law refers there are slight changes in phraseology but none in meaning.

14. "The said Court of Probate shall and hereby are fully empowered to order and make a just distribution of the surplusage or remaining goods and estate of any such intestate, as well real as personal in manner following: That is to say one-third part of the personal estate to the Wife of the Intestate (if any be) forever, besides her dower or thirds in the housing and lands during life, where such wife shall not be otherwise endowed before marriage; and all the residue of the real and personal estate by equal portions to and among the children and such as shall legally represent them (if any of them be dead) other than such children who shall have any estate by settlement of the Intestate in his lifetime, equal to the other's share; children advanced by settlement or portions not equal to the other shares; to have so much of the surplusage as shall make the estate of all to be equal; except the eldest then surviving (where there is no issue of the first born or any other eldest son) who shall have two shares or a double portion of the whole, and where there are no sons the daughters shall inherit as co-partners."

15. Deut. xxi. 17.

16. Another clause of the Act makes this clear. "Unless where all the parties interested in any estate being equally capable to act, shall mutually agree of a division among themselves and present the same in writing under their hands and seals, in which case such agreement shall be accepted and allowed for a settlement of such estate and be accounted valid in law." Winthrop said the same in his Memorial to the committee of the Privy Council. "The Memorialist begs leave further to observe to your Lordships that the pretended custom of distributing intestate real estates amongst all the children was no otherwise introduced than by the consent of parties when lands in those parts were of little or no value." *Talcott Papers*, I, p. 394.

ple universally imploy'd in husbandry; thereby considerable quantities of provisions are rais'd, and from our stores the trading part of the Massachusetts and Rhode Island are supply'd, the fishermen are subsisted, and the most of the sugars in the West Indies are put up in casks made of our staves. By means of this custom his Maj'ties subjects are here increased, the younger brethren do not depart from us, but others are rather encouraged to settle among us, and it's manifest that New England does populate faster than the Colonies where the land descends according to the rules of the common law. And such measures as will furnish with the best infantry does most prepare for the defence of a people settled in their enemies country. If this custom be, so ancient and so useful, *non est abolenda, sed privare debet communem legem.*"[17]

Such were the conditions out of which the intestate law grew, and such were the reasons for its embodiment, after sixty years of customary use, into law. Economists can find evidence here for the study of land-appropriation in a new country; students of the history of law will be interested in the growth of customary law; but for us the interest is of a different character. The law was clearly contrary to the corresponding law in England. Certain disaffected ones in the colony, opposed to the government,[18] and overzealous in finding flaws in colonial law and administration, and ever ready to exhibit such discoveries to the authorities in England, began to question the validity of the custom even before it became a law. This was done by Governor Talcott himself in 1691,[19] and by Major Palmes in 1698,[20] while in Massachusetts Dudley complained of the law in 1693.[21] The question was not destined, how-

17. *Talcott Papers*, I, pp. 145-146, Cf. 188-189.

18. Major Palmes refused to pay his dues because he considered the government restored after the Revolution of 1688 "no government." Conn. *Col. Rec.*, IV, pp. 325-326.

19. It is not unlikely that there were other early unrecorded protests against the custom, though probably not many, if there were any, before 1688. Gershom Bulkeley speaks as follows in his "Will and Doom," "if a Man dye Intestate they will and do . . . . distribute his lands among sons and daughters, &c., as if they were pots and kettles. . . . So that their law will not allow an heir or Inheritance at the Common Law which is another repugnancy to the Law of England." It is an interesting fact that Governor Talcott himself, who afterwards so loyally defended the intestate law, should have petitioned the legislature in 1691 when but twenty-two years old against the equal division of his father's estate, and should have claimed possession of the real estate by right of primogeniture. *Talcott Papers*, I, p. xix.

20. Palfrey, IV, p. 491.

21. "For want of which [i.e. the same English laws] there are different laws

ever, to become prominent for nearly thirty years, but it early became of importance as part of a larger question, the forfeiture of the charters and the proposal to unite the charter and proprietary colonies to the Crown. The agitation to produce this latter result seems to have grown out of the desire to unite the colonies of Northern America under one military head,[22] and was increased by the controversy over the right of appeal to the King in Council and the dissatisfaction arising therefrom. In Massachusetts a law had been passed regarding appeals, but it was annulled, altered, re-enacted, and again annulled.[23] New Hampshire refused an appeal in the Allen case in 1701;[24] Connecticut an appeal in the Hallam case in 1699;[25] but in each of these cases the King in Council granted the petition for an appeal, resting the decision on the plea that it was the inherent right of his Majesty to receive and determine appeals from all his Majesty's colonies in America.[26] Connecticut, on the other hand, based its determination to resist such appeal upon its willingness that the Privy Council should be the interpreter of the colony's law.[27]

and forms of administration very disagreeably not (only) in lesser matters but even in the descent of estates at the common law." Dudley's "Paper on the Governments of New England, New York, etc." *B. T. Papers, New England, vol.* 7. F. 13.

22. The period from 1695 to 1715 was a time of trial for the colonies. They were attacked by the French, were in constant trouble from the Indians, were disturbed by the many irritating reports of royal officers and merchants in the colonies, and were not sufficiently established to resist encroachment and to maintain a position of self-reliance. As a result, they were often in distress, and it is little wonder that many in New England and New York petitioned for a stronger central government. In 1697 Harrison, Ashurst, Sewell of Salem and others petitioned for a union of colonies, the Board of Trade thought that security could be obtained in no other way, the Lords Justices favored the scheme, and, in consequence, although the agents of New Hampshire, New York and Connecticut opposed the plan, New Hampshire, Massachusetts and New York were joined in 1697 under one governor, and with Connecticut and Rhode Island were placed under Bellomont as their military head. The year before an admiralty system had been erected for the colonies by commission under the seal of the Admiralty of England. In the North courts were erected at Boston and New York.

23. Palfrey, IV, pp. 172-174, 200.

24. *Ibid.*, pp. 218-219.

25. Caulkins, *History of New London*, pp. 222-227.

26. Palfrey, IV, p. 224.

27. In a deposition taken before Governor Cranston of Rhode Island two men, Fitch and Mason, said that they had heard Governor Fitz John Winthrop say, "I (or we) will grant no appeals for England but I (or we) will dispute it with the King, for if we should allow appeals I will not give a farthing for our charter." *B. T. Papers, Proprieties*, O. 39.

It was not difficult to find additional charges. Complaints were made that the colony broke the Navigation Acts, harbored pirates, neglected to take the oaths required by law, encouraged manufactures, were negligent in military duties and in the erection of fortifications, encroached on the jurisdiction of the Admiralty, and opposed the authority of its officers, protected escaped soldiers, seamen and servants,[28] and failed to comply with certain requirements of the home government—as in the case of the proclamation regarding coin, the instructions to naval officers, the command to aid New York with quotas of men against the French and Indians—etc. Through the influence of Dudley and the pertinacity of Edward Randolph, for it was he who personally led the campaign in the lobby of Parliament,[29] a bill was brought forward in 1700-1701 for reuniting to the Crown the governments of several colonies and plantations of America—Massachusetts Bay, New Hampshire, Rhode Island and Providence Plantations, Connecticut, East and West New Jersey, Pennsylvania, Maryland, Carolina and the Bahamas and St. Lucia Islands—on the ground that "the severing of such power and authority from the Crown and placing the same in the hands of subjects hath by experience been found prejudicial and repugnant to the trade of this Kingdom and to the welfare of his Majesty's other plantations."[30] The bill, however, by reason of "the shortness of time and the multiplicity of other business,"[31] failed to pass, but the Board thinking it very likely that it would come up again for consideration, desired from the colonies all possible information that would aid in the matter. From 1701 to 1706 charges continued to be sent in. Quary, Bass, Congreve, Larkin, Dudley, and Cornbury all drafted lists of complaints. The Board in a representation to the Council in 1703 expressed its opinion "that the great mischief can only be remedied by reducing these colonies to

28. Letter from the Board of Trade to Governor Blakeston of Maryland. *B. T. Papers, Maryland, Entry Book*, B. ff. 88-90. Winthrop in his complaints probably did little more, if we may judge from what we are told of them in Talcott's reply, than voice the complaints current among those opposed to the colonial administration. *Documents relating to the Colonial History of New York*, IV, p. 1079.

29. Randolph's bill of expenses incurred amounted to £96. 11. 6. *B. T. Papers, Proprieties*, G. 20.

30. The text of the Act is to be found in *B. T. Papers, Proprieties, Entry Book*, C. ff. 426-430.

31. Board of Trade to Governor Blakeston. *B. T. Papers, Maryland, Entry Book*, B. ff. 86, 88.

an immediate dependence on the Crown."[32] For Connecticut it was a time of anxiety. The influence of the Hallam case, of the controversy over the Narraganset country and the boundary line with New York, of the case of the Mohegan Indians,[33] of the petition of the English Quakers against a Connecticut law, was to keep certain aspects of Connecticut's management steadily before the Board of Trade and to lead to what were often serious misrepresentations to the home authorities. In consequence Connecticut got a bad name. In 1704 the colony narrowly escaped having a governor put over it[34] through the authority of the King in Coun-

32. *B. T. Papers, Plantations General, Entry Book,* C. f. 240. Every effort was made to discover charges particularly against Connecticut and Pennsylvania. In 1703 Penn wrote to the Crown, "I observe your bent is extremely strong to bring all proprietary governments under the disposition of the Crown." *B. T. Papers, Proprieties,* M. 19.

33. It is interesting to note that the quarrels in the colony which brought it to the attention of the Board were in large part agrarian. This was but natural in a community where husbandry was dominant. Talcott said as late as 1728 "many of the actions here (in Connecticut) are conversant about nothing else" (than the titles of land). *Talcott Papers,* I, p. 157. The Hallam appeal rested on the denial of a devise of land to "the ministry" of the colony, on the ground that it was either in violation of the Statute of Mortmain, or, if it could not be so construed, it was a devise to "the ministry" recognized by the laws of England, that is, the ministry of the Episcopal Church. As all towns in Connecticut made grants to "the ministry" or to "the church," a decision in Hallam's favor would have made havoc with ecclesiastical land titles in the towns. Caulkins, *History of New London,* pp. 222-227.

34. The Board of Trade sent a representation based on the charges of Dudley and Cornbury to the Privy Council. The Council sent it to Northey and Harcourt, the Crown lawyers. They replied advising that a governor be placed over both Rhode Island and Connecticut. This opinion was reported to the Board and was communicated to the agents of the colonies. A hearing was appointed at which they were to state why, in point of law, the Crown should not appoint governors over these colonies during the war. The hearing appointed for Nov. 30, 1704, was put off from week to week until Feb. 12, 1705. In the meantime Lord Cornbury sent over Gershom Bulkeley's "Will and Doom" to strengthen the case against Connecticut. The work was received Jan. 16, 1705. It is probable that at the hearing the agents were able to show the inexpediency, if not illegality of a military governor, for on the day of the hearing the Council, evidently convinced that the matter could be best attended to by Parliament, directed the Board to draw up a list of charges, which was done, the chief source being the letters of Cornbury and Dudley. The order in Council also instructed the Board to transmit the list of charges to the Governor of New York and New England. This was done April 18, 1705, and Cornbury was ordered to send copies to Connecticut and Rhode Island, where public depositions were to be made as to the truth or falsity of the charges. (*Documents relating to the Colonial History of New York,* IV, p. 1141). Upon the evidence thus received the Board based its representation of Dec., 1705, in consequence of which an Order in Council was issued directing

cil. But that body evidently preferred that Parliament should take the matter in hand, and in 1706 a bill similar to that of 1701 was introduced. It passed the House of Commons but failed of passage in the House of Lords.[35]

The long list of charges against the proprietary and charter governments already on the books of the Board was continually supplemented by additional charges from Congreve,[36] Dudley, Quary, Gauden and others.[37] The failure of the bill of 1706 was a severe blow to its supporters, and the colony for several years experienced a relief from its anxiety. In 1715 the matter came up again because of the complaints regarding banks, naval stores, the trouble with Carolina, etc., and the House of Commons appointed a committee composed of members of the Board of Trade "to in-

the Board to lay before her Majesty the misfeances of the charter governments. (*B. T. Journals*, 18, f. 153). This report was sent to Mr. Secretary Hedges. He in answer sent back a draught of a bill relating to the uniting of the colonies to the Crown. After some alteration, Feb., 1706 (f. 219), this bill was introduced into Parliament. *B. T. Papers, Proprieties*, M. 47; *Journal*, 18, ff. 177-178, 252, 281; 20, ff. 9, 11.

35. Palfrey, IV, pp. 368-369. See previous note.

36. Charles Congreve to the Board of Trade, Dec. 4, 1704. This letter containing a list of complaints against Connecticut was written at the order of the Board. *B. T. Papers, Proprieties*, M. 49.

37. Quary to Board of Trade, Jan. 10, 1708-9. *B. T. Papers, Plantations General, Entry Book*, D. ff. 200, 205. The following extract will show the nature of Quary's misrepresentations. The important fact to be noted is that the Board had faith in Quary. He was in high favor with the members and they listened with gravity to his suggestions and to the information which he gave. *B. T. Journal*, vol. 15, minutes for June 26, and succeeding dates, 1703, "I attended the Governor Colonel Winthrope, who received me very kindly and desired me not to look too narrowly into the mistakes of that government. I quickly found that there was good reason for that caution for on examining the custom-house I found nothing but confusion and roguery. I was apprised of many dishonest practices acted in that place before I went but did not expect to have found matters so very bad. The person that acts as collector was one Mr. Withred, a pillar of their church, but a great rogue, for there is no villainy that a man in his post could do but was constantly practiced by him. . . . It would tire your Lordship to give you a history of the illegal trade carried on and encouraged in this government from Curaçoa, Surinam and other places. . . . This is a very populous country, able to raise 10,000 effective men and yet would never assist their neighbors in defending their frontiers from the public enemy, who hath destroyed whole towns and carried away the inhabitants for want of a regulated government and militia. . . . I have no hope of preventing illegal trade in that government whilst it is in the hands of those people." *B. T. Papers, Plantations General, Entry Book*, D. ff. 200-205.

"Memorial from Mr. Stephen Gauden, relating to the misfeances of Carolina and other Proprietary Governments, whereby they Forfeit their Charter." July 25, 1716. *B. T., Proprieties*, Q. 81.

spect into the miscarriage and to prepare a bill to resume the grants of the proprietary governments."[38] Again a list of charges was prepared,[39] but, whether another failure was feared[40] or a juster policy decided upon, a different plan was tried for Connecticut. The committee of the Privy Council directed the Board of Trade to inquire of the colony—through Jer. Dummer, the agent in London—whether it would be willing to surrender its charter peaceably. Connecticut's answer is a masterpiece of firmness and politeness and, although in the name of the Governor and Company, was undoubtedly written by Saltonstall.[41] He commends the justice and honor of the ministry in thus referring the question to the corporation, a method wise and just, possessing not the least appearance of force and terror. He contrasts it with previous methods unreconcilable with common rights, law and custom, of which the colonies had had full experience. This spirit of fairness he attributes to the existing King and Ministry, who, though unlimited and subject to none, yet observed the limits of wisdom and justice, and were tender of what others should enjoy as well as of their own prerogative; who did not make use of their power to terrify the colony out of its rights and property, but gave it leave to speak for itself. After these quieting words, the Governor and Company regret that they cannot choose that resignation of their rights which the King and Ministry think might be best for them, and conclude this portion of the letter with the following instructions to the agent: "You are therefore hereby directed in plainest terms to acquaint their Lordship that we can't think it our interest to resign our charter. But on the contrary, as we are assured, that we have never by any act of disobedience to the Crown made any forfeiture of the privileges we hold by it, So we shall endeavor to make it manifest and defend our right whenever it shall be called in question."

The limits of this paper will not allow a further discussion of the attitude of the home government toward the Colony. It is,

38. *B. T. Journal*, 25, f. 216, Aug. 11, 1715.

39. *B. T. Papers, Proprieties, Entry Book*, F. ff. 464-465.

40. This may be inferred from Gauden's Memorial: "The committee appointed by the Parliament . . . seemed somewhat at a loss how to fix proper causes and reasons for the doing" [of that for which they were appointed].

41. "Letter from the Governor and Company of Connecticut relating to the surrender of their charter to the Crown by G. Saltonstall to Mr. Jer: Dummer, their agent, dated Oct. 28th, 1723, from N. Haven." *B. T. Papers, Proprieties*, R. 49.

however, fundamentally important that we should appreciate the relations which had previously existed, and the one-sided character of the information which the Board of Trade, the Privy Council and even Parliament itself received. The mere titles of the papers containing charges against the proprietary and charter governments cover twenty-one pages of an entry book. Regarding Connecticut there is almost nothing to relieve the unfavorable impression received by the Board, except a letter now and then from the Governor, and the answers to the queries that were occasionally sent to the colony. The references to Connecticut in the Journal are rare, and generally relate to some complaints against her. It is difficult to determine how far the Board believed the statements sent it, but its representations do not show any inclination to lighten the impression which the letters from the colonies give.

This was the position that Connecticut occupied in the sight of the home authorities when John Winthrop, a grandson of one Connecticut Governor and nephew of another, denying the validity of the intestate law, claimed all the real estate of his father who had died in 1717, and, ignoring the right which he had of appeal from the Court of Probate to the Court of Assistants, expressed his determination to appeal to the King in Council. This determination was carried out, and as the result of Winthrop's efforts the intestacy law was annulled by an Order in Council Feb. 15, 1728, as contrary to the laws of England and not warranted by the charter.[42] The case was a private one and the colony was not heard in the matter. There is no doubt that the defendant, Lechmere, was inadequately defended by some one little versed in the colony's affairs, that his evidence was far from complete, his purse far from full, and that he was especially in want of "a good sword formed of the royal oar."[43] Winthrop, on the other hand, was ably defended by Attorney General Yorke and Solicitor General Talbot.

42. The decree is printed in full in *Conn. Col. Rec.*, VII, *Appendix*. *Mass. Hist. Soc. Collections*, 6th ser. vol. V, pp. 496-506. It will be impossible to give here even an outline of the facts of the case. See *Talcott Papers*, I, pp. 94 note, 187, 241. *Mass. Hist. Soc. Proc.*, March, 1893, pp. 125-127. *Conn. Col. Rec.*, VII, p. 572 ff. That there was considerable justice in Winthrop's position becomes evident when we know of the contents of Wait Winthrop's will and of Lechmere's impecunious condition. *Mass. Hist. Soc. Collections*, 6th ser. vol. V, pp. 367 (note)-370; also Winthrop's letter to Cotton Mather, pp. 425-428. The most detailed account of the case is to be found in the same volume, pp. 440-467.

43. *Talcott Papers*, II, pp. 77-78, 136. *Conn. Col. Rec.*, VII, p. 191 note. *State Archives, Miscellanies*, II, doc. 313.

The Committee of the Council did not call in the assistance of the Board of Trade, and there are no documents bearing on this phase of the case among their papers. Winthrop did not rest his case solely upon the question of the validity or invalidity of the law, but he repeated most of the charges, which were already familiar to the Council and its committee, and thereby, as Mr. Parris said, "very much assisted his case."[44] The legal aspects of the trial have attracted but a small amount of attention from historians, for the incidents were neither dramatic nor politically exciting, yet there were involved in the case principles of great moment to the colonists, questions, the solution of which was to affect the future relations between them and the home government.

The effect of the vacating of the law shows at once that the Privy Council acted without a reasonable understanding of the matter at issue. It based its opinion upon the literal interpretation of the charter from its own point of view, and was entirely without an honest appreciation of the equity in the case.[45] Two conditions, defensible in themselves, had come into conflict. For the moment the customary law of one country, arising from one set of historical circumstances, was to be enforced in another country, the agrarian and economic life of which had brought into existence a customary law very different. The common law of England and the common law of the colony did not agree. The latter did not represent the defiant will of a body of law-makers, it represented a principle of land-distribution which the experience of the colony had shown to be best adapted to its own prosperity and continued existence. This becomes clearer when we note what would have been the economic effects of voiding the intestate law.

The first result would have been a general unsettling of titles to lands left intestate or alienated after intestate settlement. This was due to the fact that a large majority of the people consisted of farmers and agriculturists, possessing little personal estate.[46]

44. *Talcott Papers*, II, p. 77.

45. Govr. Talcott recognized the unfairness of the decision from the standpoint of equity, when he said in a letter to the Board of Trade Nov. 4, 1731, "Your Lordships will be best informed of the reason, necessity and usefulness of our laws by considering the state and circumstances of our country so many ways differing from that of England." *B. T. Papers, Proprieties*, S. 36. *Talcott Papers*, I, p. 250; II, p. 225. It is worthy of notice that Winthrop's own counsel declared against the judgment of the Council afterwards. *Talcott Papers*, II, p. 72.

46. *Talcott Papers*, I, p. 234.

Many of these settlements reached back to the beginnings of the colony, and the invalidating of titles would have affected large numbers of descendants who would thus have been liable to ejection at the instance of the eldest heir.[47] Such ejectment concerned the younger sons and the female heirs, for whom under such conditions there would be no place in the colony.[48] Even if the titles to estates already settled in the Court of Probate should be allowed to stand, yet there were many estates of twenty or thirty years standing that had never been settled, and more of a later date, so that the suffering would only be limited, not ended. Furthermore, litigation would have at once ensued, which would have involved the colony in an economic loss greater than that entailed in a resistance to the decree. The agrarian system of the towns would have given to this litigation a curious complexity. Quarrels were certain to arise within the towns themselves regarding the ownership of the common and undivided lands.[49] Would the title rest with the heirs at common law of those who received by grant from the King, that is, the patentees, or with those who as proprietors and contributors to the common fund purchased the lands from the Indians, and received their shares according to the size of their families and the amount of their subscription?[50] Judges, too, in

47. *Talcott Papers*, I, p. 146.

48. *Ibid.*, I, pp. 122, 146.

49. In the *Middletown Mss. Proprietary Records* there is "An Account of the Interest of the Several Proprietors of the Common and Undivided Lands [computed] according to the Custom of Deviding Intestates in the Colony of Connecticut." Dec. 28, 1733. A study of the lists herein contained shows graphically the practical working of the intestacy law. In 1673 a list of proprietors had been drawn up, 52 in number, with real estate "rights" in the undivided lands ranging from £224 to £24. In 1733 this list was revised, and it was found that by constant subdivision of "rights" through purchase, bequest and intestacy settlement, the number of proprietors had increased to 328, the number of "rights" to 386 (circa) ranging in value from £103 to 9sh. with by far the greater number valued at less than £5. An examination of such lists proves how impossible it would have been to carry out the Order in Council voiding the law. The Middletown proprietors paid no attention whatever to the king's decree.

50. *Talcott Papers*, I, p. 177. It is not unlikely that considerable trouble might have been caused had this feature of the case been brought to the attention of the authorities at home. It might have been decided in favor of the Patentees if we may judge from the legal opinion of Attorney-General Northey, Aug. 7, 1703, upon an Act of New Hampshire for Confirmation of Town Grants, "it is fit that same be repealed for that it confirms all grants of lands that have heretofore been made unto any person or persons by the inhabitants of the respective towns within that Province or by the selectmen or a committee in each Town without having any regard to or saving of the right of any persons

settling all these disputes, would have been thoroughly perplexed as to whether they should obey the decree, in which case the foundation of the colony would have been "rip't up from the bottom and the country undone;"[51] or whether they should disregard the decree, and so bring down upon the colony the loss of its charter.

But the injustice would have concerned others besides those holding lands derived from intestate settlements. Creditors who had taken lands in payment of debts—a procedure not in favor with the colony because of the cheapness of lands—would be defrauded, unless the lands, which might have considerably improved in their hands, had been made chargeable for the original loan and the improvements.[52] Furthermore, the will and intent of many who had died intestate might have been frustrated, inasmuch as they, trusting in the colonial custom, with which they had been perfectly satisfied, had made no will.[53]

In addition to these results, so contrary to justice and equity, certain economic consequences would have inevitably followed the carrying out of the Order in Council, consequences detrimental not merely to the colony, but, judging from the standpoint of her clearly avowed colonial policy, to England as well. The voiding of the law meant the abatement of husbandry. The towns of all New England, and of Connecticut in particular, were, at this stage of their development, predominantly agricultural. The results of such abatement would be a desertion of lands, a lessening of population, and a decrease in the supply to the neighboring provinces, which, engaged in trade and fishery, were dependent on Connecticut for provisions.[54] It was a clever stroke on the part of the colonial supporters of the law when they showed that its confirmation was adapted to the furthering of England's policy, and that its vacation was to the injury of that policy. Voiding the law would lead to manufacturing, for the younger sons from sheer necessity, driven from agriculture, would turn to trade and manufacturing, or else would be obliged to leave the country.[55] Thus, by this argument, England was placed on the horns of a dilemma as re-

---

who might be entitled to the same before the making such grants." *B. T. Papers, New England,* M. 46.

51. *Talcott Papers,* I, p. 177.
52. *Ibid.,* I, pp. 122, 146-147.
53. *Ibid.,* I, pp. 144, 189, 234.
54. *Ibid.,* I, p. 147.
55. *Talcott Papers,* I, pp. 147, 189; II, pp. 245-248.

gards the colonies, either beggary or insufficient population on the one side, or the promotion of trade and manufactures on the other. This, as Law surmised, "was a tender plot," and there is no doubt that as an argument it was frequently repeated in order that it might be "thôt of at home."[56] These economic results are sufficient to show that the law was an organic part of the life of the colony. Indeed, as Talcott said in a later letter to Francis Wilks in London, "we cannot think our law will be looked upon to be contrary to the law of England for the colony could not have been settled without it."[57]

The colony immediately made every effort through its agents, Dummer, Belcher, and Wilks, to defend the law if possible. There was reason for hope in such action from the fact that the Massachusetts law of 1692, after which the Connecticut law has been modeled, with one amendment, one addition, and three explanatory acts had been confirmed by the Crown.[58] Furthermore, the law was a general one in New England and, if the Order in Council were to be insisted on, it might endanger the titles to a considerable amount of New England real estate; and it would seem incredible that the home government could persist in so crippling the colonies.[59] Therefore the colony was justified in believing that, if all the arguments were fairly presented to the Lords of Trade, the good offices of that Board might be obtained.[60] This was an important step, for by the report of the committee of the Council the matter had been referred to the Board.[61]

The strongest argument against the law was that it was contrary to the law of England, and in the discussion which followed the colony exerted all its strength to minimize the force of this argument. The question is an important one in itself, but the value of the discussion lies in the expression of opinion on the part of the English and the colonial authorities regarding the interpretation

56. *Ibid.*, I, p. 123.

57. *Ibid.*, II, p. 246.

58. *Ibid.*, II, p. 79, *Mass. Hist. Soc. Proc.*, 1860-62, p. 72-73.

59. *Talcott Papers*, I, pp. 153-154, pp. 77-85. Governor Talcott says that the law had been sent over with other laws "some thirty years ago," by Gov'r Winthrop and that as nothing was said about the law then the colony had reason to think itself safe. There is a mistake here somewhere; the law was passed in 1699 and Gov'r Winthrop sent over the Book of Laws as an enclosure in his letter of Oct. 27, 1698. *B. T. Papers, Proprieties* 2A. It may be that he is referring to the October order as revised in 1673.

60. *Talcott Papers*, I, pp. 174, 249.

61. *Ibid.*, I, pp. 200-201. *B. T. Papers, Proprieties*, R. 108.

and strict construction of the phrase "contrary to the law of England." There were three views held regarding the English law in the colonies, as to how far it was binding there, and to what extent the colonial corporations had been invested by their charters with law-making powers. The first of these opinions was held by all those who were opposed to the colonial prerogatives, such as Palmes, Hallam, Gershom Bulkeley, in his "Will and Doom," Winthrop the appellant, in his "Complaint" and "Memorial," Dudley and others. According to this view the colonies were erected as corporations within the kingdom of England; they held by and were subject to the laws of that kingdom, and their legislative power extended to the making of by-laws and ordinances only for their own good government, provided the same were not contrary to the law of England.[62] From this point of view all laws passed by the colonial assemblies which were of a higher character than by-laws, and which, even within that limit, touched upon matters already provided for by English common or statute law, were illegal. The colonies were as towns upon the royal demesne.

The second view was expressed by the agent of Connecticut, Francis Wilks, and was doubtless held by those at home who, with English proclivities, were nevertheless well disposed toward the colonies. According to this view, it followed that when the colonists came to America they brought with them the common law to which they were entitled as Englishmen, and such part of the statute law as was in force before the settlement of the plantations took place. To this body of law, written and unwritten, binding on the colonies, were to be added all such later Acts of Parliament as expressly mentioned the plantations, and such Acts as had been

62. *Talcott Papers*, I, p. 393. Dudley in his letter to the Board of Trade expresses this view. "On the part of the Crown it would be provided [in case a union of colonies was affected] that the laws of England, common and statute, which have hitherto always been or ought to have been the laws of all those provinces, should be so declared and the government there directed to present to the King not Magna Charta or chapters of capital laws, but such by-laws as the several provinces in their settlements require, which are not provided for by the common and statute law of England." *B. T. Papers, New England*, vol. 7, F. 13. For Dudley's motives see Palfrey IV, pp. 367-368. Bulkeley said in his "Will and Doom," "We think that the colony of Connecticut is de Jure (we wish we could say de facto) as much subject to the Crown of England as London or Oxford." Again, "forgetting . . . that their Courts are but inferior Courts and their laws not laws properly so called or parcel of the Laws of England but only By-Laws, i.e. the Local, private and particular orders of a corporation."

re-enacted for the colony by her own legislature.[63] But no other statutes passed since the settlement could be held as binding. Therefore, according to Wilks, that law was contrary to the law of England which was contrary to the common and statute law prior to the settlement, or to the statute law made afterwards which expressly mentioned the plantations.

Both of these views, however, were strictly opposed by the colony. To the statement that the common and statute law existent at the time of the settlement was in force in the colonies, the answer was made that the charter nowhere directed the administration to be according to one law or another, whether civil, common, or statute law;[64] that by a decision of the Council itself an uninhabited and conquered country was to be governed by the law of nations and of equity until the conqueror should declare his laws,[65] and that if such declaration had not been made, then it was evident that the law of equity and of nations governed and not the common or statute law of England.[66] Therefore, the colony argued, English common law could be binding beyond the sea only in case it had been accepted by the colonist's own choice.[67] From the nature of the laws passed, it is evident that the colonial government never considered the common law to be in force within its jurisdiction, and in this belief it said it had never been corrected or otherwise instructed from the throne. In this connection Governor Talcott pertinently asks, "And why should we be directed to make laws not contrary to the laws of England if they were our laws, for what propriety can there be in making that a directory to us in making a law which was our law before we made it."[68] As this was the case, it is evident that something more was implied in the charter than the making of by-laws. In that document was proposed an object, the religious, civil, and peaceable government of the colony, which could not have been attained by the passing of by-laws. The charter implied a power to enact in the colony that which was law in England and also any good and wholesome law

63. *Talcott Papers*, I, p. 274.

64. *Ibid.*, I, pp. 149, 158.

65. *Blancard v. Galdy, Salkeld's Reports*, I, p. 411. *Talcott Papers*, I, p. 144; II, Appendix, "Instruction to Agent."

66. *Talcott Papers*, I, p. 148.

67. "The common law always hath its limits environ'd by the sea." *Talcott Papers*, II, Appendix, "Instructions to Agent," p. 492.

68. *Ibid.*, II, Appendix, "Instructions to Agent." These instructions were drawn up by John Read and not by Talcott, II, 489 note.

which was not contrary to it; and such limitations could not be to by-laws only.[69] Furthermore, the colony insisted that the analogy to a municipal corporation in England was not sound, inasmuch as it was the privilege of Englishmen to be governed by laws made with their own consent.[70] The colonies were not represented as were the English towns in Parliament; therefore the only laws made with the consent of the colonies were those of their own legislatures, and those were more than by-laws. The opinion of the colony, therefore, was that the phrase, "contrary to the law of England," referred only to laws contrary to those Acts of Parliament which were in express terms designed to extend to the plantations.[71] That this had been the practice as well as the theory in Connecticut is evident from Congreve's letter to the Board of Trade, in which he says, "They allow of none of the laws of England either common or statute to be pleaded in their courts."[72]

According to the opinion held by Winthrop and Wilks the intestate law was clearly contrary to the law of England. Even Lieutenant Governor Law of the colony seems to have inclined to this view, for he came to the conclusion that the colony in acting in the past, contrary to the view expressed by Wilks, had been mistaken.[73] But Gov. Talcott was led into no such concession; he

69. *Ibid.*, I, p. 149.

70. *Ibid.*, I, p. 159; II, Appendix, "Instructions to Agent."

71. *Ibid.*, I, p. 152.

72. *B. T. Papers, Proprieties*, M. 49. See also *Talcott Papers*, I, p. 154. Gershom Bulkeley says much the same in his "Will and Doom," but facts come to us from his pen strangely distorted, while his arguments are full of pedantry and bitterness. "The case is otherwise with us, their Majesties are not yet received to reign in Connecticut, their laws are of no force or effect here." . . . "The abolition of the Common and Statute laws of England and so of all humane laws, except the forgeries of our own popular and rustical shop . . . A strange fancy that coming over from England to another of the King's dominions we should so far cease to be his subjects as that the laws of our King and Nation should not reach us." The most recent legal decision affecting our subject is that of Justice Baldwin in "Campbell's Appeal from Probate," 64 Connecticut Reports, 1894. He held that the Connecticut rule of inheritance, differing fundamentally from the rule of England, had been the uniform doctrine of the Connecticut courts (p. 290); and he gave it as his opinion "that the common law rule of the exclusion from inheritance of all tracing their descent through uninheritable blood was never in force in Connecticut" (p. 292). His decision is both historically and judically sound.

73. *Talcott Papers*, I, p. 121. It was Jonathan Law who in 1731 drafted the "Act for the Settlement of Intestate Estates," which was to take the place of the old Act. It excluded females from the inheritance, but admitted the younger sons to inherit with the eldest son, as co-heirs. This did not better matters at all for it was equally contrary to the common law of England with

stood firmly on the ground already taken, and adroitly persisted in maintaining the complete validity of the intestate law. He probably realized that under the circumstances concession was more dangerous than resistance, and that to accept Wilk's theory would be to strike a blow at the absolute integrity of the charter. "We would," he writes, "with the greatest prostration request your Majesty, that when we find any rules of law needful for the welfare of your Majesty's subjects here, which is not contrary to and agrees well with some one of the Tryangles of the law of England, as it then is, or heretofore had been, when England might have been under the like circumstances in that particular, which we are when we make the law, that it might not be determined to be contrary to the law of England."[74]

The opinions of the English lawyers of this period, so far as I am able to discover them, are neither definite nor complete. In a report to the Board of Trade, Attorney General Yorke and Solicitor General Talbot upheld the colony's position regarding by-laws. They affirmed that the assembly of the colony had the right by their charter to make laws which affected property, on condition that such laws were not contrary to the law of England; but, although it seems probable that they intended "law of England" to cover the whole law, they did not make it clear what they meant by this term.[75] Yet these same lawyers in a later judgment declared that in one particular case, the barring of an heir to entailed lands lying in the plantation by a process of fine and recovery in England, the common law did not extend to the plantations, unless it had been enacted in the plantation where the entailed lands lay.[76] The Board itself supported the colony against adverse criticism[77] when it stated that according to the charter the laws were not repealable by the Crown, but were valid without royal confirmation unless repugnant to the law of England.[78] The

the older Act. *State Archives, Civil Offices*, II, doc. 169. *Foreign Correspondence*, II, doc. 146. See Wilks's remarks upon this Act. *Talcott Papers*, I, p. 241.

74. *Talcott Papers*, I, pp. 149-150.

75. *B. T. Papers, Proprieties*, R. 130. Aug. 1, 1730.

76. *Talcott Papers*, I, p. 238. II, Appendix. "Instructions to Agent," p. 493.

77. *Ibid.* I, p. 152, Winthrop's 8th Complaint. II, pp. 75-76, Parris, Opinion.

78. "Copy of a Representation of the Board of Trade to the House of Lords" Jan. 23, 1733-34. *British Museum*, 8223 e-15. Mentioned by Wilks, *Talcott Papers*, I, p. 294. In 1760 the Board took a different view "supporting his Majesty's right to examine into every provincial law and to give or to withhold his negative upon any good reasons which may be suggested to him

most definite expression of opinion, however, was adverse to the view which the colony took. Mr. West, in a judgment rendered regarding admiralty jurisdiction in the plantations, took the ground that wherever an Englishman went there he carried as much of law and liberty with him as the nature of things allowed; that, in consequence of this, the common law of England was the common law of the colonies, and that all statutes in affirmance of the common law passed in England antecedent to the settlement of any colony were binding upon that colony. He also held, as did Wilks, that no statutes made since the settlements were in force unless the colonies were particularly mentioned.[79] His view, which I do not doubt was very generally held by English lawyers outside of the colony, was simply a legal opinion, and was probably based on little real knowledge of the subject to which it referred. We are, therefore, fortunate in having another and different view of the matter of greater practical value. In 1773 the legal advisor of the Board, Francis Fane, returned to the Board his comments upon the first installment of the laws of Connecticut and he completed his examination of the entire 387 laws in 1741. In this report opinion came face to face with facts, and the lawyer realized the anomaly of attempting to force English law upon a people whose conditions of life were in so many particulars different from those at home. In his comment upon the intestate law Fane notices that it was different from the law of England, but it is evident that this aspect of the case troubles him little. He is chiefly concerned with matters of rule, form, and procedure, and it is in these particulars that his real objection to the law lies. He recommends the repeal of the Act,[80] but would substitute another law "either as it is now done in England or by such other methods as may best fit the province where this law is to take effect." In this statement there was for the colony a world of meaning. Furthermore, in his criticism of the later amendments and additions to the law he says nothing about their being contrary to the law of England; his

by the wisdom of his Privy Council or by his own royal prudence and discretion." *B. T. Papers, Proprieties, Entry Book*, I, ff. 299-307; Cf. opinion of House of Lords, 1734, *Talcott Papers*, I, p. 297.

79. "Mr. West's Report relating to the Admiralty Jurisdiction practiced in the Plantations." June 20, 1730. *B. T. Papers, Plantations General*, L. 10.

80. Fane evidently took it for granted that the Connecticut laws could be repealed by the King in Council. It is not probable that the Board had instructed him on that point.

recommendations for repeal are based upon the ground of uncertainty or upon some other defect of the law which would naturally attract a lawyer. An analysis of his comments upon the remaining 384 laws[81] gives us approximately the same result. The laws recommended for repeal were too strict, severe or unreasonable, incomplete or not severe enough, inexact, giving too much power to certain bodies, etc. In only one instance is a law declared contrary to the law of England, and then it is the legal principle implied in a part of the law that a man can be convicted on a general presentment which is declared repugnant. It is true that in a number of cases he recommends the repeal of a law which is different from the law of England, but it is not on the ground of its difference that the recommendation is made; it is because the law is unsatisfactory from a legal standpoint and would not be a good law in any civilized community. In nine cases, however, he considers the colony's convenience, and recommends the acceptance of the law, even though it would not have been proper for England or was not so good as the corresponding law in England. In these instances he recognizes the principle that the colony was generally the best judge of its own law, and practically concedes two of the points for which the colony contended, the principle of equity and that of custom. Fane's comments are uniformly fair and reasonable, and contain not a trace of animus toward the colonies.[82]

The circumstances and discussions thus far outlined are necessary to an understanding of the influences that acted upon the Board when it came to draw up its representation to the committee of the Council upon the petition of Belcher and Dummer.[83] In

81. The following is an analysis of the report:

There are in the list 387 Acts and 3 Resolutions. Of the Acts 312 are good, proper, well contrived for the purpose intended, reasonable, containing nothing amiss, fit to be confirmed, open to no objection or agreeable to the conveniences of the colony, and 75 are open to objection and should be repealed. Of the latter 28 are too severe or unreasonable, 2 are not severe enough, 9 are too loose, inexact, or uncertain, 6 give too much power to the selectmen, the county court or the court of assistants, 3 omit certain necessary definitions or limitations of the corresponding English law, 7 are different from the law of England and for the object intended inferior to the English law, 2 are incomplete in themselves, 9 concern Bills of Credit, 3 the intestate law, 5 are good in part and I has been repealed. It would be worth while as a commentary upon Gershom Bulkeley's "Will and Doom" to compare his partisan arraignment of the Connecticut laws with the judicial criticisms of Francis Fane.

82. "Francis Fane on the Connecticut Laws." *B. T. Papers, Proprieties,* V. 19-27.

83. The order of events may be briefly given. The petition was sent to the

this petition the colony begged the King to confirm by an order in Council to the inhabitants of the province the lands already distributed under the intestate law, to quiet them therein, and to enable them to divide the lands of intestates in the same manner in the future.[84] The colony had already discussed at considerable length the wording of the petition, debating whether it would be best to ask for a confirmation by an Order in Council, or to apply for leave to bring forward a bill in Parliament. Belcher strongly advocated the latter method.[85] Talcott in a forcible communication presented his fears of Parliament in case the matter were brought to its attention, and he had good reason to fear if we are to judge from later events. He was a prophet in his apprehension that it might lead Parliament to inquire whether the government had not accustomed itself to take the same liberty of making other laws contrary to the law of England; and, further, that it might lead Parliament to the opinion that the charter had not made them a government or province but only a corporation. Yet, on the other hand, it was equally true that neither the petition of Belcher nor the introduction of a bill in Parliament was needed, if that body had desired to end the privileges of Connecticut in 1730 as it practically did those of Massachusetts in 1774.[86]

King in February, 1730; it was referred to the Committee on Appeals Apr. 10, and to the Board of Trade Apr. 15. The Order in Council and the Petition were read before the Board Apr. 21, and the letter of Inquiry was sent to the Crown lawyers the next day. The Memorial of Winthrop in reply to the Petition was received and read on the 28th, and was sent to the Crown lawyers two days after. On the 13th of May, the Crown lawyers not having replied, a letter was sent to remind them of the Board's request. Finally, on Aug. 1, they replied and their report was read Aug. 13, when the preparations for the representation to the Committee of the Council were begun: a draught of the representation was ordered on Nov. 12, and on the 18th a letter with the Petition and the Memorial was sent to Francis Fane. He replied on the 21st and his report was read on the 24th and the work upon the draught was continued. On Dec. 2, the agents, Dummer and Wilks with Winthrop, were summoned before the Board, and appeared and presented their case on Friday, the 4th. On the 8th the draught of the representation was agreed upon, and on the 31st it was signed. *B. T. Papers, Proprieties, Entry Book*, H, ff. 10-11, 23, 39. *Journal*, 40. ff. 90, 97, 104, 111, 209, 221, 295, 299, 303, 312, 316, 322, 339.

84. *B. T. Papers, Proprieties*, R. 108. I have used the copy of the petition sent down from the committee to the Board of Trade, instead of the transcript enclosed by Belcher in his letter to Talcott, Feb. 10, 1730, and printed in the *Talcott Papers*, I, pp. 187-190.

85. *Talcott Papers*, I, pp. 167-168.

86. *Talcott Papers*, I, pp. 175-179. The history of the relations between Parliament and the proprietary and charter colonies since 1701 shows the accuracy of Talcott's judgment. The representation of the Board of Trade upon

It is not quite clear to which conclusion the agents arrived, though in the petition upon which the Board based its representation, confirmation was asked for by an Order in Council.[87] This request at once raised an exceedingly important question expressive of the political change which had come over England since the Revolution of 1688. Could the King by virtue of his prerogative and without the assistance of Parliament grant the wish of the colony? To this Attorney Francis Fane answered, at the request of the Board, as follows: "I cannot pretend to say whether the King by virtue of his prerogative can do what is desired by the petitioners. But I must submit it to your Lordship's consideration supposing the King had a power by his prerogative of gratifying the request, whether under the circumstances of this case it would not be more for his Majesty's service to take the assistance of Parliament, as that method will be the least liable to objection as well as the most certain and effectual means of gratifying the request of the petitioners."[88] That this was the opinion widely held among English lawyers is evident from Belcher's letters, in which he mentions Lord Chancellor King and the counsel which he had secured as inclined to this view.[89]

With this opinion of its legal advisor before it, the Board summoned to its presence the agents of the colony and Winthrop and listened to the arguments on both sides.[90] It then finished the

---

the petition, the resolution of the House of Lords and the revival of the effort to introduce a bill into Parliament in 1731 to unite Connecticut and Rhode Island (*Talcott Papers*, I, p. 221) were a speedy fulfilment of Talcott's fears. There is history here to be written. See Judge Chamberlain's remarks, *op. cit.*, pp. 131-133.

87. The petition upon which the Board based its representation contains the words "pray your Majesty to be pleased by your Order in Council to confirm," the petition which Belcher enclosed to Talcott says "pray that you would be pleas'd to give leave that a bill may be brought into this present Parliament of Great Britain to confirm." It is evident that the latter was the form originally intended to be used (*Talcott Papers*, I, pp. 184, 191). But probably Talcott's fears of Parliament, and particularly the pressure of more weighty matters upon Parliament just at that time, induced a change, and the petition was altered and request for a confirmation by Order in Council inserted instead. (*Ibid.*, I, p. 197).

88. *B. T. Papers, Proprieties*, R. 132.

89. *Talcott Papers*, I, pp. 167, 168, 184, 259.

90. The minute in the Board of Trade Journal is as follows: "Mr. Dummer and Mr. Wilks attending, as they had been desired with Mr. Winthrop, their Lordships desired to know from them how the colony of Connecticut would be affected by the annulling the Act for settling intestate estates. And Mr. Dummer acquainted the Board that the colony would be reduced to the utmost

draught of its own representation. Many influences underlay the wording of that report, influences which it has been the purpose of this paper to disclose. The report was the resultant of at least three forces: first, the desire to gratify the colony in confirming the lands already settled under the intestate law, for Dummer had ably presented the inconveniences which would follow the upholding of the decree of the Council; secondly, the determination to syncopate the privileges of Connecticut on the ground that she had been too independent of the Crown, and had too long a list of charges against her to escape some limitation of her powers; and thirdly, the conviction, in view of the changing constitutional relations of King and Parliament, that the only safe method whereby such end could be accomplished was to apply to the King for leave to bring in a bill for that purpose.[91] A few extracts from the report will exemplify this. After recommending compliance with the request of the colony, the Board adds, "And we think this may be done by his Majesty's royal license to pass an Act for that purpose with a saving therein for the interest of John Winthrop, Esq. But we can by no means propose that the course of succession to lands of inheritance should for the future be established upon a different footing from that of Great Britain. In return for so great a favor from the Crown we apprehend the people of Connecticut ought to submit to the acceptance of an explanatory charter whereby that colony may for the future become at least as dependent upon the Crown and their Native Country as the people of Massachusetts Bay now are whose charter was formerly the same with theirs. And we think ourselves the rather bound in duty to offer this to his Majesty's consideration because the people of Connecticut have hitherto affected so entire an independence of Great Britain that they have not for many years transmitted any of their

confusion if their estates as they now hold them should not be secured to the present possessors, their tenures being liable to be reversed or at least to be disputed in a manner that cannot fail to be expensive and vexatious. Upon the withdrawal of these gentlemen their Lordships agreed to consider the matter further at another opportunity." *B. T. Journal*, 40, f. 316. It is a little remarkable that the clerk of the Board makes no mention of Winthrop's speech, for in Wilks's report of the interview we are told that he spoke at some length. *Talcott Papers*, I, pp. 217-218. Perhaps Mr. Winthrop had overreached himself. (*Ibid.*, pp. 166, 171).

91. Judge Chamberlain says that this recommendation of the Board marks a changing constitutional policy in the direction of parliamentary supremacy over the colonies which finally led to the severance of the empire. *Op. cit.*, pp. 134, 136.

laws for his Majesty's consideration nor any account of their public transactions. Their governors whom they have a right to choose by their charter ought always to be approved by the King, but no presentation is ever made by them for that purpose. And they, thô required by bond to observe the laws of Trade and Navigation, never comply therewith, so that we have reason to believe that they do carry on illegal commerce with impunity, and in general we seldom or never hear from them except when they stand in need of the countenance, the protection or the assistance of the Crown."[92]

With this report the case of Winthrop vs. Lechmere, growing as it did, out of the land system of the New England colonies, has brought us step by step dangerously near to the principles and theories which underlay restriction on the one side and revolution on the other. How far this particular case and the discussions which grew out of it aided in the shaping of those principles, we need not attempt to discover. As part of the larger question of the uniting of the colonies and the annulling of the charters, its influence was direct and definite. After 1700 the fact of parliamentary supremacy was proven each time an effort was made to limit the independence of the proprietary and charter colonies and to bind them more firmly to the Crown; and at the same time the continuance of such efforts for thirty years increased the familiarity of Parliament with the task of controlling the colonies. In this the English authorities were not showing themselves either arbitrary or despotic. The Board of Trade, the Crown lawyers, even the Privy Council acted according to their convictions, which, though honest, were based undoubtedly upon insufficient and *ex parte* information. Connecticut's policy of reticence was in part responsible for this; she had made it possible for her enemies to fill the minds of the home authorities with suspicion, and there was just enough truth at the bottom of the charges for them to be extremely effective. Other colonies as well were on the black list of the Board. Among intelligent Englishmen both in and out of Parliament there was a strong feeling that some of the colonies were not acting consistently with the interests of England, and needed the strong hand of Parliament to curb them, even to the taking away of their treasured privileges.[93]

92. *B. T. Papers, Proprieties, Entry Book*, H. ff. 25-27. Cf. Wilks's statement in *Talcott Papers*, I, pp. 217-219, 222.

93. See the representation of 1733 and the resolution of the House of Lords

But the blow was not to fall yet. Parliament was perhaps not yet prepared to intervene in the management of colonial affairs, however general the opinion seemed to be that it had a right, in view of the events of 1688, to assume this function of the royal prerogative. Although for thirty years ample opportunities for so doing had been given, yet the rights and privileges of the charter colonies remained unimpaired. Perhaps the colonies had given insufficient provocation; if so, time would soon render the provocation greater, not because of any defiant act of the colonies but because of the inevitable tendency of their economic development. The intestacy law is but a straw showing the direction of the wind; it has a legal stamp upon it but it is in origin and effect an economic measure.

The representation of 1730, followed soon after by that of 1733, resulted in a vehement body of resolutions of the House of Lords, but no further effect was seen. One session of Parliament passed and still another, but, as no steps were taken pursuant to the resolutions, the colony began to breathe more freely. That it would have resisted the acceptance of an explanatory charter is evident; it is fortunate that it was never called upon to put the matter to the test. While the fate of Connecticut was thus hanging in the balance, another case, that of Phillips vs. Savage, was carried by appeal from the Superior Court of Massachusetts to the King in Council.[94] Here a decision in favor of the intestacy law gave new courage to Connecticut, and in another private suit, that of Clark vs. Tousey, the matter was again brought before the King in Council. The

(*Talcott Papers*, I, p. 297), where strong language is used. Wilks reports a speech made one day in the House of Lords to the same effect (*Ibid.*, I, pp. 294-295). The opinion of intelligent Englishmen can be inferred from an extract from Salmon's Modern History published in 1739. "The laws [of the charter governments] are liable to be repealed and their constitution entirely altered by the King and Parliament; which, one would think, should render them extremely cautious in making laws that may prove disadvantageous to their mother country . . . for they may very well expect that when this shall be done to any great degree the Parliament will keep a severe hand over them and perhaps deprive them of their most darling privileges. It may be found expedient hereafter also for their own defence and security to appoint a viceroy or at least a Generalissimo in time of war . . . Or at least it may be found necessary to make all the colonies immediately dependent on the Crown, as Virginia, Carolina and New York are: for the charter governments are not to be depended on in such exigencies." *Modern History* by Mr. Salmon, III, p. 568 (London, 1739).

94. For the case of Phillips vs. Savage see *Mass. Hist. Soc. Proc.* 1860-1862, pp. 64-80, 165-171.

appeal was dismissed, however, by the Privy Council in 1745 not through any decision as to the right or wrong of the case, but because of the fact that Clark had not prosecuted the appeal within a year and a day as required by the Council. Connecticut accepted the dismissal as a decision in her favor, although it was in fact nothing of the kind. It ended the matter only because no one dared to make another appeal and the question never came up again.[95]

With this dismissal the colony returned, to all outward appearance, to the position that it had occupied seventeen years before. But this was not true in fact. Seventeen years of experience with England's policy, years of argument and controversy, had enlarged the mind and toughened the sinews of Connecticut's leaders, and had formed a body of tradition, made up of higher reverence for the charter and higher regard for its integrity, to be handed down to the succeeding generation. It was not the influence of any theory of the fundamental rights of man, or of any inherent hostility to England that underlay the attempt of Connecticut to keep her charter and to preserve her privileges; it was the determination to maintain at any cost the integrity of the colony and the welfare, happiness, and prosperity of its people. In the issue which arose in 1730, as well as in that which arose in 1765, it will be found that economic causes and conditions drove the colonists into opposition to England quite as much as did theories of political independence or of so-called self-evident rights of man.

We have now followed step by step this important question from its starting point in the land system of New England to its final issue in the prerogatives of Crown and Parliament. The land system, representing the pre-feudal idea rather than the feudal, was reproduced in America with some important changes. Out of this sprang the law of intestacy, differing in principle from that of England which rested upon feudal law. This difference between the common law of the two countries was taken advantage of by certain disaffected ones of Connecticut who sought to benefit themselves by appealing to England against the colonial law. This matter, at first private, touching the lands and interests of but a few persons, became of wider importance by the vacation of the law by the King in Council. By this the agrarian harmony of Connecti-

95. The proceedings of the Privy Council upon the appeals of Clark and Tousey are to be found in *Conn. Col. Rec.* IX, pp. 592-593.

cut, and possibly of New England, was threatened. This roused the colony, and the issue became a part of the larger question of the relations of the proprietary and charter colonies to the Crown. This made the matter of importance not merely to Connecticut and New England, but to the other colonies of this class as well. But the influence of the Winthrop case did not stop here; it passed even higher, and raised the question of fundamental importance to all the colonies as to the constitutional relations of Crown and Parliament. The settlement of this question foreshadowed the action which Parliament was to take forty years after.

XIV

*Law Enforcement in Colonial New York: An Introduction**

JULIUS GOEBEL, JR.

The prospects of independence so lately declared were dark, indeed, when in 1777 the embattled New Yorkers resolved as a part of their constitution that the acts of the provincial legislature, and such parts of the common law and the statutes of England and Great Britain as "together did form the law of the . . . colony" on the day of the battle of Lexington, were to be the law of the new state.[1] It is impossible not to believe that this was done for pressing immediate need, when one sees how the records of the country Sessions courts break off at various dates, with the "style" of the ensuing term written out ready for the next court, but never again to be held in the name of the King; when one reads how clerks of the peace inquire of the distracted Provincial Congress whether precepts should be sent out for grand juries; and when one reflects that while a Tory might demand justice no better and no worse than that which a county committee might accord him, those who were steadfast in rebellion must have a forum with a due process of law not different from that to which they were accustomed. The colonists were in no doubt as to their desires. They had declared in 1774 that they were entitled to the common law, and there had been a persistent sense of grievance that they were being ousted of their right by Crown and Parliament. Inevitably the new constitution of New York had to take care that there would be no

* "Introduction," by Julius Goebel, Jr., is reprinted with the permission of The Commonwealth Fund from Julius Goebel, Jr., and T. Raymond Naughton, *Law Enforcement in Colonial New York: A Study in Criminal Procedure (1664-1776)* (New York, 1944), xvii-xxxvi.

1. Art. 35, 1 *Laws NY* (1813 rev.) 41.

tampering with something that seemed a part of the freedom for which men had shown themselves ready to die.

The article by which the constitution of 1777 declared the law of the new state was at the moment itself a terse bill of rights in its implicit assertion of what had hitherto been withheld—the declarations and statutes which protected the subject in England (yet which in spite of colonial claims did not extend overseas) and so much of constitutional right as was imbedded in the common law. Equally significant is the manner of expression—"as together did form the law of the said colony." This is not the triumphant cry of sudden victory after long denial. It is the sober recognition of achievement, an affirmation that New York would use in the future what it had wrought for itself in the past.

The People of the State, then, were compacting for nothing new. The judges of the Supreme Court of Judicature had long read in their commissions that they were to judge by the law of the Province as well as by the law of England. The rules of practice of the Circuit had stated explicitly the primacy of the former:

> That in all Such Cases that shall Come before this Court wherein there may arise any difficulty, whether the Same are to be Proceeded in according to ye Laws of This Province or according to ye Laws of England, itt is always to be understood & itt is hereby declared, that this Court will Proceed in all Such Cases in manner following, that is to say: where ye Laws of this Province have made any Provision therein, that then in Such Cases ye Court will Proceed according and not otherwise and that wherein ye Laws of this Province are Silent ye Court will be regulated by ye Laws of England.[2]

No one who has troubled to look at the judicial records for the weeks when the up-river farmers were hurrying to humble Burgoyne,[3] and later when their Orange County brethren were weighing the misdeeds of Claudius Smith and his savage Cowboys,[4] can doubt that proceedings were conducted in a manner no different from that of a few years earlier. It could not be otherwise, for the judges who held court for the People and the lawyers who attended

2. *Ms. Rules for the Court of Oyer and Terminer* (Redmond-Livingston Mss.).

3. *Ms. Mins. SCJ 1775-81* (Engr.) 107, Sept. 9, 1777.

4. *H.R. Pleadings* (unnumbered) "At a Court of Oyer and Terminer and General Gaol Delivery . . . in and for the County of Orange . . ." (Jan. 13, 1779). On the Cowboys, Ruttenber, *History of the County of Orange* (1875) 91.

had been blooded in courts of the same name and the same jurisdiction when process still ran in the name of King George.

The reception article of 1777 was written at a time when the common law was still the stone from which the edifice of our law was built, and had not yet become the dab of mortar to mortise the strawless brick of unremitting statutory production. The provincials having labored for better than a century in the construction of this edifice were intent upon its preservation. For them there were no dreams of a formative era to come—a brave new world into which Americans were to march from out the thickets of a frontier jurisprudence. Their formative era was behind them, the years when the law of England had been molded to their needs, if not utterly to their desires. This they were committing to posterity, by good fortune unaware that scholars were to make of them and their knowledge figures as clownish as a Dogberry or a Justice Shallow.

With the passing of the years, the reception article, which has weathered successive constitutional revisions, has come to be regarded in the courts as a sort of let-pass for judicial excursions into the realm of English law books instead of into the less easily penetrable reaches of our colonial legal practice. The explicit reference to the provincial status quo of 1775 has usually been conveniently overlooked. When it has been necessary to a decision that a common law rule be settled, it has been siphoned out of English books without reference to possible colonial aberrance, or has been sublimated out of that mythical general common law so beloved of legal sentimentalists. This is an affront to American tradition, no less than an evasion of what the New York constitution in no uncertain language has directed.

The judicial approach to legal-historical problems just described is quite general and is one of some antiquity, for it runs back to the time of unhappy succession when the dynasty of Blackstone lawyers finally took command of our courts. It has been subjected to virtually no criticism; indeed it has of late been connived at by scholars who have carelessly assumed that the cold facts of history are matters susceptible to the brilliant artifices of jurisprudence. One cannot otherwise charitably explain the striking and uttering of that false coinage, the "frontier theory" of American law, and that equally spurious piece, the "formative era," *post* 1783.

The conversion of Turner's frontier theory to the use and behoof of the law has been chiefly the doing of a distinguished jurist whose words, often and attentively listened to, merit examination.[5] He has averred that the history of the common law in America "begins for practical purposes after the Revolution" for he denies that the colonists brought with them and cultivated the common law in the New World, insisting that this doctrine has been overthrown by a study of colonial records and legislation. Beguiled by certain reflections of the sociologist Sumner, this jurist has asserted further that "many crudities in judicial organization and procedure are demonstrably legacies of the frontier."[6] Administration of justice in colonial America is described as "initially executive and legislative" and "these types of non-judicial justice persisted well into the last century." Indeed, the law of New York is alleged by him to have been "so completely at large," as late as 1791, that "the genius of a Kent was needed to make the common law the law of the State."[7]

Having thus dismissed to outer darkness the century and more of colonial legal development, this same writer in a recent expansion of his thesis that the formative era of American law occurs after the Revolution has offered some further explanation of the ban. The colonists, he says, claimed in the year 1774 to be entitled to the common law, but "it was not easy in the colonies to find out what that law was."[8] This difficulty he ascribes to the fact

5. Professor Roscoe Pound first stated his views in *The Spirit of the Common Law* (1912) 112 *et seq.* This was followed by the article, Judge Story in the Making of the Law, 48 *American Law Rev.* 676, 680 (1914). Reiteration in *An Introduction to American Law* (1924) 20-21; Comparative Law in the Formation of American Common Law, 1 *Actorum Academiae Universalis Jurisprudentiae* 183 (1928); *History and System of the Common Law* (National Law Library, 1939) 98; What of Stare Decisis? 10 *Fordham Law Rev.* 1, 4 (1940). Professor Pound's views are canonized by Aumann, *The Changing American Legal System* (1940) c. IV. Pound has added further glosses in his *Contemporary Juristic Theory* (1940) 25 and in *Law and Federal Government, Federalism as a Democratic Process* (1942) 25. The most extraordinary of these recent additions is that the Privy Council deprived Pennsylvania of courts for twenty years!

6. Pound, *The Spirit of the Common Law* 113 *et seq.*

7. *Ibid.* 11. Other adherents of the frontier theory: Radin, *History of Anglo-American Law* (1936) 22; Morris, *Studies in the History of American Law* (1930) 17; Paxson, Influence of Frontier Life on the Development of American Law, 13 *Reports State Bar Assn. of Wisconsin* 474 (1919-21). In Beutel, Colonial Sources of Negotiable Instruments Law, 34 *Illinois Law Rev.* 134 (1939), the variant "pioneer" society is used. Paxson has been widely cited. He is the leading lay preacher of "frontierism" but his paper shows no signs that professional data were examined.

8. Pound, *The Formative Era of American Law* (1938) 8.

that even by the year 1775 Americans themselves had published a mere handful of law books and there were available no printed reports of provincial decisions. The implications of this statement both as to what went before and as to what happened later are obvious.

The "frontier" and the "formative era" theories in combination result in this—that the law of the colonial period is relegated to the antiquarian, and the law of post-Revolutionary time is enthroned as the true American law. The emphasis laid upon the practicality of this severance has its attractions for lawyers, and so far as the profession is concerned this ruthless dichotomy will probably be assured a longer life than it deserves. Its acceptance by scholars is a question of a different order. For them no considerations of plausibility, of convenience or of practicality can validate an historical hypothesis or interpretation which is based upon inconclusive, or unexamined, data. There can be no dalliance with probability when proof positive may be lying grimly in wait. It is with facts, therefore, and their probative effect that we must concern ourselves. The details of these as they relate to the applicability of a frontier theory to New York are presented in the body of this volume. Here we shall merely enter a general denial, and outline our objections. But before we proceed to this, it is necessary that two fundamental questions of terminology be determined.

In the first place, it must be settled how the word "American" is properly used in connection with the development of our law. Since considerations of time and place, of motion and repose are involved, conventional juristic concepts are of little avail. If one nourishes a mystical belief in the essential unity of the common law wherever carried,[9] this has implications of immutability or universality which obscure the effects of migration and stamp the law with an indelible Anglicism. If, less imaginatively, one regards the law as what the sovereign wills, this requires that the law of the colonies and English law be taken as identical, and the Revolution thus becomes the instant of transubstantiation. The problem, however, is one of accounting for historical reality and it is more profitably approached as one in the mutations of a transplanted culture. Like every bit of Old World civilization brought overseas, the law underwent a process of indenization, of

9. For example, Pound, *The Spirit of the Common Law* 1 *et seq.*; Pound, What is the Common Law? in *The Future of the Common Law* (1937) 10 *et seq.*

acquiring a New World identity. This process was profoundly affected by the accidents of settlement, the separateness of the provinces and the intense particularism which prevailed, so that nowhere did it proceed at the same pace or run the same course. In some places the intellectual pull of the motherland was stronger; in others the effects of the sea change were more immediate. English officials did not delude themselves with a belief that the law which was being administered in the several plantations was identical with English law, and they were well aware of the differences between the various provincial systems. This sense of difference was no less acute in the colonies. Neither the continental label on the map nor the fact that the inhabitants were all subjects of the Crown supplied a *principium unitatis.* The culture of the settlers, and so their law, polarized in the jurisdictions where they lived. It is "American" because the history of these lusty polities is severally the history of America. Their several achievements even when they seem most English in substance and flavor are the blood and bone of American civilization and are not to be interred as a defunct bit of Empire history.

We must next inquire, what of the expression "common law"? No excursion into our colonial legal past can be undertaken unless the implications of the term are settled. It is a fact worth noticing that in the royal charters which from time to time passed the seals, the clauses dealing with the law invariably employ the expression "laws of England." The intendment of this, as we shall see, was not to effect an introduction of that law but to set a standard for colonial action. The phrase, owing to the extraordinary diversity of jurisdiction in England, actually implied an infinite variety of choice wider than if the expression "common law" had been used, and failure to take notice of this has been the undoing of many an unwary prowler into the past. A man presented at an English leet had rights different from a man presented at Sessions. A fellow tried at a Gaol Delivery must be alert that the powers of Oyer and Terminer were not used. The litigant in Common Bench faced a different *cursus curiae* from the one in King's Bench or Exchequer. No doubt a Yorkshireman who never attended a court more august than a Quarter Sessions or a County Court conceived that what he there learned was "common law," and so the Londoner who ventured into Old Bailey. The realm was a honeycomb of jurisdictions and the course of proceeding in inferior courts had not been reduced to uniformity any more than had the procedure of the central courts. It is true the law practiced in these latter courts is generally spoken of as the common law, a manner of thought which makes plausible the ever-ready "test" for anything colonial—is it to be found in Coke or Blackstone? For the provincials, however, the easy way of modern scholarship was not yet open. To the making of their law they could bring only the viewpoints of their generation and their immediate experience with some part of the "law of England." This last, we think, is a consideration of decisive importance as we come now to assess the validity of the frontier theory in relation to the law. Inevitably one asks, was that which an emigrant brought with him of his mind's goods so ephemeral, his hold upon it so tenuous, that it was promptly overwhelmed by the rigors of his place of settlement?

Both the first and second stages of the reception of English law in New York Province (the first, 1664-1683; the second, 1684-1776) that we are about to consider establish how tough-minded the settlers were, and how few concessions were made to the circumstances of place. Things were done during the first stage that to the uninitiated may seem to prove the disintegrating effects of the frontier, but the "true inwardness" of affairs (as the Puritans would put it) is not discovered by merely taking a view of the terrain and what was there built. This problem of approach was considered by us over a decade ago when we undertook in relation to a New England colony to examine the thesis that because of the grim dangers lurking in the American forests when the first settlements were made, a special frontier jurisprudence developed.[10] It was indicated that various dispositions at Plymouth resembled in remarkable degree the practices in English local courts—the manorial, the borough, the county and Session courts—the type of law-enforcing institution with which these humble people were familiar. In short, the characteristics of their law were mainly determined not by what was here but by what they had already experienced.

But the New England soil, despite its name, has too long been venerated as the seed-bed of American culture for our suggestion that there was less originality and spontaneity than is commonly

10. Goebel, King's Law and Local Custom in Seventeenth Century New England, 31 *Col. Law Rev.* 416 (1931). Our theory was first advanced in *Some Legal and Political Aspects of the Manors in New York* (1928) but without the full critical apparatus.

supposed to be welcomed.[11] The offense of our suggestion may, therefore, be moderated by what is offered in this volume respecting the enforcement of the criminal law in New York during the first epoch following its conquest. Using, as a base, matter from New England codes that had its origin in English usages, the Duke of York's lieutenants with great skill promoted as the provincial law the little they knew of English local administration. One will find few reminiscences of Coke in what was done, but much of it will responsively footnote *The Countrey Justice.* The system of law thus introduced endured for two decades, and since in many details it revived, as was designed, "memories of old England," the new order of the conqueror operated acceptably.

This artless adaptation of the practices of English inferior courts by lay persons whose resources were mainly their recollections was without doubt intended to be an accommodation with the laws of England. New York's first book of laws directed that its provisions were to be supplemented by reference to the "lawes of England,"[12] and the provincial records are replete with particular proofs. In this process of unguided assimilation there inhered potentialities for a highly original development of provincial law. But the course of history was to be otherwise. Upon the arrival of Governor Thomas Dongan in 1683 an elected assembly enacted a new judicature law and during the following spring a change of profound importance occurred. Within a few short months the whole procedural apparatus is renovated, the practices and forms of the English central courts come into use—the second stage of reception which will endure until the Revolution is under way.

Although the growth of procedure after 1684 is of infinitely greater professional significance than the initial experiments with the law, we have dwelt upon the stage of first reception in New York because writers have failed to recognize that there was a reception of English law at so early a date. Hence they have found in crudities imported from the County of Kent, or Bedfordshire or elsewhere, inspiration for the fantasm of the frontier. To the accomplished student of Coke, these crudities (which have their

11. Cf. I Chafee and Morison, *Records of the Suffolk County Court 1671-80* (1933) xxxii. But no effort was made to test our theory against the materials there edited. Aumann, in *The Changing American Legal System* 58, views our findings with great reserve. His verdict is a "not proven" so far as abandonment of the "accepted view" is concerned.

12. 1 *Col. Laws NY* 45 (1665).

parallel in other provinces) have been so striking that they have even been made to speak for the remainder of the colonial period.[13] Since there exists no reliable record study of eighteenth century colonial law for any American jurisdiction, this assumption has gone unchallenged. Thus the developments after 1783 can be made to take on a quite overpowering, but none the less distorted, significance.

It is tempting if one lives in an oasis to imagine the surrounding desert green; yet we will not speak for other American plantations, we can speak only for New York. Illusions created and fostered respecting the state of colonial law that make the period following the Revolution the "formative era" of our law have no substance so far as this Province is concerned. To find the Exchequer process of "extent" employed in 1691 abandoned, resumed and again abandoned is warning of native experiment with ancient molds. To discover the medieval *distringas nuper vicecomitem* pounced on to force an errant ex-sheriff to account is no less enlightening. To observe the institution of nisi prius jurisdiction with the complicated panoply of issue rolls, fictive jury process and *posteas* let loose in the early 1700's against the yeomen of sparsely settled counties suggests that law enforcement even in the early eighteenth century is not in the hands of ignoramuses but of people who are using English law for the good government of the Province. If one must speak solemnly of a formative era, it begins in New York on that remote day in 1684 when English indictment, English process and English forms of recordation moved in to say. There were few who at that moment knew the import of these devices or how they were to be used, but on all sides the magistrates and attorneys set about to cut a substantive law to fit what they had to use as due process.

No branch of the law has more to tell us in its working than

13. A striking example of this is the use by Thurman Arnold and Fleming James, Jr. (*Cases and Materials on Trials, Judgments and Appeals* [1936] 243-246) of excerpts and summary from an unpublished modern study on colonial procedure. From the matter printed and the author's conclusions it appears that only early seventeenth century materials were used, for it is averred that anything resembling English forms did not come into use until 1760! Arnold and James accept this without any qualification. Tricked by this bit of "history," Walton Hamilton, in The Law and Mr. Blackstone, 39 *Col. Law Rev.* 736 (1939) could say: "America was ready and waiting; the *Commentaries* appeared with no rival to dispute its claims; Blackstone mounted a waiting and empty throne."

the criminal law of how the business of adaptation and adjustment proceeded. This is especially true of the initial stages, for its matter was too urgent to await the immigration of skill and learning. Indeed, the criminal law remains something to which learning comes slowly and sporadically, the provincial bar having but a casual connection with its growth, since it is only the Crown that is entitled to be invariably represented. The felonies were still a preserve as restricted to defense counsel as were the hunting grounds of the Indian to the colonists, and in the misdemeanor field the lawyers' pickings for a long time were as lean as the quitrents paid to the King. For all that, the procedural apparatus was set up with rapidity and nearly in its entirety, as if, wanting the protection of skilled judges, there was safeguard in the forms themselves. During the brief regime of Jacob Leisler (1689-1691) the common law forms which had been in use for five years were displaced by the earlier primitive types. The experience of those tragic months made the inhabitants glad enough to revert to the "known forms of English law." This welcome was no mere superstitious totemism. The freeman was perforce a courtgoer and was aware that justice not dispatched by tested instruments was vulnerable. It is impossible to read the case of *King v. Bayard* (1702)[14] and not be struck with this awareness that proper forms were the sinews of the individual's protection. And when one compares the account of this New York trial with the English cases in the same volume of the *State Trials* the conclusion is inescapable that the colonials were by this time almost as knowledgeable as the men at home. This report was not just a carefully prepared affair for the purpose of influencing opinion. Minutes of proceedings held a year or so later at the General Sessions for Ulster County with motions to postpone trial, presentments put into indictment form and a motion in arrest based upon nice technical reasons, testify to the extent of common law procedural reception.

Once common law forms become seated, the second stage of reception passes into a phase that may be described as one of selective reproduction of English legal institutions at large. This is essentially a process of imitation, quickened from time to time by the arrival of able craftsmen—the judge Mompesson, the lawyers Alexander, Murray and Smith, and the two Attorneys General, William and John Tabor Kempe. It is a process that can be mea-

14. Cf. 14 Howell, *State Trials* 486.

sured and understood only by examination of the records, the minutes, *posteas*, judgment rolls, pleadings and briefs. And it can be assessed only by a painstaking scrutiny of everything available on contemporary English practice which, as to their Sessions and Assizes, is, alas, only too meager.

The records of the Supreme Court and the General Quarter Sessions of the Peace for the City and County of New York are the sources for appraising the best of professional development of provincial law. In the capital were congregated the most skillful lawyers, and from the beginning of the eighteenth century onward, these courts were peopled by men who had legal training. These urban sources standing alone are traverse enough of the stuff propagated as American legal history. They reveal that in one outpost of Europe litigation was conducted as skillfully as at York or Bristol, and that the picture of an oafish frontier jurisprudence is a mirage of writers who have never blown the dust from indictment, pleading or judgment roll.

The penetration of the countryside proceeds at greater leisure, but eventually with considerable completeness. From the records, the story there is obviously different and involves factors that have commonly been overlooked. The business of a General Sessions in the country was mainly the charge of the justices of the peace, and of those unsung heroes—the clerks of the peace. In the early eighteenth century, professional contacts were casual—a lawyer deputized by the Attorney General will now and again appear for the Crown, and occasionally a city barrister will make the arduous journey to Southold or to Kingston. After 1750 there is a Deputy Attorney General in most counties, and there are local lawyers like Moss Kent in Dutchess or Peter Yates in Albany who occasionally appear at Sessions although their chief business is in the local Common Pleas. By this time, however, the patterns are set and it has been largely the work of laymen, the squires on the bench, the clerks and the freeholders from whom the juries are picked.

In some few instances nearly all the documents relating to a prosecution in these inferior courts have been preserved—from the first complaint, through the meeting of the justices who examine witnesses, the warrant to take the offender, the indictment, subsequent process and the minutes of the General Sessions where trial is finally had. There is nothing very complex about the procedure. What is noteworthy is the businesslike way in which everything is done—the meeting minuted, the examinations carefully taken, the precepts in the correct form—no different from what it would have been in English Yorkshire or Sussex, and all without benefit of schools of law administration or watchful bar associations.

There is some inkling of how the *ordo judiciorum* spread. In 1738 James Livingston sent to "Cozen Henry" in Dutchess County a bill for Jacob's *Law Dictionary*, Bohun's *Declarations* and *The Clerk's Instructor*.[15] Henry Livingston had become clerk of the peace in 1737, and he was still in the office when Howe's men came staggering into White Plains.[16] Henry's monument is unique—a formidable array of papers filed in the Dutchess County Court House and divers nicely written volumes of minutes. They bear witness as few muniments now can of the part that the ordinary man of substance had in the spread of English law and the English way of doing things. In this process, as we have suggested, the freeholders all shared. They were a minority in every county, but because they were propertied they had to bear responsibility. They were enormously litigious as the civil records show. That they had a canny flair for finding their way in procedure is indicated in the spread of the plea *nolo contendere*, and the development of appeals from justices' orders.

Sessions business on the judicial side, as already remarked, was not intricate in New York, but neither was it in the English shires. There was not an enormous amount to master, and the technicalities were not beyond the grasp of a persistent courtgoer. Furthermore, as we shall describe, a Supreme Court judge came down annually on circuit, with the hardier members of the bar at his heels, and at a Court of Oyer and Terminer and General Gaol Delivery and a Court of Causes brought to Issue in the Supreme Court gave demonstration of the metropolitan way. For things not rightly done at Sessions or beyond its jurisdiction, or likely to be muddled, there was the writ of certiorari, and by a diligently fostered system of removals the finger of the central authorities was kept upon local courts. For the foolish, incompetent or knavish official there was the information, the attachment for contempt or the Governor's power of removal. But all of this was monitory or corrective. The task of building a provincial law into the lives of

15. In a letter of April 24, 1738, *Livingston Mss.* 1.

16. He was made clerk of the peace by the State May 8, 1777 (1 *Journal of the Provincial Congress* [1842] 917).

the farmers and villagers was done chiefly by themselves. The motto which the Richmond clerk inscribed in his record book is testimony of their intentions:[17]

Quid faciunt Leges ubi sola pecunia regnat
Aut ubi paupertas vincere nulla potest.

The fact that attendance upon the courts and participation in the administration of the law, especially in the country, was an incident of the freeman's duty as much as the paying of rates, does not wholly account for the spread and assimilation of English practices. On both levels—the usage in inferior courts and the infinitely more intricate practice of superior courts—the reception of English law was furthered, as already noticed in the case of Henry Livingston, by the use of English law books. Provincial patriotism in New York never went the length of exacting that only products from the presses of William Bradford or James Parker were to be studied and used in the courts. And since the intellectual home of colonial lawyers was still centered in the dingy streets about the Inns of Court, they read and cited what lawyers did at home. That is why James Alexander, William Smith, Joseph Murray, Richard Nicholls and other New York attorneys collected every book they could lay their hands on; why James De Lancey, Chief Justice of New York, was among the original subscribers to Viner's *Abridgment;* why nearly every early treatise used in the preparation of this volume bears the name of an eighteenth century New York practitioner. And lest this state of civilization here be thought exceptional, the library of Thomas Bordley of Maryland,[18] of William Samuel Johnson of Connecticut,[19] and the commonplace book of young Thomas Jefferson are thought-provoking exhibits to the contrary.

English law books were prized in New York because it was from English precedent that provincial law was built. To the extent, as in the case of General Sessions, that a virtual counterpart existed in England, the authority and jurisdiction of the colonial court could be developed into close resemblance with the aid of a Lambard, a Dalton, a Nelson or a Shaw. But in the case of the

17. *Ms. Mins. Richmond Co. Sess. 1710/11-1744* 45.

18. To Mrs. J. Montgomery Gambrill who is preparing a biography of Bordley we are indebted for a view of this inventory.

19. Now reposing in the Law Library, Columbia University.

Supreme Court, endowed with the powers of King's Bench, Common Bench and Exchequer, the question of source was complicated. If a second process was needed to summon jurors, should it be the *distringas* of King's Bench or the *habeas corpus* of Common Bench? Should an Exchequer information be brought on a forfeited bond, or a *scire facias,* and if the latter what leeway should defendant have—that given by the Barons or that given by the Lords Justices? Such were the types of problems with which both lawyers and judges had to grapple, and inevitably they saw the springs from which they must draw as the sum of available learning on English law and practice.

The lawyers' solution of their immediate problem of accommodating the usage of English courts to a different jurisdictional scheme and altered circumstances posits for the legal historian the basic question of the second stage of reception in New York—how much was copied and what was innovation? To questions of this sort the answer is often difficult to give, but so far as our proof permits we have sought to show what the New Yorkers created and what was docilely accepted. The record in this relation is not a matter of boasting for those who honor the American genius for originality. The criminal law and procedure more than any other part of English law needed purging, but beyond abandoning some of the more barbarous incidents and making numerous small procedural changes the judiciary was acquiescent.

This matter of innovation during the eighteenth century is affected somewhat by acts of assembly. Some of these provincial statutes merely parroted Acts of Parliament which did not extend to the plantations, and some were novel. But it was unusual for anything markedly original to become law, for throughout the colonial period the spirit of adventure languished under the cloud of the royal power of disallowance. Notable, of course, in the criminal field are the provincial acts setting up special machinery for the trial of slaves, and those for the summary trial of offenses below the degree of grand larceny where the accused could not give bail (1732). These latter statutes are the most striking in a steady stream of legislation extending summary jurisdiction, a trend characteristic also of contemporary English penal enactment, which certainly affected thinking in New York. As matter of sheer bulk the multiplication of penal acts was perhaps the most important contribution of the provincial legislature to the criminal procedure, and it is this bulk which has led to misunderstanding and misinterpretation—indeed, has colored the whole approach of lawyers to the problem of colonial criminal law.

The valiant service which a massing of colonial statutes can perform is illustrated by the effects produced in an academic sortie made some years ago against a privilege of jury trial in misdemeanors.[20] A seemingly impressive record of colonial indifference was achieved by the mere volume of the matter cited on the extension of summary jurisdiction, but no effort at a serious investigation of the circumstances relating to these enactments was undertaken. Instead, certain conjectures were made, such as the explanation that the statutory development in New York was due to the efforts of the royal administrators to cope with a heterogeneous population. Considering the continuous state of tension in the relations between the governors of New York and the assemblies, this seems an unsupportable hypothesis and would hardly have been proffered if the authors had done more than shepherd their statutes. The legislation of another age has meaning only if examined in connection with the social, economic and political factors which conditioned the enactment. The material which we have examined indicates that the problem of vagabondage and the desire to relieve legislators' local budgets of the costs of detention and relief led the New York legislators to favor summary trial.[21] Unquestionably, too, the limited franchise and the composition of the provincial legislature were factors of importance. The common man, who had no vote, had nothing to say about the making of these laws. It was he who felt the flick of summary justice, and his opinion about it is apparent in the mock trials of Justice Peters and Justice Hough conducted by the rioters in Dutchess and in Cumberland counties. Although when the war came he shouldered a musket to fight for his beliefs, he had nothing to say about the cautious "jury trial as heretofore used," the form in which the Constitution of 1777 guaranteed his right. And fifty years were to pass before his voice was entitled to be heard. Against this background one cannot help feeling uneasiness when historical research is confined to the text of enactments alone,

20. Frankfurter and Corcoran, Petty Federal Offences and the Constitutional Guaranty of Trial by Jury, 39 *Harvard Law Rev.* 917, 945 (1926).

21. *Infra* [Goebel and Naughton, *Law Enforcement in Colonial New York*] 117, 382, 606 *et seq.*

particularly if the levy of defunct statutes is made for the defeasance of a living constitution.

This specimen of legal historiography with its one-sided emphasis upon statutes, its bland disregard of circumstance, is typical of a prevailing mode of history writing by lawyers. We are in such fundamental disagreement with this manner of approach that we must consider at some length the postulates of method. The historical writing to which we take exception (and other examples will shortly be given) is flawed by two assumptions, both tacit, both indefensible. In the first place, it is assumed that command of contemporary law qualifies for expert opinion on the law of Coke's day or of Holt's. This fallacy seems to stem from a confusion of the scholar with that of the judge. In the case of the judge who is presumed to know the law and who, to determine what has been settled as law, must fix the genealogy of a rule, the fiction is tolerated that the law is ageless. So, if he has something to say about old law, not merely *obiter*, even if he is wrong as a matter of fact, his statement stands as valid until overruled, for the judge is making a pronouncement of law. On the other hand, no presumptions protect the historian of the law, and by no fiction can his mastery of Abbot's *Forms* validate what he may say about Coke's *Book of Entries.* The end of his inquiry is not to formulate a rule of law by reference to the past—it is to uncover the state of the law at a given time. He should know that this is but an inquiry into facts even although these facts are rules of law, incidents of practice and the circumstances relating to them. The legal historian is exactly in the position of a witness on foreign law at trial—he must qualify for the time of which he speaks, as the foreign expert qualifies for the law of the place.

The second and no less unwarrantable assumption relates to the matter of proof. In the teeth of everything a lawyer knows about the nature and quantum of proof these writers, when they deal with historical matter, cleave to a scintilla of evidence theory. They take a proposition as proven with the minimum of citation. A rule of law will be bottomed on a single case or statute; judicial practices will be settled by reference to statutes alone. This is the way of advocacy, not of scholarship. It is the method of forensic combat, not the method of investigation. The ends of legal history are not served by the mere establishment of a *prima facie* case. There is no adversary to whom the burden of proof or the duty of going forward with the evidence can be shifted. A legal historical investigation is not to be conceived as the hasty assembling of matter for a trial memorandum, but as being in the nature of inquest of office at which the available and relevant data will be collected and made of record.

Unhappily, relevance has been predetermined by availability and availability has come to mean what stands in cold print on library shelves. So it has happened that, because the acts of colonial legislatures are ordinarily accessible, lawyers who write about early American law are prone to regard a mere polling of colonial acts as an adequate method of composing legal history. No one writing today of the Volstead Act and its satellites would risk the criticism that would be properly his by failing to consider the actualities of enforcement, and the pathological aspects of the national thirst. That the judicial records of the colonial period should be overlooked by a brief writer is forgivable: that they should be ignored by lawyers who purport to write history is not.

The work of the provincial legislatures, considerable though it seems, was but a single factor in the complicated pattern of law-making, law transfer and law administration. If the New York Acts of 1732 are to be used as proof of a prevailing indifference to jury trial, surely the records of their enforcement are relevant, and equally the opinion of John Tabor Kempe. If one undertakes to give an account of the office of provincial Attorney General, clearly some reason must be offered for a failure to have fingered the papers of Alexander, Bradley and the two Kempes.[22] If an author devotes a long chapter to colonial appellate procedure, since matters of practice are involved, he does not discharge his burden by marshalling the statutes and leaving untouched the teeming records of what the courts were doing.[23] In the chancery of Clio there are no letters patent to pardon such misprisons.

That compositions which so depart from standards maintained in the discussions of contemporary legal problems should be tolerated by the bar is a strange circumstance which can only be attributed to the training which produces a peculiar confinement of

22. Cf. Hammond, *The Attorney General in the American Colonies* (Anglo-American Legal History, Series 1, no. 2) 1.

23. Pound, *Appellate Procedure in Civil Cases* (1941) c. III. The short page on the bill of exceptions (p. 94) is a particularly glaring example of how little the solution of hard problems is furthered by the employment of a bad method.

lawyers' critical faculties. From incessant harping upon the distinction, the "common law rule" versus the present state of the law in a particular jurisdiction, lawyers have come to view the common law as a vast immobile corpus in which neither the pulse of time stirs, nor the nerves of circumstance. For anything so old, so ossified, awareness that the law in action and the law in the books are not always identical is of no moment. If Coke or Hale or Blackstone will yield a premise, a bit of dialectical skill can lend it momentary dynamic strength. To a profession which asks so little, a string of ancient statutes with a case or two thrown in is respectable historical achievement.

The lawyers having shown themselves indifferent to proving title to the rich and often exciting land of the law's past, it has become a sort of *res nullius* awaiting an occupant. Although these vacant acres can be properly husbanded only by those who are technically equipped for the task, lay historians, led on by the classification of the law as a social science, have attempted to take seisin.

We have in another place expressed our doubts on the competence of laymen to manage a task for which the lawyer alone is trained.[24] It is difficult enough for one who can step blithely through the mazes of the New York Civil Practice Act to overcome the ambuscades of William Tidd or John Impey. The layman who starts his march into seventeenth or eighteenth century procedure with a staff no stouter than Blackstone's *Commentaries* will soon discover himself in the thorns. To be sure there is no virtue in knowing that *po. se cul.* indorsed on the back of an indictment signifies that a defendant has pleaded the general issue and that a jury has convicted him, but one can make misleading generalizations if one is unaware.[25] There is no great harm in believing that a cause initiated by presentment may be a civil action, but it is a belief an editor of legal records should not entertain.[26]

Our animadversions on the writing of legal history by laymen have earned us reprimand.[27] It is, of course, an American assump-

24. In 43 *Amer. Hist. Rev.* 403 (1938), a review of *Records of the Vice-Admiralty Court of Rhode Island* (edited by D. S. Towle, with an introduction by C. M. Andrews, 1936).

25. *Infra* [Goebel and Naughton, *Law Enforcement in Colonial New York*] 585 n. 147.

26. Morris, *Select Cases of the Mayor's Court of New York City 1674-1784* (1935) 742n.

27. C. M. Andrews in 4 *Colonial Period of American History* (1938) 222 n. 1. Particulars of this replication to our criticisms in the *Amer. Hist. Rev.* (*supra*

tion of long standing that given a book or two a man of parts can qualify, if not as a lawyer, at least as a jurist. Lieutenant Governor Cadwallader Colden, in 1764, succumbed to this delusion,[28] but others have learned no lessons from his discomfiture.[29] The bracketing of the law with economics, politics, sociology and whatever other "social sciences" there be, has not *eo ipso* supplied a visa for that terrible and wonderful land charted by Williams in his notes to Saunders. Nevertheless, there have been passages undertaken within its borders and things have been told by these intrepid travellers that make strange listening to one accustomed to the tongue that lawyers speak.[30] Indeed, it is evident that having failed to master the language of the law these historians have failed to penetrate into the realm of its concepts and usages.

The misuse of legal terms is no small distemper which the physic of the dictionary will soon make right, for it casts an informed and critical reader into a mood of doubting the validity of any conclusions that may be offered on any points of law and practice. If one is bred in the law, this is disturbing, because inevitably one's judgment is affected by functional considerations. Our law is one of the few occupations of man where history is of direct and specific utility. Traditionally it is by an inquiry into what the law was or has been that the solution of present perplexities is sought. The further back in time this quest is pressed, the more difficult is the finding, and it is then that the aid of the legal historian is sought. Where

n. 16) are dealt with *infra* [Goebel and Naughton, *Law Enforcement in Colonial New York*] 44 n. 216; 307 n. 96. Mr. Andrews failed to grasp, and hence to answer, our objection to generalizations about colonial law at large on the basis of matter plucked here and there from various jurisdictions. His charge that we have not seen as many documents relating to the vice-admiralty jurisdiction as he has we admit. But we do not accept the inference he seems to draw that the mere viewing of a mass of material entitles one to speak with not-to-be-disputed authority on a technical subject. Mr. Fredrick Wiener, in a review of the same book (*supra* n. 16), expresses opinions similar to ours (50 *Harvard Law Rev.* 1213 [1937]).

28. In the case of Forsey v. Cunningham, *infra* [Goebel and Naughton, *Law Enforcement in Colonial New York*] 235 n. 37.

29. Historians should find food for reflection in the comments of John Watts written to Governor Monckton January 10, 1765 (*Letter Book of John Watts* [61 *NYHS Colls.*] 321).

30. A common law judged "estopped" a vice-admiralty court (*Records of the Vice-Admiralty Court of Rhode Island* 45). In English law before a man need answer a presentment a court officer "had to" frame an indictment (Scott, *Criminal Procedure in Colonial Virginia* [1930] 72). A sworn information in a rape case is referred to as a *qui tam!* (Farrell, *The Superior Court Diary of William Samuel Johnson* [4 American Legal Records, 1942] xxxix).

such an historian, therefore, undertakes to speak of the past, since it is something a future court may need and use, he assumes a responsibility not lightly to be dismissed. This is a moral obligation the implications of which are far-reaching, for not only must the judge put trust in his word, but the parties litigant whose rights and whose fortunes will be affected by it. Once it is accepted and woven into the fabric of a precedent, it becomes something upon which still others will place reliance. This obligation is of a different order than any imposed by the self-discipline of scholars in the fields of political or economic history. Their code is their own to make and enforce. No man's rights are affected by their mistakes of facts or their misinterpretations of data. The social effects of their work lie beyond the horizon of the moment. A generation can be led by scholarly skepticism to an attitude of cynical irreverence for the achievements of its forefathers and no one can be made chargeable, for when conversion is complete, no one will by that time care. But the historian of the law must be mindful of the especial fealty which he owes. The penalties *pro stultiloquio* have long since vanished, but with digest and citator, those pitiless Mendelian registers of the law, the strain conceived by an historian's sin can be uncovered and his credit forever impaired.

Whether or not lay historians are sensible of the privity which exists between the work of legal scholars and the work of the courts, they have indicated unwillingness that the standards of the profession be applied to them. Apparently the immunity which they have properly enjoyed in their incidental use of legal materials for the writing of political history is supposed to extend to their ventures into the body of the law itself.[31] Indeed, it has been suggested that they are privileged because it is not legal, but institutional, history which they are writing. Such evasive pleading meets none of the issues we have raised respecting competence and responsibility. In the end they must be judged by what they do and not by what they may pretend to have been about.

American legal history is in its infancy, and if it is to be reared in accord with the high standards which have prevailed in the

31. The distinction was clearly recognized by Herbert Osgood who used legal sources with the greatest discretion in the preparation of his incomparable institutional histories. His sober note on legal history (1 *The American Colonies in the Seventeenth Century* [1930 ed.] 182, n. 2) should be compared with C. M. Andrews' protestations of competence to write on "historical law" (4 *Colonial Period of American History* 222, n. 1).

writing of English legal history, the matter of tutelage is crucial. We cannot aspire to Maitland's insight, his felicity of expression, but we can at least emulate his patience, his candor and his industry. These are the virtues essential to the study of our own law, for the first duty of those into whose cure it is committed must be the reconstruction of the practice in each colony. All question of technical competence aside, the writings of institutional historians do not inspire confidence that such preliminary labor will be done. In their haste to exploit quickly the new and fascinating addition to the social science family, they have failed to hold discrete the legal developments in each colony, and seduced by their belief in a general colonial history they have indulged in dangerous generalization. We think this no less a demonstration of unfitness than the light-hearted misuse of legal terms. With their first footsteps in Contracts I, lawyers have been schooled to hold singular the several American jurisdictions, and the evidence is overwhelming that the same attitude prevailed in the plantations. Because the colonies each tapped in the same cellar is no reason to assume that each drew in the same amount and of the same vintage, or that the wine bottled in New York was identical with that in South Carolina. Process of New Jersey courts did not run in New York. Jefferson of Virginia, in his catalogue of 1783, classifies the statutes of Massachusetts, Connecticut and other states together with those of Barbados and Bermuda, and calls them "Foreign Law," because that is what they in fact were to him.[32]

Nevertheless, despite what is a basic postulate of our system of public and private law, the records of various colonies have been culled here and there to produce a never existent common American rule.[33] If something is practiced in Massachusetts, it is regarded as valid for any other jurisdiction.[34] The sour complaints of royal officials are whipped together to produce a composite and unflattering picture of the colonial bench and bar at large.[35] Even the barriers of time are lightly leapt, and the legal institutions of the seven-

32. I am indebted to Marie Kimball for the list. She informs me that the list is not later than 1783 and probably was compiled between that date and 1770 when Jefferson's first collection of books was destroyed by fire. On Jefferson's legal training cf. her excellent book, *Jefferson: The Road to Glory 1743-1776* (1943) c. V.

33. Morris, *Studies in American Law* (1927) c. I.

34. Hockett, *Constitutional History of the United States* (1939) 39 *et seq.*

35. Labaree, *Royal Government in America* (1932) 382 *et seq.*

teenth century settlers are spoken of as if they remained impervious to the changes which the next century brought.[36]

Synthesis of the sort described may be proper fare for the alimentation of the social historians who function in a pleasant anarchic world of their own.[37] What sustenance such confections can furnish to a lawyer who, for his bread, must settle whether the Statute of Frauds was observed in New York Province, or whether under the constitution there is historical warrant for a blue ribbon jury is open to doubt. Where the common law reception statute or constitutional article makes specific reference to the state of the law in the colony, this calls for an inquiry into facts, which, once established, can be argued as a once applicable rule of law. Such inquiry is not concluded by forays into the pantries of other provinces. The judge who would accept in lieu of a documented statement of colonial practice in his own jurisdiction the mince of the institutional historians or the fragile meringues of social historians does the law no service.[38]

If we have seemed to speak sharply regarding the well-intentioned efforts of amateurs in the law to re-create a part of culture that only the technician is equipped to handle, this should be attributed to a certain pedantic attachment to truth, and a fear that the already deplorable historiography of lawyers will be worsened by acquaintance with the fantastic Pandects of colonial law fabricated in the studies of laymen. The practitioner has been criticized for the narrowness of his approach to legal-historical problems, and rightly so. The ambit of his researches has been fixed by the digests and so far as these will carry him, he can produce something workmanlike for judicial advisement. In the limbo of colonial practice

36. Reinsch, The Common Law in the Early American Colonies in *Select Essays in Anglo-American Law* (1908) 367, 371, 410 *et seq.*

37. Compare the matter set forth about the law in Adams, *Provincial Society 1690-1763* (1927) 14, 278; Wertenbaker, *The First Americans 1607-1690* (1929) 209 *et seq.*

38. In National Labor Relations Board v. Air Associates Inc., 121 *Federal 2nd* 586 (1941) respondent claimed that the trial examiner had been biassed and it had thus been deprived of a fair trial. On the point of procedural due process the brief of respondent referred to cases running back to the sixteenth century, and cited considerable material on colonial practice. The court brushed aside this matter, and under a misapprehension that one case (2 Rolle, *Abridgment* 668 H 1, *Dyer* 367, pl. 40) involved the Statute of Liveries delivered a discourse on that statute buttressed by citation of a galaxy of college textbooks. The method of this opinion should be contrasted with the mastery historical exposition of Chief Justice Stone in C. J. Hendry Co. v. Moore, 318 *U.S.* 133 (1943).

on which digests are silent, the lawyer is nearly helpless. He has consequently proceeded as if he were charged with the abatement of a nuisance, rather than with the delicate task of reconstructing ideas and procedures at least as complicated as the present system of law. The pressure of practice is such, however, that unless scholars trained in the law will undertake the burden of making available to the profession the record of colonial achievement, the choice of American lawyers will remain between the chance and unreliable gleanings of laymen, and the scarcely more reliable assumption that the *Commentaries* of Blackstone are a summation of provincial American usage.

It is in discharge of what we conceive to be the duty of the lawyer-historian that this book has been undertaken. Only one sector in the vast battlegrounds of seventeenth and eighteenth century law—the enforcement of the criminal law—has been chosen for reduction. But it is one of perennial interest, for the basic problem of civilized people, the security of man's person and property against his predacious fellows, and the no less important corollary, the protections of the individual against whom the weapons of society may be directed, are still matters of lively concern. Two considerations determined the selection of this problem: in the first place the desirability of filling in what has hitherto been a blank; in the second place the fact that in this relation the provincial records are fecund sources of information. During the late seventeenth and eighteenth centuries, the English Crown law, except as occasionally modified by statute, was nearly static. Its introduction and development in New York were consequently chiefly matters of practice and administrative detail. And since throughout the period the criminal law was still a first instance jurisprudence, that is to say, a part of the law rarely subjected to the corrective effects of the appellate process, the absence of those precious gems, the reasoned opinions of the judges hearing a cause by way of error, is of small consequence. Indeed, we believe that what has here been threshed out of the apparent chaff of minute books, pleadings, briefs and judgment rolls, should once and for all dispose of the fatuous preconception that colonial legal history cannot be written because there are not sufficient provincial decisions.

The manner in which the widely scattered sources upon which our conclusions are based has been reduced to order could no doubt have been improved upon. Indeed, we suspect that our regard for

Serjeant Hawkins' *Pleas of the Crown* has predisposed us to his ideas of systematizing a subject not without its confusions even in England. The clarity of that eighteenth century practitioner's approach, as yet unhampered by the coils of juristic fashion—whether natural law, realism or sociological jurisprudence—inevitably possesses attractions to those who must establish a method for an historical enterprise of some complexity. Our problem was from the first complicated by the fact that since the death of Herbert Osgood, our greatest colonial historian, the study of political institutions on the basis of native materials has sadly languished. It therefore became necessary to settle numberless details, particularly of local administration, without which one cannot understand the actual functioning of royal government in America. What was begun as a study in procedure has thus overflowed into peripheral and incidental matter which a lawyer may think dispensable. He may find his solace, however, in the minutiae of process and similar matter which have been set forth in all their arid detail. Of such dull stuff as the use of *alias* and *pluries*, of bench warrants and estreats, the reception of English law consisted. It is futile to speak in generalities of reception, unless such prosy particulars of practice are first determined.

So far as the sources and the limitations of a procedural study have permitted, it has been sought in this work to take account of the various factors in the life of the colonists that helped to mold the criminal law, and which gradually gave a peculiar provincial cast to what was received. At this late date, however, too much has perished for us to answer with precision the exiguous command of the commission of oyer and terminer—*per quam vel per quem cui vel quibus quando qualiter et quomodo*—a formula for historical inquiry hard to excel, and hard to discharge.

Finally, it is proper we speak of our illusions regarding the utility of a study of this sort. The citizen must seek the most immediate protections of his right not in the federal constitution but in the fundamental law of his state. Whatever may be the case in other jurisdictions, the constitution of the state of New York in the article on jury trial, the article on the jurisdiction of the Supreme Court and others have raised a beckoning finger to the past and thus will not suffer the deeds of colonial lawyers and judges to sleep in death. The days of judgment when happenings in the reigns of our one-time Kings must be accounted for have become rarer than they were in the youth of the Republic, but they may still be days of moment. At no time, perhaps, since Sir Guy Carleton sailed out of New York Bay, is the substance of what was then joyfully celebrated more close to becoming shadow. Whatever of freedom we have sought to protect by law has been something wrested by the individual with or without benefit of judges, and it behooves us not to forget. Restless lie the bones of Martin Marprelate who printed his tracts under English hedges, of Francis Makemie whom Lord Cornbury had prosecuted for unlicensed preaching on Long Island, since Rosco Jones' conviction for peddling religious tracts without a license was sustained by the highest court in our land.[39]

It is the tradition of our law that examples may prevail, if reason does not suffice.[40] This we think is peculiarly apposite in respect of the citizen's right where the dry phrases in which his protections are cast will succumb to the compulsion of logic unless their meaning as the distillation of past happening is kept clear. Only thus can there be intelligent choice when the moment comes to decide whether there is more virtue in losing touch with the past than in harkening to its lessons. The alien corn which seems so ravishing to many of our generation may be more green than the fields so long and so toilfully ploughed, but there have been good harvests here and the tale of the reapings may move men to cherish the old seed.

39. Jones v. City of Opelika, 316 *U.S.* 584 (1942). Since this volume went to press the Supreme Court on rehearing reversed the judgment in this case (63 *Sup. Ct. Rep.* 890 [1943]). We have not changed our text as we are not persuaded the disturbance precipitated in 1940 by the decision in Minersville School District v. Gobitis, 310 *U.S.* 586, has subsided. In the Gobitis case Mr. Justice Stone was the solitary dissenter. The court divided 5-4 in the first Jones case. Shortly thereafter Mr. Justice Byrnes, who had concurred with the majority, resigned. This judgment was reversed (5-4) when his successor, Mr. Justice Rutledge, sided with the previous dissenters. Under the circumstances one cannot yet be easy that the issue of religious liberty is safely placed beyond future unsettlement.

40. *Dialogus de Scaccario* (Hughes, Crump and Johnson, eds., 1902) I, xii.

XV

*The Rise of the New York Bar: The Legal Career of William Livingston**

MILTON M. KLEIN

On the eve of the American Revolution, the legal profession in New York possessed both social prestige and political power. The terms "lawyer" and "merchant," Crèvecoeur noted in his *Letters from an American Farmer*, were the two "fairest titles" in colonial urban society. In New York, the "Dominion of the Lawyers" was a ceaseless complaint of one loyal servant of the King. Lieutenant Governor Cadwallader Colden warned the English authorities that the New York bar, with their landlord allies and their friends in the Assembly, comprised a "faction" that was at once "formidable and dangerous to good Government" and a major threat to the "Powers of the Crown."[1]

During the earlier years of the eighteenth century, however, both bench and bar had been generally held in low repute. Merchants regarded lawyers jealousy as potential rivals for political power; the rural population eyed them with suspicion as agents of the hated landlord class; and the great proprietors themselves were resentful of legal experts who could find flaws in long-accepted land titles and transform a peaceful countryside into a bedlam of litigation. Both merchants and landlords, accustomed to handling their own legal affairs or to entrusting them to lay colleagues, pro-

* "The Rise of the New York Bar: The Legal Career of William Livingston," by Milton M. Klein, is reprinted with permission of the *William and Mary Quarterly*, 3d Ser., XV (1958), 334-358.

1. St. Jean de Crèvecoeur, *Letters from an American Farmer* (London, 1782), p. 47. Colden to the Earl of Halifax, Feb. 22, 1765, *The Colden Letter Books, 1760-1775* (New-York Historical Society, *Collections*, 1876, 1877 [New York, 1877, 1878]), I, 469-471.

tested the professionalization of the law into a "Mysterious Business"; and they denounced it as a "System of confounding other People and picking their Pockets."[2]

The legal community helped to provide ammunition for its critics. Many of its members were poorly trained; legal fees were high; barratry was not uncommon. Even members of the profession conceded the charges. One young law clerk, disgusted with the subject matter of his studies—a "dry and insipid Science"—and with the apprenticeship system for training lawyers, confessed publicly: "There is perhaps no Set of Men that bear so ill a Character in the Estimation of the Vulgar, as the Gentlemen of the Long Robe."[3] A few years later, the same critic, now a lawyer himself, expressed his contempt for the "unletter'd Blockheads of the Robe" in stronger language and with a literary scalpel that had been honed by experience:

> Some Lawyers at the op'ning of a Cause,
> Set out with mighty Pomp to gain Applause,
> But finding instantly their Want of Skill,
> With *Hums* and *Haws*, their Declamations fill.
>
> * * * *
>
> While others blund'ring fearless of Disgrace,
> Recite in *Trespass*, and join *Debt* and *Case*.
> Thus want of Learning, join'd with want of Sense,
> Is the most certain Source of Impudence.[4]

The transformation of the law in colonial New York took place about the middle of the century, coincident with a period of marked business expansion. Heightened commercial activity produced an astonishing increase in litigation, and this, in turn, created an enlarged demand for legal services. The minute books of the pro-

2. *Letter Book of John Watts* . . . (New-York Historical Society, *Collections*, 1928 [New York, 1928]), p. 13. Anne Grant, *Memoirs of an American Lady* . . . (New York, 1901), II, 152. On the state of the law in early eighteenth-century New York, see *Select Cases of the Mayor's Court of New York City, 1674-1784*, ed. Richard B. Morris (Washington, 1935), pp. 52-56, and *History of the State of New York*, ed. A. C. Flick (New York, 1933-37), III, 34-36.

3. William Livingston to Noah Welles, July 24, 1745, Johnson Family Papers, Yale University. *New-York Weekly Post-Boy*, Aug. 19, 1745.

4. [William Livingston], *The Art of Pleading, In Imitation of Part of Horace's Art of Poetry* (New York, 1751), pp. 7-10. For the authorship of this anonymous publication, see Theodore Sedgwick, Jr., *A Memoir of the Life of William Livingston* . . . (New York, 1833), p. 448*n*, and William Livingston, Jr., to William Paterson, May 29, 1801, Livingston MSS., New-York Historical Society.

vincial courts mirror the intensification of legal activity. In the Supreme Court of Judicature, the apex of the colony's common law structure, some fifty-one cases were on the docket for the summer term in 1724. Ten years later, the number had risen to 107; and by 1751, the figure was 144.[5] The New York City Mayor's Court, a court of petty jurisdiction in which most of the city's civil litigation was settled, showed a corresponding expansion. During the month of June in 1720, for example, the court had forty-six cases before it; in June of 1730, ninety-eight; and in the same month during 1751, no less that 268.[6]

At about the same time, the legal system itself underwent a metamorphosis, becoming so much more disciplined and specialized that laymen could no longer master it without professional training. As the bar became financially more attractive, men of greater ability and education entered its ranks; and by their achievements and their learning they helped to overcome much of the public hostility formerly directed against the profession.[7]

The representatives of the new bar were young men of talent and education. Many of them held baccalaureate degrees from colonial colleges, and all received training in the offices of able attorneys. Among the newcomers were William Smith, Jr., future historian of New York; John Morin Scott, subsequently a leader of the Sons of Liberty; Whitehead Hicks, later mayor of New York; and William Livingston. As the most important and influential member of the emergent lawyer class, Livingston's legal career warrants attention in its own right and as an illustration of the rising power and prestige of the entire bar in the second half of the eighteenth century.

Livingston entered the legal profession with advantages not shared by all of New York's young attorneys. Born in Albany in 1723, the youngest of the six sons of Philip Livingston, the second lord of the Livingston Manor, William Livingston was reared in

5. Minute Book of the Supreme Court of Judicature, 1723-1727, pp. 75-97; 1733-1739, pp. 103-123; 1750-1754, pp. 59-78, Hall of Records, New York City.

6. Mayor's Court Minutes, 1718-1720, pp. 358-360; 1720-1723, pp. 1-2, 8-10; 1729-1734, pp. 76-86; 1750-1751, pp. 321-333, Hall of Records, N.Y.C.

7. The same process was going on in other colonies. See Richard B. Morris, *Studies in the History of American Law . . .* (New York, 1930), pp. 62-66. Charles Warren, *A History of the American Bar* (Boston, 1911), pp. 16-17. Paul M. Hamlin, *Legal Education in Colonial New York* (New York, 1939), pp. 3-6, 115-116.

"ease and affluence."[8] He secured his formal education in Albany grammar schools and at Yale, from which he graduated in 1741. His legal apprenticeship was served under the two most prominent attorneys of the province, James Alexander and William Smith, Sr., both of whom were on intimate personal terms with the Livingston family. Livingston's apprenticeship under two attorneys was not a matter of choice. He began his clerkship under Alexander, but two intemperate publications which he sent to the New York press resulted in his peremptory discharge. One was a withering indictment of the legal apprenticeship system and the other an equally devastating personal attack on Mrs. Alexander for her social pretentiousness.[9] Livingston was then sent to Smith's office to complete his legal studies.

Livingston fretted about the inadequacy of the training he received as a law clerk, but his masters were men of broader learning and greater legal knowledge than any other attorneys in the colony. They both possessed libraries of more than ordinary size and breadth, and Smith offered his apprentices a set of "Directions relating to the Study of the Law" which provided the rudimentary framework of a law course.[10] Livingston was so impressed with it that he later adopted it for the training of his own clerks.[11]

As a member of a socially prominent and wealthy family, Livingston possessed the further advantage of a ready-made source of legal business among his own kinsmen, all active as merchants and landowners. His family was linked by blood or marriage with virtually every name in the provincial aristocracy: Schuyler, Van Rensselaer, Van Cortlandt, Beekman, Cuyler, Van Brugh, Bayard, De Peyster, and Ten Broeck; and his own marriage in 1747 to

8. Livingston to Alida Hoffman, Oct. 29, 1782, Livingston Papers, Box 13, Massachusetts Historical Society.

9. The two articles appeared in the *New-York Weekly Post-Boy*, Aug. 19, 1745, and Mar. 3, 1746.

10. Hamlin, *Legal Education*, pp. 76-78, 80-82, 171-176, 182-192. Hamlin (pp. 61-62, 82) attributes this law course, erroneously, to William Smith, Jr., and dates it about 1756. Actually both Smith and Livingston were introduced to it in the elder Smith's office much earlier. In 1747 the younger Smith sent it to a Connecticut friend who sought help in studying law. See George C. Groce, Jr., *William Samuel Johnson; A Maker of the Constitution* (New York, 1937), p. 20*n*.

11. Livingston's version may be found in his Lawyer's Book of Precedents, pp. 139-142, New York State Library, Albany. With minor variations, it is the same as the one in the younger Smith's Commonplace Book, William Smith Papers, IX, Miscellania A, New York Public Library. Smith's version appears in Hamlin, *Legal Education*, pp. 197-200.

Susanna French brought him new family connections in New Jersey as well as New York: with the Philipses, Reades, Van Hornes, and Brockholsts.

Despite these impressive advantages, Livingston suffered the same early disappointments as beginning lawyers of a later day. Prospective clients beat no busy path to his door. His first business consisted largely of drawing up wills, indentures, deeds, and bonds—chiefly for relatives and close friends. A week after receiving his license to practice,[12] he entered the first receipt in his account book: "For drawing several deeds between Volkert Pothout and Robert Benson—£3.8.0." The entry was the sole one for the month. It was followed by others of a similar nature: "For drawing Aunt Vetch's will—£2.10"; "From Mother Livingston for sundries—£9.0.3"; "From Brother Robt. for sundries—£5.10." For November 1748, his first month as a lawyer, Livingston's receipts added up to less than five pounds; for December they totaled only one. Not until three months after receiving his license did Livingston make his first appearance in the Supreme Court; seven months later he pleaded his first case in the Mayor's Court.[13] After two years of practice, his earnings averaged only about eight pounds a month.[14]

With characteristic impatience, Livingston attributed his slow start to the defects of his clerkship, which had emphasized the theoretical at the expense of the practical side of the law, and to the competition of "pettifoggers." There was more justification to the latter complaint than the former, although Livingston probably exaggerated the extent. The courts had prescribed rather exacting qualifications for the admission of lawyers, but these efforts—designed to limit the size of the profession as much as to raise its level—were frustrated by legislative enactments, the necessity of accepting lawyers who had been licensed in other colonies, and open defiance of the courts' rulings, particularly in the rural districts.[15]

12. Livingston secured his license on Oct. 14, 1748, and was admitted to the bar by the Supreme Court four days later.

13. "Cost books of Cases in which William Livingston appeared as Counsel before the New York Supreme Court," I, 1-2, New York Public Library. Mayor's Court Minutes, 1749-1750, p. 197 (Aug. 29, 1749).

14. Account Book, 1748-1773, Livingston Papers, Box 9, Mass. Hist. Soc. Livingston figured his receipts from October 1748 to September 1750 as £215 12*s.* 9*d.* and his expenses as £19 7*s.* 5*d.*

15. Hamlin, *Legal Education*, pp. 35-36. Morris, *Mayor's Court*, p. 53. George William Edwards, *New York as an Eighteenth Century Municipality, 1731-1776* (New York, 1917), pp. 32-33.

When an Albany colleague complained in 1755 of the large number of "Mountebank Lawyers" in that city, Livingston expressed his sympathy, adding that New York, too, was "crowded with practitioners."[16]

Livingston voiced his irritation in the medium he knew so well, the press. With William Smith, Jr., he addressed a series of letters to the *New-York Gazette* castigating the "Low Characters" who were tarnishing the reputation of the entire legal profession and excoriating the men who sat on the bench of the rural courts. Two years later, the charges were repeated in an essay on "Abuses in the Practice of the LAW" which appeared in Livingston's newspaper-magazine, the *Independent Reflector*.[17] In verse, Livingston burlesqued the "Geniusses" who had suddenly emerged from "Obscurity and Silence" as "sage and infallible Oracles of the Law" without benefit of schooling or experience; and with grim humor he warned prospective barristers to

> Avoid, avoid, the inextricable Snare,
> Nor madly venture to approach the Bar;
> But instant clipping vain Ambition's Wing,
> Turn *Carman, Cobbler, Fiddler,* any Thing.[18]

By 1752 Livingston should have had considerably less cause for complaint, for by then both his reputation and his business had been well advanced. Two years earlier the New York Assembly had commissioned him and William Smith, Jr., to revise the laws of the province, offering £280 for the editorial job.[19] The appearance of the work in 1752 brought the compilers the approbation not only of their colleagues at home but also of the Board of Trade in England. The Board had been critical of the confused state of the colony's statutes and had long urged a revision. The new volume was such a success that when the Board's secretary wrote to New York some years later for three or four copies, he was told that the whole edition had been "sold off."[20] A second volume, also pre-

16. Livingston to James Stevenson, Apr. 18, 1754, Mar. 28, 1755, Letter Book A, 1754-1770, Livingston Papers, Mass. Hist. Soc.

17. *New-York Gazette*, Feb. 18, Apr. 1, 1751. *Independent Reflector*, XXXV, July 26, 1753.

18. *The Art of Pleading*, pp. iv, 11.

19. *The Colonial Laws of New York from the Year 1664 to the Revolution* . . . (Albany, 1894), III, 832-835.

20. *Colden Letter Books*, I, 84. William Smith Papers, I, "1753." The work bore the title *Laws of New-York, from the Year 1691, to 1751, Inclusive* . . .

pared by Livingston and Smith, brought the codification up to 1762.[21]

Family business of a larger nature than an occasional will or bond soon raised Livingston's spirits and fattened his purse. In 1751 he was offered a general retainer by his cousin, Robert G. Livingston, and the latter's father-in-law, Colonial Henry Beekman, to serve as their counsel "in every action to be commenced or defended concerning the[ir] premises" in Ulster and Dutchess Counties.[22] James Alexander retained him in important litigation, and Mrs. Alexander forgot Livingston's unseemly behavior during his clerkship sufficiently to employ him to dispose of her first husband's estate.[23] His brothers, Peter, John, and Philip, all prominent New York merchants, engaged him in debt-recovery actions against other local tradesmen; Cousins Robert and James Livingston of New York City and Cousin Henry Livingston of Poughkeepsie contributed additional business; and from the distaff side of the family, Aunt Mary Brockholst, Aunt Joanna Philipse, and brothers-in-law David Van Horne and David Clarkson provided still other cases. The Livingston Manor itself offered a lucrative source of law business, but after 1759 this had to be shared with Robert Livingston's son-in-law, James Duane.[24] With his sources of practice thus enlarged, Livingston's income rose to £217 by 1751, and a year later it mounted further to £358.[25]

Like most New York lawyers, Livingston undertook some practice outside the city. He appeared in the higher county courts—Sessions, Common Pleas, and the Mayor's Court of Albany—and accompanied the judges of the Supreme Court as they rode the circuit, once in the spring and again in autumn. These excursions

(New York, 1752). The publisher was James Parker. See *New-York Gazette*, Jan. 28, 1751, Apr. 27, Aug. 10, 1752.

21. *Laws of New-York, from the 11th Nov. 1752, to 22d May 1762 . . . Digested by William Livingston, and William Smith, Jun.* (New York, 1762). The publisher was William Weyman. For this supplement, Livingston and Smith received about £59 each. See Livingston Account Book, 1748-1773, entry of Jan. 12, 1764.

22. Livingston, Law Register, 1750-1762 [1753], pp. 41, 51, Livingston Papers, Mass. Hist. Soc. William Livingston to Peter V. B. Livingston [August 1751], Vol. A, *ibid.*

23. Law Register, 1750-1762 [1753], pp. 51, 53, 101-102. Livingston, Supreme Court Cost Books, I, 32-33, 48-49.

24. Edward P. Alexander, *A Revolutionary Conservative, James Duane of New York* (New York, 1938), pp. 40, 42-46.

25. Account Book, 1748-1773.

into the country were tiring to the bench and to the bar,[26] and Livingston enjoyed circuit riding only when he could visit boyhood friends in Albany or on the Manor or when, during a political campaign, he could mix his law work with electioneering. As his reputation and his practice grew, he declined to accept cases in the rural courts unless old clients insisted on his services.[27]

It was in New York City, however, that ambitious lawyers secured the bulk of their business. Here were concentrated the ablest of the colony's lawyers and the most important courts. The presence of the governor and his Council, the Assembly, the Supreme Court of Judicature, the Mayor's Court, and the Court of Vice-Admiralty lent to the provincial capital an air of political as well as judicial distinction. The city's many tribunals provided opportunities for a varied practice, and Livingston's was of just such a diversified nature.

Civil rather than criminal cases occupied most of his professional attention. As in other colonies, a New York attorney's practice involved largely matters of real estate, probate, trade, and business; and Livingston was most frequently engaged in actions to collect debts, compel the enforcement of contracts, punish recalcitrant tenants, solve land titles, and clear estates in the process of administration.[28] Then, as now, much of a lawyer's business was performed outside the courtroom. Wills were drawn, deeds prepared, and indentures written, all for relatively small fees. Court costs were usually high, but popular hostility to the legal profession kept counsel's fees at a level that lawyers considered "nig-

26. In an illustrative year, 1754, the Supreme Court held sessions at Orange Town on June 1; at Poughkeepsie, June 3; at Kingston, June 6; and at Albany, June 11. In the fall, the court sat in Queens County on Sept. 3; in Suffolk on Sept. 10; in Kings on Sept. 17; and in Westchester on Sept. 24. Supreme Court Minute Book, 1754-1757, pp. 18, 52.

27. Two such requests, in 1772 and 1773, were honored, even though in the latter year Livingston had already moved to Elizabethtown, N. J. See Abraham Yates to Livingston, May 18, 1772, Beverly Robinson to James Duane, Mar. 25, May 8, 1773, Duane Papers, New-York Historical Society; Robinson to John Thomas, May 8, 1772, Robinson to Livingston, Aug. 27, 1773, Philipse-Gouverneur Family Papers, Columbia University.

28. An incomplete survey of litigation in seven American colonies, excluding New York, shows that in the mid-1730's matters of real estate, probate, and business comprised 47.4 per cent of all cases of record. The percentage was probably greater during the next few decades. See Alfred Smith Faught, "Three Centuries of American Litigation," *Temple University Law Quarterly*, XIII (1939), 501, 504.

gardly."[29] Fees were fixed by the legislature and the courts, and the schedules were enforced strictly. In the Supreme Court, for example, no more than six shillings was permitted as a retainer, three shillings for drawing up a plea, and a like sum for making out a writ. A maximum of four pounds was allowed for all attorney's charges in normal proceedings, five pounds in the case of special verdicts or special pleadings. In the lower courts, the fees were smaller: only twenty shillings for prosecuting an action to judgment, less if the case terminated in some other way.[30]

Livingston's law papers help to establish the extent of his practice but disclose little concerning the nature of his cases or his working methods. Briefs were rarely prepared; few have survived. Many cases were settled out of court, the New York judicial system making frequent use of the Dutch institution of arbitration which obviated court proceedings by referring the case to the decision of an impartial third party. Livingston, like other New York lawyers, was employed on such occasions as court-appointed referee, and at other times his own cases were settled in the same way.[31]

The high cost of justice served to discourage court proceedings. A hostile critic of the legal profession estimated in 1764 that the "Expense of Law suits in this Province yearly amounts to more than four times the support of Government."[32] Merchants used informal methods to collect debts from delinquent customers in order to avoid disagreeable and costly law suits. Livingston took pains to assure his merchant clients that they could depend on his prosecuting no one "while there is any Probability of recovering the Debt without the Trouble and Expence of an Action at Law." The latter was a "troublesome" business that ought to be avoided

29. In Livingston's Book of Precedents (pp. 410-436), the list of fees for various judicial officials took up twenty-seven pages. Included were fees of sheriffs, criers, clerks, judges, sergeants-at-arms, notaries, surveyors, doorkeepers, solicitors, coroners, masters, recorders, mayors, and the attorney general.

30. *Ibid.*, pp. 412-414. Henry W. Scott, *The Courts of the State of New York* . . . (New York, 1909), p. 143. Julius Goebel, Jr., and T. Raymond Naughton, *Law Enforcement in Colonial New York, A Study in Criminal Procedures (1664-1776)* (New York, 1944), pp. 731 ff. Morris, *Mayor's Court*, pp. 169-171.

31. See, for example, Supreme Court Minute Book, 1756-1761, p. 229, 1757-1760, pp. 153-154; "Report of Referees, McMillan ads. Lynch," Oct. 22, 1764, bound in the New-York Historical Society copy of John W. Francis, Old New York, III, 429; Morris, *Mayor's Court*, pp. 551-565.

32. Colden to Lords Commissioners for Trade and Plantations, Aug. 9, 1764, *Colden Letter Books*, I, 342.

if there were "any apprehensions of not succeeding in the prosecution of the Action." He had given his London clients complete satisfaction over a two-year period "tho' I never actually sued but one Man."[33] But, he warned his English clients, they had better not depend on their New York friends to act in their behalf. Merchants were not likely to use strong measures against their own colleagues in the business community. Lawyers could press for payment more vigorously since "People do not expect the same Complaisance from Gentlemen of our Profession whose peculiar business it is to put the Law in full force."[34]

During the course of his practice, Livingston gave ample evidence of his effectiveness in prosecuting recalcitrant debtors as well as in conciliating them. The years from 1753 to 1755 witnessed a rash of debt-recovery actions. Trade fell sharply during this period; both English and colonial merchants were caught with overextended credits. London business houses dunned their New York correspondents for payment, and the latter, in turn, pressed the local tradespeople for settlement. Livingston profited doubly from the squeeze, being retained by merchants in England and in New York. "Times are so bad with us," he wrote to an Albany colleague in the spring of 1754, "that I have letters of attorney . . . against no less than twelve merchants."[35] Forty-three of Livingston's fifty appearances in the Supreme Court during the spring, summer, and fall terms of 1754 were on behalf of merchants seeking debt recoveries.[36] His receipts reflected the volume of this type of litigation, amounting in 1754 to almost £450, the peak income of his legal career thus far.[37]

Lawyers benefited from the flood tide as well as the ebb of commerce, and the years of the French and Indian War proved especially remunerative to the legal community. New York City became the hub of the imperial supply line to the colonies, and the

33. Livingston to John Strettell, Apr. 17, 1754, to Joseph Richardson, May 8, 1754, to Timothy Forbes, June 7, 1755, Letter Book A, 1754-1770, Livingston Papers, Mass. Hist. Soc.

34. Livingston to Strettell, Apr. 17, 1754, *ibid.*

35. Livingston to James Stevenson, Apr. 18, 1754, to Thomas Monkland, May 24, 1754, *ibid.*

36. Supreme Court Minute Book, 1754-1757, pp. 33-35, 62-63, 73-75. See also William Livingston to Henry Livingston, Aug. 14, 1754, Letter Book A, 1754-1770, Livingston Papers, Mass. Hist. Soc.

37. Account Book, 1748-1773. Receipts for the period September 1753 to September 1754 were £442 8*s*. 9*d*.

upsurge of business ended the city's "bad times." Lawyers reaped the harvest of maritime litigation that followed, much of it stemming from ship seizures, captured cargoes, and the suppression of the illicit trade with the French and Dutch West Indies. Maritime cases were heard in the Court of Vice-Admiralty, which sat in New York City. Livingston was among the few attorneys who virtually monopolized the practice of this court.[38] Although maritime cases constituted but a small portion of Livingston's total practice, the financial returns were disproportionately large since the established schedules of fees did not apply in the Vice-Admiralty Court. The value of the ships and cargo in dispute determined counsel's fees. In one privateering case alone, Livingston earned £196 3*s.* 8*d.*[39] Great issues were seldom debated in the Vice-Admiralty Court, but on one occasion Livingston's arguments resulted in narrowing the interpretation of the unpopular Acts of Trade and in removing jurisdiction over certain maritime cases from the admiralty to the common-law courts.[40]

Next to commercial litigation, suits involving real property comprised the bulk of Livingston's law practice. His dockets were filled with the names of wealthy landowners whom he represented in ejectment proceedings against their tenants: the Livingstons, Morrises, Philipses, Robinsons, Van Rensselaers, and De Lanceys. That Oliver De Lancey, a political archfoe of the Livingston family, should retain William as his legal counsel merely demonstrated the degree to which political antipathies could be submerged when common economic interests were at stake.[41] During the large-scale agrarian disturbances on the great Hudson Valley estates in the late 1760's, Livingston made over fifty appearances in the Supreme Court as counsel for landlords in actions against defiant tenants.[42] Not infrequently, he acted on his own behalf, for by this time he

38. *Reports of Cases in the Vice Admiralty of the Province of New York and in the Courts of Admiralty of the State of New York, 1715-1788*, ed. Charles M. Hough (New Haven, 1925), pp. xxiv-xxvi.

39. Account Book, 1748-1773.

40. Hough, *Admiralty Cases*, pp. xx and note, 82-83. The incomplete record of admiralty proceedings published by Hough includes twenty-one cases between 1754 and 1762 in which Livingston acted as counsel.

41. See, for example, Supreme Court Minute Book, 1762-1764, p. 29.

42. *Ibid.*, pp. 69-72, 85, 159, 228-230, 346-347, 403, 422, 424, 428; 1764-1767, pp. 11, 38-39, 71-74, 90; 1764-1766, pp. 224-226, 300; 1766-1769, pp. 375-376. On the tenant uprisings of 1766, see Irving Mark, *Agrarian Conflicts in Colonial New York, 1711-1775* (New York, 1940), ch. v.

was not only an ally of the landed aristocracy but a landowner as well.

Livingston's propertied clients included Jerseyites as well as New Yorkers. James Alexander, his old law teacher, was one of the East Jersey Proprietors, and these landowners were almost constantly engaged in litigation with small holders who refused to acknowledge the title of the proprietary group. Livingston, with William Smith, Jr., was frequently engaged by the proprietors in suits against tenants and squatters. One such action, in 1754, arose from the near-armed warfare that developed between New Yorkers and Jerseyites along the border between the two colonies. Jersey officials representing the proprietors sought to evict settlers from land claimed by the Alexander group. The settlers secured assistance from New York courts, which ordered the arrest of the Jersey process servers. Livingston successfully defended the proprietary agents, challenging the jurisdiction of the New York courts on the ground that the locus of the alleged offense was in New Jersey. Since the boundary was in dispute, Livingston's plea was valid, and his challenge had the effect of terminating the New York proceedings.[43]

Clients did not always reflect the political, religious, or social interests of their counsel. Thus while Livingston feuded bitterly with Lieutenant Governor Colden in the political arena, the latter's son employed Livingston as his attorney in Ulster County land actions.[44] And while Livingston acted on behalf of the Jersey proprietors in some cases, he represented small holders against the proprietary group in others.[45] The most prominent such case

43. The border controversy was an involved one. Not only were some settlers prosecuted by the Jersey landowners for trespass, but others who accepted Jersey titles were harassed by demands for taxes from New York officials. The 1754 suit was fought in the Orange County courts. See James Alexander to Richard Gardner, Jan. 19, 1754, Alexander to David Ogden, Jan. 29, 1754, to William Alexander, July 25, 1754, "Account of the Expenses of William Livingston, William Smith and William Alexander to Orange County Court, April-May 1754," Stevens Papers, 7607, 7974, 7555, 3570, 3571, 3573, Stevens Institute of Technology, Hoboken, N. J.; also other papers, *ibid.*, 3554, 3555, 3558, 3559; Supreme Court Minute Book, 1754-1757, pp. 44, 49; Goebel and Naughton, *Law Enforcement*, p. 314*n*, 587*n*.

44. Livingston to David Colden, Apr. 27, 1762, Colden to Livingston, Apr. 27, 1762, *The Letters and Papers of Cadwallader Colden, 1711-1775* (New-York Historical Society, *Collections*, 1917-1923, 1934-1935 [New York, 1918-1937]), VI, 155-156, IX, 184-185.

45. In 1753, for example, Livingston defended one small holder in a trespass and ejectment proceeding in which James Alexander represented the plaintiff.

was the famous suit in chancery of "John, Earl of Stair, and others v. Benjamin Bond and others." This action, prolonged and involved, was begun in 1745 and continued in litigation for over three decades. At issue was the ownership of the lands in and around Elizabethtown, New Jersey. Livingston and his colleague, William Smith, Jr., entered the case in 1750 as counsel for the "Elizabethtown Associates," the small holders who challenged the claims of the East Jersey Proprietors.

The proprietors based their title on grants from Berkeley and Carteret; the small holders had Indian deeds to prove their ownership. When common-law actions, petitions to the New Jeresy legislature, and an appeal to the Crown all failed to validate the proprietors' claim, in 1745 they instituted a proceeding in the juryless chancery court, confident of the outcome because the incumbent governor and chancellor, Lewis Morris, was himself one of the proprietary group.[46] The bill in chancery filed by James Alexander and Joseph Murray on the proprietors' behalf was an awesome document of over 160 pages which had been three years in preparation.[47] Livingston and Smith required almost two years to write their reply, a more modest effort of only forty-eight pages.[48]

The mass of laws, deeds, patents, indentures, and maps included in these two prolix documents did little to clarify or simplify the issues in dispute. To complicate matters further and to harass their opponents, Livingston and Smith filed their reply on behalf of about 450 defendants although only sixty had been named in the original bill. The purpose of this bit of legal legerdemain was to put the proprietors to "an Immense Charge to Serve all of them with the Future Necessary proofs of the Court," a trick which Alexander was quick to recognize but which he could not readily cir-

Livingston to James Alexander, Aug. 9, 1753, Alexander Papers, New-York Historical Society.

46. On the background of the case, see Donald L. Kemmerer, *Path to Freedom; The Struggle for Self-Government in Colonial New Jersey, 1703-1776* (Princeton, 1940), pp. 4-15, 187-196; Edwin F. Hatfield, *History of Elizabeth, New Jersey . . .* (New York, 1868), pp. 366-369; Edgar J. Fisher, *New Jersey as a Royal Province, 1738 to 1776* (New York, 1911), pp. 176 ff.; Herbert L. Osgood, *The American Colonies in the Eighteenth Century* (New York, 1924), IV, 27-31.

47. *A Bill in the Chancery of New-Jersey, at the Suit of John Earl of Stair and others . . . against Benjamin Bond, and some other Persons of Elizabeth-Town . . .* (New York, 1747).

48. *An Answer to a Bill in the Chancery of New-Jersey . . .* (New York, 1752). A bulky handwritten copy of the reply is in the Stevens Papers, 8094.

cumvent.[49] In addition, the defense counsel challenged the jurisdiction of the chancery court on the ground that it had been erected without royal warrant.[50]

Haggling between the opposing counsel over pretrial proceedings, demurrers, petitions, motions, and replies dragged the case out for years.[51] Parties to the original suit died; Morris was replaced by Governor Jonathan Belcher, who was known to be sympathetic to the Elizabethtown Associates; the French and Indian War diverted attention from the litigation; and despite the immense labors that had gone into the preparation of the case, it was never brought to trial.[52] Had the suit been revived after the Revolution, it would have been heard by the then governor of the state of New Jersey, William Livingston.

Criminal cases were as exceptional as outstanding civil suits in Livingston's practice. The high cost of justice deterred the employment of counsel in most criminal actions, and judicial procedure limited the role of the participating lawyers. There were few opportunities for forensic contests or the display of clever courtroom tactics. Livingston's law records reveal few criminal cases of significance. In an illustrative, if not typical, Supreme Court term, that of January 1768, Livingston made thirty-five appearances. Twenty-three were ordinary debt actions, four were ejectments, seven were testamentary causes, and one a suit for restitution. Not one of the cases was of a criminal character. During his entire career at the bar, Livingston was employed in only sixteen criminal proceedings out of a Supreme Court total of some six hundred.[53]

The few criminal cases of record in which Livingston was en-

49. James Alexander to Livingston and Smith, Mar. 3, 1752, Livingston Papers, Box 12, Mass. Hist. Soc.

50. Richard S. Field, *The Provincial Courts of New Jersey* . . . (New York, 1849), p. 122.

51. Alexander to Livingston and Smith, Mar. 3, Nov. 29, 1752; Alexander and Murray, "Notice of Motions for rules," Dec. 15, 1752, "Brief to Point out the Indulgence of the Complainants and Dilatory Proceedings of the Defendants . . . ," Dec. 1752, "Notice of Motion for March 19, 1753," Mar. 5, 1753; Livingston, Smith, and Nicoll to Alexander, Nov. 25, 1752; all in Livingston Papers, Box 12, Mass. Hist. Soc.

52. Osgood, *American Colonies*, IV, 37. Kemmerer, *Path to Freedom*, pp. 234-235. Hatfield, *History of Elizabeth*, p. 372. Field, *Provincial Courts*, p. 123. Fisher, *New Jersey*, pp. 206-209.

53. Goebel and Naughton, *Law Enforcement*, pp. 573-575. Supreme Court Minute Book, 1766-1769, pp. 373-391. Livingston, Supreme Court Cost Books, I and II, passim.

gaged attracted public attention because of the prominence of the defendants or the nature of the crime. In a celebrated rape case in 1754, Livingston was retained by four gay blades who were charged with criminally assaulting a fourteen-year-old girl. The attorney general's information alleged that the foursome "with fforce and Arms . . . did make an Assault . . . beat wound and ill-treat so that of her life it was greatly dispaired . . . Mary Anderson . . . a young Girl at the time of the Violence . . . but barely turned 14 years of Age."[54] The Crown made a strong appeal for conviction, denouncing the crime as "reprehensible" and warning that failure to punish the offenders would threaten the chastity of every woman in the city—"No mans wife or Daughter would be long secure from the brutal Attempts of lustfull and licentious people."[55]

Not content with their first offense, the defendants proceeded—according to the attorney general—to arrange a "frame-up" against the girl's mother in order to bar her testimony at the expected trial. A trumped-up charge of stealing a petticoat brought Mrs. Anderson before the city's magistrates, who adjudged her guilty and sentenced her to public whipping. Although Livingston appears to have had no part in the alleged plot, he made a vigorous attempt at the trial to bar the mother's testimony on the ground that "Having undergone a publick punishm[en]t by whipping . . . she is thereby become infamous and disqualified to be a Witness." Although the Crown managed to answer this argument satisfactorily, Livingston apparently cast sufficient doubt upon Mrs. Anderson's credibility to weaken her testimony. The trial on April 18, 1755, resulted in a verdict of not guilty.[56]

Still another of Livingston's criminal cases bears the dubious distinction of being the most confused and complicated prosecution in the colony's legal history. It arose from the Crown's efforts during the French and Indian War to curb the vast illicit trade with the enemy carried on from New York. A corps of paid informers was recruited for the purpose, and one of the most notori-

54. "The King agt. John Lawrence, Jr., Charles Arding, Cornelius Livingston, and Hendrick Oudenard," Aug. 1, 1754, Supreme Court Pleadings, K-501, K-650, Hall of Records, N.Y.C. Supreme Court Minute Book, 1754-1757, p. 53. Livingston to William Kempe, Aug. 26, 1754, Livingston Papers, Vol. A, Mass. Hist. Soc.

55. Supreme Court Pleadings, K-501.

56. *Ibid.* Supreme Court Minute Book, 1754-1757, pp. 145-146. A discussion of the case and the text of the attorney general's information may be found in Goebel and Naughton, *Law Enforcement*, pp. 262-263, 786-791.

ous of these agents was one George Spencer. To prevent his testimony from being used in future proceedings, some of the city's merchants arranged a plot designed to bring Spencer into public disgrace. The plot was executed neatly. An organized mob raided Spencer's home on the evening of November 2, 1759, dragged him outside, plied him with liquor until he was drunk, and then hauled him through the streets in a cart, showering him with blows, "filth and offal" along the route.[57]

To protect Spencer and other official informants, the attorney general, John Taber Kempe, immediately secured indictments for riot against seven persons, almost all of whom were leaders of the city's mercantile community. Livingston was retained by two of the defendants, James Duane by the others. Through successive postponements, they managed to delay the case for over a year. Kempe, irritated almost to the point of hysteria by the defense's dilatory tactics, managed to use the intervening time to pile up additional charges against the accused, adamant in his refusal to drop the prosecutions. When the first of the trials took place, in 1761, Livingston's client was acquitted; and although Kempe moved for a new trial, the court records show no evidence that his motion was granted. The other defendants presumably were the beneficiaries of Livingston's successful defense, since their cases seem never to have been tried.[58]

A few of Livingston's cases excited popular attention because important political or constitutional issues were at stake; and in such suits Livingston usually acted in association with William Smith, Jr., and John Morin Scott. Dubbed the "triumvirate" because of their joint leadership of the Livingston-Presbyterian "party," the three did not constitute a formal legal partnership; but in cases bearing political or religious overtones, they worked together. Their first public appearance as a team was made in 1754, in what appeared to be a minor debt action, but in arguing the case they transformed it into a challenge to the constitutional structure of the British Empire in America.

The suit of John Obriant *v.* William Bryant originated in-

57. Supreme Court Pleadings, K-930. Goebel and Naughton, *Law Enforcement*, pp. 280-281.

58. Livingston, Supreme Court Cost Books, I, 358, 360, II, 1-7. Supreme Court Pleadings, K-926, 930, 962, 976. Supreme Court Minute Book, 1756-1761, p. 239, 1762-1764, p. 172. Goebel and Naughton, *Law Enforcement*, pp. 282-283.

auspiciously enough in the New York Mayor's Court in March 1752. The plaintiff sued to compel payment by Bryant of a seven-year-old debt, amounting with interest to about £60. Livingston, as counsel for the defendant, secured removal of the case to the Supreme Court where, after preliminary legal maneuvering, it was tried on October 24, 1753, judgment being rendered for the plaintiff.[59] Livingston now sought, by "writ of error," to carry the case on appeal to the governor and council, based upon certain defense exceptions to the bench's ruling on the admissibility of some evidence. Despite objections from Lambert Moore, Obriant's counsel, the writ was granted, returnable before the governor in December 1754. During the interim, both sides enlisted additional counsel, Smith and Scott joining Livingston for the defense and Benjamin Nicoll assisting Moore.[60]

Obriant's lawyers introduced the broader implications of the suit in arguing that the writ of error should be quashed because the most recent royal instructions to the governor forbade appeals beyond the Supreme Court in cases involving less than £300.[61] In their rebuttal, the triumvirate protested that adherence to such instructions would virtually eliminate all appeals beyond the Supreme Court since "not one personal action in a Thousand in this Infant Country" was above £300 in value. The judges of the Supreme Court would thus be "unaccountable for their Errors and in a Vast Degree the absolute Master of the Property of his Majesty's subjects."[62] But the trio also attacked Obriant's position at its constitutional root. A writ of error, they insisted, was a writ of right; and although it may have originated by, it did not depend upon, royal instructions but was rather "part of the Political Constitution and State of this Province necessary to the Peace of his Majesty's government and advantageous to the Rights of his Subjects."

59. Mayor's Court Minutes, 1752-1753, p. 119. Supreme Court Minute Book, 1750-1754, pp. 153, 177, 263, 312-313. Supreme Court Parchment Rolls, 228-D-1, Hall of Records, N.Y.C.

60. Supreme Court Minute Book, 1750-1754, p. 336. The triumvirate also secured assistance from William Smith, Sr. See Livingston, Supreme Court Cost Books, I, 86-87.

61. Supreme Court Parchment Rolls, 228-D-1. The figure had been raised from £100 to £300 in the instructions issued to Sir Danvers Osborn, who arrived as governor in October 1753.

62. Livingston, Smith, and Scott, "Wm. Bryant agt. John Obriant, In Error," [1754?], in William Smith Papers, II, 375-380.

The triumvirate challenged the validity of the royal instruction on the ground that it was neither sanctioned by common law nor confirmed by act of Parliament or of the New York legislature. No mere instrument of imperial administration could "Destroy nor Restrain inlarge nor Abridge" a right that was "interwoven with and part of the Political Frame and Constitution of this Province." The instruction in question was a "most mischievous" one, and if upheld, would vest the judges with an "uncontrollable, absolute, and formidable despotism" over the property of British subjects and would deny the latter a constitutional right of "having Recourse where Error hath intervened."[63]

Livingston and his associates lost their case when the Council, in March 1755, sustained the validity of the royal instruction, declined to accept jurisdiction of the suit, and ordered the writ of error vacated and the original judgment affirmed.[64] The principles they invoked in arguing the case, however, were scarcely lost, for the challenge to government by instruction, the attack on arbitrary acts of imperial administration, and the presupposition of a colonial constitution formed the essence of the legal position taken by the colonists on the eve of the Revolution. In their perception of this basic weakness in the imperial system, the triumvirate anticipated the later analyses of more vigorous critics like Otis, the Adamses, Dickinson, and Jefferson.[65]

The triumvirate again raised the same constitutional question a few years later, in the celebrated case of Forsey *v.* Cunningham. This suit arose in 1763 from an altercation between two of the city's merchants, Thomas Forsey and Waddel Cunningham, in which the latter was severely wounded. Forsey instituted two actions for assault and battery against Cunningham, one civil and one criminal, winning both. The civil suit became the *cause célèbre* when Cunningham, failing to have the £1500 judgment against him set aside as excessive, appealed for a review of the case to Lieutenant Governor Colden.[66]

63. William Smith Jr., *The History of the Late Province of New-York, from its Discovery, to the Appointment of Governor Colden, in 1762* (New York, 1830), II, 204-205.

64. Supreme Court Parchment Rolls, 228-D-1.

65. In this connection, see Leonard W. Labaree, *Royal Government in America; A Study of the British Colonial System before 1783* (New Haven, 1930), ch. x, and Charles F. Mullett, *Fundamental Law and the American Revolution, 1760-1776* (New York, 1933), passim.

66. Livingston, Supreme Court Cost Books, II, 207. William Smith Papers,

The Supreme Court judges refused Colden's request for the minutes of the trial on the ground that since no errors of law were involved, "no proper writ" for sending up the record existed. Colden insisted on his right to review the facts in the case as well as the law; bench and bar almost to a man opposed Colden's action as a threat to the inviolability of jury trials; and Colden exacerbated public suspicion by insisting that as the Crown's representative, he could virtually erect courts at will and define their jurisdiction and procedure.[67] Coinciding with the news of the approaching Stamp Tax, Colden's "unseasonable Effort" to introduce a judicial innovation was viewed by the triumvirate as evidence that "the Crown is aiming to deprive the Subject of his most valuable Rights."[68]

While the legal profession pleaded the case in court, Livingston sounded the alarm in a series of newspaper essays in which he warned that Colden's "scandalous abuse of the King's name and authority" would subvert the ancient right of trial by jury and destroy the "excellency" of the British constitution. The New York Assembly added its own protest, and the Board of Trade ultimately upheld the Livingston position.[69] The triumvirate's victory had political as well as legal repercussions. The clamor over the Forsey Case helped to raise public tempers and set the stage for the Stamp Act discorders. New Yorkers viewed Colden's attitude and the new British taxes as two sides of the same coin: a tightened imperial administration; and they were as vocal in protesting the one as the other.

Commonplace rather than distinguished cases provided the measure of Livingston's professional success. An examination of his law registers for the period 1750-63 discloses a total of 1,150 cases, fully half of which were undertaken during the years of the French and Indian War, a period of intense activity for the entire

---

IV, "1764." Supreme Court Minute Book, 1762-1764, pp. 224-225, 308, 358-359, 1764-1767, pp. 18, 32. Supreme Court Parchment Rolls, 21-A-8, 28-K-9, 186-K-3.

67. "Cadwallader Colden's opinion on Appeals," [Jan. 1765], *Colden Papers*, VII, 1-7.

68. William Smith, Jr., to Gov. Monckton, Dec. 3, 1764, Jan. 25, 1765, Chalmers Papers, N. Y., IV, 14-17, New York Public Library.

69. "The Sentinel," I, II, III, *New-York Gazette*, Feb. 28, Mar. 7, 14, 1765. *Journal of the Votes and Proceedings of the General Assembly of the Colony of New-York [1691-1765]* (New York, 1764-1766), II, 803-806. *New-York Gazette*, Dec. 26, 1765.

legal fraternity. The contrast between the prewar and the war years is shown in the following table.

	Total cases	*Average annual case load*
1750-53	170	43
1753-59	433	72
1759-63	547	137

In the New York Supreme Court, Livingston's activity increased similarly. During the period 1753-59, he appeared in the Supreme Court an average of eighteen times each term; during 1759-63, that figure increased to twenty-five. From 1750 to 1760, Livingston's appearances averaged about seventy-two a year; during the three-year period 1763-65, the number almost doubled.[70]

Nevertheless, Livingston's practice was both less extensive and less lucrative than that of his colleagues of the triumvirate. During his first ten years as a lawyer, Livingston handled 257 cases in the New York Supreme Court; William Smith, Jr., had 362 during his own first decade in the law.[71] From 1760 to 1768, Livingston appeared in the Supreme Court about twenty-six times each term; Smith, forty-one; and John Morin Scott, forty-three. All three reached their peak of activity in the Supreme Court during the years 1763-65, and again the junior partners outstripped Livingston in the volume of their practice. Their appearances during this period were:

	1763	*1764*	*1765*	*Total*	*Annual average*
Livingston	146	127	141	414	138
Smith	211	167	176	554	185
Scott	167	182	226	575	192.[72]

The account book which Livingston maintained from 1748 to 1773 discloses the extent of his professional income. Although he maintained it with fidelity throughout his legal career, it may well

70. Supreme Court Minute Book, 1754-1757, 1757-1760, 1756-1761, 1762-1764, passim.

71. Livingston, Supreme Court Cost Books, I (1749-1759). William Smith, Jr., "New York Supreme Court Register A," 1750-1760, New York Public Library.

72. James Duane, another active member of the New York bar, divided his energies between his private practice and Crown prosecutions in which he served as the attorney general's deputy. In addition he was busily engaged in developing his large landholdings. Yet he managed to handle almost as many private suits during this same three-year period as did Livingston, 338 to be exact. Supreme Court Minute Book, 1762-1764, 1764-1766, passim.

err in understating his earnings. He was often lax in recording receipts and was generally haphazard about collecting debts, pressing clients for payment, and keeping straight his personal finances. The reason was his professed "aversion to Figures." "Of all Things," he once confessed, "I hate to keep Accounts." Finances represented to him a subject "more intricate" than "all the hieroglyphics of Egypt."[73]

Livingston's income paralleled his practice, although receipts often lagged behind litigation. Prior to 1752, Livingston's earnings from the law amounted to an average of about £200 a year; during the next four years, they doubled.[74]

1748-49	£ 70.9.0	1752-53	£336. 0.0
1749-50	145.3.3	1753-54	442. 8.0
1750-51	217.5.9	1754-55	406.17.11
1751-52	358.0.0	1755-56	354.12.2

The increase in litigation accompanying the outbreak of the French and Indian War was reflected in the receipts of the year 1757. For the first time, Livingston's income rose to over £1000.[75] It never sank below that level for the next decade, except during the year of the Stamp Act's operation. The closing of the courts following the enactment of the law interrupted the prosperity of the entire legal profession, and Livingston suffered with the rest of his colleagues. His income dropped precipitously from a high of £1472 during 1765-66 to a meager £425 the following year. Livingston marked the loss by the rueful comment in his "Account Book": "The small am[oun]t of this years profit owing to the Stamp Act."[76]

The reopening of the courts the next year, however, brought a "Luxuriant Harvest of Law" as the institution of long-delayed suits crowded the courts' calendars. Livingston reaped the fruit with the rest of the bar as his income again rose over the £1000 mark.[77]

73. Livingston to Henry Laurens, Apr. 27, 1778, Aug. 9, 1779, Laurens Papers, South Carolina Historical Society.

74. Account Book, 1748-1773. Livingston's personal fiscal year ran from October to September or from September to August.

75. The exact income for 1756-57 was £1071 16*s*. 5*d*.

76. The courts held no regular sessions from November 1765 to May 1766. See Morris, *Mayor's Court*, p. 48.

77. Livingston's Account Book shows an increase from £425 8*s*. 2*d*. in 1766-67 to £1015 8*s*. 8*d*. the following year. Benjamin Kissam, one of Livingston's colleagues at the bar, expressed the sentiments of the entire legal fraternity in his observation: "As upon the Repeal of the Stamp Act, we shall doubtless have a luxuriant Harvest of Law, I would not willingly, after the long Famine we

From 1769 to 1773, Livingston's practice declined steadily. The dislocations produced by the new British commercial restrictions upset normal business relations between mother country and colonies, and the law reflected the disturbance. In addition, Livingston found himself in competition with an increasing number of New Yorkers who had entered the legal profession. Finally, he had already begun a voluntary contraction of practice in anticipation of his forthcoming removal to Elizabethtown, New Jersey.

At the time of his retirement from active practice in 1772, Livingston had acquired an estate variously estimated at between £6000 and £8500, together with extensive property holdings of uneven value. This did not constitute great wealth in a city where commercial fortunes of £10,000 were not uncommon, but Livingston believed the sum sufficient to permit him "with justice to my dear children [to] go into the country, where the interest . . . would more than maintain me."[78] Other New York lawyers of the day profited more handsomely from their profession. During his best five years, Livingston's income from the law averaged £1287; James Duane's was over £1400. In his best year, Livingston earned £1472; Duane bested that figure by almost £400; William Smith, Jr., declined a place on the Supreme Court bench because its £500 salary would be less than half of his average income from private practice.[79] John Tabor Kempe, New York's attorney general from 1759 to the end of the Revolution, managed to average about £884 annually from his private law practice; Livingston, during twenty-four years at the New York bar, averaged only £695 annually.[80]

Some New York lawyers developed secondary economic inter-

had, miss reaping my part of the crop." Kissam to Jay, Apr. 25, 1766, in *The Correspondence and Public Papers of John Jay . . .*, ed. Henry J. Johnston (New York, 1890-93), I, 3.

78. Sedgwick, *Livingston*, p. 158 and note. Virginia D. Harrington, *The New York Merchant on the Eve of the Revolution* (New York, 1935), p. 19. The £6000 estimate was made in 1774 by Rev. Ezra Stiles; the higher figure was Livingston's own. See *The Literary Diary of Ezra Stiles . . .*, ed. Franklin B. Dexter (New York, 1901), I, 635-636.

79. Account Book, 1748-1773. Alexander, *James Duane*, pp. 36-37. William Smith Papers, IV, "5 June, 20 July 1763." Smith to Monckton, July 20, 1763, Chalmers Papers, N. Y., IV, 11. Livingston's best five years were 1758-59, 1759-60, 1760-61, 1763-64, and 1765-66. In the latter year he reached his peak income, £1472 9*s*. 3*d*. Duane's in 1753 was £1860 13*s*. 3½*d*.

80. Catherine Snell Crary, "The American Dream: John Tabor Kempe's Rise from Poverty to Riches," *William and Mary Quarterly*, 3d Ser., XIV (April 1957), 184.

ests. Smith held the positions of clerk in Chancery and clerk of Queens County; Duane was deputy to the provincial attorney general; and both, along with John Morin Scott, speculated actively in land and accumulated vast holdings in New York and Vermont. Livingston neither sought nor secured judicial office, and although he was considered among the landed aristocracy of the colony, his property brought him few financial dividends. Even if such auxiliary enterprises had turned out more successfully, Livingston's carelessness would probably have dissipated the gains. "The truth is," he once wrote, that "I do not set a proper value on Money, and tho' I may soon be in the way of getting it, I dispair of ever attaining the Art of keeping it."[81] Thirty years later he was forced to confess that "tho' it has been for many years my profession to manage other people's affairs, I never had any sagacity about my own."[82] The executors of his estate, struggling to repair the damage done by Livingston's lifetime of casual record keeping and over-indulgence with debtors, could well agree with his daughter Susan when she observed: "Papa was too lenient, he suffered every one to do as they pleased with his property."[83]

Neither the extent of his practice nor his income reflect adequately Livingston's influence in the law. He was active in every effort to raise professional standards and to improve legal education. He urged stricter requirements for admission to the bar—including a system of public examinations—in order to prevent the influx of untrained practitioners; he attacked the county courts for permitting unlicensed attorneys to practice before them.[84] He joined with other New York lawyers in 1756 in demanding a bachelor's degree of all future apprentices; and when this stipulation proved too stringent to enforce, he reluctantly agreed to relax the requirement to two years of college.[85] The requirements for admission to practice were ultimately fixed by the Supreme Court,

81. Livingston to Noah Welles, Dec. 16, 1751, Johnson Family Papers.

82. Livingston to Rev. John Witherspoon, May 10, 1781, Livingston Papers, Box 13, Mass. Hist. Soc.

83. Susan Livingston Symmes to William Livingston, Jr., Sept. 3, 1802, Livingston Papers, Box 6, Mass. Hist. Soc.

84. *Independent Reflector*, XXXV, July 26, 1753.

85. "Articles of Agreement entered into by the Gentlemen of the Law . . . respecting Clerks," 1756, in Livingston's Book of Precedents, pp. 493-494. "Law Society Agreement as to Clerks," July 1764, William Smith Papers, No. 201. Hamlin, *Legal Education*, pp. 38, 160-161. Hamlin mistakingly believed the James Alexander copy of the 1756 agreement (New-York Historical Society) to be the only one extant.

and they were more liberal than Livingston would have liked: a five-year apprenticeship for those without college training, and a three-year clerkship for college graduates.[86]

With Smith and Scott, Livingston drew up a "Plan for a regulation of the several Rates of Business in the Profession" aimed at preventing fee-cutting wars among the city's better attorneys.[87] He urged reform of the rural courts and higher qualifications for justices of the peace, and when the New York Assembly passed legislation extending the jurisdiction of the local justices, he fought it unsuccessfully all the way to the Privy Council in England.[88] He criticized the delays in the chancery courts, demanded speedier trials in the Supreme Court and the Mayor's Court, and pleaded for improvement in the quality of juries.[89]

In his own office, Livingston provided his clerks with an elementary course of study and an extensive library, a double advantage not extended to most apprentices in colonial New York. The reading program was patterned after the one Livingston had used during his own clerkship. Its prescriptions for studying not merely law but also geography, history, divinity, and rhetoric were intended to "make a compleat Lawyer" and to "contribute their part to the perfecting a Scholar."[90] Livingston's library itself was evidence enough of the catholicity of his literary tastes and the breadth of his intellectual interests. The imperfect remnant which was inventoried in 1790, upon his death, showed over five hundred volumes. Law, political theory, and history made up about half of its contents; the remainder included the classics, poetry, contemporary English and French literature, essays, and science.[91]

The capstone of Livingston's efforts to improve the legal pro-

86. Supreme Court Minute Book, 1766-1769, p. 180 (May 1, 1767).

87. "New York City Bar Agreement Dated November 26, 1756," in Hamlin, *Legal Education*, p. 162. "A Regulation for the Taxation of Costs in the Supream Court . . . ," Aug. 1, 1757, William Smith Papers, IX, Miscellania A.

88. Smith, *History*, I, 311. *Independent Reflector*, XLII, Sept. 13, 1753. *Journal of the Legislative Council of the Colony of New-York [1691-1775]* (Albany, 1861), II, 1323-26. David Jones to Robert Charles, Apr. 26, 1760, William Smith Papers, No. 191. "Draft of Protest agt. the Act to continue the £5 Act," n.d., *ibid.*, No. 197.

89. *Independent Reflector*, XXVIII, XXX, XXXV, June 2, 21, July 26, 1753. "The Watch Tower," XXXVI, *New-York Mercury*, July 28, 1755.

90. "Some Directions relating to the Study of Law," in Livingston's Book of Precedents, pp. 139-142.

91. "List of Books found in the library of his late Excellency William Livingston, Esqr. . . . , [1790?]," Livingston Papers, Box 4, Mass. Hist. Soc.

fession in New York was the law society which he helped to found in 1770 and of which he became the first president. It was "The Moot," patterned after the Moot of Gray's Inn in England. Meetings were professional rather than social, and its regular sessions were devoted to formal debates on technical questions in law and to discussions of large questions of professional policy. Younger members of the bar received there virtually the benefits of a graduate education in law, and veteran lawyers and even justices of the Supreme Court sought the collective judgment of the Moot on knotty legal questions. As a kind of seminar in legal education and an instrument for correcting defects in the province's legal system, the Moot was unique among colonial law societies.[92]

Had Livingston devoted his full energies to his profession, his place in American legal history would now be far more secure than it is. But he spread his abilities capriciously, shifting rapidly from one passionate attachment to another, giving each of his interests a large measure of his creative capacities but neglecting to focus his full talents on any single one. He learned to paint and sketch; he studied foreign languages; he wrote and published poetry—of sufficient importance to make him colonial New York's leading poet; he was an accomplished essayist and journalist and an avid horticulturist; he was a vigorous early exponent of public education.

His liberalism propelled him into the political struggle between the Livingston-Whig party and the De Lancey-Tory faction, and his barbed pen became a potent weapon in the Livingston armory. His anticlericalism spurred him to lead two bitter contests against the Anglican Church, one over the attempts to found King's College under Episcopal control, the other over the proposal to establish an American Episcopate. His affection for the Empire made him a champion of the colonial forces which demanded vigorous prosecution of the French and Indian War; his attachment to America led him to resist, with equal vigor, the postwar measures to tighten the reigns of imperial control. When he retired in 1772 to his country retreat at Elizabethtown, New Jersey, he paused only momentarily before embarking on yet another full career—as a delegate to the Continental Congress, commander of the New Jersey militia, first Governor of the State of New Jersey and its

92. The constitution and the proceedings of the Moot are contained in the "Moot Debating Club Minutes," 1770-1775, in the New-York Historical Society.

political chief through the Revolution, one of the ablest war propagandists on the American side during that conflict, and a member of the Constitutional Convention. And if his legal reputation suffered any neglect, it was merely the happy consequence of his distinction in so many other fields.

XVI

*Legalism versus Revolutionary Doctrine in New England**

RICHARD B. MORRIS

No exposition of New England's intellectual *milieu* in the Revolutionary Era can progress far without being confronted with a significant paradox. That the front rank in leadership in the cause of political independence should have been assumed by a group of men who were largely responsible for bringing America into subjection to the reactionary legal system of England prevailing in the eighteenth century, that Revolutionary ideals should have blossomed in the barren soil of the common law—these are the twin phenomena which challenge historical explanation.

Ever since Edward Burke made the discovery that the "untractable spirit" of the colonists, indicated in their devotion to "liberty according to English ideas and on English principles," was inspired in no small part by the widespread study of the law,[1] historians have assigned to the camp of independence the colonial lawyers, placemen of the crown excepted.[2] Although the lawyers

* "Legalism versus Revolutionary Doctrine in New England," by Richard B. Morris, is reprinted with permission from the *New England Quarterly,* IV (1931), 195-215.

This paper was read at a meeting of the American Historical Association in Boston, December 29, 1931.

1. Hugh Law, Ed., *Burke's Speeches and Letters on American Affairs* (London, 1908), 91, 94, 95.

2. George Bancroft, *History of the United States,* Epoch III, Chapter 37; James Kent, *An Address before the Law Association of the City of New York* (New York, 1836), 14, 15; Lorenzo Sabine, *Biographical Sketches of Loyalists of the American Revolution* (Boston, 1864), I, 59, *et seq.*; George O. Trevelyan, *The American Revolution* (New York, 1899), Part I, 102, 103; Charles A. Beard, *Rise of American Civilization* (New York, 1930), 100-103.

as a group can not fairly be given a distinct party label, they have left for us an anomalous record of their activities.

Too often has the legal practitioner succumbed, in the words of Judge Cardozo, to an "insularity of mind that perceives in every inroad upon habit a catastrophic revolution." In modern American history the members of the bar, with certain notable exceptions, have formed a bulwark of conservatism. It would be difficult to find a parallel in contemporary life to the role which the provincial legal profession, complacently intrenched amid the forces of reaction in eighteenth-century law, played in instigating revolution. For the purposes of this paper, illustrations have been drawn largely from the profession and the practice of the law in Massachusetts.

The seventeenth century in New England is the miraculous era of law without lawyers. While it is true that seventeenth-century codification was effected by men who had had some legal training, the members of the profession in actual practice were inconsequential. Yet the absence of the professional class was to a considerable degree accountable for the liberation of American law from many of the shackles of English medievalism. The reformation of English law in England in the eighteenth century was largely an academic subject confined to pamphlets; in New England it was a real reformation espoused by courts and legislatures. Many of the archaisms of the English procedural law and of the law of evidence were abandoned, and a simplification of legal remedies was effected. Some of these reforms carried over into the following century, and Jeremiah Dummer, in his skillful tract in defence of the New England charters,[3] pays glowing tribute to the facility and economy with which redress might be had in the New England courts as a result of intelligent procedural reforms. The revolt from the common law was clearly seen in the New England legal practices governing the distribution and alienation of land, providing for divisible descent in intestate succession and the assimilation of realty and personalty for that purpose,[4] in a humanizing of the English criminal punishments, particularly in the case of crimes against property, where the influence is directly attribut-

3. Jeremiah Dummer, *A Defence of the New-England Charters* (London, 1721), 37, *et seq.*

4. *The Charters and General Laws of the Colony and Province of Massachusetts Bay* (Boston, 1814), 230-232: Act of 1692; see also Richard B. Morris, *Studies in the History of American Law* (New York, 1930), Chapter II.

able to theological ideals, in a liberal civil divorce law, and in a partial, at least, legal emancipation of the married woman.

The close of the seventeenth century was marked in New England by a conflict in the law between the forces making for change and progress and the forces making for static security and conservation. The compromise which was affected in the eighteenth century was largely a victory for the forces of reaction and brought about the widespread adoption of common-law practices. It marked the removal of the hand of theology from the law and a victory of the secular influences. The basis for this reaction can be found in the new policy of constructive imperialism introduced at the end of the century with the right of royal disallowance and judicial review; and in the growth of the proprietary and mercantile classes, whose influence was directed toward the maintenance of stability and conservatism and toward the adoption of the more technical legal system of England necessitated by the rapid growth of business.

No one factor was more significant in this reaction than the rise and influence of the New England Bar. For several generations the profession's influence had been curbed, and only after many years did it acquire sufficient prestige to break down the barriers of popular distrust.

By the Massachusetts law of 1701 and the Connecticut act of seven years later[5] attorneys were recognized as officers of the courts, and an oath of office was required of them upon admission to practice. The comparatively small number of competent lawyers of scholarship and integrity were outnumbered in all the New England colonies by a host of parasitic pettifoggers, encouraged by the practice of filling writs by sheriffs and their deputies. Shoemakers, wigmakers, and masons procured deputations from the sheriffs and stirred up petty and contemptible litigations.[6] John Adams' own town received especially unpleasant notoriety on this account. "As litigious as Braintree," became proverbial. And

5. *Charters and General Laws*, 369; *Public Records of the Colony of Connecticut* (Hartford, 1850-1890), V, 48.

6. Undoubtedly it was this increase in the litigious spirit which moved the versatile Cotton Mather to project in 1719, in addition to numerous organizations for effective lobbying and for suppressing vice, his Society of Peacemakers, which aimed to "divert Law-suits" and promote arbitration. Samuel Mather, *The Life of the Very Reverend and Learned Cotton Mather* (Boston, 1729), 48, 56.

Adams declaims against "the dirty dabblers in the law."[7] As early as 1730 a Connecticut statute, in order to eliminate this evil, restricted the number of attorneys to eleven, an act which was repealed after a short experiment,[8] and in statutes passed in 1742 and 1758 Massachusetts forbade sheriffs and their deputies from filling writs or giving legal advice.[9] Connecticut passed similar legislation at the same time.[10] Prompted by the instinct of self-preservation, the Bar Association, or the exclusive guild of trained attorneys, was founded in Massachusetts about 1760.[11] "They swarm and multiply," complained Adams only six years later of young attorneys who were seeking admission to the bar.[12] Rather rigid standards were drawn up; for example, the rules determined upon by the bar of Essex County, in 1769, prescribed three years of study with a barrister before admission to the Inferior Court, two more of practice in the lower courts before being admitted to the Superior Court as an attorney, and another two years in practice before the Superior Court as a prerequisite to the status of barrister. A further step to dignify the bench and bar was taken a few years earlier when, in 1762, the pageant of the common law was introduced into the courts of Massachusetts, judges and lawyers clothing themselves in austere judicial gowns and wigs.[13]

The elevation of the trained lawyer in the esteem of the community was accompanied by the growth of his political influence. The political role of the professional lawyers in the first quarter of the eighteenth century had been negligible. They remained obscured by the shadow of the Massachusetts Colony act of 1663, whereby attorneys were forbidden to sit as deputies in the General Court.[14] As late as 1729 Rhode Island introduced this restriction, and although the act was repealed at the next session, it was at

7. Charles Francis Adams, Ed., *The Works of John Adams* (Boston, 1856), II, 92; also 89, 90.

8. *Connecticut Public Records*, VII, 279; 358 (1731).

9. *Charters and General Laws*, 540, 617.

10. *Connecticut Public Records*, VIII, 458-459 (1742).

11. Adams, *Works*, II, 58 *n.*; Charles Warren, *History of the American Bar* (Boston, 1911), 83, *et seq.*; Frank W. Grinnell, *The Commonwealth History of Massachusetts* (New York, 1927-1930), III, 163, 174.

12. Adams, *Works*, II, 197.

13. Adams, *Works*, II, 133 *n.* Two years later this practice was emulated in the New York Supreme Court. New York Public Library: The William Smith Papers.

14. *Records of Massachusetts* (Boston, 1853), II, 279; *Charters and General Laws*, 98.

various times reintroduced.[15] "I do not recollect," writes Thomas Hutchinson, "that the town of Boston ever chose a lawyer to represent it under the second charter, until the year 1738, when Mr. John Read was chosen . . . Lawyers have ever since taken the lead, and been much employed in the publick measures of this, and of the other colonies, and of the continental congresses."[16]

The trained hand of the lawyer was soon apparent in the large-scale reception of the English legal system. Following a century distinguished for revolutionary legislation, the eighteenth century in England was, from the point of view of the output of statutes, virtually stagnant. Law reform was chiefly directed by way of Chancery rather than through common-law channels. Uninfluenced, in the main, by liberative currents, the English lawyer concerned himself with formalism and metaphysical subtlety, and looked upon the law and the constitution as a system of "petrified perfection" and finality. The English system of pleading, which was introduced in New England, is prime evidence of this condition. This system, according to Maitland, "forced our common law into a prison-house from which escape was difficult,"—and no less so in America than in England.

According to all accounts, the early lawyers in New England seemed to take malevolent delight in confounding the court with technical distinctions and in seizing every opening to wrangle over trivialities.[17] While at the turn of the century there was no disposition to encourage special pleading, its introduction, contrary to the spirit of previous procedure, is attributed to Paul Dudley and John Read.[18] By the Revolutionary Era, where a captain of militia was sued as a "yeoman" instead of a "gentleman,"[19] or

15. S. G. Arnold, *History of Rhode Island* (New York, 1859-1860), II, 98; *Rhode Island Colonial Records* (Providence, 1856-1865), IV, 430.

16. Thomas Hutchinson, *History of Massachusetts Bay* (London, 1828), III, 104 *n.*; G. B. Reed, *Life of John Read* (Boston, 1903); Justin Winsor, Ed., *A Memorial History of Boston* (Boston, 1887), IV, 571, *et seq.* In 1731, Connecticut exempted attorneys from militia duty. *Connecticut Public Records*, VII, 344, 345.

17. Train *vs.* Parks (1723), MSS. Massachusetts Superior Court of Judicature (1721-1725), Folios 94, 95, and MSS. files, No. 13, 734 (3); William D. Northend, *Address before the Essex Bar Association, December 8, 1885* (Salem 1885), 40, 41.

18. Joseph Willard, *An Address to the Members of the Bar of Worcester County, Massachusetts, October 2, 1829* (Lancaster, Mass., 1830), 32.

19. Bromfield *vs.* Lovejoy (1767) Josiah Quincy, Jr. (Samuel H. Quincy, Ed.), *Reports of Cases . . . in the Superior Court . . . of Massachusetts Bay, 1761-1772* (Boston, 1865), 237; also Spooner *vs.* Burt, Hampshire Common Pleas (1762), 33.

where the exact distinction in name or place was not entirely sufficient to avoid the slightest ambiguity, the writ would abate. Rights and duties were often based upon the quicksands of such hairsplitting distinctions.[20] Despite Otis's plea that "abatements at this day are rather odious than favored,"[21] he was as adept in the use of the plea as any attorney in the Province.[22] In their efforts to obliterate all vestiges of the heretical practices of the previous century, the legal profession, under the leadership of John Read, banished the informal action on the case for the recovery of real property;[23] but instead of adopting the more modern personal action of ejectment to try title to realty, they resorted to the ancient writs of entry and other real actions, which were obsolete in the mother country.[24] In their assiduous devotion to the principles of the common law, they evinced a conservatism in real property law which shocked even Chief Justice Hutchinson, and resulted in the perpetuation of primogeniture in entailed estates.[25] The Bar in New England appears to have deserted the cause of economic liberalism, leaving the field in the Revolutionary Era to the Church. Contrary to the spirit of these decisions were the New England sermons in this period, urging the equitable division of property and free tenure of land in order that "the landed interest" might not be "engrossed by a

20. New England was by no means the only offender. In the middle and southern colonies technicalities often obstructed the course of justice. Anderson *vs.* Livre Cognau (1714) MSS. Mayor's Court (New York City) Records (1710-1715), Folio 448; Slye *vs.* Bowlings Executors (1698) MSS. Maryland Court of Appeals Records, H. D. No. 1, Folios 136-147; Lynes *vs.* Rozier (1710) *ibid.*, Folios 180-187. On the other hand, the Massachusetts Act of 1701, providing that circumstantial errors should not cause an abatement (*Charters and General Laws*, 364), was anticipated in more general terms by the Virginia law of 1658 (Hening, *Statutes of Virginia*, I, 486); and the southern colonies in the eighteenth century appear to have been far ahead of New England in the development of summary civil procedure. *Yale Law Journal*, XXVIII (1928-1929), R. W. Millar, "Three American Ventures in Summary Civil Procedure," 195-197; 215.

21. Zuill *vs.* Bradley (1762); Ballard *vs.* McLean (1764), Quincy, *Reports*, 6, 106.

22. Adams, *Works*, II, 70, 71.

23. See also Tyler *vs.* Richards (1765), where, despite laxity of pleading in the past, the court construes *indebitatus assumpsit* strictly; see also Pynchon Executor *vs.* Brewster (1766), Quincy, *Reports*, 195, 224.

24. Asahel Stearns, *A Summary of the Law and Practice of Real Actions* (Hallowell, 1831), 74, 75, 78, 463; Willard, *Worcester Bar*, 37; James D. Hopkins, *An Address to the Members of the Cumberland Bar* (Portland, 1833), 23.

25. Baker *vs.* Mattocks (1763), Quincy, *Reports*, 69; and other cases analyzed in Norris, *Studies*, 95, *et seq.*

few."[26] Further testimony to the extent of the legal reaction is found in the restoration of the technical rules of evidence at common law, especially those listing various types of experiential incapacity and restricting hearsay evidence within fixed limits.[27] The humanizing forces in the early criminal law were counteracted now by increases in the penalties for crimes against property in emulation of the harsh English statutes.[28] To offset this, another archaic practice, the privilege of clergy, was introduced.[29] But the claim was seldom raised, and the Boston Massacre brought forth legislation depriving persons of "clergy" in the capital offense of burglary.[30] Finally, the grounds upon which absolute divorces were granted, as a matter of practice, at least in Massachusetts, were sharply curtailed.[31]

The question might pertinently be raised whether the lawyers who embraced the cause of independence likewise sought to liberalize the private law in the course of their practice. The records of the Superior Court of Judicature of Massachusetts for the Revolutionary Era reveal no evidence of this. The reactionary side was argued by the so-called radical lawyers without any apparent qualms of conscience, and arguments in favor of economic reform and of breaking with the common law came from the mouths of men who were later known as loyalists.[32] However, in the *causes célèbres,*

26. See Morris, *Studies*, 97; Alice M. Baldwin, *The New England Clergy and the American Revolution* (Durham, N. C., 1928), 128.

27. Nathan Dane, *Abridgment and Digest of American Law* (Boston, 1823), VI, 404, *et seq.*; Adams, *Works*, II, 138; Wrentham Proprietors *vs.* Metcalf (1763), Wiswall *vs.* Hall (1763), Quincy, *Reports*, 36, 27; Morris, *Studies*, 59, 60.

28. Larceny: Compare Massachusetts act of 1646 with subsequent acts of 1692, 1716, and 1736. *Charters and General Laws*, 57, 238, 415, 509. Robbery: Compare acts of 1642 and 1647 with later acts of 1711 and 1761. *Ibid.*, 56, 392, 644. Compare also Hutchinson's charge to the Grand Jury (1768), Quincy, *Reports*, 260, 261, and "Diary of John Quincy Adams," 2 *Procs.* Mass. Hist. Soc., XVI, 313, 318; also Edward Field, Ed., *State of Rhode Island and Providence Plantations* (Boston and Syracuse, 1902), III, 433, 436.

29. Quincy, *Reports*, 53 *n.*; John Adams, *Works*, II, 534; Emory Washburn, *Judicial History of Massachusetts* (Boston, 1840), 194.

30. *Procs.* Mass. Hist. Soc., LXI, 154-181: A. L. Cross, "Benefit of Clergy in American Criminal Law"; *Acts and Resolves*, V, 64, 65.

31. Adultery is the principal ground for divorce in the suits found in "Divorce, 1760-1784," MS. Volume in the Suffolk Court House, Boston, Massachusetts. Cf. especially Ford *vs.* Ford (1771), *ibid.*, Folios 66-68.

32. Baker *vs.* Mattocks (1763); and compare especially as regards Otis's position with Banister *vs.* Henderson (1765), and Dudley *vs.* Dudley et al. (1762); Elwell *vs.* Pierson (1763); Oliver *vs.* Sale (1762), Quincy, *Reports*, 69, 119, 140, 12, 42, and 29.

involving the great constitutional issues, the division in the ranks was patent. The brilliant, impassioned, and unstable Otis and his amiable associate, Oxenbridge Thacher, the author of *Sentiments of a British American* (1764), were retained by the merchants of Boston and Salem to argue against the legality of the Writs of Assistance in the Paxton's Case.[33] It was John Adams who argued the suit for a penalty against a custom-house officer for taking greater fees than were allowed by law. Again Adams and Otis, together with Gridley, patriarch of the bar, represented Boston at the time of the Stamp Act in support of a petition before the Governor and Council requesting the opening of the courts. The defence of Warren, implicated in the Berkshire Riots, devolved upon the leader of the Whig cause in western Massachusetts, Joseph Hawley, a scholar and man of integrity.[34] And Otis and Adams again joined forces in 1769 in the Court of Vice-Admiralty in defence of Michael Corbet and three other sailors charged with killing Lieutenant Panton.[35]

A second question logically arises: did the lawyers, as a group, embrace the cause of independence, and, if not, what were the motives which can account for the schism? In the early sixties the Massachusetts Bar was united. Its meetings were so harmonious that Pratt, when about to leave its happy atmosphere for the less felicitous chief-justiceship in New York, advised his colleagues: "Brethren, above all things, forsake not the assembling of yourselves."[36] John Adams, in his diary for January, 1765, gives an account of the founding of Sodalitas, a club of Boston lawyers organized to discuss and study legal problems, and comprising Adams, Fitch, Dudley, Otis, Thacher, and Auchmuty,[37] two of whose members later became pronounced loyalists; and this informal organization can be paralleled in other colonies.

The passage of the Stamp Act served further to cement the bonds of unity within the profession. Lawyers looked upon that measure as a deliberate attack upon them. The courts of justice

33. (1761), Quincy, *Reports*, 51.

34. (1767), Quincy, *Reports*, 248; See also Hawley MSS., New York Public Library and files of the *Boston Evening-Post* for 1767.

35. Adams, *Works*, II, 224-226, 526-534; Hutchinson, *History of Massachusetts Bay*, III, 231.

36. Adams, *Works*, II, 58 *n.*

37. Adams, *Works*, II, 146, *et seq.* Six of the ten members of the Bar whom Adams mentions as dining together in 1769 later because loyalists. *Ibid.*, 221, 223.

were closed and clients vanished. Debtors grew insolent, creditors furious, and lawyers poorer.[38] Even Jared Ingersoll of Connecticut, who was later convinced of the propriety of the Stamp Act, and became a stamp distributor, helped prepare anticipatory arguments against the measure.[39]

When the initial wave of resentment subsided, many lawyers refused to follow John Adams and his colleagues in their resistance to the Declaratory Act and later measures, and gradually attached themselves to the prerogative side. Friendships were broken, and recrimination supplanted harmony. Of the twenty-six barristers practising before the Superior Court of Judicature in 1762,[40] ten joined the loyalist side during the War of Independence. According to the conservative estimates of Sullivan,[41] out of thirty-six barristers and twelve attorneys who were practising in the Province at the outbreak of the war, thirteen were loyalists. These figures can not be reconciled with the fact that twenty-four barristers and attorneys of the Province signed the testimonial to Governor Hutchinson, May 30, 1774, evincing upon his removal their respect and esteem.[42] And a careful survey reveals that at least twenty-five, or about one-half, of the lawyers in the Colony can definitely be listed on the side of the Crown.[43] The depleted ranks were rapidly replenished by attorneys recruited from the patriotic party. Between the years 1775 and 1784, forty-three attorneys were admitted to the bar, only ten less than the total number admitted between 1731 and 1772, and almost twice the number gaining admission during the first thirty years of the eighteenth century.[44]

In determining a motive for the action of the loyalist members of the bar, the facts leave us little choice. Referring in his *Speech on Conciliation*, to the training of Americans in the law, Burke submitted, with a broad hint, the idea that "when great honors

38. Adams, *Works*, II, 155, 156.

39. L. H. Gipson, *Jared Ingersoll* (New Haven, 1920), 124.

40. Quincy, *Reports*, 35.

41. William Sullivan, *An Address to the Members of the Bar of Suffolk County, Massachusetts, March, 1824* (Boston, 1825), 38-39..

42. Peter Force, *American Archives* (Washington, 1837-1846), Series Four, I, 363.

43. Mills and Hicks, *British and American Register, with an Almanack for the year 1775* (Boston, 1774), 60; E. A. Jones, *Loyalists of Massachusetts* (London, 1930), Chapters XIII and XIV, 315, 316, whose listings need slight correction.

44. "List of Attorneys" in Supreme Judicial Court, Boston, Massachusetts.

and great emoluments do not win this knowledge to the service of the state, it is a formidable adversary of government." Crown officials in New England hardly needed this suggestion. A thinly disguised attempt to win the bar to the prerogative side manifested itself in royal *largesse* bountifully bestowed upon the profession. In this way, Adams charges, three of his most intimate friends, Jonathan Sewall, Samuel Quincy, and Daniel Leonard, were "seduced from his bosom" by Hutchinson.[45] Sewall, a brilliant and engaging lawyer, switched to the prerogative side when the Otises evidenced opposition in the General Court toward a private petition which he sponsored. Not being a man of wealth, the successive positions which fell to him—Solicitor-General, Advocate-General, and the lucrative posts of Judge of Vice-Admiralty and Attorney-General—completed the conversion.[46] When, in 1769, Hutchinson planned to procure the Attorney-Generalship for John Worthington with an increase in salary from £200 to £300 a year, he insinuated by way of inducement: "I fancy there is more in it than is generally known, *or Sewall would not be so fond of it*."[47] Robert Auchmuty, a ranking member of the Massachusetts bar, who, in historic memorials, has suffered unduly from the vitriolic pen of Adams, received the post of Advocate-General and succeeded Chambers Russell as Judge of the Vice-Admiralty Court. The annual compensation of £600 for the latter office may well have been attractive to one who continually "scolded and railed" about the comparative lowness of attorney's fees.[48] Another distinguished loyalist, James Putnam, the most noted lawyer in Worcester County and the preceptor of John Adams, was the last Attorney-General of Massachusetts under the Crown. Nor was this policy pursued merely to reward loyalist proclivities. Negotiations were carried on with the most prominent lawyers of the Whig cause. In 1768 Adams, for example, refused the Advocate-Generalship.[49] Hutchinson insinuates that in the Boston Massacre Case, Captain Preston and the soldiers, who engaged John Adams and Josiah Quincy, were told "to stick at no reasonable fee for that purpose," although it is clear

45. Adams, *Works*, X, 194, 231.

46. *Ibid.*, II, 78, 251; James H. Stark, *Loyalists of Massachusetts* (Boston, 1907), 454, 457; Jones, *Loyalists of Massachusetts*, 258, 259.

47. G. A. Ward, Ed., *The Journal and Letters of Samuel Curwen, an American in England, 1775-1783* (Boston, 1864), 677.

48. Adams, *Works*, II, 197, 198; Jones, *Loyalists*, 12-17; Stark, *Loyalists*, 301-305.

49. *Ibid.*, II, 210, 211.

that the actual compensation which these two courageous men received was a trifle in comparison with the services they rendered.[50] Of the twenty-five loyalist lawyers, at least seventeen were, prior to the War of Independence, important placemen of the Crown,[51] and not less than four others, including the author of *Massachusettensis,* were subsequently rewarded with valuable appointments in Canada or the West Indies.

Finally, social and family ties stand out as appreciable influences in effecting the secession from the ranks of the Revolutionary lawyers. On the loyalist side, the Olivers intermarried with the Hutchinsons; the Lyndes were related to the Olivers; the Putnams were allied by marriage with the Chandlers; the Blisses and the Uphams with the Murrays; and Boutineau's son-in-law was the perpetrator of the infamous attack on Otis—to mention a few instances.

Many circumstances following the passage of the Stamp Act served to keep the Whig lawyers united in their resistance to the power of the prerogative. Imputations of sordid motives, raised by loyalist historians, have carried little conviction. The charge was commonly made against James Otis that his subsequent public course was dictated solely by revenge for his father's disappointment at not being made Chief Justice. This allegation, as Josiah Quincy aptly suggests, "may be classed with Disraeli's insinuation that John Hampden's refusal to pay ship money was occasioned by an ancient grudge against the sheriff who levied it."[52] Adams, according to Hutchinson, was resentful at the failure of Governor Bernard to award him a justiceship of the peace.[53] Hawley, temporarily disbarred from practising before the Superior Court because of his communication to the press in the Berkshire Riot Case, was charged by the Lieutenant-Governor with bearing toward him special animus.[54] The thesis that Whig and Tory lawyers were engaged in legal feuds in their private practice is even more tenuous. Isolated instances may be found. Ruggles divided the practice of the law in Sandwich with the elder Otis and later became the younger Otis's opponent in the General Court;[55] and

50. *Ibid.*, II, 231.

51. W. H. Whitmore, Ed., *The Massachusetts Civil List* (Albany, 1870).

52. Quincy, *Reports*, 411.

53. Hutchinson, *History*, III, 296, 297. This charge was completely refuted by Adam's own account of Sewall's bid.

54. Hutchinson, *History*, III, 175; E. D. Brown, MS. Life of Joseph Hawley.

55. Adams, *Works*, II, 67, and *n.*; William Tudor, *The Life of James Otis* (Boston, 1823), 231, 232.

Worthington was generally on the opposing side of lawsuits brought by Hawley in Hampshire.[56] It is perfectly clear, however, that the Whig lawyers became increasingly resentful of a policy which systematically discriminated against them in the award of lucrative and influential places to men of no greater competence, a policy which culminated in the unwise nepotism of the clan Hutchinson. Adams complains: "Is not this amazing ascendancy of one family foundation sufficient on which to erect a tyranny? Is it not enough to excite jealousies among the people?"[57]

An incalculable influence in directing the energies of the Whig lawyers toward the curtailment of the power of the prerogative, particularly in admiralty, was their retention by the merchants. Gridley, Thacher, Otis, Adams, Kent, Dana, and Hawley numbered the influential merchants among their clients. In defending their clients against informations for smuggling, the Whig lawyers raised the great constitutional defences, such as that of John Adams in the Hancock prosecution in the case of the Sloop *Liberty*. After James Otis's Writs of Assistance speech in 1761, the Hancocks lost no opportunity in recommending him as a lawyer to their commercial associates in England having business transactions here. Hutchinson writes that Otis and Adams, men who "had no concern with commerce," "mixed with merchants and had great influence among them." More directly, Peter Oliver, in 1784, charged that Otis "engrafted his self in the Body of Smugglers, and they embraced him so close, as a Lawyer and an usefull Pleader for them that he soon became incorporated with them."[58] John Rowe, among others, on frequent occasions retained Otis, Adams, and even Hawley, whose clients for the most part were farmers and artisans. And yet, after handling John Hancock's legal affairs for three or four years, Adams, in 1772, learned to his chagrin that his client had purchased twenty writs from Samuel Quincy, the Tory, and was inspired to lament on the mutability of the legal and commercial world.[59]

56. E. D. Brown, Life of Hawley (MS.).

57. Adams, *Works*, II, 150, 151.

58. British Museum: Egerton MSS., No. 2671 (Library of Congress Transcripts).

59. Bishop *vs.* Brig "Freemason" (1763); Sewall *vs.* Hancock (1768), Quincy, *Reports*, 387, 457; Adams, *Works*, II, 215, 306; A. E. Brown, *John Hancock: his Book* (Boston, 1898), 33; Hutchinson, *History*, III, 89, 201; *Letters of John Rowe*, 27, 28; E. D. Brown, Life of Hawley (MS.).

The Records of the Court of Vice-Admiralty in the Province of Massachusetts Bay, available in the Supreme Judicial Court, throw scant light on this

To treat here the evolution of the constitutional principles of the Whig lawyers, would be a work of supererogation; but from a consideration of their social and intellectual *milieu*, the operation is apparent whereby the reactionary common law was used as a weapon for effecting constitutional emancipation and local autonomy.[60] By strict adherence to the historic common law, these lawyers disputed the authority of the prerogative courts, notably admiralty,[61] challenged the Navigation Acts upheld therein, opposed the introduction in these courts of a legal system foreign to the common law, contested the denial of trial by jury,[62] and denied the right of judges to hold office during the pleasure of the King.[63] They buttressed their arguments with citations of rare common-law and statutory sources. Adams imported from London a set of the British Statutes at Large, which he erroneously believed to be the only complete set available throughout the colonies. Rather than have an English statute relating to impressment in America disclosed, the court in Lieutenant Panton's case, Adams charges, permitted the action to be dismissed.[64] When, in 1774, the question was raised of instituting in the House of Representatives impeach-

question for the Revolutionary Era. The five MS. volumes available, cover the periods, 1718-1726, 1726-1733, 1739-1745, 1743-1765, and 1765-1772. This last volume is merely a minute book of little value and the names of the proctors are not mentioned. Likewise the file papers of the Superior Court of Judicature on the eve of the Revolution are stereotyped and unilluminating in character. For lawyers employed in Connecticut admiralty cases, see Hough, *Cases in Vice-Admiralty and Admiralty* (New Haven, 1925), and New York Public Library admiralty papers. For Rhode Island, see transcript of proceedings in the Vice-Admiralty Court, 1756-1758, Library of Congress.

60. *Harvard Law Review*, XLII (1928), E. S. Corwin, "The 'Higher Law' Background of American Constitutional Law," 401.

61. Scollay *vs.* Dunn, Quincy, *Reports*, 74; MSS. Massachusetts Supreme Court Judicature (1763-1764), Folio 107.

62. The loyalists who sought redress in a court of law, according to Daniel Leonard, "had the whole Whig interest to combat; they gathered like a cloud and hovered like harpies around the seat of justice." No greater evidence of this political dictatorship of justice could be found, Leonard felt, than in the grand and petit juries. "It is difficult to account for so many of the first rate whigs being returned to serve on the petit-jury at the term next after extraordinary insurrections, without supposing some legerdemain in drawing their names out of the box. It is certain, that, notwithstanding swarms of the most virulent libels infested the province, and there were so many riots and insurrections, scarce one offender was indicted, and I think not one convicted and punished." *Massachusettensis* (London, 1776), 21, 22, 70, 71. This charge John Adams vigorously refutes: *Works*, IV, 73, "Novanglus."

63. Joseph Hawley MSS., New York Public Library, for Hawley's indebtedness to John Adams (Folio 87).

64. Adams, *Works*, II, 224-226; IX, 317-319; X, 204-210.

ment proceedings against the judges, Hawley was instructed by Adams in the precedents afforded in his volumes of *State Trials* and the works of Selden.[65] At one time Adams threw the court into confusion by quoting from Moore's *Reports*, which he believed no man in the Province at that time had ever read,[66] and in the trying days of September, 1775, Hawley wrote Mrs. Adams that "the Publick have great need of two volumes of Mr. Adams English Statutes at Large containing the acts of 27 Edw. II and 32 Hen. VIII."[67] With one hand, Adams, in his *Novanglus*, repudiates the common law, with the other he draws most heavily upon common-law precedents in support of his revolutionary point of view and demands for the colonists the liberties of the British Constitution.

That their constitutional position was not an inescapable consequence of their exposure to the common law, it is only fair to conclude. In England the legal profession was solidly arrayed on the side of imperialism,[68] and there is no doubt but that, as Jefferson testifies, many young American lawyers, "seduced by the honeyed Mansfieldism of Blackstone, began to slide into Toryism." Yet it does seem that the Whig lawyers acted with plausible consistency in erecting a code of political liberalism upon the legal foundations of social reaction to which they were devoutly attached. In reality they were fighting for the common law and the common law remained inviolate.[69] Save for minor reforms, such as the abolition of slavery and a slight modification of the laws of descent and distribution, the War of Independence had virtually no effect upon the system of private law administered in New England. Technical pleadings, ancient real actions, unenlightened penal conditions, inequitable rules relating to legal persons survived.[70] In the decade that followed, the legal profession, which had hailed the common

65. *Ibid.*, II, 330.

66. Adams, *Works*, II, 313.

67. *Ibid.*, II, 336.

68. D. M. Clark, *British Opinion and the American Revolution* (New Haven, 1930), 186. Occasional English arguments on the American side of the constitutional issue are discussed in *Political Science Quarterly*, XLV (1930), 548-579: C. F. Mullett, "English Imperial Thinking, 1764-1783."

69. This veneration for the Constitution and the law is one of the chief characteristics of eighteenth-century English Whiggery. W. A. Holdsworth, *Some Lessons from our Legal History* (New York, 1928), 97.

70. See *Collections*, Mass. Hist. Soc., 72, *The Warren-Adams Letters*, I, 234-236 for the letter of Abigail Adams to Mercy Warren, Braintree, April 27, 1776; and Adams to Sullivan, May 26, 1776, Adams, *Works*, IX, 375.

law as the guardian of constitutional rights, now defended it as the protector of creditors' privileges.[71]

71. On constitutional questions it is clear that a minority, led in Massachusetts by Joseph Hawley, favored more extensive social and political reform. See M. C. Clune, Ed., *Smith College Studies in History* (Northampton, 1917), III, No. 1: "Joseph Hawley's Criticism of the Constitution of Massachusetts"; Hawley MSS., New York Public Library. On the economic side, the paper-money party was successful in winning over a number of prominent attorneys, although Trevett *vs.* Weeden undoubtedly represents the sentiment of the New England bar as a whole. John Bach McMaster, *History of the United States* (New York, 1883), I, 338, *et seq.* Illustrative of the public distrust of the conservatism of the bar are the expressions in *Providence Gazette,* March 15, 1778, and the legislative action recorded in *Rhode Island Colonial Records,* X, 271.

XVII

*The Process of Outlawry in New York: A Study of the Selective Reception of English Law**

MARK DeWOLFE HOWE

It has been said that "one of the chief difficulties confronting a student of our legal history is that the whole subject of the reception of English law, both common and statutory, was not thought out in any consistent way, but was left unsettled and in the air."[1] It is doubtless true that during the colonial period the selective reception and discriminating rejection of English law had, in large part, been the product of empiricism, and that coherent theory had done little to clarify the nature of the process.[2] Some of the colonies, however, were aware of the importance of the problem. The preamble to an act of the Provincial Assembly of South Carolina of 1712 recited that "many of the statute laws of the Kingdom of England or South Britain, by reason of the different way of agriculture and the differing productions of the earth of this Province from that of England, are altogether useless, and many others, (which otherwise are very good) either by reason of their limitation to particular places, or because in themselves they are only executive

* "The Process of Outlawry in New York: A Study of the Selective Reception of English Law," by Mark DeWolfe Howe, is reprinted with permission from the *Cornell Law Quarterly*, XXIII (1937-1938), 559-573. Copyright 1938 by Cornell University.

1. Cardozo, C. J., in Beers v. Hotchkiss, 256 N. Y. 41, 54; 175 N. E. 506 (1931).

2. See REINSCH, *The English Common Law in the Early American Colonies* in 1 SELECT ESSAYS IN ANGLO-AMERICAN LEGAL HISTORY (1907) 367; Pope, *English Common Law in the United States* (1910) 24 HARV. L. REV. 6; Dale, *The Adoption of the Common Law by the American Colonies* (1882) 21 AM. L. REG. (N. S.) 554; MORRIS, STUDIES IN THE HISTORY OF AMERICAN LAW (1930).

by such nominal officers as are not in or suitable for the Constitution of this Government, are thereby become impracticable here."[3] The legislature, recognizing this situation, re-enacted one hundred and sixty-seven British statutes which, upon the recommendation of Chief Justice Nicholas Trott, were found to be applicable to the condition of the colony.[4] The tenth section of the act by which these laws were received within the colony provided that "all the statute laws of the Kingdom of England which are not enumerated and made of force in this Province by this act . . . are hereby declared impracticable in this Province."[5] Three years later the legislature of North Carolina made a similar, though far less thorough, effort to accomplish the same purpose, and in general descriptive terms listed the British statutes which were to be treated as operative in the Province.[6]

In other colonies where no conscious effort to specify the operative English statutes was made, the process of reception was summarized by generalizations.[7] In 1774, Governor Tryon of the Province of New York reported to the King that "the common law of England is considered as the fundamental law of the Province, and it is the received doctrine that all the statutes (not local in their nature, and which can be fitly applied to the circumstances of the Colony) enacted before the Province had a legislature, are binding on the Colony. . . ."[8] Rebellious Americans, though they

3. Stat. No. 322, 2 Statutes at Large of South Carolina, p. 401.

4. *Ibid.* A valuable discussion of this legislation may be found in McCRADY, HISTORY OF SOUTH CAROLINA UNDER THE PROPRIETARY GOVERNMENT, 1670-1719 (1897) pp. 247-248, 517 *et seq.*

5. *Ibid.*

6. Laws of North Carolina, 1715, Ch. 31, Sec. 7. This act provided that "all statute Laws of England, made for maintaining the Queen's Royal Prerogative, and the Security of her Royal Person, and Succession of the Crown, and all such Laws made for the Establishment of the Church, and the Laws made for the Indulgence of *Protestant* Dissenters, and all Laws providing for the Privilege of the People, and Security of Trade; as also, all Statute Laws made for limitation of Actions, and preventing of vexatious Law Suits, and for preventing Immorality and Fraud, and confirming Inheritances and Titles of Land, are and shall be in Force here, although this Province, or the plantations in general, are not therein named."

7. We are not here concerned with the analogous though essentially dissimilar problem of determining which British statutes, enacted after the foundation of the colonies, were there applicable. That that problem was one of which the colonists were aware is evidenced by such legislation as that of New York in 1767 by which a series of recent English statutes were extended to the province. 4 COLONIAL LAWS OF NEW YORK, 953 (Ch. 1327).

8. 1 DOCUMENTARY HISTORY OF NEW YORK (1849) 752, 754.

might find the general formula adequate, not surprisingly changed the emphasis of its implications. In the Declaration of Civil Rights of the Continental Congress it was asserted that "the respective colonies are entitled to the common law of England . . . [and] to the benefit of such English statutes as existed at the time of their colonization; and which they have, by experience, respectively found to be applicable to their several local and other circumstances."[9]

Such generalizations as these survived the revolution and acquired constitutional dignity. The thirty-fifth article of the New York Constitution of 1777, as finally adopted, provided that "such parts of the common law of England, and of the statute law of England and Great Britain, and of the acts of the legislature of the Colony of New York, as together did form the law of the said colony on the nineteenth of April in the year of our Lord one thousand, seven hundred and seventy-five, shall be and continue the law of this State, subject to such alterations and provisions as the legislature of this State shall, from time to time, make concerning the same."[10] The sweeping simplicity of this language inevitably concealed important and difficult questions,—just those questions which during the colonial period had been left "unsettled and in the air." What portion of the common law, and precisely which statutes had formed part of the colonial law on April 19, 1775? Who was to decide these issues, the legislature, the courts, or the legal scholars of the future?

The New York legislature in 1786 endeavored to answer certain of these questions. The preamble to an act of that year recited that "such of the said [English] statutes as have been generally supposed to extend to the late Colony, and to this State, are contained in a great number of volumes; and those statutes . . . are conceived in a stile and language improper to appear in the statute books of this state."[11] Because it was deemed desirable that some definition of

9. 1 JOURNALS OF THE CONTINENTAL CONGRESS, 1774-1789 (W. C. Ford ed. 1904) 69.

10. As originally introduced in the convention the clause provided for the reception of the common law *in toto.* It provided that "the Common Law of England and so much of the Statute Law of England and Great Britain as have heretofore been adopted in practice in this State . . . shall until altered or repealed by a future Legislature of this State continue to operate and be of force and effect." The changes made in the final draft were adopted from an amendment offered by Robert Yates. 1 LINCOLN'S CONSTITUTIONAL HISTORY OF NEW YORK (1906) 540-541.

11. 1786 N. Y. Laws, c. 35.

the operative British statutes should be made, and that language and style should be adapted to local needs and tastes, it was enacted that Samuel Jones[12] and Richard Varick,[13] Esquires, should "reduce into proper form under certain heads or titles of bills all the said statutes . . . and lay the same bills before the legislature . . . to the intent that when the same shall be completed . . . none of the statutes of England or of Great Britain shall operate or be considered as laws of this State."[14] The two men were also to submit for re-enactment any colonial acts which were believed to have been in force when the revolution started. Finally they were to publish these re-enacted laws, together with such additional statutes as might in the interval be passed by the legislature.[15] Although the Jones and Varick revision was not published until 1789, the heaviest portion of their work was apparently performed within the allotted time of two years. During the sessions of 1787 and 1788 many English statutes were adopted by the legislature,[16] and in 1788 it was enacted that after the first of May, 1789, "none of the statutes of England or of Great Britain shall operate or be considered as laws of the State."[17] This legislative elimination of English statutory law was made permanent by the second state constitution of 1821.[18]

The work of Jones and Varick was not unparalleled. We have seen that South and North Carolina during the colonial period had each endeavored to accomplish the same purpose. With political independence achieved it was natural that renewed attempts to limit and define the operative British statutes should be made.

12. See 10 DICTIONARY OF AMERICAN BIOGRAPHY (1933) 197.

13. See 19 DICTIONARY OF AMERICAN BIOGRAPHY (1936) 226.

14. N. Y. Laws 1786, c. 35, Sec. 1.

15. *Ibid.* Section 2.

16. In Harmon v. Peats Co., 216 App. Div. 368, 214 N. Y. Supp. 353 (1926), *reversed on other grounds*, 243 N. Y. 473, 154 N. E. 314 (1926), it was held that the English Statute of Frauds, which had constituted part of the common law of the Province, had not, for conflict of laws purposes, become statutory law by its specific re-enactment on the recommendation of Jones and Varick in 1787. *Cf.* Burns Mortgage Co. v. Fried, 292 U. S. 487, 54 Sup. Ct. 813, 78 L. ed. 1380 (1934).

17. N. Y. Laws 1788, c. 46, Sec. 37.

18. By Section 13 of Article Seven of the Constitution of 1821 it was provided that "such parts of the common law and of the acts of the legislature of the colony of New York as together did form the law of the said colony on the nineteenth day of April one thousand seven hundred and seventy-five . . . and such acts of the legislature of this state as are now in force shall be and continue the law of this state. . . ." It is, of course, noticeable that this section nowhere mentions the statutory law of England.

In 1776 the Virginia Assembly appointed a commission of five, among whom was Thomas Jefferson, whose duty it was to submit to the legislature for revision and enactment such statutes, British and local, as were believed to be desirable.[19] Three of the commissioners carried out the task, and in 1779 submitted the laws which they had chosen.[20] During the sessions of 1785 and 1786 the most important of the bills were enacted, but their passage was spasmodic, and in 1786 it was necessary to appoint a special committee to consider those bills which had not yet been enacted into law.[21] In North Carolina there was published in 1792, at the request of the legislature, a volume of those English statutes which were believed to have been operative there prior to the revolution.[22] The preface to this volume expressed vividly the American desire to destroy, so far as possible, the British legal inheritance. The day was fondly anticipated when the people would "shake off this last seeming badge, and mortifying memento" of dependence on England.[23] The process of statutory specification continued into the nineteenth century. In 1807 the legislature of Pennsylvania requested the judges of the Supreme Court to determine which English statutes were then in force.[24] The judges' report was presented to the legislature in the following year, and was accompanied by a revealing introductory explanation of the character of the work

19. 9 HENING, STATUTES AT LARGE 175. The preamble contains an interesting recital of the reasons for the legislation: "*Whereas* on the late change which hath of necessity been introduced into the form of government in this country it is become also necessary to make corresponding changes in the laws heretofore in force, many of which are inapplicable to the powers of government now organized, others are founded on principles heterogeneous to the republican spirit, others which, long before such change, had been oppressive to the people, could yet never be repealed while the regal power continued, and others, having taken their origin while our ancestors remained in Britain, are not so well adapted to our present circumstances of time and place, and it is also necessary to introduce certain other laws, which, though proved by the experience of other states to be friendly to liberty and the rights of mankind, we have not heretofore been permitted to adopt. . . ."

20. See 12 HENING, preface. Also see Jefferson's account of the commission's work in his *Autobiography*, (P. L. Ford ed. 1914) p. 66 *et seq*. The three revisers were Jefferson, George Wythe, and Edmund Pendleton. George Mason and Thomas L. Lee, not being lawyers, excused themselves from taking part in preparing the revision. *Ibid.* p. 68.

21. 12 HENING, 409.

22. FRANCIS-XAVIER MARTIN, COLLECTION OF THE STATUTES OF THE PARLIAMENT OF ENGLAND IN FORCE IN THE STATE OF NORTH CAROLINA (1792).

23. *Ibid.* p. iv.

24. 8 STATUTES AT LARGE OF PA. p. 418. (Ch. 1831).

which had been done.[25] Shortly after the revolution a similar program of reception was instituted in Maryland.[26] It finally bore fruit in 1811 in the publication by Chancellor Kilty of a volume of British statutes considered applicable to Maryland.[27]

Any consideration of local efforts to absorb specific English statutes into the body of American written law must be treated in the light of this national endeavor. It is for this reason that a brief description of the general tendency has prefaced our examination of a neglected passage in American legal history. Our purpose is modest: to discuss with some care the re-enactment in New York State of a series of English statutes concerning outlawry, a process which, in civil cases, has generally been believed never to have constituted a part of American law. We shall see later how that instance of legislative reception was related to the work of Samuel Jones and Richard Varick. Their revision of the laws of New York has never received the detailed attention which it deserves.[28] It is

25. The report is reprinted in an appendix to 3 BINNEY at p. 593. The Pennsylvania judges, like the New York legislators, found the language of the ancient British statutes unsatisfactory for American purposes. "In perusing the statutes referred to in the report, the legislature will perceive, that in many of them the language is uncouth, and unsuited to our present form of government." *Id.* at p. 597. Jefferson in characteristic terms described the same aspect of English statutes, "which, from their verbosity, their endless tautologies, their involutions of case within case, and parenthesis within parenthesis, and their multiplied efforts at certainty, by *saids* and *aforesaids*, by *ors* and *ands*, to make them more plain, are really rendered more perplexed and incomprehensible, not only to common readers, but to the lawyers themselves." *Supra* note 20, at p. 70.

26. See the two legislative resolutions (No. 10, Nov. Sess., 1794, and No. 22, Nov. Sess., 1809) reprinted in an appendix to Volume 7 of KILTY, HARRIS AND WATKINS, LAWS OF MARYLAND.

27. An annotated edition of Chancellor Kilty's Collection was published in 1870 by J. J. Alexander.

28. No more misleading summary of the provisions of the constitution of 1777 and of the work of Jones and Varick could well be devised than that the New York Board of Statutory Consolidation which, in its report to the legislature in 1908, stated that "the first state constitution of 1777 had been in force but nine years when a revision of the laws was directed by the legislature. The state was then governed by the common law of England and Great Britain and the acts of the legislature of the colony of New York, except as abrogated by the constitution of 1777 or modified by the state legislature. In 1786 Samuel Jones and Richard Varick were appointed to 'collect, revise and digest' the acts of the colony of New York and the laws of the state passed since the Revolution." 1 MCKINNEY'S CONSOLIDATED LAWS OF NEW YORK, Annotated, pp. 1-33 at p. 2. Similarly hasty summaries of the Jones and Varick revision may be found in BUTLER, THE REVISION OF THE STATUTES OF THE STATE OF NEW YORK AND THE REVISERS (1889) p. 5, and in Arnot, *The Progress of Law Reform in New York* (1909) 43 AM. L. REV. 53. Chancellor Kent refers to the "enlightened

hoped that a brief consideration of one small aspect of their work will not only indicate the importance of their labors, but will cast light upon the larger process of statutory reception as a whole.

It is well known that the technicalities of common law pleading put formidable difficulties in the way of a plaintiff who wished to bring suit against joint contract debtors, one or more of whom was beyond the reach of process.[29] Because the obligation was joint, all debtors must be made parties defendant, and all defendants must be brought into court. If the plaintiff failed to join one of the debtors the promise declared on might be successfully traversed, or, after the time of Lord Mansfield, the claim would be dismissed on a plea in abatement. The logic of these technicalities may well have afforded scholastic satisfaction to judges and lawyers, but the plaintiff who found himself without remedy because one of his joint debtors was able to elude the sheriff would find small comfort in the procedural symmetry of justice. It was imperative, therefore, that some weapon from the armory of the common law should be given to this plaintiff. Pollock and Maitland have stated that the weapon which the courts gave to him was "as clumsy as it was terrible."[30] That weapon was the process of outlawry.

Although there is no need here to discuss in detail the intricate confusion to which English courts had, by the 18th century, brought the process of outlawry, a brief suggestion of its characteristics is essential for our purposes.[31] As applied to criminal proceedings its nature is not unfamiliar, at least in its more romantic aspects. A defendant who had been indicted or appealed of treason or felony and who eluded capture, or could not be found within the county where he stood charged, might through outlawry proceedings be put outside the king's peace and beyond his protection. In its early form the proceeding was instituted by the issuance of a writ of

and chastened spirit of moderation" which inspired the New York revisions of 1801 and 1829 (for the former of which he was himself largely responsible), but makes no mention of the Jones and Varick revision. 1 KENT'S COMMENTARIES 473, note b.

29. 2 WILLISTON, CONTRACTS (Williston and Thompson rev. ed. 1936) § 327.

30. 2 POLLOCK & MAITLAND, HISTORY OF ENGLISH LAW (1898) 579.

31. My summary of the nature of proceedings to outlawry is based primarily upon the following sources: 3 BLACKSTONE'S COMMENTARIES 297 *et seq.*; VINER'S ABRIDGMENT, Title Outlawry; 3 HOLDSWORTH, HISTORY OF ENGLISH LAW (1923) 604 *et seq.*; Thompson, *The Development of the Anglo-American Judicial System. Part I. History of the English Courts to the Judicature Acts* (1932) 17 CORNELL L. Q. 9 at pp. 12, 13; TIDD'S PRACTICE (2nd Am. ed.) 125 *et seq.*; MORRIS, THE EARLY ENGLISH COUNTY COURT (1926).

exigent from the court in which the defendant was appealed or indicted. By that writ the sheriff of the county was commanded to call the defendant at successive sittings of his county court, and if he did not appear judgment of outlawry was pronounced against him. The antiquity of the proceedings is evidenced by the fact that they took place in the ancient county court to the exclusion of the royal courts.[32] There, although founded on the sheriff's acts, the judgment was entered by the coroners. The effect of the judgment was to deprive the defendant of substantially all of his civil rights, —his chattels were forfeited to the King, his lands escheated, and, until the 14th century, he might on discovery be killed by anyone.

Successive statutes in the reigns of Henry the Sixth,[33] Henry the Eighth,[34] and Elizabeth[35] gave the defendant somewhat greater assurance that if outlawry proceedings were instituted he would hear of them. By these statutes it was provided that in addition to the writ of exigent there should issue a writ of proclamation directing the sheriff of the county where the defendant resided to make three proclamations ordering his appearance on pain of outlawry. These proclamations were to be made both in the sheriff's court and at the door of the local church after Sunday service. The defendant was also, through a writ of error, allowed to have a judgment of outlawry reversed.[36] Parliamentary solicitude for the rights of the defendant in outlawry proceedings was supplemented by the courts. Even such thick-skinned officials as the English judges found the unfairness of the proceedings offensive. To allow such severe punishments to be visited upon a person whose defense was never heard was, after all, out of line with a growing common law tradition. Such considerations as these led the courts to protect the rights of outlawed defendants by means of artificial technicalities. The most minute error in Latin spelling or grammar was enough to invalidate the entire elaborate proceedings.[37]

32. 1 HOLDSWORTH 8.

33. 8 HENRY VI, c. 10, Sec. 2.

34. 6 HENRY VIII, c. 4.

35. 31 ELIZABETH, c. 3, Sec. 1.

36. The fictitious character of the whole elaborate procedure and the unreality of the protection which was afforded the defendant were recognized by Parliament in the 19th century. See 9 HOLDSWORTH 254-256.

37. In Markham v. Gargrave, Palm. 121 (1620), *infra nominata* was misspelt *infra noninata* and *waviata* appeared as *wamata* in the writ of exigent. These errors were enough to invalidate the whole proceedings. In Griffith v. Thomas, Style 334 (1652), it was held that "there is a fault in the outlawry, for in the

By the time of Bracton, outlawry had been used in civil actions based on trespasses *vi et armis.* A series of statutes extended its application to all civil cases in which the writ of capias was permitted. The procedural requirements were substantially the same in civil and criminal proceedings, and the plaintiff who wished to assert a claim against an absent defendant would have to pick his way through a mesh of details. When the capias was returned *non est inventus*, an alias writ was issued, and after that was similarly returned, a pluries was issued. Upon the return of *non est inventus* to this writ the plaintiff would obtain his writs of exigent and proclamation, and these the sheriff would execute as in the criminal proceedings. Finally, if the defendant did not appear, the county court entered judgment of outlawry against him. In civil cases, of course, the consequences were not as drastic as in criminal proceedings, for although there was a similar forfeiture, the judgment did not operate as a conviction for crime.

Terrible and clumsy as these proceedings in many instances may have been, it is evident that in one situation they served a useful purpose. As we have seen, persons holding a claim against joint debtors were frequently unable to make service upon all of the necessary parties defendant, and the logic of pleading required that the action be abated unless the impossible were achieved. It was in such cases that outlawry seemed to justify itself, for it enabled the plaintiff, by destroying the rights of a joint debtor who was outside of, or concealed within, the jurisdiction, to sue the others upon whom service could be made. If the absent co-debtor had been outlawed a plea in abatement would not lie. The severity of a judgment of outlawry was very great, but the injury which technical rules of pleading might do a plaintiff was some justification for its use in proceedings against joint debtors. It was only when the rules of pleading had been greatly liberalized that Parliament abolished outlawry proceedings in civil cases.[38]

This brief account of the characteristics of English proceedings to outlawry will afford an adequate background for the consider-

writ to the sheriff it is *praecipipimus vobis*, instead of *praecipimus vobis* . . . Roll, Chief Justice, If the word be *praecipipimus*, then there is no command to the sheriff, for that word signifies nothing, therefore let the outlawry be reversed. . . ."

38. 42 and 43 VICT., c. 59, Sec. 3 (1879). As to the more recent status of outlawry in criminal proceedings in England, see Richards, *Is Outlawry Obsolete?* (1902) 18 LAW Q. REV. 297.

ation of that passage in American legal history which is our principal concern. It has been said that "the process of outlawry in civil cases seems to have been unknown in the United States"[39] and that "it appears that outlawry has never been known on this side of the Atlantic."[40] Such assertions have ample and distinguished judicial authority behind them. In *Harker v. Brink*,[41] the Supreme Court of New Jersey had before it for consideration the so-called Joint Debtor Act of that state. The statute was derived from a colonial act of 1771 which, after its preamble reciting that "the proceedings to outlawry against persons who cannot be taken by process not being in use in this Colony . . . ," provided a remedy for creditors who held claims against joint debtors, some of whom were beyond the reach of process.[42] The court, in discussing that statute, asserted, with perhaps some local pride for New Jersey's priority, that "a provision of similar import, and almost identical in phraseology, was enacted in New York as early as 1789."[43] *Blessing v. McLinden*[44] was a later New Jersey decision in which the court, examining further the history of the Joint Debtor Act, again referred to the colonial act of 1771 and called particular attention to its preamble. The *McLinden* case, primarily because of its detailed analysis of the history of the legislation, has frequently been cited by courts and writers. In part, at least, because of the quoted preamble from the act of 1771, the local fact that outlawry was unknown during the colonial period has been generalized into a broad assumption. In *Kittredge v. Langley*,[45] Chief Judge Cardozo, after citing *Blessing v. McLinden*, refers to a Rhode Island[46] and a Massachusetts[47] decision, and asserts that "the process of outlawry is one unknown to our law."[48] We have pointed out the fact that the New Jersey court, in *Harker v. Brink*, had claimed priority

39. Magruder and Foster, *Jurisdiction over Partnerships* (1924) 37 Harv. L. Rev. 793, 799.

40. Holdoegel, *Jurisdiction over Partnerships, Nonpartnership Associations and Joint Debtors* (1926) 11 Iowa L. Rev. 193, 197.

41. 24 N. J. Law 333 (1854).

42. Allinson, Acts of the General Assembly of the Province of New Jersey, 1702-1776, c. 543.

43. *Op. cit. supra* note 41, at 348. The New York statute referred to is in N. Y. Laws 1788, c. 46.

44. 81 N. J. Law 379, 79 Atl. 347 (1911).

45. 252 N. Y. 405, 169 N. E. 626 (1930).

46. Nathanson v. Spitz, 19 R. I. 70, 73, 31 Atl. 690 (1895).

47. Tappan v. Bruen, 5 Mass. 193 (1809).

48. *Supra* note 45, at 413.

over New York in the adoption of a joint debtor act. The New York court, by its failure to cite any earlier New York statute, seems to acknowledge that claim. Undoubtedly the attention of neither court was called to the New York colonial act of 1756[49] which provided substantially the same relief against joint debtors as that which New Jersey adopted fifteen years later.[50] But what is of importance to us—beyond incidentally determining which state may properly claim the distinction of priority—is the fact that the New York colonial act was prefaced with precisely the same recital as that which introduced the New Jersey statute. Had the court wanted some authority to establish the proposition that outlawry was never known in New York, it might have referred to the recital in the act of 1756 that it was not then known in the colony. We shall presently see how conclusive that evidence would have been.

What was it that led the American colonists to repudiate the traditional procedure of outlawry which, during the 17th and 18th centuries was of unquestionable importance in English law? Of course no conclusive answer to that question can be given; the factors which brought about the rejection of particular elements in English law are multiple and uncertain. In the case of outlawry, however, our cursory examination of its character may afford some explanation. Its clumsiness and its severity were noted by Pollock and Maitland; and American courts, in somewhat more American terms, have emphasized the same deficiencies. It has been described as "contrary to the spirit and principles of our government"[51] and "inconsistent with our institutions and repugnant to our constitu-

49. 4 Colonial Laws of N. Y., c. 997.

50. The New Jersey act lacked the final proviso of the earlier New York law, which limited the plaintiff's right of execution to the property jointly owned by all defendants and the individual property of such defendants as had been served with process. The New York act stated that the plaintiff, subject to that restriction, might have judgment and execution against "the joint debtors named in the process. . . ." The New Jersey act of 1771, as printed by Allinson, stated that judgment and execution might be had against "the joint debtors named in the proofs. . . ." The New Jersey court in Ford v. Munson, 1 South. 93 (1818) discussed an amendment of 1797, by which the word "proofs" was changed to "process," as in the New York law. The court suggested that the change was the result of an error in engrossing the 1797 law. In view of the fact that the New Jersey act of 1771 was, with the exception of the concluding proviso, copied verbatim from the New York act of 1756 it seems not unlikely that the legislative error was made not in 1797 but in 1771.

51. McCall v. Price, 1 McCord (S. C.) 82, 83 (1821).

tion and laws . . . ,"[52] and "not only dilatory and expensive to plaintiffs, but harsh and oppressive to nonresident defendants."[53] Despite the high-sounding considerations thus emphasized it is not improbable that its inconvenience to plaintiffs was the principal reason for its repudiation. Although, as we have seen, it possessed some justification when applied to claims against absent joint debtors, the joint debtor acts and other procedural devices seemed to destroy whatever claim to utility it possessed.

In view of the more or less frequent dicta that outlawry was alien to American traditions and of the express recital in the preambles of the colonial acts of 1756 and 1771, it is, perhaps, not surprising that writers and judges have recently assumed that outlawry was never known in the United States. The New York constitution of 1777, by its cautious provision for the selective reception of English law, seemed to provide a sanction for the permanent repudiation of practices such as outlawry which are "inconsistent with our institutions." The development of legal practices is not, however, as simple as we could sometimes wish. In 1787 the legislature of New York adopted an elaborate statute making detailed provision for outlawry proceedings in civil and criminal cases.[54] Because the law, with minor changes, was in effect for some forty-three years[55] it is manifestly inaccurate to say that outlawry as an incident of civil process was never known in this country.[56]

In an appendix to this article [omitted here] are printed Chapter Nine of the Laws of New York of 1787 and the various English statutes upon which that act was apparently based. No useful purpose would be served by making a detailed examination of the various similarities between the American and British legislation,—the resemblances are evident without specific emphasis. Our pri-

52. Dale County v. Gunter, 46 Ala. 118, 140 (1871).

53. Harker v. Brink, *supra* note 41, at 351.

54. N. Y. Laws 1787, c. 9.

55. The statute was repealed by Ch. 21, Sec. 1, Para. 57, Laws of N. Y. 1828, the repeal to be effective in 1830. In 1801 the act had been amended in small respects. See Laws of New York 1801, c. 51.

56. Several Virginia statutes indicate that outlawry in civil proceedings was for a time in force in that colony. See acts of Feb. 27, 1752 and Dec. 22, 1788, in 6 HENING 334 and 12 HENING 730, 736. See also Moss v. Moss's Administrator, 4 Hening and Munf. 293 (1809). Outlawry in criminal cases was recognized in Virginia after the Revolution. See Commonwealth v. Hale, 2 Va. Cas. 241 (1821); Commonwealth v. Haggerman, *ibid.* p. 244; Commonwealth v. Anderson, *ibid.* p. 245. British proceedings to outlawry in civil cases seem to have been adopted in no statutory revision.

mary concern is not to discuss the details of practice outlined in the New York act but to consider how the legislature came to adopt the statute. In view of the condemnation which proceedings to outlawry have commonly received from American courts, it is desirable to determine why the legislature of a recently rebellious colony, presumably anxious to rid itself of a cumbersome and confused inheritance, saw fit to adopt the elaborate and medieval process of outlawry. Were there no conflicting evidence it could be most persuasively argued that the outlawry statute was unrelated to the work of Jones and Varick. It will be remembered that in 1786 they were directed by the legislature to "collect and reduce into proper form . . . and lay" before the legislature for enactment such English statutes "as have been generally supposed to extend to the late Colony." In the preamble to the Joint Debtor Act of 1756, it was recited that the proceeding to outlawry against persons who cannot be taken by process was not in use in the colony. That act was still in force in 1772, for in that year Peter Van Schaack was directed by the legislature to publish a collection of colonial laws then in force,[57] and in his volume, published in the following year, the Joint Debtor Act was printed in full, with its preamble.[58] Furthermore, in a statute passed on March 9, 1774, it was stated that certain "disorderly Practices are highly Criminal and . . . it is indisputably necessary for want of Process to Outlawry (which is not used in this Colony) that special provision be made for bringing such offenders in future to trial. . . ."[59] Certainly these legislative recitals indicate that the process of outlawry was unknown in New York during the colonial period.[60] The possibility that at some time between March, 1774, and April, 1775, the elaborate proceedings were adopted by the colony and left no trace in local records is so remote as to be negligible. If English statutes concerning out-

57. 5 Colonial Laws of N. Y. Ch. 1543, p. 355.

58. Laws of N. Y., 1691-1772, p. 352. This colonial joint debtor act was reenacted almost verbatim by Sec. 23 of Chapter 46 of the Laws of 1788. Shortly afterward the criminal act was repealed. N. Y. Laws 1788, Ch. 73, Sec. 1.

59. 5 Colonial Laws of N. Y. Ch. 1660. See also the recital in a special act for outlawing Phillip French and Thomas Wenham passed on April 30, 1702. It was there stated that "the want of Process of outlawry in Criminal and Civil Causes is a manifest defect in the Execucon of the Law within this Province." 1 Colonial Laws of N. Y. Ch. 105.

60. For one case in which the Court of Quarter Sessions of New York City seems to have outlawed a defendant in criminal proceedings, see Queen v. Rideout (1708), reprinted in Goebel, Cases and Materials on the Development of Legal Institutions (1937) pp. 403-404.

lawry were not in force in New York when the revolution commenced, then Jones and Varick had not been directed to submit them to the legislature for re-enactment.

This is the logic of the argument which might be urged to deny that the act of 1787 was related to the work of Jones and Varick. Logic, however, cannot refute the testimony of contemporary records. In the Journal of the New York Assembly for January 13, 1787, appears the following entry: "Mr. Jones, pursuant to the law for revising the laws of this State, laid before the House the following bills, viz., . . . A bill entitled *An act declaring what process may be issued in certain Personal Actions, and for regulating outlawries. . . .*"[61] On that day the bill was read for the first time and ordered to a second reading.[62] Two days later the second reading occurred,[63] and on the 25th the engrossed bill was read a third time in the Assembly.[64] On January 27, the Senate resolved that the bill should pass without amendment.[65] On February 5, in the Assembly, "a message from the Honorable the Council of Revision, was delivered by the Honorable Mr. Chief Justice Morris, that it does not appear improper to the Council, that the bill entitled, *An act declaring what process may be issued in certain Personal Actions, and for regulating Outlawries* . . . [and other named bills] should respectively become laws of this state."[66] And thus the statute concerning outlawry was adopted as part of the law of New York.

My purpose, as I have said, is not to discuss the details of the statute, as they relate either to criminal or civil proceedings. Some considerations of the imitative and creative aspects of the law will, however, reveal the character of the work of Jones and Varick. The first and second sections, though not directly traceable to parliamentary acts, contain a brief statement of the existent English law as summarized by Coke, Blackstone, and Viner. In many ways the second section is the most interesting. There was no English statute conferring jurisdiction in outlawry proceedings upon the County Courts, for the obvious reason that their jurisdiction in such cases was pre-Norman in origin. It will be remembered that the ancient

61. JOURNAL OF THE ASSEMBLY OF THE STATE OF N. Y., 10th Session, 1787, p. 5. At that time Samuel Jones was a member and Richard Varick the speaker of the assembly, *ibid.* p. 3, 4.

62. *Ibid.*

63. *Ibid.* p. 8.

64. *Ibid.* p. 22.

65. JOURNAL OF THE SENATE OF N. Y., 10th Session, 1787, p. 15.

66. *Op. cit. supra* note 59, at p. 36.

County Courts derived from the shire moots presided over by the sheriffs, and that although their jurisdiction was frequently confirmed by Parliament and the king, in origin it was independent of both. The New York Constitution of 1777 had referred to the courts of common pleas and of general sessions as county courts,[67] and it has been suggested that they may have had some connection historically with the ancient county courts of England.[68] If that connection had been recognized it would have been simple and natural for the legislature in 1787 to give the common pleas and general sessions jurisdiction to conduct outlawry proceedings. Instead, the second section of the act provided that the sheriff of each county, or his deputy, should on the first and third Monday of every month, hold a court to be known as his County Court. Here, as in England, he was to demand persons on the exigents and pronounce judgment of outlawry against those who did not appear. In one respect only was the practice of this court to differ from that followed in England; the sheriff himself might pronounce judgment. That act need not, as in England, be performed by the coroners. The striking fact, therefore, about the second section of Chapter Nine is its imitative adoption of British procedure; although one would expect that Jones and Varick and the legislature would, if outlawry were to be adopted, have fitted it into the existing judicial machinery of the state, instead, they transplanted to American soil the English tribunals which traditionally had exercised jurisdiction in such proceedings, and did so despite the fact that these ancient courts performed no other function in the new society.

Each section of the act from the third through the seventh reenacts almost verbatim various English statutes from the time of Edward I to that of William and Mary. If Jones and Varick, in submitting the statute to the legislature for enactment, went farther than they had been told to go, they did far less than had been requested in the way of altering the British "stile and language" which had been declared by the legislature to be "improper to appear in the statute books of this State." There was, to be sure, a certain amount of creative enactment in the statute; the last two sections evidence a marked departure from English practice. The

67. See Articles 24, 25 and 28 of Constitution of 1777. See also People v. Albany Common Pleas, 19 Wend. 27 (1837).

68. RADIN, ANGLO-AMERICAN LEGAL HISTORY (1937), p. 174.

provisions for jury trial of the issue of damages were probably unknown in English outlawry proceedings, as were those stating that the satisfaction of the plaintiff's claim would render the judgment of outlawry totally inoperative.

In endeavoring to understand why the legislature deemed it desirable to provide for such process in civil actions it is important to remember that the extent of relief which could be obtained under the Joint Debtor Act was very limited. It was useful only when one or more of the joint debtors could be served with process. Moreover, execution could be had only against property jointly owned and the individual property of the defendants who were brought into court. The process of outlawry, on the other hand, would permit recovery against any debtor, who could not be served, whether he was jointly indebted or not, and, as provided for in New York, it apparently permitted the satisfaction of the claim out of the individual property of the absent defendant. There were certainly theoretical advantages in the process of outlawry which relief under the Joint Debtor Act would not afford, and the elimination of the severe forfeitures which in England accompanied outlawry even in civil actions, made its unfairness to defendants much less real than under British practice. Although against an absconding or concealed debtor, solely indebted, the creditor might obtain relief by proceedings *quasi in rem*,[69] the intricacies of the procedure were such that creditors might well prefer some alternative remedy—a process which would obviate the necessity of an attachment being made in the first instance. Perhaps it is not surprising, therefore, that Jones and Varick felt that it would be desirable to make provision for the broader remedy, and in view of the peculiar safeguards afforded the defendant, it may not be strange that the vigilant Council of Revision allowed the statute, without questioning, to become law.

During the years when the statute was in force there were only occasional judicial references to its provisions. Three reports in Coleman and Caines' Cases indicate that the courts were aware of the possibility of a plaintiff proceeding to outlawry against an absent defendant[70]—one indicating that it might be used in circum-

69. Act of April 3, 1775, 5 COLONIAL LAWS OF N. Y. 807 (Ch. 1731). This statute was re-enacted on April 14, 1786; see Laws of N. Y. 1786, c. 24.

70. Heyers v. Dening, Coleman and Caines' Cases 75 (1799); Jackson v. Cooper, *ibid.* at 154 (1803); Shaw *et al.* v. Colfax *et al.*, *ibid.* at p. 450 (1805).

stances also covered by the Joint Debtor Act.[71] The only detailed discussion of its character that has been found is in *Roosevelt v. W. & L. Crommelin*,[72] a case in which it was held to be applicable to proceedings against residents of Mississippi for the enforcement of rights in a bill of exchange drawn by the defendants in Mississippi. It is to be hoped that some day sheriffs' records may be discovered which will cast more light on the details of the procedure in both civil and criminal cases than is given by the bare provisions of the statute itself. John A. Dunlap, in his *Treatise on the Practice of the Supreme Court of New York*, published in 1821, discusses the local statute in some detail, but indicates that it was seldom used.[73] Its repeal in 1828, effective in 1830, was due apparently to a characteristically American combination of practical and theoretical considerations. The report of the statutory revisers submitted to the legislature in 1828 stated that the proceeding to outlawry "is so tedious and expensive, that it has become obsolete, or if resorted to, it must be for purposes inconsistent with justice."[74]

The provisions of the New York statute may well be deserving of more detailed consideration that I have given them. A reading of the statute and a comparison of its provisions with those of the English acts will suggest many questions which I have neither touched upon nor answered. I believe, however, that the simple facts established in this study are of some significance. We have seen that outlawry was an unknown process in the colonial period of New York's legal history, and we have determined that Samuel Jones and Richard Varick, going beyond the obligations imposed upon them in 1786, submitted to the legislature an elaborate statute making provision for that imported remedy. Their suggestion, combining imitative and creative elements, was found acceptable by the legislature and the Council of Revision and yas adopted as a part of the law of New York.[75] This neglected instance of selective

71. Shaw *et al.* v. Colfax *et al.*, *supra* note 70.

72. 18 John Rep. 253 (1820).

73. Volume 1, p. 138 *et seq.* The process as used in New York is also briefly discussed in 1 BACKUS, DIGEST OF LAWS RELATING TO SHERIFFS (1812) 111.

74. N. Y. Revised Statutes, Reports of the Revisers, Benjamin F. Butler, John Duer and John C. Spencer, 1826-1828, Part III, Ch. VI, Title VI, Article Second, Sec. 7, p. 56.

75. In the sketch of Samuel Jones in the Dictionary of American Biography (*supra* note 12), the author quotes a passage from the New York Legal Observer for October 1853, in which Jones was described: "His learning was vast. His principles . . . were ultra-conservative. . . . He was the man above all

reception is of far more than local significance, and I suspect that when a detailed and comparative study of other similar efforts is made the broader relevance will be self-evident. It does not seem improbable that other post-revolutionary revisers may also have endeavored, under the guise of re-enactment, to achieve what a Marxist might term a counter-revolution in our law. The fact that the ancient remedy was too novel for Americans also possesses its historical importance. The erstwhile rebels, led by Jones and Varick, had turned to England for guidance. In 1828 the British remedy was found to be unwieldy, extravagant and unfair. Accordingly, they abandoned the imported process and relied upon the sufficiency of the remedies which Yankee ingenuity could provide. "It required time and experience to ascertain how much of the English law would be suitable to this country."[76] Jones and Varick endeavored to set aside the verdict of experience, but time proved their effort to have been in vain.

---

others to adapt the system of laws to the new condition of things, . . . and on every subject of that description the Legislature followed him implicitly, while upon any subject connected with politics, they were sure to be on the other side, with entire unanimity."

76. Tilghman, C. J., in Guardians of the Poor v. Greene, 5 Binney (Pa.) 554, 558 (1813).

XVIII

*Thomas Jefferson and Blackstone's Commentaries**

JULIUS S. WATERMAN

The lectures of Blackstone, begun at Oxford in 1753, were the first to be delivered on English law in any university, and with their publication from 1765 to 1769, brought renown[1] to one whose success before had been in college administration and not in law.[2] Nevertheless, the published lectures met with criticism in England. Jeremy Bentham, a student of Blackstone who listened "with rebel ears," soon wrote an attack[3] on the constitutional principles of the Commentaries, described as "the most trenchant critique ever penned by a youthful pupil on the doctrines of a celebrated teacher whose dogmas were accepted by the learned world as profound

* "Thomas Jefferson and Blackstone's Commentaries," by Julius S. Waterman, is reprinted by special permission of the *Illinois Law Review* (Northwestern University School of Law), XXVII (1933), 629-659.

1. "[Blackstone] whose works have had beyond comparison a more extensive circulation, have obtained a greater share of esteem, of applause, and consequently of influence . . . than any other writer who on that subject has ever yet appeared." *Bentham* "A Fragment on Government" (ed. Montague 1891) p. 94.

2. For the life of Blackstone see *Odgers* "Sir William Blackstone" (1918) 27 Yale L. J. 599; (1919) 28 id. 542. *Holdsworth* "Sources and Literature of English Law" (1925) pp. 155-161, explains the nature and purpose of the Commentaries. See also *Holdsworth* "Charles Viner" (1923) 39 Law Q. Rev. 17-46.

3. *Anon.* "A Fragment on Government" (1776). See also *Bentham* "A Comment on the Commentaries" (ed. Everett 1928); *Bentham* "Usury" (1787) letter IX; *Riddell* "Bentham on Blackstone: A Review" (1929) 15 A. B. A. Jour. 676; *Alexander* "Bentham" (1929) 7 N. Y. U. L. Rev. 141; "Bentham, Blackstone and the New Law" (1926) 21 ILLINOIS LAW REVIEW 302; *Atkinson* "Bentham" (1905).

truths."[4] And before that, Joseph Priestley,[5] the scientist, who was also a dissenting minister and a friend of the colonies, in a "very angry pamphlet" had denounced Blackstone's comments on "the virulent declamations of peevish non-conformers."[6] These constituted the immediate adverse reaction in England to Blackstone's work,[7] though "Junius" had already criticised some of Blackstone's political acts.[8]

The Commentaries in America

It was in thinly settled colonial America that the Commentaries received most acclaim. By 1776 nearly twenty-five hundred copies were in use here, one thousand five hundred of which were the American edition of 1772;[9] a sale which Burke in 1775 in his speech on "Conciliation with the American Colonies" said rivaled that in England.[10] It would seem that the publication of a survey

4. 1 *Blackstone* "Commentaries" (ed. Jones 1915) p. xxiv, quoted from *Dicey* "Blackstone's Commentaries" (1909) 54 Nat. Rev. 653.

5. For the life of Priestley in the United States see *Adams* "Thomas Jefferson and the University of Virginia" Circulars of the U. S. Bureau of Education (1888) Vol. I p. 46.

6. 4 *Blackstone* "Commentaries" (ed. Jones 1915) *p. 50 n. 3. Infra note 102.

7. See also *James Sedgwick* "Remarks on the Commentaries of Blackstone" (1800); *Rowe* "Vindication of the Commentaries of Blackstone against the Strictures Contained in Mr. Sedgwick's Remarks" (1806); *Cartwright* "An Appeal on the Subject of the English Constitution" (1797) pp. 28-29. Lord Ellenborough in 1812 said: "Blackstone, when he compiled his lectures was comparatively an ignorant man. . . . It might be said of him, at the time he was composing this book, that it was not so much his learning that made the book, as it was the book that made him learned." 23 *Hansard* "Parliamentary Debates" p. 1083.

8. "Junius' Letters" (ed. Wade 1894) Vol. I p. 165, reads: "Doctor Blackstone is solicitor to the Queen. The Doctor recollected that he had a place to preserve, though he forgot that he had a reputation to lose. We have now the good fortune to understand the Doctor's principles as well as his writings. For the defense of truth, law, and reason, the Doctor's book may be safely consulted; but whoever wishes to cheat a neighbor of his estates, or to rob a country of its rights, need make no scruple of consulting the Doctor himself." Another letter of 1769 reads: "The respect due to his [Blackstone's] writings will probably increase with the contempt due to his character, and his works will be quoted when he himself is forgotten or despised." "Junius' Letters" Vol. II p. 268. Blackstone was also involved in an unfortunate situation in supporting the government in its rejection of John Wilkes as a member of the House of Commons. See *McCamic* "The First Edition of Blackstone's Commentaries" (1926) 33 W. Va. L. Q. 287.

9. 1 *Hammond* "Blackstone" (1890) p. ix; *Baldwin* "The American Judiciary" (1905) p. 9.

10. "The Works of Edmund Burke" (Bohn 1864) Vol. I p. 467.

of English law, based on introductory lectures, should have been a matter of small importance in colonial America. But a few excerpts will reveal an effect hardly to be imagined by the Oxford law lecturer.[11]

> "The widespread influence of his [Blackstone's] book on the eve of independence furthered the process of the reception of the English law in the legal system of the colonies; after the Declaration of Independence it helped check the tendency to adopt French law[12] in the older states. . . ."[13]
>
> "The fact that such a large mass of legal detail was made available in one work, in an interesting and easily mastered

11. Lord Redesdale remarked in *Shannon* v. *Shannon* (1804) 1 Schoales & Lefroy 324, 327 that Blackstone did not consider his book as an authority.

12. For hostility after the American Revolution to English law see the non-citation statutes in (1800) Laws of N. J. p. 436 par. iv; (1807) Kentucky Acts ch. 7 p. 23; (1812) 5 Laws of Penn. p. 125. See *Hickman* v. *Boffman* (Ky. 1808) Hardin 356, 372, where Henry Clay was stopped from reading from 3 East, an English report of 1803. "Let us, Americans, then duly appreciate our own government, laws and manners; and be what we profess, an independent nation; and do not plume ourselves upon being humble imitators of foreigners, at home and in our own country; but let our manners in all respects be characteristic of the spirit and principles of our independence. . . . To these [principles] we ought to resort and not to foreign systems, to lay a foundation to establish a character upon, and to rear a system of jurisprudence purely American, without any marks of servility to foreign powers or states; at the same time leave ourselves open to derive instruction and improvement from the observations, discoveries, and experience of the literati, in all countries and nations, respecting jurisprudence and other useful arts and sciences." 1 Root (Conn. 1798) intr. pp. xiii-xiv. In his address as Governor of Virginia in 1810, Judge John Tyler in attacking the alleged superiority of the common law of England said: "Shall we forever administer our free republican government on the principles of a rigid and high tone monarchy? . . . Let a stranger go into our courts, and he would almost believe himself in the Court of the King's Bench." He also objected to taking up the time of the court "in reconciling absurd and contradictory opinions of foreign judges, which certainly can be no part of an American judge's duty." "Letters and Times of the Tylers" (1884) Vol. I pp. 260-261. In a letter to Judge Tyler in 1812 Jefferson pointed out the undesirability of adopting "the civil code" but said "I admit the superiority of the civil over the common law code, as a system of perfect justice." *Jefferson* "Writings" (ed. Washington 1861) Vol. VI p. 66. See infra notes 30, 85a. See also *Kent* "An American Law Student of a Hundred Years Ago" in "Select Essays in Anglo-American Legal History" Vol. I pp. 837, 843; *Pound* "Judge Story in the Making of American Law" (1914) 48 Am. L. Rev. 676, 686; *Pound* "Spirit of the Common Law" (1921) pp. 115-116; *Gray* "Nature and Sources of the Law" (1921) p. 245, n; *Warren* "History of the American Bar" (1911) ch. 10; *Baldwin* "The American Judiciary" (1905) p. 14.

13. *Hazeltine* "Blackstone" 2 Encyc. of Social Sciences (1931) 581. See also *Hamilton* "Charles Viner and the Common Law" (1928) in Senate Document 161, 70th Cong., 1st Sess. p. 10.

form, made Blackstone's work particularly useful in eighteenth-century America. The Commentaries served as the principal means of the colonists' information as to the state of English law in general."[14]

". . . this work became at once the standard authority upon law in every American court, and especially in the great number of small courts of original common-law jurisdiction. . . . The effect was, that upon all questions, of private law at least, this work stood for the law itself throughout the country, and at least for a generation to come exercised an influence upon the jurisprudence of the new nation, which no other work has enjoyed, and to which no other work can possibly now obtain."[15]

"Blackstone provided an admirably comprehensive, lucid and up-to-date systemization of the English common law, suitable alike as a reference authority for the courts and as a text-book for students. The easiest course to pursue was to follow him in all cases where constitutions or legislatures had not spoken. . . . This admirable systemization of the confused mass of English precedents exerted a profound influence upon the legal development of this country. . . . It is hardly an exaggeration to say that what we actually took over from England was simply Blackstone."[16]

14. *Plucknett* "A Concise History of the Common Law" (1929) p. 207. For the paucity of reports and other law books see *Reed* "Training for the Public Profession of the Law" (1921) p. 111; *Warren* "History of the American Bar" (1911) ch. 8; *Dane* "Digest of American Law" (1823) intr.; *Story* "Miscellaneous Writings" (1835) p. 333. In (1928) 28 Col. L. Rev. at 405, n. 25 it is said: "The meagerness of American law libraries contributed, of course, to account for the almost Scriptural authority of Blackstone in our early law." For the tardy adoption of the common law of England in this country and the influence of Story and Kent see *Pound* "Some Parallels from Legal History" (1924) 10 A. B. A. Jour. 547, 551; *Warren* "History of the American Bar" (1911) intr.; *Morris* "Studies in the History of American Law" (1930) ch. 1; *Goebel* "King's Law and Local Custom in Seventeenth Century New England" (1931) 31 Col. L. Rev. 416; *Pound and Plucknett* "Readings in the History and System of the Common Law" (1927) pp. 306-314; *Reinsch* "The English Common Law in the Early American Colonies" in "Select Essays in Anglo-American Legal History" Vol. I pp. 367-415; *Story* "Constitution" (5th ed. 1891) pp. 109-112; infra notes 85a and 120.

15. 1 *Hammond*, supra note 9. "Its [the Commentaries] universal use and adoption in the several colonies have given him [Blackstone] in this country an influence in moulding its laws and jurisprudence which hardly ever fell to the lot of a law giver, and which certainly was never so extensively enjoyed by an unauthoritative law writer": *Dillon* "The Laws and Jurisprudence of England and America" (1895) p. 298. See also *Zane* "The Story of Law" (1927) pp. 358-359.

16. *Reed*, supra note 14, pp. 110-111. Cf. *Pound* "Interpretations of Legal

Not only did the work thus influence the law as applied in the courts but it affected as markedly the development of professional legal training in America. In the words of James Bradley Thayer: "It was the great experiment in the university teaching of our law at Oxford, in the third quarter of the eighteenth century, and the publication, a little before the American Revolution, of the results of that experiment, which furnished the stimulus and the exemplar of our own early attempts at systematic legal education."[17] And for those who desired quick and easy admission to the bar the Commentaries, a student's book in its inception, was of incomparable aid.[18]

Even more striking was the effect of the Commentaries on the political philosophy of some of the leaders of American thought. The significance of this influence has been thus stated by Mr. George Wickersham:

> "Paradoxically, those same Commentaries furnished to the American Colonies a most effective weapon in their revolution against the mother country. . . . The philosophy of the Declaration of Independence usually is ascribed to Locke and Paine. But it appears to me that one may clearly trace the influence of Blackstone's Commentaries on the mind of Jefferson, in the affirmations of the Declaration that all men are born with certain inalienable rights. . . . The counts in the indictment of George the Third, contained in the Declaration of Independence, in the main are sustained by Blackstone's description of the rights of Englishmen and the principles of the British Constitution. . . . Little did the Great Commentator realize when he read his lectures to a

History" (1923) p. 52 to the effect that *Coke's* "Institutes" became the basis of the common law of America.

17. *Thayer* "The Teaching of English Law at Universities" in "Legal Essays" (1907) pp. 367-368. 1 *Blackstone* "Commentaries" (ed. Jones 1915) p. xxix; *Odgers* "Blackstone" (1919) 28 Yale L. J. 542, 566; *Plucknett*, supra note 14 p. 207; *Oliphant* "The New Legal Education" The Nation (1930) Vol. 131 p. 493; *Hamilton* "Charles Viner and Our Common Law" (1928) p. 10, supra note 13; *Pound* "Criminal Justice in America" (1930) pp. 82, 106; *Holdsworth* "Sources and Literature of English Law" (1925) p. 159.

18. Infra notes 30, 47 and 146. See *Knapp* "Sketches of Eminent Lawyers" (1821) p. 62: ". . . many old lawyers who were in full practice when Blackstone's Commentaries first appeared in this country, were frequently heard to regret and complain that he should have so simplified and arranged his subject, and so clearly explained the principles of law, that the same amount of knowledge which had cost them years to collect, might be obtained in a short time."

polite and scholarly audience at Oxford of the weapon he unwittingly was forging for the Colonists in North America. . . . That the monarchical Blackstone so practically contributed to the establishment of Democracy in America, Mr. Thorpe[19] declared to be a paradox without parallel in history. But if the Commentaries furnished Jefferson and the other signers of the Declaration of Independence with suggestion and authority for the principles they asserted, they also furnished invaluable suggestion to the framers of the Constitution of the United States. . . . The legal conception and institutions of the Constitution reflect the teaching of the Commentaries. The Common Law as Blackstone set it forth became the fundamental law of America."[20]

It is strange that this product of one of the Tory group[21] in

19. 1 *Thorpe* "Constitutional History of the American People" (1898) pp. 39-40. "As being the highest authority on the laws of England, his [Blackstone's] book was apparently followed by the makers of the Constitution in all branches of their work, and with a fidelity which has even called forth criticism from modern English writers": *Stevens* "Sources of the Constitution of the United States" (1894) p. 48. See also *Ford* "Alexander Hamilton" (1920) p. 217; *Schuyler* "The Constitution of the United States" (1923) p. 154. See "Documentary History of the Constitution" (1900) Vol. III p. 636: "Mr. Dickinson mentioned to the House [Constitutional Convention of 1787] that on examining *Blackstone's* 'Commentaries,' he found that the term 'ex post facto' related to criminal cases only; that it would consequently not restrain the states from retrospective laws in civil cases, and that some further provision for this purpose would be requisite." Cf. *McGovney* "Cases on Constitutional Law" (1930) p. 1115 n. 7; 1 *Blackstone* "Commentaries" (ed. Jones 1915) *p. 46 n. 10; *Calder* v. *Bull* (U. S. 1798) 3 Dall. 386.

20. *Wickersham* "Presentation Address of Blackstone Memorial" (1924) 10 A. B. A. Jour. 576-578. Cf., however, an opposite view, as concerns Jefferson, in the text of this article, by reference to note 130, infra. *Martin* "Study of the American Constitution" (1926) pp. 289-290 says that Blackstone's definition of liberty influenced American legal thinking and his interpretation of liberty found its way into the Declaration of Independence. See also *Pound* "Some Parallels from Legal History" (1924) 10 A. B. A. Jur. 547, 552.

21. "Blackstone by his famous treatise confirmed the ruling classes of England in their overweening conceit of power and flattered them by expressing entire content with the law and constitution of England, as they then existed. He was an opponent of every suggested reform, and as a critic put it, 'toadied to the sinister interests and mischievous prejudices of the party in control.' In examining the part that the lawyers played in bringing on the Revolution, we find ourselves placing well known names under indictment, the names, for example, of Thurlow, Wedderburn, Mansfield, and Blackstone, the most conspicuous legal lights of their day": *Andrews* "The Colonial Background of the American Revolution" (1924) pp. 208-209. *Odgers* (1919) 28 Yale L. J. 542, 565 says Blackstone was a Whig but a "bit of a toady" and gave too glowing a description of landed aristocracy, the nobility, and the King in whom there was no folly nor weakness and who could never mean to do an improper

England, an exponent of conservative legal thought,[22] who believed the English constitution could hardly be praised enough[23] and who felt that the rights of Englishmen were the best birthright and noblest inheritance of mankind,[24] should have been studied so earnestly by colonial America during its struggle against England. Even stranger was its influence in the new nation which stood for political principles which were in marked contrast to those of the dominant group with which the commentator was associated in England.[25] But the need felt by law students and members of the profession for some modern authoritative material could overcome prejudices against the work, even among those who might grasp its political implications, since it was an easily available treatment, presented in systematic form and understandable language.[26]

JEFFERSON'S ATTACKS ON THE COMMENTARIES

But, even in America there were those[27] who challenged the Blackstone influence and the most significant member of this group

thing. See 1 "Commentaries" *p. 246. See in *Stockdale* v. *Hansard* (1839) 9 Ad. & E. 1, 120, the remarks of Lord Denman, C. J., on Blackstone's opinion as a judge of the Court of Common Pleas in *The Case of Brass Crosby* (1769) 3 Wils. 188, 204: "But it must be confessed that his remarks on the state of public feeling rather evince the spirit of a political partisan than the calmness and independence which becomes the judicial seat. We know now, as a matter of history, that the House of Commons was at that time engaged, in unison with the Crown, in assailing the just rights of the people. Yet that learned Judge proclaimed his unqualified resolution to uphold the House of Commons, even though it should have abused its power; rebuked the murmur and complaint which its proceedings had justly excited . . ." Lord Erskin said: "Mr. Justice Blackstone (is) by no means biased towards democratical Government. . . .": *The King* v. *Shipley* (1784) 4 Doug. 73, 111.

22. *Dillon*, supra note 15 p. 297.

23. "Of a constitution so wisely contrived, so strongly raised, and so highly finished, it is hard to speak with that praise, which is justly and severely its due . . .": 4 *Blackstone* "Commentaries" *p 443. *Dicey* "Law and Opinion in England" (1905) p. 62 refers to the period from 1800-1830 as one of "old Toryism" or "Blackstonian optimism."

24. 4 *Blackstone* "Commentaries" *p. 443.

25. "Junius Letters" (ed. Wade 1894) Vol. II p. 268, June 6, 1769, said of Blackstone: "There is a man, for instance, . . . who is not ashamed to maintain an oral doctrine directly opposite to that which he had written, nor to deceive the representative, after instructing the collective body of the nation. This man would willingly have accommodated his authority to the purposes of the administration . . ."

26. Supra note 14.

27. Infra note 118 for attacks by Mr. Justice James Wilson.

was Thomas Jefferson. His attacks were not prepared in the scholarly manner of Jeremy Bentham, nor were they published in a work devoted to a criticism of the Commentaries,[28] but were generalizations occurring in letters written over a period of years.

In 1812 Jefferson wrote to Judge John Tyler:

> "The exclusion from the courts of the malign influence of all authorities after the *Georgium sidus* became ascendant,[29] would uncanonize Blackstone, whose book, although the most elegant and best digested of our law catalogue, has been perverted more than all others, to the degeneracy of legal science. A student finds there a smattering of everything, and his indolence easily persuades him that if he understands that book, he is master of the whole body of law. The distinction between these, and those who have drawn their stores from the deep and rich mines of Coke Littleton, [sic] seems well understood even by the unlettered common people, who apply the appellation of Blackstone lawyers to these ephemeral insects of the law."[30]

Another view appears in a letter written two years later:

> "Blackstone and Hume have made Tories of all England, and are making Tories of those young Americans whose native feelings of independence do not place them above the wily sophistries of a Hume or a Blackstone. These two books, but especially the former, have done more towards the suppression of the liberties of man, than all the millions of men in arms of Bonaparte, and the millions of human lives with the sacrifice of which he will stand loaded before the

28. Supra note 3.

29. This was directed at Mansfield's "innovations" on the common law. See infra note 88.

30. *Jefferson* "Writings" (ed. Washington) Vol. VI pp. 65-66. This letter of June 17, 1812, was in reply to one of Judge Tyler, Federal District Judge in Virginia, of May 17, 1812, who sat with Marshall in *Livingston* v. *Jefferson* (1811) 1 Brock. 203, Fed. Cas. No. 8411. Jefferson was asked to express his view on "common law rights" as set forth by Marshall: "Letters and Times of the Tylers" (1884) Vol. I pp. 263-264. For Jefferson's views see infra note 85a. In the decision, favorable to Jefferson on the point of procedure, Marshall relied on Blackstone, describing his "elementary" work as an authority from which no one could lightly dissent. While Marshall approved the recent opinions of Mansfield, he felt it necessary to follow the older English cases in point and not his "modern" attempts to overrule it. *Beveridge* "Marshall" (1919) Vol. IV p. 113 says: "Marshall, by innuendo, blames Jefferson for invoking, for his own protection, a technicality of that very common law which the latter had so often and so violently denounced."

judgment seat of his Maker. I fear nothing for our liberty from the assaults of force; but I have seen and felt much, and fear more from English books, English prejudices, English manners, and the apes, dupes and designs among our professional crafts."[31]

Again, in a letter to Madison, in 1826, in speaking of the appointment of a law professor in the University of Virginia, which was just beginning to offer instruction, Jefferson said:

"In the selection of our Law Professor,[32] we must be rigorously attentive to his political principles. You will recollect that before the Revolution, Coke Littleton [sic] was the universal elementary book of law students, and a sounder whig never wrote, nor of profounder learning in the orthodox doctrines of the British constitution, or in what were called English liberties. You remember also that our lawyers were then all whigs. But when his black-letter text and uncouth but cunning learning got out of fashion, and the honied Mansfieldism of Blackstone became the student's horn-book, from that moment, that profession (the nursery of our Congress) began to slide into toryism, and nearly all the young brood of lawyers now are of that hue. They suppose themselves, indeed to be whigs, because they no longer know what whigism or republicanism means. It is in our seminary that that vestal flame is to be kept alive; it is thence it is to spread anew over our own and the sister States."[33]

These attacks, and one in 1810,[34] centered on two issues, undesirability of the book as a law text and its harmful political in-

31. *Jefferson* "Writings" (ed. Washington) Vol. VI p. 335, a letter to Horatio G. Spafford, March 17, 1814. From the complete letter it seems Jefferson refers to Blackstone rather than Hume in the second sentence. For other attacks on Hume, who was one of Jefferson's "favorite enemies," see *Jefferson* "Common Place Book" (ed. Chinard 1926) pp. 12, 52, 374, and infra notes 77, 80.

32. Jefferson in 1818 secured as the first professor for the University of Virginia, the scientist, economist, and legal writer, Thomas Cooper of Pennsylvania and England, who was appointed "professor of chemistry and of law." Opposition by the clergy of Virginia led him to resign before the University opened. For the later life of Cooper see *Adams*, supra note 5, p. 109; *Malone* "Thomas Cooper" (1926); *Meriwether* "History of Higher Education in South Carolina" Circulars of the U. S. Bureau of Education (1888) Vol. I pp. 143-183; 25 Fed. Cas. p. 644.

33. *Jefferson* "Works" (ed. Ford Vol. XII p. 456. See *Madison* "Writings" (1910) Vol. IX p. 218, for correspondence with Jefferson on the selection of law texts and a law professor for the University of Virginia.

34. Infra note 48.

fluence. Jefferson's interest in legal education may aid in explaining the attacks on the Commentaries as a text. Jefferson disapproved of law office study[35] though other means of instruction were hardly available.[36] In 1779, through his efforts while Governor of Virginia, the first collegiate professorship of law in this country was created at William and Mary College.[37] Later, as one of the founders of the University of Virginia, Jefferson was instrumental in establishing a "school of law, politics, and history" there.[38] This belief in the benefits to be found in university training explains why Jefferson thought that law students who had not had its advantage should spend several years in private reading of law books and works in other fields. To this end he frequently prepared lists of readings for law students. In 1790 his list included Blackstone.[39] In 1814 he revised another list prepared "near 50 years ago,"[40] and included such works as Tooke's "Diversions of Purley," "a theory of language hung on a legal squabble,"[41] the works of Kames, a Scottish legal writer whose idea on equity Blackstone disliked,[42] and the sceptical works of Priestley;[43] yet strangely enough he also listed the Commentaries and described it as "the inimitable Commentaries of Blackstone" and "the last perfect digest of both branches of law, common law and chancery." Whether this description appeared in the list of "near 50 years ago" and was copied in 1814 by oversight is not clear. It is to be noted,

35. In 1790 Jefferson said: "It is a general practice to study law in the office of some lawyer. . . . This indeed gives to the student the advantage of his instruction. But I have never seen that the services expected in return have been more than the instructions have been worth." "Works" (ed. Ford) Vol. VI p. 71. Jefferson studied in the office of Chancellor Wythe. *Jefferson*, op. cit., Vol. I p. 6.

36. *Reed*, supra note 14, p. 423.

37. *Warren*, supra note 14, p. 343. The first occupant was Chancellor Wythe and the second St. George Tucker: "Great American Lawyers" (1907) Vol. I pp. 67, 88; infra note 44.

38. *Adams*, supra note 5, p. 135.

39. *Jefferson* "Works" (ed. Ford) Vol. VI pp. 71-73.

40. Op. cit. Vol. XI pp. 420-426.

41. *Newman* "The Idea of a University" (1912) Disc. IV p. 96. Tooke was an English liberal, a friend of the colonies, an enemy of Mansfield, and a constant critic of the English government during the American Revolution: *Yarborough* "John Horne Tooke" (1926) ch. 5.

42. 3 *Blackstone* "Commentaries" (ed. Jones 1915) *p. 442 n. For Jefferson's debt to the works of Kames see *Jefferson* "The Common Place Book" (ed. Chinard 1926) intr. pp. 16-19; *Chinard* "Jefferson and Dupont de Nemours" (1931) intr. p. lxii. Infra note 87.

43. Supra note 5.

however, it was St. George Tucker's republicanized edition which Jefferson approved in 1814,[44] and that in the same year he stated that the original work was superficial and to be read only after Coke and other digests.[45] He added that while it was "lucid in arrangement, . . . correct in its matter, classical in style, and rightfully taking its place by the side of the Justinian Institutes,"[46] it was like them only an elementary book and that "the great mass of law books from which it was extracted was still to be consulted on minute investigations."

In 1810 Jefferson had said of the Commentaries as a text:

> "I have long lamented with you the depreciation of law science. The opinion seems to be that . . . everything which is necessary is in him, and what is not in him is not necessary. I still . . . [advise young men] Coke's[47] Institutes and reports are their first, and Blackstone their last work, after an intermediate course of two or three years. It is nothing

44. For the influence of *Tucker's* "Blackstone" see *Reed*, supra note 14, pp. 116-117. For further discussion of *Tucker's* "Blackstone," which perhaps explains why Jefferson continued to recommend the Commentaries when he was attacking the original work, see infra note 149. Wythe also used the Commentaries as the basis of his lectures at William and Mary: *Reed*, supra note 14, p. 116. In November, 1810, Judge Tyler, then Governor of Virginia, wrote to Jefferson about publishing Wythe's lectures, quoting Judge Spencer Roane, that they were "not a mere servile copy of Blackstone." "Letters and Times of the Tylers" (1884) Vol. I p. 249.

45. "The laws of England may be likened to a road divided into distinct stages, at each of which a review is taken of the road passed over so far." Bracton, Mathew Bacon, Coke and Blackstone were the reviewers: *Jefferson* "Writings" (ed. Washington) Vol. VI p. 291, in a letter to Cooper in 1814.

46. The reference to Justinian was prompted by the fact that the letter was an acknowledgment of a copy of *Cooper's* "Institutes of Justinian." See infra note 75.

47. Jefferson, as a law student, referred to Coke as an "old dull scoundrel" and said "I do wish the Devil had old Coke." *Jefferson* "Works" (ed. Ford) Vol. I p. 436, a letter of December 25, 1762. See also *Parton* "Jefferson a Student of Law" (1872) 29 Atlantic Monthly 179. It might be said that Jefferson could not consistently admire Coke since the latter had supposedly advocated both "parliamentary sovereignty" and the "supremacy of a fundamental law," neither of which Jefferson perhaps approved. Jefferson could approve, however, of Coke's stand in the controversy with James I and his views that the common law owed little to the Normans and that the immemorial rights of Englishmen were merely declared by the Magna Carta. In *Coke* "Third Institute," Pref., he says: "And (to speak what we think) we would derive from the Conqueror as little as we could." See *Mackay* "Coke-Parliamentary Sovereignty or the Supremacy of the Law?" (1924) 22 Mich. L. Rev. 215; *Plucknett* "Bonham's Case and Judicial Review" (1926) 40 Harv. L. Rev. 30; *McIlwain* "The High Court of Parliament and Its Supremacy" (1910) ch. 2; *Holdsworth* "History of the English Law" (1924) Vol. V pp. 428, 475.

more than an elegant digest of what they will have acquired from the real fountains of the law."[48]

But the attacks on the Commentaries, begun forty years after the work appeared in America, were not confined to its qualities as a text. In 1814 Jefferson expressed dread of its effect on the political philosophy of young students.[49] In this regard Jefferson was disturbed over the Introduction, Book One on persons and Book Four on public wrongs,[50] though he does not refer to particular passages of the work.[51]

How can one explain Jefferson's fear of Blackstone's political influence? Jefferson, unlike the conservative Blackstone, was an agrarian democrat,[52] influenced by an early frontier environment.[53] He distrusted a strong central government and was never aligned with the propertied classes, the ruling families, and the religious leaders.[54] He had little concern for stable government, desired a

48. *Jefferson* "Works" (ed. Ford) Vol. XI p. 142 n, a letter to Judge Tyler. In 1817 Story said that while the Commentaries was a summary sketch, the work should not be condemned as superficial, too general, too elementary, for these objections were founded on a general misconception of it: *Story* "Miscellaneous Writings" (1835) p. 230. See also *Holdsworth*, supra note 2.

49. Supra note 31. In 1814 Jefferson also said: "I join in your reprobation of our merchants, priests, and lawyers for their adherence to England and monarchy, in preference to their own country and its constitution. . . . I ascribe much of this [as concerns lawyers] to the substitution of Blackstone for my Lord Coke, as an elementary work." "Writings" (ed. Washington) Vol. VI p. 334.

50. *Cartwright* "An Appeal on the Subject of the English Constitution" (1797) p. 28: "So little had it occurred to Blackstone, to form an idea on our constitution, as anything distinct from our law, that in the index to his four volumes, the word 'constitution' does not so much as hold a place; and it will be seen by any attentive reader that the want of this discriminating idea betrays him into frequent inconsistencies." *Dicey* "Constitutional Law" (4th ed. 1893) p. 7: "Of constitutional law as such there is not a page to be found in his [Blackstone's] Commentaries. The matters which appear to belong to it are dealt with by him in the main under the head of Rights of Persons." Cf. *Austin* "Jurisprudence" (ed. Campbell 1874) Vol. II p. 173. On conflicting American and English ideas of the British constitution see *Van Tyne* "The War of Independence" (1922) ch. 9.

51. For exception to one passage see infra note 106.

52. *Parrington* "The Colonial Mind" (1927) pp. 342-356. "The abolition of primogeniture removed the feudal and unnatural distinctions which made one member of every family rich, and the rest poor, substituting equal partition, the best of all Agrarian laws": *Jefferson* "Works" (ed. Ford) Vol. I p. 77.

53. *Bowers* "Jefferson and Hamilton" (1925) pp. 95-98; *Dodd* "Statesmen of the Old South" (1917) pp. 3, 4, 23; *Turner* "The Frontier in American History" (1920) p. 250.

54. For Jeffersonian democracy see *Merriam* "American Political Theories"

government responsive to the popular will in each of the three branches,[55] and thought an occasional disturbance good for society.[56] He regarded the revolt from England as a social reformation and wished to eradicate every fiber of feudalism and to lay the foundation of a republican government.[57] To accomplish this in Virginia he had proposed as early as 1776 a system of general education,[58] a revision of its laws,[59] the disestablishment of the church, the passage of statutes on religious freedom, and the abolition of entails and primogeniture.[60] Hardly had the Revolution begun when he

(1924) ch. 4; *Beard* "Economic Origins of Jeffersonian Democracy" (1915); *Hansen* "Liberalism and American Education in the 18th Century" (1926) p. 179; *Parrington* "The Romantic Revolution, 1800-1860" (1927) p. 19.

55. In 1789 Jefferson said that "the people should participate in all three branches of the government to ensure honest administration; this is done by the election of the executives, the legislators and by the jury system." Further, he thought that the juries should be judges of the law when they suspect that the judges are biased and thus "they have been the firmest bulwarks of English liberty." *Jefferson* "Works" (ed. Ford) Vol. V p. 483. Infra note 85.

56. "And what country can preserve its liberties if their rulers are not warned from time to time that their people preserve the spirit of resistance? . . . The tree of liberty must be refreshed from time to time with the blood of patriots and tyrants." *Jefferson* "Works" (ed. Ford) V p. 362, a letter of 1787.

57. See *Hirst* "Jefferson" (1926) p. 130; *Muzzey* "Jefferson" (1918) ch. 3; *Chinard* "Jefferson" (1929) pp. 86-108.

58. *Adams* "Thomas Jefferson and the University of Virginia" (1888); *Honeywell* "The Educational Work of Jefferson" (1931); *Arrowood* "Jefferson and Education in a Republic" (1930); infra notes 68 and 69.

59. In October, 1776, Jefferson, as a member of the Virginia House of Delegates, "moved and presented a bill for the revision of the laws of Virginia." *Jefferson* "Works" (ed. Ford) Vol. I p. 67; (1776) 9 Hening Va. St. at L. p. 175. In this revision he proposed jury trials in chancery and a reformed criminal code: *Jefferson*, op. cit., pp. 57-78. *Kean* "Jefferson as a Legislator" (1887) 11 Va. L. J. 705, discusses Jefferson's reforms. One of the committee proposed that Blackstone's work be used as the basis for the revision. "Writings" (ed. Washington) Vol. VI p. 66.

60. "I considered four of these bills, passed or reported, as forming a system by which every fibre would be eradicated of ancient or future aristocracy; and a foundation laid for a government truly republican. . . . To these might too be added, as a further security, the introduction of the trial by jury into the Chancery courts, which have already ingulfed and continue to ingulf, so great a proportion of the jurisdiction over our property." Autobiography (1821), *Jefferson* "Works" (ed. Ford) Vol. I pp. 77-78. Jefferson succeeded in having passed three important acts: the abolition of entails, (1776) 9 Hening Va. St. at L. p. 226; abolition of primogeniture and establishment of equal partitions of estates, (1785) 12 Hening Va. St. at L. p. 138; and the "restoration" of the right of religious liberty and the disestablishment of the Church of England, (1776) 9 Hening Va. St. at L. p. 164; (1785) 12 Hening Va. St. at L. p. 184; (1789) 2 Sheperd Va. St. at L. p. 149.

resigned his seat in the Continental Congress and returned to Virginia to institute these social reforms.[61]

With the establishment of the republic his fear of the lawyers[62] and their political philosophy increased.[63] He had no desire to protect the propertied class against the masses[64] by a system of checks and balances[65] but wished to protect the individual from the tyranny of church and state.[66] Therefore, when the Federal Constitution was drafted without a bill of rights he urged that one be added.[67] He did not fear the masses and was willing to entrust them with the experiment in democratic government. But, that it might succeed, education was necessary,[68] and equally important was the nature of that education[69] and especially that of the young lawyers[70] who were to be leaders in the new government. Clearly

61. As to the Marshall attitude toward Jefferson for ignoring the revolutionary cause and returning to Virginia to devote himself to reforms see *Beveridge* "Life of John Marshall" (1916) Vol. I pp. 126-131.

62. *Warren* "Jacobin and Junto" (1931) ch. 6 on "Jefferson and the Law Craft." North Carolina is at present in the most dangerous state. The lawyers all tories, the people substantially republican, but uninformed and deceived by the lawyers, who are elected of necessity because few other candidates": *Jefferson* "Works" (ed. Ford) Vol. IX p. 129, a letter of 1800. While Jefferson was a lawyer by training he discontinued the practice after seven successful years, 1767 to 1774. *Didier* "Jefferson as a Lawyer" (1903) 15 Green Bag 153; *Davis* "Thomas Jefferson, Attorney at Law" (1927) 13 A. B. A. Jour. 63.

63. "As an intellectual he [Jefferson] had none of the lawyer's complacency with legal principles, or conceit of the law's sufficiency; and as a democrat he would not yield sovereignty into the hands of the judiciary. He had no veneration for the Common Law of England; it had grown up by slow accretions during centuries of absolutism; how should it be expected to answer the needs of a freer age." *Parrington* "The Colonial Mind" (1927) p. 352.

64. Supra note 55.

65. See *Smith* "Spirit of the American Government (1907) for the dread of popular control.

66. In 1800 Jefferson wrote: "I have sworn upon the altar of God eternal hostility against every form of tyranny over the mind of man." "Works" (ed. Ford) Vol. IX p. 148.

67. *Jefferson*, op. cit., Vol. I p. 118.

68. "I have great confidence in the common sense of mankind in general; but it requires a great deal to get the better of notions which our tutors have instilled into our minds while incapable of questioning them, and to rise superior to antipathies strongly rooted." *Jefferson*, op. cit., Vol. IX p. 143, a letter of 1800.

69. In 1810 Jefferson wrote to Judge Tyler: "I have indeed two great measures at heart without which no republic can maintain itself in strength. 1. That of general education, to enable every man to judge for himself what will secure or endanger his freedom. 2. To divide every county . . . that all the children of each will be within reach of a central school . . ." *Jefferson*, op. cit., Vol. XI p. 143 n. See also Vol. IV p. 64 and Vol. IX p. 103; supra note 58.

70. "Works" (ed. Ford) Vol. XI p. 488; supra note 33.

the social reformer in conservative colonial Virginia of 1776 and the opponent of the pro-English Federalists in the new republic could find little to praise in the political philosophy of Blackstone, the eulogist of an English society and government which had as its foundation the protection of the propertied class.

To understand completely Jefferson's antagonism toward the Commentaries one must be familiar with his theory of history, which rested on the conflict between Saxon and Norman, Whig and Tory, "Republican" and Federalist, and on the Saxon origin of ancient liberties and the subsequent destruction of them by English kings and wily Norman lawyers.

It may be contended that Jefferson's reaction to Blackstone was due to his anti-English prejudices, and that his stay in France from 1784 to 1789 had made him a disciple of French schools of thought.[71] But his views on history were formed in his student days long before he journeyed to France,[72] as can be gathered from his "Common Place Book."[73] A letter of October 25, 1825, shows that he still clung to them in his old age.[74]

It was Jefferson's view that the common law ended with the Magna Carta, that subsequent development came by way of statute law,[75] and that the common law, the rights of Englishmen, and

71. Supra note 49. For references to the French influence on Jefferson see *Beveridge* "Marshall" (1916) Vol. I pp. 303-304; *Fay* "Revolutionary Spirit in France and America" (1927) p. 222; *Parrington* "The Romantic Revolution" (1927) p. 10; *Jones* "America and French Culture" (1927) p. 550 n. 114. That the French influence on Jefferson's ideas was less than has been asserted see *Bowers* "Jefferson and Hamilton" (1925) pp. 96-101; *Chinard*, infra note 72, ch. 2; *Jefferson* "Common Place Book" ed. intr. p. 63; *Chinard* "Jefferson and Dupont de Nemours" (1931) intr. p. xii.

72. *Chinard* "Jefferson" (1929) pp. 28-33; *Jefferson* "Common Place Book" (1926) pp. 63-65; *Dickinson* "Administrative Justice and Supremacy of the Law" (1919) p. 96 n. See *Corwion* "The Higher Law Background of American Constitutional Law" (1929) 42 Harv. L. Rev. 149, 170 n. 66 for a resumé of Jefferson's theory of history.

73. "Common Place Book" (1926) ed. intr. pp. 4-14; *Chinard* "Jefferson" (1929) pp. 48-49. For the formative years of Jefferson's life see *Chinard*, supra note 72, pp. 18-33. See op. cit. p. 84 for the influence of Jefferson's Scottish teacher. See also supra note 42.

74. See infra note 77. Jefferson prepared "An Essay Towards Facilitating Instruction in the Anglo-Saxon" and recommended that the language be taught in the University of Virginia: *Jefferson* "Writings" (Memorial ed.) Vol. XVIII pp. 356-411; *Adams*, supra note 5, pp. 92, 140.

75. "Writings" (ed. Washington) Vol. VI pp. 292, 315. Because of this view Jefferson desired a translation of Bracton as the best evidence of the common law. See also op. cit. Vol. VII p. 207, a letter of 1821; Vol. IX p. 485, an observation of 1812; and supra note 46. "Such a conspectus of the history of England

the English constitution were Saxon in origin. His theory was that after the Norman Conquest English history was a struggle by the people against the Plantagenets, the Tudors, and the Stuarts[76] for a restoration of their ancient rights; that the Whigs deduced their rights from Saxon sources while the Tories turned to the Norman influence which had overcome Saxon laws;[77] and that the American colonists had assumed the long lost rights of the Saxons[78] and had

---

[a struggle by the people to secure a restoration of their ancient rights] was neither new nor original; it was one of the favorite contentions of the English jurists during the Eighteenth Century, and nowhere perhaps is it more forcibly developed than in the last chapter of Blackstone's Commentaries": *Chinard*, supra note 72, p. 31. See *Blackstone* "Commentaries" Vol. IV *p. 413, where it is said that the Norman jurist extracted the most slavish doctrines and oppressive consequences out of the primitive simplicity of the feudal law which was intended as a law of liberty by the first Saxon invaders who brought the system with them. He also said that the jury was the most important guardian of public and private liberty and that we owe it to our Saxon ancestors. See infra note 89 for a similar theory presented by "Junius" in 1770. This theory of the importance of the Saxon element in the common law appeared in a charge to a Federal grand jury in 1793, wherein Mr. Justice Wilson of the Supreme Court said: "The common law, as now received in America, bears, in its principles and in many of its more minute particulars, a stronger and a fairer resemblance to the common law as it was improved under the former [the Saxons], than to that law as it was disfigured under the latter [the Normans] . . . It was this spirit [of liberty] which dictated the frequent and formidable demands on the Norman princes, for the complete restoration of the Saxon jurisprudence. . . . There is, by the way, a pleasure in reflecting on such important renovations of the venerable Saxon government; and in discovering that our national constitution is rendered illustrious by the antiquity, as well as by the excellence, of some of its leading principles." *Wharton* "State Trials of the United States" (1849) pp. 61-65.

76. Of English liberties he said they "are not infringements merely of the king's prerogative, extorted from our princes by taking advantage of their weakness; but a restoration of that ancient constitution, of which our ancestors had been defrauded by the art and finesse of the Norman lawyers, rather than deprived by force of the Norman arms." "Common Place Book" p. 192. See also pp. 56-57.

77. "Whig historians of England, therefore, have always gone back to the Saxon period for the true principles of their constitution, while the tories and Hume, . . . date it from the Norman conquest, and hence conclude that the continual claim by the nation of the good old Saxon laws, and the struggle to recover them, were 'encroachments of the people on the Crown, and not usurpations of the Crown on the people.' . . . If first read, Hume makes an English tory, from whence it is an easy step to American Toryism [Federalism]." *Jefferson* "Writings" (ed. Washington) Vol. VII p. 414, a letter of Oct. 25, 1825.

78. In 1776, as a member of a congressional committee, Jefferson designed a shield for the new nation, placing on it "Hengist and Horsa, the Saxon chiefs from whom we claim the honor of being descended, and whose political principles and forms of government we have assumed." *Jefferson* "Works" (ed. Ford) Vol. II p. 45 n; *Chinard* "Jefferson" (1929) p. 86.

won a victory in the war against the English king and his lawyers. Now in the new nation the ancient conflict was resumed in the struggle between the Federalists and the "Republicans" and in this contest the arch apostles of Toryism[79] to be overcome by the "Republicans" were Blackstone and Hume.[80] The Commentaries, the embodiment of the anti-republican influences of Norman, Tory, and their American descendant—Federalism—was spreading in the young nation the political principles of these aggressors upon ancient Saxon liberties.

A further explanation of Jefferson's antagonism toward Blackstone is perhaps to be found in his opinion of Mansfield. Mansfield was Chief Justice of England from 1756 to 1778, a member of the English cabinet or closely associated with it prior to the Revolution,[81] legal adviser to the group which was determining

79. "For in truth, the parties of Whig and Tory are those of nature. They exist in all countries, whether called by these names, or by those of Aristocrats and Democrats, . . . Ultras and Radicals, Serviles and Liberals." *Jefferson* "Works" (ed. Ford) Vol. XII p. 323. See also *Jefferson* "Writings" (ed. Washington) Vol. VII p. 391, a letter of 1825.

80. "The elegant one [History of England] of Hume seems intended to disguise and discredit the good principles of government." *Jefferson* "Works" (ed. Ford) Vol. X p. 416, a letter of 1807. In this letter Jefferson recommends a republicanized version of *Hume's* "History." See also supra note 31. "Hume, the great apostle of toryism, says 'it was the people who encroached upon the sovereign, not the sovereign who attempted as is pretended, to usurp upon the people.'" Hume also derided the idea "that the people are the origin of all just power." Jefferson therefore said of Hume: "And where else will this degenerate son of science, this traitor to his fellow man, find the origin of just powers, if not in the majority of the society? Will it be in the minority? Or in an individual of that minority?" "Writings" (ed. Washington) Vol. VII p. 356, a letter of June 5, 1824, to John Cartwright, an English friend of the colonial cause. See "Life and Correspondence of Major Cartwright" (1826) Vol. II pp. 265-278, to the effect that this letter of Jefferson was sent to Bentham by Cartwright. See also supra note 50; *Hirst* "Jefferson" (1926) pp. 555-556.

81. See *Hansard* "Parliamentary History" Vol. XVIII pp. 266-282, for attacks in Parliament in 1775 on Lord Mansfield for having drawn acts obnoxious to the American colonies and for serving both as Chief Justice and as a member of the "cabinet." In the debates is a defense of these bills by Mansfield. In (1899) 107 Law Times 325, Mansfield was referred to as the chief support of Lord North's government and as a political chief justice. The impropriety of his serving in the "cabinet" and as Chief Justice in the trials for seditious libel is also discussed. *Campbell* "Lives of the Chief Justices" (1873) Vol. III p. 361 says it seems hardly credible that Mansfield should have been present at the cabinet deliberations over prosecutions for seditious libel as the proceedings were likely to come before him and therefore he must have been struck with the impropriety of taking part in originating them. For Mansfield's views on the British Empire, the relation of the colonies to Parliament, the doctrine of virtual representation, and internal and external taxation, as expressed in party

England's colonial policy,[82] and the patron of Blackstone.[82a] As early as 1788 Jefferson expressed fear of the "sly poison" of Mansfield's legal innovations.[82b] In attacks on Mansfield Jefferson usually mentioned Blackstone as having been his abettor.[82c] The "judicial freedom of decision" which chancery judges practiced,[83] and which Mansfield had imitated in a court of law, aroused Jefferson. Therefore, in a constitution for Virginia drafted by him as far back

---

debates in Parliament, see *Marks* "England and America" (1907) Vol. I pp. 46-48; *Andrews* "American Law" (1900) p. 54; *Roscoe* "Eminent British Lawyers" (1830) p. 191; 1 *Blackstone* "Commentaries" (Andrews' Cooley 4th ed. 1899) *p. 109 n. 2.

82. "Thus throughout the whole of the great struggle for independence, into which the colonists were driven, Lord Mansfield opposed every measure which might have prevented the result he so greatly deprecated. . . . While in politics, Lord Mansfield was thus adverse to those liberal principles which might have taught him to view the resistance of the colonies in another light, in matters of religion his opinions were fortunately of a much more tolerant character": *Roscoe* "Eminent British Lawyers" (1830) p. 191. *Lucas* "Lord North" (1913) Vol. II p. 1775; *Van Tyne* "The War of Independence" (1922) pp. 196-223; *Clark* "British Opinion and the American Revolution" (1930) p. 242; *Becker* "The Eve of the American Revolution" (1918) p. 109; *Campbell*, supra note 81, p. 405; 17 Encyc. Brit. (11th ed. 1910) p. 600.

82a. For Mansfield's influence on Blackstone's career see *Holdsworth* "Blackstone" (1927) 7 Ore. L. Rev. 155, 157; infra notes 87, 92, 120, 124. For Mansfield's commendation of the Commentaries as a text and his reference to the uncouth, crabbed author, Coke, see (1873) 18 Albany L. Jour. 220, 221. Compare, however, Bentham's view of Mansfield's attitude on Bentham's attacks on the Commentaries: *Bentham* "Works" (1843) Vol. I p. 246. See also *Holdsworth* "Blackstone's Treatment of Equity" (1929) 43 Harv. L. Rev. 1, 7, 11; *Holliday* "Mansfield" (1797) p. 89.

82b. In October, 1788, Jefferson wrote: "So evident a heresy [the case of the interrogatories in Pennsylvania] in the common law, ought not to be tolerated on the authority of two or three civilians, who happened, unfortunately, to make authority in the courts of England. I hold it essential, in America, to forbid that any English decisions since the accession of Lord Mansfield to the bench, should ever be cited in a court; because, though there have come many good ones from him, yet there is so much sly poison instilled into a great part of them, that it is better to proscribe the whole." *Jefferson* "Writings" (ed. Washington) Vol. II p. 487. See also infra note 87.

82c. See infra note 87 for a letter of 1789 in which Jefferson states that Mansfield's views had been "admirably seconded by the celebrated Dr. Blackstone." See supra note 33 for a reference in 1825 to the "honied Mansfieldism of Blackstone." 3 *Hammond*, supra note 9, p. 604 of the editor's notes.

83. For opposition to "chancery" in the colonies see *Goebel* "Materials on Legal Institutions" (1931) p. 362; *Pound* "Spirit of Common Law" (1921) p. 53; *Pound* "Interpretations of Legal History" (1923) p. 103; 3 *Blackstone* "Commentaries" (ed. Jones 1915) *p. 428 n; 1 Root (Conn. 1789) intr. xiv; "Great American Lawyers" (1907) Vol. I pp. 444-449. For the history of some early chancery courts see "Great American Lawyers" (1907) Vol. I p. 76; *Story* "Miscellaneous Writings" (1835) p. 268. See also *Warren* "History of the Federal Judiciary Act of 1789" (1923) 37 Harv. L. Rev. 49, 96.

as 1776 he provided for jury trials in chancery.[84] He did this because the jury was that "inestimable institution," which curbed the judges and represented the people in the judicial branch.[85] It was this "judicial freedom" that had led the American courts to consider the common law of England as "a birthright or an inheritance,"[85a] thereby adopting a body of law of questionable merit to govern the people, when it ought to have been left for the legislative branch to enact it in such part and of such a period as it saw fit.

In England the prototype of the uncontrolled usurper of legislative powers was Mansfield. It was he who by his innovations had tended to turn law courts into those distrusted courts of equity and to take them out of "the pale of juries."[86] A free country could in

84. *Jefferson* "Works" (ed. Ford) Vol. II p. 177; Vol. I p. 60. Supra notes 59 and 60.

85. *Jefferson*, op. cit., Vol. V p. 224; First Annual Presidential Message, *Jefferson* "Works" (ed. Ford) Vol. IX p. 340. Supra note 55.

85a. Jefferson's opposition to the view that the common law of England was "a birthright or an inheritance" and therefore the law of the several states, rested in part on the fact that he did not believe the people should be governed by laws that their respresentatives had not adopted. Jefferson wrote to Judge Tyler in 1812: "I deride with you the ordinary doctrine, that we brought with us from England the common law rights. This narrow notion was a favorite in the first moment of rallying to our rights against Great Britain. But it was that of men who felt their rights, before they had thought of their explanation. The truth is, that we brought with us the rights of men, of expatriated men." *Jefferson "Writings"* (ed. Washington) Vol. VI p. 65. Again: "the common law of England was not our 'birthright,' a conceit as inexplicable as the trinity, but [came] by adoption." A letter of June 13, 1822, op. cit., Vol. VII p. 251. For a similar idea see the remarks of John Adams in "Novanglus" in 1774, *Adams* "Works" (1851) Vol. IV p. 122. Jefferson also did not believe that Congress, much less the federal courts, had the power to make the common law of England federal law. *Jefferson* "Works" (ed. Ford) Vol. IX pp. 73, 76, 87, in a letter of 1799. Contrast this view with that of the Chairman of the Congressional Committee, to consider the extension of the Sedition Act of 1798, which was in effect for two years, who stated that the statute should be continued since the federal common law crime of seditious libel, which was based on the law of England prior to the Revolution, was ameliorated by the Sedition Act and was therefore more objectionable than the statute: "Annals of 6th Congress" (1799-1801) pp. 916-917, debate of Jan. 21, 1801. For the Sedition Act see (1789-99) 1 U. S. St. at L. 596; infra notes 152b, 155. Cf. *Story* "Constitution" (5th ed. 1891) sec. 151. For the identification in colonial times of the rights of man and the common law rights of Englishmen see *Pound* "Judge Story" (1914) 48 Am. L. Rev. 676, 681; *Pound* and *Plucknett* "Readings" (3d ed. 1927) p. 309; *Pound* "Spirit of the Common Law" (1921) p. 100; *Pound* "Interpretations of Legal History" (1923) p. 41; *Morris* "Studies in American Law" (1930) p. 67. See also supra note 30.

86. "The only natural improvement of the common law, is through its homogeneous ally, the chancery, in which new principles are to be examined, con-

no wise tolerate such action.[87] Accordingly, to rid American law of the example of Mansfield, and of his poisonous decisions, Jefferson contended that no English authorities prior to the accession of George III in 1760 should be cited in American courts.[88] In 1789 Jefferson classed Mansfield and Blackstone, who had been closely associated in England, as opponents of "republicanism." Political radicals of the times in England, as "Junius" and Horne Tooke, likewise regarded them as part of the political group which had supported the odious domestic and colonial policies of the English government. "Junius" denounced Mansfield for destroying Saxon rights and the Saxon spirit of liberty by his treatment of juries,[89]

cocted and digested. But when by repeated decisions and modifications, they are rendered pure and certain they should be transferred by statute to the courts of common law, and placed within the pale of juries." *Jefferson* "Writings" (ed. Washington) Vol. VI p. 66, a letter of 1812 to Judge Tyler.

87. "Lord Mansfield, a man of the clearest head and most seducing eloquence . . . has been able since his admission to the bench of judges in England, to persuade the courts of common law to revise the practice of construing their text equitably. The object of former judges has been to render the law more and more certain. That of this personage to render it more incertain [sic] under pretense of rendering it more reasonable. . . . His plan of rendering the chancery useless by administering justice in the same way in the courts of common law has been admirably seconded by the celebrated Dr. Blackstone, a judge in the same department, who has endeavored to prove that the jurisdiction of the Chancery is chaos, irreducible to a system, insusceptible of fixed rules, and incapable of definition or explanation. Were this true, it would be a monster whose existence should not be suffered for one moment in a free country wherein every power is dangerous which is not bound up by general rules." *Jefferson* "Works" (ed. Ford) Vol. IV p. 479, a letter of 1789. See also (1932) 81 U. Pa. L. Rev. 115, 117. See 3 *Blackstone* "Commentaries" (ed. Jones 1915) *p. 432-442, and editor's notes which give an opposite view of chancery to that which Jefferson attributes to Blackstone. See also supra note 82a.

88. "We may doubt, therefore, the propriety of quoting in our courts English authorities posterior to the Declaration of Independence, or rather to the accession of that King, whose reign, ab initio, was the very tissue of wrongs which rendered the Declaration at length necessary. The reason for it had inception at least as far back as the commencement of his reign. This relation to the beginning of his reign, would add to the advantage of getting us rid of all Mansfield's innovations, or civilizations of the common law." *Jefferson* "Writings" (ed. Washington) Vol. VI p. 65, a letter to Judge Tyler in 1812. See also supra notes 30, 33.

89. "In contempt or ignorance of the common law of England, you have made it your study to introduce into the court where you preside measures of jurisprudence unknown to Englishmen. . . . Who ever heard you mention Magna Carta or the Bill of Rights with approbation or respect? By such treacherous arts the noble simplicity and free spirit of our Saxon laws were first corrupted. The Norman conquest was not complete until Norman lawyers had introduced their laws and reduced slavery to a system. This one leading principle directs your interpretation of the laws and accounts for your treatment of juries

and Horne Tooke said of Mansfield he wished the common law knew as little of Mansfield as did Mansfield of the common law.[90] There were others in America who thought of Mansfield as one of the leaders in England who opposed the colonies and who were hostile to the principles of personal liberty.[91] Perhaps Jefferson's dislike of Mansfield as early as 1788, for his part in the Revolution and for his alleged anti-republican principles, may have been the start of his adverse views on Blackstone, as he often associated the two.[92] One must also recall the part Mansfield played as judge, from 1770 to 1777, in the trials for seditious libel[93] in England

. . . Instead of those certain positive rules by which the judgments of a court of law should invariably be determined, you have fondly introduced your own unsettled notions of equity and substantial justice. Decisions given upon such principles do not alarm the public so much as they ought . . . In the meantime the practice gains ground; the Court of King's Bench becomes a court of equity; and the judge, instead of consulting the law of the land, refers only to the wisdom of the court and the purity of his own conscience." "Junius' Letters" (1894) Vol. I pp. 308-309, a letter of 1770 on the conduct of Lord Mansfield in cases of seditious libel. See also *Campbell* "Lives of the Chief Justices" (1873) Vol. III p. 337.

90. *Yarborough* "John Horne Tooke" (1926) p. 86 cites an address in which Tooke attacked Mansfield for his exercise of discretionary powers, for acting as in chancery and for setting aside jurymen. For bitter English newspaper attacks on "that crafty and cruel Caledonian Judge,"—"the bloodthirsty Mansfield,"—see *Trevelyan* "The American Revolution" (1908) Vol. III p. 184; *Hinkhouse* "The American Revolution in the English Press" (1926) p. 78 n. 1.

91. In a letter to Mr. Justice Story in 1829 John Quincy Adams said: "You speak in terms of unqualified admiration of Lord Mansfield . . . Is not Lord Mansfield most responsible of all men of that age, for the war of the American Revolution? Was he not originally a Scottish Jacobite, with the principles of Sir Robert Filmer ["Patriarchia; or the Natural Power of Kings" (1680)] bred in the bone? Did he not carry them to the grave, and how much of them did he introduce into his system of Commercial Law, and fly-blow into the Common Law?" *Story* "Life and Letters of Joseph Story" (1851) Vol. II p. 12. Adams also wrote to Story that the common law was a system "more than sufficiently poisoned by the feudality of the Norman conquest, but still illuminated with principles favorable to personal liberty, at least with jury trial and the habeas corpus. These were unknown to the Roman law, and if Lord Mansfield did not expunge them from the law of England, it was not for want of his exertion to do so. His principles, in our controversy with Great Britain, flowed naturally from his fountain of Roman law, which knew as little of the link between taxation and representation as of habeas corpus and jury trial": op. cit., p. 20. See *Tyler* "Literary History of American Revolution" (1905) Vol. I p. 216; Vol. II p. 200 for attacks in current writings on Mansfield.

92. 1 *Blackstone* "Commentaries" (ed. Jones 1915) p. xx; "Mansfield—Political Chief Justice" (1899) 107 Law Times 325; supra note 82a.

93. For Mansfield's part in the political libel cases of his day see 19 *Howell* "State Trials" pp. 1075-1138, the trial of John Wilkes in 1770; 20 op. cit., pp. 803, 867, the trial of John Almon in 1770 for selling "Junius' Letter to the King"; and 20 op. cit., pp. 651-803, the trial of John Horne in 1777 for his

which involved the friends of America and the radical opponents of the government's colonial policy—Wilkes and Tooke.[94]

It is therefore strange that Jefferson, with his dread of anti-republican influences, should have delayed until 1810 to condemn the Commentaries. Perhaps Jefferson's activities in national politics from 1790 till 1810 required so much time that it was not until retirement that he was able to resume his discussion of legal questions. By 1810 he had shifted from attacks on Mansfield to those on Blackstone, for then the Commentaries perhaps seemed a more harmful influence than Mansfield's judicial decisions.

The Source of Jefferson's Views on the Commentaries

Were the views of Jefferson on the Commentaries original[95] or did he receive his inspiration to battle against the work from some contemporary critic? Dr. Priestley[96] might have affected Jefferson's views on Blackstone as it was upon his sceptical works that Jeffer-

remarks on the English troops in America. See also *Campbell* "Lives of the Chief Justices" (1873) Vol. III p. 446; *Bleackley* "Life of Wilkes" (1917); *Yarborough* "Life of John Horne Tooke" (1926) p. 85; *Stephen* "History of the Criminal Law" (1883) Vol. II ch. 24; *Roscoe*, supra note 82, p. 219. *Bentham* "The Elements of the Art of Packing as Applied to Special Juries, Particularly in the Cases of Libel Law" (1820) p. 72, states that the chief purpose of packing was crushing the liberty of the press. Beveridge states that the juries were "packed" by the Federalists in the trials for libel under the Sedition Act of 1798: "Marshall" (1919) Vol. III p. 42 n. 1. Bentham also assailed Mansfield for his view that liberty of the press consisted in merely having the privilege to print without license. See *Rex* v. *Woodfall* (1770) 20 *Howell* "State Trials" 895, 903, a trial for publishing "Junius' Letter to the King" wherein Mansfield made the statement in the charge to the jury. See 4 *Blackstone* "Commentaries" *p. 151 for the same statement of the law. See "Junius' Letters" (1894) p. 94 for an attack on Mansfield for his charge to the jury in the trials of Wilkes and of Almon, supra, to the effect that it had nothing to do except determine the fact of printing and publishing and the innuendos. Cf. *Forsyth* "History of Trial by Jury" (1875) p. 223.

94. For the seditious libel trials in the United States in Jefferson's time see *Bowers* "Jefferson and Hamilton" (1925) ch. 17; *Nelles and King* "Contempt by Publication" (1928) 28 Col. L. Rev. 401-409; *Nelles* "The Summary Power to Punish for Contempt" (1931) 31 Col. L. Rev. 956; *Beveridge* "Marshall" (1919) Vol. III ch. 1; infra note 156. "It is probable that no one thing contributed more to inflame the public mind against the Common Law than did the insistence of the American courts on enforcing the harsh doctrines of the English law of criminal libel—that truth was no defense, and that the jury could pass only on the fact of publication and the application of the innuendo": *Warren*, supra note 14, p. 236. Infra notes 152 et seq.

95. Supra note 73.

96. Supra note 5.

son based his ideas on religion.[97] Though Jefferson wrote often to Priestley, and as early as 1800 was discussing with him a professorship in the proposed University of Virginia,[98] the published works of Jefferson do not refer to the dispute between Priestley and Blackstone in 1769.[99] Jefferson,[100] as did Priestley, thought "that in every country and in every age, the priest has been hostile to liberty."[101] In view of these facts it seems odd that Jefferson did not discuss with Priestley his early debate with Blackstone as to whether "non-conformity was a crime," which appeared in 1772 in a separate volume as an appendix to the first American edition of the Commentaries.[102] But it seems that Priestley had forgiven Blackstone before Jefferson began to attack him.[103]

Jefferson also discussed the Commentaries with Dr. Cooper in 1814.[104] In a letter of that year[105] he attacked a passage from Blackstone to the effect that Christianity was a part of the common law.[106] Jefferson, relying on his theory of history, insisted that during the final two hundred years of Saxon paganism there developed a common law in which Christianity had no part.[107] The view that Christianity was an integral part of the common law, he declared, "was the most remarkable instance of judicial legislation that has ever occurred in English jurisprudence or perhaps in any other" and revealed "the pious disposition of the English judges to connive at the frauds of the clergy, a disposition which has often

97. *Jefferson* "Works" (ed. Ford) Vol. XI p. 333; op. cit. Vol. IX p. 457; *Randall* "Jefferson" (1888) ch. 14.

98. *Jefferson* "Works" (ed. Ford) Vol. IX p. 97.

99. Infra note 102.

100. Supra note 97.

101. *Jefferson* "Writings" (ed. Washington) Vol. VI p. 334.

102. Blackstone said: "I must beg leave to inform Dr. Priestley, since it seems he is yet to learn it, that *non-conformity* is still a crime by the laws of England." "An Interesting Appendix to Blackstone's Commentaries" (1772) Vol. V p. 40.

103. Priestley in 1778, some years after his tilt with Blackstone, prepared a course of lectures on the laws of England. It does not appear that he attacked the Commentaries but cited it apparently with approval: *Priestley* "Observations on Education" (1778) pp. 280-334.

104. Supra notes 45 and 75; see also note 32.

105. *Jefferson* "Writings" (ed. Washington) Vol. VI p. 315.

106. 4 *Blackstone* "Commentaries" *p. 59 reads: "Christianity is a part of the laws of England."

107. For Jefferson's essay on this topic see *Jefferson* "Reports" (Va. 1829) pp. 137-142; "Common Place Book" (1926) pp. 351-363; *Jefferson* "Works" (ed. Ford) Vol. I pp. 453-464; *Jefferson* "Writings" (ed. Washington) Vol. VII pp. 359-361.

rendered them faithful allies in practice."[108] But since these letters to Cooper nowhere refer to any of the latter's ideas concerning Blackstone, it may be inferred that Jefferson's antagonism drew little inspiration from this source.[109]

To what extent was Jefferson influenced by Bentham, a contemporary legal reformer, with whom he had much in common? Jefferson was active in the revision of the laws of Virginia and had drafted a proposed criminal code[110] and like Bentham he desired to use reason rather than precedent as the test of schemes for bettering the lives of those governed.[111] Nevertheless, the writings of Bentham are not included in the readings prepared by Jefferson for law students, though the suggestions covered many fields of learning.[112] Jefferson must have heard of Bentham's attacks on the Commentaries and known of his books since as early as 1802[113] some of Bentham's books were to be found in France, a country with whose intellectual life Jefferson kept in close touch. In 1814 Albert Gallatin, Secretary of the Treasury under Jefferson, wrote a letter to the Governor of Pennsylvania concerning codification and public education which Bentham had publicly recommended to the governors of the American states.[114] In addition both Priestley and Cooper, correspondents of Jefferson, were familiar with the works of Bentham before they left England. Bentham, in fact,

108. Supra note 105, p. 311; "Works" (ed. Ford) Vol. I p. 453 n; *Hirst* "Jefferson" (1926) p. 35. Jefferson's "infidel utterance" was cited as authority by counsel for the defense in an indictment for blasphemy in *State* v. *Thomas Jefferson Chandler* (Del. 1837) 2 Harr. 553. Clayton, C. J., denounced Jefferson's views. See *Wright* "John Middleton Clayton" in "Great American Lawyers" (1908) Vol. III p. 417. For another attack on this view of Jefferson see "Life and Letters of Joseph Story" (1851) Vol. I pp. 430-434; "Memoirs of John Quincy Adams" (1876) Vol. VIII p. 291.

109. *Cooper* "The Law of Libel and the Liberty of the Press" (1830) does not condemn the Commentaries and makes only a slight reference to the work, despite the fact that Cooper discussed aspects of the law of libel on which the Commentaries might have been considered "anti-republican." See *U. S.* v. *Cooper* (1800) Fed. Cas. No. 14,865 for Cooper's trial for seditious libel. See also *Cooper* "Justinian" *p. 634.

110. Supra notes 59 and 60.

111. *Jefferson*, op. cit., Vol. IX p. 104.

112. Supra notes 39 and 40.

113. *Dillon* "The Laws and Jurisprudence of America and England" (1895) p. 337 n. For the dates of Bentham's works see *Halévy* "Philosophic Radicalism" (trans. Morris 1928) p. 527.

114. See *Bentham* "Papers Relative to Codification and Public Instruction Including Correspondence with Divers Constituted Authorities in The American United States" (1817).

felt indebted to Priestley for one of his fundamental philosophic principles.[115] Edward Livingston, who prepared certain codes for Louisiana, stated that he had received the inspiration for his work from reading Dumont's edition of Bentham.[116] Aaron Burr, while in England in 1808, became an associate of Bentham and referred to his works with praise.[116a] From these facts it seems that Jefferson likewise should have been familiar with Bentham's writings. But if Jefferson's failure to refer to Bentham in his correspondence can be relied upon it seems that he was not influenced by Bentham's attacks on Blackstone.

There was an American who had announced his fear of Blackstone's anti-republican views before Jefferson did and from whom Jefferson might have drawn his ideas about Blackstone. This was James Wilson, a signer of the Declaration of Independence, a member of the Constitutional Convention of 1787, the first professor of law in the present University of Pennsylvania and a member of the first Supreme Court of the United States.[117] In 1774 in an address "On the Nature and Extent of the Legislative Authority of the British Parliament"[118] Wilson took exception to statements of Blackstone that there is in every state a supreme and uncontrolled authority, that this "absolute despotic power" is vested in Parliament,[119] and that the colonies as a part of the British Empire and as conquered territory[120] were subject to the control of such a

115. *Malone* "Thomas Cooper" (1926) p. 14. For Bentham's obligation to Priestley see (1926) 21 ILLINOIS LAW REVIEW 302, 307.

116. *Hunt* "Edward Livingston" (1864) p. 96; *Bentham* "Works" (ed. Bowring 1843) Vol. XI pp. 23, 51.

116a. "Memoirs of Burr" (ed. Davis 1837) Vol. II p. 414.

117. "Great American Lawyers" (1907) Vol. I p. 214.

118. This address was published in pamphlet form in 1774. See *Wilson* "Works" (ed. Bird Wilson 1804) Vol. III pp. 203-246 for the address. See also *Wilson* "Works" (ed. Andrews 1895); *Adams* "Selected Political Essays of James Wilson" (1930); *Adams* "Political Ideas of the American Revolution" (1922) ch. 7, on "The Legal Theories of James Wilson"; *Konkle* "Joseph Hopkinson" (1931) ch. 4.

119. 1 "Commentaries" *pp. 49, 51, 108, 160.

120. For Blackstone's view that the American colonies are to be deemed conquered territory and that the common law of England has no authority there, see 1 "Commentaries" (ed. Jones 1915) *p. 107 and notes. Cf. *Story* "Constitution" (5th ed. 1891) sec. 151. See *Wilson* "Works" (ed. Andrews 1895) Vol. I p. 19 notes 1 and 2, where the editor alleges that after the first edition, Blackstone, at the suggestion of Mansfield, changed his text on the power of Parliament over the colonies. Andrews in speaking of the power of Parliament over the American colonies says: "The similarity of the doctrines of Mansfield and Blackstone suggests the query as to whether Mansfield was fol-

parliament. Certainly this was a view which the rebellious colonists and the founders of the nation, who believed that all government is founded on the consent of the governed, could not approve.[121] This address of Wilson, which centered largely upon a refutation of the Commentaries, was not based upon the right of revolution but was a legal argument to show that though the American colonies were a part of the British Empire, owing allegiance to the Crown, they were not subject to parliamentary control.[122]

By 1790 Wilson was delivering lectures to law students and had turned from a refutation of Blackstone's conception of the British Empire to a treatment of the despotic and absolute principles which appeared in the Commentaries.[123] Wilson's attack in these lectures began with the often quoted definition that municipal law is "a rule of civil conduct, prescribed by the supreme power in a state."[124]

---

lowing Blackstone, or Blackstone was quoting the opinion of his influential friend. An examination discloses that Blackstone re-edited volume I in 1776, within a year from its first publication; and while there was nothing on this subject which would seriously have incensed an American reader, although he clearly erred in claiming the colonies as occupying conquered territory—the significance of which was that the inhabitants of conquered territory could not claim the rights of constitutional representation as a part of the common law —the subject was entirely changed in the second edition to conform to the opinion of Mansfield and the predominant ministry in England." "American Law" (1900) p. 55. In *Blackstone* "Tracts" (1771) p. 17, in the essay on "An Analysis of the Laws of England" prepared about 1776 it is said "our plantations abroad, are governed by their own laws; but are bound by acts of the British Parliament, if specially named therein." In the Commentaries the phrase "governed by their own laws" does not appear. See 1 *Hammond* "Blackstone" (1890) pp. 275-285 of the editor's notes, and *Tucker* "Blackstone" (1803) Vol. I pt. 1, editor's app. p. 381 for a discussion of Blackstone's views of the control of Parliament over the American colonies and the authority of the common law in the colonies.

121. 1 *Hammond* "Blackstone" (1890) p. 112 of the editor's notes.

122. For a discussion of the colonial conception of the British Empire see *Carpenter* "American Political Thought" (1930) p. 32; *McIlwain* "The American Revolution" (1923); *Schuyler* "Parliament and the British Empire" (1929); *Parrington* "The Colonial Mind" (1927) pp. 179-190; *Hirst* "Jefferson" (1926) p. 70; *Van Tyne* "The War of Independence" (1922) ch. 8.

123. See "Great American Lawyers" (1907) Vol. I, p. 212; 1 *Hammond* "Blackstone" (1890) p. 112 of the editor's notes.

124. 1 "Commentaries" *p. 44. See also *Wilson* "Works" (ed. Andrews 1895) Vol. I p. 54 n, where the editor alleges that Blackstone, who was a protegé of Mansfield, was probably influenced by him in formulating this definition; supra note 120. 1 *Hammond* "Blackstone" (1890) p. 112 of editor's notes, points out that Judge Zephaniah Swift, 1759-1823, in "The System of the Laws of Connecticut" (1795) and St. George Tucker in his edition of the Commentaries (1803) Vol. I pt. 1 *p. 53 n. 10 and pp. 3-6 of the editor's app. disagree with Blackstone's definition. At the time Swift prepared his work it is said he repre-

Wilson objected to the idea that "law" presupposes some supreme power as it contained the germ of divine right, assumed the existence of despotic government, and denied that social compact theory of a state which traces the authority of law to the consent of the governed.[125]

In speaking of Blacksone's view of an uncontrolled power which prescribed the law, Wilson said:

> "If the doctrines insinuated in the definition of law can be supported on the principles of reason and science, the defense of other principles, which I have thought to be those of liberty and just government, becomes—I am sorry to say it —a fruitless attempt."[126]
>
> "As I have mentioned Sir William Blackstone, let me speak of him explicitly as it becomes me. I cannot consider him a zealous friend of republicanism. One of his survivors or successors in office, has characterized him by the appellation of an anti-republican lawyer. On the subject of government, I think I can plainly discover his jealousies and attachments. . . . As author of the Commentaries he possesses uncommon merit. . . . In public law, however, he should be consulted with a cautious prudence. . . . On every account,

sented the school of legal thought which desired to create a system of jurisprudence purely American. See "Great American Lawyers" (1907) Vol. II p. 117.

125. *Wilson* "Works" (1804) Vol. I p. 66.

126. *Wilson*, op. cit., Vol. I p. 68. Wilson's adverse reaction to Blackstone's theory of the uncontrolled power of a sovereign was set forth in an opinion, holding that a state was not immune from suit in a federal court by a citizen of another state. The opinion, in part, reads: "The law, says Sir William Blackstone, ascribed to the King, the attribute of sovereignty; he is sovereign and independent, within his own dominions. . . . Hence it is, that no suit or action can be brought against a King, even in civil matters; because no court can have jurisdiction over him; for all jurisdiction implies superiority of power. This last position is only a branch of a much more extensive principle, on which a plan of systematic despotism has been lately formed in England, and prosecuted with unwearied assiduity and care. Of this plan, the author of the Commentaries was, if not the introducer, at least the great supporter. He has been followed in it by writers later and less known; and his doctrines have, both on the other and this side of the Atlantic, been implicitly and generally received by those who neither examined their principles nor their consequences. The principle is, that all human laws must be prescribed by a superior. . . . another principle, very difficult in its nature and operations, forms, in my judgment, the basis of sound and genuine jurisprudence; laws derived from the pure source of equality and justice must be founded on the consent of those whose obedience they require. The sovereign, when traced to the source, must be found in the man." *Chisholm* v. *Georgia* (1793) 2 Dall. 419, 458. See 1 *Blackstone* "Commentaries" (ed. Jones 1915) *p. 243 n. 5.

therefore, he should be read and studied. He deserves to be much admired; but he ought not to be implicitly followed."[126a]

Wilson again condemned this definition in even stronger terms, saying that Blackstone "has defined municipal law, as applied to the law of England, upon principles to which I must assign the apithets dangerous and unsound. It is of high import to the liberties of the United States, that the seeds of despotism be not permitted to lurk at the roots of our municipal law."[127] He also objected to Blackstone's view that English liberties were human in origin[128] for he believed that they were natural rights and not subject to the supreme power which Blackstone said existed in every government.[129]

At this point it is well to consider the statement that Jefferson in drafting the Declaration of Independence was influenced by the Commentaries[130] and used it as authority to support his views. Jefferson could have found support for his "natural rights" theory[131] in Blackstone's well-known statement of the supremacy of the law of nature over human laws.[132] Such a phrase, perhaps added by Blackstone for ornament,[133] could have been used by those seeking legal support for the right of resistance against what was considered the wrongful exercise of power by the English parliament.[134] But

126a. *Wilson*, op. cit., Vol. I pp. 21-22.

127. *Wilson*, op. cit., Vol. I p. 179.

128. 1 "Commentaries" *p. 127.

129. *Wilson*, op. cit., Vol. II pp. 456-475. For further attacks by Wilson on the basis that Blackstone relied inconsistently on divine right and absolute power and also on a compact theory, see 1 *Hammond* "Blackstone" (1890) pp. 111-117 of the editor's notes, and *Andrews* "American Law" (1900) p. 46 n. 1.

130. Supra note 20.

131. See *Haines* "Revival of Natural Law Concepts" (1930) pp. 54, 56 for Jefferson's views on natural rights and the law of nature. See also *Wright* "Natural Law in American Political Theory" (1923) 4 S. W. Pol. Science Q. 202.

132. "This law of nature, being coeval with mankind and dictated by God Himself, is of course superior to any other. . . . no human laws are of any validity, if contrary to this. . . ." 1 *Blackstone* "Commentaries" *p. 41.

133. *Pollock* "The History of the Law of Nature" (1901) 1 Col. L. Rev. 11, 31, says this phrase was added for ornamentation. *Haines* "The Law of Nature" (1915) 25 Yale L. J. 617, 622 points out that this statement of the supremacy of a fundamental law was later ignored by Blackstone in discussing parliamentary sovereignty. See 1 "Commentaries" *p. 91.

134. "Nor is Blackstone's appeal to men of all parties difficult to understand. Eloquent, suave, undismayed in the presence of palpable contradictions in his pages . . . he is the very exemplar of legalistic and judicial obscurantism." *Corwin*, supra note 72, pp. 365, 405. For examples of inconsistencies in Blackstone's legal and political philosophy see 2 Encyc. of Social Sciences pp. 580-581.

"the law of nature" and "natural rights" were concepts which were so current at the time[135] that it scarcely seems that Jefferson in presenting them, in his "Summary View of the Rights of British America"[136] in 1774 and in the Declaration of Independence in 1776, depended on Blackstone's chance statement. James Wilson in his address of 1774[137] cited Blackstone to the effect that there is a fundamental law of nature which is superior to human law,[138] but it is clear that Wilson quoted the phrase merely to confront the English leaders with the authority of one of their own group and not as the source of his inspiration. Rather than state that it was Blackstone who influenced Jefferson in his phrasing of the Declaration of Independence it may be more safely said that he was influenced by James Wilson, who had criticised Blackstone's work several years before the drafting of the Declaration. Just what influence Wilson's address of 1774 had upon Jefferson is difficult to determine.[139] A portion of it appears in "The Common Place Book" but whether it was known to Jefferson before or after 1776 is not clear,[140] as the date of this citation is uncertain. Jefferson, however, should have been familiar with Wilson's law lectures of 1790 and 1791, given in Philadelphia, as he was living there as the time as Secretary of State and no doubt heard references to the addresses by a member of the Supreme Court. Perhaps Jefferson attended the opening lecture, as it is said the cabinet did.[141] To what extent Jefferson's views were influenced by Wilson perhaps cannot be determined; though it is certain that Wilson expressed his fears to law students twenty years before Jefferson began his attempt to stem the tide of Blackstone.[142] It does not appear, however, that Wilson spoke of the work as elementary and superficial

135. *Haines*, supra note 131, pt. 1.

136. *Jefferson* "Works" (ed. Ford) Vol. II p. 53.

137. Supra note 118.

138. *Wilson* "Works" (1804) Vol. III p. 206.

139. "Common Place Book" (1926) intr. pp. 4-14, 39-44; *Becker* "The Declaration of Independence" (1922) p. 105; *Adams* "Political Ideas of the American Revolution" (1922) ch. 7; *Chinard* "Jefferson" (1929) pp. 71-78; *Dana* "The Declaration of Independence" (1899) 13 Harv. L. Rev. 319.

140. "Common Place Book" art. 832.

141. (1900) 34 Am. L. Rev. 481, 483; *Wood* "History of University of Pennsylvania" (1833) p. 101.

142. See *Andrews* "American Law" (1900) p. viii: "by the use of the Commentaries as the first book, the minds of students have been filled with ideas and principles not at all adapted to, and indeed in direct conflict with, the fundamental principles of American law; as there has been no corrective, these impressions cling to them after they have become lawyers."

as did Jefferson in later years[143] but approved it outside the field of public law.

Another source of Jefferson's antagonism toward the Commentaries may have been St. George Tucker's republicanized edition of Blackstone published in 1803.[144] In his preface Tucker speaks of the law student laying aside that "rich mine of learning,"[145] Coke on Littleton, for Blackstone's Commentaries and that "this sudden revolution in the course of study may be considered as having produced effects almost as pernicious as the want of a regular and systematic guide, since it cannot be doubted that it has contributed to usher into the profession a great number, whose superficial knowledge of the law has been almost as soon forgotten as acquired."[146] This was the same idea expressed by Jefferson in 1812 in speaking of "Blackstone lawyers" as "ephemeral insects of the law."[147] While Tucker and Jefferson were in accord on this point, Tucker thought that Blackstone's work was more than an elementary digest, for he described Blackstone as uniting the talents of a philosopher, an antiquarian, an historian, a jurist, and a classicist.[148]

In the preface to his edition Tucker praised the recent legislation in Virginia instituted by Jefferson as a means of fostering a republican government.[148a] Moreover, he added to the original work lengthy appendices which discussed the sovereignty of the people, the introduction of the common law of England, freedom of the press, the bill for the more general diffusion of knowledge in Virginia, the right of expatriation, the virtues of the jury system, and Jefferson's act directing the course of descent in Virginia. These appendices contained views which were in harmony with Jefferson's; they expressed respect for his reforms in Virginia and showed a devotion to "republican" principles; they republicanized this English treatise to meet the needs of American law students. Thus they may have called the attention of Jefferson to the harmful influence of the original work. Further, it may be that Tucker's

143. Supra notes 30 and 48.

144. Supra note 44.

145. Jefferson used this same figure of speech in 1812, nine years later, in referring to Coke. See supra note 30.

146. *Tucker* "Blackstone" (1803) Vol. I pt. 1 p. iv.

147. Supra note 30. Cf. note 18, supra.

148. *Tucker*, op. cit., p. vi. For Jefferson's praise of the Commentaries see supra note 46.

148a. *Tucker*, op. cit., editor's app. p. 444.

edition explains Jefferson's willingness in 1814 to recommend the Commentaries as a law text, for it was this edition which Jefferson approved in his list of that year.[149]

It is difficult, therefore, to determine whether Jefferson's reaction to the Commentaries expressed current views or if certain writers influenced him. It can be said that others before Jefferson had attacked the work for its reactionary influence, as others have since,[150] but few, if any, had dwelt upon its undesirability as a text on account of its superficial treatment of the law.

Conclusion

Were the fears of Jefferson as to the influence of the Commentaries justified? Did the work contain such anti-republican principles as were used to thwart Jefferson's ideals? Is it possible to find in the decisions, briefs, and debates, instances where the work was used to establish principles contrary to Jefferson's? In Jefferson's writings no such instances are referred to, though he might have been aware of them. A few will be set forth showing such a reliance upon the Commentaries as might have aroused Jefferson. In all fairness, however, it must be said that the fact that the Commentaries was used as authority does not mean that those

149. Supra note 44.

150. "Blackstone caught and expressed the spirit of his time with consummate skill, but he caught it only just in time. Hardly was his ink dry when Bentham sounded a blast that rudely disturbed the supposed finality of the common law, and (what was even a greater matter) the independence of the United States, insured the free and ample development of English legal ideas in directions and for purposes as yet unknown": *Pollock* "The Law of England" (1887) 3 L. Q. Rev. 343, 344. "It was during our Revolutionary struggle, . . . that Blackstone's Commentaries were written and published, and in weighing what he says about the common law it must be constantly borne in mind that he was a Tory of he strictest sect, and was an ultra believer in the divine right of kings, and of kingly prerogatives. While Blackstone is perhaps the greatest law commentator of the world on the law in general, what he says, when he comes to treat of prerogatives and governmental power, must be scrutinized very closely, when we, Americans, come to apply it to our own affairs under our free institutions": *Thomas* "The Law of Constructive Contempt" (1904) p. 22. "Blackstone was a Tory lawyer, who interpreted the British constitution by a narrow legalism that was obsolete before the Commentaries came from the press": *Parrington*, supra note 52, p. 280. See also *Gettell* "History of Political Thought" (1924) pp. 287, 343. "To Blackstone the field of English law seemed a paradise filled with everything to delight the eye and mind; to Bentham it was a howling wilderness, full of all sorts of unclean birds and ravening beasts": *Dillon* "The Laws and Jurisprudence of England and America" (1895) p. 307. Supra notes 22 and 23.

citing the work necessarily approved its implications nor that they were opposed to "republican" principles. Jefferson cited the work repeatedly in 1771 when he was attempting to prove that the General Court of Colonial Virginia, composed of the Governor and his Council, had jurisdiction over ecclesiastical matters.[151]

In 1799 Mr. Justice Iredell of the Supreme Court of the United States cited Blackstone as authority for the principle that the liberty of the press consisted merely in being privileged to publish without a license.[151a] In a charge to a grand jury he quoted at length from the Commentaries, after reading the following statement:

> "The definition of it [liberty of the press] is nowhere more happily or justly expressed than by the great author of the commentaries on the laws of England, which book deserves more particular regard on this occasion, because for nearly thirty years it has been the manual of almost every student of law in the United States, and its uncommon excellence has also introduced it into the libraries, and often to the favorite reading of private gentlemen; so that his views of the subject could scarcely be unknown to those who framed the Amendments to the Constitution and if they were not, unless his explanation had been satisfactory, I presume the amendment would have been more particularly worded, to guard against any possible misunderstanding."[152]

On February 25, 1799, the Report of the Committee on the Repeal of the Sedition Act, which disapproved of repeal, was debated in the House. The Committee was of the opinion that the Sedition Act was constitutional, despite the first amendment of the Federal Constitution, and that in the absence of such a federal statute seditious libel would be punishable by the federal govern-

151. *Godwin* et al. v. *Lunan* (1771) Jefferson's Reports (Va.) 96; *Barton* "Virginia Colonial Decisions" (1909) Vol. I p. 208. For the only other legal argument of Jefferson extant, see "Works" (ed. Ford) Vol. I p. 470 n.

151a. 4 "Commentaries" *p. 151.

152. *Wharton* "State Trials of United States" (1849) p. 478. See a charge to a state grand jury in 1798 on freedom of speech and of the press by Judge Alexander Addison who said "that liberty of the press is precisely as stated by Sir William Blackstone." Addison (Pa. 1800) 270, 281. For early cases in which the English law of libel was not followed see *People* v. *Croswell* (N. Y. 1804) 3 Johnson's Cases 336; *Comm.* v. *Clapp* (1808) 4 Mass. 163; *Warren*, supra note 14, pp. 236-239; *Cooper* "The Law of Libel and the Liberty of the Press" (1830) pp. 80-87. See also infra note 160a.

ment since it was a common law crime.[152a] But in reply John Nicholas of Virginia contended that the definition of freedom of the press, namely permission to print without a license, should be traced to its source and that was Blackstone.[152b] Tucker in 1803 stated that this definition of liberty of the press "was only to be found in the theoretical writings of the English commentators."[152c]

In the trial of William Duane[153] for contempt by publication in 1801 the prosecution quoted from the Commentaries[154] to the effect that it was contempt to speak disrespectfully of the judges acting in their judicial capacity, that truth would not be a defense, and that the court had the power to proceed summarily by attachment for contempt. Jefferson in criticizing this case said: "Have not the Whig lawyers of England always denied that the publication of truth could be either a contempt or a libel" and "if the printing of truth may be a contempt in England, can it be in the United States the constitution of which inhibits any law abridging the freedom of the press."[155] It seems that Blackstone's questionable statement that the judiciary had the power to punish summarily for contempt by publication came from Tory sources and originated in the struggle over freedom of speech and press in which Mansfield played such an unfortunate part.[156]

152a. For the act see 1 U. S. St. at L. 596. For the debates see "Annals of 5th Congress" (1797-1799) Vol. III pp. 2985-3008. See also supra note 85a and infra note 155.

152b. "Annals of 5th Congress," op. cit., p. 3008. The Commentaries was cited as authority of this definition in the debates on the passage of the Sedition Act: "Annals of 5th Congress" (1797-1799) Vol. II p. 2148. See *Carroll* "Freedom of the Press in the Federalist Period; The Sedition Act" (1919) 18 Mich. L. Rev. 615, 630-634, on the Blackstonian doctrine of liberty of the press.

152c. *Tucker* "Blackstone" (1803) Vol. I pt. 2, editor's app. p. 18.

153. *Hollingsworth* v. *Duane* (C. C. 1801) Wall. 77, Fed. Cas. No. 6616.

154. 4 *Blackstone* "Commentaries" *pp. 285-286.

155. *Jefferson* "Works" (ed. Ford) Vol. IX p. 257 n. The Sedition Act of 1798, which was not involved in the *Duane* case, provided that truth was a defense and that the jury "shall have a right to determine the law and the fact, under the direction of the court, as in other cases." (1798-1799) 1 U. S. St. at L. 596. See also supra notes 85a and 152a.

156. *Nelles and King*, supra note 94, pp. 405, 408; *Fox* "History of Contempt of Court" (1927) pp. 20-21; *Frankfurter and Landis* "Power of Congress Over Procedure in Criminal Contempt" (1924) 37 Harv. L. Rev. 1010, 1046 n. 128. It appears that the passage in the Commentaries on attachment for contempt, differing from Blackstone's statements in his earlier lectures, rested on an undelivered opinion in 1765 of Mr. Justice Wilmot in a case of libel for comments on Mansfield's conduct of the proceedings against John Wilkes. While the opinion, in a proceeding which was abandoned by the Crown, was not printed until 1802, it seems that this undelivered judgment was the authority for Black-

In an attachment for contempt by publication of one Oswald, counsel for the state cited Blackstone as authority for this method of proceeding, and later as a member of the state assembly, to which had been presented a memorial complaining of the punishment of the offender, the same gentleman again relied upon Blackstone "in support and illustration of his sentiments upon liberty."[157]

Thus, in charges to the grand jury, congressional debates, and in arguments of counsel have been found instances which reveal that perhaps the Commentaries did have an anti-republican influence. Yet each involved the related issues of liberty of the press, seditious libel, contempt by publication, summary punishment, and the right of jury trial. This would seem to furnish Jefferson little support for his fierce attacks. But in the struggle for political democracy which was being waged in England and America in the years following 1760, these issues were considered vital in securing political liberty under supposedly tyrannical administrations. It was these—freedom of the press and trial by jury—to which De Lolme, in 1807,[158] a French student of English political institutions, said the English people were most thoroughly wedded and which were of the greatest advantage to public liberty. It was the opinion of St. George Tucker that freedom of the press was "the solid and immovable basis both of the state and federal government."[159] And Marshall, Pinckney and Gerry, as envoys to France, wrote Talleyrand in 1798 that there was no right "of which the importance is more deeply impressed on the public mind, than the liberty of the press."[160]

Alexander Hamilton in 1804, as counsel for the defense in an indictment for libel (by which Jefferson, when President of the United States, was the person attacked), argued:

> "The check upon the press ought to be deposited, not in a permanent body of magistrates, as the court, but in an occasional and fluctuating body, the jury, who are to be selected by lot. Judges might be tempted to enter into the views of government, and to extend, by arbitrary constructions, the

stone's views, as he submitted parts of the Commentaries to Wilmot for criticism: "Memoirs and Notes of Opinions of Wilmot" (1802) pp. 71, 243.

157. *Respublica* v. *Oswald* (1788) 1 Dall. (1 U. S.) 319, 321, 329a.

158. *De Lolme* "The Constitution of England" (1807) pp. 187, 424. This work first appeared in 1784.

159. *Tucker* "Blackstone" (1803) Vol. I pt. 2, editor's app. p. 16.

160. "Annals of 5th Congress" (1797-1799) Vol. III p. 3449.

laws of libels. . . . In England trial by jury has always been cherished as the greatest security of the subject against the oppression of government; but it never could have been a solid refuge and security, unless the jury had the right to judge of the intent and the law."[160a]

Though Jefferson's reaction to the supposedly anti-republican Commentaries cannot be traced to definite parts of the work or to specific effects, yet as one who adhered to the political principles of revolutionary days he saw grave danger in the influence of Blackstone, whose book was spreading insidiously the doctrines of English Toryism in the new nation. However, it would seem that the outcome of controversies over freedom of the press, seditious libel, contempt by publication, and right to trial by jury, would have been the same if the Commentaries had not been written.[161] For the struggle, which Jefferson so vividly described, between Saxon and Norman, Whig and Tory, "Republican" and Federalist, would have gone on, with "anti-republicans" finding authority for their views though the Commentaries was not at hand to quote. And despite the fact that Jefferson won his battle at the polls in national elections, the judiciary, a branch of the Federal government he feared, enabled the constitutional principles of Federalism, which Jefferson viewed as the American descendant of Norman and Tory ideas, to survive long after his agrarianism had been worsted.

Perhaps it was Story and Kent, two great American commentators, authorities on constitutional law, teachers of law, powerful instrumentalities for bringing the common law of England into our own law and in directing the course of American legal thought, who eventually defeated Jefferson's designs on the common law of

160a. *People* v. *Croswell* (N. Y. 1804) 3 Johnson's Cases 353, 355. Supra note 152. Blackstone also said the jury system was the glory of the English law, that Rome and Carthage fell because they were strangers to trial by jury, and that the jury was the surest guardian of public justice": "Commentaries" Vol. III *pp. 379-380; Vol. IV *pp. 349, 414. In the debate of 1788 in the Virginia Convention for the adoption of the Federal Constitution, Patrick Henry objected to its adoption because of lack of assurance of jury trials in civil cases and cited "the sentiments of the learned Judge Blackstone, so often quoted on the subject": *Elliot* "Debates" (1836) Vol. III p. 544.

161. For an opposite view see *Holdsworth* "Blackstone" (1927) 7 Ore. L. Rev. 155, 157, 160, who says: "If the Commentaries had not been written when they were written I think it would be very doubtful whether you [the United States] . . . would have so universally adopted our common law. Most of us now agree that the laws of England have departed further from Blackstone than your laws have departed over here.

England as interpreted by Blackstone. Two excerpts reveal that it may have been these disciples of Blackstone who achieved victory for the Tory public law of England through the medium of judicial supremacy in our governmental system:

> Kent who was "a disciple of Locke and Blackstone, remodeling seventeenth-century liberalism into eighteenth-century conservatism, . . . was concerned to erect the barriers of the Common Law about the unsurveyed frontiers of the American experiment, assigning exact metes and bounds beyond which it should not go. Like John Marshall and Joseph Story he was expert in devising legal springes to catch unwary democrats, and while the Jeffersonians were shouting over their victories at the polls, he was engaged in the strategic work of placing the Constitution under the narrow custodianship of the English law."[162]
>
> "In the year 1833 he [Story] published his Commentaries on the Constitution, the fruit of long labors, which was at once accepted throughout the North as a classical authority, and which has held its ground pretty well since. . . . Story was steeped in the Common Law and his thinking reveals the strong influence of Blackstone. In passing through the mind of the great Tory commentator, English constitutional theory had received a pronounced Tory bias, and something of this remains after filtering through the mind of Story. . . . With its pronounced bias The Commentaries [of Story] must be regarded as a partisan document, which like The Federalist has grown in authoritativeness with the triumph of its party principles."[162a]

Another quotation reveals that there are legal scholars of today who agree with Jefferson in his attitude on the effect of Blackstone's work. Two writers have said:

> "It is a commonplace that the political or social attitude roughly represented by the old-time Federalism has tended

162. *Parrington* "The Romantic Revolution in America, 1800-1860" (1927) p. 197. See also "Letters and Times of the Tylers" (1884) Col. II p. 322; "Great American Lawyers" (1907) Vol. II p. 498.

162a. *Parrington*, op. cit., pp. 301-302. A review of Story's Commentaries said: "Earnestly do we desire that it may perform the salutory office of aiding to win back the judgments of our Southern brethren to the sound doctrines of 1789." (1834) 38 North American Review 63, 84. Marshall said that Story's book, south of the Potomac, would be considered an infidel political work: *Warren* "The Supreme Court" (1932) Vol. I p. 779. See also *Konkle* "Joseph Hopkinson" (1931) pp. 280-283.

to prevail in constitutional adjudication. Entrenched in the judiciary, even after the *debacle* of 1800, Federalism naturally felt a broad scope of judicial power as in itself an excellence to be conserved. Potentially inconsistent provisions in bills of rights were reconciled by construing them, so far as possible, as guaranteeing only the rights and privileges of British subjects at common law. And it is significant that our courts took their common law of personal and civil liberty, including rules which were then even in England controversial or insecure, from the Tory Blackstone rather than from such Whig jurists as Erskine and Lord Camden. Even yet, for example, it is possible to doubt whether the Blackstonian theory, of freedom of the press as consisting merely in freedom from censorship prior to publication has become entirely obsolete in our jurisprudence."[163]

Perhaps the "canonization" of "the honied Mansfieldism" of Blackstone and the triumph of Blackstonian conservatism over the "suspicious realism" of Jefferson have been for the best. But the odd twists which time makes of the serious efforts of those who labor to produce certain ends, as shown by what history has done to the unsuspecting Blackstone and the ever watchful Jefferson, are of interest.

It is alleged that Blackstone's lectures for university law students became a political weapon in the hands of the American opponents of England's colonial policy in depriving his country of one of her greatest foreign possessions.[164] The text, having served such a fatal purpose, became in turn legal scripture which tended to bring into the thought of the judiciary of the new democratic nation many reactionary principles of public law of Tory England, of dubious soundness even when written, and was one of the means of bringing into the constitutional theory of the new nation principles which the King's armies could not force upon colonial America. Then these lectures, the first of their kind in England, given to stimulate university teaching of the common law,[165] while they fostered professional legal education here, became a horn-book which served to crowd the profession with those "ephemeral in-

163. *Nelles and King*, supra note 94, p. 405. See also *Black* "Judicial Mileposts on the Road to Absolutism" (1932) 81 U. Pa. L. Rev. 160, 163.

164. Supra note 20.

165. 1 *Blackstone* "Commentaries" *pp. 29-31.

sects" whom Jefferson called "Blackstone lawyers."[166] And Jefferson, who opposed Blackstone's work because it was superficial and anti-republican, saw the first occupant of the first university chair of legal instruction in this country,[167] and one established by his efforts, rely upon the work, though not with servility, as the basis of his instruction. He also saw the successor of that first occupant publish a republicanized edition, which, it has been said, "fixed the Blackstone tradition in this country" in law teaching and which became "the core of the whole legal system" by making "the common law of the country simply Blackstone."[168]

So the youths of America, whom Jefferson desired to protect against the political influence of the Tory lawyer, whether in the law school which Blackstone's lectures inspired or in the law office, a place of study to which both Blackstone and Jefferson objected,[169] did not escape the subtle influence of his work. That despotic definition of law,[170] so objectionable when considered in the light of "good republican principles," was learned by thousands of unsuspecting young lawyers in the years to come, who no doubt became good citizens of the republic despite their knowledge of that dreaded definition of their art.

166. Supra note 30.
167. *Warren,* supra note 14, p. 343.
168. *Reed,* supra note 14, pp. 111-112, 116-117. Supra note 44.
169. 1 *Blackstone* "Commentaries" *p. 32; supra note 35.
170. Supra note 124.

XIX

*Delaware Cases, 1792-1800**

ZECHARIAH CHAFEE, JR.

Between approximately 1792 and 1830 several Delaware lawyers compiled elaborate notebooks of the cases that they argued or witnessed in different courts, with occasional additions from similar reports made by others. The volumes under review by Professor Chafee reprint these notebooks as edited by Daniel J. Boorstin. The notebooks are particularly important, because they contain the court's statement of law and the reasoning of the judges, which are generally missing from earlier court records. Professor Chafee chose to base his review only on the material before 1801, because of the comparative scarcity of other printed judicial opinions during the eighteenth century. In the section of the review which is here reprinted, the author is primarily concerned with the sources of Delaware law.

Bench and Bar

Let us now turn to the strictly legal aspects of this newly published Delaware material. It reveals a mature bench and bar in full operation. The attorneys are not just amateurs with a gift of gab like the Rhode Island lawyer of the same period, who learned his profession by going out into his garden and addressing five cabbages in a row for the judges and twelve other cabbages in a row for the jury, and then found when he got into the court room

* This excerpt from a Book Review by Zechariah Chafee, Jr., of Daniel Boorstin, ed., *Delaware Cases, 1792-1830*, 3 vols. (St. Paul, Minn., 1943) is reprinted with permission from the *Harvard Law Review*, LVII (1944), 407-426. Copyright 1944 by the Harvard Law Review Association.

that the cabbages were still there.[1] These Delaware attorneys, to borrow Professor Wambaugh's favorite phrase, make a noise like a lawyer. They behave like a regular bar, so much so that sometimes two or three lawyers are needed to argue for one client. Where did they obtain the necessary preparation? Apparently, it was not until 1802 that a rule of court required an applicant for admission to prove that he had "studied the law with assiduity under the direction of some practising attorney or gentleman of the law, in the United States for the term of two years after his arrival at the age of 21 years."[2] Yet very likely this rule merely codified what most embryo Delaware lawyers were doing already. It is plain that the learning and reasoning ability displayed in argument after argument in these volumes could not have been acquired without prolonged and diligent work.

The courts show a similar maturity. The elaborate rules of court printed in the first volume provide for numerous exigencies, and their language has a thoroughly modern ring. The judicial opinions are well reasoned. Their learning is accompanied with frequent flashes of hard sense which deserve study by judges of our own time. Perhaps a judge could breathe more freely in the days when he was not weighted down by thousands of volumes of law reports, treatises, encyclopedias, and digests. Another sign of maturity is the frequent notation of a division in the court, with a dissenting opinion often presented.[3] A court during the early years of its work may very well be content to make a record of the

1. Updike, Memoirs of the Rhode Island Bar (1842) 24.

2. Rules of the Supreme Court, 1 Del. Cas. xliv (1802). Regular clerkship of three years was required when legal studies were begun during minority. A rule of the Court of Chancery in 1818 required solicitors in that court to study three years and take an examination. *Id.* at xlvii. In the same year a rule of the Court of Common Pleas also required three years of law study in Delaware, but added: "This rule shall not affect the case of gentlemen resident of the state, who have gone or may go abroad to continue their legal education, or gentlemen members of the bar of Pennsylvania or Maryland, who have practised law two years in the Supreme Courts of either of those States." *Id.* at xxxiii. The statement by Charles Warren that "In Deleware, three years' study was prescribed" is perhaps based on the rules just cited, or he may have had access to some earlier rule of court. Warren, History of the American Bar (1911) 202.

3. Examples of such cases are: Field v. Turner, 1 Del. Cas. 150, 1 *id.* 434 (1797); Bucchannan v. Huffington, 1 Del. Cas. 174 (1798); State v. Bender, 1 Del. Cas. 16, 1 *id.* 337, 1 *id.* 478, 1 *id.* 660, 2 *id.* 9 (1793); Brown v. Hodgson, 1 Del. Cas. 380 (1795); Trustee of Loan Office v. Maxwell, 1 Del. Cas. 472 (1797); State v. Smith, 1 Del. Cas. 416, 1 *id.* 480, 2 *id.* 68 (1796).

actual decision without more. The next step is to express the reasons which make that decision prevail, even if they were not acceptable to all the judges. Finally, when the judicial process is well developed, judges become conscious of the desirability of giving the bar the benefit of the reasoning of the minority.[4]

Occasionally the notebooks enliven the learned discussion by injecting some court room incident. Judge Johns was absent during a term of the Court of Quarter-Sessions, "neither in sickness nor trouble . . . but increasing his estate."[5] One surmises that the learned judge was speculating in Western lands. James Wilson, whose *Red Book* reveals him as an able lawyer with an engaging personality, speaks occasionally of attacks of bad health; perhaps this explains why he left the law for the ministry after sixteen years of practice. "Having opened the argument, and being much exhausted by the heat of the day, I could not take the arguments of other counsel but will subjoin extracts from my own notes."[6] After the elaborate arguments about the complex devise of "Cheat, now called Honesty," he writes: "Being unwell and late at night I went to bed." Apparently he did not stay up to hear the charge of Chief Justice Read, which leaned toward his opponent, the plaintiff; but he awoke next morning to hear good news. The jury had disregarded the judge's charge, and Wilson's closing entry on this case reads: "Notwithstanding, a verdict by as intelligent a jury as was ever impanelled in Sussex was given for the defendants."[7] Still, Wilson bore no grudge against the judge. A year later, he notes at the end of another case, where the prosecutor's second cousin once removed was excluded from the jury on Wilson's objection: "N.B. Chief Justice Read gained great esteem for his impartiality and candor in this decision." Wilson, however, did not gain much by purging the jury, because it found his client guilty of assault and battery and the fine was $60.[8] Wilson shows the judges as anxious to push work along. Judge Bassett and Judge Rodney upset the usual leisureliness of lawyers by adopting

4. See Wambaugh, Study of Cases (2d ed. 1894) §§ 47, 107; Note (1893) 27 Am. L. Rev. 87.

5. Waller v. Dunnaho, 1 Del. Cas. 165 (1797).

6. Wright's Lessee v. Cannon, 1 Del. Cas. 227, 228 (1796). Fortunately the arguments of other counsel were preserved for us by Bayard and Judge Rodney. 1 *id.* 368, 2 *id.* 55.

7. Burton's Lessee v. Prettyman, 1 Del. Cas. 56, 58 (1795).

8. State v. Turner, 1 Del. Cas. 94, 1 *id.* 390 (1796).

a rule of court which allowed only one continuance for any case.[9] A judge might take an odd short cut to save time. In a jury trial, one of the two judges was examined as a witness and then returned to the bench.[10] And the judges were quick to cut short unprofitable arguments: "Sir, you may save yourself any trouble on that point."[11]

Sources of Law

Whence did these lawyers and judges derive their law? Partly, of course, from the Delaware statutes, of which more hereafter; but these failed to provide rules for much of the litigation reported in this work, so resort to some kind of unwritten law was inevitable. What was the source of this unwritten law of Delaware?

As to the actual period of statehood here covered, the documents are explicit. The Delaware Constitution of 1776 declares:

> The common law of England, as well as so much of the statute law as have been heretofore adopted in practice in this state, shall remain in force, unless they shall be altered by a future law of the Legislature; such parts only excepted as are repugnant to the rights and privileges contained in this constitution and the declaration of rights, &c. agreed to by this convention.[12]

The common law of England, thus recognized as binding in 1776, was kept in force by the later Constitution of 1792:

> All the laws of this state, existing at the time of making this constitution, and not inconsistent with it, shall remain in force, unless they shall be altered by future laws; and all actions and prosecutions now pending, shall proceed as if this constitution had not been made.[13]

Notwithstanding the apparent simplicity of these provisions, they raise several fascinating problems, of which a few can be briefly suggested.[14] (1) Did "the common law of England" describe

9. Lowry v. Insley, 1 Del. Cas. 249 (1799). Compare Rule 13 of the Supreme Court, 1790. 1 Del. Cas. xxxviii.

10. Peery's Lessee v. Burton, 1 Del. Cas. 74 (1795).

11. Laws v. Davis, 1 Del. Cas. 256 (1800); see Brown v. Brown, 1 Del. Cas. 188 (1798).

12. Art. 25, reprinted in 1 Del. Laws, 1776, appendix p. 89.

13. § 10, reprinted in 1 Del. Laws, 1792, pp. xlvi-xlvii.

14. See Pope, *The English Common Law in the United States* (1910) 24 Harv. L. Rev. 6.

an assemblage of specific decisions reprinted in hundreds of volumes of English law reports, or a single system of principles and rules of action? By the first view each English decision was binding law as much as a Delaware decision; but by the second view the English cases merely evidence the underlying body of doctrine. Furthermore, under the first view the English common law was taken over in a frozen form, something that was solid and incapable of alteration, so that whatever came afterward would have to be a different thing, namely, Delaware common law; whereas the second view permitted the imported principles and rules of action to be further developed by Delaware judges to meet future needs. (2) As of what date was the English common law adopted? The corresponding contemporary enactment in Virginia specifies 1607, the date of the settlement of Jamestown,[15] but the Delaware constitution is silent on this question. Should we read in 1681, the date of Penn's charter, or 1776, when Delaware became independent and established this constitution; or was it a timeless system? This problem affects the force of English decisions at various periods, *e.g.*, between 1681 and 1776, and between 1776 and 1943. Is a Delaware court bound to follow some wooden English legal doctrine of the seventeenth or eighteenth century which has long since been modified or discarded in England? Or should it concur with Commissioner Roscoe Pound of Nebraska, which also took over the "common law of England" without a date, that this phrase did not petrify the law, as embodied in judicial decisions at any one time, but included "all judicial improvements and modifications in this country and in England, to the present time, so far as applicable to our conditions"?[16] (3) Is "the common law" limited to the decisions or doctrines of the Courts of Common Pleas, King's Bench, and Exchequer; or does it also include those of Chancery, Admiralty, and the ecclesiastical judges?

Leaving these problems to Mr. Boorstin with the hope that his

15. Ordinances of Virginia Convention, 1776, § 6, reprinted in 1 VA. REV. CODE (1819) c. 38. On the adoption or rejection of British statutes, see *id.* c. 40, reprinting the act of 1792.

16. William v. Miles, 68 Neb. 463, 93 N. W. 682 (1903). See GRAY, NATURE AND SOURCES OF THE LAW (2d ed. 1921) 244. Nebraska, as part of the Louisiana Purchase, had once been under the civil law in some sense, so that the problem of the introduction of the common law was not quite the same there as in Virginia or Massachusetts. Although Delaware had the Swedes and Dutch before Penn, I doubt whether a previous thin sprinkling of Continental Europeans had any material effect on the law brought by a wave of English speaking settlers.

forthcoming commentary will be able to note some cases contributing to a solution, I turn to a related problem which has aroused considerable controversy. What sort of unwritten law existed in an American colony between its settlement by Englishmen and its express recognition of the common law by some enactment like that of Delaware's that "The common law of England . . . shall remain in force"? These words treat the common law, however defined, as nothing new. Apparently the people wanted to keep something they had long possessed. But how long? A natural inference from such a provision is that it sought to preserve the law which had been brought over from England by the first settlers, except as it had been modified by local statutes or was unsuited to regional conditions. This is the orthodox legal theory, backed by the authority of Mr. Justice Story.[17] In Delaware and Pennsylvania it derives some support from William Penn's charter of 1681:

> . . . the Lawes[18] for regulateing and governing of Propertie, within the said Province, as well for the descent and enjoyment of lands, as likewise for the enjoyment and succession of goods and Chattells, and likewise as to felonies, shall be and continue the same as shall bee for the time being, by the general course of the Law in our Kingdome of England, untill the said Lawes shall be altered by the said William Penn, . . . and by the freemen of the said Province, their Delegates or Deputies. . . .[19]

Did this "general course of the Law in our Kingdome of England," which William Penn was to take with him to replace whatever law the Swedes and the Dutch had previously enjoyed on the Delaware, coincide with the "common law of England" which was

17. Van Ness v. Packard, 2 Pet. 137, 144 (U. S. 1829) ("Our ancestors brought with them its general principles, and claimed it as their birthright. . . ."); 1 STORY, CONSTITUTION (2d ed. 1851) §§ 156-57; see Chief Justice Shaw in Commonwealth v. Chapman, 13 Metc. 68 (Mass. 1848).

18. The word "Lawes" can hardly be limited to statutes. This would be inconsistent with the last clause of the quoted passage, which specifically deals with provincial legislation and permits it to depart from English law, and contrary to Erie R. R. v. Tompkins, 304 U. S. 64 (1938). Note that the Penn charter omits the requirement of the 1629 and 1691 charters for Massachusetts, where colonial legislation must not be "contrarie to the lawes of . . . England." And the 1620 Patent of the Council for New England reads "not contrary to the Laws and Statutes of . . . England," which furnishes a fresh argument for *Erie R. R. v. Tompkins.*

19. Reprinted in MACDONALD, SELECT CHARTERS ILLUSTRATIVE OF AMERICAN HISTORY, 1606-1775 (1904) 187.

recognized a century later by the first state constitution? Hardly so, if "the common law" describes only an assemblage of specific English decisions. The great Quaker did not intend to fill much-needed cargo space on the *Welcome* with a complete set of law reports including Serjeant Maynard's recently published edition of the Year Books. He did not order Siderfin's folio to follow by next year's ship as soon as it was off the press. But if we define "the common law of England" as a system of principles and rules of action, then it does come close to "the general course of the Law in . . . England." For such a law only a few treatises like Coke's *Institutes* and Dalton's *Justices of the Peace* needed to be taken aboard; the rest of the system could be carried in men's heads. Such an unwritten law might gradually change with the passage of time. Colonists would go to England to study law at the Inns of Court and return with many law reports for their libraries. Proprietors and British officials would cite court decisions in their disputes with the settlers. (We must not assume that colonial law depended merely on the will of the colonists.) Thus, the original system of principles would eventually absorb big chunks of case law. Yet at no point in the process would there be a sharp break or any sense of something new. The lawyers who helped put "the common law of England" into the Constitution of 1776 may have felt that they were simply preserving what Delaware had always had since William Penn landed in 1682. And it is arguable that according to the standards of a world of mutability they were right. "The test of personal identity . . . lies . . . in its life—in the continuity of its life."[20]

The orthodox theory of Story has been vigorously attacked by two groups of writers.[21] Both groups insist that the English common law was in large measure an alien system in the colonies for several decades after their settlement. As to what law did prevail in its stead, these two modernist theories diverge.

First, Paul Reinsch in 1899 and Charles J. Hilkey in 1910[22] contended that the early settlers lived under a sort of folk law

20. Haldane, *arguendo*, in Free Church of Scotland v. Overtoun, [1904] A. C. 515, 609.

21. See Chafee, Book Review (1936) 41 AM. HIST. REV. 766; 1 RECORDS OF THE SUFFOLK COUNTY COURTS, 1671-1680 (1933) xxviii.

22. Reinsch, *The English Common Law in the Early American Colonies*, in 1 SELECT ESSAYS IN ANGLO-AMERICAN LEGAL HISTORY (1907) 367, 369; Hilkey, *Legal Developments in Colonial Massachusetts, 1630-1686*, in 37 STUDIES IN HISTORY, ECONOMICS AND PUBLIC LAW (1910) 157.

created by themselves in response to their peculiar conditions. Reinsch describes it as a "period of rude, untechnical popular law," partly embodied in brief codes like the dooms of the Anglo-Saxon kings, which departed from the models of the common law, and partly in an unwritten law which had "no reference to that system." Although Reinsch and Hilkey concede that the settlers were influenced by their former contact with English law, they assert that the colonists "did not consider English law binding."[23] Insofar as the settlers needed to use past experience for obtaining rules of law, they took them from the Old Testament and not from English sources. Finally, so Reinsch says, this period of self-made law was "followed, as lawyers became numerous and the study of law prominent, by the gradual reception of most of the rules of the English common law," a process somewhat resembling the historic reception of Roman law into Germany and Scotland during the Renaissance.[24]

On the other hand, Julius Goebel, Jr., in 1931[25] refused to assume that our ancestors left behind them practically all the legal portion of their cultural heritage and suffered a complete sea-change. *Coelum non animum mutant qui trans mare currunt.* So he concludes that they did bring with them the very law they had known in England. But their English law, he maintains, was not the common law—the decisions and doctrines of the King's courts in London. The law with which humble emigrants had grown up was the customary law administered in the English local courts—those in the county towns and boroughs and manors. It was to these courts that the small farmer or artisan would turn if he wished to replevy his cows or to collect a bill, and that turned upon him if his hogs were unringed or if he put his garbage in the street.[26] This transplantation of local institutions and customary law was,

23. See Hilkey, *op. cit. supra* note 69, at 300; Reinsch, *op. cit. supra* note 69, at 369.

24. Reinsch, *op. cit. supra* note 69, at 370. On the reception of the Roman law, see Maitland, *English Law and the Renaissance,* in 1 SELECT ESSAYS IN ANGLO-AMERICAN LEGAL HISTORY (1907) 168, 170-75; GRAY, NATURE AND SOURCES OF THE LAW (2d ed. 1921) 320.

25. Goebel, *King's Law and Local Custom in Seventeenth Century New England* (1931) 31 COL. L. REV. 416. See also the introduction to MORRIS, SELECT CASES OF THE MAYOR'S COURT OF NEW YORK CITY, 1674-1784 (1935); Haskins, *The Beginnings of the Recording System in Massachusetts* (1941) 21 B. U. L. REV. 281 (pointing out the influence of borough and manorial customs).

26. Goebel, *op. cit. supra* note 72, at 420.

he says, the basic factor in the colonial law of the seventeenth century. Eventually—here Goebel does agree with Reinsch—as the administration of justice became professionalized, "the Leviathan common law was set in motion." Yet the seventeenth century "gave us legal institutions which the common law never succeeded in smothering."[27]

It is too early to pronounce a verdict among these contesting theories until much more evidence is available. When we do have abundant materials in print and more unpublished manuscripts have been subjected to thorough examination by scholars, we may find that all three theories are partly true. It may turn out that Winthrop, Penn, and the rest brought over the common law as a body of principles, and not as the mass of case law which Story knew; that it was always binding on the settlers, but required to be supplemented from other sources of unwritten law in order to meet their increasingly complex needs, with which local legislation could not possibly keep pace. Reinsch and Goebel and the other modernists have supplied valuable information about these auxiliary sources of colonial law, but have perhaps exaggerated their importance and understimated that of the common law. According to this surmise, there was no late "reception" of the common law in the colonies. It was there from the start in some form, yet not the same form. I have already suggested that it underwent a continuous reception as the growth of law libraries and serious legal students brought more and more case law and detailed doctrines from England. Such a developing common law would naturally play an increasing part in the administration of justice outside the scope of colonial statutes; and it would gradually tend to displace whatever existed of home-made law or English local law. The long process can be considered at an end when the records show judges and lawyers in an American court reasoning like their contemporaries in an English court and citing cases and treatises freely.[28] Yet something may still remain of the factors stressed by

27. *Id.* at 420, n.9, 448.

28. Lawyers apparently cited cases for some time before judges began to do so. Several of the earliest volumes of American law reports print rather elaborate arguments of counsel and yet contain no judicial opinions. See, *e.g.*, the pre-Revolutionary Maryland cases in volume one of the reports of Howard & McHenry. The nearest approach to judicial opinions at this time in Maryland seems to be the printed memorandum in several cases by Daniel Dulany, an eminent lawyer, who was often consulted either by counsel or by the court. For examples, see West v. Stigar, 1 H. & McH. 247 (Md. 1767); Somerville v.

Reinsch and Goebel, especially in petty litigation and in situations where English rules of action are plainly unsuited to American conditions. Also, new factors alien to the common law may appear; for example, the continental law which lawyers began studying in the Revolutionary period or the civil law doctrines prevailing in territory annexed from France or Mexico.

This surmise may be called the synthetic rubber hypothesis because it endeavors to combine several elements with an elastic common law. Indeed, there is less antagonism among the three theories already advanced than appears at first sight. It is largely a question of more or less, for everybody now agrees that the common law had some influence from the start and that early colonial courts acted somewhat differently from the royal courts in England. If this synthetic rubber hypothesis really serves as a useful starting point for future inquires into American legal history during the seventeenth and eighteenth centuries, as I venture to think, then the task of an investigator is much harder than formerly. He can no longer be content with assembling data in support of a single monopolistic factor which he happens to favor, and add a grudging sentence or two conceding that the common law or some independent competitor did also operate in some minor fashion. Instead, he will search for the existence of several possible factors—generalized common-law principles; English case law; English local law; home-made law, with specific reference to colonial conditions; continental law. He will endeavor to determine the relative weight of each factor and judge whether its trend is upward or downward. He will look for the emergence of a new factor and note the signs of approaching death in an old factor. These are all phases of the central problem, the relations and divergences between the judicial process in England and in English-speaking North America.

Delaware Cases ought to furnish useful help in such investigations. Any new evidence about eighteenth-century American law will be welcomed, but these books have three special advantages. First, they concern one of the middle colonies. Hitherto, the con-

---

Johnson, 1 H. & McH. 348 (Md. 1770). When the judges sought Dulany's advice, they appear to have followed it in their decision without giving their own reasoning. Dulany was then something like a commissioner of today, who aids a court of last resort to clear its docket by writing an opinion which the court adopts. In Delaware also, arguments of counsel apparently came earlier than judicial opinions. See *Re* Cahoon, 1 Del. Cas. lxii (1771).

troversy about the nature of colonial law has largely concentrated on one region in New England. Hilkey's conclusions are largely based on data from Massachusetts Bay, while Goebel draws his mostly from Plymouth. Neither colony is altogether typical of what went on along most of the Atlantic coast.[29] The early theocracy in the Bay Colony might produce a hostility toward the common law and a courage for independent lawmaking which would not operate among English emigrants generally. The early piety, communism, and simplicity of life in Plymouth lessened the importance of law. The settlers in Delaware were more like our present-day selves. Undoubtedly Delaware was so closely linked with Pennsylvania that we cannot form an adequate picture of its colonial law until we know more about what went on in the courts of the larger colony, but the existing evidence should justify guarded conclusions.

Second, the cases come from all kinds of courts. We can watch many judges doing work comparable to that done in the King's Bench or the Common Pleas. This is not true of the Suffolk County Court or the Mayor's Court of New York City, where questions of law would not arise frequently and where local law might easily loom large just as it did in the contemporary Mayor's Court in London.[30] Such minor colonial courts may suggest a greater disregard of the common law in this country than was actually the case. The scholar is on more familiar ground when he reads a decision of the Delaware High Court of Errors and Appeals or even a *per curiam* opinion or set of opinions *en banc* in a lower Delaware court comprising several judges.

Third, it is unusual to find decisions on points of law so soon after the settlement of an American colony. Of course, the Virginia and Maryland law reports have several cases earlier in date than 1771, when Mr. Boorstin's cases begin, but Virginia and Maryland were founded many decades before Delaware, so that they had a long opportunity for legal development. The year 1771 is only ninety years after Penn's charter, only seventy years after the three Delaware counties set up their separate assembly. By 1792 we have continuous reporting of a term of court in Wilson's *Red Book.*

29. Goebel, of course, is well aware of this possibility, as shown by his references to New York. *Op. cit. supra* note 72, at 420, n.9. Reinsch's essay surveys all the colonies, but Massachusetts furnishes his best arguments.

30. See MORRIS, *op. cit. supra* note 72.

Either date brings us within the span of one human life from the beginning of Delaware's legal history. The importance of this fact will shortly be made clear.

Let us now examine the bearing of the Delaware cases on three of the points which seem worth investigating as part of the problem of the origins of the law of any American colony. (1) Did the alleged "reception" of the common law ever take place, and if so when? (2) To what extend do lawyers and judges rely on cases and treatises? (3) What traces of a law different from the English common law exist in either judicial decisions or statutes?

(1) *Did the alleged "reception" of the common law ever take place, and if so when?* The most vulnerable point in the two modernist theories is their assumption of a break with the past at some midway point in the legal history of every American colony (or state). Its unwritten law is surely the English common law when printed judical opinions begin. If this same colony had a system alien to the common law for a considerable period after its settlement, then there must have been a fairly definite transition when the new law imported from England replaced bodily the old law which the colonists had known for decades. It is worth while, therefore, to examine the court records of Delaware or any other colony for substantially contemporaneous evidence of this epoch-making event.

Of course, this alleged transition was not the act of a day, like the periodic oscillations of unhappy Alsace from the Code Napoleon to the German Code and vice versa. The process of shifting over may have occupied several years, like the reception of the Roman law to which it has been compared. But we have abundant proof of the reception of the Roman law into any given country of Europe from the men who lived through it; we know what they thought about it; historians can give its approximate dates. Have we similar proof of the "reception" of the English common law in any given American colony? Do we learn from that generation or the next just when and how it happened? Unless the common law was always considered to be in force (which these modernist writers deny), one would suppose that contemporaries, especially lawyers, would be greatly impressed by the arrival of a complete new system of law from overseas and the simultaneous rejection of the law of their ancestors. They would comment on this striking event in their letters and diaries, they would get it into histories, they and their children would speak of it for years afterwards, just as they remembered the Great Awakening and we remember the Great Depression.

The survival of such contemporaneous evidence would be particularly probable in Delaware because of the shortness of its legal history before Mr. Boorstin's cases begin. We have only about a century at our disposal between Penn's settlement and the systematic reporting of Wilson's *Red Book* and Bayard's notebook in 1792. If Delaware ever had an alien system of law, either a rude popular law or English local and customary law, and if this system lasted for a considerable period as the modernist writers say, then there would not be enough of the century left for lawyers to have time to forget this old law. The fact of its disappearance and the arrival of a new system would be recent history.

If we assume for the sake of argument that Delaware did have a reception of the English common law, what was its date? Hilkey and perhaps Reinsch place the Massachusetts reception around 1691, the epoch of Andros and the provincial charter, seventy years after Plymouth Rock; Goebel places it in New York as shortly after 1700. A later date would be probable in immature Delaware, close enough to 1792 to be well within the limits of oral transmission. Moreover, Pound[31] pushes down the reception in all the colonies much farther; it began in the middle of the eighteenth century and got an impetus from the publication of Blackstone's *Commentaries* in 1765, about the time that Wilson and Bayard were born. However you take it, Delaware lost its supposed alien system of law only a few decades before 1792.

Lawyers and judges are great hands for recalling the law of their youth and passing it on to younger men. Quite a little about the Rhode Island law before the Civil War was passed on to me by James Tillinghast, my senior partner's father, and I should have learned a good deal more of this if (as in the Delaware of 1792) there had been very few printed lawbooks to distract my mind from conversation. During the last decade of the eighteenth century, a Delaware judge's memory, thus reinforced, could easily range back over the whole legal history of the three lower counties

31. SPIRIT OF THE COMMON LAW (1922) 115-16. Blackstone must have greatly influenced the growing use of English case law, which will be discussed shortly. Pound's fuller account of the late eighteenth century takes a position similar to the hypothesis suggested in this review. POUND, FORMATIVE ERA OF AMERICAN LAW (1938) 6-13.

since 1701. Indeed, we have seen Chief Justice Read recalling the story of ancient surveys before Penn landed.[32] Judge Johns, on hearing a Delaware case mentioned, immediately recalled that it was decided "before the organization of the present judiciary system."[33] Given the inclination of judges today to recite how a Federal Rule of Civil Procedure has replaced New Equity Rule *x* and how that superseded Old Equity Rule *y*, it stands to reason that, if the whole ancient law of Delaware had been superseded within a century or much less, then Read or some other judge would have found an opportunity to mention such a cataclysm more than once in these Delaware cases. Yet I have not found in them the slightest hint that Delaware ever had any law except the common law of England.

This silence is especially significant in cases which involved old transactions soon after the settlement of Delaware. For example, the supreme court passed on the validity of executory devises in wills of 1695 and 1728.[34] If Delaware ever had a "reception" of the English common law, these two wills very likely preceded that event. It was surely arguable that their validity ought to depend on the rules of the ancient system and not on the subsequently imported common law. Such a nice problem of conflict of laws in time would hardly have been overlooked by acute lawyers like Bayard and Wilson. Instead, the arguments of counsel and the charge of the court cited English cases and treatises, plainly showing that they regarded the English common law as the only law of Delaware since Penn landed.

All this leans in support of the synthetic rubber hypothesis. The inference that there was no colonial reception of the common law, however, does not exclude the possibility of a reception of English case law, for that is quite a different matter. A colony might start with a body of proprietary or legislative statutes which left little need at first for unwritten law; generalized common law principles would suffice. Probably lawyers did not cite cases or even know them. As litigation became more complex and legal knowledge grew, these principles would become clothed with English case law. Thus, the late eighteenth century saw in America a

32. *Cf.* Burton's Lessee v. Prettyman, 1 Del. Cas. 363, 364-5 (1795).

33. Chambers v. Smack, 1 Del. Cas. 503, 1 *id.* 259 (1800).

34. Burton's Lessee v. Prettyman, 1 Del. Cas. 268 (1800) (this same will appears in several cases between these parties concerning "Cheat, later called Honesty"); Conwell's Lessee v. Conwell, 1 Del. Cas. 72, 1 *id.* 377 (1795).

gradual systematization of the common law, expedited by the publication of Blackstone and comparable to Lord Nottingham's systematization of equity. But this would not seem like any break with the past; case law would not be regarded as new law. The bar and bench were steeped in the Blackstonian philosophy that cases do not make new law but merely expound old principles.[35] They would think it entirely natural to cite cases in 1800 about a will of 1695, although a Delaware court of 1695 would not have cited cases. This change in professional attitude would come almost unconsciously and would not excite attention like the arrival of a new body of law. The increase of technicality from year to year would be imperceptible, just as the ritualistic English clergyman moved the Communion table in the central aisle of his parish church a foot eastward each week until he made it an altar without anybody in his evangelical congregation realizing what had happened.

(2) *To what extent do lawyers and judges rely on cases and treatises?* If the foregoing conjectures be worth serving as a basis for inquiry, then the examiner of a given body of American court records before 1801 can take the existence of the common law *in some form* for granted, and proceed to ascertain what form it assumes in his material. One significant point will be the use made of precedents and treatises.

Cases are often cited in these Delaware volumes, though perhaps not so much as today. These are mostly from English reports. Citations occur in arguments of counsel in 1771[36] and continue thereafter. Perhaps judges did not adopt the practice of giving opinions until later, or else the note takers did not bother to write down what they said. In any event, the earliest judicial opinions here reported are in 1793, but we find almost all of them abstaining from citations, with only two exceptions.[37] It may be significant that in both these cases the judge who cited precedents was Chief Justice Read of the supreme court. Perhaps he introduced the practice to the bench. In 1794 the court of common pleas observed: "Pow. Con. 333 is a book not cited, but is decisive of the point."[38]

35. 1 BL. COMM. *69.

36. *Re* Cahoon, 1 Del. Cas. lxii (1771). See note 28 *supra* as to the absence of judicial opinions in the reported early cases in Maryland.

37. Hall v. Field, 1 Del. Cas. 11 (1793); Gilpin v. Gilpin, 1 Del. Cas. 343 (1793).

38. Moore v. Wright, 1 Del. Cas. 22, 23 (1794).

By 1796 the same court was reconciling an apparent conflict in the English authorities and distinguishing cases cited by the counsel against whom the court was deciding.[39] Read, however, was the main citer on the bench for two or three years. I surmise that lawyers of the eighteenth century behaved like lawyers of today more closely than the bench behaved like our judges, and that arguments of counsel were elaborate for a considerable period during which the court was still merely noting its decision without giving reasons. Eventually the happy thought struck judges that they had the last word and could do some reasoning about the case as well as the lawyers could. After all, each judge had been a lawyer once and knew how to talk that way, and he had read his cases too. Thus, the judicial opinion may have been mainly the outgrowth of the arguments of counsel, though it must owe something to the interruptions from the bench during arguments which are so noticeable in the Year Books.

Delaware cases are cited much less often. A given notebook sometimes reports counsel as relying on an earlier case in the same notebook or trying to distinguish it. This occurs in the chain of cases already discussed on the competency of a Negro to testify against a white man.[40] Occasionally a Delaware case outside the notebooks is mentioned by a judge from his personal experience, possibly twenty years before.[41] Very likely he had been of counsel in the case in his days at the bar. Thus Chief Justice Read said in 1793: "I have heard the former Chief Justice complain that the struck juries stood too long"; and then Read limited them to one term.[42] In an 1800 case involving the admissibility of entries in a shopbook, Chief Justice Johns said:

> This is a case of great importance. Neither my brother nor myself recollects any determination on the express point since the organization of the present courts. I do recollect a single case in New Castle County before the existence of the present judiciary system. I was of counsel in the case of

39. Simpson v. Helford, 1 Del. Cas. 400, 1 *id.* 494 (1796). In the second report of this case, Helford is spelled Hillford.

40. State v. Bender, 1 Del. Cas. 16 (1793), citing Collins v. Hall, 1 Del. Cas. 8 (1793), a case in a different court and county.

41. Marine v. Stayton, 1 Del. Cas. 116 (1797); Collins v. Rigua, 1 Del. Cas. 141, 2 *id.* 78 (1797); Pope v. Jones' Executors, 1 Del. Cas. 399, 1 *id.* 493 (1796); see cases cited *infra* notes 42, 43.

42. Burton's Lessee v. Prettyman, 1 Del. Cas. 11, 2 *id.* 4 (1793).

> *Boggs and Lewden* to which I have alluded and which was decided in 1784. . . . the point whether money could be charged in an account was barely moved and not insisted on by William Tilghman, of counsel for the plaintiff. I afterwards asked the counsel on both sides, *viz*, the late Chief Justice Read and William Tilghman, their opinion in relation to the charge of a cash item—and they disagreed.[43]

These references fall short of the kind of state case law we have today. There is an air of reminiscence about them like a college student's "Way back in my freshman year." The judges are appealing to the wisdom of their predecessors rather than to a binding authority, such as they recognize in English decisions. Although Delaware was moving toward its own system of judicial precedents, it could hardly attain this mature stage of legal development until Delaware law reports were generally available to the bench and bar.

Decisions in other states (or colonies) are also cited with a rarity which was natural when few law reports had been printed. When the assignee of a bond found the obligor insolvent and sued the assignor to get back the consideration paid, plaintiff's counsel cited the *American Museum* to show that the assignee had won a similar case in Charleston, South Carolina, and argued:

> It is of the utmost importance to the United States aggregately and individually, that the judiciary tribunals of the union as well as those of the states respectively should harmonize in their determinations upon points accompanied by an identity of circumstances, in order that the common law may be the same throughout the whole.[44]

In deciding this suit in favor of the assignee, Chief Justice Read distinguished two Pennsylvania cases reported by Dallas.[45] Again, in the Burton litigation over "Cheat, now called Honesty," Read stated that plaintiff's counsel had read a case from Pennsylvania (apparently unreported) showing the necessity of deriving titles

43. Chambers v. Smack, 1 Del. Cas. 503, 503-504, also reported in 1 *id.* 259 (1800).

44. Gravinston v. Freeman, 1 Del. Cas. 102, 105, also reported in 1 *id.* 488 (1796). Clayton's notebook comments that the Charleston decision had been overruled in South Carolina by a dictum.

45. Pennsylvania cases in Dallas are also cited in Wright's Lessee v. Cannon, 1 Del. Cas. 42 (1794), 1 *id.* 227, 2 *id.* 55 (1796); Nandine v. Darrach, 2 Del. Cas. 131 (1800).

from the proprietary.[46] Here was a point of law obviously common to both of the states founded by Penn. When the quarter-Asiatic woman was freed from slavery, Chief Justice Bassett mentioned a similar Maryland case, without giving any citation.[47]

Treatises are frequently cited. This indicates well-stocked law libraries. Probably some of the books mentioned were American, for several titles appear on Eldon James's list of legal treatises printed in this country before 1801.[48] We find citations, however, in cases before 1801 of books like *Bacon's Abridgement, Comyn's Digest,*[49] *Doctrina Placitandi, Fearne on Contingent Remainders, Hawkins' Pleas of the Crown, Morgan's Essays,* and *Viner's Abridgment.* Eighteenth-century Delaware lawyers were evidently investing heavily in treatises and reports imported from England, either directly or through booksellers in Philadelphia. Carlyle defined a university as a great collection of books, and the same may be said of the common law when it takes the form of a system of case law and detailed doctrines. Until very many books were brought across the Atlantic, the common law in this country must have been mainly a body of general principles. The law grew with law libraries.

Mr. Boorstin will be able to give us much definite information about the use of precedents in his commentary. This will include the period after 1800, which is neglected in this review. It will be interesting to see whether the nineteenth-century Delaware cases reveal three tendencies which *a priori* seem probable: a lessened deference to English cases subsequent to independence; more frequent citation of Delaware cases as the earlier notebooks circulated in manuscript; and many citations of cases in other states with the increase of their published law reports.

(3) *What traces of a law different from the English common*

46. Burton's Lessee v. Prettyman, 1 Del. Cas. 154 (1797).

47. Phillis v. Lewis, 1 Del. Cas. 417 (1796).

48. James, *A List of Legal Treatises Printed in the British Colonies and the American States Before 1801*, in HARVARD LEGAL ESSAYS (1934) 159. Mr. Boorstin's table of abbreviations, 1 Del. Cas. liii, shows the following books which are also on James' list: BECCARIA ON CRIMES AND PUNISHMENT; BURN'S JUSTICE OF THE PEACE; BLACKSTONE'S COMMENTARIES; BULLER'S NISI PRIUS; VALETTE'S DEPUTY COMMISSARY'S GUIDE WITHIN THE PROVINCE OF MARYLAND; ESPINASSE'S DIGEST OF NISI PRIUS; GILBERT ON EVIDENCE; MITFORD'S EQUITY PLEADING; WATSON ON PARTNERSHIP. Of course, some of these may not have been cited in Delaware cases until after 1800.

49. The Irish edition of 1793.

law exist in either judicial decisions or statutes? Although these Delaware cases show no conscious recognition of an original alien system of law, as pictured by Reinsch and Goebel, or even of the preceding period of less technical law envisaged by my synthetic rubber hypothesis, still these cases may perhaps reveal survivals from an earlier time. In considering how far Delaware law had departed from English models, we can consider first the unwritten law, and then statutes.

The unwritten law, so far as substantive rules go, shows few traces of having been moulded by local conditions. The only case I have noted as raising the possibility of a divergence from English decisions decided to follow them. In arguing that crops passed to a devisee along with the land on which they were growing when the testator died, Wilson for the devisee had cited English authorities.[50] Ridgely and Bayard for the executors answered: "if the law be so in England, it cannot be so here. . . . Although there may be no Act of Assembly which expressly changes the law in this point, yet we differ in many points of practice from the law of England without the authority of an Act of Assembly, as in the taking in execution growing corn, which cannot be done in England." Wilson replied: "Wills are construed here by the same rules and have the same effect they have in England. . . . If there can be shown a different practice countenanced by the courts, we must sumbit to it, but as none such can be shown, it is better that the law should be left settled, as [it] has been for centuries in England."[51] Chief Justice Bassett charged according to English law in favor of the devisee, who got a sizable verdict of £135.[52]

Of course, some English doctrines of substantive law were sure to prove unacceptable under the different circumstances of an American colony. The most obvious situations of this sort, like the distribution of intestate property, would probably produce appropriate colonial legislation (of which more hereafter). Hence, it is conceivable that not many situations demanding a non-English rule of action would be left over for the unwritten law to handle during the eighteenth century. Later, as affairs got more complex, new points of divergence would become articulate which were not

50. Waples v. Waples, 1 Del. Cas. 203, 1 *id.* 463, 2 *id.* 107 (1798). The authorities cited were Cro. Eliz. and Co. LITT.

51. 1 Del. Cas. at 204-206.

52. A new trial was sought for misdirection, but the outcome is not stated.

covered by statutes. Then American substantive case law would start to diverge from its English counterpart much more noticeably than it did before 1801. This seems a point worth inquiry.

Civil procedure offers very different possibilities. This probably differed a good deal at the very start from English procedure,[53] being in a general way much simpler and influenced by the reforms of the Commonwealth period,[54] which disappeared in England for a hundred and seventy years after the restoration of Charles II. Consequently, the eventual absorption of English case law on procedure into our law just when Bentham was excoriating it was nothing short of a calamity, from which it has taken us over a century to recover. If only some American legal writer of ability had set himself soon after 1800 to do for civil procedure at law what Story did for equity and Edward Livingston for criminal law! He might have systematized the simple remedies and court rules which had come to us from colonial times and shaped them sensibly to handle the controversies of a new century. Such a treatise might have had a wide influence and give us a native straightforward procedure, endowed with sufficient toughness to withstand the invasion by Meeson and Welsby and Chitty and a host of similar heartless technicians. Instead, the outworn formalities of English common-law actions were welcomed by the litigants and lawyers of the young republic. The litigiousness which had been our besetting sin since the seventeenth century[55] made us grasp eagerly the new foreign weapons which enabled us to fight each other bitterly and endlessly over the distinctions between trespass and trespass on the case, the defenses available under the general issue, and the formal steps necessary to perfect a writ of error as contrasted with an appeal or a new trial.[56]

The Delaware cases before 1801 have not yet plucked the fatal tree of knowledge. Although the forms of action seem more differentiated than in seventeenth-century Massachusetts where almost every suit was an action on the case, the traditional names are still

53. See 1 RECORDS OF THE SUFFOLK COUNTY COURTS, 1671-1680 (1933) xxxviii-lvi.

54. See Robinson, *Anticipations under the Commonwealth of Changes in the Law*, in 1 SELECT ESSAYS IN ANGLO-AMERICAN LEGAL HISTORY (1907) 467.

55. See 1 RECORDS OF THE SUFFOLK COUNTY COURTS, 1671-1680 (1933) xxxvi.

56. See POUND, APPELLATE PROCEDURE IN CIVIL CASES (1941) 106-320, for the unbelievable technicalities of appellate review.

little more than mere labels,[57] and pleadings count for even less. The divergences from English practice, however, seem to receive little attention from the Delaware courts. In the only instance of judicial comment noted, Chief Justice Read said as to views by juries: "granting of views here is of course, but not so in England, for they are not granted there but upon sufficient cause shown, and I think they are often improperly granted here in cases where it is not necessary."[58] He afterwards added: "in a course of forty years' (I think) practice, I have never known but one case where a view was necessary."

The statutes cited in these volumes are mainly Delaware legislation, but there are references to acts of Parliament, which I shall discuss later. Colonial statutes, as I have already suggested, probably are more responsive to American conditions and show more marked departures from English models than does colonial unwritten law. The Connecticut statute distributing intestate land among all the children is a famous example.[59] Reinsch's strongest arguments for a home-made law are based on colonial legislation. Yet in Massachusetts, at least, this was not the rude popular law which he indicates; by 1660 the Bay Colony had a surprisingly mature and comprehensive body of statutes, and it was more influenced by English law than Reinsch concedes.[60] And early Delaware law derived from Pennsylvania, which Reinsch himself describes as "fitted out with the most complete system of colonial codes."[61] Mr. Boorstin's commentary will doubtless discuss some of the Delaware statutes involved in his cases with respect to their maturity and their relation to contemporary English law. This review will not go into these interesting problems or analyze any specific statute, but will merely speak of a few interesting cases which show how local legislation generally was handled by judges.

The possibility that an old statute may become obsolete without express repeal was raised in one case. The plaintiff, a creditor of the decedent, had levied execution on the premises under a

57. See, however, Polk v. Coston, 1 Del. Cas. 276 (1800), where the judicial distinction between trover and case deprived the gullible Polk of the value of his hogs.

58. Polk's Lessee v. Minner, 1 Del. Cas. 59, 61 (1795).

59. Andrews, *The Influence of Colonial Conditions as Illustrated in the Connecticut Intestacy Law*, in 1 Select Essays in Anglo-American Legal History (1907) 431.

60. See Plucknett, Book Review (1930) 3 New Eng. Q. 157.

61. *Op. cit. supra* note 69, at 396.

judgment against the administrator and bought in at the sheriff's sale. The defendant claimed the same land as purchaser at a later administrator's sale held under a court order. Wilson and others for the plaintiff relied in part on a Pennsylvania statute of 1700, passed before Delaware was separated.[62] Ridgely and Bayard answered:

> The Act of Pennsylvania of 1700 could not be considered as the law of this state. It was not found among our laws, and the statute book of Pennsylvania could be no proof of the Laws of Delaware. Many laws had existed not contained in our statute book. They had been repealed or become obsolete from non-user. It would be possible from ancient editions of the laws to show acts not now in force, but where no memorials could be found to evidence their repeal. The statute book had always been considered as containing the body of the legislative acts in force; and it would be dangerous to go beyond it; as the persons as well as property of the citizens might be made dependent on laws which it would require the diligence of an antiquarian to have any knowledge of.[63]

Several cases bear on the respect which the courts should show to the legislature in construing statutes. On the question whether a statute imposing certain formalities upon actions against an executor or administrator applied to a suit against a living obligor who died *pendente lite,* Chief Justice Bassett said:

> I conceive the Act does not apply to this suit; and the Legislature must have had a prophetic spirit to have formed the Act to this case. Inconveniences may arise, but they will not warrant the court to apply the law to a case not within it. Our powers are judicial, not legislative. Nothing further is necessary to entitle plaintiff now to recover than was necessary when suit was brought.[64]

And in another case Ridgely argued:

> We are not to contradict the legislature, nor refine upon a law already plain; if they enact a foolish law, if their ideas

62. See 2 Del. Cas. 58nn. for probable citations of the legislation.

63. Wright's Lessee v. Cannon, 1 Del. Cas. 368, 1 *id.* 227, 2 *id.* 55 (1795). The reports conflict as to the result. See the appendix on "Desuetude of Statutes in the United States" in GRAY, NATURE AND SOURCES OF THE LAW (2d ed. 1921) 329. See also *id.* at 189-97.

64. Brown v. Brown, 1 Del. Cas. 188, 191 (1798).

> are plain, it is the law and binding. It is dangerous to assume an unlimited power of construction, for it is upon the law our rights hang and society depends.[65]

The separation of powers, however, did not prevent the court from letting statutory interpretation be shaped by the fact that the act had been drawn by a judge before he came on the bench:

> . . . it is beyond all doubt that at the time of passing the Act for the more easy and speedy recovery of legacies the legislature well knew a legacy could not be recovered at common law. There were then two gentlemen in the House whose legal abilities have never been questioned, one of whom must have penned this Act. (The persons here alluded to were the two Chief Justices of Pennsylvania and Delaware—Hon. Thomas McKean and Hon. George Read, Esquires.)[66]

Chief Justice Read, the very man who drew a statute, was obliged as a judge to construe it, and remarked, with the pride of an obstetrician recognizing the scar of his first Caesarian: "This Act is the first I ever drew."[67]

The same case discusses the interesting question whether a legislature can construe a prior statute. When such an interpretative statute was cited against him, Bayard argued: "That Act was passed since this action. The legislature can make laws but have no right to pass an opinion upon the law." But Wilson later replied that the act was binding as "a legislative construction, though passed since this action was brought."[68]

British statutes raise special difficulties,[69] which are related to the general problem of the binding effect of English law in the colonies. According to Blackstone, these colonies, like Ireland, were "not bound by any acts of parliament unless particularly named."[70] Such an express extension to America occurred very rarely, and not

65. Laws v. Davis, 1 Del. Cas. 256, 258 (1800).

66. Simpson v. Hillford, 1 Del. Cas. 494, 496, also reported in 1 *id.* 400 (1796).

67. Browne's Executors v. Derickson, 1 Del. Cas. 171 (1798). For Read's further participation in statutory drafting, see Laws v. Davis, 1 Del. Cas. 256 (1800).

68. Wright's Lessee v. Cannon, 1 Del. Cas. 42 (1794), 1 *id.* 227 (1796). Bayard gives the date of the second phase of this litigation as 1795. See 1 *id.* 368.

69. See Sioussat, *The Theory of the Extension of English Statutes to the Plantations*, in 1 SELECT ESSAYS IN ANGLO-AMERICAN LEGAL HISTORY (1907) 416; GRAY, NATURE AND SOURCES OF THE LAW (2d ed. 1921) 196.

70. 1 BL. COMM. *108.

in any of the English statutes cited in the cases under consideration.[71] American lawyers disliked Blackstone's theory,[72] and yet the colonists were unwilling to go to the opposite extreme of being automatically subject to every act of Parliament. For example, the Pennsylvania Quakers objected to the application of English statutes requiring dissenters to take an oath of allegiance and disqualifying Quakers from giving evidence in criminal cases or holding office.[73] And it is inconceivable that the colonists came under the harsh eighteenth-century British legislation which imposed the death penalty for scores of new offenses. The result of this conflict was a confusing compromise. Some English statutes were applied, others were not; and it was hard to say which was which. The Delaware Constitution of 1776 prolonged this vagueness by continuing in force "so much of the statute law as [has] been heretofore adopted in practice in this state."

Certainly Blackstone's theory is not accepted in the Delaware cases noted as citing English statutes. It is true that not one of these statutes was actually enforced in a case, but they were not treated as conclusively inapplicable because of their failure to mention the colonies. Instead, their rejection was usually based on their inconsistency with specific Delaware legislation. Typical reasoning runs: "Lands in England cannot be sold for debt; by our Acts of Assembly here it can."[74]

In the most interesting of these cases, trover for a female slave, the plaintiff's claim to ownership by purchase was questioned because he showed nothing to take the sale out of Section 17 of the Statute of Frauds.

> *Sed, Per Curiam.* The 29 Car. II, c. 5 . . . does not extend to this country. Certain parts of the Statute have been adopted as the law of the state by an Act of Assembly [1 Del.

71. Wright's Lessee v. Cannon, 1 Del. Cas. 42 (1794) (incorrectly citing on ejectment 11 GEO. II, c. 19, §§ 12, 13 (1738), 1 *id.* 227 (1796) (citing Statute of Frauds), 2 *id.* 55 (1796) (pre-Jamestown statutes on sale of land for debts); Laws v. Davis, 1 Del. Cas. 256 (1800) (citing 13 ELIZ., c. 10 (1570) against long ecclesiastical leases); Jacobs v. Aydlotte, 1 Del. Cas. 443 (1797) (incorrectly citing Statute of Frauds).

72. See 1 STORY, CONSTITUTION (2d ed. 1851) §§ 155-58.

73. See Shepherd, *History of Proprietary Government in Pennsylvania*, in 6 STUDIES IN HISTORY, ECONOMICS AND PUBLIC LAW (1896) 351 *et seq.* This book has useful material on the early legal history of Delaware.

74. Peery, *arguendo*, in Wright's Lessee v. Cannon, 1 Del. Cas. 42, 49 (1794).

Laws 327],[75] and to say the parts not enacted by law were in force here would be to say the Act of Assembly is nugatory, and that the same law would have existed if it had not been made. Bills of sale are usually made use of to pass such property, but they are not necessary.[76]

75. This Delaware "Act about contracts and assumptions" dealt only with guaranties, promises by executors and administrators, and agreements upon consideration of marriage or concerning any interest in land or not to be performed within one year. The requirements varied somewhat from the Statute of Frauds. It repealed only an earlier act of the same title, which I have not been able to identify.

76. Jacobs v. Aydlotte, 1 Del. Cas. 443 (1797). The report mistakenly refers to § 6 of the Statute of Frauds instead of § 17.

Glossary

Meanings assigned in this glossary were selected for the primary purpose of explaining usage in the seventeenth and eighteenth centuries for both English and American law. The meanings are therefore primarily historical rather than contemporary in application. This selective glossary is not a substitute for such essential reference volumes as *Black's Law Dictionary* by Henry Campbell Black, fourth edition (St. Paul, 1951), which provided the basis for the glossary.

A mensa et thoro—A kind of divorce which is rather a separation of the parties by law than a dissolution of the marriage.

A vinculo matrimonii—A term descriptive of a kind of divorce which effects a complete dissolution of the marriage contract.

Abatement—A plea which, without disputing justice of plaintiff's claim, objects to place, mode, or time of asserting it; it allows plaintiff to renew suit in another place or form, or at another time, and does not assume to answer the action on its merits, or deny existence of particular cause of action on which plaintiff relies.

Action—A form of suit in a court of law.

Affirmation—A solemn religious declaration that is substituted for an oath, especially by those having conscientious scruples against taking an oath.

Alias—A second writ issued where one of the same kind has already been issued in the same cause without having been effective.

Assigns, assignees—Those to whom property shall have been transferred.

Assizes of Jerusalem—A code of feudal jurisprudence prepared by an assembly of barons and lords A. D. 1099, after the conquest of Jerusalem. It was compiled principally from the laws and customs of France.

Assumpsit—A form of action which lies for the recovery of damages for the non-performance of a simple contract.

Audita querela—The name of a writ constituting the initial process in an action brought by a judgment defendant to obtain relief against the consequences of the judgment, on account of some matter of defense or discharge arising since its rendition, and which could not be taken advantage of otherwise.

Barratry—The criminal offense of frequently exciting and stirring up quarrels and suits either at law or otherwise.

Benefit of clergy—Originally an exemption from punishment by the secular courts that was accorded to clergymen, and later extended to a larger segment of the population and made more specialized in the offenses it applied to, thereby mitigating the extreme rigor of the criminal laws.

Bill of exceptions—A formal written statement of the objections taken by a party during the trial of a cause to the decisions, rulings, or instructions of the trial judge.

Capias—The general name for several species of writs, the common characteristic of which is that they require the officer to take the body of the defendant into custody. The writ *capias ad respondendum*, usually simply termed a *capias*, required the defendant to be safely secured so that he could appear in court on a certain day to answer the plaintiff in the action.

Certiorari—An original writ commanding judges or officers of inferior courts to certify or to return records or proceedings in a cause for judicial review of their action.

Chancery—A court of equity, or the system of jurisprudence administered in courts of equity. In England the Court of Chancery possessed the highest equitable powers and jurisdiction.

Chattel—An article of personal and movable property.

Collateral heir—Hereditary succession in a line of descent connecting persons who are not directly related to each other as ascendants or descendants, but whose relationship consists in common descent from the same ancestor.

Conveyance—In real property law, a transfer of legal title to land, but popularly used by lawyers to denote any transfer of title.

Coparceny, coparcenary—An estate where lands of inheritance descend to several persons in common.

Copyhold—A species of customary estate in England or estate at the will of a lord, the only visible title to which consists of the copies of the court rolls made by the steward of the manor when a tenant is admitted to any parcel of land.

Coram Mayor—Before the mayor or chief magistrate of a city.

Coverture—The condition or state of a married woman.

Crimen improbissimum—Literally, "most unjust or wicked crime or offense."

Cursus curiae—The practice of the court.

Curtesy—The estate to which by common law a man is entitled, on the death of his wife, in the lands or tenements of which she was seised in possession in fee simple or in tail during her coverture, provided they have had lawful issue born alive which might have been capable of inheriting the estate.

Customal, custumal—A written collection of the usages or customs of a manor or some locality, having the force of law there.

De ventre inspiciendo—A writ to inspect the body of a woman who claims or pretends to be pregnant to see whether she is with child.

Demurrer—A demurrer to evidence is an objection or exception by one of the parties in an action at law, to the effect that the evidence which his adversary produced is insufficient in point of law (whether true or not) to make out his case or sustain the issue. This proceeding is analogous to a demurrer to a pleading.

Deodand—In English law any personal chattel which was the immediate occasion of the death of any reasonable creature, and which was forfeited to the crown to be applied to pious uses and distributed in alms by the high almoner.

Devise—A gift of real property by the last will and testament of the donor; a testamentary disposition of land or realty.

Devisee—The person to whom lands or other real property are devised or given by will.

Dicta—Gratuitous opinions of a judge, which do not embody the resolution or determination of the court, on matters not necessarily involved in the case or essential to its determination.

Dispositive—Having to do with the disposition or direction of something.

Distringas—In English practice a writ directed to the sheriff of the county in which a defendant resides, or has any goods or chattels, commanding him to distrain upon the goods and chattels of the defendant for forty shillings in order to compel his appearance.

Distringas nuper vicecomitem—A writ to distrain the goods of one who lately filled the office of sheriff to compel him to do some act which he ought to have done before leaving the office.

Dower—A species of life estate to which every married woman is entitled on death of her husband, intestate, or in case she dissents from his will, out of the lands and tenements of which he was seised in fee during the marriage.

Ejectment—At common law a mixed action which lay for the recovery of the possession of land and for damages for the unlawful detention of its possession. It came to be adopted as the usual method of trying titles to land.

Embracery—An attempt to influence a jury to one side or the other.

En banc—The court sitting as a whole.

Encumbrances—An encumbrance is a claim, lien, charge, or liability attached to and binding real property.

Entail—A fee abridged or limited to the issue or certain classes of issue, instead of descending to all the heirs.

Equity—A system of jurisprudence administered by certain tribunals, sometimes distinct from the common law courts, and empowered to decree "equity" in the sense of justice as ascertained by natural reason or ethical insight, but independent of the formulated body of law.

Escheat—In feudal law an escheat was an obstruction of the course of descent, and consequent ending of the tenure, by some unforeseen contingency, in which case the land naturally reverted back to the original grantor.

Evidentiary—Necessary to prove the essential or ultimate fact; affording evidence.

Exchequer—In England the jurisdiction of the Court of Exchequer, one of the four superior courts at Westminster, extended to revenue cases arising out of the non-payment or withholding of debts to the Crown, and by gradual extension to all suitors in personal actions.

Execution—A writ of execution put in force the judgment or decree of a court.

Exigent—In English practice a judicial writ made use of in the process of outlawry, commanding the sheriff to demand the defendant from county court to county court until he be outlawed.

Fee, fee simple—A freehold estate in land; an estate of inheritance without condition, belonging to the owner, and alienable by him or transmissible to his heirs absolutely and simply.

Fee tail—A freehold estate in which there is a fixed line of inheritable succession limited to the issue of the body of the grantee or devisee, and in which the regular and general succession of heirs at law is cut off.

Felony—A crime of graver or more atrocious nature than those designated as misdemeanors. Generally an offense punishable by death or imprisonment in a penitentiary. At common law an offense also occasioning total forfeiture of either land or goods.

Feme covert—A married woman.

Frankalmoigne—In English law a spiritual tenure whereby religious corporations held land of the donor to them and their successors forever.

Freebench—A widow's dower out of copyholds to which she is entitled by the custom of some manors.

Gavelkind—A species of socage tenure common in Kent in England, where among other things, the lands descend to all the sons or heirs of the nearest degree together.

Holographic—A will or deed written entirely by the testator or grantor with his own hand.

In capite—In chief; tenure *in capite* was a holding directly from the king.

In forma pauperis—Describes permission given to a poor person to sue without liability for costs.

Indebitatus assumpsit—That form of the action of *assumpsit* in which the declaration alleges a debt or obligation to be due from the defendant, and then avers that in consideration thereof he promised to pay or discharge the same.

Institutio heredis—In Roman law the appointment of the *heres* in the will. It corresponds very nearly to the nomination of an executor in English law.

Intestacy, intestate—The state or condition of dying without having made a valid will.

Leet—In English law the name of a court of criminal jurisdiction held once a year in early times within a particular hundred, lordship, or manor.

Messuage—A dwelling house and the adjacent buildings.

Misdemeanor—Offenses of less consequence than felonies.

Mulct—A fine imposed on conviction of an offense.

Nisi prius—The *nisi prius* courts are such as are held for the trial of issues of fact before a jury and a presiding judge.

Nolo contendere—"I will not contest it." The name of a plea in a criminal action having the same legal effect as a plea of guilty.

Non est inventus—"He is not found." The sheriff's return to process requiring him to arrest the body of the defendant, when the latter is not found within his jurisdiction.

Non liquet—"It is not clear."

Non vult ulterius prosequi—"Do not wish to follow up or pursue further."

Nonfeasance—Nonperformance of some act which ought to be performed; omission to perform a required duty at all.

Novel disseisin—A writ of assise which lay for the recovery of lands or tenements, where the claimant had been lately dispossessed.

Nugatory—Futile, ineffectual, invalid.

Nuncupative will—An oral will declared or dictated by the testator in his last sickness before a sufficient number of witnesses, and afterwards reduced to writing.

Ore tenus—Orally.

Outlawry—A process by which a defendant or person in contempt on a civil or criminal process was declared out of the protection or aid of the law.

Oyer and terminer—A court for the trial of cases of treason and felony, formerly used only on particular occasions, as upon sudden outrage or insurrection in any place.

Pendente lite—Pending the suit; during litigation.

Per curiam—A phrase used in the law reports to distinguish an opinion of the whole court from an opinion written by any one judge.

Per testes—To prove something in solemn form by calling the witnesses before the court.

Personalty—Personal property; chattels.

Pluries—When an original and *alias* writ have been issued and proved ineffectual, a third writ, called a *pluries* writ may frequently be issued. It is to the same effect as the two former.

Postea—In common law practice a formal statement which gives an account of the proceedings at the trial of the action.

Primogeniture—The superior or exclusive right possessed by the eldest son to succeed to the estate of his ancestor in right of his seniority by birth to the exclusion of younger sons.

Pro re nata—Adapted to meet the particular occasion.

Pro stultiloquio—Literally, "penalties for foolish talking."

Pro tanto—For so much; for as much as may be; as far as it goes.

Quasi in rem—A technical term used to designate actions instituted against the defendant personally, though the real object is to deal with particular property or subject property to the discharge of claims asserted.

Qui tam—An action brought by an informer who shares in the penalty.

Quo warranto—An ancient writ against a defendant inquiring by what warrant or authority he has claimed, usurped, or exercised any office, privilege, or franchise.

Realty—Real property, such as land.

Recovery—The obtaining of some right or property by the judgment of a court, as the result of an action brought for that purpose.

Remembrancing—Recording, recollecting, remembering; as by means of a written record, for example.

Replevin—An action brought to recover possession of goods unlawfully taken.

Resiant—A resident; continually dwelling or abiding in a place.

Scire facias—A judicial writ, founded upon some matter of record, such as a judgment or recognizance and requiring the person against whom it is brought to show cause why the party bringing it should not have advantage of such record.

Seisin, seized—Possession of land in fee simple.

Service—In legal practice the exhibition or delivery of a writ, notice, injunction, etc., by an authorized person, to a person who is thereby officially notified of some action or proceeding in which he is concerned.

Socage—A species of tenure in England whereby the tenant held certain lands in consideration of certain inferior services of husbandry to be performed by him to the lord of the fee. In free socage the services are not only certain but honorable.

Stare decisis—The policy whereby courts agree to abide by or adhere to decided cases or precedents.

Supersedeas—In practice the name of a writ containing a command to stay or temporarily suspend the proceedings at law.

Testamentary—Pertaining to a will or testament. In English law testamentary causes are matters relating to the validity and execution of wills.

Traverse—In the language of pleading, a traverse signifies a denial. A *special traverse* is a peculiar form of denial, the design of which is to explain or qualify the denial, instead of putting it in the direct and absolute form.

Traverse jury—A petit jury; a trial jury.

Trespass *vi et armis*—The common law action for damages for any injury committed by the defendant with direct and immediate force or arms against the plaintiff or his property.

Trover—In common law practice an action which became the remedy for any wrongful interference with or detention of the goods of another.

Ut de corona—As of the Crown.

Utlagatum capias—In English practice a writ which lies against a person who has been outlawed in an action, by which the sheriff is commanded to take him and keep him in custody until the day of the return, and then present him to the court, there to be dealt with for his contempt.

Wager of law—In old practice the giving of sureties by a defendant in an action of debt, that at a certain day assigned he would take an oath in open court that he did not owe the debt, and at the same time bring with him eleven neighbors who should swear that they believed he said the truth.

Writ of entry—A real action to recover the possession of land where the tenant or owner has been disseised or otherwise wrongfully dispossessed.

Writ of error—A writ issued from an appellate court directed to the court of record, requiring the judges to remit to the appellate court the record of an action before them, in which a final judgment has been entered, in order that examination may be made of certain errors alleged to have been committed.

Index

D

E

F

Q

R

www.ingramcontent.com/pod-product-compliance
Lightning Source LLC
LaVergne TN
LVHW090255210926
848480LV00001B/25